JBoss in Action

JBoss in Action

CONFIGURING THE JBOSS APPLICATION SERVER

JAVID JAMAE
PETER JOHNSON

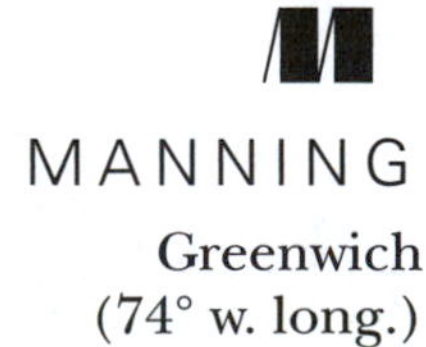

MANNING
Greenwich
(74° w. long.)

For online information and ordering of this and other Manning books, please visit www.manning.com. The publisher offers discounts on this book when ordered in quantity. For more information, please contact

Special Sales Department
Manning Publications Co.
Sound View Court 3B fax: (609) 877-8256
Greenwich, CT 06830 email: orders@manning.com

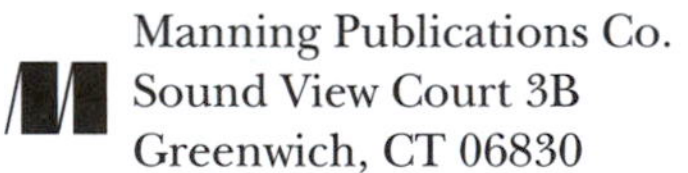

Manning Publications Co.
Sound View Court 3B
Greenwich, CT 06830

Development Editor Nermina Miller
Copyeditor: Andrea Kaucher
Typesetter: Gordan Salinovic
Cover designer: Leslie Haimes

ISBN 978-1-933988-02-3
Printed in the United States of America
1 2 3 4 5 6 7 8 9 10 – MAL – 14 13 12 11 10 09

brief contents

contents

preface

As a consultant, I worked at many different software shops, and grew tired of seeing people reimplement the same code over and over again. I knew there had to be a faster and better way to write business applications than reimplementing security frameworks and remoting frameworks for every project. Code reuse was the whole appeal of OO programming, right?

I started working with WebSphere in 2001—which led me to learn more about the J2EE specification. I was fascinated by the idea that my knowledge of the standard was portable; I could go to different companies that used J2EE application servers, and focus on learning and programming business code rather than tinkering with mediocre, homemade frameworks that would occupy my time and give me little portable knowledge, which is of paramount importance as a consultant.

I wanted to experiment with WebSphere at home but found the lack of project and code transparency frustrating. I came across JBoss and spent many hours experimenting and learning about EJBs, JNDI, security, and class loading. Although I'd used open source frameworks, I had never taken advantage of pouring through the forums and code to learn and discuss the framework. I had taken advantage of the free price of open source, but not the freedom to distribute, examine, improve, and modify the code. I finally started understanding the benefits of this model.

I started working with JBoss on a few projects in 2002 and wrote a couple JBoss-related articles in 2004. Then, toward the end of 2005, two interesting things happened at around the same time. First, the consulting and training company that I was working for became a JBoss Partner (before the Red Hat acquisition) and asked me to take ownership of the partnership and to start teaching JBoss courses. Second, I got a call from an Acquisitions Editor (the person who finds writers for the publisher) at Manning asking if I had any leads on somebody who would be interested in writing a book. She had run across my JBoss articles and thought I might be a good person to ask. I thought that writing a book would be as easy as writing a series of technical articles, so I offered to write the book myself. And after a little bit of convincing, I got the job.

At that point, I had to decide what the book would cover and who it would target. Although I appreciated that the JBoss AS code and documentation was open, having read through much of the JBoss AS documentation and books, I just wasn't satisfied with the style, quality, and expected audience of the material. Most of the documentation seemed overly esoteric and (in my opinion) geared more toward developers of the application server itself, not necessarily toward the users. But I also didn't want to write another book on how to develop Java EE applications. Plenty of books and articles had already done that in an application server–agnostic fashion. I saw little benefit in writing another book on the specification with some bits and pieces of JBoss AS mixed in. I decided that the book should be geared toward developers and administrators who want to learn how to configure the application server.

After knowing whom the book was geared toward, I had to decide what version of the software to cover. When I started, JBoss AS 4 was widely deployed; but, because JBoss AS 5 was originally supposed to be released in 2006, I opted to cover JBoss AS 5 so that the book wouldn't be outdated as soon as it was published.

Deciding whom the book would be geared toward and what version I wanted to cover was relatively easy. Writing the book was a whole different game! I didn't appreciate the myriad facets of an application server I'd have to understand in order to write a comprehensive book. An application server is like a universe, and few people are masters of more than a few parts of that universe. Although I had a good understanding of many parts of JBoss, I quickly realized that I had to learn a lot more. Another challenge was that I was covering JBoss AS 5, which was actively being developed. Every time I thought I had something figured out, it changed. I ended up spending an enormous amount of time trying to work around bugs in beta releases and trying to keep up with design discussions on the developers' forums.

In July of 2006, I realized I was in way over my head. I still thought that the JBoss AS 5 release was around the corner, so I told Manning that I wanted to bring somebody in to help me get the book out on time. I called everybody I knew and I scoured through the JBoss forums looking for people. I had a few leads, but I was most impressed with Peter Johnson. I found him on the forums, answering question after question. He provided detailed explanations, gave plenty of references and background, and used eloquent language.

After talking to Peter, I realized that he had significant experience with JBoss AS. He works for Unisys, which has been a JBoss Partner since JBoss AS 3.2.3 came out, and was technical lead for the team that evaluated JBoss AS for its enterprise readiness. The lack of a decent administrative interface to JBoss AS was one of his concerns, which caused him to lead a team that developed an administration console which was open-sourced by Unisys and made available for JBoss AS versions 2.2.7 through 4.2.3. He and a few of his coworkers also worked with the JBoss admin console team on a proposed admin console that was to come out with JBoss AS 5, but was later dropped in favor of Embedded Jopr.

Unisys, as a good corporate citizen in the open source community—not just taking but also giving back—allowed Peter and his coworkers to participate in various ways, such as providing patches to improve performance of JBoss AS and PostgreSQL. Having been a teacher in a former life, Peter knew that the best way to learn a new topic is to try to explain it to others. He hung out in the forums, seeing what kinds of questions people asked, trying out what he thought were the solutions, and posting answers when he felt he could offer help or insight. By participating in the forums, he could kill two birds with one stone: give back to the open source community and gain a deeper understanding of JBoss AS.

Peter was excited to join the project, and we seemed to agree on almost everything. We shared the same vision for the audience and direction of the book, and he dove right into writing, pushing out chapter after chapter, and providing me with great feedback on what I had already written.

With my background teaching JBoss courses and Peter's fervent dedication to the online forums, we had experience fielding many common questions. We decided to focus the book on the most common things that new and intermediate users of JBoss AS try to configure. For the most part, each chapter provides you first with background information and then with specifics on configuring common things for the part of the application server covered by the chapter.

As for JBoss AS 5, the release date kept getting pushed back. This was expected because the application server underwent several major architectural and infrastructural changes. As I write this preface in December of 2008, the GA release of JBoss AS 5 has just been released. We're expecting a final release in January 2009, which should coincide with the U.S. print version of this book. Peter and I have been working long and hard on this project, and we hope that you find that it answers most of your basic questions and gives you enough background to figure out the ones that it doesn't.

JAVID JAMAE

acknowledgments

We've learned firsthand that it takes a village to publish a book. Although we get the privilege of seeing our names on the front cover, dozens of other people have contributed to putting it all together. We'd like to thank everyone at Manning, especially our publisher, Marjan Bace, and our development editors, Howard Jones, Joyce King, Jackie Carter, and Nermina Miller (we were really hard on our editors, so we went through a lot of them), for their continuous support and help on so many aspects of the manuscript. Thanks also to the others at Manning who worked with us in different stages of the project: Andrea Kaucher, Katie Tennant, Gordan Salinovic, Gabriel Dobrescu, Steven Hong, Leslie Haimes, and Mary Piergies.

Many reviewers read the chapters during various stages of completion and provided valuable feedback and input that helped to make the book what it is today. We would like to thank Anil Saldhana, Tray Scates, David Strong, Scott Dawson, Patrick Dennis, Norman Richards, Andrew C. Oliver, Scott Stirling, John Tyler, Nathan Slippen, Michael Abney, Deepak Vohra, TVS Murthy, Sumit Pal, Bas Vodde, Goldy Lukka, and Riccardo Audano. We especially want to thank David Strong and Rod Coffin who provided detailed notes on things that needed to be corrected. Rod also did a final pass through the manuscript just before publication, ensuring that the technical content and code were up to date and correct.

Thanks to Vo Blinn, Bongos, Robert Jackson, Alan C, Jan Nielsen, James Hood, Vulinh Nguyen, and many others for picking up the book as part of the Manning Early Access Program (MEAP), and providing input such as spelling corrections, references to sections that had moved or been deleted, and input on various topics that they'd like to see covered.

Javid Jamae

To my wife Elizabeth—I love you, and I couldn't have done this without you. Words cannot express my gratitude. To my kids Austin, Sina, and Kian—I'm glad I'll have much more time to spend with you now. Thanks to my parents for all their support. And a big thanks to my in-laws Jack and Pam for helping us out so much over the course of the last several years.

Thanks to all the folks at Manning (especially Andrea and Nermina) for helping form the book into what it is. Thanks to Rod Coffin for his excellent technical review of the book. And last but not least, thanks to Peter for joining me to write this book. It's been a pleasure working with you.

Peter Johnson

I would like to thank my wife Sandy for her support and understanding over the course of this project. You are my number one cheerleader, and I love you for it. I also want to thank my daughters, Cheryl and Alexa, who provided welcome diversion when I needed to step away from the book.

I also want to thank Tony Sarris, my manager at Unisys, and the rest of the Unisys management team, for supporting me in this effort.

I had several technical reviewers of my chapters that I want to thank. Julien Viet took time off from coding the JBoss Portal to review the portal chapters. Tray Scates and Scott Dawson reviewed and provided technical input for all of the chapters that I wrote. I even want to thank Jim Fontana for reviewing the chapter that did not make it into the book. Those are the breaks, Jim.

Finally, I would like to thank my mom and dad, Erika and Jerry, who at a very early age taught me that one plus one was zero with one to carry.

about this book

One of the things you quickly realize when you work with any of the technologies covered by the Java EE umbrella is that many things are part of the specification, and some things are left as "implementation details" or left up to the implementer's discretion. In practice, this means that any time you learn a Java EE technology, besides learning the fundamentals about that technology, you also need to learn how to apply or configure the technology in the environment in which you wish to deploy it. If your deployment environment of choice is the JBoss Application Server, then this book is for you because it covers those areas that are outside the scope of the specifications.

In this book, we cover a wide variety of technologies and show you how to configure those technologies specifically for use in the JBoss Application Server. Naturally, this can't be done in a vacuum, so we provide simple examples that illustrate the technology and then walk you through the steps necessary to configure things such as deployment descriptors, access control, and encryption. Our intent isn't to describe every nuance of any particular technology. For that, we recommend that you read books particular to those technologies (and we provide references at the end of most chapters). Instead, use this book to learn how to use the technology within the JBoss Application Server.

We believe that you learn more by trying things out for yourself than by reading about how it's done. By keeping our examples simple, we're able to provide complete source code, including configuration files, within the book itself. If you want, you can try the examples using only the text in the book. All you need is a text editor. But we don't provide build scripts in the book; instead, we provide diagrams showing the contents of the resulting packages (JAR, WAR, EAR, and so on). We assume that you can use whatever tools you're familiar with to compile and package the applications.

Audience

As programmers at heart, we wrote the book from a programmer's point of view. Any programmer that uses the JBoss Application Server in his or her daily routine will benefit from reading this book. But we went beyond mere coding to look at what it takes to get an application configured and into production.

With its focus on configuration topics, this book is also ideal for use by system administrators who need to configure and deploy applications to the JBoss Application Server. Many of the chapter introductions guide administrators, pointing out the sections on which they should focus.

Roadmap

This book is divided into four parts. Part 1 covers JBoss Application Server (JBoss AS) basics. Here's where you're introduced to the application server, how it's configured, and how applications are deployed; you're also given an overview of security. Part 2 gets into individual Java EE technologies, such as web applications, enterprise applications, and messaging, and describes their configuration in detail. Part 3 covers the JBoss Portal, describing portal administration and configuration. Finally, Part 4 covers topics that you'll want to consider when going into production—things such as performance tuning, clustering, and a whole checklist of other items.

Chapter 1 gives you a 10,000-foot view of JBoss AS by showing you how to download, install, run, and deploy into it. You'll learn about the installation structure and where important server configuration files go. We also provide you with some history and an architectural discussion to give you a broader background on the product.

Chapter 2 provides a first look at configuring the application server. The techniques you learn here will be useful in the chapters that follow. You'll learn how the application server is architected and, from there, how you go about configuring it. The chapter continues by describing various configuration topics not covered elsewhere and concludes with a look at some of the tools you can use to administer the application server.

Chapter 3 discusses deploying applications and contains a discussion of class loaders. From the JBoss forums, we've gleaned some of the common deployment errors that crop up and have provided solutions to those issues. We end the chapter describing how to deploy data sources and Hibernate archives.

Chapter 4 introduces you to security in JBoss AS. We start with a general overview of basic security concepts such as authentication and authorization. We then discuss how these concepts are implemented in JBoss AS. Finally, we show you how to configure security in JBoss, demonstrating how you can access security data from a database, LDAP, or other security datastores. After reading this chapter, you should have a general understanding of how to configure security in JBoss.

Chapter 5 discusses the JBoss AS web application server, known as JBoss Web Server. First, you'll learn how to build and deploy web applications. Then, you'll learn the basics on how to configure web applications and JBoss Web Server. Finally, we build on the basic configuration knowledge to show you a number of practical things that you can configure in your web applications.

Chapter 6 merges the discussions in chapter 4 and chapter 5 to show you how to configure security for web applications. We'll teach you how to use all the standard web authentication models and how to tie them into your own security datastore. We'll also teach you how to use secure public-key communication to encrypt access to your site.

Chapter 7 talks about EJB applications and the EJB server, the heart of JBoss AS. We show you how to structure, deploy, and configure EJB applications. Then, we show you how to configure the application server, enabling you to do things such as change the communication transport and secure EJB applications.

In chapter 8, you'll learn about configuring JBoss Messaging, which is the JMS-compliant messaging server bundled with the JBoss Application Server. The chapter starts off describing JMS and how JBoss Messaging is architected. We present a simple messaging client application and then expand it to include a message-driven EJB and a message-driven POJO. We use this client to describe messaging configuration topics such as changing the messaging store to use another database, defining your own destinations, providing access control, and encrypting messaging data.

Chapter 9 covers JAX-WS–based web services. After a brief introduction into web services, we present a simple POJO-based web service and its client. We expand the example by converting the web service into an EJB, and developing a C# client for the web service. We use the example to describe various configuration topics such as describing the web service using both annotations and descriptor files, configuring access control, and using WS-Security to both encrypt and sign web service messages.

Chapters 10 and 11 provide an introduction into the JBoss Portal. Chapter 10 starts with a description of portals in general and the JBoss Portal in particular. We explain how to install the Portal and set it up to use a database. Then, we provide an example portlet that's a little more complex that the other examples in this book because we want to highlight various portlet coding techniques. We then use the example to describe how to configure the Portal to include the portlet, using both configuration files and the Management Portlet. In chapter 11, you'll learn how to use the Content Management System (CMS) that comes with the JBoss Portal, and how to define access control for your portal and portlets. The chapter ends with a section that puts everything you learn together to create a custom portal.

Chapter 12 introduces clustering in JBoss AS. This chapter talks about the basics of clustering and shows the location of all the configuration files and how to configure the underlying clustering services. You'll set up a simple cluster in this chapter and learn how to configure JGroups and JBoss Cache.

Chapter 13 builds on this background from chapter 12 to show you how to configure clustering for specific services. You'll learn how to configure HTTP load balancing and HTTP session replication, how to cluster session EJBs, how to cluster entities, and how to configure high-availability JNDI.

In chapter 14, we present ways to assess the performance of your deployed applications and practical steps for improving the performance. We examine performance using a holistic approach, looking at tuning the hardware, operating system, database, JVM, application server, and your application. We give detailed information on properly sizing the Java heap, and tips on how to interpret thread dumps to pinpoint performance issues within your code.

We end the book in chapter 15 with a checklist of items you'll want to consider when moving your applications into production. Besides referring you back to prior chapters for topics we've already covered (such as clustering and performance tuning), we cover such topics as selecting the proper platform (operating system, JVM, and application server), running multiple instances of the application server on a single host, slimming the application server by removing services you don't need, securing or removing the default applications, replacing the Hypersonic database with a production-worthy database, configuring the application server to run as a service so that it will start up automatically when the server is booted, and configuring JSP compilation.

Appendix A discusses JNDI. First, you'll learn about how to configure the Environment Naming Context, allowing you to define local names for your resources and beans. Then, we show you how to explore what's in JNDI by using the JMX console.

Appendix B covers last-minute changes to JBoss AS that were made too late to be included in the earlier chapters because they had already gone to the printer. We held off on sending this appendix to the printer for as long as possible to get you all of the latest JBoss AS developments.

Source code conventions and downloads

The source code for the various examples in this book is available for download from www.manning.com/JBossinAction. After downloading the zip file, unzip it, and open the index.html file in the base directory using your favorite browser. (We recommend Firefox.) That file provides all the information you need to build, deploy, and experiment with the examples. And we provide build scripts!

All source code in listings or in text is in a `fixed-width font like this` to separate it from ordinary text. Occasionally, text or commands that should be all on one line are wrapped to two or more lines. In such cases, the continuation lines begin with a continuation character (➥,) as in this example:

```
$JAVA_HOME/bin/java -classpath .:/home/jbia/jars/log4j.jar
➥     org.jbia.example.Client arg1
```

Pay close attention to the continuation characters when used in an XML file listing. Often, the service reading the XML won't trim whitespace characters from the text, causing the text to be misinterpreted. For example, consider the following example XML:

```
<some-stuff>
➥   really great stuff
➥   </some-stuff>
```

You should type it, as follows:

```
<some-stuff>really great stuff</some-stuff>
```

Most example commands are provided in an operating system–neutral fashion rather than showing the command twice, once for Windows and again for Linux. Consider the following generic command:

```
wsrunclient -classpath target/dist/client.jar org.jbia.ws.Client
```

Notice two things: First, we provide the script name without any suffixes or prefixes, and we use forward slashes as directory separators in file names. This command would be entered in Windows as

```
wsrunclient -classpath target\dist\client.jar org.jbia.ws.Client
```

And in Linux as

```
./wsrunclient.sh -classpath target/dist/client.jar org.jbia.ws.Client
```

Unless otherwise specified, all relative paths are within the JBoss Application Server installation directory. In addition, we use the text *xxx* to mean any of the configurations within the server directory. As an example, if you install JBoss AS at c:\jboss-5.0.0.GA, then the text server/xxx/conf/jboss-service.xml refers to the files c:\jboss-5.0.0.GA\server\default\conf\jboss-service.xml, c:\jboss-5.0.0.GA\server\all\conf\jboss-service.xml, and to any similarly located jboss-service.xml files in other configurations you might have in the c:\jboss-5.0.0.GA\server directory.

Code annotations accompany many of the listings, highlighting important concepts. In some cases, numbered bullets link to explanations that follow the listing.

If you have the PDF version of this book, beware of copying example code from the PDF file to a command line or text editor. For example, the dash character (-) within the PDF file is typically not the dash character (ASCII character 0x2D) expected by software. You've been warned.

On versions of JBoss middleware

Writing a book about a version of the JBoss Application Server that hasn't reached general availability (GA) is a calculated risk. When we started this project in the summer of 2006, 4.0.4 was the latest version with talk of the 5.0 version being released early in 2007. We figured that by the time we got the book done, 5.0 would be out. Well, in the spring of 2007, 4.2.0 came out, and 5.0 was only at beta 2. We put the book on hold until 5.0 beta 3 came out; when beta 4 came out soon after, it had so many changes that once again we put the book on hold until CR1, and then verified again on CR2 before starting to send the chapters to the printer.

Although we've endeavored to ensure that the configuration settings we provided will be correct for the final release, there are no guarantees. We recommend that you check the website for the book (www.manning.com/JBossInAction) for any addendums. But, we will ensure that the source download works correctly with JBoss

AS 5.0.0.GA within two or three weeks after it's released. Check the index.html file in the source code download for the exact version that it works with.

JBoss Portal is a different story. The chapters on the portal are based on the 2.6.4.GA release running on JBoss AS 4.2.2, and were later verified with JBoss AS 4.2.3 and Portal 2.7.0. As of this writing, there's no clear roadmap of which version of the Portal will work with JBoss AS 5.0.0.GA. We will put a notice in the Author Online forum when this situation changes.

Author Online

Purchase of *JBoss in Action* includes free access to a private web forum run by Manning Publications where you can make comments about the book, ask technical questions, and receive help from the authors and from other users. To access the forum and subscribe to it, point your web browser to www.manning.com/JBossinAction. This page provides information on how to get on the forum once you're registered, what kind of help is available, and the rules of conduct on the forum.

Manning's commitment to our readers is to provide a venue where a meaningful dialogue between individual readers and between readers and the authors can take place. It isn't a commitment to any specific amount of participation on the part of the authors, whose contributions to the book's forum remain voluntary (and unpaid). We suggest you try asking the authors some challenging questions, lest their interests stray!

The Author Online forum and the archives of previous discussions will be accessible from the publisher's website as long as the book is in print.

About the authors

Javid (pronounced JAW-veed) Jamae has been a programmer his whole life, starting on Applesoft BASIC at a young age and dabbling with a myriad different programming languages before getting paid to write code in Java in the late 90s. Working as a consultant, trainer, and software coach for several years, Javid had the opportunity to work on many different projects in many different industries. Javid has also published many Java-related online and print articles over the last several years. Javid lives in Houston with his wife and three kids and is currently plotting ways to start the next multi-billion-dollar software company.

Peter Johnson started his computer career in 1980 supporting a COBOL accounting package running on a Burroughs mini-computer. He started working in Java in 1998, and was lead designer on projects such as a JDBC driver for the DMSII database that runs on Unisys mainframes. For the past several years, he has been chief architect on a team that analyzes performance of Java applications on large-scale Intel-based machines (8 to 96 CPUs) and evaluates various open source software for enterprise readiness. Peter speaks often about Java performance and JBoss technologies at industry conferences such as the Computer Measurement Group conference, Linux World, and JBoss World.

About the title

By combining introductions, overviews, and how-to examples, the *In Action* books are designed to help learning and remembering. According to research in cognitive science, the things people remember are things they discover during self-motivated exploration.

Although no one at Manning is a cognitive scientist, we are convinced that for learning to become permanent it must pass through stages of exploration, play, and, interestingly, retelling of what is being learned. People understand and remember new things, which is to say they master them, only after actively exploring them. Humans learn *in action*. An essential part of an *In Action* book is that it's example-driven. It encourages the reader to try things out, to play with new code, and explore new ideas.

There is another, more mundane, reason for the title of this book: our readers are busy. They use books to do a job or solve a problem. They need books that allow them to jump in and jump out easily and learn just what they want just when they want it. They need books that aid them *in action*. The books in this series are designed for such readers.

about the cover illustration

The figure on the cover of *JBoss in Action* is a “Sword-bearer to the Grand Signior.” The illustration is taken from a collection of costumes of the Ottoman Empire published on January 1, 1802, by William Miller of Old Bond Street, London. The title page is missing from the collection and we have been unable to track it down to date. The book’s table of contents identifies the figures in both English and French, and each illustration bears the names of two artists who worked on it, both of whom would no doubt be surprised to find their art gracing the front cover of a computer programming book...two hundred years later.

The collection was purchased by a Manning editor at an antiquarian flea market in the “Garage” on West 26th Street in Manhattan. The seller was an American based in Ankara, Turkey, and the transaction took place just as he was packing up his stand for the day. The Manning editor did not have on his person the substantial amount of cash that was required for the purchase and a credit card and check were both politely turned down. With the seller flying back to Ankara that evening the situation was getting hopeless. What was the solution? It turned out to be nothing more than an old-fashioned verbal agreement sealed with a handshake. The seller simply proposed that the money be transferred to him by wire and the editor walked out with the bank information on a piece of paper and the portfolio of images under his arm. Needless to say, we transferred the funds the next day, and we remain grateful and impressed by this unknown person’s trust in one of us. It recalls something that might have happened a long time ago.

The pictures from the Ottoman collection, like the other illustrations that appear on our covers, bring to life the richness and variety of dress customs of two centuries ago. They recall the sense of isolation and distance of that period—and of every other historic period except our own hyperkinetic present.

Dress codes have changed since then and the diversity by region, so rich at the time, has faded away. It is now often hard to tell the inhabitant of one continent from another. Perhaps, trying to view it optimistically, we have traded a cultural and visual diversity for a more varied personal life. Or a more varied and interesting intellectual and technical life.

We at Manning celebrate the inventiveness, the initiative, and, yes, the fun of the computer business with book covers based on the rich diversity of regional life of two centuries ago, brought back to life by the pictures from this collection.

Part 1

The JBoss Application Server

The book is about configuring the JBoss AS and the applications deployed to it. We start the book with a quick introduction into the JBoss Application Server (JBoss AS). Chapter 1 gets you up and running with a simple web application. It also describes the directories and files that are part of the JBoss AS distribution. Those descriptions will come in handy in the following chapters when we look at many of the files and directories in more detail.

Chapters 2 through 4 provide overview information—general things that you'll need to know as you read the rest of the book. Chapter 2 provides an overview of what configuration means within JBoss AS. Chapter 3 covers how to deploy applications; almost all the other chapters rely on this knowledge as you deploy web application, enterprise application, web services, and even portlets. Finally, chapter 4 discusses how security works within JBoss AS. Security is also a topic that we return to time and again in later chapters as we tell you how to secure web applications, EJBs, web services, and so on.

1 Vote for JBoss

This chapter covers

- Installing JBoss AS
- Exploring the JBoss Directory Structure
- Starting and stopping the Server
- Deploying and undeploying applications

In 2005, I (Javid) attended the Houston JBoss User Group meeting to watch a presentation on the Enterprise Java Beans 3.0 (EJB3) specification. The speaker was wearing a T-shirt with *Vote for JBoss* printed across the front. This was a reference to the movie *Napoleon Dynamite,* a cult-hit comedy in which the main character, Napoleon, a nerdy high-school student, sports a shirt with the words *Vote for Pedro* printed on the front to support his friend's campaign for student-council president. Although the T-shirt was intended as a parody of popular culture, it stimulated me to think about the words *Vote for JBoss* more literally.

Voting is part of the democratic process, but the word also has capitalistic significance. In capitalism, people vote with their wallets; so it's easy to vote for JBoss because it has a free, open source license, costing nothing to download, install, and use. Thousands of programmers vote for JBoss every year. As a reader of this book, you're one of those who voted for JBoss and are probably interested in finding out more about the JBoss products and how to work with them.

To open this chapter, we talk about what JBoss is and why it's so popular. The rest of the chapter guides you on how to dive in and get started with the JBoss Application Server (JBoss AS). We discuss how to install, how to start and stop, and how to deploy a basic application into the server. We also explore the structure of the application server and show you how to configure the server to suit your needs.

1.1 Introducing JBoss

When Java first came out in 1996, many people created their own application infrastructures from scratch, reinventing the wheel for many aspects of their applications. The Java 2 Enterprise Edition (J2EE) specification—the predecessor to the current Java EE specification—aimed at creating a standardized application framework for enterprise applications development.

In 1999, Marc Fleury started a small open source project called JBoss, which provided an implementation of the Enterprise Java Bean (EJB) portion of the J2EE specification. As the project became popular, the developers started selling documentation, consulting services, and training. By 2001, Fleury and company incorporated as the JBoss Group, LLC, and started offering developer support services in 2002. In this same timeframe, they made available JBoss AS 3, which emerged to become a full-fledged J2EE application server that was competitive with proprietary application servers such as WebSphere and WebLogic.

NOTE The name of the project was originally EJBoss (Enterprise Java Beans Open Source Software). Sun didn't like the use of their EJB trademark, so the *E* was dropped from the project name, making it *JBoss*.

The JBoss Group, LLC, became a corporation under the name JBoss, Inc., in 2004. With the introduction of JBoss AS 4, JBoss, Inc., started offering production support services for enterprises. JBoss AS 4 has become a popular application server and is still widely deployed throughout the industry. JBoss, Inc., also expanded its offerings to more than an application server. Many of the components that ran within JBoss AS could be run independently outside of JBoss AS, such as JBoss Cache, Hibernate, jBPM, and JBoss Rules.

Red Hat, Inc., bought JBoss, Inc., in April 2006. The popularity of JBoss AS continues to rise with the new and innovative features in JBoss AS 5. Although the majority of this book covers JBoss AS 5, select chapters cover other hot technologies, such as JBoss Portal, that can run on top of the application server.

So what exactly is JBoss, and why do you need it? Let's look at what JBoss is and why it has become so popular in the industry.

1.1.1 What is JBoss?

The word *JBoss* is used to refer to several things: the division of Red Hat that develops software products, the trademark used for all the products that the group makes, and an application server. When people use the term *JBoss,* they're usually referring to JBoss Application Server, commonly abbreviated as JBoss AS. Throughout this book, we use the term *JBoss AS* to refer to JBoss Application Server version 5 or specify if we mean otherwise. In order to avoid confusion between the term JBoss, the application server, and JBoss, the division of Red Hat, we use the term *Red Hat* to refer to the company that makes JBoss products.

JBoss AS is a Java Enterprise Edition 5 (Java EE 5)–compliant application server. A Java application server standardizes the application development architecture. It does this by defining several *component models*—standards that developers can use to develop *components*. These components can be deployed into an application server using a standard *deployment model*. When the components are running in the server, the server provides a set of *services* that are made available to the components.

The application component models include standards such as Enterprise JavaBeans (EJBs), Java Server Pages (JSP), and servlets. Some examples of Java EE services that are available to these components include remoting, security, transaction management, persistence, messaging, resource pooling, concurrency control, naming and directory services, and deployment.

An *application server* is a place to run your Java code. What do we mean by this? Without an application server, you'd write your application code and start your application using a main method. Somewhere in your application you'd need to start all the various services that you might need to access (for example, a database connection pool; a transaction manager; clustering services; security services). The left side of figure 1.1 shows an example of the code you'd have to write to start all the services that you reference.

The left side of the figure shows an application with domain code and code that integrates into various frameworks that provide services to the domain code. In this style, you write code to integrate with the various services and, perhaps, the services themselves.

The right side of the figure shows how things work in an application server environment. With an application server, you write your application code using a standard component model, package it into a standard archive format, and then deploy the archive into the application server, which starts your application and all services that your

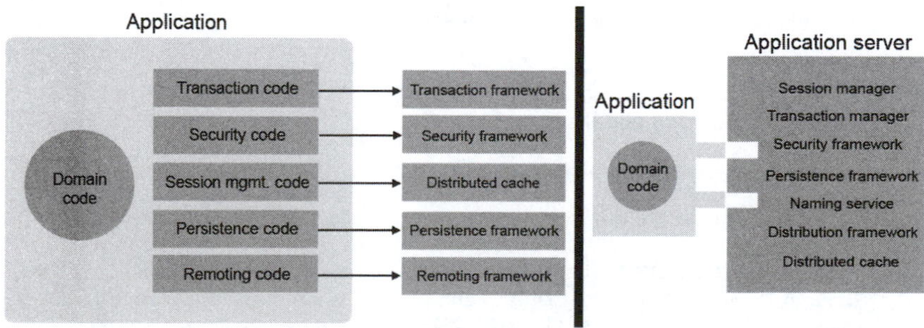

Figure 1.1 The left side shows an application that runs outside of an application server. The right side shows an application that plugs into the application server.

application needs to access. Because you're working within a standardized framework, the services are typically made available to your code transparently. You only have to provide metadata—in the form of annotations or Extensible Markup Language (XML)—to hook the services into your components; no code is typically necessary.

Programming with the Java EE standard and using an application server can drastically reduce the amount of integration code and configuration that you'd otherwise need. In addition, it often prevents you from having to write application services from scratch. Java EE 5 defines many components and services; a list can be found on the Sun website, http://java.sun.com/javaee/technologies/.

Besides JBoss AS, Red Hat provides several software products that you can use either on top of the application server or independently in your own application environment. Let's explore this set of products.

1.1.2 Exploring the JEMS lineup

JBoss AS is the core product in Red Hat's suite of Java middleware products that they collectively call the JBoss Enterprise Middleware Suite (JEMS). All the other JEMS products integrate with the JBoss AS, and many of them can also run outside of the application server in Java SE applications. Table 1.1 summarizes the various JEMS technologies and tells you where you can learn more about them.

Table 1.1 Technologies in Red Hat's JEMS

Technology	Summary	Chapter(s)
JBoss Microcontainer	The configuration framework used to wire together JBoss AS services. The microcontainer can also be used as a general purpose dependency injection framework.	2
Hibernate	An Object-Relational Mapping (ORM) tool used to implement the persistence portion of the EJB3 specification.	3, 7
JBoss SX	A role-based declarative security service used by many JBoss AS services.	4, 6, 7, 8, 11
JBoss Web Server	A fast, native Web server that also enables usage of web technologies such as servlet, JSP, and JavaServer Faces (JSF).	5, 6, 12–13
EJB Server	An implementation of the EJB3 specification.	7
JBoss Messaging	A JSR-914–compliant Java Messaging Service (JMS) messaging server.	8
JBoss Portal	A JSR-168–compliant portal server.	10–11
JBoss Clustering	A self-forming clustering framework.	12–13
JBoss Cache	A transactional, distributed, in-memory cache used by many JBoss AS services.	12–13
JBoss Transactions	A distributed transaction technology supporting Java EE, Common Object Request Broker Architecture (CORBA), and Web Services standards (formerly Arjuna Transaction Service Suite). The JBoss Transactions service is used by many JBoss AS services.	Not covered
JBoss Rules	A JSR-94–compliant rules engine (formerly Drools).	Not covered

Table 1.1 Technologies in Red Hat's JEMS *(continued)*

Technology	Summary	Chapter(s)
jBPM	A full-featured business process management (workflow) engine.	Not covered
Red Hat Developer Studio	A set of plug-ins that extends the Eclipse development platform to enable web application development.	Not covered
Seam	An application integration framework that can reduce boilerplate code used to write many web applications. This framework is the underpinning of the proposed WebBeans Java specification (JSR 299).	Not covered
JBoss AOP	An aspect-oriented-programming framework.	Not covered

Many of these technologies are so involved that they warrant their own books. Unfortunately, we can't cover every technology listed in table 1.1; and those that we do cover can only have one or two chapters dedicated to them. Most of this book focuses on the core application server services and a subset of the most popular products that build on top of it. While we're on the topic of popularity, let's talk about why JBoss AS is so popular.

1.1.3 Why is JBoss AS so popular?

In addition to license costs, the real cost of adopting a new product is a function of many things, including how long it takes to learn, how easy it is to use, the quality of the product, and the quality of support. Companies pay for training and support, so they can survive those last-minute issues that inevitably arise a week before a critical release. Some people even view a free license as a con when evaluating products because of stereotypes that open source software products are low-quality hacks that ultimately result in high cost and risk for the company. "How could it possibly be good if they're giving it away for free?" some may ask.

But JBoss AS doesn't fit this stereotype. More and more companies are choosing JBoss AS as a production application-server platform, and some research (such as that from BZ Research) shows that JBoss AS is a market leader in the Java application server space. Why is JBoss AS so popular?

NOTE Unfortunately, most major market-share research studies have excluded Red Hat's JBoss AS because they generate their statistics based on license sales. Red Hat doesn't charge per license for JBoss AS, making it difficult to compare apples to apples. But a few survey-based research studies have been done that show usage percentages that include JBoss AS. A December 2005 survey by BZ Research concludes that JBoss AS is tied for first with IBM at about 37% each. BEA and Oracle follow at about 27% each. (These numbers add up to more than 100% because some companies use more than one brand of application server.)

We argue that it's not only cost that makes JBoss AS so popular. The success of JBoss AS is a result of producing a competitive product and being open source. You may wonder how one Java EE–compliant application server can compete with another. They're all following the same specification, so how can one be better than another? The same ways that 802.11-compliant wireless router manufacturers and HDTV manufacturers compete: price, features that go above and beyond those defined in the specification, ease of use, time to market, and support.

The Java EE specification standardizes many things, but not everything. JBoss AS has many easy-to-use features that go above and beyond the Java EE specification. For example, setting up a JBoss AS cluster requires minimal configuration. JBoss AS is also good at staying ahead of the curve when new technology specifications come out. For example, JBoss AS has had support for Java SE 5.0 and EJB3 since 2005, while other major players dragged their feet for two or more years.

JBoss AS also has the advantage of being an open source software application. What advantages does Red Hat's open source model give JBoss AS over other proprietary application servers? Consider this: A programmer can download JBoss AS, install it, start it, and deploy an application into it in under 10 minutes, all without worrying about obtaining a license. Programmers find that it's easy to experiment with JBoss AS and learn how to use it. They also love the fact that it's free. Many have never used JBoss AS on a production application but have tinkered around with it out of curiosity or for side projects. They often use JBoss AS to learn how to do Java EE development at home, even though their work environment may be running on a proprietary application server.

Programmers are able not only to play around with JBoss AS but also to have a view into the JBoss AS project's transparent development process. They can view the bug-tracking database, read about designs for upcoming features, and look through the developer forums to see what the lead developers of the different product modules are discussing. They can also look through the code to understand it, to debug issues, or to learn how JBoss AS works. Best of all, they can contribute to the process on several different levels. They can report, comment on, and discuss issues with the developers who are working on them. If there's a bug in a feature of JBoss AS that they're using, they can patch it and submit it for acceptance into a future release. Or, if they're particularly devoted, they can become regular contributors and take on programming tasks.

Because of the participatory nature of open source, large communities form around such popular products. JBoss AS has a large, international community that provides support through user groups, forums, and wikis. It's often easier to find this type of free public support for large open source applications than it is for proprietary applications. Because popular open source products like JBoss AS have a user base that's significantly larger and more involved than proprietary competitors, bugs are often found and patched faster in open source applications than in proprietary applications.

JBoss AS isn't the only open source application server out there. Other open source application servers include WebSphere Community Edition (CE), Geronimo, and GlassFish. All of these have their pros and cons. WebSphere CE and Geronimo are both generally behind the pack as far as adoption of new technologies and specifications, but they do offer strong administration consoles. GlassFish is another Java EE 5–compliant application server, but JBoss AS has been around longer and is considered to be a more mature product in several areas.

Okay, that's enough philosophizing about the virtues of open source. After all, we're geeks and we just want to dive in and start using the technology.

1.2 Installing JBoss Application Server

Installing JBoss AS is simple. When you go to the JBoss AS download site, you have the option to download JBoss AS as a zip file or to install it using an installation wizard, called the JEMS Installer. The fastest and easiest way to install JBoss AS is to download the binary distribution and unzip it to a directory on your machine. This isn't a bad thing to do if you're trying to get a running application server quickly—what the standard installation is intentionally designed for. But this is at the cost of having an installation with all security turned off, and many development-centric features (such as hot deployment) turned on. If you go this route, you have to secure and customize your server's configuration when you're ready to put your server into production.

As we discuss in section 1.3.6, JBoss AS is built on a modular architecture that allows you to run only the particular services that you need for your application environment. Using the JEMS Installer allows you to select only the services that you want running in your server. As we discuss in chapter 15, you can remove services manually (called *slimming* the server), but the installer can make it easier because you don't have to keep track of which services have dependencies on other services. The installer also allows you to secure the prepackaged management applications that ship with JBoss AS.

Whether you use the installer or install JBoss AS from the binary distribution, the nice thing about the JBoss AS installation is that there are no hidden files or settings that end up in places that you don't know about—such as the system registry in Windows. JBoss AS and all of its configuration files are contained entirely under a single directory structure. If you want to uninstall JBoss AS, you delete the entire directory structure. If you want to move the installation somewhere else, you move the entire directory structure. After you have a customized configuration on one machine, it's best to duplicate the existing configuration on other development or production machines rather than trying to manually re-create the configuration or trying to rerun the installer.

As we'll discuss in section 1.3.8, one of the best things to do is to version-control the entire server structure (or at least the configuration directory). If you choose to use the installer, our recommendation is to use it to install JBoss AS on a single machine, customize the server's configuration, version-control the configuration, and then check out the latest configuration on other machines. This helps you ensure that your server configuration is exactly the same across installations.

In this section, we'll discuss how to prepare for installing JBoss AS and how to install JBoss AS using either the binary distribution or the installer.

1.2.1 *Preparing for the installation*

If you have the Java Development Kit (JDK) or Java Runtime Environment (JRE) installed, you're pretty much ready to run JBoss AS. Previous versions of JBoss AS required a JDK because it comes with a Java compiler whereas the JRE doesn't. JBoss AS needs a compiler in order to dynamically compile JSP files at runtime. JBoss AS 5 now ships with a library called the Eclipse JDT (from Eclipse IDE fame) that can compile Java code at runtime; therefore, a JDK isn't required to run JBoss AS 5. That being said, if you install JBoss AS 5 in a development environment, you may need a JDK installed on your machine to develop Java applications if you don't use an IDE, like Eclipse, with its own compiler library.

Most people use Sun's Software Development Kit (SDK), but we discuss how to select a different platform in chapter 15. After installing the JRE or the SDK, the only other thing you need to remember to do is set up an environment variable called `JAVA_HOME` that points to the root directory of your SDK or JRE installation. Depending on how you installed the SDK or JRE, you may already have this environment variable configured. In that case, you're good to go. If you don't, you'll have to learn how to set environment variables for your OS.

For Windows XP systems, right-click My Computer and select the Properties option from the context menu (or hold the Windows key down and press the Pause/Break button). After the System Properties window comes up, click the Advanced tab and then Environment Variables. Figure 1.2 shows you the applicable screens. Setting environment variables on most other versions of Windows is similar to Windows XP.

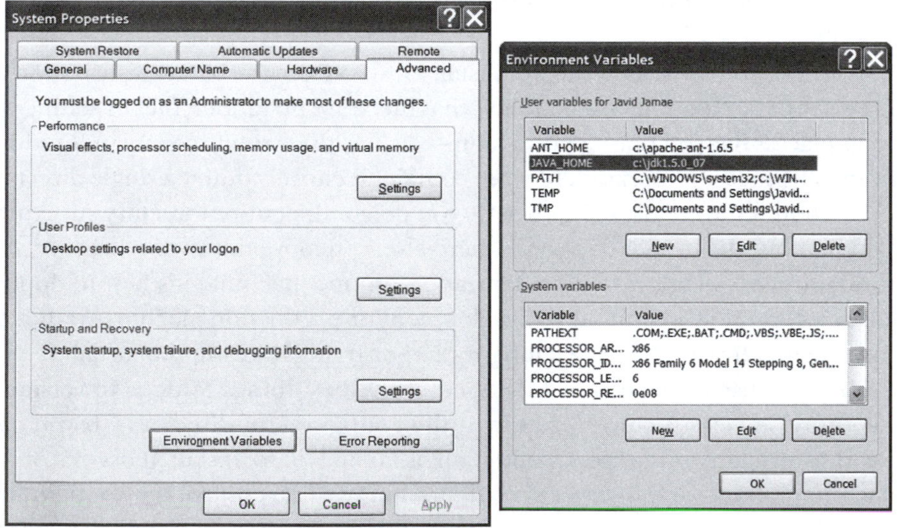

Figure 1.2 You can use the Environment Variables dialog under Windows XP's System Properties to configure the `JAVA_HOME` environment variable.

For UNIX-type systems, add a set command to the startup script that sets up your environment. You might also have to export it, as follows:

```
set JAVA_HOME=/usr/home/jdk1.5.0
export JAVA_HOME
```

After setting the JAVA_HOME directory, you can download either the binaries or the installer for JBoss AS from the JBoss website.

1.2.2 Installing from the binary distribution

Installing from the binary distribution is easy because there's no installation; first, you download the distribution archive (a zip file), and then you unzip it into a directory. That's all that you need to do. You can download the binary distribution from http://labs.jboss.com/jbossas/downloads. If you want to jump ahead, you can start the server by going into the bin directory and executing either the `run.bat` for Windows or the `run.sh` for UNIX. On UNIX you may have to make the shell scripts executable first.

JBoss runs on top of a Java Virtual Machine (JVM), but some things are done better with native operating system functionality. For example, web pages can generally be served with better performance when using native libraries. Running an application as an operating-system service is also more easily accomplished with native support. For these things, JBoss provides a supplementary library called JBoss Native that can be downloaded and unzipped into your application server's bin directory. You can download JBoss Native from http://labs.jboss.com/jbossweb/downloads/.

See the references section at the end of this chapter for links to the JBoss wiki that explain how you can use the JBoss Native library.

1.2.3 Using the JEMS Installer

To download the installer, go to http://labs.jboss.com/jemsinstaller/. From that page you should be able to download the latest JEMS Installer, which comes in the form of an executable JAR file. If your OS's window manager is configured correctly, you can start the installer by double-clicking the JAR file. Otherwise, you may have to specify a program to open it with or execute the JAR from the command line as follows (substituting your specific file version in for the *X.X.X*):

```
java -jar jems-installer-X.X.X.jar
```

Because we're not sure exactly what the order of the screens will be in the JBoss AS 5 installer, we'll just cover some basic things that should be available. First, you should be able to specify an installation directory. Everything that gets installed is relative to this directory; like in the binary installation, you don't have to worry about configuration files and libraries being placed in various places throughout your system. If you install to a Windows machine, the installation path defaults to C:\Program Files (with a space). If you've been programming in Java for a while, you've likely been burned once or twice by libraries or code that had problems working with paths that include spaces. We recommend, out of sheer paranoia, that you change this default to point to a directory that has no spaces in its name.

> **Note**
>
> At the time of writing this book, the installer was unavailable for JBoss AS 5 CR1. We anticipate that the installer will be available with the general availability (GA) release of JBoss AS 5. We assume, based on conversations with the folks at Red Hat, that the installer won't change much between JBoss AS 4 and JBoss AS 5. Also note that JBoss AS 4 didn't include the JBoss Web Server as a web container; it used Tomcat. The difference is that the JBoss Web Server can be configured to use the JBoss Native library for your OS to make the server run faster. The JBoss AS 5 installer may automatically detect your OS and install the appropriate JBoss Native library. Because the installer was not available, we don't cover the installation of the JBoss Native library in this book.

You should also be able to pick the type of server configuration that you want to install, as shown in figure 1.3. A *configuration* is a set of services that runs in your server. You'll notice that you have several configurations to choose from. After you select the configuration, you're given a list of services (called *packs* in the installer) with check boxes next to them. You can use these check boxes to enable or disable individual services. The installer should also allow you to specify a name for you configuration. We talk about server configurations more in section 1.3.6.

If you know what type of database you're going to use, you should be able to configure a data source. This allows you to enter all of your data source driver and connection information and generate a –ds.xml file in your deploy directory. We discuss data sources in chapter 3.

Another thing you should be able to configure with the installer is deployment isolation (also called call-by-value semantics). If you plan on loading different versions of the same class files in different applications running within the application server, then you might want to enable deployment isolation, which causes JBoss AS to keep

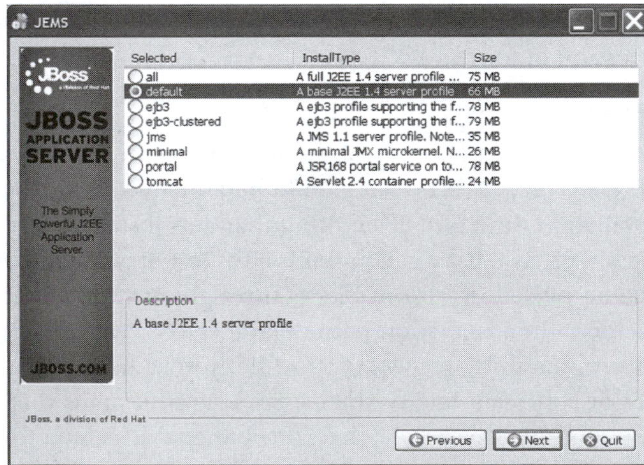

Figure 1.3 Prepared configurations available through the installer

individual class-loading caches for each application and search those caches first before going to the global class-loading repository. This may cause a performance decrease, so you may want to consider running different application server instances for applications that need separate class loaders. If you don't enable this feature, you can still configure an individual application to have an isolated class loader. We take an in-depth look at class loading and how to configure it in chapter 3 (section 3.2).

Another thing you should be able to configure is security. The installer should let you disable or secure various services such as the JMX management consoles and the HTTP tunneling service. By default, most services and applications aren't secured but should be before going to production. We talk about this more in chapter 15.

Whether you've used the binary distribution or the installer, all your JBoss AS files are under one installation directory. If you look in this directory, you'll see that the file structure for the installation is straightforward. Let's walk through it.

1.3 Exploring the installation

All files needed to start and use JBoss AS exist in a single directory structure. Understanding the directory structure makes configuration and deployment easier. It also lays a foundation for the rest of the book, so let's explore it.

Figure 1.4 shows the top-level JBoss AS directory structure.

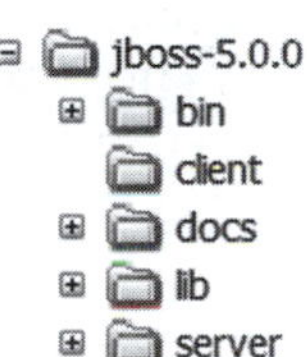

Figure 1.4 The top-level directories in the JBoss AS directory structure

Throughout the rest of the book, we refer to directories under this structure relative to the root directory. For example, there's a directory called default under the server directory in figure 1.4. The default directory has a directory called deploy. We refer to that directory as server/default/deploy.

Let's delve into the contents of each of these directories.

1.3.1 The bin directory

The bin directory contains all the binaries and scripts that you need to start and stop JBoss AS. Section 1.4 covers the details of how to start and stop the server. The scripts are all available in both the Windows .bat format and the UNIX .sh format.

This directory also contains other scripts used for various purposes. Table 1.2 lists these other scripts and tells you where we talk about them.

Table 1.2 Scripts that are available in the bin directory

Script	Description
`twiddle`	A command line Java Management Extension (JMX) client. We discuss this further in chapter 2 (section 2.3.2) and chapter 3 (section 3.1.1)
`probe`	A utility used for discovering JBoss AS clusters. We don't discuss this particular script elsewhere in the book.

Table 1.2 Scripts that are available in the bin directory *(continued)*

Script	Description

`wsconsume`
`wsprovide`
`wsrunclient`
`wstools`
	A series used for Web Services. We talk about these further in chapter 9 (section 9.2.2).

1.3.2 The client directory

The client directory contains libraries that you may need to communicate with JBoss AS from a client application. These libraries aren't loaded by the server directly but by client programs running in a different JVM process than JBoss AS. These applications are often called *standalone clients* or *remote clients*. Standalone clients include most client applications (excluding web browsers). Some examples of remote clients include standalone GUI clients (for example, Swing; Abstract Windows Toolkit, or AWT; and Standard Widget Toolkit, or SWT), remote Web Services clients, remote web containers (like a standalone instance of Tomcat), and JMS clients. Remote clients typically call EJBs, Web Services, or JMS queues and topics that are running on the server.

The libraries in the server's client directory are used by standalone clients to make remote calls to JBoss AS possible. Many web applications never use the libraries in the client directory. This is because the client libraries are generally for remote access to a server. In many web applications, the web-tier code and the EJB code are often collocated in the same server and share the same set of server libraries. Web browsers can communicate with the web tier over HTTP and don't need any of the client libraries packaged with JBoss AS. The web tier can then communicate with the EJB server making local calls because they're both running in the same JVM instance.

If you're running a standalone client application, you have to determine which libraries you need and make them available in your standalone client application's `CLASSPATH` environment variable. Some people choose to include all the Java Archive (JAR) files that are in the client directory in their client class path, whether they need them all or not. This often involves copying them all into the client application's packaging structure or pointing the class path to a JBoss AS installation on the machine with the client code. Another way to do this is to use the jbossall-client.jar JAR file in the client directory. This JAR file contains a META-INF/Manifest.mf file that contains class path references to all the client JAR files, so you only have to include a single client JAR file in your class path. But keep in mind that some IDEs don't handle class path references well (or at all.)

If you don't want to use all the client libraries, you have to rely on your compiler to determine what compile-time class dependencies you have and include the appropriate JAR files from the client directory that have those class files. In addition to the compile-time dependencies, you may also have some runtime dependencies. Those usually surface in the form of a stack trace when you first start your application or while you're testing it. You also have to find the appropriate JAR files for the runtime dependencies and add them to your client's runtime class path. If you need some help locating the JAR file containing a specific class, chapter 3 (section 3.3.1) introduces a utility that can help with this. Again, you might choose to package the libraries that you depend on in your client application's packaging structure or point your class path to a local JBoss AS install on the machine running the client code.

1.3.3 The docs directory

Contrary to many people's first assumptions, there are no user manuals, reference guides, or javadocs for the application server in the docs directory. These have to be downloaded from the jboss.com website as referenced at the end of this chapter. The docs directory contains the following:

- Document Type Definition (DTD) files and XML schemas for the configuration files that JBoss AS uses
- Configuration examples for various J2EE and JBoss AS services
- Licenses for various libraries included in JBoss AS
- Unit test results from the tests run against the server for the particular release

One popular directory under this structure is the docs/examples/jca directory. This directory contains examples of different data source configuration files for different databases. For example, if you're using the MySQL database, you can copy the mysql-ds.xml file from this directory into the server/xxx/deploy directory and modify the data source configuration as described in chapter 3 (section 3.4.1). This will make a MySQL data source available for access in JBoss AS's Java Naming and Directory Interface (JNDI) server.

1.3.4 The lib directory

The lib directory contains libraries that JBoss AS needs to start the core application server. You shouldn't need to put anything in this directory. If you have a library that you want to share across the application server, you can put the library in the lib directory for your server configuration (under the server directory). We talk about this directory further in section 1.3.7.

1.3.5 The server directory

No files exist directly in the server folder, but the directory has one or more subdirectories. Each subdirectory contains what is called a *server configuration.* When you start JBoss AS, you start a particular server configuration. Each configuration contains a set of services and applications that are started when the server starts.

Other application servers have a fixed set of services that run when you start them; but with JBoss AS, you can configure your application server to be as big or as small as you want it to be by adding or removing different services and applications from your configuration.

Each configuration directory has several subdirectories, the main ones being conf, lib, and deploy. Let's try to understand server configurations a little better, and then we'll explore the configuration structure in section 1.3.7.

1.3.6 Understanding server configurations

Many of the leading proprietary application servers come with a fixed set of services that can't be extended or reduced. JBoss AS, on the other hand, isn't an application server with a fixed set of services. JBoss AS is designed to be as big or as small as you want it to be. At its core, JBoss AS is a *microcontainer*, the foundation architecture into which you can plug only the services that your applications need, gaining the advantage of running fewer components on the server. This reduces your server's memory footprint and allows it to start, and perhaps run, faster. Running fewer services also means that you can have less concern for security vulnerabilities due to services that bind to ports on your machine.

Figure 1.5 shows you how the microcontainer runs on top of the JVM and how the various application-server services plug in to the microcontainer. Application code then gets deployed into the server and uses the various services.

When you start JBoss AS, you're always starting a *server configuration*. A server configuration is a directory structure under the application server's server directory that contains code, libraries, and configuration files for a set of services and applications that run when the server starts.

JBoss AS provides you with server configurations that you can use as starting points. You want to pick a server configuration that's closest to your needs and then add, remove, and configure services as necessary. Some of the features that ship with the standard installation are less used and more often removed. We talk about how to remove these services in chapter 15 when we talk about *slimming*, or reducing the size of, the server.

The binary distribution of JBoss AS comes with three configurations: *default*, *minimal*, and *all*. The root of each configuration is a subdirectory under the server directory in the JBoss AS directory structure. As we discuss in section 1.4, when you start JBoss AS using the start script, it starts the default configuration unless you specify otherwise.

Table 1.3 summarizes the three configurations that are available with the binary JBoss AS distribution.

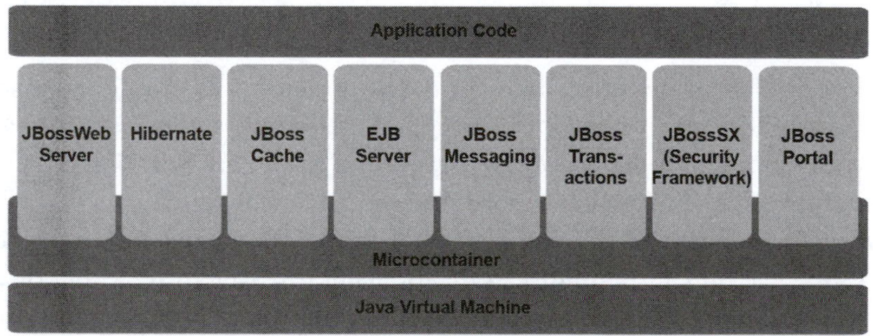

Figure 1.5 Services running on top of the microcontainer

Table 1.3 The three server configurations that ship with the binary distribution of JBoss AS

Configuration	Description
default	Includes all necessary services to bring up a fully compliant Java EE 5 server. This configuration doesn't include clustering services.
minimal	Starts a minimal set of services including the microcontainer, some deployers, and the JNDI service.
all	Starts all services that ship with JBoss AS, including the clustering services.

The configurations that come with the binary distribution can—and should—be customized. The installer creates a customized configuration. We discuss customizing the configuration in section 1.3.8.

Throughout the book we refer to files that could be in one or more server configurations. If a file can only be found in a specific server configuration, we refer to that configuration specifically. For example, the following file can only be found in the *all* server configuration:

server/all/deploy/cluster/cluster-jboss-beans.xml

If the file can be found in multiple server configurations, then we use an *xxx* in place of the server configuration directory when we refer to it. For example, the following file can be found in the *default* and the *all* configurations:

server/xxx/deploy/hsqldb-ds.xml

Now that you understand what the configurations are, let's take a look at what the directory structure for a configuration looks like.

1.3.7 Exploring the configuration structure

There are four main directories under each configuration: conf, deploy, deployers, and lib. Figure 1.6 shows the structure of the default configuration.

Figure 1.6 The directory structure of a server configuration before starting the server for the first time. After you start the server for the first time, several temporary directories are additionally created.

In addition to the directories shown in figure 1.6, the first time you start a configuration, JBoss AS creates several additional directories that contain temporary files and log files. These generated directories are data, log, tmp, and work. Let's walk through each of the existing and generated directories to see what's inside them.

THE CONF DIRECTORY

Each configuration has a conf directory that holds files used for server-wide configuration. Some of the important files that you may need to modify are listed in table 1.4.

This directory is only scanned once, during the server's boot sequence, so any changes that you make here aren't picked up until you restart the server.

Table 1.4 Some of the main configuration files found in the server/xxx/conf directory

File	Description
bootstrap.xml	Defines core microcontainer services that start when the server first starts
jboss-service.xml	Defines core JMX services that start when the server first starts
jboss-log4j.xml	Configures logging, which we discuss further in chapter 2
login-config.xml	Configures authentication and authorization modules for security, which we describe in chapter 4
standardjboss.xml	Used to configure the various EJB containers, which we talk about in chapter 7

THE DEPLOY DIRECTORY

The deploy directory is where applications and services are deployed. This is where you can deploy any application packages—for example, JAR, Web Archive (WAR), or Enterprise Archive (EAR)—that you create. It also means that many services that are running in your server configuration are deployed in this directory.

Deploying applications into JBoss AS involves copying them into the deploy directory. JBoss AS detects deployments made to this directory while the server is running and dynamically deploys the applications to the server. We discuss this further in chapter 3.

THE DEPLOYERS DIRECTORY

The deployers directory contains all the JBoss AS services that are used to recognize and deploy different application and archive types. For example, the ejb3.deployer directory contains libraries and configuration files necessary for starting the service that deploys EJB3 applications that you deploy into the deploy directory. We talk about deployers in chapter 3.

THE LIB DIRECTORY

The lib directory holds server libraries that are shared across all services and applications within a configuration. If you have a library that you want to share across multiple applications within your server, this is a good place to put it. A common example of a library that you'd want to share in this fashion is a database driver. If your library is pertinent to a single application, then you might decide to package it with your application archive.

THE GENERATED DIRECTORIES

JBoss AS generates several directories the first time you start a configuration. These directories are as follows:

- *data*—Used by services and applications that need to write to the file system for storing temporary data. One of the main things that uses this directory is the Hypersonic SQL Database (HSQL DB), which is the default data source that's configured in JBoss AS.
- *log*—Holds three log files: boot.log, server.log, and audit.log. The boot.log file is a temporary log file used to do logging from the time JBoss AS starts until the logging service is enabled, giving you a view into errors that may occur

before the logging service has had a chance to start. The server.log file is the log file that log4j (the main logging service of JBoss AS) is configured to write to. We discuss logging and log4j more in chapter 2. The audit.log file can be found under this directory's security subdirectory. The security service logs all security-related log files to this file to make it easier to audit security error.

- *tmp*—Stores temporary data by various services.
- *work*—Used by JBoss Web Server (the web container that comes prepackaged with JBoss AS) to store compiled JSP files and other temporary data.

1.3.8 Customizing your configuration

If you use the installer, you inherently create your own customized configuration, albeit one that you'll likely configure further after the installation process is complete. As we discussed earlier, while you're going through the installer, you can select a name for your customized configuration. We recommend changing the name to something other than *default* to communicate the fact that the configuration that you've created isn't the default server configuration.

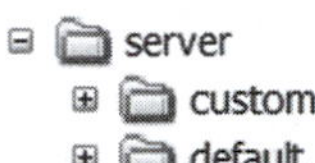

Figure 1.7 To create a custom configuration, start by copying one of the prepackaged configurations under the server directory.

If you've manually installed JBoss AS using the binary distribution, you can create your own configuration by making a copy of one of the prepackaged configuration directories under the server directory. For example, you could copy the *default* directory (and all of its contents recursively) to a directory called custom, as shown in figure 1.7.

This copy can then be modified by changing configuration files or adding and removing applications and services that you may or may not need. Using one of the prepackaged configurations is the quickest way to get up and running, but they have settings that may not be desired in a production environment. For example, a secured management console might slow you down in a development environment, so security is disabled by default; but, you should secure or disable the management consoles when you go into production.

A version control system is a great tool for managing, backing up, and replicating your configuration because it prevents you from having to manually install and customize a configuration in order to run an application in a new environment. Some teams choose to version-control the entire JBoss AS distribution rather than only the configuration directory. This isn't a bad idea because you can ensure that any new machine that you set up has exactly the same environment as that in which you performed your development and testing. Having the entire JBoss AS distribution in version control also lets you go back to old labels that may have run on old versions of JBoss AS.

Many teams keep parallel configuration structures for different environments. You can also create variables for parameters in your configuration that JBoss AS will fill in with system properties provided on the command line or in properties files. We talk about this more in chapter 2.

Now that you have a good background on the contents of the JBoss AS installation, let's learn how you can start and stop the application server.

1.4 Starting and stopping the server

After installing JBoss AS, you can open a console window on your computer and navigate to the bin directory to run the scripts that allow you to start and stop your server. During development, you'll likely start and stop the server from a console window periodically as you make configuration changes. Running in the console window allows you to see logging information as the server starts and runs.

After your application is in a production environment, you don't want the server to go down when you accidentally close a console window or log off a user. In this case, you want to run JBoss AS as a process that runs in the background on your operating platform. In a Windows environment, this is known as running the server as a *Windows Service*. In UNIX, this is known as running it as a *daemon*. We show you how to do this in chapter 15.

Let's discuss how to start the application server.

1.4.1 Starting the server

To start JBoss AS using the default configuration, open a command window and navigate to the bin directory, and then issue the following command:

```
./run.sh     <-- On UNIX
run.bat     <-- On Windows
```

After running the start script, the server logs quite a few messages to the console window. The tail end of the console output should look similar to what is shown in listing 1.1.

Listing 1.1 Output from starting the default configuration

```
16:59:55,102 INFO  [TomcatDeployment] deploy, ctxPath=/, vfsUrl=ROOT.war
16:59:56,258 INFO  [Http11Protocol] Starting Coyote HTTP/1.1 on http-
   127.0.0.1-8080
16:59:56,414 INFO  [AjpProtocol] Starting Coyote AJP/1.3 on ajp-127.0.0.1-
   8009
16:59:56,430 INFO  [ServerImpl] JBoss (Microcontainer) [5.0.0.CR1 (build:
   SVNTag=JBoss_5_0_0_CR1 date=200806301254)] Started in 1m:57s:188ms
```

The last line of the output indicates that the server has started and tells you how long it took to start. This doesn't necessarily mean that every application and service was started successfully. Scrolling back through the output might yield a stack trace or some warn-level or error-level log messages. At this point, with a standard install, there should be no error messages or stack traces when you start JBoss AS. As you can see, it starts relatively quickly when there are no user applications deployed to the server.

NOTE The startup time on JBoss 5.0.0 CR1 was about 54 seconds on a dual-core Intel machine with 2 gigs of RAM that was running Windows. The startup time for JBoss 4.2 was less than 20 seconds. We anticipate that the startup time will improve significantly with either the GA version of JBoss AS 5 or one of the first minor releases that comes out shortly after.

When you try to bring JBoss AS up in a console window, we highly recommend that you bring up the console window first, navigate to the bin directory, and then execute the start script from within a console window. We don't recommend starting any of the scripts in the bin directory by double-clicking them from a GUI.

There are two primary reasons for avoiding this. First, during development, it's useful to see log messages and standard output in a console window. Double-clicking the script may cause it to run without a console window (depending on the way your environment is set up). This means you'd have to pull up the log file in a separate console window or text editor and make sure you have a way to refresh the log file as it's appended to—a popular UNIX command to use is `tail`. Many text editors also have auto-refresh features that detect if the file has been updated and automatically scroll to the bottom of the file.

The second disadvantage to double-clicking the start script from a GUI is that, even if a console window does come up in your environment, terminating the server process may cause the console window to close immediately. This prevents you from scrolling through the console window history to read logging and console output. If you bring up a console window and start the server by manually executing the script, terminating the process will merely take you back to the command prompt, allowing you to still scroll through the history.

Another thing that you may want to do is increase the *scroll buffer* (sometimes called the *screen buffer*) on your console window. This tells the console window how much history to keep as the screen fills up and starts scrolling. Sometimes error messages are accompanied by long stack traces. If your buffer size is inadequate, the beginning of your stack trace may scroll out of your buffer, causing much frustration and hair pulling. If you can afford the memory, set the limit to be infinite or the maximum possible (9999 lines on Windows). But don't panic if important log information scrolls off the screen because you can always pull up the server log file to look back at your output. The logs are in the log directory of the server configuration, which we discussed in section 1.3.7. We talk about how to configure logging in chapter 2.

In this section, we've explored how to start the default configuration. If you create a configuration using a different name or want to run a different prepackaged configuration, you'll have to specify the configuration name when you run the start script. Let's take a look.

1.4.2 Starting an alternative configuration

To start JBoss AS with a configuration other than the default configuration, you have to provide the `-c` parameter to the start script. For example, you start the all configuration as follows:

```
./run.sh -c all      <-- On UNIX
run.bat -c all      <-- On Windows
```

This causes JBoss AS to read all the configuration files it needs from the server's server/all directory. It writes any temporary files to directories under the configuration as well.

TIP Many people initially assume that they can bring up multiple instances of JBoss AS on the same machine by starting two different server configurations in different console windows. Although you do have to start different server configurations, you also have to worry about what OS ports the different services bind to and make sure that they don't conflict. We talk about how to bring up multiple nodes on the same machine in chapter 15.

Now that you've seen how to start both the default configuration and an alternative configuration, let's talk about how to verify that the server is running properly.

1.4.3 Verifying that the server is running

The last line of the output after running the start script gives you an indication that the server has started. Another way to see the application server in action is to navigate to http://localhost:8080/. Figure 1.8 shows you this page, which contains links to useful online resources and some of the prepackaged applications that ship with JBoss AS.

The JBoss Online Resources section gives you a list of useful links from the JBoss AS website. If you have questions about JBoss AS, these are generally good places to look—but only after looking through your copy of *JBoss in Action*, of course.

WARNING When JBoss AS starts up, it binds to *localhost* by default. Older versions of JBoss would bind to the address *0.0.0.0*. Because of this change, you can't access JBoss AS locally by using your machine name. For example, to verify the server is running, you can't go to http://myhostname:8080; you have to go to http://localhost:8080 or http://127.0.0.1:8080. You can also bind your server to a specific IP address when it starts up. See chapter 15 for further discussion on binding.

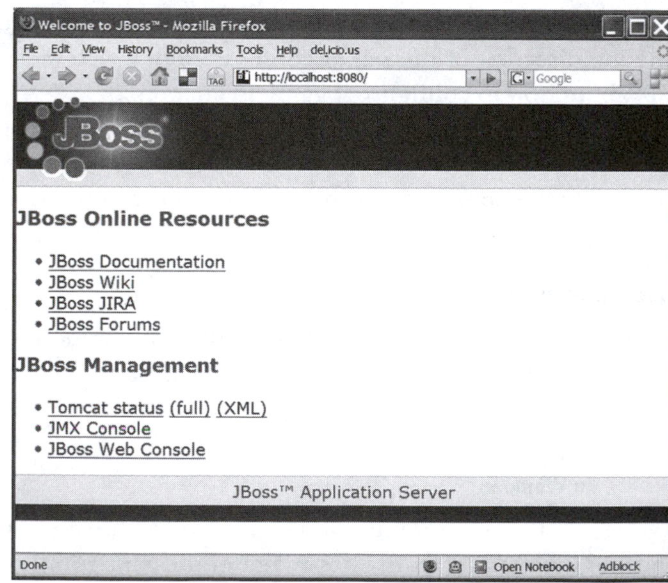

Figure 1.8 You can see the Welcome page from a web browser after the server starts.

The JBoss Management section gives you links to different web-based management applications that come prepackaged with JBoss AS. The Tomcat Status web application gives you status information on the JBoss Web Server, which is built on top of Tomcat. We talk about the JBoss Web Server in chapter 5. The JMX Console gives you a view into the services and applications running on JBoss AS. If you click the JMX Console link, you can try it out. We discuss the JMX Console application in detail in chapter 2.

Now you know how to start the server and verify that it's running. Let's learn how to shut it down.

1.4.4 Stopping the server

Shutting down JBoss AS is as easy as starting it. The shutdown scripts are also in the bin directory. To shutdown JBoss AS, you can run the following command:

```
> ./shutdown.sh -S      <—— On UNIX
> shutdown.bat -S      <—— On Windows
```

If you run JBoss AS in a console window, you have to bring up another console window to execute the shutdown script. If you don't run as a service, you can easily kill the process from the command window by issuing a termination command (Ctrl-C in most OSs). When you do this, JBoss AS executes the same shutdown thread that gets executed by running the shutdown script.

1.5 Deploying to the server

Now you know how to install, start, and stop JBoss AS. But what good is an application server with no applications? After you've written an application, you have to know how to put it into the application server. This is called *deploying* an application to the application server. Deploying and undeploying applications in JBoss AS can be done entirely through filesystem operations. To deploy an application you copy it (or move it) into the deploy directory of the server configuration in which you want the application to run. To undeploy an application, you remove it from the deploy directory. Figure 1.9 shows you where the deploy directory is relative to the server's default configuration.

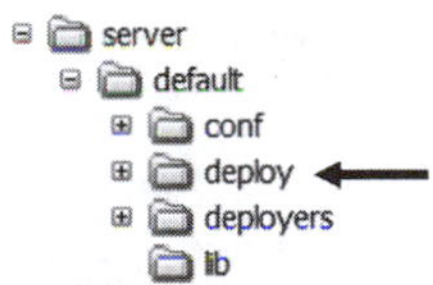

Figure 1.9 You can deploy an application to the server by copying it into the deploy directory, and you can remove an application by deleting it from the deploy directory.

NOTE Unfortunately, one thing that JBoss AS truly lacks is a good administrative console. Most things in JBoss AS are accomplished through filesystem or JMX operations. For example, configuration changes are made by changing flat text files, and you deploy and undeploy through filesystem copy and delete operations or through JMX operations. This can be disheartening for those who lean on GUIs to guide them through these things. Many JBoss AS proponents argue that you don't need the GUI because many activities can be automated by using scripts or build tools that hook into JBoss AS using filesystem or JMX operations.

You can deploy applications to JBoss AS even while it's running; the application server dynamically picks up deployments. In chapter 3, we explore ways to configure the frequency and location at which deployments are scanned.

If you don't have a good grasp on how deployment works, don't worry; chapter 3 is entirely devoted to deployment. At this point we want to get you up and running, so we're more interested in how to deploy an application.

Let's walk through a step-by-step example in which we'll build and deploy a simple Hello World! web application into JBoss AS. After deploying the application, we'll verify that the deployment worked by accessing the application through a web browser. The first thing you need to do is build the application.

1.5.1 Creating the application

The Hello World! application is so simple that it requires only two files: a servlet class and a web configuration file. First, create a directory called helloWorldBuild where you'll build and stage the application. Make this directory structure look like figure 1.10.

Listing 1.2 shows you the source for the `HelloWorldServlet.java` class. Create this class, and put it in the directory structure, as shown in figure 1.10.

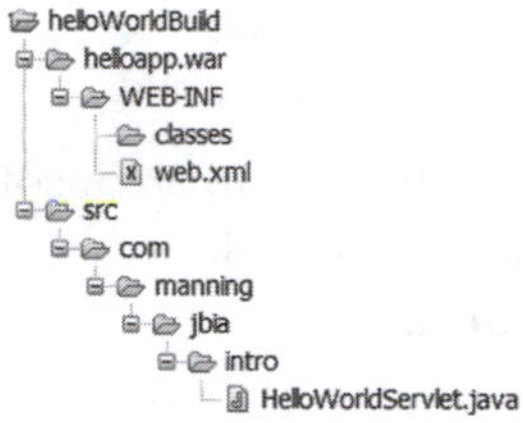

Figure 1.10 The contents of the directory structure you'll use to build the Hello World! application.

Listing 1.2 The source code for the HelloWorldServlet.java servlet

```
package com.manning.jbia.intro;
import java.io.IOException;
import java.io.PrintWriter;
import javax.servlet.ServletException;
import javax.servlet.http.HttpServlet;
import javax.servlet.http.HttpServletRequest;
import javax.servlet.http.HttpServletResponse;
import javax.servlet.http.HttpSession;
@SuppressWarnings("serial")
public class HelloWorldServlet extends HttpServlet
{
  @Override
  public void service( HttpServletRequest request,
                   HttpServletResponse response )
       throws ServletException, IOException {
    PrintWriter out = response.getWriter();
    out.println( "<html><body>Hello World!</body></html>" );
    out.close();
  }
}
```

This file merely prints out the words *Hello World!* in the body of an HTML page that's sent to the user in response to any call to the servlet. The other file that you need to create is the standard deployment descriptor, web.xml, a configuration file that JBoss

AS uses when deploying the web application. Listing 1.3 shows you what the web.xml file looks like for our application.

Listing 1.3 The code for the web.xml file

```
<web-app version="2.5"
      xmlns="http://java.sun.com/xml/ns/javaee"
      xmlns:xsi="http://www.w3.org/2001/XMLSchema-instance"
      xsi:schemaLocation="http://java.sun.com/xml/ns/javaee
         http://java.sun.com/xml/ns/javaee/web-app_2_5.xsd">
  <servlet>
    <servlet-name>Hello Servlet</servlet-name>
    <servlet-class>
      com.manning.jbia.intro.HelloWorldServlet</servlet-class>
  </servlet>
  <servlet-mapping>
    <servlet-name>Hello Servlet</servlet-name>
    <url-pattern>/sayhello</url-pattern>
  </servlet-mapping>
</web-app>
```

Again, create this file, and put it in the directory structure, as shown in figure 1.10. After all the files are in place, pull up a console window, and go to the helloWorldBuild directory. In that directory, execute the following command to build the servlet class (use backslashes if you're running Windows):

```
javac -classpath [path-to-jboss]/server/default/lib/servlet-api.jar -d
➥helloapp.war/WEB-INF/classes src/com/manning/jbia/intro/*
```

Make sure that you replace `[path-to-jboss]` with the path to your JBoss AS installation. After this command runs, the WEB-INF/classes directory should contain the compiled HelloWorldServlet.class file (under its appropriate package).

At this point, the application is built, and you can deploy it into the application server. Let's see how.

1.5.2 Deploying the application

Before deploying the application, pull up another console window and start JBoss AS, as described in section 1.4.1. After the server has started, place the console window so that it's visible in the background of your screen because you'll want to see what happens in the server when the application is deployed.

The helloapp.war directory is an exploded web application package structure. We talk about archived and exploded packaging in chapter 3. You can move this entire directory structure into the deploy directory. You can do this manually through your OS's GUI by dragging and dropping the entire directory structure as shown in figure 1.11.

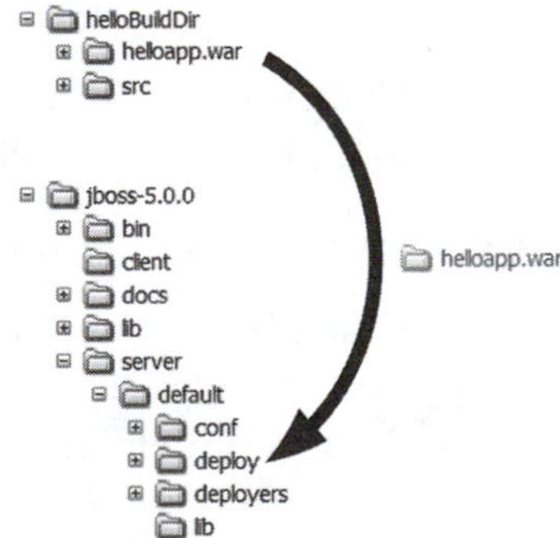

Figure 1.11 You can deploy the sample application by moving the helloapp.war directory into the deploy directory under the default server configuration in JBoss AS.

Remember to keep the JBoss AS server console visible as you do this so that you can see the output when the deployment occurs.

TIP When you copy an application into the server as an exploded directory structure, it's possible for the deployment descriptor to get copied before all the application resources are copied. This can be bad because JBoss AS triggers deployments based on detection of or updates to the deployment descriptor; so, the server may try to deploy an incomplete application. On some OSs, you can avoid this by doing a move rather than a copy because a move is treated as an atomic operation. That means that none of the files is made available until all of them are available. If the server does try to deploy a partially-copied application, then you can redeploy it by updating the appropriate deployment descriptor as we discuss in chapter 3.

You should see some messages in the server console that indicate that JBoss AS automatically detected that the application was put into the deploy directory and deployed it. The console should displayed something like the following:

```
08:36:07,687 INFO  [TomcatDeployment] deploy, ctxPath=/helloapp,
  vfsUrl=helloapp.war
```

Now pull up a web browser and navigate to the following URL:

http://localhost:8080/helloapp/sayhello

The page that pulls up should have the output shown in figure 1.12.

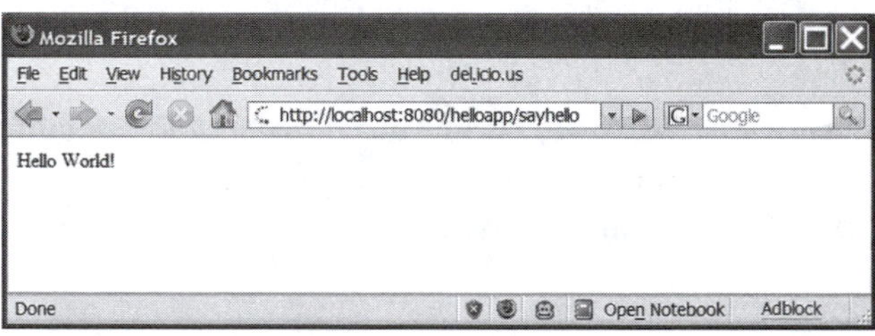

Figure 1.12 After deploying the sample web application, you can navigate to this page to make sure the application is running properly.

Now that you know how to deploy the sample application into the application, let's try to undeploy the application.

1.5.3 Undeploying the application

Undeploying an application is as simple as deploying it. We delete the archive file or exploded directory from the deploy directory. If you delete the helloapp.war file from the server/default/deploy directory while the server is still running, you'll see the following console output:

```
13:27:40,750 INFO  [TomcatDeployer] undeploy, ctxPath=/helloapp,
  vfsUrl=helloapp.war
```

This output tells us that JBoss removed the helloapp.war application from the server.

1.6 Summary

This chapter focused on getting you up and running quickly with JBoss AS in a development environment. We started off by giving you some background on JBoss, explaining what it is, what other products are in JEMS, and looking at why the JBoss products are so popular.

You then learned how to install JBoss. We started by discussing what you needed to obtain before installation, and then explained how to do an installation using both the standard binary distribution and the installer. We compared the tradeoffs between these two installation processes and gave recommendations on the various installation options in the installer.

After installing JBoss, we gave you a tour of the JBoss installation by walking you through the different directories, stopping to examine key files in each. We started at the top level and then dove into the various directories in the server configurations. We explained why you'd want to create your own custom server configuration and walked you through how to do it.

After examining the server structure, we showed how to start and stop JBoss from the command line. We demonstrated how simple it is to start the default server configuration, and then we showed how to start an alternate configuration. Before explaining how to stop the server, we discusses a few things you can do to verify that the server started properly. In chapter 15, we build on this section to show how you can start JBoss as a system service.

Finally, we gave an overview on how to deploy applications into the server by walking you through how to build a simple Hello World! web application and put it in the server configuration's deploy directory. After showing how to test the application, we demonstrated how removing an application involved removing the file from the deploy directory.

Now that you've learned about the structure of the application server, how to start and stop it, and how to deploy and undeploy applications, let's learn more about how to manage and configure the server.

1.7 References

The JBoss AS documentation—http://labs.jboss.com/jbossas/docs

The BZResearch website—http://www.bzresearch.com

"Where Is Open Source in the App Server Surveys?"—http://java.sys-con.com/read/45075.htm

Interview with Marc Fleury on the history of JBoss—http://news.com.com/2008-1082-994819.html

Adding Apache Portable Runtime to a Web Server by installing the JBoss Native library—http://www.jboss.org/community/docs/DOC-9912

Running JBoss as a service on Windows using the JBoss Native library—http://www.jboss.org/community/docs/DOC-11932

2 Managing the JBoss Application Server

This chapter covers

- Examining the JBoss AS architecture
- Configuring JBoss AS
- Examining the administration tools
- Exploring various MBeans

The journey of a thousand miles starts with a single step; this adage from the *Tao Te Ching*, the book central to the Taoist school of Chinese philosophy, describes this chapter fairly well. *JBoss in Action* is all about managing the JBoss Application Server, and in this chapter, you take your first steps in such management, continuing your journey throughout the rest of the book.

JBoss AS provides a good out-of-the-box experience for application developers. You can download the application server, install it, run it, and even deploy applications to it, usually without having to do any configuration changes. It just runs.

After a while, you might want to do things like change the ports used, add new services or remove unwanted services, or change various configuration options; to do this, you need to know where to make such changes. Knowing how the application server is architected will clarify why the configuration is spread out among dozens of files instead of centralized in one location. Therefore, we start with a description of how JBoss AS is architected, and from there look at some files that govern the server configuration.

2.1 Examining the JBoss Application Server architecture

JBoss AS isn't a monolithic application that performs all the functions required of a Java Platform, Enterprise Edition (Java EE)-compliant server. Nor is it a conglomeration of components that provide those functions. Instead, it's a large collection of independent and interdependent components, each of which focuses on a specific area of Java EE functionality.

Earlier versions of JBoss AS were built around a Java Management Extension (JMX) kernel. This kernel provided a basic set of functionality, and all services supplied with the application server were written as Managed Beans (MBeans) that plugged into the JMX kernel. This loosely connected architecture enabled new services to be easily added. In addition, unwanted services could be easily removed. The end result was a customized server that provided only the services you needed, resulting in an efficient use of computer memory and hard drive space.

With the 4.0.3 release, JBoss AS started migrating to a microcontainer architecture. The microcontainer enables new services to be written using Plain Old Java Objects (POJOs) rather than as MBeans. The 5.0 release of JBoss AS takes a major step on the migration path, with the microcontainer being a visible component of the architecture.

NOTE Martin Fowler describes the origin of the term *POJO* in this way: "The term was coined while Rebecca Parsons, Josh MacKenzie and I were preparing for a talk at a conference in September 2000. In the talk we were pointing out the many benefits of encoding business logic into regular Java objects rather than using Entity Beans. We wondered why people were so against using regular objects in their systems and concluded that it was because simple objects lacked a fancy name. So we gave them one, and it's caught on very nicely."

Because the 5.0 release uses the microcontainer-based architecture, we describe that first and, after that, look into JMX. You'll find that JMX still plays a significant role in the application server.

2.1.1 Understanding the microcontainer

The JBoss Microcontainer is a dependency injection framework similar to the Spring Framework. With it you can do the following tasks (among others):

- Specify objects to be instantiated
- Provide constructor parameters when instantiating objects
- List property values to set (such as object A has a property which is a reference to object B)
- Specify dependencies among objects (such as object X must be created before object Y)

This new microcontainer architecture has several benefits over the old JMX kernel architecture. First, it's much lighter because it doesn't have to support JMX, allowing you to build even smaller minimal configurations. Second, services built on top of the microcontainer can be deployed standalone, within another application server such as BEA's WebLogic Server, or even within a web server such as Tomcat. For example, the EJB3 container could be deployed on the Tomcat web server because the EJB3 container is based on the microcontainer.

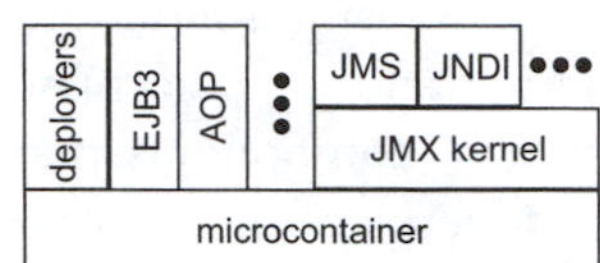

Figure 2.1 A simplified view of the JBoss AS 5.0 architecture, showing several services that rely only on the microcontainer and other services that still rely on JMX

Because not all services have been ported to the microcontainer, the JMX kernel still plays a major role in the architecture, as illustrated in figure 2.1. The JMX kernel is one of the primary POJOs defined to, and created by, the microcontainer.

Eventually, in some future release, JBoss AS will be entirely microcontainer based and have an architecture similar to that shown in figure 2.2. JMX is transitioning from being the underlying architecture of the application server to one of the services deployed to the microcontainer to manage and monitor components.

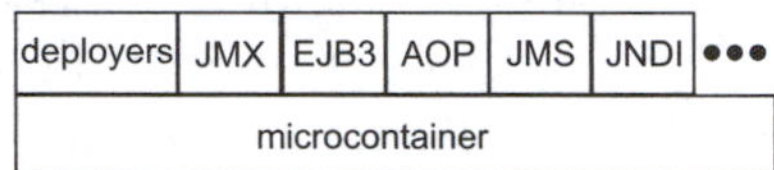

Figure 2.2 A simplified view of the eventual JBoss AS architecture, showing how all services will rely entirely on the microcontainer

UNDERSTANDING THE BEANS CONFIGURATION FILE

You can use bean configuration files in the server/xxx/conf directory to configure the microcontainer. Most bean configuration files follow the pattern *-jboss-beans.xml, but the bean primary configuration files found in the server/xxx/conf directory don't follow this pattern. An excerpt from the server/xxx/conf/profile.xml file, which highlights many of the bean definition capabilities of the microcontainer, appears in listing 2.1.

Listing 2.1 Excerpt from profile.xml file

```
<deployment xmlns="urn:jboss:bean-deployer:2.0">
 ...
 <bean name="ProfileService"                    ❶
       class="org.jboss.system.server.profileservice.     ❷
➥     basic.MetaDataAwareProfileService">
  <constructor>
   <parameter>...</parameter>                          ❸
  </constructor>
    <property name="profileRoot">                      ❹
➥   ${jboss.server.home.dir}</property>
  ...
 </bean>
...
 <bean name="VFSDeployerScanner" class="...">
  <property name="profileService"><inject bean="ProfileService"/>     ❺
  </property>
```

```
    <property name="URIList">
     <list elementClass="java.net.URI">
      <value>${jboss.server.home.url}deployers/</value>      ❻
     </list>
    </property>
   </bean>
   ...
  </deployment>
```

The profile.xml configuration file declares multiple beans using the `<bean>` tag. Each bean has a name ❶ and a class that implements the bean ❷. You can use constructor injection to specify parameters to pass to the constructor when the bean is created ❸, setter injection to specify initial values for bean properties, or both for the standard data types ❹ and for collections ❻. In addition, you can specify that one bean references another using the `<inject>` tag to inject a bean as either an initial property value ❺ or as a parameter to a constructor (not shown).

EXAMINING THE MICROCONTAINER CONFIGURATION FILE

The primary beans configuration file for the application server is located at server/xxx/conf/bootstrap.xml. This file includes other bean configuration files, which in turn define a series of POJOs or JavaBeans that provide services such as the following:

- *The Profile Service*—Provides basic profiling information on the loading of services. For example, the Profile Service provides the "Started in 99s.999m" message in the output log when the application server has fully started.
- *The JMX Kernel*—Implements the JMX kernel.
- *Several beans related to the deployers*—Include the Main Deployer, which manages all the deployers.

2.1.2 Understanding JMX

The JMX specification, defined by Java Specification Request 3 (JSR 3), concerns managed JavaBeans, or MBeans. To create an MBean, all you need to do is define an interface and a class that implements the interface (the specification states the interface must be named XxxMBean and the class named Xxx, where Xxx is any name). Once an instance is created, it can be registered by name with the MBean server.

Once registered, any JMX client can access the MBean by name via the MBean server. In addition, the JMX client can request information about the MBean and can make requests to the MBean, but only through the MBean server. Note that the client never accesses the MBean. This interaction is illustrated in figure 2.3.

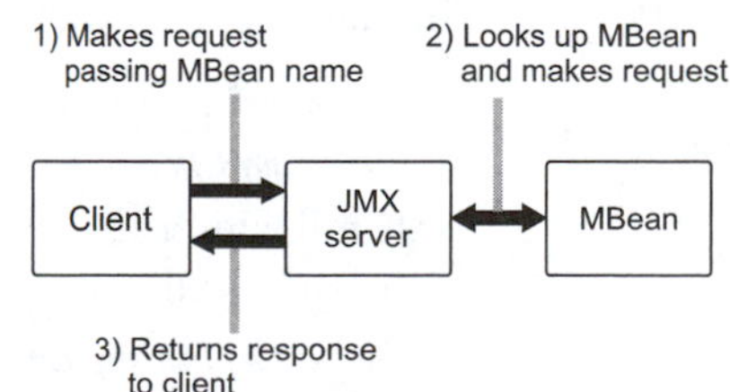

Figure 2.3 Accessing an MBean via the JMX server

In the application server, the service deployer instantiates the MBeans, based on the contents of the jboss-service.xml file that accompanies the service or the various *-service.xml files that appear in the deploy directory, and registers the MBeans with the MBean server provided by the application server. Other applications, including other services, can then access the services of those MBeans via the MBean server. This mechanism provides for loosely coupled services that can be easily replaced.

UNDERSTANDING MBEAN NAMES

We mentioned that MBeans get registered by name and that clients can look them up by name, but we've not yet defined what an MBean name is. It's not a simple text string. Instead, it's a multipart name consisting of the following:

- A domain (similar to a package name for a Java class)
- One or more key properties (each of which is a key value pair)

When expressed as a string, the name starts with the domain, followed by a colon, followed by the key properties separated by commas. Figure 2.4 illustrates an example MBean name written as a string.

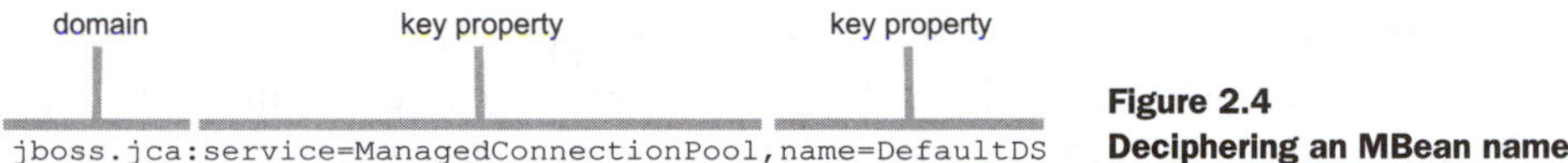

Figure 2.4 Deciphering an MBean name

Note that the ordering of the key properties is irrelevant. The following text strings, when used as MBean names, denote the same MBean:

```
jboss.jca:service=ManagedConnectionPool,name=DefaultDS
jboss.jca:name=DefaultDS,service=ManagedConnectionPool
```

Now that you have some background about MBeans, let's look at the primary descriptor file used by JBoss AS to define MBeans and, indirectly, to declare services.

EXAMINING THE JMX KERNEL DESCRIPTOR FILE

The server/xxx/conf/jboss-service.xml file is the primary descriptor file used to declare MBeans to the JMX kernel. This file, and its layout, is specific to JBoss AS. You can use a different descriptor file by setting the `jboss.server.root.deployment.filename` system property to the filename and setting the `jboss.server.config.url` system property to the directory containing that file. Note that, if you do the latter, all configuration files that typically appear in the server/xxx/conf directory must appear in the directory specified by `jboss.server.config.url`.

The jboss-service.xml file defines a number of MBeans, including the following:

- *The logging service.*
- *The thread pool*—Used to supply threads to run the various services. You can easily tell which services use the thread pool by noting the `ThreadPool` property on the other MBeans.
- *The Java Naming and Directory Interface (JNDI)*.
- *Various MBeans for managing security*—Include Java Authentication and Authorization Service (JAAS).

- *Various MBeans related to accessing JMX services.*
- *Various MBeans related to the remoting service*—Enable remote access to local services. These services play a role in almost all remote access to the application server, including messaging and EJB access.

2.2 Configuring the application server

Besides the jboss-service.xml file covered in the previous section, services deployed to the application server can embed a META-INF/jboss-service.xml into their archives or a separate *-service.xml file that declares the MBeans for that service. For example, the Universally Unique ID (UUID) generator defines its MBeans in the server/xxx/deploy/uuid-key-generator.sar/META-INF/jboss-service.xml file. As another example, the various *-service.xml files found in the server/xxx/deploy/messaging directory define the MBeans used by the messaging service.

These configuration files aren't the only ones used to configure services. Each service can define its own configuration file(s), beyond the XML files used to define the MBeans for the service. For example, the server/xxx/conf directory contains many configuration files, which are described in table 2.1.

Table 2.1 Files in the conf directory

File	Description
bootstrap.xml	Used by the microcontainer to load the initial set of POJOs. This file is a master file that includes the following files: aop.xml, classloader.xml, deployers.xml, jmx.xml, and profile.xml.
jacorb.properties	Used to configure the Java Object Request Broker (JacORB) service, which is used when clustering application servers.
jax-ws-catalog.xml	Used to map XML metadata names to local metadata descriptor files—both Document Type Definition (DTD) and XML Schema Definition Language (XSD)—in the docs/dtd and docs/schema directories. This is a required catalog to support Java API for XML-based Web Services (JAX-WS).
jbossjta-properties.xml	Used to configure the Java Transaction API (JTA) service.
jboss-log4j.xml	Used by the logging service to define the logging settings.
jboss-minimal.xml	A variation of the jboss-service.xml file configured for a minimal application server configuration. This file is never used.
jboss-service.xml	Used by the JMX kernel.
jndi.properties	Used by the JNDI service to define default properties.
login-config.xml	Used by the security service to define login modules.
standardjboss.xml	Used by the EJB service to define configuration settings.
standardjbosscmp-jdbc.cmp	Used by the EJB service to define type mappings for various databases for use with Container Managed Persistence (CMP) for EJB 2.x entity beans.

We cover many of the configuration files in other chapters in this book, but there are a few that we don't cover later that are worth looking at here. The topics we examine include configuring logging, configuring directory locations using system properties, and defining additional system properties.

2.2.1 Configuring logging

The application server uses log4j, an open source logging framework, to do logging. The log4j configuration file is located at server/xxx/conf/jboss-log4j.xml.

By default, two appenders are defined: one for the console, which is set to log entries identified as level info or higher priority, such as warning and error entries; and one for the server/xxx/log/server.log file, which is set to log all levels. In addition, various category settings define the trace level for various packages to limit the amount of logging accomplished.

Some of the logging configuration changes that you might want to make include the following:

- Specifying a rolling log file
- Limiting the amount of logging produced
- Adding logging for your application
- Defining a new log file

Each of these topics is covered in the following text.

ROLLING THE SERVER LOG FILE

The server.log file is created new each time the server is launched, and grows until the server is stopped or until midnight. This behavior, although appropriate for a development environment, isn't optimal for a production environment. In production, you should specify a rolling log file that creates a new log file when it reaches a certain size. Listing 2.2 shows how you can change the appender for the server.log file to create, at most, 20 log files of 10 megabytes (MB) in size each. All the changes are highlighted.

Listing 2.2 Defining a rolling log appender

```
<log4j:...>
 <appender name="FILE"
class="org.jboss.logging.appender.RollingFileAppender">     <- Uses rolling appender
 <errorHandler .../>
 <param name="File"                                         (1) Location of log file
 value="${jboss.server.log.dir}/server.log"/>
 <param name="Append" value="true"/>                        <- Appends to existing file on startup
 <param name="MaxFileSize" value="10MB"/>                   <- Limits log file size to 10 MB
 <param name="MaxBackupIndex" value="20"/>                  <- Keeps only last 20 log files
 <layout .../>
 </appender>
 ...
</log4j>
```

We didn't change the `errorHandler` or `layout` settings from the default. By the way, the various appenders defined in the `org.jboss.logging.appender` package are simple subclasses of the log4j appenders defined in the org.apache.log4j package that automatically create the server/xxx/log directory.

The system property jboss.server.log.dir defines the location of the log file ❶.

LIMITING LOGGING

If the server log file grows too rapidly, or you want to suppress messages displayed on the console log, you can change the logging options to reduce the amount of logging.

As an example, assume that your application uses Hibernate. You might find that the log file quickly grows in size, reaching way over 100 MB within minutes. Looking at the log file, you see many log entries that look like those in listing 2.3.

Listing 2.3 Too much logging

```
2007-... DEBUG [org.hibernate.transaction.JTATransaction] commit...
2007-... DEBUG [org.hibernate.jdbc.JDBCContext] successfully ...
2007-... DEBUG [org.hibernate.impl.SessionImpl] opened session ...
2007-... DEBUG [org.hibernate.transaction.JTATransaction] Looking...
```

You can easily prevent the log from containing these entries by editing the jboss-log4j.xml file. As shown in listing 2.4, you can prevent the log from containing these DEBUG entries by adding a new category entry to the jboss-log4j.xml file and setting the priority to INFO.

Listing 2.4 Shrinking the log file

```
<log4j:configuration ...>
 . . .
 <category name="org.hibernate">        <-- ❶ Identifies package to log
  <priority value="INFO"/>              <-- Suppresses DEBUG log entries
 </category>
 . . .
</log4j:configuration
```

The category name ❶ comes from the name between brackets in the log file. Note that, in the log entries presented, this name begins with org.hibernate. If you, instead, wanted to remove the transaction-related logging output, use a category name of org.hibernate.transaction.

You can add similar category entries to remove other output from the log or to reduce the level of logging performed by one of the services. For example, to set logging from JBoss Messaging to the warning level or higher, add the following categories to the jboss-log4j.xml file, as shown in listing 2.5.

Listing 2.5 Limiting messaging logging to warning or higher

```
<log4j:...>
 ...
 <category name="org.jboss.messaging">
  <priority value="WARN"/>
 </category>
 <category name="org.jboss.jms">
```

```
  <priority value="WARN"/>
 </category>
</log4j>
```

Note that JBoss Messaging uses two primary packages, meaning we had to declare two categories. How did we know this? We looked at the class names for the entries that appeared in the server log. Although the server log shows the full package and class name, the console log shows only the class name; therefore, you should always use the names in the server log to determine the logging category names.

Finally, you can limit what logging information shows up in a log file or on the console by changing the value of the `Threshold` parameter for an appender. For example, you can limit the console log output to errors by changing the jboss-log4j.xml file as shown in listing 2.6.

Listing 2.6 Limiting console logging to the error level

```
<log4j:...>
 ...
 <appender name="CONSOLE" ...>
  ...
  <param name="Threshold" value="ERROR"/>
 </appender>
 ...
</log4j>
```

Conversely, if you want all logging information to show up on the console, you could change the level to `TRACE`, or even remove the `Threshold` parameter entirely.

LOGGING YOUR APPLICATION

If you use log4j or Apache Jakarta Commons Logging within your application, you can log your application by adding category entries to the jboss-log4j.xml file. For example, if your application uses the package name `org.jbia`, you can log the classes in that package and its subpackages by adding a category to the jboss-log4j.xml file, as shown in listing 2.7.

Listing 2.7 Defining logging for your application

```
<log4j:...>
 ...
 <category name="org.jbia">
  <priority value="DEBUG"/>
 </category>
</log4j>
```

The debug—and higher—messages show up in the server.log file, and the info—and higher—messages show up in the console log.

DEFINING A SPECIFIC LOG

In one way, the server.log file is great because all the log information is in a single location. But the downside is that, at times, searching for data within it is akin to finding a needle in a haystack. There are times when you'd like to log specific messages to a particular file. For example, suppose you want to log all info messages from all classes in the `org.jbia` package to a file named jbia.log. Listing 2.8 shows the entries you need to add to the jboss-log4j.xml file to accomplish this task.

Listing 2.8 Creating a log file specific to an application

```
<log4j:...>
 ...
 <appender name="JBIA" ...>                    ❶
  ...
  <param name="File"
   value="${jboss.server.log.dir}/jbia.log"/>  ❷
  ...
 </appender>
 ...
 <category name="org.jbia">                    ❸
  <priority value="DEBUG"/>                    ❹
  <appender-ref ref="JBIA" />                  ❺
 </category>
</log4j>
```

We give the appender a unique name, `JBIA` in this example ❶, so that we can reference it later. The `File` parameter identifies the log file name ❷. We specify the category ❸ and priority ❹ to identify what we want to log, and then we reference the appender ❺ that we named earlier ❶. We did not provide the entire appender configuration as it's the same as for the `FILE` appender that already appears in the jboss-log4j.xml file, except the name attribute is set to `JBIA` instead of `FILE`.

These examples are some of the things you can accomplish with changing the logging configuration. To find out everything that you could do, refer to the log4j documentation or obtain a book on log4j.

2.2.2 Configuring directory locations

In chapter 1, we described the various default directories used by the application server; you *can* change those locations. Table 2.2 lists various system properties that define those locations, specifies the default value for each directory, and describes the purpose of that directory.

Table 2.2 System properties that define directory locations

Property	Default location	Description
`jboss.home.dir`	-installation directory- Examples: /opt/jboss-5.0.0.GA c:\jboss-5.0.0.GA	Directory where the application server is installed. This is a read-only property and can't be set from the command line.
`jboss.home.url1`	-installation directory- Examples: file://opt/jboss-5.0.0/ file:/c:/jboss-5.0.0.GA/	URL variant of jboss.home.dir.

Table 2.2 System properties that define directory locations *(continued)*

Property	Default location	Description
`jboss.lib.url`	<jboss.home.url>lib/	The directory containing JAR files used to bootstrap the application server.
`jboss.patch.url`	-none-	Directory, or file, containing patches to the application server classes. The class loaders will look for classes in this location first before accessing the JAR files in the lib or server/xxx/lib directory.
`jboss.server.base.dir`	<jboss.home.dir>/server	The directory containing the server configuration directories.
`jboss.server.base.url`	<jboss.home.url>server/	URL variant of jboss.server.base.dir.
`jboss.server.home.dir`	<jboss.server.base.dir>/default	The directory containing the server configuration being run.
`jboss.server.home.url`	<jboss.server.base.url>default/	URL variant of jboss.server.home.dir.
`jboss.server.config.url`	<jboss.server.home.url>conf/	The directory containing configuration information.
`jboss.server.data.dir`	<jboss.server.home.dir>/data	The directory where application-specific data is kept.
`jboss.server.lib.url`	<jboss.server.home.url>lib/	The directory containing JAR files used by the application server.
`jboss.server.log.dir`	<jboss.server.home.dir>/log	The directory where the server log is placed.
`jboss.server.temp.dir`	<jboss.server.home.dir>/tmp	The directory used as a temporary work area.

Some locations have both a *dir* and a *url* variant; if you want to change the location of such a directory, you should set both properties. For example, to change the location of the server directory, you must set both the `jboss.server.base.dir` and the `jboss.server.base.url` system properties. You can change any of the locations by providing the system property on the command line or by editing the run script file. For example, you could change the location of the log file to place it on another disk by using this command:

```
run -Djboss.server.log.dir=d:/log
```

In addition, the application server uses other system properties of interest, which are given in table 2.3.

Table 2.3 Other system properties

Property	Default value	Description
`jboss.server.name`	default	The name of the server configuration. This property corresponds to the value of the `-c` option to the run script.
`jboss.bind.address`	127.0.0.1	The IP address to which the application server is bound. This property corresponds to the value of the `-b` option to the run script.

You can query the system properties from your application. For example, if you need to keep a file containing data somewhere, you can get the `jboss.server.data.dir` system property and then save your data file within a directory under that location.

2.2.3 Defining system properties

Some properties that are kept in XML configuration files might change based on the environment in which you're running. For this reason, the application server provides support for variable substitution in configuration files. This means that a configuration file can use a variable in place of providing a value for a given configuration property. Then, when the configuration file is loaded by the application server, it substitutes the variable with the value that was provided for the variable. A common use of this capability is to reference the various system properties defined in the previous section.

Variables take the following form:

```
${some.property.name:the_default_value}
```

This means that the value of the property is `some.property.name`, and if no property is provided by the user, the value `the_default_value` will be used as a default. The system properties can be provided by the user when the application server is started by using the `-D` option as follows:

```
./run.sh -Dsome.property.name=8000
```

In addition, you can set system property values in the run.conf and run.bat script files.

System properties can also be provided using the System Properties Service. This service enables you to list several system properties in the server/xxx/deploy/properties-service.xml configuration file or to load system properties from one or more .properties files. Listing 2.9 shows an example configuration.

Listing 2.9 Configuring the System Properties Service

```
<mbean code="org.jboss.varia.property.SystemPropertiesService"
     name="jboss:type=Service,name=SystemProperties">
  <attribute name="URLList">
    http://somehost/some-location.properties,
    ./conf/somelocal.properties
  </attribute>
  <attribute name="Properties">
    first.property=This is the first value
    second.property=This is the second value
  </attribute>
</mbean>
```

❶ Locations of properties files

❷ Defines system properties

The `URLList` attribute block ❶ points to properties files that contain system properties. You can provide a URL or a directory relative to the root of the server configuration. If you provide multiple entries, separate them with commas.

The `Properties` attribute block ❷ configures properties directly in the service configuration. Each property must be specified as a name/value pair on a separate line.

So far, we have presented all configurations as text files, so if you want to make any configuration changes, you have to use a text editor. But JBoss AS comes with several tools you can use to modify the configuration using JMX. We cover those tools next.

2.3 Exploring the management tools

JBoss AS comes with several tools you can use to modify the configuration, such as the JMX Console and twiddle. These tools are generic JMX tools used to view and modify MBeans.

Another alternative, which we don't cover in this book, is the JBoss Operations Network (JBoss ON), which is a web-based tool that provides a single point of administration for an enterprise that has deployed JBoss AS. You can use JBoss ON to monitor things such as multiple application servers, multiple Tomcat servers, and even the systems on which the servers are running. JBoss ON is available only with a paid JBoss AS support subscription.

JBoss AS 5.0 has a new administration console which is a subset of the administration functionality found in JBoss ON. You can use this administration console to configure data sources and message destinations. We don't cover the administration console in this book because, as of this writing (JBoss AS 5.0.0.CR2 is the current version), the administration console still isn't available. The administration console will either come with JBoss AS 5.0.0.GA or will be available as a separate download.

2.3.1 Using the JMX Console

The most useful tool from a developer's perspective is the JMX Console, a web application that can read, display, and update MBeans. To access the JMX Console, when an application server is running, enter the following URL into a browser:

http://localhost:8080/jmx-console

The main page of the JMX Console, also known as the *agent* view, lists all the MBeans registered to the application server (see figure 2.5). Note that the MBeans are grouped by namespace.

Each MBean is listed as a link which, when clicked, displays details about that MBean. For example, figure 2.6 shows the data displayed for the connection pool for the `DefaultDS` data source.

The top half of the MBean details page displays a table listing the property values for the MBean. If a property is writeable, the value is presented in a form field. You can change the value and click the Apply Changes button at the bottom of the table to change the value of the property.

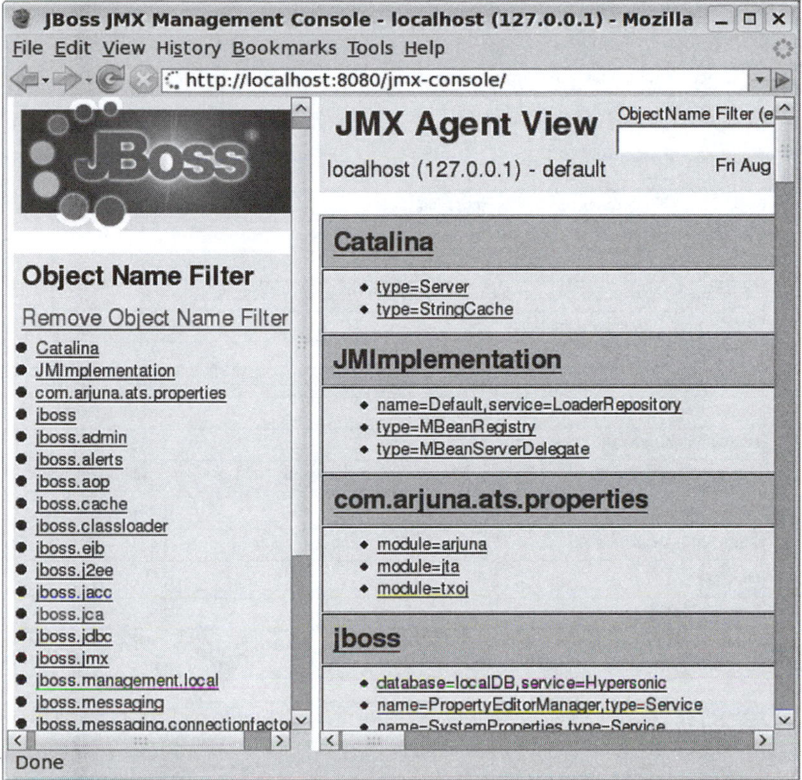

Figure 2.5 The JMX Console main page, showing some of the accessible MBeans

The bottom half of the MBean details page displays a table containing the various operations supported by the MBean. There's an Invoke button for each operation that, when clicked, invokes the operation. If the operation accepts parameters, a list of parameters is presented with fields where you can enter in each parameter value; object-valued parameters can't be entered, but you can enter almost anything else.

WARNING Needless to say, the ability to invoke any MBean operation gives you great power. But as Spiderman learned, with great power comes great responsibility. Make sure you understand the ramifications of invoking an operation before you do so. You wouldn't want to, for example, invoke the `halt` operation on the `jboss.system:type=Server` MBean unless you wanted to stop the application server.

Although the JMX Console is a convenient tool for a developer, it's not an adequate tool for managing the application server. For example, a single data source is represented by four MBeans, each of which appears in the agent view with different links; there's no single page from which a data source can be managed.

Additionally, any changes made using the JMX Console are transient. If you restart the application server, all changes are lost. This is because the JMX Console only calls

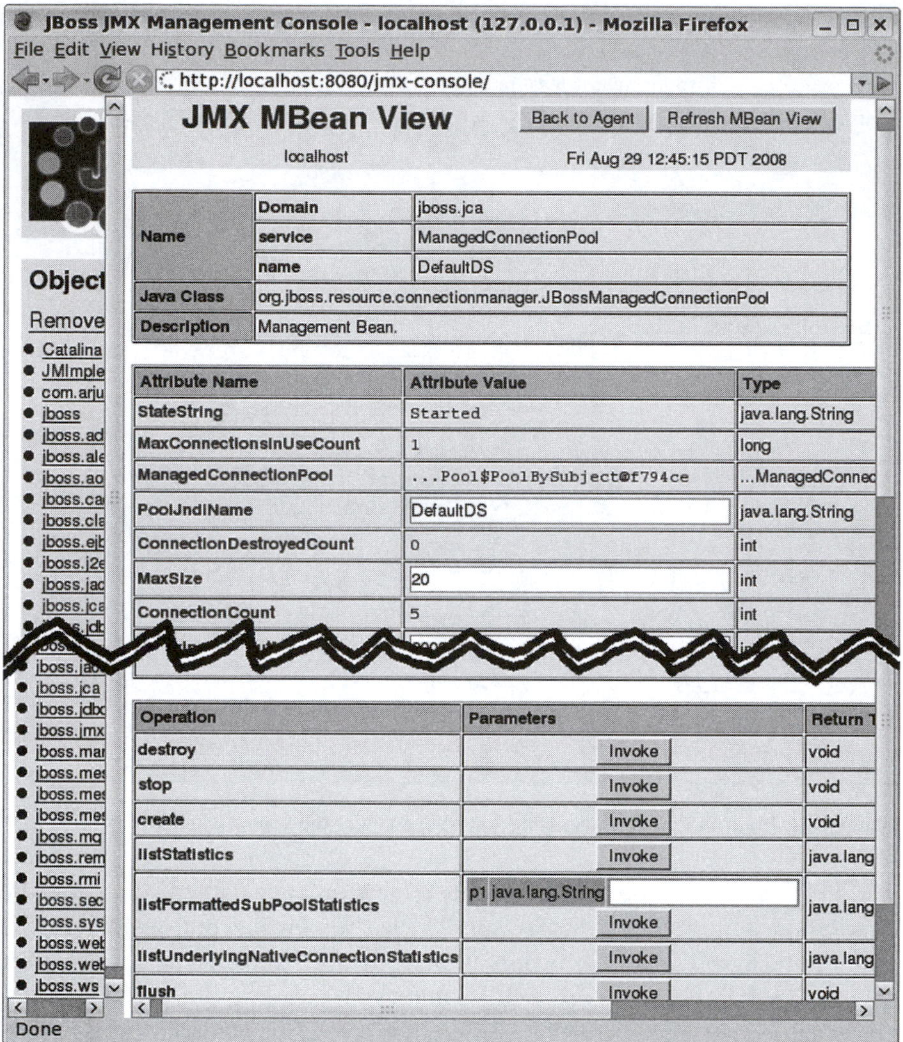

Figure 2.6 A JMX Console MBean detail page, showing information about the `DefaultDS` data source

on the MBeans to change property values; it doesn't modify the XML configuration files used to initialize the MBeans when the application server starts.

Finally, you can edit only MBean properties marked as writeable; therefore, some configuration settings, such as port assignments, can't be changed.

2.3.2 *Using the twiddle utility*

If you're anti-WIMP (windows, icons, menus, pointers) and prefer the power of a command line, rejoice—for a command-line tool, named twiddle, has the same power and flexibility of the JMX Console. The twiddle utility is well documented in the application server documentation; there are even examples of common twiddle usage, so we'll not repeat them here and, instead, urge you to read the documentation.

In addition, twiddle provides an extensive help system. To get basic help, a list of commands, or a detailed description of a command, enter one of the following:

```
twiddle
twiddle --help-commands
twiddle -H=<command>
```

One of the benefits of using twiddle over the JMX Console is that you can invoke twiddle from a script, automating many management tasks. Like the JMX Console, any changes made to MBeans via twiddle are transient and aren't retained when the server is restarted. But you could build a script that starts the server and then runs various twiddle commands to set the desired properties.

One of the best features of twiddle is that it's open source. Because the source is accessible, you can use it as an example of how to programmatically access MBeans. The main class can be found in the source distribution at console/src/main/org/jboss/console/twiddle/Twiddle.java, and a class for each command can be found in the console/src/main/org/jboss/console/twiddle/command directory. These classes illustrate how you can write your own programs to manipulate JMX MBeans. Of particular interest is the method `Twiddle.createMBeanServerConnection`, which shows how to access the MBean server, and the `execute` method in each of the command classes, such as `GetCommand`, which illustrates how to manipulate MBeans.

Now that you know how to access MBeans using both the JMX Console and twiddle, let's look at some MBeans that contain information that you might be interested in.

2.4 Examining interesting MBeans

Throughout this book we refer to various MBeans that are of interest for each topic that we cover. We also mention significant properties and operations that you might want to use to manage the MBeans. You can use the JMX Console to examine and play with those MBeans. Let's look at a few MBeans that aren't covered by the other topics in this book and highlight some of the things you can do with them. The ones that we cover here include the following:

- `jboss:type=Service,name=SystemProperties`—Enables you to examine the system properties
- `jboss:service=JNDIView`—Enables you to view the contents of JNDI
- `jboss.system:type=Log4jService,service=Logging`—Enables you to change the logging levels
- `jboss.system:service=ThreadPool`—Enables you to change the thread pool size
- `jboss.system:type=Server`, `jboss.system:type=ServerConfig`, and `jboss.system:type=ServerInfo`—Provide a wealth of information about the server

This list isn't complete; a lot of MBeans provide a lot of information, and many of them provide means to change the settings of the underlying services. One way of building your vocabulary is to learn a new word each week and make the effort to include that word in your writing and speaking. Similarly, you can learn more about managing the application server by spending some time each week getting to know a new MBean and the capabilities or information it puts at your mouse pointer. Therefore, consider the following as only a small introduction into the MBean possibilities.

2.4.1 Viewing system properties

The `jboss:type=Service,name=SystemProperties` enables you to examine the system properties. The `showAll` method returns a collection of system properties. The output from the `showAll` method as seen in the JMX Console is shown in figure 2.7. The list of properties is in alphabetical order. Well, actually, it's ASCII order.

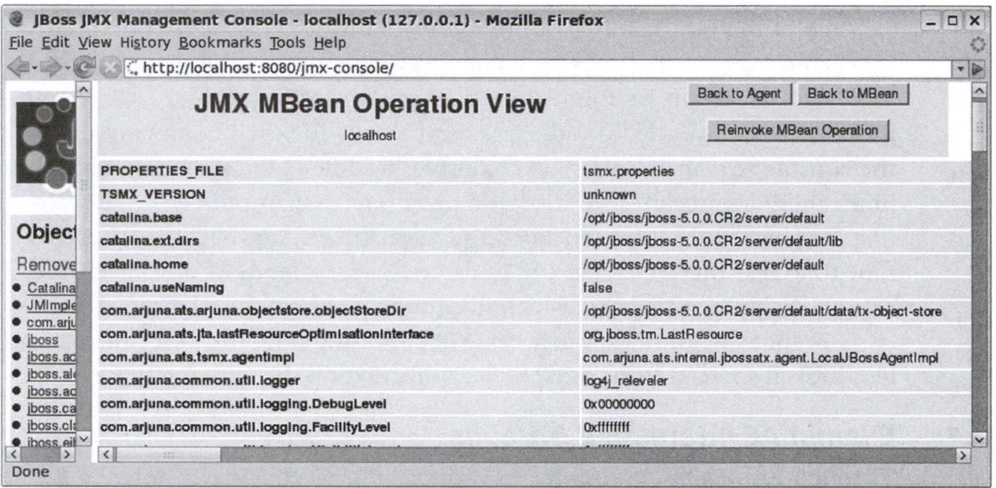

Figure 2.7 Viewing the system properties in the JMX Console

The system properties come in handy when they're used to identify locations or other things within the various descriptor files. You saw an example of this earlier in section 2.2.1 when we used the `jboss.server.log.dir` property to identify the location of the log file. You can do the same thing within your applications descriptor files such as jboss-web.xml or jboss-service.xml.

2.4.2 Viewing the JNDI namespaces

The `jboss:service=JNDIView` MBean enables you to view the contents of JNDI. As shown in figure 2.8, the `list` method returns a collection containing all the JNDI namespaces, the names in each namespace, and the class for each name and namespace.

Sooner or later, when looking up an object in JNDI, you'll get a *class cast* exception or, perhaps, a *name not bound* exception. When that happens, you now know where to look to view the names and namespaces.

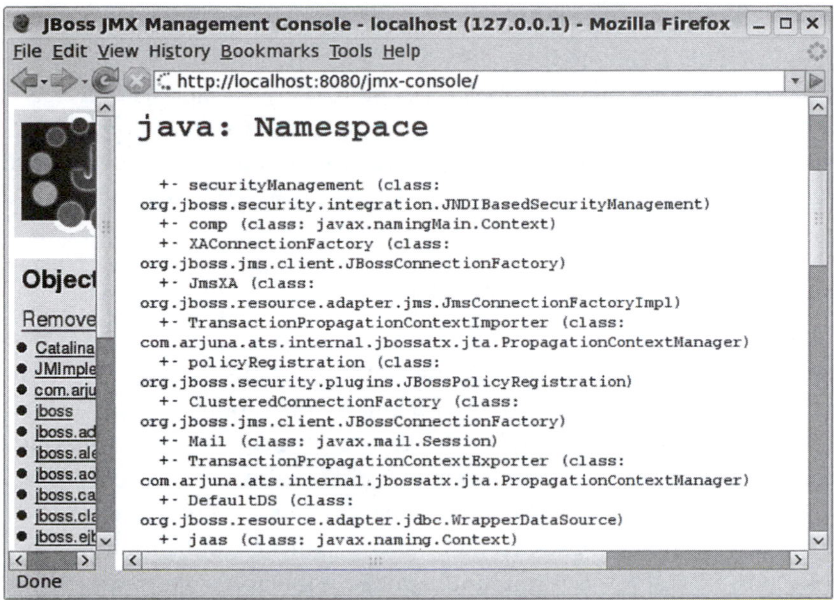

Figure 2.8 Viewing the JNDI namespace using the JMX Console

2.4.3 *Changing the logging levels*

The `jboss.system:type=Log4jService,service=Logging` MBean enables you to change the logging levels. If you prefer something a little more interactive, this MBean enables you to change various logging settings. You can capture and output in the log files output normally written to standard out and standard error; you can even decide what level output to log, as illustrated in figure 2.9.

This example shows how to use the JMX Console to set the level of logging for Hibernate to INFO.

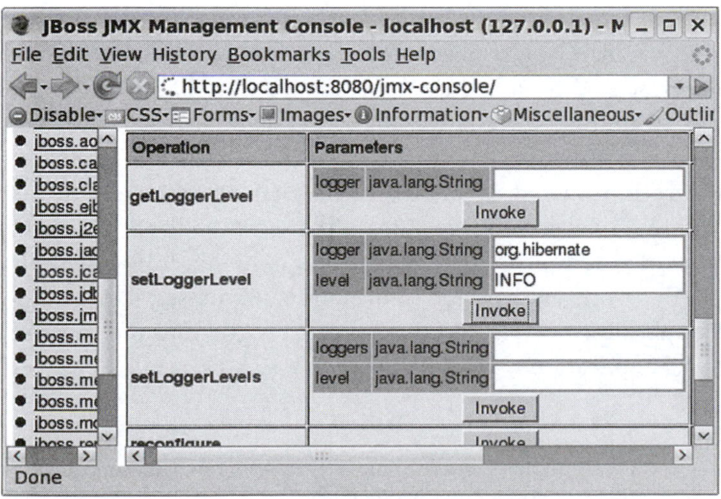

Figure 2.9 Using the JMX Console to change the log settings

2.4.4 Increasing the thread pool size

The `jboss.system:service=ThreadPool` MBean enables you to change the thread pool size. If you find that the response time on your application has suddenly increased, it could be that there aren't enough threads to handle the requests. You can use this MBean to view how many requests are waiting for a thread (the `QueueSize` attribute), and if a large number of requests are waiting, you can increase the maximum number of threads available by changing the `MaximumPoolSize` attribute value.

2.4.5 Obtaining application server information

The `jboss.system:type=Server`, `jboss.system:type=ServerConfig`, and `jboss.system:type=ServerInfo` MBeans provide a variety of information about the application server. Almost everything you might want to know about the application server is kept here, things such as the build level of the application server, operating system information, the server configuration name and its directories, Java Virtual Machine (JVM) information, host name, heap memory available, and much more.

You've now completed the first step on your journey and should understand the basic concepts behind configuring and managing the application server. In the chapters that follow, as we go over various services and components provided by the application server, we continually return to the theme of management and configuration, pointing out specific configuration files and their settings.

2.5 Summary

In this chapter, you learned that JBoss AS is a set of components built on top of a POJO microcontainer, with other components built on top of the JMX kernel that runs on top of the microcontainer. You also learned that each component is configured using its own configuration XML file; therefore, you can easily change the configuration using a basic text editor. Can you say: vi? Or if you're running on Windows, you can use Visual Notepad.

You also examined some of the tools provided by JBoss AS to change the configuration. One, the JMX Console, was web based, and the other, the twiddle utility, uses a command-line interface. Although these tools do let you change the configuration settings of MBeans at runtime, the changes aren't persistent because they're lost when the application server is restarted.

Finally, you were introduced to some MBeans that provide helpful information about the application server, such as the MBeans that give the list of names in the JNDI namespace or a list of system properties. In the chapters that follow, we call out even more MBeans used to manage or get information about services or applications deployed to the application server. And that's a great segue into the topic of the next chapter—deploying applications.

2.6 References

log4j documentation—http://logging.apache.org/log4j/docs/documentation.html
JMX specification—http://jcp.org/en/jsr/detail?id=3

3 Deploying applications

> ***This chapter covers***
> - Understanding application deployment
> - Understanding class loading
> - Fixing common deployment errors
> - Deploying miscellaneous applications

In a way, JBoss AS is much like a new house that you've purchased. The house has floors, doors, windows, walls and a roof, all of which correspond to the services provided by JBoss AS. Although these things do keep the rain off of your head and shield you from the wind, they don't add character to a house; they don't make it a home.

To make a house into a home, you add the furnishings, the decorations, and other items that give both purpose and character to each room. Similarly, you have to add applications to JBoss AS to provide it with personality, utility, and purpose. As a table, chairs, and dinnerware can transform an empty room with four walls into a dining room in which to entertain friends or family, a well-crafted web application deployed to JBoss AS can convert it into an inviting website for your customers to visit.

The whole purpose of an application server is to run applications. But before you can run those applications, they must be deployed. This chapter discusses the types of applications (and we use that term loosely) that can be deployed and how deployment works within the JBoss AS. Let's look, first, at what it means to deploy an application.

3.1 Understanding deployment

Deployment consists of two phases. First, you notify the application server, either directly or indirectly, of an application to deploy. Second, the application server performs the necessary steps to make that application ready for use.

JBoss AS uses a plug-in deployer architecture where separate deployers are responsible for deploying applications of different types. This makes the deployment architecture modular and enables you to easily define new types of applications.

3.1.1 Deploying an application

Perhaps the simplest way to deploy an application is to place it in the server/xxx/deploy directory. If the server is running, the deployment scanner scans this directory periodically, and if it sees any new or updated applications, it deploys them. If the server isn't running, the deployer scans the directory when it starts.

If the application is updated—for example, by copying a newer version of the application with a more recent timestamp to the deploy directory—then the deployment scanner undeploys the old application before deploying the new. One side effect of this undeploy/deploy action is that any current application state is lost, including any session state for active users. Therefore, it's not a good idea to use hot deployment in a production environment unless you're absolutely sure that you won't interrupt the existing sessions. After all, if you drop the session state for a thousand customers, you'll either receive a lot of angry emails or phone calls or suddenly find yourself without any customers at all.

Undeploying an application is easy: remove the application from the deploy directory. The next time the deployment scanner runs, it notices that the application no longer exists and undeploys it.

An alternate mechanism to deploying an application is to use the `deploy` or `redeploy` operation of the `jboss.system:service=MainDeployer` MBean. You can use either the JMX Console or twiddle to invoke this method. You could, for example, use twiddle to deploy a file named myapp.ear, located in a directory named /some/path, by entering the following at a command prompt (all on one line):

```
twiddle invoke "jboss.system:service=MainDeployer"
➥           deploy /some/path/myapp.ear
```

The application to be deployed must be accessible to the server because the application server deploys the application in its current location; this method doesn't copy the application to the server configuration's deploy directory, meaning that in the example the application is deployed from where it's located—at /some/path/myapp.ear. Additionally, because the application isn't copied to the deploy directory, if you restart the application server, the application is no longer deployed. Use the `undeploy` method on the same MBean to undeploy an application deployed in this manner.

If you use a script to start the application server, you can always add twiddle statements to deploy the desired applications. Two positive notes about this mechanism: you can use it in the case where the JBoss AS installation directory has been marked as read-only (because the application isn't copied to the deploy directory), and you can use it to deploy applications even if the hot deployer has been turned off.

NOTE Astute readers are probably wondering about Java Specification Request 88 (JSR-88), which defines Java EE application deployment. You will be happy to know that JBoss AS supports JSR-88. But you'll be unhappy to know that it has a few problems which prevent us from recommending its use. First, no tool uses JSR-88; if you want to use JSR-88 to deploy an application, you have to write code. Second, applications deployed using JSR-88 are placed into the tmp directory and aren't redeployed when the application server is restarted. Therefore, you have to redeploy the applications when the application server is restarted.

3.1.2 Understanding application packaging

When you deploy an application, you always deploy the application's package. A package can be either an archive file or an *exploded* directory. An archive is a file such as a Web Archive (WAR) or Enterprise Archive (EAR) file. But, what is an exploded directory? Let's look at an example. Assume you have an application that consists of an EJB Java Archive (JAR) file and a WAR file containing a web interface. You can package these files into an EAR file—let's call it myapp.ear—and copy the myapp.ear file to the deploy directory. That's an example of deploying an archive file. Or, you can place the JAR and WAR files in a directory named myapp.ear and copy the whole myapp.ear directory to the deploy directory. This is an example of an exploded directory. You could go even further and unpack the WAR file, the JAR file, or both. Figure 3.1 illustrates the files on disk in both deployment scenarios.

You might ask: which is the preferred mechanism? Both have their good and bad sides. With a single archive file, there's only one file to deal with, and there's not the possibility of the application being partially deployed because one of the files was deleted (as an example).

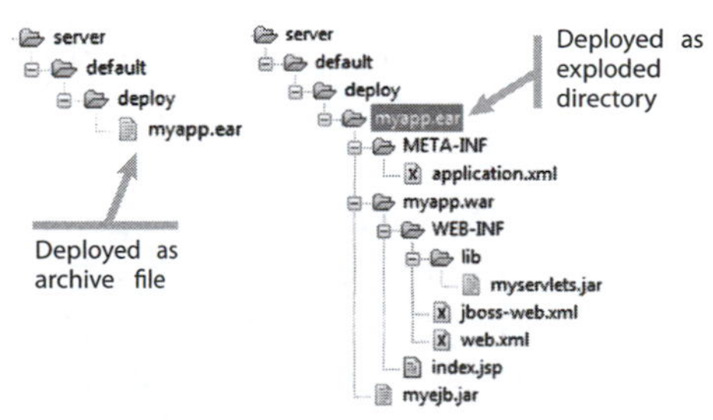

Figure 3.1 Deploying an archive file vs. an exploded directory

There are several advantages to having an exploded directory. First, all the configuration files and deployment descriptors are in plain view and can be easily edited. If you edit the primary descriptor for an application, such as the application.xml file within an EAR, then the hot deployer redeploys the application. Table 3.1 lists the primary descriptors for each application type.

Second, you can change JSPs, style sheets, and various other text files, and the application automatically starts using them

Application type	Primary descriptor
WAR	WEB-INF/web.xml
EAR	META-INF/application.xml
SAR	META-INF/jboss-service.xml
JAR	META-INF/ejb-jar.xml
RAR	META-INF/ra.xml

Table 3.1 Primary descriptors for various application types

(though for a style sheet or image file, the client might have to hit the browser refresh button to see the update). Third, you can easily add new files. For example, you might have a doc directory that contains PDF files and a servlet that generates a web page of links to those files based on the contents of the doc directory. Adding a new PDF is easy: copy it to that directory. The downside to exploded deployment is that you have to contend with multiple files instead of a single file.

One other thing to note: if you deploy an archive file, the deployer unpacks the file into the server/xxx/tmp/deploy directory using a generated name based on the archive filename, such as myapp28562-exp.ear for the previous example. This directory contains the exploded version of the archive, although any JAR files are left as they are and aren't unpacked. Before you think that this is convenient and provides you with the best of both worlds, realize that, when the application server is restarted, most of the contents of the server/xxx/tmp/deploy directory are deleted. Therefore, you should never rely on the contents of anything in the server/xxx/tmp directory. After all, there's a reason that it's named tmp!

3.1.3 Understanding application types

As we mentioned in the introduction to this chapter, we use the term *application* in a broad manner. So, what is an application? According to Webster, one of the definitions for application is *a use to which something is put.* You can infer that to mean that an application is any use to which you put the application server, or an application is anything that performs a useful function that you can deploy to the application server.

Two primary types of applications are business applications and services. A business application provides a business function, typically to end users, whereas a service provides functionality that supports other applications. Often, *application* is used to refer to only business applications, but in this chapter, we'll use application in the general sense.

Webster's definition provides a lot of leeway in what is considered to be an application, but that's good because JBoss AS supports a large number of different application types. How does it distinguish between one type of application and another? It uses the suffix for the application's file or directory name. Table 3.2 lists the various suffixes, describes their purposes, and provides the chapter or section where the application type is covered in more detail.

With so many application types, how does the application server know in which order to deploy them? That's the question we answer next.

Table 3.1 Application types and their suffixes

Suffix	Application type	See
.deployer -deployer-beans.xml	Defines an application deployer, which is used to deploy a specific type of application. These application types show up only in the server/xxx/deployers directory.	Section 3.1.5
.aop -aop.xml	Defines aspects to apply to classes that extend or add functionality to those classes.	—
.sar -service.xml	Defines a service, which adds functionality to the application server.	Chapters 7 and 8
-jboss-beans.xml	Defines POJOs for the microcontainer.	Chapter 2
.rar	Defines a resource adaptor, which is used to connect to enterprise information systems using the Java Connector Architecture (JCA).	—
-ds.xml	Defines a data source, which is used to access data in a database.	Section 3.4.1
.har	Defines a Hibernate archive, which is used to access a database using Hibernate.	Section 3.4.2
.jar	Defines a collection of EJBs that provides business logic for an application. Could also be a class library, but those typically are packaged within other applications or are placed in the server/xxx/lib directory as opposed to being placed in the server/xxx/deploy directory.	Chapter 7
.zip	The deployer examines the contents of the zip file to determine what type of application it contains and then deploys the application using the proper deployer. For example, if the zip file contains WEB-INF/web.xml, it deploys the file as a web application. But there's one oddity: the default context for a WAR deployed as a zip file is the full filename, such as http://localhgost:8080/someapp.zip.	—
.war	Defines a web application, which provides a web interface for an application or a web service.	Chapters 5 and 9
.wsr	A JBoss-specific archive that defines a web service. Use this suffix to deploy the web service after all the WAR files have been deployed.	Chapter 9
.ear	Defines a Java EE application, which is a collection of EJBs, WAR files, and class libraries.	Chapter 7
.bsh	Defines a service using bean shell script.	—
.last	Treated as a directory (or archive file) of applications to be deployed. The contained applications are deployed last, in the order given by their suffixes.	Section 3.1.4

3.1.4 Understanding deployment ordering

During initialization, or when the deployer is presented with multiple applications to deploy, deployment is performed in a specific order based on the application type. It just so happens that table 3.2 lists the application types in the default order in which they're deployed.

Conveniently, the *.last archive is deployed last. If you have an application that needs to be deployed after everything else is deployed, create a directory named, for example, doit.last in the server/xxx/deploy directory and place your application into that directory. Then you can rest assured that all the other applications are deployed before your application.

DEALING WITH NESTED APPLICATIONS

You can create an application that contains embedded applications. The obvious example is an EAR file which can contain both JAR and WAR files. But you're not limited to that; you could have a JAR that contains a SAR that contains a—well, you get the idea. How do these Russian-doll-styled applications figure in the deployment ordering?

NOTE A Russian doll is a set of dolls (usually wooden) of decreasing size that can be nested one inside another. This principle, when used in design, is known as the *matryoshka* principle. The nesting of packages is similar in concept.

First, the outer application type determines the order of the deployment among all applications at that level. Then, when it comes time to deploy the Russian-doll-styled application, the innermost application is deployed first. If there are multiple applications at any level, the suffix ordering applies. Figure 3.2 illustrates the ordering of the deployment of a hypothetical set of applications. The number next to each application identifies its relative deployment ordering.

Having said this, there are ways to override the order of applications deployed in a Russian-doll-styled application. For example, within an EAR file the META-INF/application.xml file defines the ordering applied to the embedded applications. The later chapters on the application types cover any such ordering mechanisms.

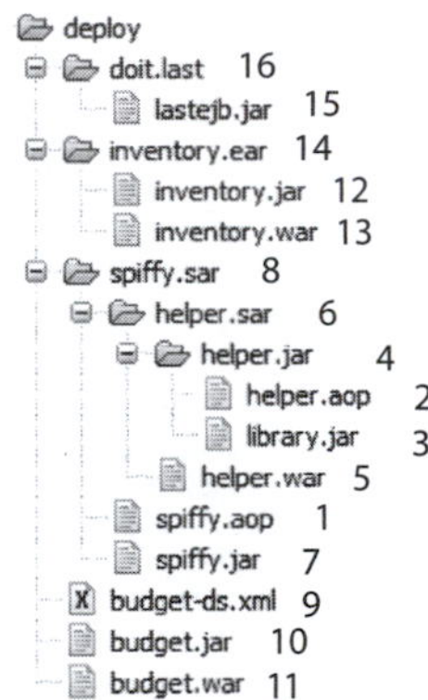

Figure 3.2 Deployment ordering with Russian-doll-styled applications

3.1.5 Deployment configuration options

The deployer is configured via the deployers.xml and profile.xml descriptor files, both found in the server/xxx/conf directory. This file defines several POJOs that manage various deployment responsibilities. Table 3.3 identifies each of these POJOs and highlights some of the more interesting configuration properties provided by each one.

Table 3.2 Deployer POJOs configuration properties

Bean	Property	Description
`MainDeployer`	`structuralDeployers`	A list of beans that define the high-level classification of the kinds of things that can be deployed. For example, a number of file types are packed archives and are listed for the `JarStructure` bean. These are defined by a set of file extensions such as .zip, .ear, and so on. Or text files that define services, such as *-ds.xml and *-service.xml, which are defined for the `FileStructure` bean.
	`deployers`	A list of the various deployers. These deployers handle the files that were identified by the `structuralDeployers`. Think of it this way: the `structuralDeployer` property identifies all the file types that are of interest, whereas the `deployers` property identifies the services that deploy each of those file types.

`DeploymentFilter`	`prefixes`
	`suffixes`
	`matches`
		Identifies which files or directories can be ignored by the deployer. The `matches` property matches a full, simple directory or filename, whereas the other two properties match prefixes or suffixes. Each is a list of comma-separated strings. Notice that the items listed reflect things such as temporary files created by editors or other software, work files or directories used by source control systems such as Subversion, and so on.

`VFSDeploymentScanner`	`URIList`	A list of locations that the deployer scans for applications to deploy. See the section after this table for an example.
	`URIs`	Same usage as `URIList`, but the list is provided as a single, comma-separated string of values.
	`recursiveSearch`	Indicates whether the scanner should recursively search subdirectories for applications to deploy. Only used when a directory name doesn't have a dot in it. For example, various messaging service descriptors are located in the server/xxx/deploy/messaging directory. As long as this property is `true`, which is the default value, the messaging directory is scanned for applications to deploy. If this property is set to `false`, that directory isn't scanned, possibly causing significant problems if you plan on using the messaging service. This setting doesn't affect exploded application directories, such as jmx-console.war, because they always have dots in their names.

Table 3.2 Deployer POJOs configuration properties *(continued)*

Bean	Property	Description
`VFSBootstrapScanner`	(same as for `VFSDeploymentScanner`)	Locations to be scanned as part of the bootstrap process. Unless you want to change how bootstrapping is done, you shouldn't change this.
`VFSDeployerScanner`	(same as for `VFSDeploymentScanner`)	Locations to be scanned for the various deployers.
`HDScanner`	`scanEnabled`	Set this to `true` (default) to enable the hot deployer and to `false` to disable it. When set to `false`, applications are deployed only when the server is started or when the deploy method on the `MainDeployer` MBean is called.
	`scanPeriod`	The number of milliseconds the hot deployer waits between performing scans. The default is 5000 milliseconds (5 seconds). This value is ignored if `scanEnabled` is set to `false`.
	`scanThreadName`	You can use this to change the name of the thread from its default of HDScanner. The thread name enables you to identify the hot deployer thread if you should take a thread dump.

As noted in the table, you can specify multiple deployment locations. Perhaps the best way to see how to do this is by an example.

USING MULTIPLE DEPLOYMENT LOCATIONS

Let's assume that you prefer to deploy your applications to a directory other than the default server/xxx/deploy directory. For example, directory access might be set so that you only have read-only access to the application server installation directory, and you can't write to the deploy directory. In such a case, you can modify the configuration to also deploy files placed at /opt/deploy (as an example) by setting the `URIList` property of the `VFSDeploymentScanner` bean as shown in listing 3.1.

Listing 3.1 Deployment directories in profile-service.xml

```
<deployment xmlns="urn:jboss:bean-deployer:2.0">
  ...
  <bean name="VFSDeploymentScanner" ...>
    ...
    <property name="URIList">
      <list elementClass="java.net.URI">
        <value>${jboss.server.home.url}deploy/</value>
        <value>file:/opt/deploy/</value>
      </list>
    </property>
  </bean>
</deployment>
```

Note the trailing slash used for /opt/deploy/. It signifies that the defined location is a directory that should be scanned for applications to deploy. If the trailing slash is missing, the location is assumed to be a single application—either an archive file or an exploded directory—to deploy. In that case the location would have to have one of the accepted suffixes, such as /opt/someapp.war.

With the above change, you can now place applications in the /opt/deploy directory, and they're treated as if they were placed in server/xxx/deploy. They're even automatically redeployed when the server is restarted.

One of the concerns you'll have when deploying an application is where to place the JAR files required by that application. Should they be packaged with your application, placed in the server/xxx/lib directory, or added to the class path? Before we can answer this question, you first need to understand how the class loader works—the topic of our next section.

3.2 Understanding class loading

The JBoss AS documentation contains a detailed description of how the application server loads classes. In addition, several wiki pages describe class loading and solving problems with class loading. Rather than repeat that text here (which in programming circles is known as reuse, but in literary circles is known as plagiarism—with apologies to the great Lobachevsky), we take a slightly different tack.

NOTE JBoss AS 5.0 introduced a new class loader based on the new Virtual File System (VFS). The VFS was implemented to simplify and unify file handling within the application server. The new class loader, named the VFS Class Loader, uses VFS to locate JAR and class files. Even though this represents a significant change in how classes are loaded in JBoss AS 5.0, the resulting behavior is much the same as for prior versions of JBoss AS.

The JBoss AS documentation gets down into some nitty-gritty details concerning class loading and can overwhelm you if you're first encountering the topic. Therefore, we describe a more simplified view of how the application server loads classes. We should point out that the simplified view might not fit all cases, so if you run into one of those cases, we encourage you to read the JBoss AS documentation to more fully understand class loading. Hopefully, after reading our simplified introduction, you'll find the in-depth details easier to digest.

We start with a description of the class loaders because the application server uses many class loaders so that it can properly differentiate between classes, if required. Then we go into class scoping, which enables the application server to differentiate among classes. Finally, we look at loader repositories, which enable several class loaders to share or isolate classes.

3.2.1 Understanding multiple class loaders

The application server uses multiple class loaders, each of which load a specific set of classes. Part of the reason for doing this is to separate the various applications that are deployed. For example, if there were only a single class loader, and one application needed a specific version of a class and another application needed a different version, then you could have a problem. One application would have to use the wrong version, possibly resulting in errors. By utilizing multiple class loaders, each application can load its own version of the class.

The application server keeps track of all the class loaders and implements rules that define not only which class loader loads a given class, but also whether classes loaded by one class loader have access, or visibility, to classes loaded by another class loader. Figure 3.3 provides a simplified view of such class visibility; each box in the diagram represents a class loader. In the diagram, classes at a certain level have visibility to other classes at the same level and to classes in a lower level, but they don't have visibility to classes at a higher level.

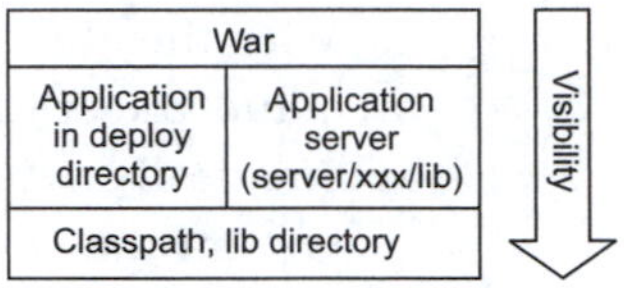

War	
Application in deploy directory	Application server (server/xxx/lib)
Classpath, lib directory	

Visibility

Figure 3.3 A simplified view of class visibility, where classes in files or directories higher in the diagram can reference classes in directories lower in the diagram.

TIP No applications have visibility to classes within a WAR file that, by the servlet specification, are required to be separate. You can change that behavior by setting the `useJBossWebLoader` property of the `WarDeployer` bean in the server/xxx/deployers/jbossweb.deployer/META-INF/war-deployers-jboss-beans.xml file to `true`. If that doesn't give full visibility, you might also want to set the `java2ClassLoadingCompliance` property of that same bean to `true`. The war-deployers-beans.xml file contains descriptions of the usage of both of these properties.

At the lowest level are the classes in the class path, including basic Java Virtual Machine (JVM) classes (such as those in `rt.jar`) and the boot classes for the application server found in the lib directory. The next level consists of all the classes for deployed applications and the application server classes found in the JAR files in the server/xxx/lib directory. The topmost level represents classes in a WAR file, which could be in the deploy directory or within an EAR or Service Archive (SAR) file.

This visibility of classes comes in handy if you want to share large class libraries among several applications. Doing so cuts down on the amount of memory needed to run those applications. The downside is that, if two deployed applications require different versions of a class library, they won't be able to run this way. To get these two applications to deploy properly, you'll need to know about scoping.

3.2.2 Scoping classes

You can specify that a particular application should have its own class loader repository and prefer using its own classes over those available in other applications. This is known as *scoping*. You do this by defining a class loader repository in one of the JBoss AS–specific configuration files. First, let's look at an example of configuring class scoping, and afterwards we'll describe loader repositories.

To do scoped class loading for a SAR file, modify the META-INF/jboss-service.xml file to contain the following:

```
<service>
  <loader-repository>jbia.loader:loader=Loader1</loader-repository>
  ...
</service>
```

For an EAR file, modify the META-INF/jboss-app.xml file to contain the following:

```
<jboss-app>
 <loader-repository>jbia.loader:loader=Loader2</loader-repository>
 . . .
</jboss-app>
```

And for a WAR file, modify the META-INF/jboss-web.xml file to contain the following:

```
<jboss-web>
 <class-loading>
  <loader-repository>jbia.loader:loader=Loader3</loader-repository>
 </class-loading>
 . . .
</jboss-web>
```

The only part of the name that's important is the loader attribute; you can name the rest anything you want. For example, each of the following is valid:

```
<loader-repository>foo.bar:loader=some.stuff</loader-repository>
<loader-repository>com.myorg:loader=org.ear</loader-repository>
```

Additionally, if your application uses different versions of JAR files available in the server's server/xxx/lib directory, you can set the `java2ParentDelegation` class loader repository property to `false` to force the application server to use the classes in your JAR files instead. Here's how it would look in a SAR archive's META-INF/jboss-service.xml file; it's similar for the other files.

```
<service>
  <loader-repository>jbia.loader:loader=Loader1
   <loader-repository-config>java2ParentDelegation=false
     </loader-repository-config>
  </loader-repository>
  . . .
</service>
```

The tags used in the previous configuration files refer to loader repositories, not to class loaders. So, what are loader repositories? We answer that question next.

3.2.3 Understanding loader repositories

You might wonder how class loader repositories relate to class loaders and if they're the same or different. Well, they're different. The application server creates many class loaders, one for each application. If you run the JMX Console, you can see them about one-third of the way down on the agent view page. Their names all begin with `jboss.classloader:id=`.

In addition, the application server maintains several loader repositories, which are locations from which the application server can load classes. One loader repository might be used by one class loader while another is used by several class loaders. For example, although there's a separate class loader for each deployed application, they all use the same loader repository. Or if you define a loader repository for an application then the class loader for that application uses its own class loader repository.

If you define a loader repository for an application, the class loader for that application gets its own repository. The end result is that classes within that application prefer classes inside the application to classes outside the application. As a side effect, classes in other applications don't have visibility to classes within that application. Think of it as a one-way mirror wrapped around the application—it can see out, but nobody can see in.

Figure 3.4 illustrates class preferences with and without using a loader repository. JAR file three.jar is in the server/xxx/lib directory and contains version 1 of class C, whereas EAR files one.ear and two.ear are in the server/xxx/deploy directory, and contain classes A and B, respectively. In addition, two.ear contains version 2 of class C. To ensure that the classes in two.ear pick up the correct version of class C, a loader repository is declared within two.ear. When class A references class C, it gets the one in three.jar, but when class B references class C, it gets the one in two.ear. Using EAR files is an example; we could have used SAR, JAR, or any other archive type. And the result would be the same.

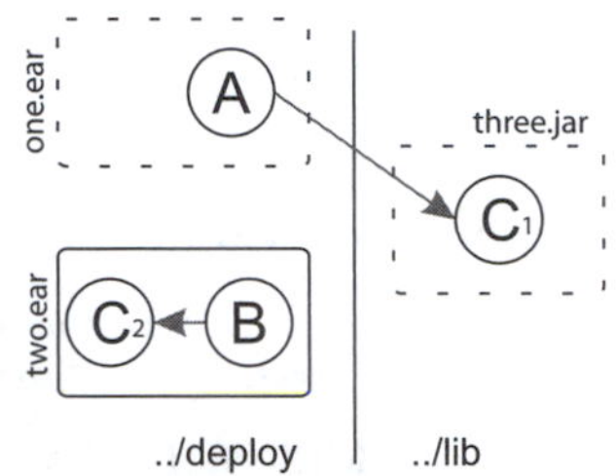

Figure 3.4 An example of how class loader repositories affect class access, where classes A and B each reference the expected version of class C

As we mentioned earlier when we started this discussion on class loading, what we have presented here is a simplistic view of how the application server deals with class loading. For more in-depth knowledge, we recommend that you read the JBoss AS documentation. But you should now be able to figure out most of the common problems associated with class loading.

3.3 Fixing common deployment errors

Application deployment is one area where it appears that Murphy's Law rules: inevitably, something will go wrong. But when it does, you can console yourself with knowing that you're not the only one to have such misfortune; a quick browse through the JBoss online user's forums reveals that many others have been visited by Murphy also. We've gleaned some of the more common deployment problems from the forums, and we provide suggested solutions for correcting the following issues:

- Class not found exceptions
- Duplicate JAR file errors
- Zip file errors
- Class cast exceptions

3.3.1 Class not found exception

A `ClassNotFoundException` error usually is caused by one of two issues. The one that probably comes to mind immediately is that you're missing a JAR file. The typical solution is to find which JAR contains that class and to include it in your WAR or EAR file. One solution is to use Ant with the following class path:

```
<path id="classpath">
  <fileset dir="/" includes="**/*.jar" />
</path>
```

For those of you not inclined to take such drastic measures, the jarFinder utility is for you. You can use it to search through a directory of JAR files (including subdirectories) looking for a class, a property, or any other kind of file, with a given name.

You can download the source for jarFinder at http://www.isocra.com/articles/jarFinder.php. The files also appear in the source for this book. Once you download it, unzip it and build it using the provided build.xml Ant script. The resulting class files appear in the classes subdirectory, which you must include in the class path. Here's an example of running the utility to locate the `org.jboss.aop.advice.Interceptor` class within the JBoss installation directory:

```
java -cp classes com.isocra.utils.jarSearch.DirectorySearcher
➥        $JBOSS_DIR org.jboss.aop.advice.Interceptor.class
```

Once you locate the JAR file that contains the class, you should include it in your application. If you have a client application with this problem, then you should include the JAR file in your client's class path.

The often-overlooked root cause is that the wrong class loader is looking for the missing class. For example, a servlet in your WAR file invokes an EJB located in a JAR file in the EAR file that, in turn, attempts to access a class in the WAR file. The issue here is that the classes in the EAR file don't have visibility to the classes in the WAR file.

The solution is fairly simple: move the JAR file to a lower level in the class visibility hierarchy. For the example, you move the classes out of the WAR file and into the EAR file. You might have to repackage your classes because you should keep the servlet classes in the WAR file. Now the servlets and the EJBs have access to the classes.

A variation of this problem for a client application occurs when the text *no security manager* appears, as follows:

```
javax.naming.CommunicationException [Root exception is
java.lang.ClassNotFoundException: org.jbia.SomeMissingClass
(no security manager: RMI class loader disabled)]
```

A Google search would seem to indicate that you need to set up a security manager, but that's typically not necessary. Instead, the solution is to make the necessary JAR file available in the class path for the client application.

3.3.2 Duplicate JAR files

Another common problem is including a JAR file in your application that's already provided in the application server's server/xxx/lib directory (or even elsewhere, such as the tag library JAR, jstl.jar, which is provided in the server/xxx/deploy/jbossweb.sar directory). Sometimes this isn't a problem, but if you get a `ClassCastException`, you might look to see if you're packaging JAR files that are already supplied by the application server.

A variation of this problem happens when you include the log4j.jar file in your application. Then, you get the following error:

```
10:42:50,093 ERROR [STDERR] log4j:ERROR "org.jboss.logging.util.Only
OnceErrorHandler" was loaded by [org.jboss.system.server.NoAnnotatio
nURLClassLoader@1de3f2d].
10:42:50,249 ERROR [STDERR] log4j:ERROR Could not create an Appender
. Reported error follows.
10:42:50,249 ERROR [STDERR] java.lang.ClassCastException: org.jboss.
logging.appender.DailyRollingFileAppender
```

In either case, the solution is simple: remove the offending JAR file from your archive, or define a separate class loader repository for the application.

3.3.3 Zip file errors

Archive files are in a zip file format, and the zip file classes provided by the JVM are used to unpack such archives. A variety of exceptions are thrown when the zip file classes have problems unpacking files. These problems typically occur if an archive is being copied to the deploy directory, and at the same time, the hot deployer runs and attempts to deploy a partially copied file.

Assume you have a WAR file that's 10 MB due to the number of JAR files you need to include. Also assume that when you copy the file over a network to the deploy directory, it takes the file 20 seconds to copy. Recall that the hot deployer runs every 5 seconds, so we can guarantee you that the hot deployer will attempt to deploy the file before it has been completely copied. The result—a zip file error.

A variation of this problem happens when deploying an exploded directory; all the files aren't copied before the hot deployer runs, and you get a missing file error. But when you look for the file, there it is. Unfortunately, cursing the hot deployer does you no good.

The solution is to not copy anything into the deploy directory. Instead, copy the application package into a temporary location on the same hard drive partition as the deploy directory. Then once the copy is complete, move the package to the deploy directory. Such a move, because it's on the same partition, is atomic.

3.3.4 Class cast exception

Class cast exceptions can be caused by a variety of problems. The most obvious is that the object you're attempting to cast isn't of the type you thought. You can easily determine this by examining the class of the object you're attempting to cast, either through using a debugging tool or by adding logging code to your application to print out the class of the object. But there are two other subtle causes that can take place when using an application server.

First, you might be getting an object, such as an EJB, from JNDI and then attempting to cast the resulting object. For example, consider the following code to access an EJB:

```
Context ctx = new InitialContext();
MyEjb ejb = (MyEjb)ctx.lookup("MyEjb");
```

One potential problem in this code is that you used the wrong JNDI name to look up the EJB. For example, by default, the EJB has the name *MyEjb/local*. In this case, what gets returned by the lookup method is a JNDI Context object—hence, the class cast exception. The solution is to use the full EJB name, as follows:

```
MyEjb ejb = (MyEjb)ctx.lookup("MyEjb/local");
```

A second potential problem is that the name of the EJB might be *MyEjb*, but that's for the remote interface. In this case, you have to use the narrow method on the `RemoteObject` class as follows:

```
Object obj = ctx.lookup("MyEjb");
MyEjb ejb = (MyEjb)RemoteObject.narrow(obj, MyEjb.class);
```

Another subtle cause for the class cast exception might be that the object was created using one class loader, and you're attempting to cast it within a class loaded by another class loader. For example, assume you obtained a collection called `coll` and are extracting `org.foo.Widget` objects out of it using the following code:

```
Object obj = coll.get(i);
log.debug("obj=" + obj.getClass());
org.foo.Widget w = (org.foo.Widget)obj;
```

When it executes, the code prints the following line in the log file:

```
...obj=org.foo.Widget
```

Yet, the third line of the code causes a class cast exception.

This usually happens if you package, within your application, a JAR file that's already provided by the application server. The object was probably created using the class as defined in the application server, and then the cast is being done using the class definition from your application. Even if the two classes are identical, because they're handled by different class loaders, they're considered to be different classes. The solution is to either identify a separate class loader repository for your application or to remove the duplicate class library from your application.

3.4 Deploying miscellaneous applications

You should now know all about deploying applications to the application server. You're even prepared for a visit from Murphy. In the chapters that follow, we cover several types of applications. But before we get to them, some application types don't need a whole chapter to describe, so we cover them here. These applications are data sources and Hibernate archives.

3.4.1 Deploying data sources

At some point in time, you'll want to access data in a database, and you'll require some mechanism to do this. Your application could use Java Database Connectivity (JDBC) to access the database directly; but, that has one fairly major problem—establishing a connection with the database is an expensive operation. And with a web application, you might find that a significant amount of time is spent hitting the database, so you might want to avoid having to frequently reestablish connections.

The solution to this problem is to let the application server manage your database connections using a data source. The application server can then manage the database connections by pooling them and by providing connections to the application when it needs them. The question then becomes: how does one declare, or deploy, a data source to the application server?

The answer is to create, and then deploy, a *-ds.xml file. You can use any name for the file that you like, as long at the suffix is *–ds.xml*. Listing 3.2 shows an example.

Listing 3.2 Example *-ds.xml file

```
<datasources>
  <local-tx-datasource>
    <jndi-name>MySqlDS</jndi-name>
    <connection-url>jdbc:mysql://mysql-hostname:3306/jbossdb
➥  </connection-url>
    <driver-class>com.mysql.jdbc.Driver</driver-class>
    <user-name>x</user-name>
    <password>y</password>
    <min-pool-size>5</min-pool-size>
    <max-pool-size>20</max-pool-size>
    <idle-timeout-minutes>0</idle-timeout-minutes>
    <blocking-timeout-millis>5000</blocking-timeout-millis>
    <exception-sorter-class-name>
➥  org.jboss.resource.adapter.jdbc.vendor.MySQLExceptionSorter
➥  </exception-sorter-class-name>
    <check-valid-connection-sql>SELECT COUNT(*) FROM FooBar
    </check-valid-connection-sql>
    <metadata>
      <type-mapping>MySQL</type-mapping>
    </metadata>
    <connection-property name="xxx" type="java.lang.String">yyy
➥  </connection-property>
  </local-tx-datasource>
</datasources>
```

The <local-tx-datasource> tag defines a particular type of data source that handles local transactions. Three different data source types are available, each of which handles transactions differently. Table 3.4 describes each type.

Table 3.3 Data source transaction types

Tag	Description
<local-tx-datasource>	Identifies a data source that uses transactions, even distributed transactions within the local application server, but doesn't use distributed transactions among multiple application servers.
<no-tx-datasource>	Identifies a data source that doesn't use transactions. This option isn't shown in the example, but would appear in place of the <local-tx-datasource> tag.
<xa-datasource>	Identifies a data source that uses distributed transaction among multiple application servers. This option isn't shown in the example, but would appear in place of the <local-tx-datasource> tag.

Which transaction type should you use? In most cases, you'll use `<local-tx-datasource>` because it handles transactions within a single application server. If you're clustering your application servers or wanting to use distributed transactions among multiple application servers, then you should use `<xa-datasource>`. Note that both `<local-tx-datasource>` and `<xa-datasource>` handle distributed transactions involving multiple data sources. The difference is that `<local-tx-datasource>` handles them only within a single running application server, whereas `<xa-datasource>` handles them among many running application servers. On the other end of the spectrum, if your applications only read from the database, then using `<no-tx-datasource>` would be appropriate.

NOTE XA is an API defined by The Open Group's Distributed Transaction Processing model. This model provides communications mechanisms between a Transaction Monitor and several resource managers, which perform updates against databases. The Transaction Monitor is responsible for coordinating the individual transactions handled by the resource managers to ensure transactional semantics when multiple resource managers are involved in a single transaction.

Within the transaction type, you can specify a wide variety of configuration options. Table 3.5 describes the various configuration options in the *-ds.xml file. A complete set of configuration options, along with a description of each option, can be found in the docs/dtd/jboss-ds_5_0.dtd file.

Table 3.4 Data source configuration options for *-ds.xml

Tag	Description
`<jndi-name>`	Name used to look up the data source in the JNDI namespace. The *java:* prefix is automatically added to this name.
`<connection-url>`	The URL used by the JDBC driver to establish a database connection. This URL is specific to the database and the driver for the database. In the example, the name of the database is *jbossdb*, which must be a valid database in MySQL.
`<driver-class>`	The class name for the JDBC driver. Valid only for `<local-tx-datasource>` and `<no-tx-datasource>`.
`<xa-datasource-class>`	The class name for the distributed transaction data source. Valid only for `<xa-datasource>`.
`<user-name>`	The user name for making the database connection.
`<password>`	The password for the given user name.
`<security-domain>`	References a security domain that uses an identity login module defined in login-config.xml. You can use this in place of `<user-name>` and `<password>` to provide an encrypted password to the database.

Table 3.4 Data source configuration options for *-ds.xml *(continued)*

Tag	Description
<min-pool-size>	The minimum number of open connections maintained by the application server. Note that the application server doesn't open any connections until the first request for a connection, at which time it opens the specified number of connections. To establish connections when the application server is started, you can write a simple service that does nothing but ask for a connection.
<max-pool-size>	The maximum number of open connections maintained by the application server. If the application server runs out of connections, it allocates a new connection to fulfill that request, until it hits the maximum number of connection. At that point, it queues the requests until connections are freed. Therefore, it's important that applications close any connections that they obtain.
<idle-timeout-minutes>	If a surplus connection isn't in use for the specified number of minutes, then that connection is closed. Note that the number of open connections never goes below the <min-pool-size>.
<blocking-timeout-millis>	The number of milliseconds a requestor waits for a connection to become available before the wait times out. The requestor then gets an exception.
<exception-sorter-class-name>	Identifies a class used to determine if an error number returned by the database is fatal.
<check-valid-connection-sql>	Identifies an SQL to be executed when the connection is established to verify the connection's validity. In the example, `FooBar` must be a table in the jbossdb database specified in the connection URL.
<valid-connection-checker-class-name>	Identifies a class that can be used when the connection is established to verify the connection's validity. The class specified must implement the `org.jboss.resource.adapter.jdbc.ValidConnectionChecker` interface. Use this option instead of <check-valid-connection-sql> when you want to use more than a single SQL statement to check the connection's validity. Be aware that any application making a connection request that causes a connection to be established must wait until the connection checker is finished.
<type-mapping>	Used by the container-managed persistence (CMP) code to identify the database and adjust its database handling accordingly. The name use must match one of the names in the standardjbosscmp-jdbc.xml file. Additionally, you can add new entries to the standardjbosscmp-jdbc.xml to customize the database interaction. Note that this is used only for EJB 2.1, not for EJB3.
<connnection-property>	Identifies a property to pass to the `java.sql.Driver` when establishing a database connection. In the example, the property name is `xxx` and the value is `yyy`. Refer to your JDBC driver documentation for the valid properties. You can provide multiple <connection-property> entries. Valid only for <local-tx-datasource> and <no-tx-datasource>.

Table 3.4 Data source configuration options for *-ds.xml *(continued)*

Tag	Description
`<xa-datasource-property>`	Identifies a property to pass to the `javax.sql.DataSource` when establishing a database connection. Refer to the JDBC driver documentation for the valid properties. You can provide multiple `<xa-datasource-property>` entries. Valid only for `<xa-datasource>`.

`<transaction-isolation>`	Identifies the transaction isolation level to use with the database. Valid values include
	`TRANSACTION_READ_UNCOMMITTED`
	`TRANSACTION_READ_COMMITTED`
	`TRANSACTION_REPEATABLE_READ`
	`TRANSACTION_SERIALIZABLE`
	`TRANSACTION_NONE`
	Refer to your database's JDBC documentation for a description of each level and which levels your database supports. Not valid for `<no-tx-datasource>`.

You can define multiple data sources within a single *-ds.xml file, but we recommend that you define only a single data source per file. This makes the data sources easier to manage.

JBoss AS comes with a set of example *-ds.xml files for a variety of databases. You can find them in the docs/examples/jca directory, which should be your first stop when defining a *-ds.xml file. Also, we provide several example *-ds.xml files in many of the chapters in this book.

Now that you have the *-ds.xml file for your database, what do you do with it? Well, two things. The *-ds.xml file goes into the deploy directory. Yes, that's right; it's treated as an application, specifically as a service. Second, you must provide the JAR file for the JDBC driver for the database. Place the driver JAR file in the server/xxx/lib directory. Be careful with JDBC drivers that contain a version number as part of the filename—you don't want two versions of the same driver to be resident in the server/xxx/lib directory at the same time.

Once the data source is deployed, the application server creates several MBeans for the data source. These MBeans are defined in table 3.6, where *XXX* is the JNDI name for the data source.

Table 3.5 MBeans created for a data source

MBean	Description
`jboss.jca:name=XXX,` `service=DataSourceBinding`	Manages the `javax.sql.DataSource` objects.
`jboss.jca:name=XXX,` `service=LocalTxCM`	Manages the connection manager, which is responsible for the connection pool. You can use this MBean to manage various aspects of distributed transactions, such as the local XA resource transaction timeout value. Created only for `<local-tx-datasource>`.

Table 3.5 MBeans created for a data source *(continued)*

MBean	Description
jboss.jca:name=XXX, service=XATxCM	Manages the connection manager, which is responsible for the connection pool. You can use this MBean to manage various aspects of distributed transactions, such as the distributed XA resource transaction timeout value. Created only for <xa-datasource>.
jboss.jca:name=XXX, service=NoTxCM	Manages the connection manager, which is responsible for the connection pool. Created only for <no-tx-datasource>.
jboss.jca:name=XXX, service=ManagedConnectionFactory	Manages the connection factory, which creates database connections.
jboss.jca:name=XXX, service=ManagedConnectionPool	Manages the pool of database connections. You can use this MBean to monitor the number of active connections and even change the min and max connection count.
jboss.jdbc:service=metadata, datasource=XXX	You can use this MBean to change the type mapping. Doesn't appear if the data source is defined as a no transaction data source.

When you deploy a *-ds.xml file to the deploy directory, that data source is available to all applications deployed to the application server. You can also package the *-ds.xml file with your application. Let's look at how to package a data source in an EAR file as an example.

PACKAGING A DATA SOURCE IN AN EAR FILE

In chapter 7, we describe how to package web applications and EJBs into an EAR file. You can also place the *-ds.xml file in the EAR file.

For example, assume that the web application is packaged in inventory.war, and the EJBs are packaged in inventory.jar. You could place those archives and the data source descriptor into a single EAR file that has the contents illustrated in figure 3.5.

In addition, because the *-ds.xml file is located within the package, you can also place the JAR file for the JDBC driver there. If you add a class loader repository to the EAR file descriptor, then only this application would have access to the JDBC driver.

Figure 3.5 The contents of the `inventory.ear` package, showing the embedded *-ds.xml file

The application.xml file enumerates the archives packaged within the EAR file, but it's a standard Java EE descriptor and, because data source descriptors aren't part of standard Java EE, they can't be referenced in that file. Instead, you use a META-INF/jboss-app.xml file which references the data source descriptor, as follows:

```
<!DOCTYPE jboss-app PUBLIC "-//JBoss//DTD J2EE Application 1.4//EN"
      "http://www.jboss.org/j2ee/dtd/jboss-app_4_0.dtd">
<jboss-app>
 <module>
  <service>inventory-ds.xml</service>
```

```
  </module>
</jboss-app>
```

Now that you have the EAR file, you can deploy it and run the application, which then uses the data source descriptor to access the database. Now let's turn our attention to deploying a Hibernate archive.

3.4.2 Deploying a Hibernate archive

Although accessing data in a database is an integral requirement for most applications, you might prefer to access the data using higher-level constructs than SQL statements, which is what you use with JDBC. Hibernate is an object-to-relational mapping (ORM) layer that enables you to use POJOs in your application while Hibernate worries about mapping those objects to tables in the relational database. Explaining what Hibernate is, how it works, and how to use it is beyond the scope of this book; for that we recommend *Java Persistence with Hibernate* by Christian Bauer and Gavin King.

JBoss AS provides a simple mechanism to support the use of Hibernate within your applications—the Hibernate archive. Creating a Hibernate archive is easy. It consists of the classes for the objects you want to persist to the database, the Hibernate mapping files for those classes, and a Hibernate service descriptor. Note that you don't have to create a Hibernate archive to use Hibernate within JBoss AS; the Hibernate archive is provided merely as a convenience if you have several applications accessing the same data via Hibernate.

You can create a Hibernate archive the following ways:

- Coding a persistent object that defines the data to store in the database
- Coding a mapping file that shows how to map the object contents to the database
- Coding the Hibernate services file which defines the Hibernate archive

Once you have the archive, you can package and deploy it. Let's look at the details for each of these steps.

CODING THE PERSISTENT OBJECT

First, you need a class to persist. For an example, let's consider a simple class that contains information about a video that you might download from a video rental website, as shown in listing 3.3.

Listing 3.3 Video.java

```
package org.jbia.har;
public class Video {
  private int id;
  private String name;
  private int minutes;
  private float price;
  /*getters and setters*/
}
```

Because the getters and setters are standard (nothing special about them!), we've omitted them to save space. Note that no special constructs or annotations are required; this looks like a standard JavaBean. The only special item is the id field because, in Hibernate, all persistable classes should have an object id.

CODING THE MAPPING FILE

Next, you need to define how the contents of the Video class are mapped to a table in the database. This is where the mapping file comes in. Listing 3.4 shows a mapping file that corresponds to the Video class.

Listing 3.4 Video.hbm.xml

```
<!DOCTYPE hibernate-mapping PUBLIC
   "-//Hibernate/Hibernate Mapping DTD 3.0//EN"
   "http://hibernate.sourceforge.net/hibernate-mapping-3.0.dtd">
<hibernate-mapping>
 <class name="org.jbia.har.Video" table="Video">
  <id name="id" type="integer" column="id">
   <generator class="identity" />
  </id>
  <property name="name" type="string" column="name" />
  <property name="minutes" type="integer" column="min" />
  <property name="price" type="float" column="price" />
 </class>
</hibernate-mapping>
```

Note the description of the id field. Setting the generator class to identity means that the database automatically assigns the object id when the object is persisted, using the database's built-in identity capability. This works for databases like MySQL. For databases that support a sequence column, you use a class value of sequence instead. Note the following example:

```
<id name="id" type="integer" column="id">
   <generator class="sequence" />
</id>
```

For various other possible values for the generator class, refer to the Hibernate documentation for details.

CODING THE HIBERNATE ARCHIVE CONFIGURATION FILE

Finally, you need a Hibernate archive configuration XML file to define the Hibernate archive. Listing 3.5 shows the XML for the video example.

Listing 3.5 video-hibernate.xml

```
<hibernate-configuration
  xmlns="urn:jboss:hibernate-deployer:1.0">
 <session-factory
   bean="jbia.har:app=Video"          ❶
   name="java:/hibernate/jbia/VideoSF">          ❷
  <property name="datasourceName">
➥   java:/jdbc/deploymentDS</property>          ❸
  <property name="dialect">
➥   org.hibernate.dialect.MySQLDialect          ❹
➥   </property>
```

```
  <property name="hbm2ddlAuto">        ❺
➥   create-drop</property>
  <property name="showSqlEnabled">
➥   true</property>
  <depends>jboss:service=Naming</depends>
  <depends>jboss:service=TransactionManager
➥   </depends>
  <depends>jboss.jca:name=jdbc/deploymentDS
➥   ,service=DataSourceBinding</depends>
 </session-factory>
</hibernate-configuration>
```

This descriptor creates an MBean, in this case named `jbia.har:app=Video` ❶. You can use any name that you like for the MBean, provided that it follows MBean naming conventions and is unique among all deployed MBeans.

The `name` attribute identifies the JNDI name for the Hibernate session factory ❷. The client uses this name to look up the session factory to work with persistent objects.

The example references the data source ❸ created in the previous section. Therefore, a Hibernate archive isn't a replacement for a *-ds.xml file; it builds on it. Because that data source uses the MySQL database, we identify it as such in the `dialect` property ❹. The Hibernate documentation lists the various dialects that are available; there's one for almost every available relational database.

The `create-drop` setting for `Hbm2ddlAuto` ❺ indicates that Hibernate automatically creates the tables described by the mapping files and drops any tables found in the database that aren't in one of the mapping files. This is a feature that would be used in a development environment, but not with a production database. The Hibernate archive deployer automatically scans the Hibernate archive looking for mapping files, *.hbm.xml; you don't have to explicitly identify those files. The Hibernate documentation describes the various other settings for the `Hbm2ddlAuto` attribute.

The attributes used in this example aren't the only possibilities. Many Hibernate properties have corresponding MBean attributes; the JBoss AS documentation has a table containing this information. Some of the Hibernate properties are handled in special ways; those properties and their special handling are provided in table 3.7.

Table 3.6 Hibernate properties that are handled specially

Hibernate property	MBean attribute	Special handling
`hibernate.cache.provider_class`	`CacheProviderClass`	If not specified, defaults to `org.hibernate.cache.HashtableCacheProvider`
`hibernate.transaction.flush_before_completion`	-none-	Always set to `true`
`hibernate.transaction.auto_close_session`	-none-	Always set to `true`

Table 3.6 Hibernate properties that are handled specially *(continued)*

Hibernate property	MBean attribute	Special handling
`hibernate.connection.agressive_release`	-none-	Always set to `true`
`hibernate.connection.release_mode`	-none-	Always set to `after_statement`

Refer to the Hibernate documentation for details regarding what these settings mean. Now that you have all the required files, you're ready to create the Hibernate archive.

PACKAGING THE HIBERNATE ARCHIVE

Compile the Java source file(s) and place them into an archive file, named video.har, as shown in figure 3.6. Note that the archive uses the extension *.har.* To build such an archive, you can use the JAR utility and name the resulting file video.har.

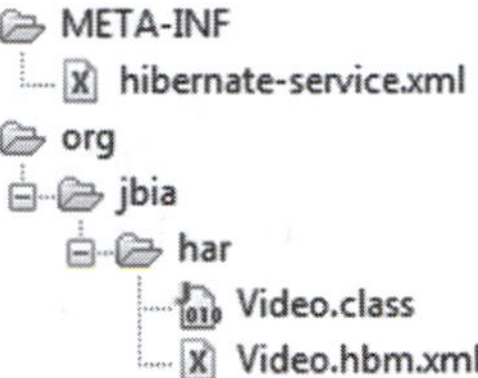

Figure 3.6 The contents of the video.har archive

The mapping file, Video.hbm.xml, must have the same base filename (*Video* in this example) as the class file and must be in the same directory as the class file. You can also include helper classes, if required; but don't provide a mapping file for any class that's not persistent.

DEPLOYING THE HIBERNATE ARCHIVE

You can deploy the Hibernate archive by copying it to the deploy directory, making the Hibernate archive an application (based on our loose definition of an application). And like other applications, you can deploy it as an archive file or an exploded directory. Once deployed, any other application deployed to the application server can access the persistent objects defined by the Hibernate archive.

CODING THE HIBERNATE CLIENT

As we mentioned earlier, the client uses the JNDI name to look up a session factory. From there, it can open a Hibernate session and use that session to manipulate persistent objects. Once the client is done, it should close the session to free it up for other clients.

Listing 3.6 shows code that can be used to look up the session factory and create the session.

Listing 3.6 Look-up of Hibernate session

```
import javax.naming.InitialContext;
import org.hibernate.SessionFactory;
import org.hibernate.Session;
...
  InitialContext ctx = new InitialContext();           ❶
  SessionFactory hsf = (SessionFactory)
    ctx.lookup("java:/hibernate/jbia/VideoSF");             ❷
  Session hs = hsf.openSession();       ❸
  try {
    /* do something with hs */
```

```
    } finally {
      hs.close();        ❹
    }
  ...
```

This Hibernate client is an application deployed to the application server; hence, no properties need to be used to obtain the initial JNDI context ❶. The client uses the JNDI name specified in the hibernate-services.xml file to look up the session factory ❷. The client then opens a session ❸, does some work, and then closes the session ❹.

Once you have the Hibernate session object, you use it as you would in a normal Hibernate program. For example, the following code would get a list of all videos, ordered alphabetically by name:

```
import org.hibernate.Query;
import java.util.List;
...
  Query q = hs.createQuery("from org.jbia.har.Video order by name");
  List l = q.list();
...
```

And the following code would create a new video and store it in the database:

```
Video video = new Video();
video.setName("Monty Python and the Holy Grail");
video.setMinutes(91);
video.setPrice(14.99f);
hs.save(video);
```

The above client code could appear in an EJB stateless session bean, and that bean could be invoked from a servlet. In chapter 7, we describe how to package web applications and EJBs into an EAR file. You can also place a Hibernate archive into an EAR file.

PACKAGING A HIBERNATE ARCHIVE IN AN EAR FILE

Packaging a Hibernate archive within an EAR file is similar to doing the same with a data source. For example, assume that the web application is packaged in video.war, and the EJBs are packaged in video.jar. You can place those archives and the Hibernate archive into a single EAR file, which has the contents illustrated in figure 3.7.

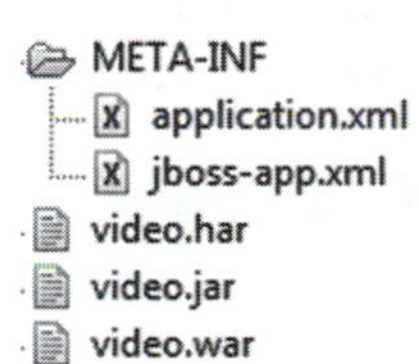

Figure 3.7 Contents of the `video.ear` package containing a Hibernate archive

The application.xml file is a standard Java EE descriptor, and because Hibernate archives aren't part of standard Java EE, they can't be referenced in that file. Instead, you use a META-INF/jboss-app.xml file to reference the Hibernate archive, as follows:

```
<!DOCTYPE jboss-app PUBLIC "-//JBoss//DTD J2EE Application 1.4//EN"
      "http://www.jboss.org/j2ee/dtd/jboss-app_4_0.dtd">
<jboss-app>
 <module>
  <har>video.har</har>
 </module>
</jboss-app>
```

Now that you have the EAR file, you can deploy it and run the application, which then uses the Hibernate archive to access the persistent objects.

3.5 Summary

In this chapter, you learned how to deploy applications, both business applications and services, to the application server. You found out that you could package an application as either an archive file or exploded directory. You became acquainted with the various application types and found out that the applications types are deployed in a specific order.

You should also have a basic understanding of how the application server loads classes and how you can scope the class loading to avoid conflicts between different versions of class libraries. You're now prepared to handle many of the common deployment errors, such as a class not found or class cast exception, or to deal with errors that result if you have a duplicate JAR file.

As an added bonus, you also found out about configuring data sources and Hibernate archives. Configuring data sources is a topic that we return to several times in the remaining chapters of this book because almost anything of interest done with an application server involves a database.

What we've given you in this chapter is the equivalent of us telling you that, in order to turn your new house into a home, you have to unload the moving van (or your buddy's pickup truck) and bring the furniture into the house. You might have even figured out that certain things go into certain rooms.

But we've not yet covered the equivalent of how to turn each room into a functional and inviting area of the house. That's what we get into in the next part of the book; we discuss specific types of applications and how to configure them for use with the application server. We tackle this job one room—we mean *application type*—at a time. But before we get there, we need to cover one more global topic that we return to in various chapters: security.

3.6 References

JBoss AS documentation—http://www.jboss.org/file-access/default/members/jbossas/freezone/docs/Server_Configuration_Guide/beta500/html/index.html

jarFinder utility—http://www.isocra.com/articles/jarFinder.php

4 Securing applications

This chapter covers

- Fundamentals of security
- Dynamic login configuration
- Secure communication
- Public-key certificates
- JBoss login modules

Security is an important part of most enterprise software applications because system vulnerabilities and loss of sensitive data can be costly. Security can be compromised in many ways: unauthorized users may access your application's data; someone may intercept a message being transmitted between two users; or hackers may expose vulnerabilities in your network or application server, giving them access to run commands on your OS.

The two main aspects to security are securing access to information inside of your application and securing access to the environment in which your application runs. Hackers could go through your application to access information or execute malicious code, or they could access the OS on which your application runs. Security must be put into place to protect both application data and the environment in which your applications are running.

Chapter 15 discusses various configuration and environment-related topics related to securing your application server and the surrounding environment. Other chapters in the book also (tangentially) discuss topics related to application server security. Table 4.1 summarizes the sections where we talk about application security for the different components and resources available in the application server.

Table 4.1 A summary of where we discuss the authentication, authorization, and secure communication for each of the major Java EE component technologies

Technology	Authentication	Authorization	Secure communication
Fundamentals	4.1.2	4.1.3	4.2
Web	6.2 and 6.5	6.3	6.4 and 6.5
EJB	7.8.3	7.8	7.8.4
Messaging	8.5.2	8.5.2	8.5.7
Web Services	9.4	9.4	9.5
Portlets	11.4	11.4	Not covered

NOTE Another security concern in application security is the ability to track and monitor user operations for accountability and auditing purposes. For example, in a payroll system, you may want to keep a log of user actions that result in a salary adjustment and make sure that you can keep track of who authorized each salary change. Security auditing and accountability is a large topic and isn't covered in this book.

In this chapter, we cover the fundamental aspects of application security including authentication, authorization, and secure communication. We also discuss JBoss AS's security implementation, called JBoss SX, and show how to configure it. Finally, we talk about the various JBoss SX security modules, which enable you to read security data from different sources such as a database or a Lightweight Directory Access Protocol (LDAP) server. Future chapters will build on this chapter to show how to enable security in web applications, EJB applications, and for JMS.

Let's explore some of the fundamentals concepts of application security.

4.1 Understanding security

To better understand the topics related to application security, we examine an enterprise application that makes use of authentication, authorization, and secure communication. After giving you a high-level overview of these security concepts, we dig further into authentication and authorization, deferring the discussion on secure communication until section 4.2 because that topic is more involved. After talking about authentication and authorization, we show how to configure security in JBoss AS and how to enable logging. Let's start with the overview.

4.1.1 Understanding application security

To understand how authentication, authorization, and secure communication fit into an enterprise application, let's look at an example of a web-based retail banking application. Figure 4.1 shows a typical request flow through the application.

Most people have accessed a web-based bank before, so this shouldn't look too unfamiliar. In the diagram, we have a bank customer (let's call her Melissa) who's trying to access her bank account through her bank's secure Java EE-enabled website. In order for customers to be able to log into the bank's website without worrying about phishing schemes or man-in-the-middle attacks, the bank has purchased a secure public-key certificate from a trusted *certificate authority* (CA). Melissa accesses the bank website and clicks on a link that should take her to her account summary ❶. This link might be something like https://www.jbossbank.com/acctSummary.

Because the page is accessed via a secured protocol (HTTPS), the server sends its secure certificate to Melissa's web browser. Melissa's browser, like all major browsers, has a list of well-known certificate authorities. On receiving the bank's certificate, her browser turns around and asks the trusted certificate authorities if the certificate belongs to the bank ❷. Assuming that one of the certificate authorities acknowledges the authenticity of the bank's certificate, Melissa's browser tries to forward her to the account summary page she originally requested. As far as Melissa is concerned, this all happens behind the scenes. She can now trust that she's accessing *her* bank and that nobody can intercept her communication with her bank. Also, as long as she accesses the bank over the secure protocol, all her communications are transferred over a secure channel.

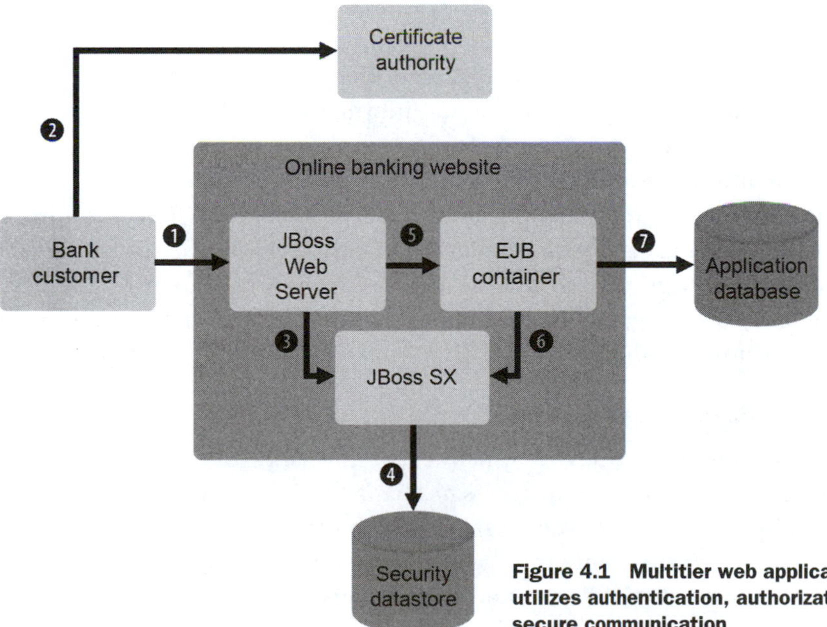

Figure 4.1 Multitier web application that utilizes authentication, authorization, and secure communication

Now that Melissa knows that she can trust the bank, the bank needs to know if it can trust her. The URL for the account summary page is secured with form-based authentication. Users also must be a part of the AccountHolder role before accessing the page. Before Melissa can access the account summary page, her request is intercepted by the JBoss Web Server web container. The container realizes that the URL that she's accessing is secured, so it checks with the security framework ❸ to see if Melissa is already logged in. After realizing that she's not, a login form is sent back to Melissa, prompting her for her username and password.

When Melissa types in her credentials and submits the form, the web container receives the form submission and passes Melissa's credentials to the application server's security framework ❸. The security framework accesses security information from a database ❹, which it queries to determine whether or not Melissa can access to the resource she's requesting. First, the security framework should *authenticate* Melissa, comparing the password she supplies against a known password to see if she should be granted access to the system at all. Then, the security framework should *authorize* Melissa, determining if her username is associated with a role that can access the resource.

Everything matches up, so the security framework returns control back to the web container. Now that Melissa's credentials have been verified, the web container forwards her request to the resource associated with the URL for the account summary. The account summary page is implemented as a servlet. In order for the servlet to render Melissa's account summary information, it needs to access her account information. The servlet makes a call to the `getAccountSummary(User u)` method on a session EJB called `Account`, which runs in the EJB container ❺. Because the EJB container runs locally, the servlet automatically propagates the security credentials.

Like the servlet, this EJB method only allows access to users with the AccountHolder role. The EJB server accesses the JBoss SX security framework ❻ to determine if Melissa is authenticated and authorized to access the resources. Again, access to the EJB method succeeds, and Melissa's account information loads from the application database ❼. After the account summary loads, control returns to the servlet, which renders the output and sends it back to Melissa, still over a secure channel.

The three main areas of application security that we see here are authentication, authorization, and secure communication. In this section, we discuss authentication and authorization in more detail. We also discuss how to configure JBoss SX and how to enable security logging. Secure communication requires more discussion and is covered in more depth in section 4.2. Let's take a closer look at authentication.

4.1.2 Understanding authentication

Authentication is the process by which a system verifies the identity of a user. In the example, when Melissa tries to access her bank's website, the site asks her for her username and password. This procedure allows the site to authenticate her as a valid user. But humans aren't the only ones whose identities are validated by software applications; programs can also try to authenticate against an application. In security parlance, *principal* refers to either a human user or a machine that's trying to prove its

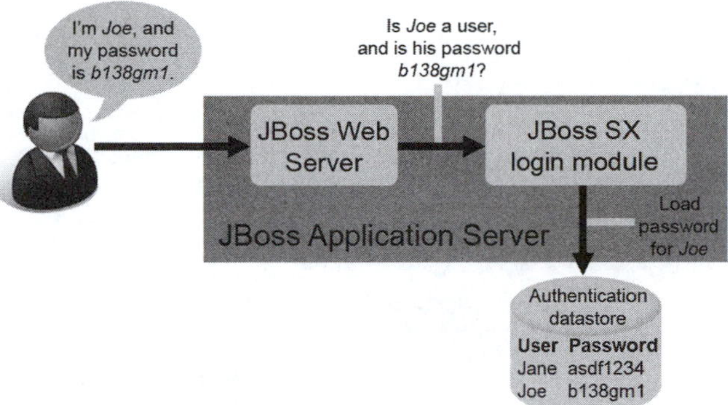

Figure 4.2 The application server authenticates a principal when it tries to access a secured resource.

identity on another system. A principal provides one or more forms of identification known as *credentials*. Possible credentials include passwords, certificates, biometric data, smart cards, physical tokens, or any other reliable form of identification.

In figure 4.2, we show a user named Joe trying to access a web resource. He provides his username and password. The server calls the JBoss SX framework to authenticate the user. The JBoss SX framework then tries to load Joe's password from a security data source and compare it to the password he provided. The security framework doesn't authenticate the user if his username doesn't exist in the data source or if his password doesn't match the one in the data source.

Security data can be kept in different data sources, so JBoss SX has different *login modules* that can read security information from different locations such as a database or an LDAP server. We discuss the different login modules that are available in JBoss SX in section 4.3.

Many cryptographic protocols provide both clients and the server with the ability to authenticate each other by using public certificates as a credential. We give you an overview of how this works when we discuss secure communication in section 4.2.

Now, let's take a closer look at authorization.

4.1.3 Understanding authorization

Authorization is the process of verifying that a principal has sufficient privileges to access an application resource. For example, a user may have access to a document management system but may not have access to look at particular documents put into the system by other users. Authorization is often achieved by assigning one or more roles to a principal and then associating one or more roles with a component or resource that a principal might want to access. When the principal tries to access the component, the system looks at the roles allowed to access the component and the roles assigned to the principal. If the principal has one of the roles assigned to the component, then he can access the component; otherwise, the principal can't access the component. This process is called role-based authorization.

Figure 4.3 shows how authorization works when our friend Joe tries to access the administrator page on the web application he's using.

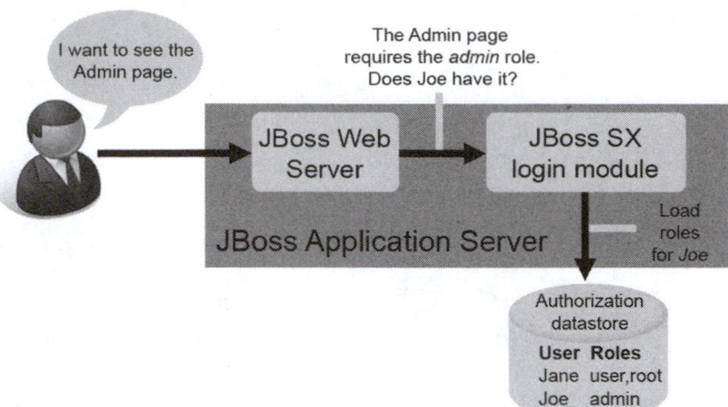

Figure 4.3 The steps involved in authorizing a user

Joe is trying to access the administrator page, which is configured to require a role of *admin*. The web container asks the JBoss SX login module whether Joe (who has already been authenticated) can access the page. The login module goes to the authorization data source, loads all of Joe's roles, and then asserts that one of those roles is *admin*.

Java EE defines declarative, role-based authorization for standard component technologies such as servlet, JSP, and EJB. Declarative authorization means that you can assign roles to components via configuration without the need to write any code. As you'll learn in chapter 7, access to EJB methods is restricted by roles defined in either annotations or a deployment descriptor. Web applications can define role access for particular URLs in deployment descriptors as well, as we discuss in chapter 6.

There are certain situations where role-based security doesn't cut it. This fact becomes evident when the security you want to apply depends on the context of the request that the user sends. Applying security based on information in the request is often called *context-based security*, or *programmatic security*. For example, you want to allow a bank employee to enter deposits under $10,000 dollars, but anything over $10,000 would require manager's approval. This type of security often involves writing code and is considered part of the business functionality of your software. Unfortunately, there's a lot of information to cover on role-based security, so we don't discuss context-based security. You can implement context-based security in several ways for each of the different component models. For EJBs, you can use JBoss SX security proxies or EJB3 interceptors. For web applications, you can use servlet filters, custom valves, or interceptors.

Now that you have some background on how authentication and authorization work, let's discuss how you can configure applications to enable these aspects of security.

4.1.4 Configuring security

Each Java EE component or resource has a different mechanism for defining security. For example, you can use a web application's standard deployment descriptor to define which authentication policy should be used and to secure individual URLs by defining roles that have permission to access them. This definition of what method to use and what should be secured is defined in each component's standard deployment descriptor. But, the Java EE specification doesn't specify the underlying security implementation; it doesn't describe where the security data should be kept, how it should be retrieved, or how it should be validated. Each application server vendor has to create its own security implementation and allow programmers to configure and use it through vendor-specific deployment descriptors.

JBoss AS's security implementation is called JBoss SX, which builds on top of the Java Authentication and Authorization Service (JAAS) to secure all the Java EE technologies running in the application server. The relationships between the major components of the security framework are shown in figure 4.4.

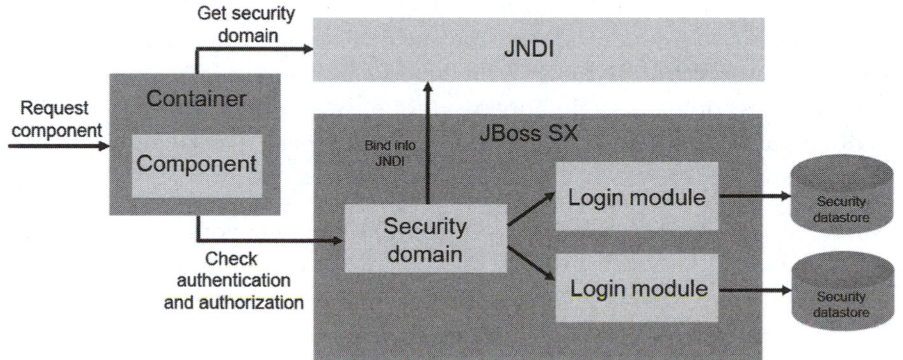

Figure 4.4 The security domain and login modules are the major components of the security framework.

When a request comes into JBoss AS, the targeted application component or resource—the web application, EJB application, JMS queue/topic, or whatever it may be—doesn't need to know where the underlying security data exists or how it's accessed. The component request is routed to a JBoss SX component called a *security domain*, an abstraction used to secure all requests made to a component. The security domain performs any necessary security checks and notifies the component whether the user can proceed or not. The security domain knows how to use one or more login modules to load security data from a data source.

Security domains are configured at the server level and can be used by any component within the server. Security domains are bound into JNDI when the server starts; pointing to the security domain's JNDI context maps a component to a security domain. You can add or modify existing security domain definitions within the server/xxx/conf/login-config.xml file.

Listing 4.1 shows an example of a security domain definition in this file.

Listing 4.1 A security domain definition in the login-config.xml file

```
<application-policy name="jmx-console">        ❶
  <authentication>
    <login-module
      code = "org.jboss.security.auth.spi.UsersRolesLoginModule"    ❷
```

```
      flag = "required">
      <module-option name="usersProperties">
        props/jmx-console-users.properties
      </module-option>
      <module-option name="rolesProperties">
        props/jmx-console-roles.properties
      </module-option>
    </login-module>
  </authentication>
</application-policy>
```

The application-policy block ❶ defines a security domain. The name attribute specifies the name of the security domain. JBoss SX uses this name to generate the JNDI context with which it binds the security domain into JNDI. In the case of this example, the name attribute is set to some-domain, so the JNDI context associated with this security domain definition would be java:/jaas/jmx-console. All security domains are bound under the java:/jaas namespace. (As we discuss in the appendix A, the java: namespace is local to the server.)

NOTE When you define a security domain in the login-config.xml file, JBoss SX doesn't automatically bind the security domain into JNDI. JBoss SX only binds a security domain into JNDI after you deploy an application that references the security domain.

You can use the login-module element in the application-policy configuration to point to one or more login modules. In the example configuration, you point to a login module of type UsersRolesLoginModule ❷. This login module loads security information from properties files on the filesystem. A typical production system uses a database or an LDAP server to hold security information. JBoss SX provides several login modules that support different backend data sources. We go through the different login modules available with JBoss SX in section 4.3.

You've learned how to configure security by adding a domain to a shared configuration file. Some people prefer to have the security configuration for their applications reside in the application archives themselves. Let's see how this can be done.

4.1.5 Dynamic login configuration

JBoss SX provides a feature called *dynamic login configuration* that allows you to define security in your application archive rather than in the server's login-config.xml file. To enable this feature, you have to create and deploy an MBean for the service to the server's server/xxx/deploy directory. The service will look like that shown in listing 4.2.

Listing 4.2 The MBean service definition for the dynamic login configuration service

```
<server>
  <mbean code="org.jboss.security.auth.login.DynamicLoginConfig"
    name="jboss:service=DynamicLoginConfig">
    <attribute name="AuthConfig">
      dynamic-login-config.xml
    </attribute>
    <depends optional-attribute-name="LoginConfigService">
```

```
      jboss.security:service=XMLLoginConfig
    </depends>
    <depends optional-attribute-name="SecurityManagerService">
      jboss.security:service=JaasSecurityManager
    </depends>
  </mbean>
</server>
```

You can name this file whatever you want, as long as you suffix it with -service.xml (for example, dynamicloginconfig-service.xml) so that the appropriate JBoss deployer picks it up and deploys it as an MBean service. You use the `AuthConfig` attribute ❶ to specify the name of the file (within your archive) that will contain your security domain definitions. The format of this file is exactly the same as the login-config.xml file we discussed in the last section, so you can copy that into your application archive and whittle it down. In listing 4.2, we configure the dynamic-login config service to look for the dynamic-login-config.xml file. If this were a WAR file, an EAR file, or any other archive, JBoss AS would look for it in the META-INF directory of that archive. You enable security for your application and point it to a security domain defined in this file.

The file that points to the AuthConfig attribute has to be available in the root of your application's class path. If you have a WAR file, you have to wrap it in an EAR file to use dynamic login configuration because the class path for a WAR file isn't accessible from outside the WAR file. You can create a JAR file in the EAR (maybe calling it resource.jar or dynamic-login.jar) that contains this file and any other resource file you may need when configuring dynamic login. Then you configure your application.xml file to know about the JAR file.

Now that you've learned about configuring security domains, we'll show how to enable logging for the various security services.

4.1.6 Logging security on the server

By default, security logging is minimal. If you want to log more security information for debugging purposes, you can add the following to your server/xxx/conf/jboss-log4j.xml file:

```
<category name="org.jboss.security">
  <priority value="TRACE" class="org.jboss.logging.XLevel"/>
</category>
<category name="org.jboss.web.tomcat.security">
  <priority value="TRACE" class="org.jboss.logging.XLevel"/>
</category>
<category name="org.apache.catalina">
  <priority value="DEBUG"/>
</category>
```

Remember to comment out the threshold parameter in the appender that you want the logging messages to appear in. We discussed logging in more detail in chapter 2. In addition to setting the log4j logging, you can set the following JVM property when you start JBoss AS to get additional logging related to SSL:

```
-Djavax.net.debug=ssl
```

Now that you have a general understanding of what authentication and authorization are and how JBoss SX enables Java EE security, let's take an in-depth look at secure communication.

4.2 Using secure communication

We often need to send data over an open network (for example, the internet), but we should be aware of three aspects of secure communication: *confidentiality, data integrity,* and *source integrity.* Confidentiality refers to protecting a sent message from being read by anybody else besides the intended recipient(s). To ensure confidentiality, the sender often encrypts messages that the recipient then decrypts. Data integrity refers to a message recipient's confidence that the message she receives wasn't manipulated while in transport. Encrypted communication protocols can also ensure data integrity.

Source integrity gives assurance to a message recipient that the message she receives is indeed from the sender that she thinks she's communicating with and not somebody else who's posing as the sender. Source integrity can be protected by using a reliable third party that assigns certificates to different people and organizations. A person who wants other people to trust him can obtain a certificate and send it to other parties who can verify the certificate owner's identity by asking the trusted third party, which is usually a certificate authority.

WARNING It's important to remember that the source that has integrity may be a machine, meaning that a non-trusted user on a trusted machine could gain access to things that he shouldn't.

Secure protocols such as Transport Layer Security (TLS) or Secure Sockets Layer (SSL) can be used to provide these three aspects of secure communication. These protocols use a combination of public and private key cryptography and digital certificates. In this section, we discuss mechanics and configuration behind these forms of cryptography.

NOTE TLS is a newer specification that's meant to be a replacement for SSL. TLS 1.0 is similar to SSL 3.0. TLS is starting to gain in acceptance and usage, but SSL is still a more dominant and well-known protocol. Because more people recognize the initialism SSL, from here on, we refer to both SSL and TLS as SSL.

Let's start by talking about the two major categories of encryption: symmetric encryption and asymmetric encryption.

4.2.1 Understanding symmetric and asymmetric encryption

Encryption is easier to understand when you consider the analogy of a lock and key. Let's say that you have a secret message that you want to mail to a friend. You put the message in a box that can be secured with a padlock. If you and your friend both have keys to the same lock, you can put the lock on the box, lock it, and send it to your friend. After receiving the box, she can open it with her key. This is how *symmetric encryption* works. A message is encrypted with a *secret key* and decrypted with the same key. As long as the key isn't compromised, the two parties can communicate securely.

Figure 4.5 Symmetric encryption uses a single secret key that both parties use to encrypt and decrypt text.

Figure 4.5 illustrates that with symmetric encryption, both parties participating in the communication use the same secret key.

The difficulty with private key encryption is the initial distribution of the shared secret key. For both parties to initially know about the key, you have to share the key in an insecure fashion. But a slightly different strategy makes secure communication possible without an initial shared key being exchanged.

Returning to our analogy, let's say that your friend has a special lock with two keys; each key can lock the padlock, but the padlock can only be unlocked with the opposite key. Now your friend makes copies of one of the keys (her public key) and gives them out to anyone and everyone. Whoever wants to send her a secret message can put the message in the box and use the public key to securely send the message. Once she receives the message, she uses the key that she didn't distribute (her private key) to unlock the padlock.

Public key encryption, or *asymmetric encryption*, uses a pair of mathematically associated keys. After a message is encrypted with one, it can only be decrypted with the other. It's also infeasible to derive one key using its counterpart, so having the public key can't help a hacker ascertain the private key. Figure 4.6 shows you the sequence of events that occurs when two parties communicate using public key encryption.

Asymmetric encryption is convenient because you don't have to worry about distributing a shared key; but, unfortunately, it's much slower than symmetric encryption. Many secure protocols (such as SSL) use public key encryption to establish a secret key

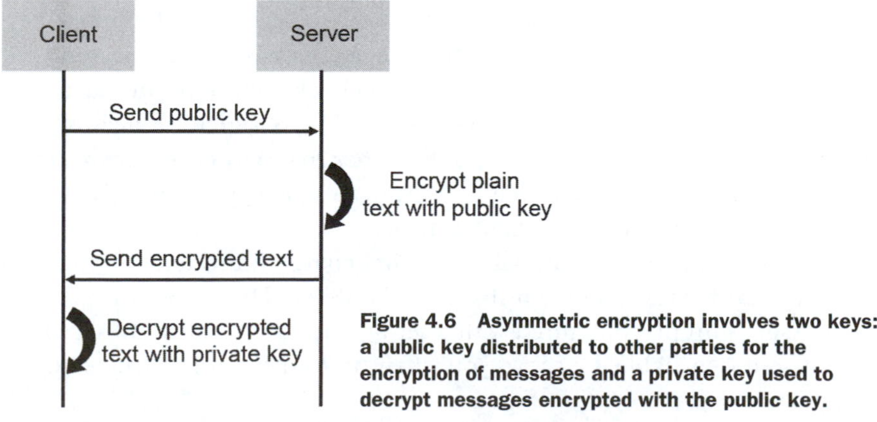

Figure 4.6 Asymmetric encryption involves two keys: a public key distributed to other parties for the encryption of messages and a private key used to decrypt messages encrypted with the public key.

when two users first negotiate a conversation, and then they use the secret key to continue the communication using symmetric encryption.

NOTE A private key is part of an asymmetric key pair. The private key should never be distributed or shared, but its public key counterpart can be shared with anybody. A secret key is used in symmetric encryption and is shared between two users. Symmetric encryption is also (confusingly) called private key encryption, even though the key that it uses is called a *secret key* and the name *private key* already has meaning in asymmetric encryption.

You've learned how symmetric and asymmetric encryption work, but secure protocols can do more than encrypt messages; they also enable source authentication.

4.2.2 Understanding certificates and source authentication

Consider another analogy. Let's say that you get a package in the mail from your bank with an unlocked padlock and a key. It's one of those special public keys that can be used for asymmetric encryption. The bank asks you to fill out some forms with personal information, lock it in the box, and send it to them. Assuming that this is a common way to send secure correspondence to your bank, you compile the information, take the locked box down to the post office, and send it to the return address that was on the package that you received. You're feeling pretty good about yourself because you sent your message securely.

A few days later, you go to check your account balance and see that your account is empty. What happened? The letter you received wasn't from the bank. A scammer conned you out of your money using a so-called *social hack*. The letter and lockbox you received looked almost identical to one you usually get from your bank. You trusted that the address that you were sending it to was your bank's, but it wasn't.

Public keys are great, but the person sending an encrypted message needs to be certain that he is sending his message to the right person. He needs a way to ensure that a public key he received is from the person he thinks it's from. In addition to encrypting a message, the SSL protocol supports authentication of both the client and the server through use of public key certificates.

A *public key certificate* is a digital certificate that consists of some information about the certificate holder's identity and a public key. To verify that the public key belongs to the user whose identity is on the certificate, a CA signs the certificate. For example, when you try to access your bank's website to check your account balance, your web browser obtains the bank's certificate and verifies its signature against the CA that signed the certificate. If the CA verifies that it has that particular certificate in its database, then you can rest assured that the certificate that you received isn't a false certificate that was created under the bank's name.

There are many publicly available CAs that charge individuals and enterprises for public key certificates. The main three are VeriSign, Thawte, and Entrust. All major web browsers ship preconfigured with a set of trusted CAs. Most JREs also ship with a list of trusted CAs. Table 4.2 shows you where to find the list of trusted CAs in different applications.

Table 4.2 Where to find the trusted CAs in different applications

Application	Where the CA information is kept
Firefox 1.0	Tools > Options > Advanced > Certificates > Manage Certificates > Authorities[a]
Firefox 1.5	Tools > Options > Advanced > Security > View Certificates > Authorities[a]
Firefox 2.0 and 3.0	Tools > Options > Advanced > Encryption > View Certificates > Authorities[a]
Internet Explorer 6	Tools > Internet Options > Content > Certificates > Trusted Root Certification Authorities
Internet Explorer 7	Tools > Internet Options > Content > Certificates > Trusted Root Certification Authorities
Java program	[JRE HOME]/lib/security/cacerts[b]

a. The menu items may be different on different platforms. For example, on Mac OS, you go to Firefox > Preferences instead of Tools > Options.

b. This isn't a plain-text file. To access the certificates in this file, you have to use a tool called *keytool*. We talk about this in section 4.2.3.

If you want a signed certificate, you must first generate a self-signed certificate and use it to create a Certificate Signing Request (CSR). The CSR (along with a few hundred dollars) is then sent to the CA who validates your identity and then sends back a signed certificate.

But, certificates don't always have to be signed by a third-party CA. Developers often create self-signed certificates for use in their development environments. An organization can also act as its own CA. The certificate is often signed by the organization, which runs its own CA server. To authenticate a certificate, the client has to recognize the private CA. A web client can add the enterprise's private CA to the web browser's list of authorities to authenticate the server. But with a Java-based client or server, either the cacerts file must be modified, or the runtime must use an alternative file. We talk about these options in section 4.2.4.

Now that you have a good understanding of how encryption, certificates, and certificate authorities work, let's look at how you can create your own certificates and get them signed.

4.2.3 Creating and signing certificates

Most JVMs ships with a command-line tool called *keytool*. This tool can be used for the following:

- Generating and storing self-signed public/private key pairs
- Generating CSRs
- Importing public certificates that you've had signed by a CA
- Importing public certificates for some other party that you trust

As figure 4.7 shows, keytool stores public/private key pairs and certificates inside of *keystores*. You can think of a keystore as a container (or a keychain) for keys. As you'll

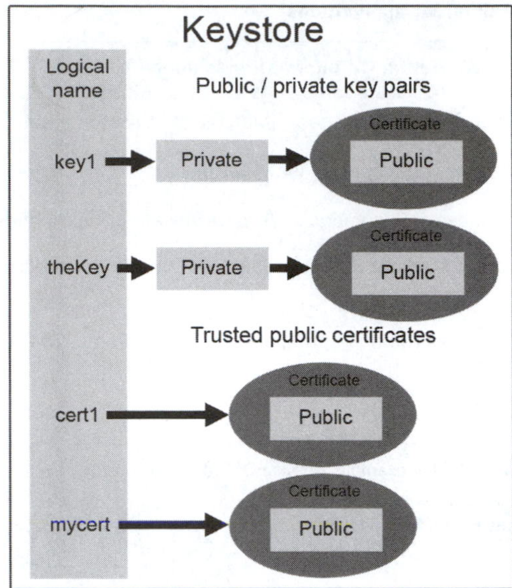

Figure 4.7 A keystore can contain your public/private key pairs, as well as other people's trusted public certificates.

learn when we discuss encryption throughout the book, different JBoss AS services utilize keystores to access keys and certificates.

You can use keytool from any directory if your system's `PATH` environment variable contains the bin directory under the root of your JDK installation. Let's look at some examples of common things that you can do with keytool. If you want to create a new private key with a self-signed certificate, you run the following command:

```
keytool -genkey -alias mykey -keyalg RSA -validity 3650 -keystore
➥ mykeys.keystore
```

When you run this command, keytool prompts you for a password for the keystore, several pieces of identifying information about you and your organization, and a password for the key that you want to create. This command generates a public/private key pair using the RSA algorithm (named using the the last initials of the three guys who invented it) that expires after 10 years with an alias of `mykey` in a keystore called `mykeys.keystore`. As you see in figure 4.7, the alias is a logical name that provides an easier way to access the key when you try to read it out of the keystore later.

If you don't specify a keystore using the `-keystore` command-line switch (`mykeys.keystore` in this example), then keytool uses a default keystore called `.keystore` in the home directory of the user running the command. The location of the home directory depends on the OS you're using.

If you want to export the CSR for the self-signed certificate you created, you issue the following command:

```
keytool -certreq -alias mykey -keystore mykeys.keystore -file getMeSigned.cer
```

When you run this command, keytool prompts you for the keystore password. After entering the password, keytool outputs a CSR that can be sent to a CA for signing.

After receiving the response from the CA, you can import the certificate into the keystore using the following command:

```
keytool -import -alias mycert -keystore mykeys.keystore -file
➥ signedCertificate.cer
```

You can also export your certificate from the keystore if you want to distribute it using the following command:

```
keytool -export -alias mykey -keystore mykeys.keystore -file mykey.cer
```

This command prompts you for the keystore password and then outputs your certificate, whereas the `certreq` command outputs a CSR.

When you're configuring certificates for Java applications, you often need to modify the cacerts file that we mentioned in 4.2.2.

4.2.4 Modifying the cacerts file

The cacerts file (referenced in table 4.2) that ships with the JRE contains a list of trusted CAs. This file is a keystore that only contains public key certificates for trusted certificates or CAs. This type of keystore is often called a *truststore*. If you're running a Java application that needs to trust a certificate authority above and beyond the ones that come prepackaged with the JRE, you have one of two choices: use a different truststore or modify the cacerts truststore.

If you want to change the certificates in the cacerts file, you import certificates into the file using the keytool command as described in the last section. For example, if you get a self-signed certificate called server.cer for the server that you want to trust, you might import it as follows:

```
keytool -import -alias myserver -file server.cer
➥        -keystore C:/jdk1.5.0_06/jre/lib/security/cacerts
```

The password that you use may differ between different JDKs and different versions. For example, the cacerts file that ships with Sun's version 1.5 JVM uses the password `changeit`.

To use a different truststore, you have to provide the following JRE arguments when you start your Java application:

```
java -Djavax.net.ssl.trustStore=<file>
➥   -Djavax.net.ssl.trustStorePassword=<pass> …
```

The `javax.net.ssl.trustStore` argument should point to the file where the alternative truststore is located. The `javax.net.ssl.trustStorePassword` argument passes the password into the truststore. The password for a truststore (as with a keystore) is the password to the file that holds the certificates, not the password for the certificates themselves. Those passwords are defined when you create the certificates.

4.2.5 Understanding certificate-based client authentication

In SSL communication, the server is required to have a certificate. In typical use (as when a user tries to access his bank's website), the server has a certificate, but the client doesn't need one. *Server authentication* occurs when the client and server are using SSL but only the server has a certificate. In this scheme, when a client tries to access a

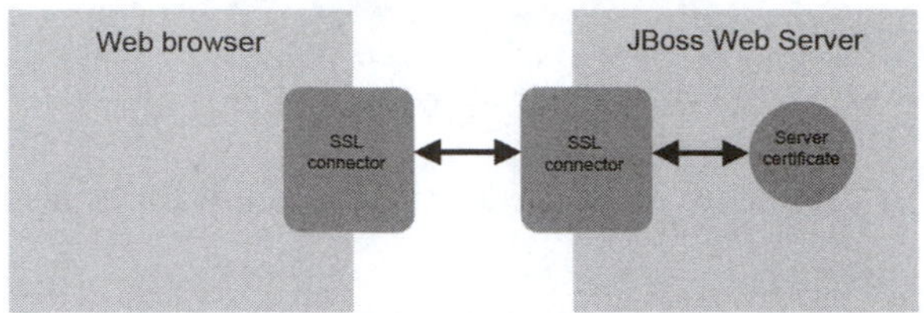

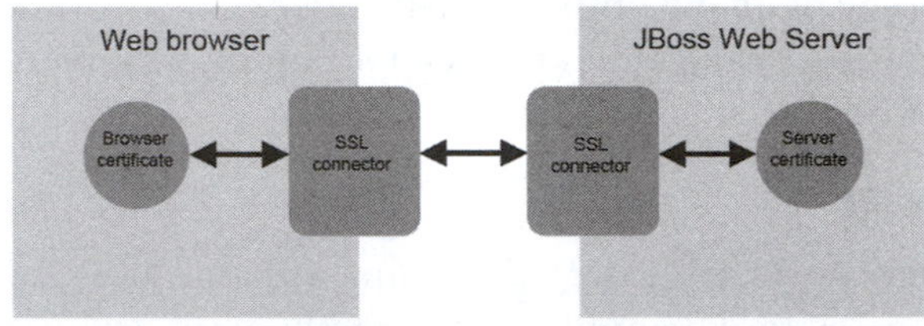

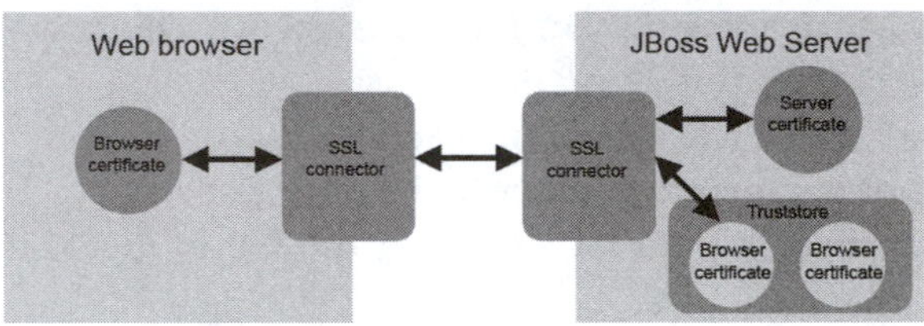

Figure 4.8 The ways that certificates can be used for authentication

server, the client verifies the server's certificate during the protocol-level handshaking, as you can see in the top diagram in figure 4.8.

SSL is capable of authenticating a client as well. Authenticating a client happens in a *mutual authentication* scheme; both the client and the server must have certificates. With mutual authentication, when a client tries to access the server, the protocol-level handshaking forces both parties to verify one another's certificates. In JBoss AS, SSL client authentication can be used to authenticate clients who are trying to access either the web container or the EJB container. For web applications, protocol-level mutual authentication can be configured using the HTTP connector as discussed in chapter 6 (section 6.4.3). The middle diagram in figure 4.8 shows that both the client and the server need to have certificates in order to have mutual authentication. Table 4.3 summarizes the differences between server authentication and mutual authentication.

Table 4.3 The differences between server and mutual authentication

Authentication strategy	Who wants to verify the other party's identity?	Who needs public key?
Server authentication	Client	Server
Mutual authentication	Client and server	Client and server

Mutual authentication isn't commonly found in publicly accessible web sites because all users of a website would have to create or obtain their own certificates and set them up in their browsers. Mutual authentication is sometimes used in intranet applications and in applications that need added assurance that requests coming into the system originate from a safe source. For example, a bank may implement SSL mutual authentication in an application that allows other banks to submit transactions over the internet. Although the authentication could be done by password, the certificate gives the bank more confidence about the identity of the client and also ensures that the information is encrypted before it's sent over the internet.

Many internal corporate applications use mutual authentication to allow employees to securely access their applications over the internet. In many cases, the company is its own CA and assigns keys to each employee who needs access to the internal systems.

So far, we've talked about mutual authentication at the protocol level, meaning that the client and server authenticate each other using their CAs when the protocol-level handshaking occurs. But this type of protocol authentication is different from the application-level authentication we talked about in section 4.1.2. The server can use the client's certificate as a credential for application-level authentication. Building on top of the protocol-level mutual authentication, the server can read the information off the client certificate and compare it against its own database of users. This is often called *client-certificate authentication.*

The bottom diagram in figure 4.8 shows that client-certificate authentication requires both the client and the server to have certificates. The diagram also shows that the server must have a truststore that contains all the public certificates for the clients whom it wants to trust to gain access to its applications. This truststore is a security data source that's pointed to by a JBoss SX login module in the same fashion that you'd point to a database or an LDAP server. We talk about the login module that you use to configure this in section 4.3.4. You also learn how to configure client-certificate authentication from end to end for a web application in chapter 6 (section 6.5).

What are the tradeoffs between password-based client authentication and client-certificate authentication? You can argue whether authenticating against information on a certificate provides any protection over authenticating against a user-provided password. If the client's certificate is already available in the web browser or application, then the server can automatically get the certificate and authenticate the user. The user doesn't have to stop and type in a password. Client-certificate authentication provides you with an auto-login mechanism.

But, replacing password-based authentication with client-certificate authentication isn't always a good idea. What if somebody steals the user's computer with the certificate on it? The thief wouldn't not need a password to gain access to the information the true owner of the certificate had access to. What if somebody sneaks into your office and runs a few transactions while you're out to lunch? What if somebody hacks into a bank's server that has a client certificate set up to talk to another bank's transaction system? Again, the hacker would have immediate access without the need for manual authentication. These are all considerations you have to make before choosing client-certificate authentication over password-based authentication.

We've talked about how to configure security domains, and we've also talked about how to create certificates. Often, you'll need to bring these two together to create an SSL-aware security domain.

4.2.6 Configuring an SSL-aware security domain

JBoss Web Server has built-in support for SSL through its HTTP connector, so configuring SSL for web applications is relatively simple as we see in chapter 6 (section 6.4). But, if you want to authenticate clients based on their certificate information as we discuss in chapter 6 (section 6.5), then you'll have to define an SSL-aware security domain.

Unfortunately, you can't specify an SSL-aware security domain in the login-config.xml file as we did for non-SSL security domains in section 4.1.4. To enable an SSL-aware security domain, you must also define an MBean instance of `JaasSecurityDomain` that points to a truststore. Figure 4.9 shows you the relationship between the `JassSecurityDomain` MBean and the security domain defined in the login-config.xml file.

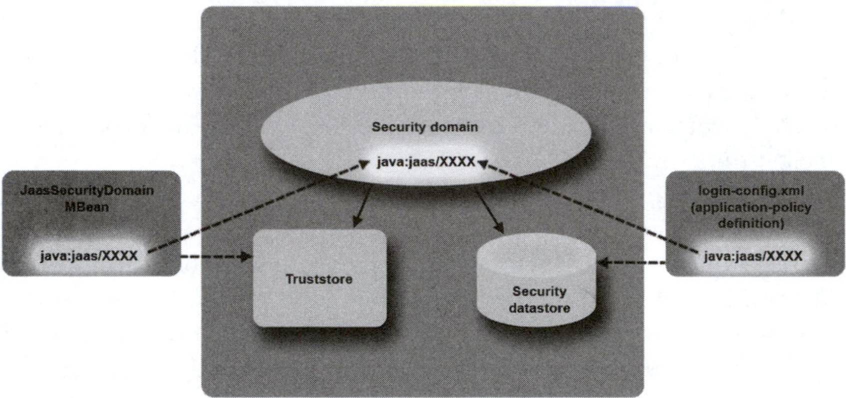

Figure 4.9 The relationship between the `JaasSecurityDomain` MBean, the truststore, the security domain, and the security datastore

To define the `JassSecurityDomain` MBean, create a file that ends in -service.xml and put it in the server/xxx/deploy directory. We talked about how services are defined using *-service.xml files in chapter 2 (section 2.2). Listing 4.3 shows what the contents of this file look like.

Listing 4.3 An SSL-aware security domain defined as an MBean

```
<server>
 <mbean code="org.jboss.security.plugins.JaasSecurityDomain"
      name="jboss.security:service=MySecurityDomain">
   <constructor>
     <arg type="java.lang.String"
        value="my-security-domain"          ❶
     />
   </constructor>
```

```
    <attribute name="KeyStoreURL">
      ${jboss.server.home.dir}/conf/server.truststore          ❷
    </attribute>
    <attribute name="KeyStorePass">servercert</attribute>      ❸
    <depends>jboss.security:service=JaasSecurityManager</depends>
  </mbean>
</server>
```

The value attribute ❶ of the constructor element is the name of the security domain you're defining. In this example, when the security domain is deployed to the server, it's bound under the java:/jaas/my-security-domain JNDI context because of the constructor argument defined on the MBean. The KeyStoreURL ❷ and KeyStorePass ❸ elements are used to define the location of the truststore and password to the truststore, respectively.

If you want your security domain to do authentication and authorization as well, you still need to define a security domain (an application policy block) in your login-config.xml file as described in section 4.1.4. The constructor argument of the security-domain in the MBean definition and the name attribute of the application-policy element in the login-config.xml file have to match up. To define an application policy for the SSL-aware security domain shown in listing 4.3, you write the following:

```
<application-policy name="my-security-domain">
...
</application-policy>
```

Now that you have a better understanding of the fundamental concepts of security and how encryption works, let's look at how to configure specific login modules.

4.3 Configuring login modules

A JBoss SX login module knows how to access a security data source in order to load a principal's password and role information. This information is then used to determine if the principal should be authenticated or authorized into an application.

Login modules are configured within security domains. In section 4.1.4, we showed how to define security domains using the .application-policy block in your configuration's server/xxx/conf/login-config.xml file. Each security domain can have one or more login modules. So far, we've only mentioned the UsersRolesLoginModule, which provides a way to read security data from a file. Table 4.4 summarizes some of the various login modules available in JBoss SX.

Table 4.4 Login modules that can be used when defining a security domain

Login module[a]	Description
BaseCertLoginModule	Authenticates client certificates. Must be stacked with another login module that does authorization.
CertRolesLoginModule	An extension of BaseCertLoginModule that authenticates against client certificates and authorizes against properties files.

Table 4.4 Login modules that can be used when defining a security domain *(continued)*

Login module[a]	Description
ClientLoginModule	Used by standalone clients that want to log into a secure server.
DatabaseCertLoginModule	An extension of BaseCertLoginModule that authenticates against client certificates and authorizes against a database.
DatabaseServerLoginModule	Loads user/role information from a database.
IdentityLoginModule	A testing login module that causes all users to authenticate with the same credentials.
LdapExtLoginModule	Loads user/role information from an LDAP server (supports hierarchical role structures).
LdapLoginModule	Loads user/role information from an LDAP server (only works with flat role structures).
RunAsLoginModule	Can be stacked with other login modules to define the run-as status that they use while they're authenticating. Useful if you need to call a secured EJB that's responsible for authenticating users.
SimpleServerLoginModule	A testing login module that allows any role with a null password to authenticate.
SRPCacheLoginModule	Used to authenticate users using the Secure Remote Password (SRP) protocol.
SRPLoginModule	Used by standalone clients that want to authenticate using the SRP protocol.
UsersRolesLoginModule	Loads user/role information from properties files.

a. All the login modules listed in table 4.4 are Java classes that exist in the org.jboss.security.auth.spi package except for SRPCacheLoginModule and SRPLoginModule, which are in org.jboss.security.src.jaas, and ClientLoginModule, which is in org.jboss.security.

Although there are many login modules, only a handful of them are widely used, so we focus on those. But don't worry too much if you're planning on using one of the login modules not covered in this book; you should be able to configure any login module based on the background in this section.

4.3.1 Using the file-based login module

The UsersRolesLoginModule stores username and role information in properties files. An example application-policy definition is as follows:

```
<application-policy name = "my-security-domain">
  <authentication>
    <login-module
        code="org.jboss.security.auth.spi.UsersRolesLoginModule"
        flag = "required">
      <module-option name="usersProperties">
        my-users.properties
```

```
        </module-option>
        <module-option name="rolesProperties">
          my-roles.properties
        </module-option>
      </login-module>
    </authentication>
  </application-policy>
```

The usersProperties and rolesProperties options point to files that should be placed in either the root of the application archive's class path or in your server configuration's conf directory. The format of the file that the usersProperties option points to should look like the following:

```
javid=passw0rd
joesmith=test1
janesmith=jb00sRul3z
```

Each line has a username and a password that are separated by an equals sign. The format of the file that the rolesProperties option points to should look like the following:

```
javid=SomeSimpleRole
joesmith=SomeOtherRole
janesmith=SomeSimpleRole,SomeOtherRole
```

In this file, each line has a username and a set of comma-separated roles that are separated by an equals sign.

If you want to associate user and role definitions with multiple security domains that use the UsersRolesLoginModule, then you can put the common users and roles in a pair of default files that are shared by all the security domains. These files can be specified by the defaultUsersProperties and defaultRolesProperties module options. As with the files pointed to by usersProperties and rolesProperties, the default files must also be in the conf directory of the server configuration or in the root directory of your application archive's class path.

Table 4.5 lists the module options that can be set for UsersRolesLoginModule.

Table 4.5 The properties that can be used with UsersRolesLoginModule

Module option	Description
usersProperties	The properties file that contains usernames and passwords.
rolesProperties	The properties file that contains role definitions for users.
unauthenticatedIdentity	The value of this option is used as the identity (principal name) for any source that doesn't provide any authentication information.
password-stacking	Used to configure multiple login modules. See section 4.3.5.
ignorePasswordCase	By default, passwords are case sensitive, but you can make the password comparison case insensitive by setting this option to true.

Table 4.5 The properties that can be used with `UsersRolesLoginModule` *(continued)*

Module option	Description
`defaultUsersProperties`	Specifies a default users properties file shared by multiple security domains.
`defaultRolesProperties`	Specifies a default roles properties file shared by multiple security domains.

This login module is often used in development and testing but isn't typically used in a production system. Most enterprises store their security information in a database or an LDAP directory. Let's look at how to configure the login module that reads security data from a database, and then we'll look at the one that reads security data from an LDAP server.

4.3.2 Using the database login module

Most enterprise application programmers are familiar with relational databases, so databases are a logical choice for storing security information. JBoss SX provides the `DatabaseServerLoginModule` for the purpose of loading authentication and authorization information from a database. Here's a typical `application-policy` definition using this login module:

```
<application-policy name = "database-domain">
  <authentication>
    <login-module
    code="org.jboss.security.auth.spi.DatabaseServerLoginModule"
    flag = "required">
      <module-option name="dsJndiName">
        java:/OracleDS
      </module-option>
      <module-option name="principalsQuery">
       SELECT PASSWD FROM USERS WHERE USERID=?
      </module-option>
      <module-option name="rolesQuery">
       SELECT ROLEID, 'Roles' FROM ROLES WHERE USERID=?
      </module-option>
    </login-module>
  </authentication>
</application-policy>
```

The value of the `dsJndiName` module option points to the JNDI name for the data source that contains the security information. The `principalsQuery` option defines the query that the login module executes when it tries to authenticate a principal based on this password. If this option isn't set, the login module executes the following default query:

```
select Password from Principals where PrincipalID=?
```

The `rolesQuery` option defines the query that the login module executes when it tries to authorize a principal based on her roles. If this option isn't set, the login module executes the following default query:

```
select Role, RoleGroup from Roles where PrincipalID=?
```

If you override the queries using the `principalsQuery` and `rolesQuery` options, you need to ensure the projection (the select clause) maintains the same order as the default queries; the query variables, the column names in the database, and the table names in the database can be whatever you want.

You'll notice that there's a column called `RoleGroup`. A role group is a descriptive name for the group of roles that a user belongs to. Unfortunately, Red Hat provides no clear explanation of the purpose of this column. They merely tell you that it has to be set to the value `Roles`. You can do this in several ways, but the simplest is to override the default `rolesQuery` with something similar to the following:

```
select Role, 'Roles' FROM Roles WHERE PrincipalID=?
```

Table 4.6 shows the options that can be used for this login module.

Table 4.6 The options that can be used with the `DatabaseServerLoginModule`

Module option	Description
`unauthenticatedIdentity`	The value of this option is used as the identity (principal name) for any source that doesn't provide any authentication information.
`password-stacking`	Used to configure multiple login modules. See section 4.3.5.
`dsJndiName`	The JNDI name for the data source that contains the security information.
`principalsQuery`	The query to pull back the password for the principal attempting to authenticate against the system.
`rolesQuery`	The query to pull back the role and role group for the principal attempting to authorize against the system.

4.3.3 Using the LDAP login module

Although programmers are typically more familiar with databases, many enterprises use software products that utilize LDAP for managing security information. Examples of such systems include Microsoft's Active Directory, Novell's eDirectory, and Red Hat's Fedora Directory Server. Organizations that use these systems often piggyback onto the security information stored in these servers, allowing them to maintain a single standardized security model for all of their new and existing systems. Many enterprises use LDAP for holding authentication information and a database for holding authorization information because LDAP can be difficult to set up and maintain.

We approach configuring the LDAP login module from a slightly different perspective. Unlike the database server login module where you probably define both the security information and the application data, you'll likely have to access an existing security data source that someone else set up. The first order of business is to discover where the information you're interested in is stored. In LDAP, information about a user is stored in a *user object*, and information about the groups (or roles) that a user belongs to is stored in a *group object*. If you can find your user object and the objects for the groups you belong to, then you should be able to configure the LDAP login module.

If that sounds difficult, don't worry; it's a little work, but it's doable. In the following text, we explain enough about LDAP to help you find the objects of interest and describe some tools that can help you locate the information you need. You'll then be ready to configure the LDAP login module.

UNDERSTANDING LDAP

An LDAP server maintains a tree of objects, similar to the file and directory hierarchy found on most computers or what's found in JNDI. In Java, LDAP is accessed via JNDI and represented as a JNDI directory. The information in an LDAP server can be considered to be in a tree, as illustrated in figure 4.10.

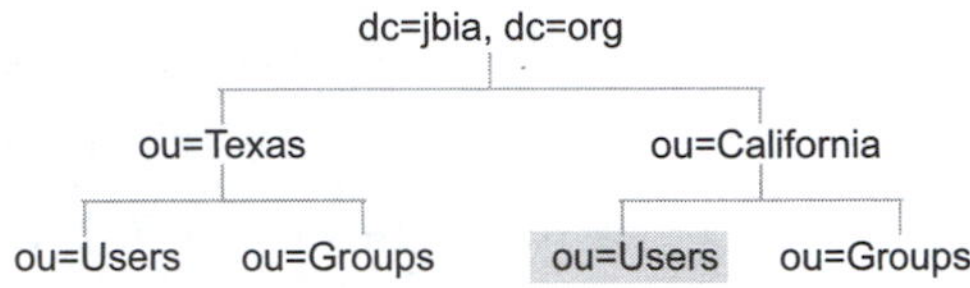

Figure 4.10 Simple LDAP directory tree

A few things to note about the tree are as follow:

- Each node has a two-part name, separated by an equals sign. The first part is an abbreviation for the type. Typical abbreviations include `dc` for domain controller, `ou` for organizational unit, and `cn` for common name. The second part is a simple name assigned to the node.
- The root node has a multipart name. The typical name is the same as the organization's website URL in reverse. An organization whose web site URL is www.jbia.org would have a root as indicated in the figure. Note that the *www* prefix is typically not used.
- The full name of an object, also known as the distinguished name (DN), is its name and all the nodes up to the root. The DN for the highlighted node is `ou=Users,ou=California,dc=jbia,dc=org`. Note that the order is from leaf node to root node.

Now that you have some knowledge of LDAP, the next thing you need is a tool that will help you find the information you need.

SELECTING AN LDAP TOOL

When browsing LDAP for the first time, you need a GUI tool because the GUI automatically performs the necessary calls to discover the contents of the directory tree. An open source LDAP browser, JXplorer, is available from Source Forge at http://sourceforge.net/projects/jxplorer/. This browser is written in Java, so it'll run on any platform.

The main benefit of using JXplorer is that you don't have to know how to form the necessary LDAP queries to browse the tree. But this is also one of the main detriments because, to configure the login module, you need to know how to fashion the proper queries. For that, a command-line tool is much better. Many LDAP implementations come with a tool that enables you to search the LDAP directory tree. Usually the tool is named *ldapsearch*. If you have such a tool available, you can use it; if not, the Sun ONE Directory Server Resource Kit 5.2.1, which is a free download available at http://www.sun.com/download/products.xml?id=3f74a0db, contains an ldapsearch tool, and is available for a wide variety of platforms. The text that follows assumes you're using the Sun tool; if you use a different tool, check with that tool's documentation for usage instructions.

If you're using Active Directory, install the support tools that come with Windows Server 2003. One of the support tools is called Active Directory Users and Computers, which displays LDAP directory trees. You can find the support tools in the support/tools directory on the CD. You can install them on Windows XP or Vista.

BROWSING THE LDAP DIRECTORY TREE

Now that you've assembled your tools, you're ready to dig into the LDAP directory tree. To get started, you need to know the following pieces of information:

- The host name for the system running the LDAP server.
- The port used by the LDAP server. Port 389 is the default port.
- If the LDAP server doesn't allow anonymous access, you'll need an account and password that has search and read access.
- The DN of the root node.

You should be able to get all of this information from the network administrator responsible for maintaining the LDAP directory tree. Whether you should bring the bribe of a six-pack of the administrator's favorite brew is up to you. If your company uses Active Directory, you can discover some of these items for yourself.

If you log into a domain on your Windows PC, you can find the host name by examining the `USERDNSDOMAIN` environment variable, which records the domain controller used when you successfully logged in. That domain controller contains the LDAP server.

Most likely, the LDAP server is running on port 389.

Most likely, your account has the necessary access rights.

Run the Active Directory Users and Computers tool, connecting to the host. It displays the DN for the root node.

After you obtain this information, you can run JXplorer and connect to the LDAP server. You'll see something similar to figure 4.11, which is an example LDAP directory tree.

The next step is to find your user object, which we've highlighted in the figure. Unfortunately, every LDAP directory tree is different, so you can either browse around or show up at the administrator's office with another six-pack. Another alternative is to use the export capabilities of JXplorer to dump the entire tree to a text file and use a text editor to search for your login id. To use the search menu, you need to know which attribute contains your login id, and you don't know that yet.

After you find your user object, scan through the data looking for your login id and note the attribute for that id. For Active Directory, that attribute is usually `sAMAccountName`. In other LDAP servers, an attribute named `uid` is often used for the login id.

When you configure your login module, you need to provide a query that can locate this user object. You now have all the information necessary to create this query, so let's see how to do it.

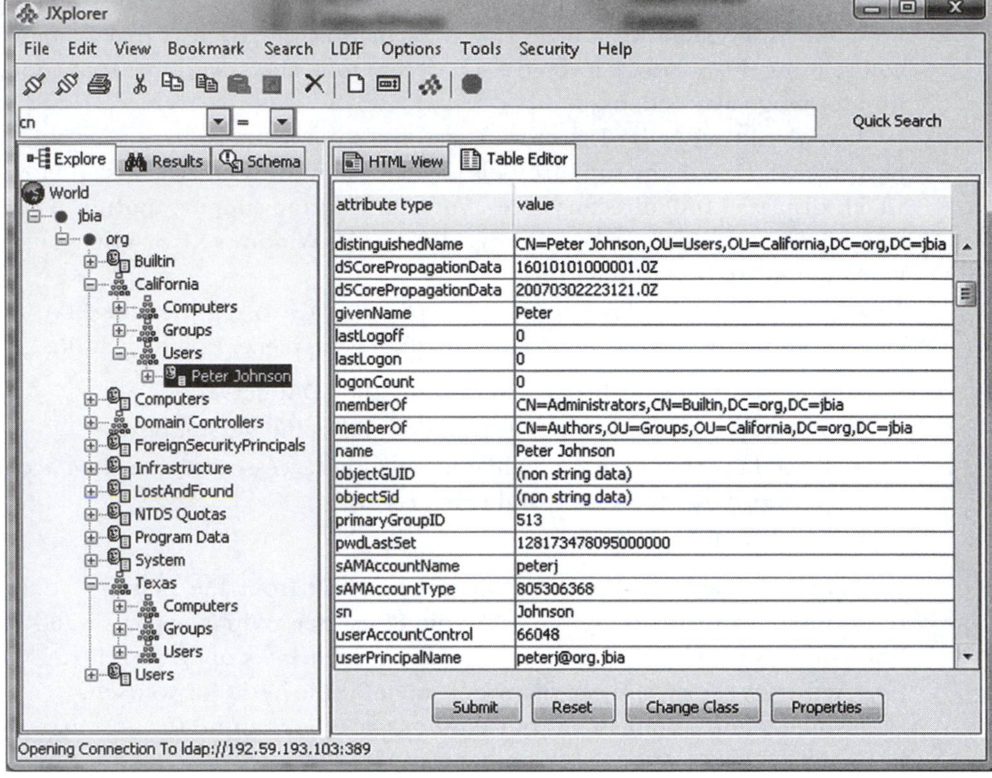

Figure 4.11 Browsing the LDAP directory tree

ESTABLISHING THE USER OBJECT QUERY

You can use the ldapsearch command line tool to construct and test the query that you need to use to locate your user object. The command line syntax is as follows:

```
ldapsearch -b <baseDN> -h <host> -D <account>
            -w <password> (<attribute>=<loginId>)
```

The options for the tool are as follow:

- `<baseDN>` is the root DN, which is `dc=jbia,dc=org` in the example.
- `<host>` is the LDAP server host name.
- `<account>` and `<password>` are the same you used for JXplorer.
- `<attribute>` is the name of the attribute containing your login id.
- `<loginId>` is your login id.

Here's an example command that works with the example LDAP directory tree:

```
ldapsearch -b "dc=jbia,dc=org" -h jbia-fs1 -D jbia\peterj
            -w javadude "(sAMAccountName=peterj)"
```

The result should be the user object. The ldapsearch tool prints out all the attributes for that object.

One thing to look out for, particularly in Active Directory, is that there could be multiple directory trees that appear as one, causing errors when you attempt to branch from one tree to another. If you get the following error, then you've run into this problem:

```
javax.naming.PartialResultException: Unprocessed Continuation Reference(s);
➥ remaining name 'dc=jbia,dc=org'
```

If this happens, you might have to use a node further down the tree. For example, in the example LDAP tree, you might have to use `ou=Users,ou=California,dc=jbia,dc=org`. If this happens, you can configure multiple LDAP login modules, one for each base DN that you can search and that contains the users you're interested in.

In addition to the user query, the login module also needs to locate the group object. Let's see how to establish a query that will do this for us.

ESTABLISHING THE GROUP OBJECT QUERY

Most likely, your user object is the member of many groups. Locating the DN for the group object may be as simple as looking for an attribute that's repeated multiple times. In Active Directory, the attribute is named `memberOf` and provides the DN for the group objects. Use the group DN to locate one of the group objects in JXplorer, and look through the attributes of the group object looking for the members of the group. In Active Directory, the member attribute contains that information. In some LDAP servers, the member attribute value is the user account id, but in other servers, such as Active Directory, the value is the user DN. You need to note which scenarios apply to your LDAP server because that will determine how you perform your search.

Search through the attributes of the group object to find one that gives the simple group name. In Active Directory, this can be either the `name` or `sAMAccountName` attribute. This name is the role name that the LDAP login module will return.

If the member attribute is the simple user login id, then you can use ldapsearch to find all the groups to which you belong. The basic ldapsearch syntax is almost the same as before.

```
ldapsearch -b <baseDN> -h <host> -D <account>
➥          -w <password> "(<attribute>=<loginId>)" <nameAttr>
```

The only differences in the values from the user query are as follow:

- For `<attribute>`, use the name of the attribute in the group object that references the users in the group. Typically, this attribute is named `member`.
- For `<loginId>`, use your account id. Note that you can't use the user object DN here, although this could be a limitation of the ldapsearch tool used.
- For `<nameAttr>`, use the attribute that contains the simple group name.

Here's an example command that works for the example LDAP directory tree if the `member` attribute for the groups uses a simple login id:

```
ldapsearch -b "dc=jbia,dc=org" -h jbia-fs1 -D jbia\peterj
➥          -w javadude "(member=peterj)" name
```

The result should be a list of the various groups to which you belong.

Now that you have the queries that yield the user and group objects, you're ready to configure the LDAP login module.

CONFIGURING THE LDAP LOGIN MODULE

We can now create an LDAP login module using all the information we've gathered so far. Listing 4.4 shows an `application-policy` configuration based on the example data that we've provided in this section.

Listing 4.4 Example LDAP login module configuration

```
<application-policy name="ldapLogin">
 <authentication>
  <login-module flag="required"
     code="org.jboss.security.auth.spi.LdapExtLoginModule">
   <module-option name="java.naming.factory.initial">
➥com.sun.jndi.ldap.LdapCtxFactory</module-option>
   <module-option name="java.naming.provider.url">
➥ldap://jbia-fs1:389/</module-option>                  ❶
   <module-option name="java.naming.security.authentication">
➥simple</module-option>                   ❷
   <module-option name="bindDN">
➥jbia\peterj</module-option>            ❸
   <module-option name="bindCredential">
➥javadude</module-option>                ❹
   <module-option name="baseCtxDN">
➥dc=jbia,dc=org</module-option>           ❺
   <module-option name="baseFilter">
➥(sAMAccountName={0})</module-option>           ❻
  <module-option name="rolesCtxDN">
➥dc=jbia,dc=org</module-option>           ❼
   <module-option name="roleFilter">
➥(member={1})</module-option>            ❽
   <module-option name="roleAttributeIsDN">
➥true</module-option>          ❾
  <module-option name="roleNameAttributeID">
➥name</module-option>          ❿
  </login-module>
 </authentication>
</application-policy>
```

In this case, we use the `LdapExtLoginModule` because it can handle hierarchical LDAP structures, a necessary quality when using Active Directory. You could use the `Ldap-LoginModule` instead, although its options are slightly different. Note the use of various name properties; as we mentioned earlier, LDAP is treated as part of JNDI. The URL ❶ comes from the hostname we used in the ldapsearch program, with the proper protocol and the default LDAP port. For this example, we use simple authentication ❷, meaning that we supply a login id ❸ and a password ❹ to log into the LDAP server. LDAP servers provide a server-specific authentication mechanism that you can use instead; you can specify that authentication name here.

The base DN ❺ and filter ❻ are the same ones that we used for ldapsearch when we looked up the user object. The login id as supplied by the user (for example, when the browser asks the user to log in) is used for the `{0}` placeholder. As configured, the user needs to supply his account name, without a domain name, to log in. For example, when asked to log in by the browser, we'd supply peterj, not jbia\peterj. The sAMAccountName contains only the basic account name, not the name in conjunction with the domain name.

Active Directory allows a user to log in using his email address, which is the value of the userPrincipalName attribute. You could require the user to use an email address to log into a web application by changing the baseFilter to be (userPrincipalName = {0}). The password would be the same as for the login id.

The role DN ❼ is the same one we used for ldapsearch when looking up the group. For the filter ❽, the user's login is used for the {0} placeholder, and the user's full DN is used for the {1} login id. Because Active Directory uses the user's DN as the value of the member attribute, we use the {1} placeholder.

When set to true, the roleAttributeIsDN option ❾ indicates that the memberOf attribute is for a user object, and the name attribute for a group is a DN, not a simple name. We also have to supply an attribute whose value is the simple group name ❿. The group names gathered by this process form the roles to which the user belongs and are used to grant access rights. If, in your LDAP server, the memberOf attribute is a simple group name and not a DN, you can set roleAttributeIsDN to false; then you don't have to supply the roleNameAttributeID option. Table 4.7 lists other module options that can be used for the LDAP login module.

Table 4.7 The options that can be used with the LdapExtLoginModule

Module option	Description
allowEmptyPasswords	Set this to true if the LDAP server allows anonymous login.
jaasSecurityDomain	The MBean name of the JaasSecurityDomain used to decrypt the password specified by bindCredential.
roleAttributeId	If roleAttributeIsDN is set to false, this is the name of the attribute of the user object that contains the role names.
roleRecursion	If the LDAP server allows groups to be part of groups, set this value to the number of nesting levels allowed. The LDAP login module will then recursively search each group for parent groups to which it belongs, adding each one to the roles to which the user belongs. The default is 0, meaning that there's no nesting of groups.
searchScope	Allows one of the following values when searching for groups: ▪ *OBJECT_SCOPE*—Searches only in the context specified by the rolesCtxDN option. ▪ *ONELEVEL_SCOPE*—Searches in the content specified by the rolesCtxDN option and one level further out (away from the root). ▪ *SUBTREE_SCOPE*—Searches in the content specified by the rolesCtxDN option and all levels further out towards all branches of the tree. This is the default.
searchTimeLimit	The number of milliseconds to allow for searching for groups or users. If the search takes longer, it's aborted. The default is 10000 (10 seconds).

Time for a short quiz: what's missing from this configuration? If you answered *the user's password*, give yourself a gold star. The configuration did have a password used to log into the LDAP server for making the queries, but this is akin to the account and password used to establish a database connection, not to authenticate a user who's logging into an application. In the database server login module, the query included the user's password, but where is it in LDAP? To answer this question, we have to tell you a little about how the LDAP login module works.

The LDAP login module performs three queries against the LDAP server to log in a user, as follows:

- The first query looks up the user object using only the login id. This search is similar to the first ldapsearch query that we showed you earlier.
- A second query is a login attempt using the user's login id and the password.
- The last query obtains the group objects.

The password is used, but you don't have to reference it in the login module. Now let's take a look at another login module that helps simplify development and testing.

4.3.4 *Using the identity login module*

It's often easier to develop and test applications when you don't have to worry about security constraints. But disabling or changing the security configuration of the application itself isn't necessarily a good idea; you're likely to forget to enable security again before you check your code back into version control. JBoss SX provides a login module called `IdentityLoginModule` that allows anybody to access the system, no matter what credentials they provide. This login module isn't meant to be used in a production environment, but it can come in handy in a development or test environment. The module can be used as follows:

```
<login-module code="org.jboss.security.auth.spi.IdentityLoginModule"
          flag = "required">
  <module-option name="principal">javid</module-option>
  <module-option name="roles">texan,newyorker</module-option>
</login-module>
```

The `principal` option is the principal that all users will be authenticated as. If this option isn't provided, it defaults to `guest`. The `roles` option is a comma-separated list of roles the principal will be assigned to.

Let's explore how login-module stacking works.

4.3.5 *Stacking login modules*

Login modules can be stacked on top of one another if you want to authenticate or authorize against multiple sources or if want to authenticate from a different source than you authorize from. You can define two login modules in an `application-policy` definition as shown in this example:

```
<application-policy name="my-stacked-policy">
  <authentication>
    <login-module
```

```
      code="org.jboss.security.auth.spi.UsersRolesLoginModule"
      flag = "required">
      ...
    </login-module>
    <login-module
     code="org.jboss.security.auth.spi.DatabaseServerLoginModule"
     flag="required">
      ...
    </login-module>
  </authentication>
</application-policy>
```

One login module uses the `UsersRolesLoginModule`, and the other uses the `DatabaseServerLoginModule`, as defined by the code attribute for each login module. In this case, both login modules have their `flag` attributes set to `required`. The `flag` attributes specify which login modules are necessary and/or sufficient for authentication. The following are possible values for the `flag` attribute, taken directly from the JBoss AS documentation:

- *`required`*—Requires that the login module succeeds for the authentication to be successful. If any required module fails, the authentication will fail. The remaining login modules in the stack will be called regardless of the outcome of the authentication.
- *`requisite`*—Requires the login module to succeed. If it succeeds, authentication continues down the login stack. If it fails, control immediately returns to the application.
- *`sufficient`*—Doesn't require the login module to succeed. If it does succeed, control immediately returns to the application. If it fails, authentication continues down the login stack.
- *`optional`*—Doesn't require the login module to succeed. Authentication proceeds down the login stack regardless of whether the login module succeeds or fails.

Based on the settings you use, some login modules may be reached, and others may not. Any login module that is reached and successfully authenticated against will make the authenticated principal's role information available for authorization.

If you want to authenticate against only one login module but still want to collect role information from other login modules, you could use the `password-stacking` module option on each login module as shown here:

```
<module-option name="password-stacking">useFirstPass</module-option>
```

The value `useFirstPass` is the only value that this module option can take; if you define this module option, you must use that value. Enabling this module option causes each login module to check if the user has already been authenticated by another login module. If so, then the login module will skip its own authentication and will only make its security roles available for authorization. If a login module only does authentication, such as the `BaseCertLoginModule`, then you only authorize against other login modules that it's stacked with.

Let's take a look at the BaseCertLoginModule, which you use when doing client-certificate authentication.

4.3.6 Using the client certificate login module

If you want to do client-certificate authentication, you need to specify an application-policy that knows how to read a keystore using an SSL-aware JaasSecurityDomain MBean. JBoss SX provides the BaseCertLoginModule for this purpose. This login module only knows how to authenticate against a keystore, so it must be stacked with another login module that knows how to do authorization. Listing 4.5 shows you an example of how to configure the BaseCertLoginModule stacked with the UsersRolesLoginModule.

Listing 4.5 Stacking BaseCertLoginModule with UsersRolesLoginModule

```
<application-policy name = "my-client-cert">
  <authentication>
    <login-module
       code="org.jboss.security.auth.spi.BaseCertLoginModule"
       flag = "required">
      <module-option name="password-stacking">
         useFirstPass                                         ❶
      </module-option>
      <module-option name="securityDomain">
         java:/jaas/my-client-cert                            ❷
      </module-option>
    </login-module>
    <login-module
       code="org.jboss.security.auth.spi.UsersRolesLoginModule"
       flag = "required">
      <module-option name="password-stacking">
         useFirstPass                                         ❶
      </module-option>
      ...
    </login-module>
  </authentication>
</application-policy>
```

The key module option that you must configure is securityDomain ❷. The password-stacking module option ❶ set on both login modules tells the security domain that the login modules should be stacked.

An alternative to stacking the BaseCertLoginModule is to use one of the classes that extends it. Two such login modules are the CertRolesLoginModule and the DatabaseCertLoginModule. The CertRolesLoginModule is a hybrid between the BaseCertLoginModule and the UsersRolesLoginModule. It can authenticate against a public key certificate like the BaseCertLoginModule and authorize against roles defined in a properties file like the UsersRolesLoginModule. Likewise, the DatabaseCertLoginModule is a hybrid between the BaseCertLoginModule and the DatabaseServerLoginModule, which authorizes against a database. The best place to learn about these other login modules is in the JBoss AS documentation, which we reference at the end of the chapter.

4.4 Summary

We started this chapter by discussing the fundamental concepts behind application security, including authentication, authorization, and encryption. You learned that authentication is used to determine if a principal is who he claims to be. You learned that authorization is used to determine if a principal has the authority to gain access to the resources that he's trying to access. And you learned about the importance of secure communication, particularly when the communication is going over an open network. You also saw an overview of how application security is configured in JBoss SX by defining security domains and how to enable logging so that you can debug security related issues when in development.

We then took a much closer look at secure communication. We discussed the differences between symmetric and asymmetric encryption. We talked about certificates and how they can be used with asymmetric encryption protocols to enable source authentication, and then we showed how to use the keytool utility to create your own self-signed certificates and to import signed certificates into a keystore. We also explored how certificates can be used to authenticate clients and showed how to create a security domain that uses a keystore as a security datastore.

Finally, we dove into the details behind configuring login modules, particularly focusing on how to access security information from a database and an LDAP directory.

In other chapters in the book, we show how to configure security for various components or resources. But we'll assume that you already know how to configure a security domain with a login module accessing your underlying security data as we've explained in this chapter. Table 4.1 in the beginning of this chapter summarized all the sections in the book that talk about application security. Of all of these topics, web security is by far the most involved. In fact, we had so much to write about web security that we couldn't fit it into the web chapter; we had to put it in its own chapter. The next chapter will specifically talk about configuring web applications and the web server without discussing security. We've dedicated chapter 6 to web security. After that, each chapter that talks about security will contain the discussion directly in the chapter.

4.5 References

JBoss documentation—http://labs.jboss.com/jbossas/docs
See section 5.5.3 of the Configuration Guide for a discussion of the various login modules available in JBoss.

Customizing EJB security in JBoss—http://www.javaworld.com/javaworld/jw-02-2002/jw-0215-ejbsecurity.html

Although this article references previous versions of EJB technology, you can accomplish context-based security in much the same way using EJB3 interceptors.

Part 2

Application services

Now that you have a basic understanding of how things work within JBoss AS, we'll tackle specific application types. The chapters in this part of the book cover the different types of applications that can be deployed to the application server: web applications, enterprise applications (including EJBs), messaging applications, and web services.

In each chapter, we tackle many of the same issues: what are the standard configuration mechanisms, and what additional configuration is required by JBoss AS? How do you secure the application, not just in authentication and access control, but also in encrypting the transmitted data? In fact, securing a web application is such a large topic we gave it its own chapter.

Each chapter is freestanding. You can read only the chapters you're interested in, and come back to the others when you're ready.

5 Configuring JBoss Web Server

This chapter covers

- Configuring web applications
- Configuring JBoss Web Server
- Configuring URL paths
- Configuring connectors
- Configuring web class loading
- Configuring JavaServer Faces

The most common technologies for creating Java web applications are JSPs and servlets, the standard Java EE web component technologies. These technologies can be deployed to many different web containers, but the most popular is Apache Tomcat, the reference implementation for the servlet and JSP specifications. Tomcat also doubles as a general-purpose web server that's able to do most things that popular native web servers (for example, Microsoft IIS and Apache HTTP Server) do, such as serving static content, supporting virtual hosting, supporting a Common Gateway Interface (CGI), and so on. Tomcat is written in Java, so it's portable but historically slower at serving static web pages than native web servers. Apache is also the leader in the native web server market with the Apache HTTP Server, a fast and highly scalable web server.

JBoss AS serves web applications using a new Red Hat product called *JBoss Web Server*, which combines the speed of the Apache HTTP Server with the versatility of Apache Tomcat. JBoss Web Server is built on top of Apache Tomcat 6.0 but is capable of using a native Apache library called Apache Portable Runtime (APR) to attain the speed of the Apache HTTP Server.

In this chapter, we teach you about the structure of web applications and how to deploy them into JBoss AS. We then explore how to configure web applications and the JBoss Web Server. We do cover a few aspects of web application configuration in other chapters; we discuss session persistence and replication in the clustering chapters (chapters 12 and 13), class loading and scoping web applications in the deployment chapter (chapter 3), and web application security in the web security chapter (chapter 6).

5.1 Understanding web applications

In chapter 1, we created and deployed a simple web application into JBoss AS. We won't walk you through how to do this again, but in order to understand how to configure web applications and the JBoss Web Server, it's helpful to go over the basic structure of a Java EE web application.

Java EE web applications are packaged into the WAR structure defined in the servlet specification. In this section, we'll explore the structure of a WAR package and talk about the various configuration files that web applications use.

5.1.1 Understanding the web application structure

The packaging structure for a web application is simple. To explain the structure, we'll show you the directory outline for a simple Hello World! application and discuss what files go in which directories.

Figure 5.1 shows the structure of a WAR package.

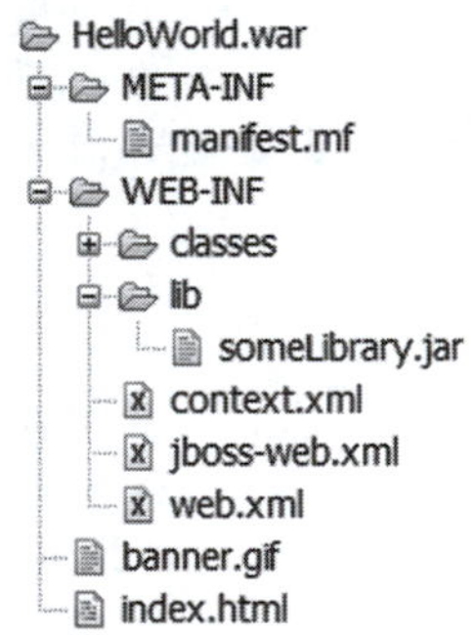

Figure 5.1 WAR archives contain Java code, presentation content, and configuration files.

The top-level folder shown in figure 5.1 defines the name of the package. If a web application is packaged as an exploded directory structure, the top-level folder defines the name of the package, which is `HelloWorld.war`. If the application were packaged as an archive, the filename for the archive file would be HelloWorld.war.

The top-level directory contains any static or presentation-specific files that your application may need. This directory might include HTML files, XML files, images, JSPs, sound clips, movie files, or other multimedia files. In this example, we see a file called index.html and another called banner.gif directly under the top-level directory. These files can also reside in subdirectories directly under the top-level directory (excluding the META-INF and WEB-INF directories).

But applications contain more than static files; they contain code and configuration as well. The WEB-INF directory of a WAR package contains all the configuration files and code for a web application. You don't want end-users to be able to access your code and configuration files through a web browser; therefore, web containers restrict external access to the WEB-INF directory.

The WEB-INF directory contains the standard and the JBoss Web Server–specific web deployment descriptors, web.xml and jboss-web.xml, as well as a Tomcat deployment descriptor called context.xml. We discuss deployment descriptors in the next section. The WEB-INF directory also contains two subdirectories, classes and lib. The classes directory holds any compiled class files that are part of your deployment, and the lib directory holds any JAR libraries that your web application code depends on.

A Java archive tool (such as `jar`, which ships with Sun's JDK) creates a file called manifest.mf that it puts in the META-INF directory. This file holds metadata about the files in the archive and can be used to provide functionality such as electronic signing, version control, package sealing, and extensions. Like the WEB-INF directory, the META-INF directory is also inaccessible from a web browser.

A web application can be packaged inside of an Enterprise Archive (EAR). We discuss this further in chapter 7 (section 7.1.3).

5.1.2 Understanding web application configuration

The servlet specification defines the structure and contents of web applications. All Java web applications must have the WEB-INF/web.xml deployment descriptor—a configuration file that provides the server with necessary information when it's deploying an application. Because the web.xml deployment descriptor is defined by the servlet specification, it's often called the *standard deployment descriptor.*

Because the standard deployment descriptor contains configuration elements that are common across all application servers, it only defines logical configuration. Each application server must provide a mechanism to realize this logical configuration; several application servers, including JBoss AS, do so by adding *proprietary deployment descriptors.* The standard deployment descriptor defines *what* should logically happen, but the proprietary deployment descriptor describes *how* it should be carried out by physically tying it to some application server logic or component.

For example, you can constrain a URL to be accessed only by a particular security role in the standard deployment descriptor. This is a logical definition of what should be secured, and so the configuration is portable across application servers. But the physical configuration in the proprietary deployment descriptor tells the server how you want to enforce the security rules by defining the source of the security data and how that data should be compared to the restricted security role.

To make life simple, JBoss Web Server provides default physical behavior for most of the logical configuration found in the standard deployment descriptor, often rendering a proprietary deployment descriptor unnecessary. When needed, JBoss Web

Server provides two proprietary deployment descriptors called jboss-web.xml and context.xml. As shown in figure 5.1, all the deployment descriptors (standard and proprietary) must reside in the web application's WEB-INF directory.

Now, let's take a closer look at each of these deployment descriptors.

THE WEB.XML FILE

Each web application must have a web deployment descriptor called web.xml located in the application's WEB-INF directory. The web.xml file holds standard configuration information for servlets and JSPs. Because this file is part of the Java EE 5 specification, it's mandatory and portable across web application servers.

Listing 5.1 shows a simple web.xml file declaring a single servlet.

Listing 5.1 Declaring servlet and URLs inside the WEB-INF/web.xml file

```
<web-app version="2.5"
      xmlns="http://java.sun.com/xml/ns/javaee"
      xmlns:xsi="http://www.w3.org/2001/XMLSchema-instance"
      xsi:schemaLocation="http://java.sun.com/xml/ns/javaee
       http://java.sun.com/xml/ns/javaee/web-app_2_5.xsd">
  <servlet>
    <servlet-name>Hello Servlet</servlet-name>
    <servlet-class>
      com.manning.jbia.HelloWorldServlet</servlet-class>
  </servlet>
  <servlet-mapping>
    <servlet-name>Hello Servlet</servlet-name>
    <url-pattern>/sayhello</url-pattern>
  </servlet-mapping>
</web-app>
```

Because this file is explained in depth in the specification, numerous books, and numerous online articles, we won't spend time explaining how to use it. One of the best places to find information on the elements in this file is in the XML schema, which is located in the server's docs/schema/web-app_2_5.xsd file.

THE JBOSS-WEB.XML FILE

JBoss Web Server uses WEB-INF/jboss-web.xml as its main proprietary deployment descriptor. Here's an example of what this file might look like:

```
<jboss-web>
  <security-domain>java:/jaas/simple-security-domain</security-domain>
</jboss-web>
```

The top-level element is `jboss-web`. This file is usually scant—or unnecessary altogether—because again, JBoss Web Server uses many intuitive defaults, obviating the need for verbose and explicit manual configuration.

Throughout this chapter, we show how to configure different elements within this file to enable various web application features. Table 5.1 gives an overview of some of the main elements that we discuss in this book.

Table 5.1 The top-level elements that can be configured in a jboss-web.xml file

Element	What is it?
`class-loading`	Used to enable isolated class loading as discussed in chapter 3 (section 3.2). Use this if you wanted to change the class loading behavior for the application but not necessarily the entire server.
`security-domain`	Specifies which security domain the application uses for authentication and authorization. We discuss this in chapter 6 (section 6.1.2).
`context-root`	Defines the root URL mapped to this application when HTTP requests come in (we discuss this in section 5.3.2). Use this if you want to use a different URL context than the implicit one (the name of the WAR file).
`virtual-host`	Specifies which virtual host the application belongs to. This must match a virtual host that was defined in the Tomcat server.xml file. We discuss this in section 5.3.1.
`use-session-cookies`	A boolean flag that indicates whether or not the session should be kept in client cookies.
`replication-config`	Specifies when to replicate the HTTP session state throughout a cluster. We talk about this more in chapter 13.
`resource-env-ref`	Maps the Enterprise Naming Context (ENC) name for a `resource-env-ref` defined in the web.xml file to the location in the global JNDI namespace. Use this if you've defined a `resource-env-ref` in the web.xml file for an application.
`resource-ref`	Maps the Enterprise Naming Context (ENC) name for a `resource-ref` defined in the web.xml file to the location in the global JNDI namespace. Use this if you've defined a `resource-ref` in the web.xml file for an application.
`ejb-ref`	Maps the Enterprise Naming Context (ENC) name for an `ejb-ref` defined in the web.xml file to the location in the global JNDI namespace.
`ejb-local-ref`	Maps the Enterprise Naming Context (ENC) name for an `ejb-local-ref` defined in the web.xml file to the location in the global JNDI namespace.
`servlet`	Used to specify servlet–specific customizations in JBoss Web Server. The only feature currently supported is the run-as-principal feature, which we don't discuss in this book.

THE CONTEXT.XML FILE

As we mentioned in the introduction to this chapter, JBoss Web Server is built on top of Tomcat. Applications running in a standalone Tomcat server can specify a proprietary deployment descriptor called context.xml. JBoss Web Server has overridden most of the configuration features of the context.xml file in the jboss-web.xml file, making context.xml unnecessary in most cases. If you're used to running standalone Tomcat servers, you'll have to get used to doing most of your application-level configuration in the jboss-web.xml file instead of the context.xml file. There are a few cases where the context.xml file is used; we talk about one of them in section 5.6 when we discuss application-level Tomcat valves.

If you're used to using Tomcat as a standalone web container, you may be used to putting this file in the META-INF directory. JBoss Web Server looks for the file in the WEB-INF directory so that all the web configuration files for an application are in one location.

Now that you've seen what is in each deployment descriptor, let's see how JBoss Web Server simplifies configuration that applies to all the applications in the server.

EXPLORING GLOBAL APPLICATION CONFIGURATION

An instance of JBoss AS can host multiple web applications. What if you have an application configuration that you want to apply to all the web applications running in your server? You could duplicate the configuration in each application's configuration files, but JBoss Web Server provides global configuration files that allow you to avoid this duplication. A *global configuration file* is one whose contents apply to all the applications in the server. For example, having a global web.xml file is the same as repeating the configuration in that file in each individual web application's web.xml file. We put a particular configuration element in a global configuration file when we know that the element applies to all the web applications.

These files are located in the directory that hosts the JBoss Web Server's deployer. Table 5.2 shows the various application configuration files and their global counterparts.

The global web.xml file allows you to apply a global configuration that would otherwise go in each application's web.xml file. The existence of a global web.xml file isn't defined by the servlet specification; therefore, it's neither standard nor necessarily portable between application servers. Likewise, the contents of the global context.xml file apply to all web applications in the server and obviate the need to define the same configuration in each application's context.xml file. There's no global configuration for jboss-web.xml, so any configuration you wish to apply to all the applications in your server must be repeated in each application's jboss-web.xml file.

It's worth looking through the global configuration files to see what types of configuration are usually defined globally. Now that you've learned about the structure of Java web applications and about the various application-level configuration files, let's take a closer look at how to configure the JBoss Web Server.

Table 5.2 The directories where the various application-level configuration files can be found

Filename	Application-level configuration (relative to your application's root directory)	Global configuration (relative to default configuration directory)
web.xml	WEB-INF/web.xml	deployers/jbossweb.deployer/web.xml
context.xml	WEB-INF/context.xml	deploy/jbossweb.sar/context.xml
jboss-web.xml	WEB-INF/jboss-web.xml	None available

5.2 Configuring JBoss Web Server

One nice thing about running in an application server environment is that the application server provides a set of services that applications can use, allowing you to focus on writing business code. You can then hook your applications into the services using the application configuration files you learned about in section 5.1. In addition to configuring applications, you may also have to configure the properties of the services themselves.

In this section, you'll learn about the various files and directories related to the JBoss Web Server. This gives you a basis for understanding how to configure the various services available to web applications.

5.2.1 Locating key directories

Figure 5.2 shows you the JBoss AS directory structure, highlighting the main directories related to JBoss Web Server and web applications deployment.

As we discussed in chapter 2, you copy your application directory to the deploy directory to deploy it into JBoss AS. In a standard binary installation, a web application called `ROOT.war` is in the deploy directory of the *default* configuration. If you start the application server and go to http://localhost:8080, you'll see the root web application.

Figure 5.2 The main directories used to configure JBoss Web Server and to deploy web applications

JBoss AS comes prepackaged with JBoss Web Server in both the *default* and the *all* configurations. The JBoss Web Server deployer lives in the jbossweb.sar subdirectory of server/xxx/deploy. The server/xxx/deployers jbossweb.deployer directory contains the necessary JAR files to deploy web applications. The following are some of the key files and directories:

- *deploy/jboss.sar/server.xml*—Primary server configuration file. Used to configure server components such as virtual hosts, protocols, ports, and request filters. We discuss this file in the next section.
- *deploy/jbossweb.sar/context.xml*—Global version of the application-level file by the same name.
- *deploy/jbossweb.sar/jsf-libs*—Directory. Contains libraries necessary for JSF development.
- *conf/web.xml*—Global version of the application-level file that we explored when we discussed application configuration.
- *deployers/jbossweb.deployer/META-INF/war-deployers-jboss-beans.xml*—Microcontainer configuration file. Used to initialize the WAR deployer. In addition to configuring WAR package deployment, this file also enables some additional server configuration such as security, class loading, and clustering.

Let's take a closer look at the server.xml and war-deployers-jboss-beans.xml configuration files because they're the primary files used for server configuration.

5.2.2 Exploring JBoss Web Server Configuration

JBoss Web Server's main configuration file, server.xml, is located in the server/xxx/deploy/jbossweb.sar directory as shown in figure 5.2. This file is used for most of the server configuration that you'll be concerned with. Because JBoss Web Server is built on top of Tomcat, this file is almost identical to Tomcat's server.xml file. Looking through the Apache Tomcat 6 documentation (reference at the end of this chapter) can help you gain a better understanding of the various configuration elements in the server.xml file. If you've configured Tomcat before, you should be comfortable with this file. If not, no sweat; we'll give you a high-level overview in this section and show you how to configure specific things in this file throughout the chapter.

The server configuration is composed of components, some of which are containers for other components. The various configuration elements in this file can be nested inside of one another in different ways. Figure 5.3 shows the acceptable nesting of these elements. For example, the Service component is a container for the Connector and Engine components.

If you open this file, you'll see code similar to that shown in listing 5.2. Almost everything is a nested subcomponent of the Service element.

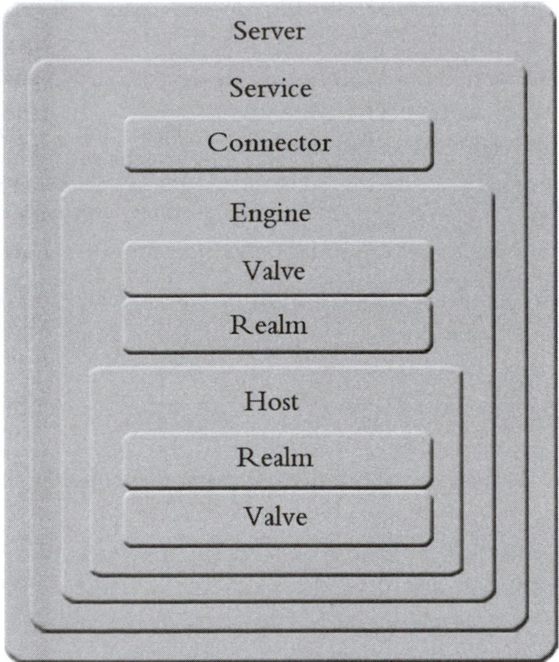

Figure 5.3 Different components in the server.xml file can be nested inside of one another.

Listing 5.2 The server.xml used to configure JBoss Web Server components

```
<Server>   ❶
  <Service name="jboss.web"      ❷
    className="org.jboss.web.tomcat.tc5.StandardService">
    <Connector port="8080" address="${jboss.bind.address}"      ❸
      maxThreads="250" strategy="ms" maxHttpHeaderSize="8192"
      emptySessionPath="true"
      enableLookups="false" redirectPort="8443"
      acceptCount="100" connectionTimeout="20000"
      disableUploadTimeout="true"/>
    <Engine name="jboss.web" defaultHost="localhost">      ❹
      <Realm className=      ❺
        "org.jboss.web.tomcat.security.JBossSecurityMgrRealm"
           certificatePrincipal=
        "org.jboss.security.auth.certs.SubjectDNMapping" />
      <Host name="www.somehostname.com"      ❻
        autoDeploy="false" deployOnStartup="false"
        deployXML="false">
        <Alias>somehostname.com</Alias>      ❼
        <Valve className=      ❽
          "org.apache.catalina.valves.RequestDumperValve" />
      </Host>
    </Engine>
  </Service>
</Server>
```

Table 5.3 summarizes the various components seen in listing 5.2. Each element is listed with a description of what the element is used for and a summary of when you might need to configure it. This file can have other elements, but they‘re rarely used. We won’t discuss them here.

Table 5.3 The configurable elements in the server.xml file

	Element	What is it?	When would you configure it?
❶	`Server`	Represents the entire servlet container.	Likely never.
❷	`Service`	Container for multiple connectors that share a single engine.	Likely never.
❸	`Connector`	Binds to a particular port and listens for requests using a particular protocol.	For any changes to the protocol or port that clients use to communicate with the web container. We discuss this in section 5.4.
❹	`Engine`	Receives and processes all requests from all connectors in the same service. The engine must be defined after all the connectors.	When you’re setting up load-balanced JBoss Web Server nodes as discussed in chapter 13.

Table 5.3 The configurable elements in the server.xml file *(continued)*

	Element	What is it?	When would you configure it?
5	`Realm`	Defines how security information (such as usernames, roles, and passwords) is handled.	If you need to change the strategy for mapping X509 certificate chains to a principal for authentication purposes. We discuss this when we talk about web security in chapter 6.
6	`Host`	Defines virtual hosts.	If you need to add or change the configuration for a domains or hostname mapped to your server. We discuss this in section 5.3.1.
7	`Alias`	Specifies an alias for `Host` element that surrounds it.	If you have multiple names for the same virtual host. We discuss this in section 5.3.1.
8	`Valve`	Intercepts requests that come into the system and executes code before the request reaches the targeted web component.	In order to add some sort of monitoring or logging capability to the web container or a particular web application. We discuss this when we talk about valves in section 5.6.

Out of the box, two connectors are defined—one that supports regular HTTP traffic on port 8080 and one that supports traffic from native web servers using a protocol called AJP on port 8009. The AJP protocol, a TCP/IP-based binary protocol, was created specifically for Tomcat as an alternative to sending HTTP messages to a web container. Because JBoss Web Server is built on top of Tomcat, JBoss Web Server supports the AJP protocol too. You use the AJP protocol when you want to front-load an application server with a native web server. The native web server must have support for the AJP protocol, usually through a plug-in called mod_jk. You can see a diagram of how this works in figure 5.10 in section 5.4, which is where we explore connector configuration in detail.

The previous example has a `Host` element, which handles all traffic to the machine intended for the www.somehostname.com domain. If you have more than one domain pointing to the IP address for a particular machine, you add different host configurations to handle them. You can also provide aliases for a given host using the `Alias` configuration element. You'll learn how to define virtual hosts in section 5.3.1.

The `Valve` element that we've defined provides us with a log of all the requests that go to the enclosing `Host` element. Valves define interceptors that can be executed as a request comes into the server. For example, if you want to log every access to a particular virtual host, you use a valve that intercepts the request and prints a message to a log file before continuing to process the request. You can define valves at the engine level or the host level, giving you the flexibility to apply a valve to the entire server or a single virtual host. You can also define them for individual applications in the context.xml file. We look at some of the valves that you can enable in section 5.6.

Now that you know how to configure the server.xml configuration file, let's explore the microcontainer configuration file for the WAR package deployer because it also has some server configuration that you might be interested in.

5.2.3 Exploring the WAR deployer configuration file

JBoss Web Server is bootstrapped when the WAR deployer is loaded. The microcontainer configuration file for the WAR deployer contains some server configuration elements that you may want to adjust. This file, war-deployers-jboss-beans.xml, is located in the server/xxx/deployers/jbossweb.deployer/META-INF directory.

This configuration file defines a bean called `WarDeployer`, the main deployer used for web applications. This deployer defines several properties that affect the way applications deploy into JBoss Web Server. Table 5.4 summarizes the main properties that you might configure.

If the `deleteWorkDirOnContextDestroy` property is set to `true`, the container deletes the directory under `server/xxx/work` that corresponds to the application when the application context is destroyed. The *application context* is an object the server creates when the application starts running and destroys when the application stops running. The object is used to store configuration and runtime information about the application. Think of it as an in-memory representation of your configuration file. The application context is destroyed when the server is stopped or when an application is removed from the server. The work directory is used by JBoss Web Server to store compiled JSP files and other temporary data. You may want to refer to these files after the server has stopped, so the default value is `false`; if you don't need these files to hang around, change this to `true`.

The rest of the configuration attributes in table 5.4 are related to class loading and are covered in section 5.5. The war-deployers-jboss-beans.xml file also contains other deployers such as the WebAppClusteringDefaultsDeployer, which we discuss in chapter 13.

Now that you have a general understanding of how web applications and JBoss Web Server are configured, let's explore some common configurations. We'll start with a discussion of configuring URL paths.

Table 5.4 Commonly modified properties under the `WarDeployer` configuration element in the war-deployers-jboss-beans.xml file

Property	What is it?
`defaultSecurityDomain`	The security domain used if you don't explicitly define one in your application's WEB-INF/jboss-web.xml. We talk about this in chapter 6 (section 6.6).
`deleteWorkDirOnContextDestroy`	Deletes the server/xxx/work directory after the application context ends.

`java2ClassLoadingCompliance`
`useJBossWebLoader`
`filteredPackages`
	These properties are used to configure class loading for web applications. We talk about these properties in section 5.5.

5.3 Configuring URL paths

An application can contain many different types of content (HTML pages, images, servlets, JSPs, and so on). You can configure a single JBoss AS instance to host multiple applications. A JBoss AS instance can also host multiple domains (or hostnames) that each run multiple applications. When a URL is sent from a user's web browser to the server, the server has to determine how to route the request to the appropriate hostname, application, and resource that the user is trying to access.

Let's dissect a URL that might be sent from a client browser to understand how the different parts of the URL help route a request to a resource on the server. Figure 5.4 shows you the five main parts of a URL and how they relate to elements within the network or JBoss Web Server.

The protocol defines how the client wants to talk to the server. Generally, we use `http`, but if we want secure communication, we use `https`. We talk about secure web communication in chapter 6 (section 6.4). The port specifies which OS port the web server is listening to requests on. If no port is specified, web browsers typically send the request to port 80. The protocol and port that a browser sends to the server determine which connector is accessed. The domain name routes a request through the internet (or intranet) to the machine hosting JBoss AS. Multiple domain names can be routed to a single server instance.

The context path tells the application server which web application the end user is trying to access. If you have multiple applications running on the same server, they should each have a unique context path so that the server can distinguish where the request should be routed. You can also bind one application in your server to the root context path, meaning that the user won't have to specify a context path to access that particular application. This shortcut is useful when you want users to access an application right when they type in your domain name.

The last part of the URL is the resource that the user is trying to access. This resource can be anything from a static HTML file or an image to a servlet or a JSP. If a static file is specified in this part of the URL, it's accessed relative to the root of your web application. If a web component (such as a JSP, servlet, or JSF page) is requested, this portion of the URL depends on the logical mapping defined in the web.xml file.

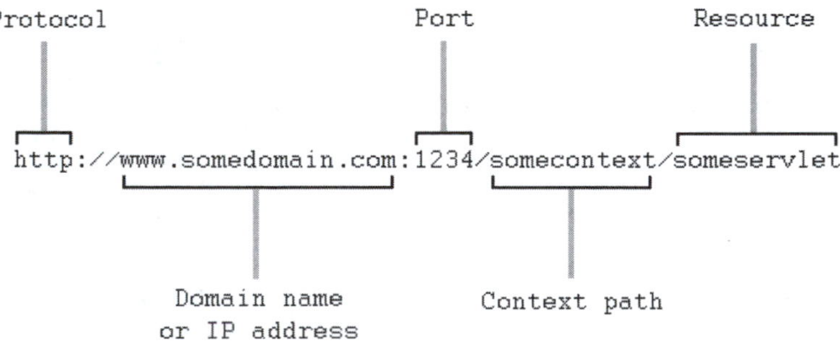

Figure 5.4 The various parts of a URL are read by the server to guide the request to the appropriate resource.

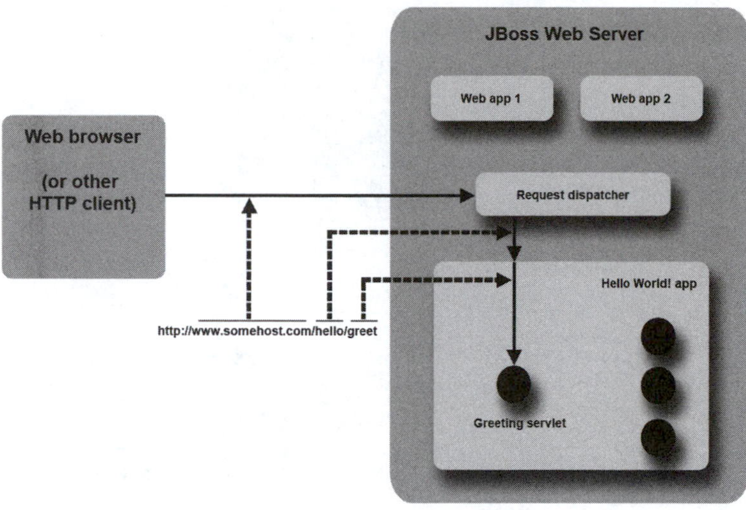

Figure 5.5 The request dispatcher routes a request to a resource by examining the URL.

When a request gets routed to JBoss AS, a component called a *request dispatcher* examines the request and decides which application and resource to forward the request to. Figure 5.5 shows how the different portions of the URL help the request dispatcher decide where to route a request.

As the figure shows, when a request comes into the dispatcher, it examines the context path and determines which application to access. It then accesses the application and forwards the request to the appropriate resource within the application.

Now that we have some background on how the server breaks apart the URL and uses it to route the request, let's take a look at how to configure virtual hosts, context paths, and resources.

5.3.1 Enabling virtual hosts

Multiple domain names or sub-domain names can point to the same instance of JBoss AS. Domain names must be registered with a Domain Name Service (DNS) server so that they can resolve to the IP address for the server. By default, if you deploy an application to the server, it's accessible on any domain name mapped to the box. For example, if you deploy an application called `bankapp.war` to a server that has the domains `www.site1.com` and `www.site2.com` pointing to it, it can be accessed using either the http://www.site1.com:8080/bankapp URL or the http://www.site2.com:8080/bankapp URL.

If you want to host different domains on the same server but only want to expose specific applications on each domain, you can configure applications to bind to specific hostnames using *virtual hosts.* A virtual host is a mechanism for segmenting the web container to expose certain applications to certain domains.

Figure 5.6 shows you a single JBoss Web Server instance running two virtual hosts—one for the `www.site1.com` domain and the other for the `www.site2.com`

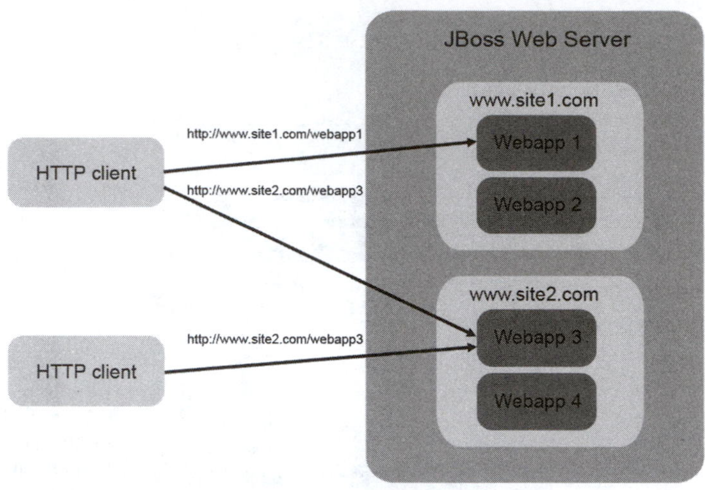

Figure 5.6 Requests going to different domain names can resolve to the same server.

domain. The different web applications running in the server are bound to the different virtual hosts. This isn't uncommon in an enterprise that has many small web applications that don't warrant the cost and overhead of their own servers.

To use virtual hosts, you have to do the following:

1. Configure the connector to use virtual hosts.
2. Define the virtual host in the server configuration file.
3. Bind your applications to the virtual host in your application configuration file.

Let's talk about each of these steps, starting with the connector configuration.

ENABLING VIRTUAL HOSTS ON THE CONNECTOR

In section 5.4, we discuss how to configure the various JBoss Web Server connectors. To enable virtual hosts, you must enable the `useIPVHosts` attribute on the connector used to access the application in question. This is a boolean attribute, so the values can be either `true` or `false`. The default value is `false`; if you set it to `true`, the connector determines the destined domain name of the incoming request and forwards it to the virtual host configured to handle that domain name.

DEFINING THE VIRTUAL HOST

In the server configuration file, virtual hosts are defined by the `Host` element in JBoss Web Server's server/xxx/deploy/jbossweb.sar/server.xml file. As you learned when we talked about the structure of the server.xml file in section 5.2.3, the `Host` element is a sub-element of the `Engine` element. You can define multiple hosts for an engine. A single virtual host definition in the server.xml looks similar to the following:

```
<Engine name="jboss.web" defaultHost="localhost">
   <Host name="localhost" autoDeploy="false" deployOnStartup="false"
         deployXML="false">
   </Host>
</Engine>
```

The `defaultHost` attribute on the `Engine` element points to the virtual host that handles requests for applications that have no virtual host binding. If you define multiple virtual hosts, one of the hosts that you define should match the `defaultHost` attribute for the engine. The `name` attribute on the `Host` element specifies the domain name that the virtual host is defined for. This should match the domain name registered with your DNS server. By default, the `name` attribute is set to `localhost`, allowing the virtual host to handle every request that comes into the server.

To define your own virtual host, you add another `Host` block to the server.xml file. Here's an example of a virtual host definition for a domain called `www.somehostname.com`.

```
<Host name="somehostname.com" autoDeploy="false"
     deployOnStartup="false" deployXML="false">
  <Alias>www.somehostname.com</Alias>
</Host>
```

The only thing that you need to change on the virtual host configuration is the `name` attribute. In this case, we also added an `Alias` sub-element. An alias is used if you want to map multiple domain names to the same virtual host configuration. An alias can be a completely different host name, or it can be used to define a domain and one or more sub-domains as in the example.

All the deployment-related attributes are set to `false` because these are Tomcat configuration attributes. JBoss AS uses its own application deployment mechanism to load web applications into memory—the WAR deployer.

Now that you've learned how to define a virtual host in the server configuration file, let's look at how to bind an application to the virtual host.

BINDING AN APPLICATION TO A VIRTUAL HOST

To bind an application to the virtual host, you need to configure the application itself. You can bind an application to a virtual host by using the `virtual-host` element in the web application's WEB-INF/jboss-web.xml file. Here's an example:

```
<jboss-web>
   <virtual-host>www.somehostname.com</virtual-host>
</jboss-web>
```

As we discussed in the last section, if you don't specify the `virtual-host` element, then requests sent to the application are handled by the virtual host defined by the `defaultHost` attribute, which is defined in the `Engine` element in the server.xml file.

Now that you've learned how to configure the host portion of a URL, let's delve more into context paths.

5.3.2 *Configuring context paths*

As shown in figure 5.7, the context path is the part of the URL that comes right after the domain name and port.

The context path points the request dispatcher to the appropriate application. JBoss Web Server makes configuring the context path for an application easy—you don't have to configure it at all! When you deploy a web application into JBoss AS, the

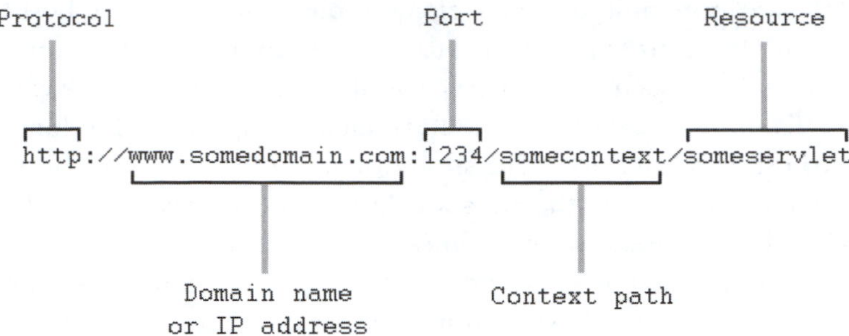

Figure 5.7 The context path directs the request to the appropriate application inside the server.

WAR deployer uses the name of the WAR package (sans the .war extension) for the context path. For example, if you deploy a WAR package named `helloworld.war` into JBoss AS, JBoss Web Server assigns the context path `helloworld` to the application.

Figure 5.8 demonstrates this relationship by showing a web package deployed in the server and how it relates to the context path in a URL used to access a resource in the application.

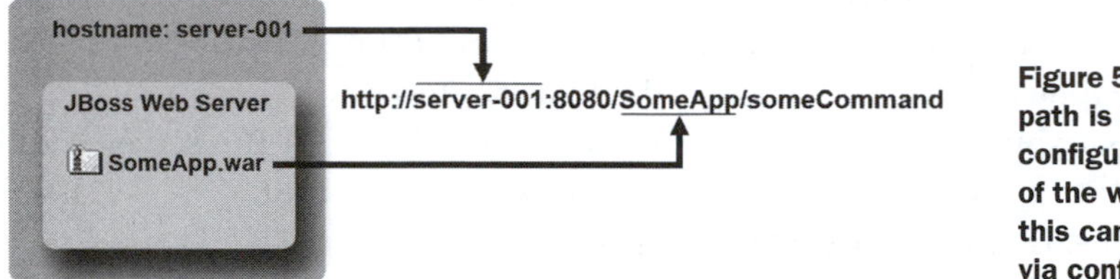

Figure 5.8 The context path is automatically configured to the name of the web package, but this can be overridden via configuration.

If you want to use a different context path for an application than the name of the web archive, you can change it through manual configuration. If you deploy your web application in a WAR package, this configuration can be done through your application's jboss-web.xml file. If you deploy your application as part of an enterprise package (EAR), you configure it in the enterprise package's application.xml file. Let's see how to do both.

CHANGING THE URL CONTEXT PATH FOR A WEB APPLICATION

If you deploy your application in a web archive, you change the context path by adding a `context-root` element in the jboss-web.xml file for your application. For example, if you have an application deployed as `helloworld.war`, but you want the context path to be `hello` instead of `helloworld`, you configure the following in the jboss-web.xml file:

```
<jboss-web>
  <context-root>/hello</context-root>
</jboss-web>
```

WARNING If you've used Tomcat as a standalone application server, you may be used to changing the context path in the server.xml file or in the context.xml file for your application. This method doesn't carry over to JBoss Web Server; you should stick with changing the jboss-web.xml file as described in this section.

The value of the `context-root` element overrides the JBoss Web Server default, which is based on the name of the WAR file. Overriding the default context root is fairly simple for enterprise applications as well.

CHANGING THE URL CONTEXT PATH FOR AN ENTERPRISE APPLICATION

We cover enterprise applications in chapter 7. But because we're on the subject of configuring context paths, it's worth mentioning how you might configure the URL context for a web application that's part of a larger enterprise application. An *enterprise application* is an application that may contain one or more web archives and/or EJB archives in one big archive file. Each enterprise application has its own configuration file called application.xml. Each web application is configured in the application.xml file under a web module element. Here's how you set the `context-root` in this file:

```
<application>
   <display-name>HelloWorldApp</display-name>
   <module>
      <web>
         <web-uri>helloworld.war</web-uri>
         <context-root>/hello</context-root>
      </web>
   </module>
</application>
```

The `context-root` element is set to `hello`, so any traffic going to the `hello` URL context is directed to the `helloworld.war` application.

Now that you know a bit about context paths, you might be curious to know how to configure an application to have no context path at all.

5.3.3 Changing the root context path

What if you have a web application that you want people to access by providing only a domain name? For example, you own the `mywonderfulbank.com` domain, and you want your users to be able to access your banking application by going to http://www.mywonderfulbank.com/. You want an application that's bound to the *root context.* The root context is the context bound to /. Think of this as a lack of a context in the URL. Out of the box, the root context points to a web application deployed under the `server/xxx/deploy/ROOT.war` package.

In chapter 1, after installing JBoss AS and starting the default configuration, we asked you to pull up a browser window and go to http://localhost:8080/. The web application that came up was the root application. You most likely want to change the default root application because you don't want it accessible in a production system. You can do this in several ways.

- *You can change the existing root application*—You can modify the existing root application or build your own and replace the existing one. This is one of the simplest approaches.
- *You can configure the context path*—When we talked about configuring context paths in section 5.3.2, you learned how to override the default context path by specifying the `context-root` element in an application WEB-INF/jboss-web.xml file. If you have another application that you want to bind to the root context, you use the following configuration:

  ```
  <jboss-web>
    <context-root>/</context-root>
  </jboss-web>
  ```

  Before doing this you should remove or rename the default root web application (`ROOT.war`) from the deploy directory.
- *You can remove the root context*—You may decide that your server doesn't need a root application at all. In that case, you can delete the default root web application from the deploy directory altogether. If a user tries to access the root context and there's nothing mapped to it, JBoss Web Server will return a blank page.
- *You can secure the root context*—You may decide that the default root application is useful, but you don't want people accessing it unless they have permission or are physically on the server. In chapter 6, we teach you how to secure a web application by restricting URLs and binding the application to a security domain. Another way to secure the root application is to bind it to a virtual host that can only be accessed when somebody is physically on the server. We talk about how to do this in chapter 15.

Now that we've discussed how to configure the URL paths, let's talk about how to configure connectors.

5.4 Configuring connectors

In section 5.3, we discussed the structure of a URL that's sent from a client browser to the server. We discussed how the domain name, context path, and resource definition in the URL helps route a request to the appropriate resource on the server. The two parts of the URL that we didn't talk about in detail are the protocol and the port. Figure 5.9 shows you where these elements are in a URL that might be sent to a web server.

The protocol portion of the URL defines the protocol over which you intend to communicate with the server. HTTP is the protocol that web browsers use to communicate with web servers. Clients communicate over HTTP or Hypertext Transfer Protocol over Secure Sockets Layer (HTTPS), or secure HTTP. The top portion of figure 5.10 shows that a web browser can communicate with JBoss Web Server over HTTP or HTTPS.

But clients don't always communicate directly to a servlet container; sometimes they communicate with a native web server, which in turn, communicates with a servlet

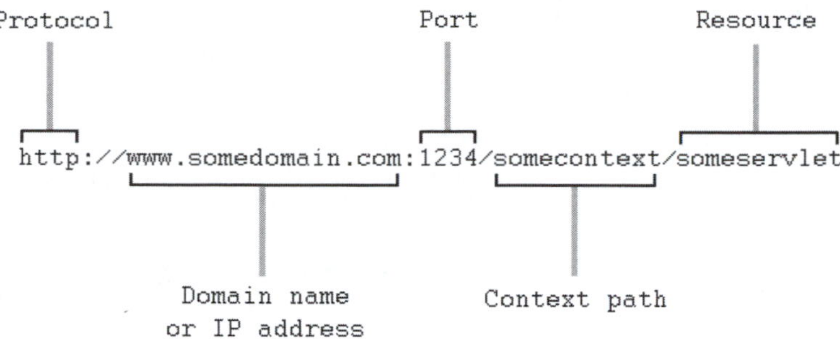

Figure 5.9 The protocol and the port are configured in the connector definition in the server.xml file.

container. The native web server can forward the HTTP request to the servlet container using either the HTTP or HTTPS protocol. But JBoss Web Server supports another protocol called AJP that allows native web servers to send the request in a binary format, which can be faster in many cases. The bottom portion of figure 5.10 illustrates the different forms of communication that can occur between a web browser and a native web server and, in turn, between a native web server and JBoss Web Server.

OSs allow multiple programs to communicate over the network. To separate the communication traffic, an OS allows different programs to bind to different TCP/IP ports. Web servers typically bind to port 80 to listen for HTTP traffic.

JBoss Web Server uses connectors to bind to particular ports and listen for traffic over particular protocols. You can configure two main types of connectors in JBoss Web Server: HTTP connectors and AJP connectors. The HTTPS protocol is supported by defining an HTTP connector with a few extra configuration attributes.

Let's take a closer look at how to configure the connectors, and then we'll discuss several common things that you can configure connectors to do.

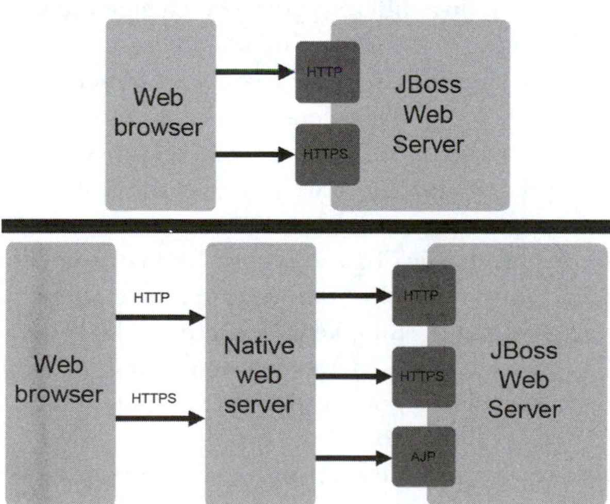

Figure 5.10 JBoss Web Server can accept HTTP or HTTPS directly from a web browser or a native web server. It can also accept AJP requests from a native web server.

5.4.1 Understanding connector configuration

In section 5.2.2, we discussed the structure of the JBoss Web Server configuration file (server/xxx/deployers/jbossweb.deployer/server.xml) and how connectors are defined as sub-elements to the `Server` configuration element. If you open the server.xml file in an out-of-the-box configuration, you see a configuration that looks similar to what is shown in listing 5.3.

Listing 5.3 Connectors configured in the server.xml file

```
<Service name="jboss.web"
      className="org.jboss.web.tomcat.tc6.StandardService">

  <!-- A HTTP/1.1 Connector on port 8080 -->
  <Connector protocol="HTTP/1.1" port="8080"
     address="${jboss.bind.address}"
     connectionTimeout="20000" redirectPort="8443" />

  <!-- A AJP 1.3 Connector on port 8009 -->
  <Connector protocol="AJP/1.3" port="8009" address="${jboss.bind.address}"
     redirectPort="8443" />

  <!-- SSL/TLS Connector configuration using the admin devl guide keystore
  <Connector protocol="HTTP/1.1" SSLEnabled="true"
     port="8443" address="${jboss.bind.address}"
     scheme="https" secure="true" clientAuth="false"
     keystoreFile="${jboss.server.home.dir}/conf/chap8.keystore"
     keystorePass="rmi+ssl" sslProtocol = "TLS" />
  -->

  ...
```

The first connector is an HTTP connector, which is configured to listen for regular HTTP traffic on port 8080. You know this is an HTTP connector because of the `protocol` attribute. The `protocol` attribute takes on a default value of `HTTP/1.1` if undefined. The `port` attribute configures the port number that the connector binds to. If you want your HTTP traffic to come in on a different port, you change the value of the port attribute. For example, if you plan on running a standalone instance of JBoss AS, you can set the port attribute to `80`, allowing clients to access your server without specifying a port; browsers send requests to port 80 by default.

You know that the second connector is an AJP connector because the `protocol` attribute is set to `AJP/1.3`. The `port` attribute tells you that the AJP connector is bound to port `8009`. The third connector is a secured HTTP connector—an HTTP connector configured to handle HTTPS traffic. To use secured HTTP, a keystore must exist. Because each JBoss AS user must create his own keystore, the connector is commented out by default. We talked about creating keystores and public-key certificates in chapter 4. We talk about how to use encrypted web communication in chapter 6.

In the next several sections, we describe how to configure various connector attributes. The HTTP and AJP connectors share most of the same configuration attributes; as we describe how to configure the attributes, assume that the configuration can apply to either connector unless we specify otherwise.

Let's start with a discussion of how to configure concurrency control in a connector.

5.4.2 Configuring concurrency

Connectors are designed to handle concurrent connections from multiple browsers. There are two main attributes that you can configure: `maxThreads`, and `acceptCount` (for the HTTP connector) or `backlog` (for the AJP connector).

- *`maxThreads`*—The maximum number of processing threads that can run concurrently. Because the server can't create any more threads, this parameter ultimately limits the number of concurrent users. If all threads are being used, it's up to the individual connector to provide queuing. If left unspecified, the default is 200 threads.
- *`acceptCount`* or *`backlog`*—Defines the length of a queue. When all request processing threads are busy, the connector starts queuing the requests. The HTTP connector uses the `acceptCount` attribute, and the AJP connector uses the `backlog` attribute. If the queue is full, the connector refuses the request. If left unspecified, the default is to queue 10 requests.

If you have a lot of concurrent users, you want to make sure that none of them is keeping a connection open for too long so that other requests can be fulfilled. Let's explore how to configure connection timeouts.

5.4.3 Configuring timeouts

Sometimes, the resource that a client is trying to access doesn't respond or responds slowly. We don't want the client to hog a connection thread indefinitely, so the connector provides a `connectionTimeout` attribute that you use to specify the number of milliseconds to wait for the requested URL after a connection is made. For the HTTP connector, the default is 60 seconds (60,000 milliseconds); for the AJP connector, the default is 0 (infinite).

5.4.4 Configuring a proxy hostname and port

If you're running behind a proxy server, you can fool your web applications into thinking that you aren't by using the `proxyName` and `proxyPort` attributes. These attributes override the values that are provided to your application when your code calls the `request.getServerName()` and `request.getServerPort()` servlet methods.

Now that we've discussed connectors and how to configure them, let's see what configuring class loading entails.

5.5 Configuring web class loading

In chapter 3 (section 3.2), we gave you a general background on how class loading works in JBoss AS. Java EE web applications don't follow the same default class loading convention that most other archive types do in JBoss AS. Web applications don't use a shared class-loader repository but delegate to the regular system class loader by default. The servlet specification recommends that web applications be isolated from one another, and Red Hat abides by this recommendation.

You can configure web applications to use a class-loader repository in the microcontainer configuration file for the WAR deployer, server/xxx/deployers/jbossweb.

deployer/META-INF/war-deployers-jboss-beans.xml. The class loading properties are part of the `WarDeployer` bean. You can configure three class loading properties: `java2ClassLoadingCompliance`, `useJBossWebLoader`, and `filteredPackages`.

The `java2ClassLoadingCompliance` property is set to `false` by default, telling the deployer to load classes from within the web application's WEB-INF/lib and WEB-INF/classes directories before trying to load them from the parent (system) class loader. The `useJBossWebLoader` property is also set to `false`, telling the container to use its regular class loader rather than a regular JBoss AS class loader that hooks into a class loader repository.

You may have a case where you want to load most of your libraries from inside of your application's WEB-INF/lib and WEB-INF/classes directories first, but you also have a subset of classes that you want to load through the parent (system) class loader first. In this case, you can leave the `java2ClassLoadingCompliance` property set to `false` but specify specific package names using the `filteredPackages` property. JBoss AS will attempt to load classes that match the packages listed under this property by going to the parent (system) class loader first. This method only works if the `useJBossWebLoader` option is `false`—that is, there's no class loader repository.

You should now have a good background on how web application class loading works in JBoss AS. Now let's talk about valves, another feature of JBoss Web Server.

5.6 Using valves

Sometimes you want to perform certain actions every time a request comes into the server. For example, you may want to log information about the request, or you may want to check the originating IP address on a request and block it if it's on a blacklist. You can program this logging or blacklisting functionality into your application code, but because it's not specific to your business logic, you might, instead, accomplish it using a *valve*, or interceptor.

TIP People using JBoss Web Server often want to know how to enable web-server–style access logging. Servers like Apache, IIS, and Tomcat standalone are configured to create log files that show information about requests made to the server. JBoss Web Server has no logging enabled by default, but it can be enabled by using the `AccessLogValve`.

JBoss Web Server provides valves that can intercept requests as they come into the server. Figure 5.11 shows how requests coming from HTTP clients are intercepted by a valve, the valve logs information about the request to a log file, and then the request continues to the destined web applications.

You can configure valves for individual applications by defining them in the WEB-INF/context.xml file. You can also define them at the server level as a subelement of an engine or a host in JBoss Web Server's server.xml file, as we discussed in section 5.2.3. Only the `CachedConnectionValve` is enabled by default, but others are available, yet commented out, in the server.xml file.

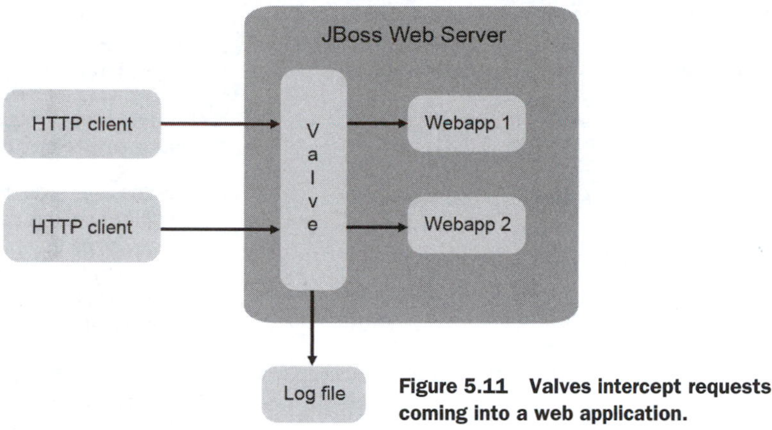

Figure 5.11 Valves intercept requests coming into a web application.

Valves are configured using the `Valve` element. The element must have an attribute called `className` that points to a Java class with the valve code. For example, imagine the following valve defined in the server.xml file:

```
<Host name="mydomain.com" ... >
  <Valve className="org.apache.catalina.valves.RequestDumperValve" />
  ...
</Host>
```

Every time a request comes into the mydomain.com virtual host, this valve prints all the request information to the console window as well as to the server/xxx/log/server.log file. Table 5.5 lists some other valves that you might find useful.

Table 5.5 Some valves that ship with JBoss Web Server

Valve name (the value of the Valve `className` attribute)	Description
`org.apache.catalina.valves.RequestDumperValve`	Logs information about a request before and after it's processed. Beneficial for debugging problems related to the request header or information on a cookie.
`org.apache.catalina.valves.AccessLogValve`	Writes to a log file that resembles a web server access log. Provides a configurable pattern syntax for customized log file formatting.
`org.apache.catalina.valves.FastCommonAccessLogValve`	Similar to the `AccessLogValve` but faster and more limited in configuration. Intended for use in a production system.
`org.apache.catalina.valves.RemoteAddrValve`	Allows filtering of requests based on the client's IP address.

Table 5.5 Some valves that ship with JBoss Web Server *(continued)*

Valve name (the value of the Valve `className` attribute)	Description
`org.apache.catalina.valves.RemoteHostValve`	Allows filtering of requests based on the client's hostname.
`org.apache.catalina.authenticator.SingleSignOn`	When the user signs into a single application, this valve automatically signs them into all other applications associated with the virtual host for which the valve is defined.
`org.jboss.web.tomcat.service.sso.ClusteredSingleSignOn`	This is the same as the `SingleSignOn` valve but enables the single-sign-on feature to work across a cluster of JBoss AS servers.
`org.jboss.web.tomcat.service.jca.CachedConnectionValve`	Automatically closes all JCA connections when the web request ends. This might be useful during development, but you'll probably want to solve the underlying problem before production and disable this valve.

All the valves that start with the `org.apache.catalina` package name are well documented in the Tomcat 6 online documentation, so we won't delve into the details on these. The ones that start with `org.jboss.web` are specific to JBoss Web Server and are well documented in the JBoss AS documentation.

Let's move on to another common area of the web server that you might want to configure when you're creating Java-based web applications: JSF.

5.7 Configuring JavaServer Faces

Earlier versions of JBoss Web Server shipped with Apache MyFaces, but it now has built-in support for JavaServer Faces using the GlassFish Mojarra JSF implementation. Mojarra is the JSF 1.2 reference implementation. If your application uses JSF, you don't have to package the core JSF libraries with your application; all you have to do to make your application use MyFaces is configure the FacesServlet in your application's WEB-INF/web.xml file as shown in listing 5.4.

Listing 5.4 Adding a servlet and servlet-mapping element to the WEB-INF/web.xml file

```
<web-app version="2.5"
   xmlns:xsi="http://www.w3.org/2001/XMLSchema-instance"
   xmlns="http://java.sun.com/xml/ns/javaee"
   xmlns:web="http://java.sun.com/xml/ns/javaee/web-app_2_5.xsd"
   xsi:schemaLocation="http://java.sun.com/xml/ns/javaee
   ➥                   http://java.sun.com/xml/ns/javaee/web-app_2_5.xsd">
  ...
```

```
  <servlet>
    <servlet-name>Faces Servlet</servlet-name>
    <servlet-class>javax.faces.webapp.FacesServlet</servlet-class>
    <load-on-startup>1</load-on-startup>
  </servlet>
  <servlet-mapping>
    <servlet-name>Faces Servlet</servlet-name>
    <url-pattern>*.faces</url-pattern>
  </servlet-mapping>
  ...
</web-app>
```

The `.FacesServlet` is a standard part of the JSF specification that enables JSF requests to be processed and handled. If you want to update or add to the JSF libraries, you can find them in the server/xxx/deploy/jbossweb.sar/jsf-libs directory. If you want to use a different implementation altogether, you can delete that entire directory and include your JSF libraries in your own application's WEB-INF/lib directory.

5.8 Summary

We started this chapter by talking about the structure of web applications and by examining the different deployment descriptors that are used for web applications that will run in JBoss AS. You learned that configuration files can be packaged in the WEB-INF directory of a web application and that global configuration files can also be used to configure application-level settings for all web applications running in the server.

After discussing web application configuration, we took a look at the configuration of JBoss Web Server. We explored where the key configuration files can be found and gave you an overview of what they contain.

Using this fundamental knowledge of configuring web applications and JBoss Web Server, we spent the rest of the chapter talking about specific and common things that you can configure when using web applications. We started by talking about URL paths and how the different parts of a URL submitted by a client are used to route a user's request to a particular piece of content. We looked at virtual hosts to see how servers can host multiple host names and then learned how to configure a virtual host and bind an application to it. We looked at context paths to see how servers can host multiple applications, and you learned how to change the context path for a web and an enterprise application. We also discussed the root context and went over several different options for changing the root context path.

After learning how to configure URL paths, we discussed JBoss Web Server connectors and how they're used to allow client requests to come in over different protocols. We discussed how to configure many aspects of communication on the connectors including concurrency, timeouts, security, virtual hosts, and proxy hostnames.

After talking about connectors, we discussed web class loading. We discussed class loading in chapter 3, but web applications have slightly different class loading rules because of the servlet specification. We gave an overview of why there are different requirements and showed how to configure different web-specific class loading parameters.

We also talked about valves and how they intercept incoming and outgoing requests to enable pre- and post-processing. We showed how to configure a valve and gave a summary of the various valves that are available in JBoss Web Server. We wrapped up the chapter with a discussion of the JSF implementation that's available and how you can enable your application to use it.

We didn't cover two major things about web applications: security and clustering. There's a lot to say about both these topics. Web security is so detailed that we devote the entire next chapter to it. We also have two chapters (12 and 13) on clustering that discuss web-related clustering topics such as HTTP session replication and load balancing.

5.9 References

Apache Tomcat 6.0 documentation—http://tomcat.apache.org/tomcat-6.0-doc/index.html

Servlet specification—http://jcp.org/aboutJava/communityprocess/mrel/jsr154/index.html

The GlassFish Mojarra project—https://javaserverfaces.dev.java.net/

Configuring JSF—http://www.jboss.org/community/docs/DOC-10837

6 Securing web applications

This chapter covers

- Configuring web security
- Web authentication
- Web authorization
- Encrypted web communication

While working on different projects, we've seen project teams spend a lot of time writing custom authentication and authorization code. But this code functions in much the same way as the security model defined by the Java EE specification. In many cases, you don't have to write custom security code for every new web application you write; the standard web security features of Java EE can obviate writing security code altogether, allowing you to add security to your application entirely through configuration.

In chapter 4, we talked about the fundamentals of JBoss security and showed you how to configure security domains and login modules. In chapter 5, we talked about the basics of web applications and how to package, deploy, and configure them. In this chapter, we bring these two concepts together, and you'll learn how to configure web security.

First, we explore the configuration files necessary to enable security; then we talk about how to enable authentication and authorization for URLs relative to your application's context path. We also look at how to enable secure communication for server authentication, mutual authentication, and client-certificate authentication.

6.1 Configuring web security

By default, web applications aren't secured. If you write a web application and deploy it to the application server without configuring security, anybody can access any URL relative to your application's context path. JBoss Web Server is also insecure by default. For example, all requests sent to your server are unencrypted because the secure HTTP connector isn't enabled. In this section, you'll learn how to configure the various server and application configuration files to enable security.

Figure 6.1 shows you which configuration files are used to configure security within the server and for applications.

Although this seems like a lot of files, each file has a specific purpose. The server.xml file configures JBoss Web Server and, in particular, can be used to define connectors, which we discussed in chapter 5. In this chapter, we'll take a closer look at how to enable secure communication by configuring this file.

In chapter 5, you also learned that each web application has a standard WEB-INF/web.xml deployment descriptor and a JBoss-specific WEB-INF/jboss-web.xml deployment descriptor. These files configure application security by defining which of your application's URLs are secured and by pointing to the security domain that should be used to enforce the security constraints.

The login-config.xml file contains security domain definitions. Security domains compare security data on incoming requests to security data kept in security datastores, which security domains access using login modules. This file isn't specific to web security but is part of the underlying JBoss SX security framework. Table 6.1 summarizes where you can find each file and what security aspects you can configure.

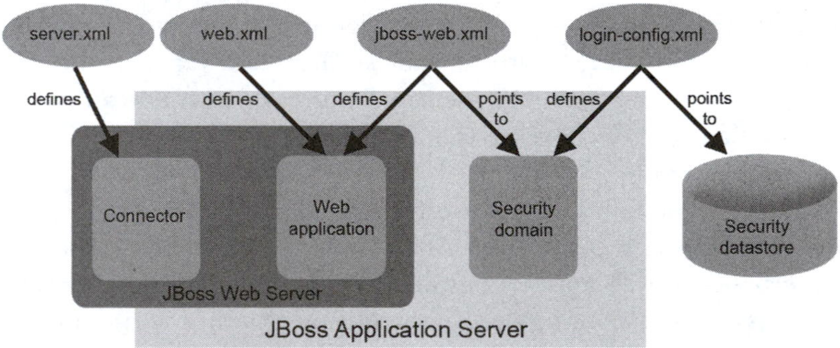

Figure 6.1 Three main files are used to configure security for web applications, in addition to the login-config.xml file, which is used to configure security domains for any application running in JBoss Web Server.

Table 6.1 The four primary configuration files used to configure web security

Configuration file	The configurable security aspects
WEB-INF/web.xml - [a]	▪ The authentication strategy (`BASIC`, `FORM`, `DIGEST`, or `CLIENT-CERT`) ▪ Which URL patterns should be restricted to which logical roles ▪ A set of logical roles
WEB-INF/jboss-web.xml - [a]	The JNDI name for the security domain that the web application should use
server/xxx/deploy/jbossweb.sar/server.xml	▪ The secure HTTP connector (SSL port, keystore file, and so on) ▪ The portion of the certificate compared during `CLIENT-CERT` authentication
server/xxx/conf /login-config.xml	▪ The definition for security domains ▪ The login module that the security domain should use

a. These files are relative to your application's directory structure, not to the server's root directory like the other files listed in this table.

You've already seen the login-config.xml file in chapter 4. Let's take a closer look at the other three files to see how you can use them to configure web security. We'll start with the web.xml file.

6.1.1 *Configuring security in web.xml*

The standard web deployment descriptor, web.xml, is used to specify application-level authentication, authorization, and encryption. Figure 6.2 shows you the general structure of the elements in the web.xml file pertinent to security configuration.

The number in the upper-left corner of each box represents the multiplicity of the element, or how many of a given element type can exist within the scope of the enclosing element. For example, only a single `web-resource-collection` can be defined inside of a `security-constraint`, but many `security-constraints` can be defined inside of a `web-app`. Listing 6.1 shows you a sample web.xml with security enabled.

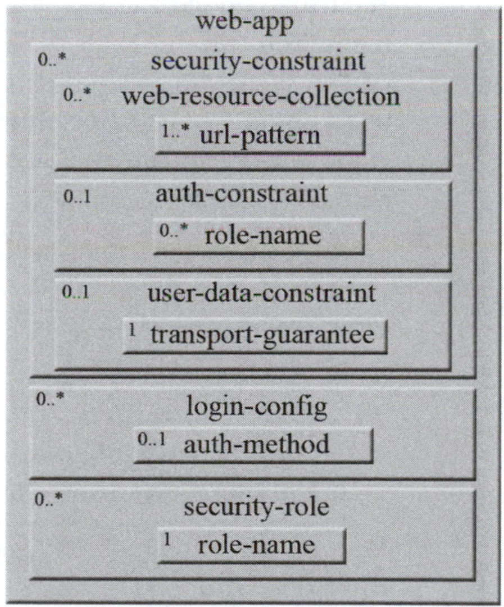

Figure 6.2 The security-related elements in the standard web deployment descriptor, web.xml

Listing 6.1 A WEB-INF/web.xml file with security enabled

```
<web-app>
<security-constraint>
  <web-resource-collection>
    <web-resource-name>Some Resource</web-resource-name>
    <url-pattern>/*</url-pattern>                              ❶
    <url-pattern>/shoppingcart/*</url-pattern>
    <http-method>GET</http-method>                        ❷
    <http-method>POST</http-method>
  </web-resource-collection>
  <auth-constraint>
    <role-name>SomeSimpleRole</role-name>           ❸
  </auth-constraint>
  <user-data-constraint>
    <transport-guarantee>
      CONFIDENTIAL                            ❹
    </transport-guarantee>
  </user-data-constraint>
</security-constraint>

<login-config>
  <auth-method>BASIC</auth-method>          ❺
</login-config>

<security-role>
  <role-name>SomeSimpleRole</role-name>         ❻
</security-role>
</web-app>
```

Security is added to specified URL patterns under the web-resource-collection element. You use the http-method element ❷ to specify which HTTP methods (usually GET or POST) you want secured for the URLs that you've defined. You define the URLs using the url-pattern element ❶. You can define more than one URL pattern for a given web-resource-collection. As per the specification, the string value of a URL pattern is treated as follows:

- A string beginning with a / character and ending with a /* suffix is used for path mapping.
- A string beginning with a *. prefix is used for extension mapping.
- A string containing only the / character indicates the *default* servlet of the application. In this case, the servlet path is the request URI minus the context path, and the path info is null.
- All other strings are used for exact matches only.

After specifying which URLs are to be secured, you need to specify which roles are authorized to access those URLs by defining roles under the auth-constraint block ❸. In listing 6.1, a role called SomeSimpleRole is defined with the role-name element. Roles are also defined separately under the security-role element ❻. We discuss authorization further in section 6.3.

If you secure a URL, it's assumed that the user who's trying to access it is authenticated. You specify authentication for the entire web application using the login-config block ❺. JBoss provides four different authentication strategies that can be defined using the `auth-method` attribute. We discuss these options further in section 6.2.

You use the `transport-guarantee` element ❹ to specify whether requests coming into the application must be encrypted or not. We discuss secure communication further in section 6.4.2.

The web.xml file is used to define what URLs are to be secured but says nothing about how to secure them. That's the job of the security domain, which you define in the login-config.xml file and point the application to in the jboss-web.xml file. Let's examine how to point to the security domain in the jboss-web.xml file.

6.1.2 Configuring security in jboss-web.xml

You can use the jboss-web.xml deployment descriptor to map an application to a security domain. Let's look at an example. Assume that you have a security domain defined in your login-config.xml file that looks like the following:

```
<application-policy name="some-domain">
  ...
</application-policy>
```

The following jboss-web.xml shows how you'd point to this security domain:

```
<jboss-web>
   <security-domain>java:/jaas/some-domain</security-domain>
</jboss-web>
```

When the security framework reads the login-config.xml file, it creates a security domain and binds it into JNDI under `java:/jaas/some-domain`. The `security-domain` element in the jboss-web.xml file merely has to point to that security domain; all this file does is map the application to the security domain. The bulk of the configuration is in the application's web.xml file and the server's login-config.xml file.

6.1.3 Configuring security in server.xml

In chapter 5, we introduced you to the server.xml file, the main configuration file for JBoss Web Server. For security purposes, you might want to configure the connector configurations in this file. In the out-of-the-box configuration, JBoss Web Server has a secure HTTP connector that's defined but commented out in the server.xml file. The configuration for this connector looks something like this:

```
<Connector protocol="HTTP/1.1" SSLEnabled="true"
        port="8443" address="${jboss.bind.address}"
        scheme="https" secure="true" clientAuth="false"
        keystoreFile="${jboss.server.home.dir}/conf/chap8.keystore"
        keystorePass="rmi+ssl" sslProtocol = "TLS" />
```

If you uncomment this connector configuration and point it to a keystore containing your server certificate, clients can access pages on your server over SSL. We talk about this further in section 6.4. This file also contains configurations that can be used for client-certificate authentication.

JBoss Web Server also defines a *realm* inside of the server.xml file. The realm integrates the JBoss Web Server into the JBoss SX security framework. The realm definition in the server.xml file looks like the following:

```
<Realm className="org.jboss.web.tomcat.security.JBossWebRealm"
  certificatePrincipal="org.jboss.security.auth.certs.SubjectDNMapping"
  allRolesMode="authOnly" />
```

The `certificatePrincipal` attribute is used for client-certificate authentication, which we talk about in section 6.5. The `allRolesMode` attribute is discussed further in section 6.3.2.

Now that you've learned about the different configuration files used to configure web security, let's take a closer look at how to authenticate web users.

6.2 Authenticating users

The great thing about Java EE authentication is that it can be applied to your application without writing any code. When a user requests a secured URL (as defined in the `web-resource-collection` in the web.xml file), the server detects if the user is logged in or not using information stored on the user's session. If the user tries to access a secured URL, the container forces the user to login using the authentication method defined for the application before displaying the page that the user requested. Figure 6.3 illustrates this sequence of events.

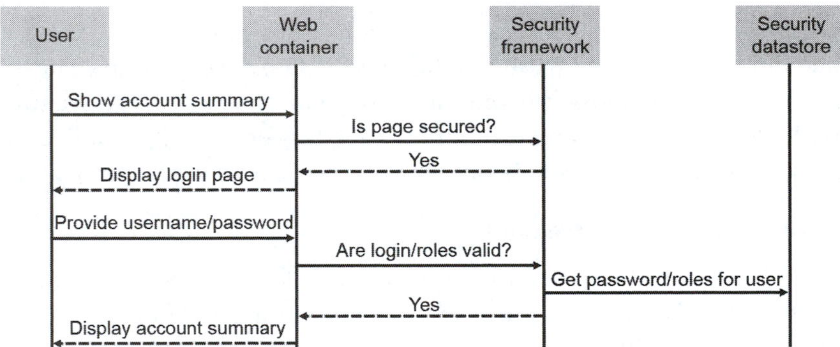

Figure 6.3 The Java EE web security process for a user who's requesting an account summary page in a web application

When users request the Account Summary page, they're not taken directly to the page. The Account Summary page is secured and only allows access to users with certain roles. Here's a description of the sequence of events in figure 6.3:

- The web container asks the security framework if the page is secured; the framework tells the container that it is.
- The container forwards a login page to the user, who fills it out and submits it back to the container.

- The container asks the security framework if the user can access the page.
- The security framework determines if the password that the user provided is the same as that stored in the security datastore; if so, it also determines if the user is authorized to access the Account Summary page.
- If everything matches up, the user is shown his Account Summary page. If not, then the user is taken to an error page.

One caveat: There's no simple way to develop a mechanism that allows users to authenticate from any given page. For example, you may try to create a website that displays a login form on the top of every page—so long as the user isn't authenticated—allowing him to login whenever he chooses. This process doesn't work because the container must intercept a call to a secured URL for the security framework to determine if the user is logged in or not, requiring you to rethink your page flow in an application.

Only being able to see a login screen after attempting to load a secured resource isn't uncommon. Take Amazon.com, for example; they don't allow you to directly login from any page. They give you a sign-in link that takes you to a login page. After logging in, you're directed to your account summary. Yes, having a login form on each page would make the login a one-step process, but this two-phase login procedure is an idiom that most web users are accustomed to. And if millions of users on Amazon.com aren't bothered by it, your users should probably be okay with it too.

One benefit to this model is that it's easier for users to bookmark pages in your application. Users should be able to bookmark URLs, even if they have to authenticate in order to get to them and then access them later. If they try to access pages that they bookmarked when they were logged in, the container prompts them to log in before forwarding them to their requested pages. If their sessions are still active, they're directed to the pages without having to authenticate again.

Now that you've seen the sequence of events that occur when a web user is authenticated, let's explore the different authentication strategies that JBoss provides.

6.2.1 Understanding the web authentication strategies

You can authenticate a user in an application in many ways, but prompting a user for a password is the most common. Java EE defines two main password authentication strategies that can be used by web applications: *HTTP basic authentication* and *form-based authentication.* A third password-based strategy, *digest authentication,* is available in JBoss but isn't required by Java EE and is less commonly used. Above and beyond these strategies, clients can be authenticated using a signed certificate with *client-certificate authentication* (also called *HTTPS client authentication*).

As we learned in section 6.1, the standard web deployment descriptor WEB-INF/web.xml defines authentication using the login-config element. Here's a reminder of what that definition looks like in the web.xml file:

```
<login-config>
  <auth-method>BASIC</auth-method>
</login-config>
```

The `auth-method` element defines the authentication strategy for the application. The allowed values are `BASIC`, `FORM`, `DIGEST`, and `CLIENT-CERT`. Table 6.2 summarizes these values.

Table 6.2 The different web authentication strategies available in JBoss

Authentication strategy	`auth-method` value	Description
HTTP basic authentication	`BASIC`	This option uses HTTP basic authentication, which causes the browser to pop up a modal dialog box prompting the user for his password.
Form-based authentication	`FORM`	Form-based authentication is similar to basic authentication, but an HTML page with a login form is sent to the browser for the user to log in with.
HTTPS client authentication	`CLIENT-CERT`	If the client has a public-key certificate, the server verifies the certificate using this strategy.
Digest authentication	`DIGEST`	This authentication mechanism causes the browser to present a dialog box in the same fashion as basic authentication, but the password is hashed in a digest that includes other information before it's sent to the server.

NOTE A web application can only have a single `login-config` block defined, so you can only have a single authentication method for the application. If you wish to have different authentication methods for different URLs in your application, you must create multiple web applications and deploy them to JBoss separately.

Basic authentication and form-based authentication are the most commonly used authentication strategies, but there are two problems with using them over regular HTTP. First, the user has no assurance of source integrity for the server. For example, how does a user know if he's accessing his bank's web site or a spoofed web site put together by a hacker? Second, the user's password is vulnerable to interception because these authentication methods don't encrypt the password when it's sent. This doesn't mean you shouldn't use these authentication strategies; it does mean that you probably want to provide access to your login page over secure HTTP (HTTPS). We discuss how to enable HTTPS to provide secure, encrypted web communication in section 6.4.

Let's take a look at how to configure basic, digest, and form authentication. Client-certificate authentication is more involved and is easier to understand after you've gained background on how to configure the HTTPS connector and to set up protocol-level client authentication. We dedicate all of section 6.5 to client-certificate authentication. We'll start with basic authentication.

6.2.2 Basic authentication

HTTP basic authentication is a *challenge-response protocol* that's part of the HTTP specification. When a user requests a secured URL, the container determines if the user has logged in yet. If he hasn't, it challenges the user to provide credentials by sending an HTTP 401 message back to the user's browser. This HTTP 401 message causes the browser to display a dialog box prompting the user for his password. Figure 6.4 shows you a dialog box that a web browser would show when it receives the 401 message.

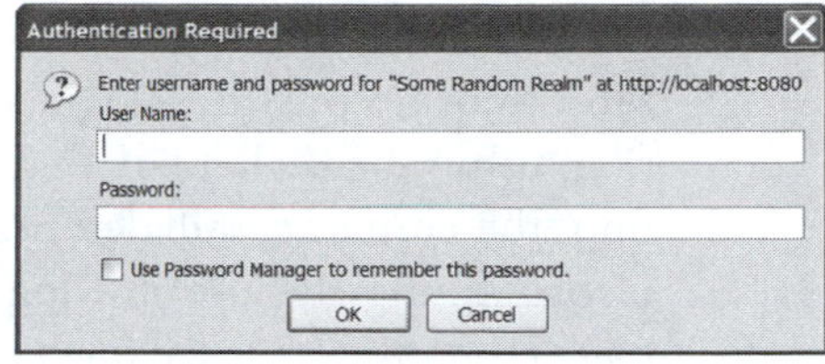

Figure 6.4 A dialog box is shown when basic authentication is used and the user's credentials are needed.

When the user fills out the username and password and submits the dialog box, the browser encodes the information (using base64 encoding) and sends it back to the web container for authentication against the security framework—the response portion of the challenge-response.

Basic authentication is configured in the WEB-INF/web.xml file using the following `login-config` declaration:

```
<login-config>
  <auth-method>BASIC</auth-method>
  <realm-name>My Site</realm-name>
</login-config>
```

The `auth-method` element specifies that basic authentication should be used. The `realm-name` element specifies descriptive text that's sent back to the client upon requesting a secured URL. This field gives the client a name to associate with the secured part of the website that he is trying to access. Most browsers display the value of the realm name in the dialog box that's shown to the user.

This strategy isn't secure when used over insecure HTTP because the password supplied to the dialog box isn't encrypted before it's sent to the server (base64 is an encoding algorithm, not an encryption algorithm). Basic authentication can be used securely with a server that enables HTTPS. In this case, the user can rest assured that the information that he's submitting over the wire is encrypted using the server's public key. We show how to configure HTTPS in section 6.4.

Browsers often cache the username and password used to log into a website. Although this may be a convenience to the user, the browser often takes the liberty of automatically retransmitting the security credentials without prompting the user again. This practice makes it difficult to enable a logout feature for your application because the browser keeps logging the user back in.

Because of the inability to control logging out and the lack of integration with a site's look and feel, we've rarely seen or used basic authentication in larger enterprise applications. That being said, basic authentication is simple to set up and is often used in smaller applications, particularly internal company applications with few users. To bypass the inability to log out and the lack of integration with a site's look and feel, use form-based authentication. Let's take a look.

6.2.3 Form-based authentication

Most websites provide a login screen that integrates with the site's look and feel rather than using the dialog box that basic authentication uses. With form-based authentication, the container still determines whether or not the user has logged in; but instead of prompting the user for login information using a browser dialog box, an HTML page containing a login form is sent. The user fills out the HTML form and submits it back to the server. This HTML page can have any format as long as it has a form that has the required form elements, as shown in listing 6.2.

Listing 6.2 An HTML form used for form-based authentication

```
<form name="loginForm" method="post" action="j_security_check">
<table>
   <tr>
      <td>User Name:</td>
      <td><input type="text" name="j_username"></td>
   </tr>
   <tr>
      <td>Password:</td>
      <td><input type="password" name="j_password"></td>
   </tr>
   <tr colspan="2" >
      <td><input type="submit" value="login"></td>
   </tr>
</table>
</form>
```

Required

As shown in the code listing, the form's action must contain the value `j_security_check` and a text box for the username and password with the name attributes set to `j_username` and `j_password`, respectively.

Form-based authentication can be enabled in web.xml using a `login-config` declaration similar to the following:

```
<login-config>
  <auth-method>FORM</auth-method>
  <form-login-config>
    <form-login-page>/restricted/login.html</form-login-page>
    <form-error-page>/restricted/bad-login.html</form-error-page>
  </form-login-config>
</login-config>
```

The value of `auth-method` must be equal to `FORM` to enable form-based authentication. The `form-login-config` element is used to define the login page that the user should be forwarded to when he's prompted for a password. It also allows you to define an error page that the user is forwarded to if the login is unsuccessful.

Like basic authentication, form-based authentication is also insecure when used over HTTP, so you may want to enable secure HTTP as discussed in section 6.4.

We've talked about basic and form-based authentication, which are both insecure. Now let's talk about digest authentication, which is similar to basic authentication, but is more secure.

6.2.4 Digest authentication

Digest authentication is a challenge-response authentication scheme like basic authentication. But with digest authentication, the password isn't sent over the network in clear text. The client uses an MD5 hashing function to hash the password (and other data) in a string known as a *digest.* The digest is then sent to the server, which compares it to a saved MD5 representation of the digest that it has in its security datastore for the user.

With basic authentication, a hacker can easily snoop a request to obtain a user's password or to perform a *replay attack.* Replay attacks occur when a hacker snoops the request and resubmits it later or modifies and resubmits it to get other information besides what was in the snooped request. Digest authentication uses a security technique called a *nonce,* or a *session token,* to make replay attacks difficult.

Although digest authentication gives you a slight security advantage over basic authentication, the advantage isn't that great. Besides the data that goes in the digest, none of the other data in the response is hashed; therefore, digest authentication isn't considered strong encryption. If you want to have truly secure access, you should make sure that your client and server are communicating over a secure channel such as SSL or TLS.

If you do decide to use digest authentication, you need to specify an authentication method in your application's WEB-INF/web.xml file similar to the following:

```
<login-config>
  <auth-method>DIGEST</auth-method>
  <realm-name>Default</realm-name>
</login-config>
```

The `realm-name` has the same purpose in digest authentication as it does in basic authentication. After defining the WEB-INF/web.xml, you also need to define a security domain in your server/xxx/conf/login-config.xml file that specifies some digest-specific options. Listing 6.3 shows you an example of the settings you could use if you define a security domain using the `UsersRolesLoginModule`.

Listing 6.3 A security domain that can be used to enable digest authentication

```
<application-policy name = "jmx-console">
<authentication>
<login-module
    code="org.jboss.security.auth.spi.UsersRolesLoginModule"
    flag = "required">
  <module-option name="usersProperties">
     props/jmx-console-users.properties</module-option>
  <module-option name="rolesProperties">
     props/jmx-console-roles.properties</module-option>
  <module-option name="hashAlgorithm">MD5</module-option>
  <module-option name="hashEncoding">rfc2617</module-option>
  <module-option name="hashUserPassword">false</module-option>
  <module-option name="hashStorePassword">true</module-option>
  <module-option name="passwordIsA1Hash">true</module-option>
```

```
    <module-option name="storeDigestCallback">
        org.jboss.security.auth.spi.RFC2617Digest</module-option>
  </login-module>
  </authentication>
  </application-policy>
```

When you store your passwords in your datastore (file, database, LDAP, and so on), you need to make sure that you store the hashed, MD5 version of the password instead of the clear text password. To obtain the hashed version of the password, you go to the server/default/lib directory and execute the following command:

```
java -classpath jbosssx-server.jar
➥   org.jboss.security.auth.spi.RFC2617Digest username realm password
```

The output for this command is your hashed password, which you store in your security datastore. Make sure that you substitute the username, realm, and password parameters with the information for the user whose encrypted password you want to determine. Also note that you'll have to put quotes around the realm if it consists of multiple words.

WARNING Many operating system command-line shells store commands in a history file to make it easier to recall previous commands. Generating the digest password from such a shell causes the username and password to be stored in the history file and, possibly, retrieved by an intruder. You might consider clearing the history file after running the command to create the digest. Also, someone snooping on a system might be able to pick up the command line that you're executing via execution of a command or utility that shows the processes running on your machine, such as the `ps` command on UNIX. To be safer, you can put the sensitive data in a file and redirect it as input into the command that creates the digest. You can lock down file permissions or delete the file after running the command to protect yourself further.

You now know how to enable authentication for web applications. Let's look at how to enable web authorization.

6.3 Authorizing users

After users are authenticated, the web container must see if they're authorized to access the information they requested. In this section, we explain the fundamentals of how to configure authorization, and then we dive into a more specific discussion on how to authorize any authenticated user to view a particular URL. Let's start with the basics.

6.3.1 Configuring authorization

Authorization for web application is specified in your application's WEB-INF/web.xml file by associating role names with URL patterns. Listing 6.4 shows you the portion of a web.xml file used to configure authorization.

Listing 6.4 The portion of a web.xml file used to configure authorization

```
<security-constraint>
  ...
  <auth-constraint>
    <role-name>SomeSimpleRole</role-name>
    <role-name>SomeOtherRole</role-name>
  </auth-constraint>
</security-constraint>
...
<security-role>
  <role-name>SomeSimpleRole</role-name>
</security-role>
<security-role>
  <role-name>SomeOtherRole</role-name>
</security-role>
```

❶ **Required role definition**

❷ **Optional role definition**

Any requests made on a secured URL defined within a `web-resource-collection` of a `security-constraint` block require the user to be a member of one of the roles specified under the `auth-constraint` block using the `role-name` element ❶. You can specify multiple roles in one `auth-constraint` block; but if you want to specify different roles for different URL patterns, you must specify multiple `security-constraint` blocks.

Later on in the file, we declare each security role that we referenced in our `security-constraint` configuration using `security-role` declarations ❷. This second definition of the role in the `security-role` block isn't generally required by JBoss Web Server but is often added so that an application is portable across the Java EE applications server. The second definition *is* necessary when we want to use a `role-name of *` (an asterisk) to grant access to any authenticated user. Let's talk about how this works.

6.3.2 *Allowing access to any authenticated user*

If you want to allow any authenticated user to access a given URL, you can specify an asterisk as your `role-name`. Listing 6.5 shows you an example of this using the `security-constraint` definition in your web.xml file.

Listing 6.5 Allowing any user to access a URL pattern

```
<security-constraint>
  ...
  <auth-constraint>
    <role-name>*</role-name>
  </auth-constraint>
</security-constraint>
...
<security-role>
  <role-name>SomeSimpleRole</role-name>
</security-role>
```

❶ **Asterisk grants access to all users**

❷ **A standalone role definition**

Notice that the value of the `role-name` attribute in the `auth-constraint` block is equal to `*` (an asterisk) ❶. But what does that mean exactly? It means that any authenticated user can access the given URLs or that you only want to allow access to user roles defined in the standalone `role-name` definitions ❷. The exact behavior can be controlled in the realm definition in JBoss Web Server's server.xml file. As we discussed in section 6.1.3, the realm definition looks like this:

```
<Realm className="org.jboss.web.tomcat.security.JBossWebRealm"
  certificatePrincipal="org.jboss.security.auth.certs.SubjectDNMapping"
  allRolesMode="authOnly" />
```

The `allRolesMode` attribute in the server.xml determines the behavior when a web application defines an `auth-constraint` block with a `role-name` equal to `*` in its web.xml file. Table 6.3 summarizes the three available settings for the `allRolesMode` attribute.

Table 6.3 The configuration options for the `allRolesMode` attribute in web.xml

`allRolesMode` option	Description
`strict`	This option interprets the servlet specification strictly by requiring that the user be in a role defined by a `role-name` element in the web.xml file (as shown in ❷ in listing 6.5).
`authOnly`	Allows any authenticated user.
`strictAuthOnly`	Because the `security-role` definition (as shown in ❷ in listing 6.5) is optional in JBoss Web Server, you can use this setting to get `strict` behavior when `security-role` elements are defined and `authOnly` behavior when none is defined.

Note that the `allRolesMode` setting is made in the server.xml file, so the settings apply to all web applications running in the server.

We've covered authentication and authorization in web applications; now let's turn to the server and see how we can secure the HTTP connector to enable secure communication.

6.4 Encrypting web communication

As we discussed in chapter 4, SSL is a certificate-based protocol that enables encryption as well as source authentication. Web applications can enable SSL to prevent eavesdropping and to assure users that the applications are hosted by the correct site.

In this section, we'll show how to enable SSL communication by defining a secure HTTP connector. After that, we'll talk about how to ensure that secure requests that go to an insecure connector get rerouted to a secure connector. We'll finish by talking about how to enable mutual authentication for greater client source integrity.

Let's start by talking about how to define a secure HTTP connector.

6.4.1 Enabling HTTPS

To handle HTTPS requests, you must do the following:

- Create or obtain a certificate for your server.
- Make sure that certificate is in a keystore.

- Define a secure HTTP connector.
- Point the connector to your keystore.

In order to enable HTTPS in JBoss Web Server, you have to obtain or create a keystore with a certificate for your server. You can create a self-signed certificate, or you can obtain a certificate from a certificate authority as we discussed in chapter 4. If you use keytool, the command will look similar to this:

```
keytool -genkey -alias serverCert -keyalg RSA -validity 1500 -keystore
➥  server.keystore
```

WARNING When you create a server keystore to be used by JBoss Web Server, you must match the keystore password and the password for the key. If you don't, you'll get an exception that looks like this: `java.io.IOException: Cannot recover key`. See the *Tomcat 6.0 SSL How-to* reference at the end of this chapter for more details.

After creating the keystore with a certificate in it, you must set up a connector in JBoss Web Server to listen for the SSL traffic. We discussed how to configure JBoss Web Server connectors in the server.xml file in chapter 5. Out of the box, JBoss Web Server's server.xml configuration file defines an HTTP connector, but it's commented out. If you uncomment this connector, you can use it to enable HTTPS for the server. Listing 6.6 shows you an example of a secured HTTP connector.

Listing 6.6 A secure HTTP connector that points to keystore

```
<Connector port="8443"
  ...
  scheme="https"          ❶
  secure="true"          ❷
  clientAuth="false"       ❸
  keystoreFile="${jboss.server.home.dir}/conf/server.keystore"       ❹
  keystorePass="serverpass"      ❺
  sslProtocol = "TLS" />       ❻
```

The `scheme` ❶ attribute defines the protocol scheme you're using. If unspecified, the default is `http`. To configure a secure SSL connector, you set it to `https`. The value of this attribute is returned when the `request.getScheme()` method is called from within your application code. Set the `secure` ❷ attribute to `true` to inform JBoss Web Server that you're configuring a secure connector. The value of this Boolean attribute is returned when the `request.isSecure()` method is called from within your application code. Set the `clientAuth` ❸ attribute to `false` if you want the client to authenticate the server's certificate. If you want to do mutual authentication, you can set it to `true`. See section 6.4.3 for further details. The `keystoreFile` ❹ and `keystorePass` ❺ attributes define the location of the keystore file containing the server's certificate and the password for the keystore file, respectively. The `sslProtocol` attribute ❻ specifies the version of the SSL protocol to use. It defaults to `TLS`.

The `keystoreFile` attribute uses a system variable called `${jboss.server.home.dir}` to reference the root directory of the server configuration that you're running. In the example, the keystore is in a file called `server.keystore` in the server configuration's conf directory. The `keystorePass` attribute should be set to the password that was created for the keystore and key pair, which JBoss Web Server expects to be the same.

After enabling this connector, clients can access your secure server using their web browsers. They should be able to point to any web application that you have running on the server and access it securely over SSL. Based on the port configured in the example, clients have to provide a URL to the browser that might look like the following:

https://www.myfakebank.com:8443/bankingapp/AccountSummary

Notice that the protocol in this URL is `https` (not `http`), and the port is set to `8443` (not `8080`, which the default HTTP connector is configured to). If you configure the connector for a different port, clients must point to that port.

Many times a secure request will get routed to an insecure connector. If this is the case, you want to make sure that the insecure connector can reroute the request to a secure connector.

6.4.2 Enabling transport guarantees

Pop quiz: Can a user access your application through different connectors? The answer is *yes*. If you have an HTTP connector and an HTTPS connector, the user could access your application through either one. But what if you want an application to only be accessed securely? Java EE defines a mechanism called a *transport guarantee* that allows you to specify this. The transport guarantee is defined in the `security-constraint` element in your application's standard web deployment descriptor, WEB-INF/web.xml.

If a transport guarantee is enabled and a user tries to access your application through an insecure connector, the connector forwards the request to the port specified by the `redirectPort` attribute. (For this to work, you have to configure a secured connector on the port that you're redirecting to.)

Let's say that you have a banking application and intend for users to access the account summary through SSL using the following URL:

https://www.myfakebank.com:8443/bankingapp/AccountSummary

What would happen if a user tried to access the account summary using the following URL instead?

http://www.myfakebank.com:8080/bankingapp/AccountSummary

By default, a user could access the account summary using either protocol. But if you want to require that the account summary URL be accessed over SSL, you can specify a transport guarantee. If your application specifies a transport guarantee for a particular URL and an attempt is made to access that URL through the HTTP or AJP connector, then JBoss Web Server forwards the request to a secure connector.

Figure 6.5 shows you the sequence of events that occurs when trying to access a URL with a transport guarantee through an insecure port.

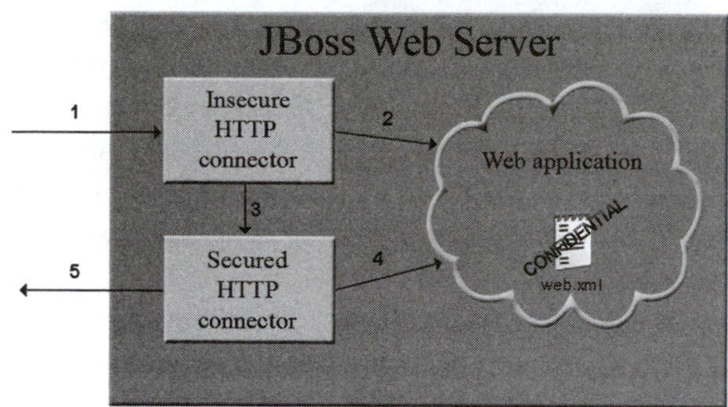

Figure 6.5 Accessing a URL with a transport guarantee through an insecure port

1. When an insecure request comes to the server, the HTTP connector handles it (the default port is 8080).
2. The connector forwards the request to the container, which detects that the destined web application is marked as having a confidential transport guarantee.
3. Further processing of the request is passed on to the redirect port defined for the insecure connector. The redirect port is set to that of the secure HTTP connector.
4. The secure HTTP connector does the SSL handshaking and then handles the request for the client.
5. The response redirects the client's browser to point to the secure protocol and port where the HTTPS connector is listening.

Both the default HTTP connector and the default AJP connector are configured to redirect to port 8443 upon receiving a secure request. Here's what the HTTP connector looks like:

```
<Connector protocol="HTTP/1.1" port="8080"
        address="${jboss.bind.address}"
        connectionTimeout="20000"
        redirectPort="8443"          ❶
/>
```

In this example, the port configured under the connectors `redirectPort` attribute ❶ is used to forward secure requests to the secure HTTPS connector configured on port 8443.

The transport guarantee itself is defined in the `security-constraint` block in your application's WEB-INF/web.xml file, as follows:

```
<security-constraint>
  ...
  <user-data-constraint>
    <transport-guarantee>
      CONFIDENTIAL
    </transport-guarantee>
  </user-data-constraint>
</security-constraint>
```

The value of the `transport-guarantee` element can be one of three options: `CONFIDENTIAL`, `INTEGRAL`, and `NONE`. A setting of `CONFIDENTIAL` specifies that the application requires that data be transmitted to prevent other entities from observing the contents of the transmission. A setting of `INTEGRAL` means that the data sent between a client and the server can't be changed in transit. As far as JBoss Web Server is concerned, if the transport guarantee is set to `CONFIDENTIAL` or `INTEGRAL`, insecure requests for the URLs defined in the `security-constraint` block get redirected to the secure connector (using SSL). Setting the transport guarantee to `NONE` is the equivalent of not setting the transport guarantee at all.

Now that you've seen how transport guarantees work, let's talk about how a server can mutually authenticate a client who has their own certificate installed in their web browser.

6.4.3 Enabling mutual authentication

So far, we've talked about server authentication, where a user validates the identity of a server's certificate and uses that certificate to communicate with the server over a secure channel. Some applications require a more secure method of authenticating clients than only a password. A client with a signed certificate provides better source integrity than only a password. As we discussed in chapter 4, SSL allows the client and the server to authenticate each other in a mutual authentication scheme. Applications that need mutual authentication are generally not public websites but intranet applications or business-to-business applications with limited numbers of users.

Figure 6.6 shows you how mutual authentication requires the clients to have certificates and requires the server to have a certificate and a truststore with the client certificates in it.

To do mutual authentication, you have to create certificates (either self-signed or purchased from a certificate authority) for your clients, typically one for each. These certificates have to be imported into the server's truststore. You can either add them to the Java Runtime Environments' (JRE) primary truststore (the `cacerts` file if you're using Sun's JRE), or you can put the certificates in a new truststore and point to it in the HTTPS connector.

We outlined how to create certificates and keystores using the `keytool` that ships with most JDKs in chapter 4. Here are the steps you take to enable mutual authentication with a self-signed client certificate:

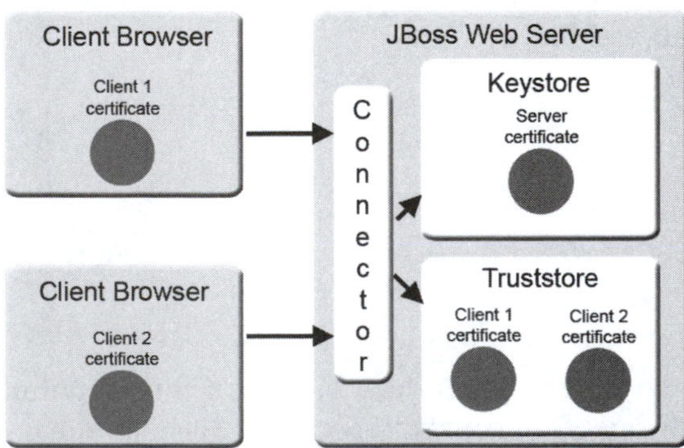

Figure 6.6 To set up mutual authentication, the client has a certificate, and the server has a certificate in a keystore and the clients' certificates in a truststore.

1. *Create a server certificate*—If you use keytool to generate a self-signed certificate on the server machine, this certificate is automatically placed within a keystore. Here's an example of the command that you'd run:

```
keytool -genkey -alias serverCertificate -keyalg RSA -validity 1500
➥         -keystore server.keystore
```

2. *Create a client certificate*—If you use keytool to generate a self-signed certificate on the client machine, this certificate is automatically placed within a keystore. Here's an example of the command that you run:

```
keytool -genkey -alias clientCertificate -keyalg RSA -validity 1500
➥         -keystore client.keystore
```

3. *Export the client certificate from the keystore (on the client)*—You export the certificate so that you can import it into a truststore used by the server. In the following example, you export the certificate to a file called client.cer:

```
keytool -export -alias clientCertificate -keystore client.keystore
➥         -file client.cer
```

4. *Import certificate into browser*—Convert the certificate to a format compatible with the client's browser (see next section) and import the certificate into the client's browser.
5. *Create server truststore*—Copy the client certificate (client.cer in this case) to the server and import the client certificate into a truststore (on the server).

```
keytool -import -alias clientCertificate -keystore server.truststore
➥         -file client.cer
```

6. *Configure the HTTPS connector*—Point to the server truststore and server keystore in the HTTPS connector definition in JBoss Web Server's server.xml file and set the clientAuth attribute to true.

```
<Connector protocol="HTTP/1.1" SSLEnabled="true" port="8443"
  address="${jboss.bind.address}" scheme="https" secure="true"
  clientAuth="true"
  keystoreFile="${jboss.server.home.dir}/conf/server.keystore"
  keystorePass="server-keystore-pass"
  truststoreFile="${jboss.server.home.dir}/conf/server.truststore"
  truststorePass="server-truststore-pass"
  sslProtocol="TLS" />
```

Note that setting clientAuth to true causes JBoss Web Server to authenticate the client's certificate at the protocol level. If the users access a secured page, they still need to provide a password to authenticate at the application level. We mentioned earlier that you might need to convert your certificate to a different format in order for your browser to support it. Let's talk about that.

6.4.4 Creating browser certificates

If you want the server to authenticate a client browser, the browser needs a certificate. Whether you create a self-signed certificate or get one from a certificate authority, you probably have to convert the certificate into a different format to import it into your browser. Most major web browsers support the PKCS12 certificate format. Although it's not difficult to do, there are quite a few steps, precluding us from covering the specifics within the scope of this book. But we do have a reference to the JBoss Wiki at the end of this chapter that shows you how to convert X509 certificates created by `keytool` to PKCS12 certificates using a tool called *openssl*. We also show you how to convert the certificate format in the source code that ships with the book.

So far, we've been using certificates to authenticate at the protocol level. If you want to use the client's certificate as the credential to authenticate users on the server, you can enable client-certificate authentication, which we'll talk about next.

6.5 Enabling client-certificate authentication

In chapter 4, we introduced you to client-certificate authentication, a mechanism by which you can use a client's public key certificate as an authentication credential. When communicating with a web server, this certificate must be installed in the client's browser. Web-based client-certificate authentication only works if a secured HTTP connector handles the client's request. Information in the certificate is passed to the security domain to authenticate and authorize the user at the application level.

NOTE Keep in mind that client-certificate authentication gives you greater source integrity but doesn't necessarily do a good job of asserting a human user's identity. For example, if you have a certificate on your machine and use it to authenticate against a server using client-certificate authentication, somebody else could sit behind the keyboard, and the server wouldn't know, care, or ask him to prove who he is. One way to verify a client certificate *and* challenge the user for a password is to set `clientAuth` to `true` in the secure HTTP connector as we discussed in section 6.4.3; then use `FORM`, `BASIC`, or `DIGEST` authentication to secure various URLs. The secure HTTP connector takes care of the source authentication at the protocol level by using mutual authentication while the application-level authentication challenges the user for a password. You have the best of both worlds. The only caveat is that all connections to the secure server require client certificates, whether or not they're going to a secured resource.

To enable client-certificate authentication, you must follow these steps:

- Enable protocol-level mutual authentication as described in section 6.4.
- Set the authentication method in your web application to `CLIENT-CERT`.
- Define a security-domain MBean that points to the keystore containing the server certificate.
- Define the security domain in the login-config.xml file.
- Point to the security domain in the applications jboss-web.xml file.
- Select a strategy for forming the principal from the certificate.

- Add principals and roles to the security datastore.
- Add the client certificate to the server's truststore.
- Create a browser certificate.

The following sections describe each of these steps in more detail.

6.5.1 Enabling protocol-level mutual authentication

Follow all the steps for enabling mutual authentication for the secure HTTP connector that we talked about in section 6.4. Note that the `clientAuth` attribute doesn't have to be set to `true` in the server.xml file in order to carry out client-certificate authentication because client-certificate authentication works at the application level, not the protocol level. The security domain in the next step takes care of the client authentication if and when it's needed. Set the `clientAuth` option to `false` if some URLs on your server should be accessible by clients without a certificate. Set it to `true` if you want all clients to at least be mutually authenticated by their browser certificates; then you can secure the URLs that you want to restrict access to in each application's WEB-INF/web.xml file.

6.5.2 Setting the authentication method

Your application's WEB-INF/web.xml must define the following `login-config` declaration:

```
<login-config>
  <auth-method>CLIENT-CERT</auth-method>
</login-config>
```

Notice the `auth-method` is set to `CLIENT-CERT`, telling JBoss Web Server to authenticate the user based on his certificate.

6.5.3 Specifying the JaasSecurityDomain MBean

As we discussed in chapter 4, to create an SSL-enabled security domain, you must define a `JaasSecurityDomain` MBean. Create a file in the deploy directory that ends in *-service.xml* (for example, mysecuritydomain-service.xml). Listing 6.7 shows you what the contents of this file should look like.

Listing 6.7 Defining an MBean to create an SSL-enabled security domain

```
<server>
  <mbean code="org.jboss.security.plugins.JaasSecurityDomain"
      name="jboss.security:service=SecurityDomain">
    <constructor>
      <arg type="java.lang.String" value="simple-security-domain"/>
    </constructor>
    <attribute name="KeyStoreURL">
       ${jboss.server.home.dir}/conf/server.truststore
    </attribute>
    <attribute name="KeyStorePass">serverpass</attribute>
```

```
      <depends>jboss.security:service=JaasSecurityManager</depends>
    </mbean>
  </server>
```

Remember the value of the `value` attribute you used for your constructor argument because you'll refer to it in the next step. Make sure that the `KeyStoreURL` and the `KeyStorePass` attributes point to the server's truststore that you created as part of the first step.

6.5.4 Specifying the security domain

Now you need to define a security domain in the login-config.xml file or in your dynamic login configuration file. You want to use the `BaseCertLoginModule` and stack it with another login module for authorization as we described in chapter 4. See an example of how this might look in listing 6.8.

Listing 6.8 Stacking `BaseCertLoginModule` with `UsersRolesLoginModule`

```
<application-policy name="simple-security-domain">
  <authentication>
    <login-module code="org.jboss.security.auth.spi.BaseCertLoginModule"
          flag="required">
     <module-option name="password-stacking">useFirstPass</module-option>
     <module-option name="securityDomain">
➥   java:/jaas/simple-security-domain</module-option>
    </login-module>
    <login-module code="org.jboss.security.auth.spi.UsersRolesLoginModule"
          flag="required">
     <module-option name="password-stacking">useFirstPass</module-option>
     <module-option name="usersProperties">myusers.properties
➥     </module-option>
      <module-option name="rolesProperties">myroles.properties
➥     </module-option>
    </login-module>
  </authentication>
</application-policy>
```

Note that the `securityDomain` module option points to the full JNDI name for the security domain. The part that comes after `java:/jaas/` must match the constructor argument that you passed into the security domain MBean you created in the last step.

6.5.5 Pointing to the security domain from the application

Now that you set up the security domain and the connector allows access over HTTPS, your web application needs to make use of the security domain. Your application's WEB-INF/jboss-web.xml file must point to the security domain, as follows:

```
<jboss-web>
  <security-domain>java:/jaas/simple-security-domain</security-domain>
</jboss-web>
```

As we discussed in section 6.1.2, you must make sure that the value of the `security-domain` element is the same as that defined in your login-config.xml file. In this case, the name attribute of the application-policy element in the login-config.xml file is simple-security-domain.

6.5.6 *Selecting a strategy for forming the principal from the certificate*

With password-based authentication, the user types in a username as a principal and a password as the credential. When implementing client-certificate authentication, it makes sense to use the certificate's public key as the credential, but what would you use as the principal itself? If you look at the structure of a certificate, you could use several parts of the certificate to represent the principal. In JBoss Web Server, you can choose which part to use by configuring the realm setting in the JBoss Web Server's server.xml file. We talked about the realm in section 6.1.3, but let's take another look at it.

```
<Realm className="org.jboss.web.tomcat.security.JBossWebRealm"
  certificatePrincipal="org.jboss.security.auth.certs.SubjectDNMapping"
  allRolesMode="authOnly" />
```

The certificatePrincipal attribute configures which part of the client's certificate should be used as the principal. Out of the box, the certificatePrincipal attribute is set to the SubjectDNMapping option shown. This option uses the certificate's entire Distinguished Name (DN) record. Table 6.4 shows you what other options you have.

Table 6.4 The different parts of the certificate that can be used for client-certificate authentication

certificatePrincipal option	Part of the certificate used as principal
org.jboss.security.auth.certs.SerialNumberIssuerDNMapping	The serialNumber and issuerDN
org.jboss.security.auth.certs.SubjectCNMapping	The value of the SubjectDN's CN element
org.jboss.security.auth.certs.SubjectDNMapping	The entire SubjectDN
org.jboss.security.auth.certs.SubjectX500Principal	The SubjectX500Principal

We recommend trying the SubjectCNMapping option because it's the easiest to set up in your underlying security datastore where you store your principals and credentials. The option you define determines what part of the certificate is parsed and passed in as the principal to the login modules that authenticate and authorize the principal. You must make sure that this part of the certificate is stored in your underlying authorization datastore as well.

6.5.7 *Adding principals and roles to the authorization datastore*

You must add the principal and roles to the underlying authorization datastore (which the login module stacked with the BaseCertLoginModule points to, as discussed in step 4). The data that you populate into the datastore depends on the strategy you selected for forming the principal name using the `certificatePrincipal` attribute described in step 6. For example, if you used the `SubjectCNMapping` option, then you add users that match the names in the Common Name (CN) element of the certificate. Let's say you have a certificate with the following output:

```
> keytool -printcert -file client.cer
Certificate stored in file <client.cer>
Owner: CN=Joe Schmoe, O=SomeCA, OU=SomeCAOrg
Issuer: CN=Joe Schmoe, O=SomeCA, OU=SomeCAOrg
Serial number: 47a22427
Valid from: Thu Jan 31 13:40:23 CST 2008 until: Sat Mar 10 13:40:23 CST 2012
Certificate fingerprints:
    MD5:  BA:82:F1:83:A8:13:82:F5:0F:67:00:99:13:48:1C:B7
    SHA1: 14:A7:00:3A:EB:EE:3D:E3:EF:67:C9:68:16:22:D3:53:ED:84:D4:4E
```

If you used `SubjectCNMapping` in your server.xml realm and a `UsersRolesLoginModule` in your login-config.xml, the property file you use to store your roles might look like this:

joe\ schmoe=rolea, roleb

The `CN` value in the certificate is Joe Schmoe, with camel-case lettering, but note the lowercase lettering to define the principal in the datastore. When JBoss parses the principal off of the certificate, it converts it to lowercase before comparing it to the value in the datastore, so you must add the name to your authorization datastore in lowercase letters. You also have to use an escape character (backslash) to support the space. You may have to do the same to support equals signs or other delimiters.

Although you stacked the `UsersRolesLoginModule` with the `BaseCertLoginModule`, you need an empty user properties file to exist. You may face a similar case for other login modules.

6.5.8 Adding the client's certificate to the server's truststore

The truststore you pointed to in step 3 is the authentication datastore, so you must import each client's certificate into the truststore. You can use the `keytool` command to do this, as follows:

```
keytool -import -alias "Joe Schmoe" -keystore server.truststore -file
➥ client.cer
```

The alias that you use must match the principal that would be parsed by the security framework. The alias acts as the principal name and the certificate acts as the credential. The value you use for the alias depends on the `certificatePrincipal` option you used in step 6. The code snippet shows what it might look like if you used the `SubjectCNMapping` value for the `certificatePrincipal`.

6.5.9 Creating a browser certificate

As described in section 6.4.4, you have to convert each client's certificate to a format that your browser can handle.

So far, we've shown you examples where applications point to a specific security domain, but you may decide that you want a particular domain applied if no application-specific security domain is specified.

6.6 Changing the default security domain

If you don't configure a security domain for an individual web application in the jboss-web.xml file but have defined security for various components in your web.xml file, then JBoss defaults to the security domain configured using the `defaultSecurityDomain` property of the `WarDeployer` bean defined in the following web server microcontainer configuration file:

server/xxx/deployers/jbossweb.deployer/META-INF/war-deployers-jboss-beans.xml

Out of the box, the default security domain is configured as follows:

```
<property name="defaultSecurityDomain">
➥      java:/jaas/jboss-web-policy</property>
```

This property points to the security domain `jboss-web-policy`, which is defined in the server/xxx/deploy/security/security-policies-beans.xml file. This security domain is an extension of the `other` security domain defined in the server/xxx/conf/login-config.xml file. The `other` security domain is configured to load usernames and roles from files using the `UsersRolesLoginModule`. If you plan on using the default security domain, you may want to define your own security domain in the login-config.xml file and point the `DefaultSecurityDomain` attribute to it. Otherwise, you might change or remove the definition for the default security domain.

6.7 Summary

We started this chapter by talking about the various configuration files used to configure security in web applications and how to tie that configuration in with the security domain configuration you learned about in chapter 4. We then gave a background on how challenge-response authentication works for web applications and talked about the three challenge-response authentication mechanisms available in JBoss Web Server. We showed how to configure basic authentication, digest authentication, and form authentication and talked about the benefits and drawbacks to each.

Next, we talked about authorization and showed how to configure role-based access for different URLs. We also showed how to configure a URL so that any authenticated user could access it, regardless of role assignment.

After learning about authentication and authorization, you learned how to encrypt web communication. We talked about how to enable HTTPS by configuring the HTTP connector to reference a secure certificate. You then learned how to enable a transport guarantee on an application to make sure that it can only be accessed over a secure channel. Last, you learned about mutual authentication and how the server can verify a browser certificate during the protocol handshaking.

Building on your fundamental knowledge of authentication and encryption, we taught you how to enable client-certificate authentication, whereby information on a client's certificate can be used as a client's credentials. You learned how to change the default security domain that web applications are configured to use.

The nice thing about JBoss security is that a user who logs in through the web tier of an application doesn't have to re-authenticate against the EJB tier. As you'll see when we discuss EJB security in the next chapter, the EJB server integrates into the same JBoss SX security framework and implements a similar configuration model.

6.8 References

Digest Access Authentication—http://www.zvon.org/tmRFC/RFC2069/Output/longContents.html

Creating a PKCS12 certificate for Firefox—http://wiki.jboss.org/community/docs/DOC-11989

Tomcat SSL How-to—http://tomcat.apache.org/tomcat-6.0-doc/ssl-howto.html

7 Configuring enterprise applications

This chapter covers

- Packaging and deploying enterprise applications
- Configuring the EJB server
- Configuring the EJB containers
- Configuring JPA / Hibernate
- EJB remoting and JNDI
- EJB security

Many small web applications can be written entirely using JSPs and servlets, packaged as a WAR file, and deployed into JBoss or even a JSP/servlet container such as Tomcat. But you should consider several limitations about this architecture if your application is going to grow to be more than a simple web application. First, if your application is going to have multiple interfaces or integration points, you'll want to separate your business logic from your web presentation code by pulling the logic out of your servlets. Decoupling the business logic from the presentation allows you, for example, to enable a travel booking site to use Web Services to call the same business logic as that used by your hotel reservations web application. Simple web applications also need a lot of boilerplate application logic that's practically the same for almost any enterprise-ready application such as security, remoting, and transaction management.

As Java-based server applications became popular in the late '90s, people realized the ubiquity of these concerns, and the EJB specification was created in response to enable server-side application component development. The current, and relatively new, version of EJB is EJB3. If you've been in the Java world for a while, you may have either used previous versions of EJB or been told to stay away from them altogether. For example, one of the main problems was that the options available for persistence left many application developers with complex and/or non-performant code, causing many people to avoid EJB persistence altogether.

By polling the Java developer community, learning from popular lightweight frameworks such as Hibernate and Spring, and taking advantage of new language features such as annotations, the specification team created the new, lightweight EJB3 specification. EJB3 applications are simple to develop and unit-test in comparison to older versions of the EJB specification. Above all, persistence is greatly improved through a completely new persistence specification known as the Java Persistence API (JPA). There's still a stigma around the standard, an unfortunate preconception because the newer EJB3 specification has tremendous benefits over the old one.

JBoss initially started as an EJB server, which is arguably its most popular feature to this day. In this chapter, we talk about how the EJB server works and how you can configure the various features to support your development and deployment needs. We focus our discussion on configuring application services related to session beans and entities. In chapter 8, "JBoss Messaging," we'll cover message-driven beans and message-driven POJOs.

7.1 Understanding EJBs

EJB 3.0 defines a model for transactional components and objects. The term *transactional* implies that the component is used to perform a cohesive set of operations that should all be part of the same logical unit of work. The term *server-side* implies that the component isn't used for user presentation, but for back-end business logic or persistence.

The EJB3 specification defines three types of enterprise bean objects: session beans, entity objects, and message-driven beans. Session beans are typically used to write business code encapsulated in a larger business transaction that may make calls to other transactional components. For example, a session bean might be used to make a reservation through a hotel reservation site. The code in the bean may check for room availability, reserve the room, and then send an asynchronous message to a third-party clearinghouse used by other reservation systems to notify them that the room has been reserved. All this might be encapsulated in a single transaction.

Entities are objects that represent domain objects mapped to the database. Entity persistence is either encapsulated by a database transaction or part of a larger business transaction. Message-driven beans are asynchronous message consumers managed by a container.

NOTE Unfortunately, the EJB3 specification is unclear about what to call the equivalent of what used to be Entity Beans in the previous EJB specifications. The specification refers to them as entity beans, persistent entities, entities, and entity objects (all lowercase common nouns). For example, section 2.4 of the EJB Core specification defines three types of *enterprise bean objects* and then refers to them specifically as *entity objects*. Articles, tutorials, and implementation documentation about EJB3 also use differing names. For example, the Hibernate documentation freely calls them *entity beans*. Because of this naming ambiguity, we stick with the common-noun form *entity* to refer to EJB3 objects used for persistence, although the term *entity bean* is also acceptable.

Figure 7.1 shows you how the various Java EE components might communicate in an enterprise application.

Servlets, JSPs, session EJBs, entities, and the entity manager are all defined in the Java EE specification. Either a rich internet application written using technologies such as Flash or DHTML/AJAX or a web service client might access session beans directly to perform business operations. Traditional web applications might go through servlets and JSPs to execute business logic. Entities can be passed around from server to client and back, but can only be persisted by an *entity manager*, which is only accessible from the server. The entity manager is typically accessed through a session or message-driven bean.

In this section, we give you background on session beans and entities. We don't give you a comprehensive background or primer on all the aspects of these technologies

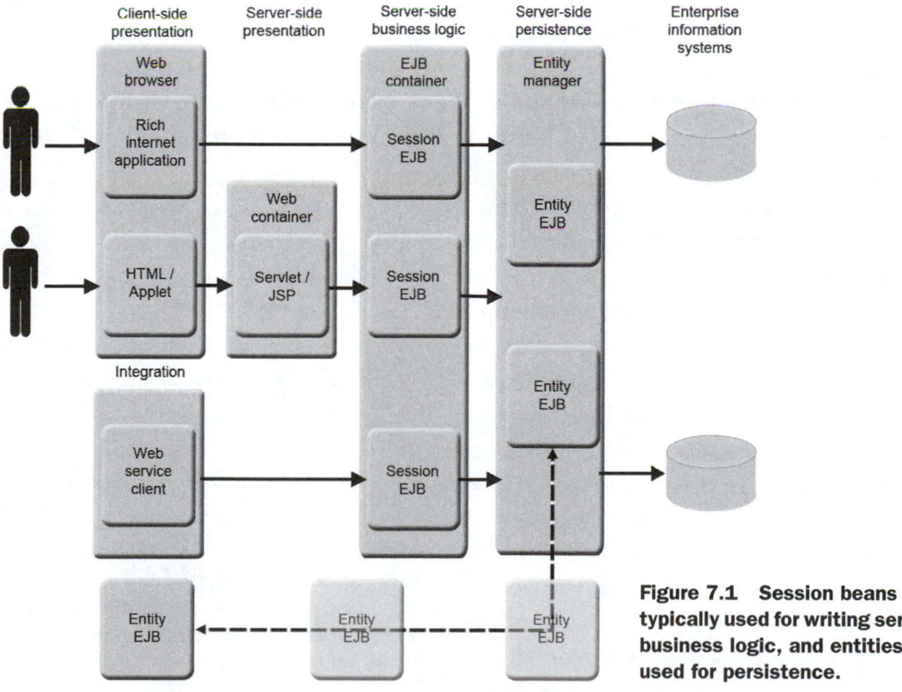

Figure 7.1 Session beans are typically used for writing server-side business logic, and entities are used for persistence.

because there's quite a bit to talk about. Our focus is on those aspects of the technologies that you may want to configure in the server.

7.1.1 Understanding session beans

Session beans are used to encapsulate business logic. The two types of session beans are stateful and stateless. As the names imply, stateful session beans (SFSBs) maintain client state across multiple requests, whereas stateless session beans (SLSBs) maintain no state across client requests.

Session beans are pre-created when the server starts and then maintained in a pool. Because SLSBs don't maintain state for individual clients, each request can grab a pre-created session bean from a pool and return it to the pool after the request is complete. Unlike SLSBs, SFSBs aren't reused between requests. SFSBs maintain a session identifier with the client that consecutive requests will use to retrieve the same bean out of the pool.

In some applications, clients keep their connections open for quite a while. If many clients are using an application, keeping connections open can lead to a large number of SFSBs staying resident in memory. To alleviate the memory footprint, the Java EE specification defines a model of passivation and activation where SFSBs are persisted to secondary storage when they're idle for a specified length of time and retrieved when accessed again.

Session beans define a *business interface*, a Java interface used to access the bean. Remote clients use a bean's business interface to make calls to the bean. The business interface for a session bean can be defined as a *local interface* or a *remote interface*. A local interface can be accessed by an EJB client located inside the application server. Examples of local clients include web applications or other EJBs running in the same application server instance. A remote interface can be accessed by remote clients that run in different processes on the machine or on a different machine that accesses the JBoss server instance over a network. Examples of remote clients include code running in other web servers or GUI clients.

It makes sense for a local client to make a call to an EJB's interface the EJB is running in the same JVM, but you might wonder how a remote client can do the same thing. JBoss makes *remoting*, the act of making remote calls, easy by allowing clients to download an object, called a *dynamic proxy*, that implements the EJB's business interface. The dynamic proxy doesn't implement the business logic for the EJB, but does know how to make a call to the server to have the EJB execute the business logic. Figure 7.2 illustrates this process.

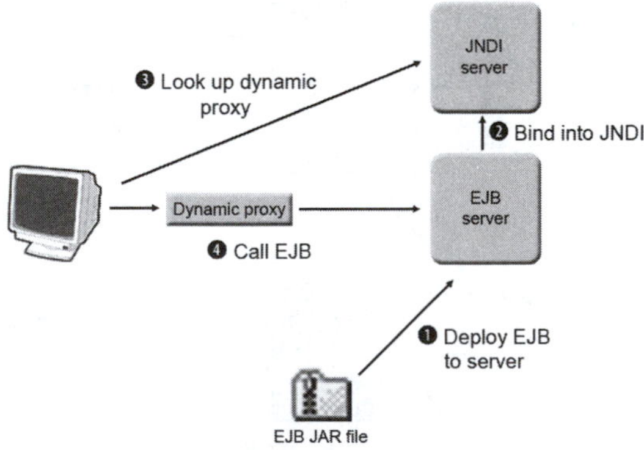

Figure 7.2 A client obtains a dynamic proxy from the server; then, it can use the proxy to make calls to an EJB.

When the EJB is deployed to the server ❶, a dynamic proxy is generated and bound into the JNDI server ❷. In section 7.4.1, you'll learn about the default binding strategy and how to change it. When the client wants to make calls to an EJB, it obtains the dynamic proxy by doing a lookup in the JNDI server ❸. The dynamic proxy shares the same business interface as the session bean, so the client pretends it's making a call to the bean ❹. The dynamic proxy takes the call and forms it into a message that can be passed over a network into the EJB server, using whatever protocol it's configured to support. When the EJB server receives the message, it calls the session bean, which executes the business logic and returns a response back to the dynamic proxy and, in turn, back to the client.

Now that you've seen how session beans work, let's see how entity persistence works by discussing Hibernate and JPA.

7.1.2 Understanding Hibernate and JPA

Entities are used to map objects in a domain model to a persistence store (generally, a relational database). Hibernate is perhaps the most popular ORM tool in the Java community. Hibernate became quite popular in the early 2000's because it's transparent, flexible, and powerful. In 2003, JBoss hired Gavin King, the lead developer for Hibernate, and several other Hibernate developers, making Hibernate a JBoss project. Gavin King then went on to join the specification team for the EJB3 specification, bringing many of the ideas from Hibernate into the EJB3 specification.

The EJB3 specification defines an ORM standard called the Java Persistence API (JPA). As you may have guessed, Hibernate now implements the JPA specification. If you want to use EJB3, you can use Hibernate as your persistence framework. If you were apprehensive to use previous versions of EJB because of the persistence mechanism, you can now feel comfortable using EJB3 entities with Hibernate. JPA is designed to be used both inside and outside of the container to give you the freedom to use it in the same way that you might currently use Hibernate or any other ORM framework.

In previous versions of EJB, entity beans were server-side components managed by the container and able to be invoked remotely by client applications. With JPA, entities are now POJOs that can be passed around between application components and back and forth between the client and server. Because they can be passed around, there's no need to make them remotely accessible.

But, you ask, "I thought the database was on the server side; how are entities persisted if the client doesn't know about the database?" In JPA, a *persistence context* manages entities and their lifecycles. In a Java EE application server, the persistence context is managed by the container. Developers can access the persistence context through an entity manager. The entity manager isn't remotely accessible to clients. Therefore, the entity object must be associated with the entity manager (on the server) before the entity manager can persist it to the database.

If you're used to using Hibernate as a standalone ORM solution, you don't have to use JPA. In chapter 3, you learned how to deploy Hibernate archives to JBoss AS. In section 7.5, we talk about how to configure JPA and how you can use and access Hibernate mappings and objects through JPA.

7.1.3 Understanding enterprise packaging

In EJB3, EJBs are packaged using a regular JAR structure. JARs that contain EJBs are often called EJB-JARs. But, in enterprise application development, applications are often composed of more than EJBs. In Java parlance, an enterprise application is one comprised of EJBs, POJOs, and one or more presentation or integration technologies.

If your application is composed of multiple archives, you can use an Enterprise Archive (EAR) to combine all of them. You can think of an EAR as an archive of archives. An EAR can contain WARs, EJB-JARs, and/or regular JARs. By using an EAR, you can deal with a single archive after your application has been built.

Figure 7.3 shows you the structure for an EAR package (as an exploded directory).

This enterprise archive is called SomeEnterpriseArchive. It contains a WAR called SomeWebArchive.war and an EJB-JAR called SomeEjbJarArchive.jar. As you see in the figure, these packages are at the top level of the containing archive. A META-INF directory is also at the top level. As with any other archives, the META-INF directory contains deployment descriptors. In the case of EARs, two deployment descriptors are used: application.xml (standard) and jboss-app.xml (proprietary).

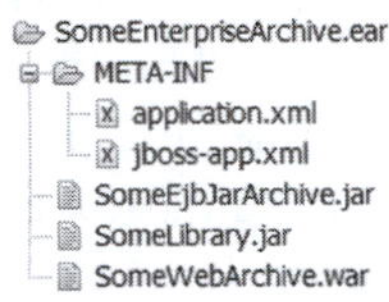

Figure 7.3 EARs are composed of other packages such as WARs and EJB-JARs.

Listing 7.1 shows you the application.xml file that would be used for the EAR in figure 7.3.

Listing 7.1 Example of application.xml file for an EAR

```
<application>
   <display-name>Some Enterprise Archive</display-name>
   <module>
      <web>
         <web-uri>SomeEnterpriseArchive.war</web-uri>
         <context-root>/myapp</context-root>
      </web>
   </module>
   <module>
      <ejb>SomeEnterpriseArchive.jar</ejb>
   </module>
</application>
```

The application.xml file is responsible for defining the archives that are part of the EAR and providing any additional information about them. For example, you can specify the `context-root` for the SomeEnterpriseArchive.war web application as shown in the example. If you deploy an EAR and specify the context root at this level, it will override any context definitions in the WAR file itself.

The jboss-app.xml file is used for several things. The main use is to configure class loading for the entire enterprise application using the `loader-repository` configuration as discussed in chapter 3. It's also used to deploy modules that are

JBoss-specific. The application.xml file can be used to deploy standard archive types, but it doesn't know how to deploy JBoss archives such as HARs and data sources as we discussed in chapter 3.

In this section, we gave you background on how session and entity EJBs work. We also showed you the structure for EJB and enterprise packages. Now let's put the knowledge to use by creating an EJB application. You can deploy the code we create in this section to the application server in order to test many of the configurations we talk about throughout the rest of the chapter. If you're not a programmer, you might want to find somebody to help you get through the next section or obtain the code that accompanies the book because it automates building and deploying the application for you.

7.2 Creating an EJB application

To get a better idea of how an EJB application works, let's create one. Again, because the focus of this book is on configuring JBoss, and not on application development, we stick with a simple Hello World! example. This will give us something that we can deploy into the container to test various aspects of JBoss configuration.

The Hello World! application will consist of a standalone client, a session bean, and an entity. The client will send strings containing greeting messages into the session bean. The session bean, called `GreeterBean`, implements the `Greeter` interface. On receiving a greeting, the session bean will create a `Greeting` entity and persist it into the database using the entity manager injected into the session bean. The client can then ask the session bean for a list of all the greetings that it has sent to the bean, at which time the session bean uses the entity manager to query the database and returns a list of `Greeting` objects to the client.

Figure 7.4 shows you the sequence of calls between components in our sample application.

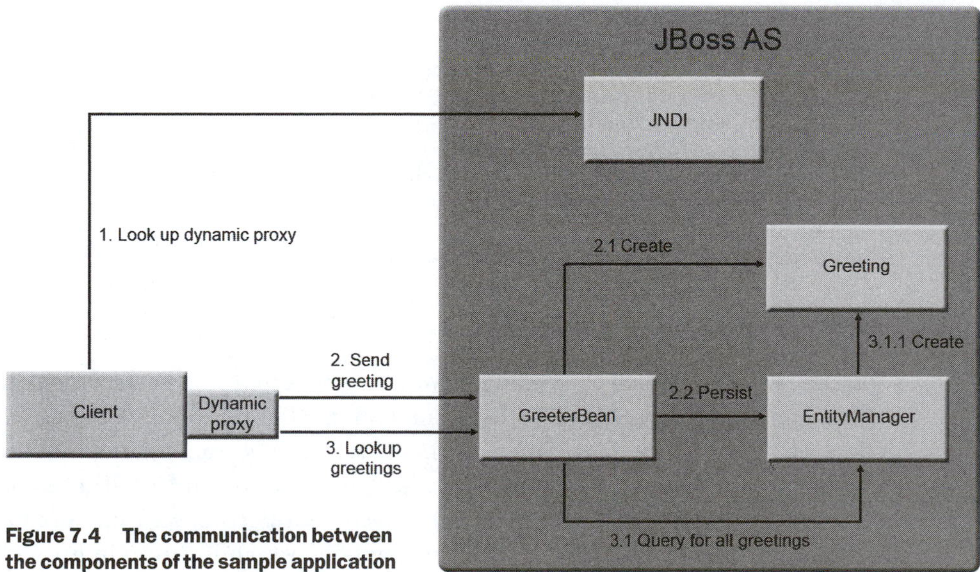

Figure 7.4 The communication between the components of the sample application

In case you're not familiar with how to read this diagram, order of calls is 1, 2, 2.1, 2.2, and so on. Now let's take a look at how to write the necessary code.

7.2.1 Coding the example application

To create the sample application, start by writing the GreeterBean session bean, which is the heart of the business logic in the application. Listing 7.2 shows you the code for the session bean's remote interface (Greeter).

Listing 7.2 Session bean's remote interface

```
package com.manning.jbia;
import java.util.List;
import javax.ejb.Remote;
@Remote
public interface Greeter {
  public void greet(String message);
  public List<Greeting> getAllGreetings();
}
```

The interface is annotated with the @Remote annotation, which tells the container that this is a remote interface. The interface defines two methods, one that allows a remote client to send greetings into the session bean and another that allows the client to retrieve all the greetings that have been sent previously. Listing 7.3 shows you the GreeterBean code that implements this remote interface.

Listing 7.3 Session bean code

```
package com.manning.jbia;
import java.util.List;
import javax.ejb.Stateless;
import javax.persistence.EntityManager;
import javax.persistence.PersistenceContext;
@Stateless
public class GreeterBean implements Greeter {
  @PersistenceContext
  private EntityManager em;
  public void greet(String message) {
    Greeting greeting = new Greeting(message);
    em.persist(greeting);
  }
  public List<Greeting> getAllGreetings() {
    return em.createQuery("from Greeting").getResultList();
  }
}
```

The GreeterBean class is annotated with the @Stateless interface, which tells the container that it's an SLSB. The bean implements the remote interface and provides code for the two methods defined on the interface. The EntityManager class variable is annotated with the @PersistenceContext annotation, which tells the container to inject an entity manager associated with the current peristance unit. Persistence units ares defined in the META-INF/persistence.xml file, which is shown in listing 7.4.

Listing 7.4 META-INF/persistence.xml file containing definition for entity manager

```
<persistence>
  <persistence-unit name="greeter">
    <jta-data-source>java:/DefaultDS</jta-data-source>
    <properties>
      <property name="hibernate.hbm2ddl.auto"
              value="create-drop"/>
    </properties>
  </persistence-unit>
</persistence>
```

This file specifies that you're using the application server's default data source by pointing to the `java:/DefaultDS` JNDI name in the `jta-data-source` element. You also enable a setting called `hibernate.hbm2ddl.auto`, which dynamically re-creates the database tables every time the application is brought up. This setting obviously isn't one that you want to enable in production, but it's useful when you're first developing or prototyping a new system.

The methods on the session bean utilize the entity manager to read and write `Greeting` objects to the database. Listing 7.5 shows you the code for the entity.

Listing 7.5 `Greeting` class defining an entity for sample application

```
package com.manning.jbia;
import java.io.Serializable;
import javax.persistence.Entity;
import javax.persistence.GeneratedValue;
import javax.persistence.Id;
@Entity
public class Greeting implements Serializable {
  private int id;
  private String message;
  public Greeting() { }
  public Greeting(String message) { this.message= message; }
  @Id @GeneratedValue
  public int getId() { return id; }
  public String getGreeting() { return message; }
  private void setId(int id) { this.id = id; }
  private void setGreeting(String message) { this.message = message; }
}
```

The entity class is annotated with the `@Entity` annotation, which tells the container that this is an entity. There are two class-level variables: `id` and `message`. The entity manager uses the `id` variable to associate the instance of the object in memory to a particular primary key in the database. The `getId()` method is annotated with the `@Id` and `@GeneratedValue` annotations to tell the entity manager that the associated field is the one that should be bound to the primary key and that the value for the primary key should be auto-generated. JPA requires a setter for each persistent attribute, but because clients don't need to change the `id` and `message` attributes, they can be left as private.

The `message` attribute stores the data that the client sends to the session bean. Because the get method is called `getGreeting()`, the field will automatically be associated with a column in the database called `greeting`. The same convention applies to the `id` field as well. The entity class implements the `Serializable` interface because you're going to pass the `Greeting` objects over the wire to the client.

Listing 7.6 shows you the client code that accesses the sample application.

Listing 7.6 Client code that calls sample application

```
package com.manning.jbia;
import java.util.Hashtable;
import java.util.List;
import javax.naming.Context;
import javax.naming.InitialContext;
public class Client {
  public static void main(String[] args) throws Exception {
    InitialContext ctx = new InitialContext();
    Greeter greeter = (Greeter)
      ctx.lookup("GreeterBean/remote");                      ❶

    greeter.greet("Hello, world!"); //English
    greeter.greet("Hola, mundo!"); //Spanish
    greeter.greet("Salam, donya!"); //Persian                 ❷
    greeter.greet("Bonjour, monde!"); //French
    greeter.greet("Ciao, mondo!"); //Italian

    List<Greeting> greets = greeter.getAllGreetings();
    for (Greeting greeting : greets) {                          ❸
      System.out.println(greeting.getGreeting());
    }
  }
}
```

The client code first loads the dynamic proxy for the `GreeterBean` from JNDI ❶ by passing in the name of the bean appended with a slash and the word *remote* (`GreeterBean/remote`). This combination is the default name that the bean gets bound to when it's deployed into the server. After loading the dynamic proxy, the client uses the `Greeter` interface to interact with the proxy. The client calls the `greet()` method ❷, passing in several "Hello, World!" greetings in different languages. Then, the client calls the `getAllGreetings()` method ❸ to load a list of all the `Greeting` objects, iterates over the list, and prints out each greeting.

To run this client code, you need to specify your JNDI properties in a file called jndi.properties located at the root of your class path. The contents of that file will look like the following:

```
java.naming.factory.initial=org.jnp.interfaces.NamingContextFactory
java.naming.provider.url=localhost:1099
```

The `java.naming.provider.url` property points to the hostname and port of the JNDI server.

And that's it. Considering the amount of code and configuration you'd have to write to produce an equivalent sample application with JDBC or even with Hibernate, EJB3 is a blessing! Now let's see how we can package our code and deploy it into the application server.

7.2.2 Packaging and running the example application

When you write an EJB and want to deploy it, you have to compile and package it. To compile the code, you need several JAR files on your build class path. With modern IDEs and build tools, it's easy to include entire directories of JAR files in your class path, so the easiest way is to add all the JAR files in the following paths under the JBoss installation:

lib
server/xxx/lib
server/xxx/deployers/ejb3.deployer
server/xxx/deployers/jboss-aop-jboss5.deployer

As we discussed in section 7.1.3, EJBs are deployed in JARs that are often called EJB-JAR archives. Packaging the EJB is almost trivial because all you have to do is create a JAR. Your compiled source code, including any directories under which your source may exist, goes directly into the top level of the JAR file. You also need to put the persistence.xml file in the META-INF directory directly under the root folder.

Figure 7.5 shows the structure of the EJB-JAR file that you need to create.

The META-INF directory doesn't need a jboss.xml or ejb-jar.xml file for this sample application.

After you create the archive, copy it in to the deploy directory of the application server. You should see a bunch of output in the console window that ends with the following lines:

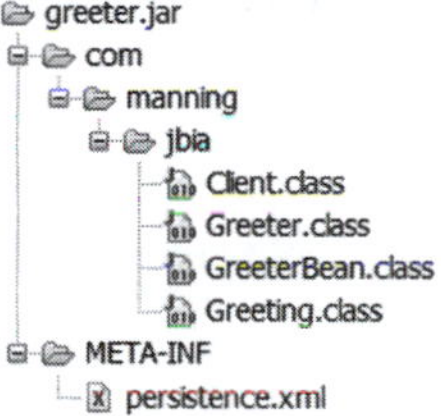

Figure 7.5 The structure of an EJB-JAR file

```
INFO [MCKernelAbstraction] installing bean:
  jboss.j2ee:jar=greeter.jar,name=GreeterBean,service=EJB3 with
  dependencies:
INFO [MCKernelAbstraction]
  persistence.units:jar=greeter.jar,unitName=greeter
INFO [EJBContainer] STARTED EJB: com.manning.jbia.GreeterBean ejbName:
  GreeterBean
```

Now, build and run the client application using a runtime class path that contains the same directories as the build class path, as well as the directory containing your client code and jndi.properties file. The jndi.properties file should be in the root of your class path. You should see the following output:

```
Hello, world!
Hola, mundo!
Salam, donya!
Bonjour, monde!
Ciao, mondo!
```

This example has given you an overview of how to create a simple EJB application. Now, let's take a more in-depth look at EJB configuration.

7.3 Understanding EJB configuration

As we've discussed throughout the book, running in an application server allows you to focus on developing components that contain business logic, while plugging into services that are already available. After you understand how to develop EJBs and deploy them into the application server, you'll want to know how to configure EJB applications and the services that they use. To gain a better understanding of how to do this, we need to explore the various application and server configuration points.

As with web configuration, there are two types of configuration: configuration of individual web applications and configuration of the JBoss EJB container. Application configuration pertains to individual EJBs and EJB archives. Examples of application configuration include defining security, defining JNDI names, enabling clustering, and defining which transport protocol a particular bean supports. Server configuration relates to behavior that applies to all applications running in the server, such as protocol settings, the default database used by entities, and class loading.

In this section, you'll learn to locate and explore the various configuration files used in the JBoss EJB container and in EJB applications. The remaining sections of this chapter will build on top of this fundamental understanding of the configuration files to teach you how to make your applications use the features available to applications running in the JBoss EJB container.

7.3.1 Where does everything go?

Before diving into an explanation of what the various configuration files do, you need to understand where the JBoss EJB container configuration files reside and where EJB applications get deployed. Figure 7.6 shows you the JBoss directory structure, highlighting the directories that are used to configure and deploy EJB applications and configure the EJB server.

```
server
  default
    conf
    deploy
    deployers
      ejb3.deployer
        META-INF
```

Figure 7.6 The directories used for EJB configuration and deployment

The conf directory contains a configuration file called standardjboss.xml. This is a global version of the proprietary deployment descriptor called jboss.xml, which we talk about in the next section. The contents of the standardjboss.xml file apply to all EJB applications deployed to the server. This file is predominately used to configure the various EJB containers for the different EJB types and the corresponding dynamic proxies that are used to access them. We visit this file several times throughout this chapter.

The deploy directory is where you deploy EJB applications. Several configuration files for various EJB services are also in the deploy directory. We discuss some of these in section 7.3.3.

The JBoss EJB server comes prepackaged in both the *default* and the *all* configurations. The EJB deployer is packaged under the deployers/ejb3.deployer directory. The ejb3.deployer/META-INF directory contains configuration files used to configure the EJB3 deployer.

Now that we know where applications can be deployed and where the server configuration files go, let's take a closer look at application configuration.

7.3.2 Configuring EJB applications

With EJB3, you can configure applications almost entirely using annotations and default conventions. You can specify configuration parameters that you want or have to configure by using annotations, and the container assumes default values for most everything that you don't explicitly specify—minimizing or, in many cases, eliminating the need for XML deployment descriptors. You can still use XML deployment descriptors in place of annotations, but the intention with EJB3 is to use deployment descriptors to override default configuration or configuration specified in annotations. This model is often called *convention over configuration.*

One great thing about EJB3 is that you don't have to specify an entire XML configuration file to override a single configuration option; you can specify only the portion of the deployment descriptor that you wish to override. In this case, the deployment descriptor is called a *partial deployment descriptor.*

When we talked about web applications in chapter 5, we discussed the differences between standard and proprietary deployment descriptors. EJB applications also have standard and proprietary deployment descriptors. Let's take a look at the deployment descriptors that EJB applications can use.

One standard deployment descriptor in an EJB application is the META-INF/ejb-jar.xml file. In EJB3, this file is largely optional because of annotations. Another standard deployment descriptor that can be defined is the META-INF/persistence.xml. This file is used to configure what are known as JPA persistence units, which we'll discuss shortly. As usual, JBoss AS provides default behavior for most configurable components and services, keeping JBoss AS-specific configuration to a minimum. When EJB application configuration is necessary, JBoss AS provides a proprietary deployment descriptor called jboss.xml.

Throughout this chapter, and in the accompanying source code for the book, we show you how to configure EJBs using annotations, but we also show you how to use the XML configuration files when it makes sense.

Figure 7.7 shows you that all the deployment descriptors (standard and proprietary) must reside in the EJB application's META-INF directory.

Let's take a closer look at each of these deployment descriptors, starting with the ejb-jar.xml file. Because ejb-jar.xml and persistence.xml are standard deployment descriptors, they're covered in depth in the EJB3 specification and in many online documents and tutorials on EJB3, so we only give you an overview of those files here.

Figure 7.7 All the deployment descriptors go in the META-INF directory of an EJB-JAR archive.

THE EJB-JAR.XML FILE

The ejb-jar.xml file is the standard deployment descriptor used to configure session and message-driven beans. As we mentioned in section 7.1.2, entities aren't managed directly by the container, they're managed by the JPA persistence context. For that reason, entities aren't configured in this file (as opposed to previous versions of EJB). Listing 7.7 shows you the outline for the ejb-jar.xml file.

Listing 7.7 Outline of a META-INF/ejb-jar.xml file

```
<ejb-jar>        ❶
  <description>Some JBoss Application</description>          ❷
  <display-name>Some App</display-name>
  <enterprise-beans>
    <session> ... </session>                                  ❸
    <message-driven> ... </message-driven>
  </enterprise-beans>
  <assembly-descriptor>
    <security-role> ... </security-role>
    <method-permission> ... </method-permission>
    <container-transaction> ... </container-transaction>      ❹
    <exclude-list> ... </exclude-list>
  </assembly-descriptor>
</ejb-jar>
```

The root element is `ejb-jar` ❶; under that is a `description` and a `display-name` element ❷. These elements are descriptive metadata fields used for logging. The main element blocks in this file are the `enterprise-beans` block ❸ and the `assembly-descriptor` ❹ block. The `enterprise-beans` block ❸ defines session and message-driven beans. To define a session bean, you define a `session` element; to define a message-driven bean, you define a `message-driven` element. These bean definitions can be used to define a bean's class, its interfaces, any other EJBs it references, which interceptors it uses, and whether the bean uses container transactions.

The `assembly-descriptor` block ❹ provides the definition for how security roles are applied to the bean method, the definition of method permissions, the definition of transaction attributes for EJBs using container-managed transactions, interceptor bindings, a list of methods to be excluded from being invoked, and a list of exception types that should be treated as application exceptions.

Now let's look at the persistence.xml file, which is used to configure entity persistence.

THE PERSISTENCE.XML FILE

The persistence.xml file is the standard deployment descriptor used to configure a JPA persistence context. You saw an example of this file when we showed you how to code the sample application in section 7.2.1. JBoss has built-in support for Hibernate as its JPA implementation, so most applications have a persistence.xml file that looks similar to that shown in listing 7.8.

Listing 7.8 The persistence.xml file used to configure JPA entity persistence

```
<persistence>
  <persistence-unit name="userDatabase">
    <provider>org.hibernate.ejb.HibernatePersistence</provider>
```

```
    <jta-data-source>java:/DefaultDS</jta-data-source>
    <properties>
      <property name="hibernate.hbm2ddl.auto" value="create-drop"/>
      <property name="hibernate.dialect"
            value="org.hibernate.dialect.HSQLDialect"/>
    </properties>
  </persistence-unit>
</persistence>
```

The `persistence-unit` block defines a persistence context. This configuration defines Hibernate as the JPA provider and points to `java:/DefaultDS`, the JNDI name for the default data source in JBoss AS. The block also defines any properties that you might want to provide to Hibernate. We talk about the persistence.xml file more when we discuss entity persistence in section 7.5.

Last but not least, let's take a closer look at the proprietary jboss.xml deployment descriptor.

THE JBOSS.XML FILE

The jboss.xml file is the proprietary deployment descriptor used to configure EJBs. The structure of the file is similar to the ejb-jar.xml. This similarity exists because the standard ejb-jar.xml deployment descriptor describes what behavior you're configuring, and the proprietary jboss.xml deployment descriptor describes how you're configuring the behavior defined in the standard deployment descriptor. Listing 7.9 shows you an example of a jboss.xml file.

Listing 7.9 The jboss.xml file used to specify JBoss AS–specific configuration for EJBs

```
<jboss xmlns="http://www.jboss.com/xml/ns/javaee"
      xmlns:xsi="http://www.w3.org/2001/XMLSchema-instance"
      xsi:schemaLocation="http://www.jboss.com/xml/ns/javaee
                        http://www.jboss.org/j2ee/schema/jboss_5_0.xsd"
      version="3.0">
  <security-domain>jbia-domain</security-domain>
  <enterprise-beans>
    <session>
      <ejb-name>ShoppingCart</ejb-name>
      <jndi-name>ShoppingCart</jndi-name>
      <clustered>true</clustered>
      <cluster-config>
        <partition-name>DefaultPartition</partition-name>
        <load-balance-policy>
           org.jboss.ha.framework.interfaces.RandomRobin
        </load-balance-policy>
      </cluster-config>
      <security-domain>overridden-domain</security-domain>
    </session>
    <session>
      <ejb-name>StatelessTest</ejb-name>
      <jndi-name>StatelessTest</jndi-name>
    </session>
  </enterprise-beans>
</jboss>
```

You can use the jboss.xml file to configure behavior that's particular to the application server, such as

- Global JNDI bindings (see section 7.4.1)
- Configuring dynamic proxies (see section 7.4.3)
- Configuring the different EJB containers (see section 7.4.3)
- Defining JBoss service objects (see section 7.6)
- Configuring the transport protocol (see section 7.7)
- Securing EJBs (see section 7.8)

We refer back to the jboss.xml file or the equivalent annotations throughout this chapter.

In this section, you learned how to configure EJB applications. Now let's talk about how to configure the EJB server.

7.3.3 *Configuring the EJB server*

Server configuration is done in either the EJB server's configuration files or in the configuration files for the various services that run on top of the EJB server. These service configuration files are deployed as services in the server configuration's deploy directory. Table 7.1 summarizes the different files that can be configured, what configuration they're available in, and what they're used for.

Table 7.1 Summary of the EJB server and various EJB service configuration files

File[a]	Configuration	What it configures
deploy/cluster/jboss-cache-manager.sar/ META-INF/jboss-cache-configs.xml	all	The JBoss Cache configuration that defines the caches for SFSB, entities, queries, timestamps
deploy/ejb3-connectors-jboss-beans.xml	default, all	The EJB connector used for remoting
deploy/ejb3-interceptors-aop.xml	default, all	All the interceptors used during EJB calls and lifecycle events, both on the client and the server side
deploy/ejb3-timer-service.xml	default, all	JBoss's implementation of the EJB Timer, a service specified by the Java EE specification that allows for EJB calls that occur based on timer events
deployers/ejb3.deployer/META-INF/ persistence.properties	default, all	Default properties used when creating a persistence unit (as defined in an application's persistence.xml file)
deployers/ejb3.deployer/META-INF/ jpa-deployers-jboss-beans.xml	default, all	The deployer used to recognize and deploy JPA archives
deployers/ejb3.deployer/META-INF/ ejb3-deployers-jboss-beans.xml	default, all	The deployer used to recognize and deploy EJB archives

a. All directories are relative to the server configuration directory.

These are all standard configuration file types that we cover in this book (-service.xml, jboss-beans.xml, -aop.xml) or are standard to Java (.properties), so we don't go into a discussion of the file structures. We refer back to these files throughout this chapter and in chapter 13 when we discuss EJB clustering.

By this point, you should have a good understanding of the configuration files used for EJB application and server configuration. The rest of this chapter will build on top of this knowledge by showing you how to configure specific behavior using the configuration files. Let's start by talking about how you can configure session beans.

7.4 Configuring session beans

When session EJBs get deployed to the server, they're automatically bound into JNDI using a default name. Changing this default binding is a common configuration. In this section, we explore how to change the JNDI binding for a bean and how to look up a bean.

We also describe how to configure the EJB container and the dynamic proxy that the client uses to call the server. These configurations will allow you to enable SFSB passivation and configure the pool size for SLSBs.

Let's first discuss how to change the JNDI binding for a session bean.

7.4.1 Changing the JNDI binding

JNDI provides a uniform way for both local and remote application components to look up references to dynamic proxies for the EJB that they need to call. As EJBs are deployed into the server, the server automatically creates the dynamic proxy for the EJB and binds it into the JNDI server. You'll need to know how to change the JNDI name for an EJB and how to look up the JNDI name from a client.

By default, when you deploy a session bean into JBoss, the JNDI name that the bean gets bound to is the name of the bean itself. For example, let's say that you deploy the SLSB, remote business interface, and local business interface shown in listing 7.10 to JBoss AS.

Listing 7.10 An SLSB and its local and remote interfaces

```
//A stateless session bean
@Stateless
public class MessagePrinterBean implements MessagePrinterRemote,
   MessagePrinterLocal {
  public void printRemoteMessage(String message) { ... }
  public void printLocalMessage(String message) { ... }
}

//A local interface
@Local
public interface MessagePrinterLocal {
  public void printLocalMessage(String message);
}
```

```
//A remote interface
@Remote
public interface MessagePrinterRemote {
  public void printRemoteMessage(String message);
}
```

When the EJB deploys to the application server, it gets bound under the name MessagePrinterBean, which the clients will use to look up the bean. If you want, you can change the JNDI binding for the bean to TextMessagePrinter instead of MessagePrinterBean through either an annotation or configuration. Let's look at how to do both, starting with the annotation approach.

CHANGING THE JNDI BINDING THROUGH ANNOTATIONS

The JNDI name for a session bean can be changed by applying one of the following annotations on the session bean class:

```
@org.jboss.ejb3.annotation.RemoteBinding
@org.jboss.ejb3.annotation.LocalBinding
```

As the names suggest, to change the remote JNDI binding, you use the @RemoteBinding annotation, and to change the local JNDI binding, you use the @LocalBinding annotation. For example, if you want to change the local and remote JNDI bindings for the message printer example listing 7.10, you could add the following annotations to the SLSB class.

```
@Stateless
@LocalBinding(jndiBinding="LocalTextMessagePrinter")
@RemoteBinding(jndiBinding="TextMessagePrinter")
public class MessagePrinterBean ...
```

If you want to bind the dynamic proxy for the session bean to multiple remote names, you can, as follows:

```
@RemoteBindings( { @RemoteBinding(jndiBinding="TextMessagePrinter"),
             @RemoteBinding(jndiBinding="AnotherName") } )
```

Here we use the @org.jboss.ejb3.remoting.RemoteBindings annotation (note the *s* at the end) to contain multiple @RemoteBinding annotations.

Now, let's see how to change the default JNDI binding for a session EJB through configuration.

CHANGING THE JNDI BINDING THROUGH CONFIGURATION

You can also change the JNDI binding for a session bean's dynamic proxy via the META-INF/jboss.xml file. Listing 7.11 shows a partial deployment descriptor that changes the default JNDI binding or overrides the ones defined by annotations.

Listing 7.11 Partial deployment descriptor that changes default JNDI binding for an EJB

```
<jboss xmlns="http://www.jboss.com/xml/ns/javaee"
     xmlns:xsi="http://www.w3.org/2001/XMLSchema-instance"
     xsi:schemaLocation="http://www.jboss.com/xml/ns/javaee
                 http://www.jboss.org/j2ee/schema/jboss_5_0.xsd"
```

```
      version="3.0">
  <enterprise-beans>
    <session>
      <ejb-name>MessagePrinterBean</ejb-name>
      <jndi-name>TextMessagePrinter</jndi-name>
      <local-jndi-name>LocalTextMessagePrinter</local-jndi-name>
    </session>
  </enterprise-beans>
</jboss>
```

The `ejb-name` element defines which session bean you want to change the bindings for. The `jndi-name` element modifies the binding for the dynamic proxy used for remote access. The `local-jndi-name` element modifies the binding for the dynamic proxy used for local access.

You've seen how to change the binding for an EJB; now let's discuss how to look up a session bean from a client.

7.4.2 Looking up a session bean

In order to call an EJB, you have to look up a dynamic proxy from a JNDI server and make a call to the proxy. As we discussed in the last section, a bean is automatically bound into JNDI by its name. If you deploy a bean called `TexanGreeter` that implements the `Greeter` remote interface, you access it in the following way:

```
Greeter myGreeter = (Greeter) ctx.lookup("TexanGreeter/remote");
```

Notice that you have to append the word *remote* after the name. If you want to look up a local interface for the same bean, you write the following:

```
GreeterLocal myGreeter =
➥ (GreeterLocal) ctx.lookup("TexanGreeter/local");
```

This time you use *local* after the bean name instead of *remote*.

If you deploy an EJB-JAR bundled in an EAR file, you need to preface the JNDI name with the name of your EAR file.

```
ctx.lookup("earfilename/BeanName/remote");
```

Now that you know how to change the JNDI binding for EJBs and look them up in JNDI, let's examine another aspect of session bean configuration—configuring the EJB containers.

7.4.3 Configuring EJB containers

In JBoss AS, there's a container definition for each type of remotely accessible EJB. It's useful to know how to configure containers and the dynamic proxies configured to call the containers so that you can control features such as session-bean pool size and SFSB passivation. In this section, we take a high-level look at how to configure the various EJB containers to help you with more specific configurations throughout the rest of this chapter.

NOTE In EJB3, an entity manager (the interface used to read/write entity objects to a database) can't be accessed remotely and isn't managed by a server container. The entity manager accesses entity objects from within a persistent context, which is an in-memory cache of entity objects synchronized to the database. A persistence context is configured in an application's META-INF/persistence.xml file. Because entities aren't managed by a server container, as we explore the container configuration, you won't see anything relating to EJB3 entities.

Both the dynamic proxy and the container for each type of EJB are defined in the server/xxx/conf/standardjboss.xml file. This file defines two main blocks: one that defines the dynamic proxies and one that defines the containers. Listing 7.12 shows you the general structure of the file.

Listing 7.12 General structure of standardjboss.xml

```
<jboss>
  <invoker-proxy-bindings>
    <invoker-proxy-binding>...</invoker-proxy-binding>
    <invoker-proxy-binding>...</invoker-proxy-binding>
  </invoker-proxy-bindings>
  <container-configurations>
    <container-configuration>...</container-configuration>
    <container-configuration>...</container-configuration>
  </container-configurations>
</jboss>
```

Each `invoker-proxy-binding` block defines a dynamic proxy and how it's associated with an invoker, a component used to configure a transport protocol. We talk about configuring the transport protocol in section 7.7. The `container-configuration` blocks configure the server container. Listing 7.13 shows you the SFSB configuration as an example.

Listing 7.13 Container configuration for SFSB in standardjboss.xml

```
<container-configuration>
  <container-name>Standard Stateful SessionBean</container-name>        ❶
  ...
  <container-interceptors>...</container-interceptors>      ❷
  ...
  <persistence-manager>
    org.jboss.ejb.plugins.StatefulSessionFilePersistenceManager       ❸
  </persistence-manager>
  <container-cache-conf>...</container-cache-conf>      ❹
  <container-pool-conf>
    <MaximumSize>100</MaximumSize>      ❺
  </container-pool-conf>
</container-configuration>
```

You know that this listing is the configuration for the SFSB container because of the `container-name` element ❶. The SLSB container has a `container-name` value of `Standard Stateless SessionBean`, so it's also easy to find.

The container configuration is primarily composed of the interceptors defined in the `container-interceptors` block ❷. The container passes incoming requests through a chain of interceptors before it reaches the EJB. Each interceptor handles different non-business concerns of the request, such as checking for security and initializing transaction management. Although you can create custom interceptors and change the order of the existing ones, we've found little use for this in practice. If you do need to extend or change the interceptors, the JBoss AS Configuration Guide (referenced at the end of this chapter) explains how to do so.

Some of the other elements in these configuration files are much more commonly changed. Let's take a look at some of these uses.

CONFIGURING THE SESSION-BEAN POOL SIZE

You can configure the SFSB and SLSB pool sizes by setting the values of the `MinimumSize` and `MaximumSize` elements under the `container-pool-conf` element ❺. The `MinimumSize` setting tells the container how many instances to bring up when the container first starts. The `MaximumSize` setting isn't a strict maximum size; it tells the pool the maximum number of instances to keep alive. If more requests come in than this maximum, the server creates more. If you want to strictly limit the number of concurrent requests to a server, you use the `strictMaximumSize` and `strictTimeout` elements as follows:

```
<container-pool-conf>
  <MinimumSize>20</MinimumSize>
  <MaximumSize>100</MaximumSize>
  <strictMaximumSize>true</strictMaximumSize>
  <strictTimeout>10000</strictTimeout>
</container-pool-conf>
```

The `strictMaximumSize` Boolean attribute tells the container to never allow more concurrent requests than the value defined in the `MaxiumSize` element (100, in this case). Requests that come in after the maximum are blocked until they timeout based on the number of milliseconds defined by the `strictTimeout` element, after which a `java.rmi.ServerException` is thrown. If the value of the timeout is 0, then it immediately times out. The maximum (and default) value is the maximum possible `Long` value which is 9,223,372,036,854,775,807 milliseconds or about 292,471,208 years.

CONFIGURING SFSB PASSIVATION

Stateful bean passivation is configured with two elements: the `persistence-manager` block ❸ and the `container-cache-conf` block. The `persistence-manager` defines which persistence manager should be used for passivation. The container uses the persistence manager to read and write passivated objects to secondary storage. The default SFSB persistence manager is the `StatefulSessionFilePersistenceManager`, which writes the session bean state to a file.

The passivation rules are defined in the `container-cache-conf` configuration block ❹. In this block, you define a cache policy and a configuration for that cache policy as shown in the following code snippet:

```
<container-cache-conf>
  <cache-policy>
    org.jboss.ejb.plugins.LRUStatefulContextCachePolicy
  </cache-policy>
  <cache-policy-conf>
    <min-capacity>50</min-capacity>
    <max-capacity>1000000</max-capacity>
    ...
  </cache-policy-conf>
</container-cache-conf>
```

The default policy is a Least Recently Used (LRU) policy called `LRUStatefulContext-CachePolicy`. If you want to disable passivation altogether, you replace the default with `org.jboss.ejb.plugins.NoPassivationCachePolicy`. This policy never writes to a secondary storage; it keeps all the sessions in memory.

If you want to write to a database or use a distributed cache for your SFSB passivation, the best bet is to use the all configuration and use a cache loader. We talk about this more when we discuss clustering in chapters 12 and 13.

We've seen how to configure session beans and their containers; now let's look at how to configure entity persistence.

7.5 Configuring entity persistence

To use EJB3 entities, you have to configure a data source and define a META-INF/persistence.xml file in your application package. We discussed data sources and how to configure them in chapter 3 (section 3.4.1); now, let's take a closer look at what's in the persistence.xml file and see what you can do with it.

When you deploy an application archive with a META-INF/persistence.xml file, the application server automatically scans the class files in the package to see if any entities are defined. It then creates a persistence context based on the configuration in the persistence.xml file, making sure to include all the entity classes that it found. Plenty of information is available on JPA configuration in the JPA specification, which is referenced at the end of this chapter.

In this section, you'll learn how to configure JPA to use Hibernate objects and mappings in JBoss. Let's start by seeing how a session bean might get a reference to a persistence context so that it can start using it to persist objects.

7.5.1 Injecting Hibernate objects

In JPA, we use the `EntityManager` class to interact with the persistence context, and we use the `EntityManagerFactory` class to create `EntityManager` instances. If you've been using Hibernate, you may have code that uses the Hibernate `Session` and `SessionFactory` objects to interact with the persistence context. Because Hibernate is JBoss's JPA implementation, if you need to access these Hibernate objects, you can do so. Not only can you access them, but JBoss even enables you to inject them directly into your EJBs, as shown in listing 7.14.

Listing 7.14 Injecting Hibernate objects into EJBs

```
import org.hibernate.Session;
import org.hibernate.SessionFactory;

@Stateful public class SomeBean ... {
  @PersistenceContext(unitName="unitOne")
  Session session;

  @PersistenceUnit(unitName="unitTwo")
  SessionFactory factory;
}
```

In this code, the same `@javax.persistence.PersistenceContext` and `@javax.persistence.PersistenceUnit` annotations used to inject `EntityManager` and `EntityManagerFactory` objects (respectively) can also be used to inject the `Session` and `SessionFactory` objects. The application server manages the lifecycle of the `HibernateSession` object the same way that it manages the lifecycle of the `EntityManager` object.

If you already have a reference to an `EntityManager` instance, you can still obtain a reference to `HibernateSession` as shown in listing 7.15.

Listing 7.15 Casting JPA objects into Hibernate objects

```
import org.jboss.ejb3.entity.HibernateSession;
import org.hibernate.Session;

...

@PersistenceContext EntityManager entityManager;

public void someBusinessMethod()
{
  HibernateSession hs = (HibernateSession)entityManager;
  Session session = hs.getHibernateSession();
  ...
}
```

You can also deploy existing Hibernate mapping files into JBoss AS, giving you a faster transition into EJB3 and JPA. Let's see how this works.

7.5.2 Deploying Hibernate mappings

Many people fear switching to JPA because they've already invested so much in creating their Hibernate mapping files. In chapter 3 (section 3.4.2), we talked about how to deploy a Hibernate archive in JBoss AS. If you don't want to use JPA or already have application code running in Hibernate, that option is great.

But if you do want to use JPA, there's one great advantage of having Hibernate as the JPA implementation for JBoss AS—you can deploy Hibernate .hbm.xml mapping files in an EJB archive, and the mapped classes can be accessed as JPA entities inside your code. The best part is that you don't have to configure anything; as long as the

.hbm.xml mapping files are in an archive that's scanned for entities, the mapped classes automatically become entities.

Now that you've learned how to configure various aspects of entity persistence, let's take a look at how JBoss AS enables you to easily define new services using service objects.

7.6 Creating JMX service objects

In chapter 2 (section 2.1.2), we talked about how JBoss AS services can plug into JBoss's management interface by defining a JMX MBean. Many applications need monitoring or dynamic management capabilities; and, if you're running in JBoss, JMX is an easy way to get this functionality. In the past, writing your own service required configuration work, but with an extension of the new EJB3 container and through the use of annotations, JBoss makes this process simple.

JBoss AS now offers a new component type called a JMX service object. Service objects are a special type of EJB that are similar to SFSB. Service objects can define local and remote interfaces, be injected into and from other EJBs, and maintain state. The main difference is that service objects are singletons; only a single instance of the service object is available in the server (for all clients) as you'd expect of a service running in the server.

7.6.1 Creating a service object

Let's look at an example of how you might use a service object. Let's say that you want to build an investment calculator that calculates the future value of an investment with a given interest rate (or growth rate). You want to implement the calculator as an SLSB where every client has its own calculator. Now let's say that the interest rate for the calculator is set on the server side by an administrator. You only want a single interest rate for all the calculators, so you want to maintain this data in a singleton. Listing 7.16 shows you the calculator class.

Listing 7.16 Code for SLSB calculator

```
@Stateless
public class StatelessCalculatorBean implements Calculator {
  @EJB(beanName = "InterestRateMBean")
  private InterestRateManager interstRateManager;
  public double calculateTotalInterest(double presentValue, int years) {
    return calculateFutureValue(presentValue, years) - presentValue;
  }
  public double calculateFutureValue(double presentValue, int years) {
    double interestRate = interstRateManager.getInterestRate() / 100;
    return presentValue * Math.pow((1.0 + interestRate), years);
  }
  public double getInterestRate() {
    return interstRateManager.getInterestRate();
  }
}
```

The remote interface that the bean uses looks like listing 7.17.

Listing 7.17 Code for remote interface

```
@Remote
public interface Calculator {
  public double getInterestRate();
  public double calculateTotalInterest(double presentValue, int years);
  public double calculateFutureValue(double presentValue, int years);
}
```

The calculator implements a remote interface with a few methods that make use of a class-level variable called `interestRateManager` that's an instance of the `InterestRateManager` interface. The field is injected into the SLSB using the `@EJB` annotation. The annotation injects a bean called `InterestRateMBean`, which is the service object that implements the `InterestRateManager` interface and manages the interest rate for the investment calculator. The management interface shown in listing 7.18 uses the `@Management` annotation to make the interface methods available through an MBean server.

Listing 7.18 `@Management` interface for sample application

```
@Management
public interface InterestRateManager {
  // Attribute
  public void setInterestRate(double g);
  public double getInterestRate();
  // Life cycle method
  public void create() throws Exception;
  public void destroy() throws Exception;
}
```

The interface for the MBean is annotated with the `@org.jboss.ejb3.annotation.Management` interface. This annotation tells JBoss AS that the interface is a management interface for a service object. Any method on the management interface that abides by the JavaBean's set and get method syntax becomes a JMX attribute on the MBean. Any other method becomes an MBean operation. Because MBeans have a lifecycle, you need to tie into the lifecycle operations with the `create` and `destroy` methods defined on the interface. Listing 7.19 shows you the code for an MBean that implements the managed interface.

Listing 7.19 MBean that manages interest rate for investment calculator application

```
@Service(objectName = "jbia:service=interestRateManager")
public class InterestRateMBean implements InterestRateManager {
  private double interestRate;
  public void setInterestRate(double interestRate) {
    this.interestRate = interestRate;
  }
  public double getInterestRate() {
```

```
    return interestRate;
  }
  // Lifecycle methods
  public void create() throws Exception {
    interestRate = 5.25;
    System.out.println("Calculator - Creating");
  }
  public void destroy() {
    System.out.println("Calculator - Destroying");
  }
}
```

The MBean class has the `@org.jboss.ejb3.annotation.Service` annotation on the class. This annotation tells JBoss AS that an instance of this class is a service object. When this object is deployed, the container maintains it as a singleton. The `objectName` attribute defines the JMX name that the service gets bound to in the JMX server. Now that you've created the code for the service object, let's see how to run it and try it out. Both the `@Service` and the `@Management` annotation classes are found in the client/jboss-ejb3-ext-api.jar file, as well as in the client/jbossall-client.jar file.

7.6.2 Running the sample application

After writing the code for the application, you need a client that can access the calculator. The main method for the client looks up the dynamic proxy for the calculator and makes calls to it as follows:

```
Calculator calc =
➥   (Calculator) ctx.lookup("StatelessCalculatorBean/remote");
System.out.println(calc.calculate(1, 10, 100));
```

If you run the code, the output is `15947.906560388028`, which you get when the interest rate is set to the default value of 0.08. Now, if you want to change this value, you do the following:

1. Go to the JMX Console: http://127.0.0.1:8080/jmx-console/
2. Navigate to the `jbia:service=interestRateManager` MBean, which is probably the only MBean listed under the `jbia` JMX domain.
3. Modify the `InterestRate` attribute.

Figure 7.8 shows you a screen shot of the JMX Console for this bean.

As you can see in the image, the `InterestRate` attribute allows you to change the interest rate for the service object, and the lifecycle methods are listed as operations. Modify the interest rate, and run the client again to see the value change.

You can also access service objects from other components besides EJBs. Let's see how.

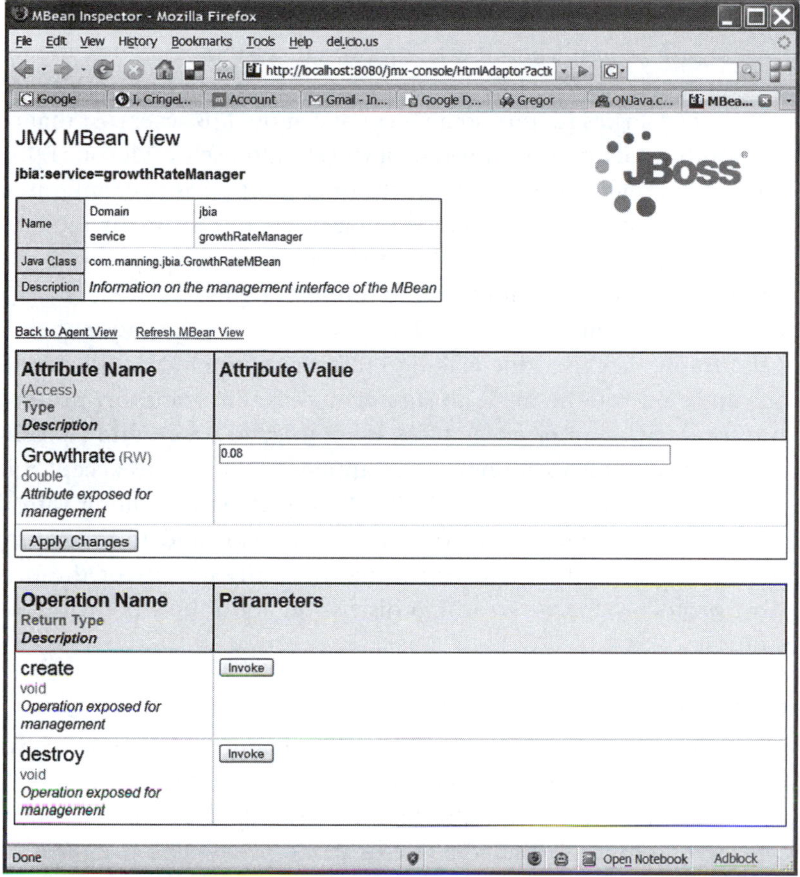

Figure 7.8 The JMX management screen for the `InterestRateMBean` MBean

7.6.3 *Accessing MBeans without injection*

In the example, you accessed the interest rate service object using EJB injection. But what if you wanted to access the service object from a non-EJB component such as a servlet or a JSP? You can access a service object programmatically using the following code:

```
MBeanServer server = MBeanServerLocator.locate();
calcManager = (InterestRateManager) MBeanProxyExt.create(
➥    InterestRateManager.class,
➥    "jbia:service=interestRateManager",server);
```

You've seen how to use service objects. Now, let's explore another important configuration related to EJBs: accessing them using different transport protocols.

7.7 Configuring the transport protocol

Many web-based Java EE applications are deployed in a topology where the web server and EJB server are collocated, obviating the need for remote calls to EJBs. But some applications and topologies require some form of remote EJB access. At that point, the question arises as to which transport protocol you should use to call your EJBs. In most cases, a standard socket-based protocol works fine. JBoss AS is preconfigured to support socket calls to EJBs. But sometimes you may want to change or reconfigure the transport protocol used for remote calls to the server. For example, you may have a network security restriction that limits you to tunneling EJB calls over HTTP.

In this section, we discuss the architecture and configuration behind JBoss Remoting, the framework used for making EJB calls remotely. You'll learn what configuration changes need to be made to support a different transport protocol. Many different transports are supported by JBoss Remoting, so we couldn't possibly cover them all. We show you how to configure the application server to accept remote EJB calls over Remote Method Invocation (RMI). This explanation, along with the overview of the architecture, should give you enough background to read through the JBoss Remoting documentation and learn how to configure any of the other available transport protocols. Let's start with a discussion about how the transport protocol configuration works.

7.7.1 Understanding transport configuration

JBoss AS uses the new JBoss Remoting framework to enable EJB remoting. Several components interact to make EJB remoting possible, as shown in figure 7.9.

As we've discussed previously, an EJB client makes calls to a dynamic proxy that has been downloaded from a JNDI server. The dynamic proxy uses the JBoss Remoting

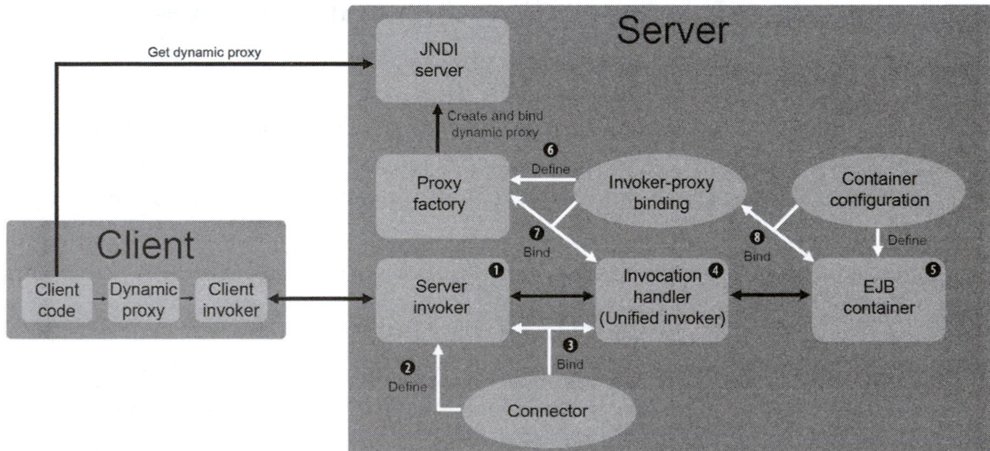

Figure 7.9 The components involved in EJB remoting. The black lines represent runtime interactions between components. The white lines show how the various configuration files define and bind the components together.

framework to call a *server invoker* ❶. A server invoker's job is to read requests on a particular transport and forward them to one or more *invocation handlers* that handle the requests. The server invoker is created by a *connector* ❷, a component configured in the server/xxx/deploy/remoting-service.xml file. When the connector component is created, it creates the server invoker and binds it (or connects it) to its invocation handlers ❸—hence, the name *connector.*

The application server defines an invocation handler known as the *Unified Invoker* ❹ that can be configured to call various EJB containers ❺ used for different types of EJBs. The Unified Invoker's configuration can be found in the server/xxx/deploy/remoting-service.xml file. (Don't get confused by the name Unified Invoker. The Unified Invoker isn't an invoker; it's an invocation handler.)

When a dynamic proxy sends a request from the client to the server, it specifies which invocation handler it wants the request directed to. The request has to carry some information that tells the server invoker which invocation handler it wants to use. The dynamic proxy is provided with this information when it's created by its *proxy factory*, the component that creates new dynamic proxies. The proxy factory is bound to an invocation handler. When the proxy factory is asked to create a new dynamic proxy, it confirms that the dynamic proxy knows how to generate requests that wind up at the correct invocation handler.

The binding between the invocation handler and the proxy factory can be done in one of two places. The default configuration for proxy factories is in the server/xxx/conf/standardjboss.xml file. The `invoker-proxy-binding` elements in this file define proxy factories ❻ and bind them to their invocation handlers ❼. This same definition and binding ❽ can also be done in an application's META-INF/jboss.xml file.

The Unified Invoker needs a way to forward to the appropriate EJB container based on the type of EJB request. This forwarding can be done in the server/xxx/conf/standardjboss.xml file or in the application's META-INF/jboss.xml file using the `container-configuration` element that we discussed in section 7.4.3. This element defines an EJB container and associates it with an `invoker-proxy-binding` that can call it.

The server/xxx/conf/standardjboss.xml (or the application's META-INF/jboss.xml file) contains the `invoker-proxy` bindings. An `invoker-proxy-binding` defines a proxy factory and binds it to an invocation handler. Listing 7.20 shows you the binding that defines the SLSB dynamic-proxy factory and binds it to the Unified Invoker.

Listing 7.20 `invoker-proxy-binding` binding to Unified Invoker

```
<invoker-proxy-binding>
  <name>stateless-unified-invoker</name>
  <invoker-mbean>
    jboss:service=invoker,type=unified</invoker-mbean>      ❶
  <proxy-factory>
    org.jboss.proxy.ejb.ProxyFactory</proxy-factory>
  <proxy-factory-config>                                    ❷
    <client-interceptors>
```

```
    ...
    </client-interceptors>          2
  </proxy-factory-config>
</invoker-proxy-binding>
```

The invoker-mbean element ❶ specifies the MBean name for the invocation handler that the proxy factory injects into dynamic proxies that it creates. The proxy-factory-config element ❷ defines the proxy factory. The same files (standardjboss.xml and jboss.xml) contain the container definitions for the different EJB request types. We looked at these in section 7.4.3. The container is tied to the invoker-proxy-binding in the container configuration's invoker-proxy-binding-name element. To bind to the invoker-proxy-binding shown in the listing, a container configuration has to have the following element defined:

```
<invoker-proxy-binding-name>stateless-unified-invoker
➥  </invoker-proxy-binding-name>
```

The invoker-proxy-binding-name element references one of the invoker-proxy-binding elements defined in the same file. This reference indirectly binds the EJB container to the invocation handler that the invoker-proxy-binding is already bound to, allowing requests coming in from the client's dynamic proxy to be routed all the way through to the EJB container.

The great thing about this architecture is that you don't have to change any of the container or proxy factory configurations to support a different transport protocol. Because of the invocation handler abstraction and the existence of the Unified Invoker, all you have to do is change the connector configuration to change the transport. Let's see how this might work.

7.7.2 Changing the transport

As we mentioned, changing the transport only requires a change to the connector configuration in the server/xxx/deploy/remoting-service.xml file. For example, if you want to change to an RMI transport instead of a socket-based transport, you change the connector configuration to look like listing 7.21.

Listing 7.21 Updated connector configuration that supports RMI transport

```
<mbean code="org.jboss.remoting.transport.Connector"
  name="jboss.remoting:service=Connector,transport=RMI"       1
    display-name="RMI transport Connector">        2

 <attribute name="Configuration">
  <config>
   <invoker transport="rmi">        3
    ...
   </invoker>

   <handlers>
    <handler subsystem="invoker">
      jboss:service=invoker,type=unified
```

```
        </handler>
      </handlers>
    </config>
  </attribute>
  <depends>jboss.remoting:service=NetworkRegistry</depends>
</mbean>
```

Changing the `transport` attribute on the `invoker` element ❸ tells the connector to create an RMI-based server invoker when the connector is created. The supported options here are `socket`, `sslsocket`, `http`, `https`, `multiplex`, `sslmultiplex`, `servlet`, `sslservlet`, `rmi`, and `sslrmi`. These options are all fully documented in the JBoss Remoting documentation referenced at the end of this chapter.

The changed display name for the MBean ❷ reflects the new purpose of the connector. You don't have to make this change, but it makes sense to have the name match what the connector does. The name of the MBean itself also changed ❶. You don't have to do this either because the MBean name is still unique in the MBean server, but it also makes more sense to do this. Remember that, if you update this name, you also want to update any references to it—for example, the Unified Invoker definition in listing 7.19 that references the socket connector's MBean name as an MBean dependency. You want to update this definition in the server/xxx/deploy/remoting-service.xml file to have the correct name in the MBean dependency, as follows:

```
<mbean code="org.jboss.invocation.unified.server.UnifiedInvoker"
    name="jboss:service=invoker,type=unified">
  <depends>jboss:service=TransactionManager</depends>
  <depends>jboss.remoting:service=Connector,transport=RMI</depends>
</mbean>
```

You should now have enough of an understanding to configure transport protocols in JBoss. If you need to use a transport that we didn't talk about, you should be able to read through the JBoss Remoting documentation and learn the details about the other transports. Now, let's build on top of what you learned about security in chapter 4 to see how security is applied to EJBs.

7.8 Securing EJBs

Any remotely accessible component requires security. Entities don't require security because they're not remotely accessible. We discuss security for message-driven beans in chapter 8, "JBoss Messaging." So we only need to cover session beans in this section.

Session EJBs can be accessed from within the application server or from remote clients. If an EJB is accessed from the integrated web container running in the same application server instance as the EJB container, then the web application doesn't have to explicitly pass the security credentials to the EJB server. In this case, the web container can call the EJB by merely looking up and calling a dynamic proxy, as we discussed in section 7.4.2. The security credentials are automatically propagated from the web container to the EJB container. Even though the web application is an EJB client, it doesn't need to pass credentials to the EJB server. If an EJB is accessed remotely from a standalone application or web container running in a different JVM process, then the security credentials have to be passed to the EJB server from the client.

Web applications enable security for particular URL patterns. EJBs, on the other hand, are secured on an individual method basis. Security can be added to EJB methods (public methods declared in the EJB's business interface) using either standard Java EE annotations or XML descriptor files. We talk about both methods in this section. Let's start with annotations.

7.8.1 Securing EJBs via annotations

The simplest way to add security to EJB methods is by using annotations. Listing 7.22 shows you an example of an SLSB that uses annotations to secure its methods.

Listing 7.22 Adding security to EJBs using annotations

```
@SecurityDomain("simple-security-domain")
@RolesAllowed( { "bank-manager", "teller" })
@Stateless
public class StatelessCalculatorBean implements Calculator, CalculatorRemote
{
  public double calculateTotalInterest(double presentValue, int years) {
    return calculateFutureValue(presentValue, years) - presentValue;
  }
  @RolesAllowed("teller")
  public double calculateFutureValue(double presentValue, int years) {
    double interestRate = 5.25 / 100;
    return presentValue * Math.pow((1.0 + interestRate), years);
  }
  @RolesAllowed("bank-manager")
  public double getInterestRate() {
    return 5.25;
  }
  @DenyAll
  public String getTheAnswerToLifeTheUniverseAndEverything() {
    return "42";
  }
  @PermitAll
  public String freeForAll() {
    return "You're in!";
  }
}
```

First, you'll notice that the `@SecurityDomain` annotation is defined at the class level and is used to specify which security domain this particular EJB class will use. The attribute in the annotation points to the name of the security domain defined in the server's login-config.xml file. Also note that you don't need to specify the `java:/jaas` prefix in the annotation.

The three annotations—`@RolesAllowed`, `@PermitAll`, and `@DenyAll`—are used to specify method-level authorization on the EJB. Table 7.2 summarizes these annotations.

Table 7.2 The Java annotations used to specify security for EJB methods

Annotation	Description
`@javax.annotation.security.RolesAllowed`	A standard EJB3 annotation used to define which roles have access to a given method
`@javax.annotation.security.PermitAll`	A standard EJB3 annotation used to signify that any authenticated user can access the method
`@javax.annotation.security.DenyAll`	A standard EJB3 annotation used to signify that no users can access the method
`@org.jboss.ejb3.annotation.SecurityDomain`	A JBoss-specific annotation used to define the security domain that calls to this bean will be routed to

The `@RolesAllowed` annotation defined at the class level specifies the default security access for all the methods in the class. Therefore, the `calculateTotalInterest()` method requires either the role `bankmanager` or `teller`. The `calculateFutureValue()` method and the `getInterestRate()` methods each define their own roles, which completely override any roles defined at the class level. If no class-level roles are defined and a method also has no roles defined, then that method can be accessed by anybody.

TIP Make sure you're referencing the correct annotation class. For example, there's an `org.jboss.annotation.security.SecurityDomain` annotation class and an `org.jboss.aspects.security.SecurityDomain` annotation class. Because they share a name and they both take the same number and type of arguments, it's easy to import the wrong class (`org.jboss.aspects.security.SecurityDomain`) when annotating an EJB with security.

If you try to access the methods on this class with different users who have different permissions, you can see what methods can and can't be accessed. For example:

```
---------------------------------------------
User: admin, Roles: bank-manager, teller
---------------------------------------------
admin could call calculateFutureValue (requires 'teller')
admin could call calculateTotalInterest (requires 'bank-manager' or 'teller')
admin could call getInterestRate (requires 'bank-manager')
admin could not call getTheAnswerToLifeTheUniverseAndEverything (DenyAll)
admin could not call freeForAll (PermitAll)
---------------------------------------------
User: bank-manager, Roles: bank-manager
---------------------------------------------
bank-manager could not call calculateFutureValue (requires 'teller')
```

```
bank-manager could call calculateTotalInterest (requires 'bank-manager' or
   'teller')
bank-manager could call getInterestRate (requires 'bank-manager')
bank-manager could not call getTheAnswerToLifeTheUniverseAndEverything
   (DenyAll)
bank-manager could not call freeForAll (PermitAll)
---------------------------------------------
User: teller, Roles: teller
---------------------------------------------
teller could call calculateFutureValue (requires 'teller')
teller could call calculateTotalInterest (requires 'bank-manager' or
   'teller')
teller could not call getInterestRate (requires 'bank-manager')
teller could not call getTheAnswerToLifeTheUniverseAndEverything (DenyAll)
teller could not call freeForAll (PermitAll)
---------------------------------------------
User: joe, Roles: customer
---------------------------------------------
joe could not call calculateFutureValue (requires 'teller')
joe could not call calculateTotalInterest (requires 'bank-manager' or
   'teller')
joe could not call getInterestRate (requires 'bank-manager')
joe could not call getTheAnswerToLifeTheUniverseAndEverything (DenyAll)
joe could not call freeForAll (PermitAll)
```

If you study the output carefully, you'll notice that some of the results are incorrect. Unfortunately, bugs in the beta version of JBoss 5 prevented us from seeing the correct output. We hope these will be fixed by the GA release.

We don't have any annotations to define authentication because we don't have different challenge-response strategies for authenticating EJB clients like we did for web clients.

There's some debate on whether security annotations should be used, or whether security configuration is better kept in configuration files because security roles may change. Our experience is that it's generally safe to define security in annotations. Security roles are logical and shouldn't change dynamically in a production system. If you need to change security roles, you'll likely want to do it as part of a full release cycle that includes running all your acceptance tests. At that point, it doesn't matter if the information is kept in deployment descriptors or in annotations. That being said, you may have environment or process constraints that force you to keep security information in deployment descriptors, so let's explore how to use them to configure security.

7.8.2 Securing EJBs via configuration

If you want to define security declaratively, you can do so in the EJB deployment descriptors: META-INF/ejb-jar.xml and META-INF/jboss.xml. You can also use the deployment descriptors to override security settings made in annotations. You can define the security domain for the entire application by using the following in the META-INF/jboss.xml file:

```
<jboss>
  <security-domain>greeterDomain</security-domain>
</jboss>
```

You can define the method-level security in your application's META-INF/ejb-jar.xml file. Listing 7.23 shows you an example of an XML configuration that adds security constraints equivalent to those specified using annotations in listing 7.22.

Listing 7.23 Security constraints defined with XML configuration

```
<ejb-jar xmlns="http://java.sun.com/xml/ns/javaee"
      xmlns:xsi="http://www.w3.org/2001/XMLSchema-instance"
      xsi:schemaLocation="http://java.sun.com/xml/ns/javaee
                   http://java.sun.com/xml/ns/javaee/ejb-jar_3_0.xsd"
      version="3.0">
  <assembly-descriptor>
    <security-role>
      <role-name>texan</role-name>
    </security-role>
    <method-permission>
      <role-name>texan</role-name>
      <method>
        <ejb-name>TexanGreeter</ejb-name>
        <method-name>sayHello</method-name>
      </method>
    </method-permission>
    <method-permission>
      <unchecked/>
      <method>
        <ejb-name>TexanGreeter</ejb-name>
        <method-name>getName</method-name>
      </method>
    </method-permission>
    <exclude-list>
      <method>
        <ejb-name>TexanGreeter</ejb-name>
        <method-name>canGreet</method-name>
      </method>
    </exclude-list>
  </assembly-descriptor>
</ejb-jar>
```

Here, you apply the same security conditions that you did in the example code with annotations in the previous section. The `method-permission` block contains `role-name` elements that specify the roles that can access the methods defined in the method block. You also use the `unchecked` attribute to get the same behavior as the `@PermitAll` annotation. And if you want to exclude a method from any access (like `@DenyAll`), you use the `exclude-list` block instead of defining a `method-permission` block.

7.8.3 Nonintegrated security

A nonintegrated client trying to access the EJB container from outside of the application server must pass security credentials to the server. Nonintegrated clients include any out-of-process applications, out-of-process web containers, or code running in other application server instances. The dynamic proxy that the client obtains from the server is responsible for propagating the principal and credential information to the server. The EJB container has a security interceptor that takes the security credentials and forwards them to the appropriate security domain to handle authentication and authorization.

The Java EE specification says that a nonintegrated client must be able to log in using JAAS, as shown in listing 7.24.

Listing 7.24 Specifying EJB security credentials using a JAAS callback handler

```
import javax.security.auth.login.LoginContext;
import javax.security.auth.callback.CallbackHandler;
import org.jboss.security.auth.callback.SecurityAssociationHandler;
...
SecurityAssociationHandler handler = new SecurityAssociationHandler();     ❶
SimplePrincipal user = new SimplePrincipal("javid");
handler.setSecurityInfo(user, "test".toCharArray());     ❹
LoginContext loginContext =
  new LoginContext("myClientDomain",
            (CallbackHandler) handler);     ❸
loginContext.login();     ❷
InitialContext ctx = new InitialContext();
CalculatorRemote calculator = (CalculatorRemote)
                ctx.lookup("calculator/StatelessCalculatorBean/remote");
```

Here you do a standard JAAS login using a JBoss implementation of the JAAS `CallbackHandler` interface called `SecurityAssociationHandler` ❶. When the `LoginContext.login()` method is called ❷, it calls the handler to get the username and password. The handler is passed in as the second parameter to the `LoginContext` constructor ❸. The principal and the password are passed in to the handler using the `setSecurityInfo()` method ❹.

NOTE If you want your client code to be completely free of all JBoss dependencies, you can write your own implementation of `CallbackHandler`. This is rather easy; see the references for a link to an article that shows you how.

JAAS requires that you define a login module for the client to use. JBoss provides a client login module called `org.jboss.security.ClientLoginModule`. To define a JAAS login module, you create a properties file (for example, named auth.conf) that looks like the following:

```
myClientDomain {
    org.jboss.security.ClientLoginModule required;
};
```

The first word in the file, `myClientDomain`, is the name of the login module (also called a *domain* in JAAS). The client code knows which domain to use because the `LoginContext` constructor takes the domain name as its first argument.

For the client to to access the properties file, you must set the `java.security.auth.login.config` system property. You pass this in as a JVM parameter, as follows:

```
java -Djava.security.auth.login.config=auth.conf MyProgram
```

You've seen how to propagate security credentials from the client to server to authenticate and authorize the client. Now, let's see how you can enable secure communication for EJB communication.

7.8.4 Securing EJB communication

Many web-based applications enable encryption on the web tier and only allow access to EJBs and other middle-tier components through the web tier. Because the communication between the web tier and the EJB tier usually happens behind a firewall, it's often unnecessary to communicate with EJBs using an encrypted protocol. But, if you're running a standalone client (such as a GUI application), it may call EJBs directly. In this case, you may choose to encrypt communication to your EJBs.

To set up secure EJB communication over SSL, you need to do the following:

1. Create a server certificate inside of a keystore.
2. Export the server certificate.
3. Import the server certificate into a client truststore.
4. Configure a connector to support SSL.
5. Point the server to the server keystore.
6. Point the client to the client truststore.

We talked about the first three steps in chapter 4. To recap, these steps go something like this:

```
1  keytool -genkey -alias serverCertificate -keyalg RSA -validity 1500
   ➥   -keystore server.keystore -keypass serverpass -storepass serverpass

2  keytool -export -alias serverCertificate -keystore server.keystore
   ➥   -storepass serverpass -file server.cer

3  keytool -import -alias serverCertificate -keystore client.truststore
   ➥   -storepass clientpass -file server.cer
```

The fourth step builds on what you learned about configuring the server invoker in section 7.7. You have to define a new JBoss Remoting connector and point your EJBs to it. You do this by creating a new *-service.xml file in the server/xxx/deploy directory as shown in listing 7.25.

Listing 7.25 Creating a connector that points to an SSL-aware server socket factory

```
<?xml version="1.0" encoding="UTF-8"?>
<server>
  <mbean code="org.jboss.remoting.transport.Connector"

   name="jboss.remoting:type=Connector,transport=sslsocket3843,
➥    handler=ejb3">
```

```
    <attribute name="InvokerLocator">
      sslsocket://${jboss.bind.address}:3843                    ❶
    </attribute>
    <attribute name="Configuration">
      <config>
        <handlers>
          <handler subsystem="AOP">
            org.jboss.aspects.remoting.AOPRemotingInvocationHandler    ❷
          </handler>
        </handlers>
      </config>
    </attribute>
  </mbean>
</server>
```

You configure the invoker with an `InvokerLocator` attribute ❶, which defines the URL that the invoker binds to. Note that the protocol is `sslsocket` and the port is `3843`. The address is set to a variable populated with the bind address set with the `-b` option when you start JBoss. An invocation handler ❷ is defined using an aspect-oriented programming (AOP)–based handler called `AOPRemotingInvocationHandler`. This handler obviates the need to explicitly point the connector to the unified invoker.

Your EJB must point to the SSL invoker. We talked about how to bind an EJB to an invoker using XML configuration earlier in the chapter. With EJB3, you can also bind your beans to an invoker using annotations. Listing 7.26 shows you an example.

Listing 7.26 Binding EJB to invoker using annotations

```
import javax.ejb.Stateless;
import org.jboss.ejb3.annotation.RemoteBinding;
import org.jboss.ejb3.annotation.RemoteBindings;

@RemoteBindings({
   @RemoteBinding(clientBindUrl = "sslsocket://127.0.0.1:3843",     ❶
            jndiBinding="StatelessSSL")
   })
@Stateless
public class GreeterBean implements Greeter {
  ...
}
```

An EJB can be bound to multiple invokers using the `@RemoteBindings` ❶ annotation, which contains one or more `@RemoteBinding` annotations. Each `@RemoteBinding` annotation defines a `clientBindUrl` attribute set to point to the `InvokerLocator` URL you defined in the connector MBean. The annotation also contains a `jndiBinding` attribute that defines the JNDI name you use to look up the bean proxy that will access the invoker. Your client application looks up the bean as follows:

```
Greeter greeter = (Greeter) ctx.lookup("StatelessSSL");
```

The `jndiBinding` attribute is optional because you can look up a bean by its default name, as we discussed earlier in the chapter. That's all the code you need; all that's left is to start your server and run your client. Start your server with the following JVM arguments:

```
./run.sh -Djavax.net.ssl.keyStore=/path/to/server.keystore
➥       -Djavax.net.ssl.keyStorePassword=serverpass -c enterprise
```

The javax.net.ssl.keyStore argument should point to the path where your server keystore exists, and the javax.net.ssl.keyStorePassword should contain the password for your server keystore.

Last, you must point your client code to the truststore using the following arguments:

```
java -Djavax.net.ssl.trustStrore=/path/to/client.truststore
➥    -Djavax.net.ssl.trustStorePassword=clientpass com.manning.jbia.Client
```

After downloading the remote proxy that points to the SSL invoker, the client can send requests to the server over SSL.

7.9 Summary

We started the chapter by giving you background on enterprise Java components and packaging. We talked about how session beans work in JBoss AS through the use of dynamic proxies. We then talked about Hibernate and JPA, giving you background on how the persistence and business side of enterprise Java fit into the JBoss world. We wrapped up the discussion by introducing you to the package structure for an enterprise application.

We walked you through how to build an enterprise application where a client could send greeting messages from a client to a server where they were persisted. The client could then load the messages, allowing you to see how session EJBs and persistent entities are built, packaged, deployed, and called in JBoss AS.

Next, we took a look at how to configure EJB applications and the application server. We talked about where all the configuration files reside and what's contained in each. For EJB applications, we looked at the standard ejb-jar.xml and persistence.xml files, as well as the proprietary jboss.xml file. For the server, we gave you an overview of the various services that are used for EJBs and showed you where to find them.

After laying a foundation for how to configure EJB applications and the various EJB containers and services, we took a closer look at session beans. You learned how to configure the JNDI bindings for the beans using both annotations and configuration files. You also learned how JBoss binds session beans into JNDI and how to load them from a client application. Then, we looked at the various EJB container configurations, and you learned how to configure session-bean pool sizes and bean passivation timeouts.

After talking about session beans, we talked about entity beans. Most of the configuration for entity persistence is done through annotations and is part of the standard specification, but you learned how to inject Hibernate objects into entities and how to deploy Hibernate mapping files that could be accessed and used as JPA entities.

Next, we talked about JMX service objects, which significantly simplify the ability to deploy MBean services in JBoss AS. You created a simple calculator management service object and injected it into a calculator EJB. You also learned how to access the MBean without injection.

After learning about service objects, you learned how to configure the transport protocol. We gave you an overview of how the transport protocols are configured for an application. Then, we showed you how you could change the configuration in your application or in the global deployment descriptor by changing the existing socket-based configuration to support RMI calls.

Last but not least, we talked about EJB security. We showed you how EJB method access could be restricted to only certain roles on the server. We also showed you how nonlocal client applications could pass security credentials to the EJB server using the `SecurityAssociation` class, JAAS, or a JNDI initial context factory. We then talked about secure EJB communication by showing you how to configure the EJB connector to support SSL.

7.10 References

Interceptor chains—http://labs.jboss.com/jbossas/docs. At the time of writing this entry, chapter 11 of the JBoss AS 5.0.0 Configuration Guide discusses customizing interceptor chains in the standardjboss. xml file.

JBoss Remoting documentation—http://labs.jboss.com/jbossremoting/docs/index.html

UnifiedInvoker guide—http://docs.jboss.org/jbossas/unified_invoker/UnifiedInvoker_guide.html

Customizing EJB security in JBoss—http://www.javaworld.com/javaworld/jw-02-2002/jw-0215-ejbsecurity. html. Although this article references previous versions of EJB technology, you can accomplish context-based security in much the same way using EJB3 interceptors.

JPA specification—http://jcp.org/aboutJava/communityprocess/final/jsr220/index.html

Invoking EJBs through SSL—http://labs.jboss.com/jbossejb3/docs/tutorial/ssl/ssl.html

Writing your own CallbackHandler to handle JAAS security for a standalone client–http://jaikiran.wordpress.com/category/jaas/

8 JBoss Messaging

This chapter covers

- Understanding messaging systems
- Developing a simple JMS client
- Using message-driven beans (MDB)
- Using message-driven POJOs
- Configuring JBoss Messaging

The previous chapters covered many examples of different types of applications that are deployed to the application server. All the applications have one thing in common—they all use synchronous communications mechanisms to interact with each other. In many cases, this is exactly what you want. For example, it makes no sense to reply to a customer query about how many items are in inventory until the inventory EJB has returned that information.

Sometimes you might prefer to communicate asynchronously with another application or with a component within the same application. For example, standard accounting business practices might require that a log is maintained of certain transactions. You might prefer that the log be written asynchronously so that you don't hold up the transaction from completing. But you still want a guarantee that the log entry is made. Messaging systems evolved to solve this kind of problem.

In this chapter, we cover the messaging system that comes with JBoss AS 5.0, JBoss Messaging. The JBoss team developed JBoss Messaging from the ground up to provide a high-performance and highly scalable messaging server. It replaces the JBossMQ messaging server that came with earlier versions of JBoss AS. We don't cover JBossMQ in this chapter, although many of the concepts and applications presented work with it also.

This chapter starts with an overview of messaging systems in general, and the Java Message Service (JMS) in particular. We then present a simple messaging client and follow that with an example EJB message-driven bean. After that we go into the architecture and configuration of JBoss Messaging. All the JBoss Messaging–specific information is located together in the second half of this chapter. If you're already familiar with JMS, you can skip ahead to section 8.1.4. If you're an administrator or a developer interested in configuring JBoss Messaging, you can skip to section 8.5

8.1 Understanding messaging systems

Messaging systems have been around for some time. Many of the larger systems vendors have provided messaging-oriented middleware (MOM) for many years, such as IBM's MQSeries. With the advent of the Java programming language, many of these MOM vendors started to provide APIs that enabled Java applications to participate in the exchange of messages. Unfortunately, every vendor had a different API, which defeated the whole write-once-run-anywhere paradigm; and so, the Java Specification Request 914 (JSR-914) expert group—led by Sun Microsystems—was formed to define a standard API for messaging, the JMS API.

Initially, the expert group imagined that JSR-914 would be used to access existing MOMs. In this way, it was akin to the Java Database Connectivity (JDBC) API, which provides an API to access relational databases. But as the Java platform matured and provided increased reliability, scalability, and performance, messaging systems built entirely in Java emerged. JBoss Messaging is one of these new-generation, pure-Java messaging systems.

The JSR-914 expert group faced two challenges—the existing MOMs used two different architectures and supported two different messaging models. The next sections examine these architectures and models.

8.1.1 Understanding messaging system architectures

As illustrated in figure 8.1, two basic architectures are used for a MOM: centralized and decentralized.

The centralized architecture uses a centralized server to which all messaging clients connect. The clients send messages to the centralized server, which is responsible for delivering the messages to the proper recipients. The use of a centralized architecture doesn't preclude clustering the server so that multiple servers share the responsibility of routing the messages—often necessary as the system outgrows the capacity of a single server. In such a case, the cluster is thought of as a centralized server.

The decentralized architecture delegates the responsibility of message handling to the clients. The client messaging components communicate with each other to pass

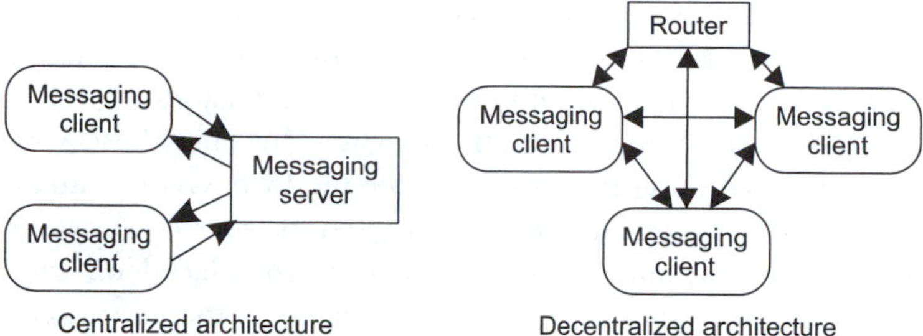

Figure 8.1 There are two message system architectures: the centralized architecture and the decentralized architecture.

messages. In some cases, a router using multicast facilitates this communication. In other cases, the client messaging component communicates directly to other client messaging components.

There are pros and cons to both architectures. With a centralized architecture, you can run the messaging server on a high-powered server with fast disks to handle the storing of messages in a database. On the other hand, every message makes at least two network hops to get to its recipient—first to the server and finally to the recipient. With a decentralized architecture, messages can go directly from originator to recipient and, when using multicast, to multiple recipients simultaneously. On the negative side, each client must run on a higher-end computer because each client computer is now charged with handling and storing messages.

8.1.2 Understanding the messaging models

There are two messaging models supported by JSR-914: *point-to-point* and *publish-and-subscribe*. With point-to-point messaging, a *sender* places messages in a *queue*, and from there, it's delivered to one *receiver*. Several senders can place messages on the same queue, and multiple receivers can receive them, but an individual message is delivered to only one receiver. Having multiple receivers is a benefit in a high-volume situation because the workload of handling the messages can be distributed among the receivers. Point-to-point messaging is illustrated in figure 8.2.

Figure 8.2 With point-to-point messaging, each message sent by a sender is placed into a queue and then handled by one—and only one—receiver.

With publish-and-subscribe messaging, a *publisher* places messages in a *topic*. Every *subscriber* registered to receive messages on that topic receives a copy of the message. Publish-and-subscribe messaging is illustrated in figure 8.3.

Figure 8.3 With publish-and-subscribe messaging, each message is placed into a topic and read by all subscribers.

The two models come in handy in different scenarios. In the earlier example of maintaining a transaction log, the point-to-point model fits best. Every EJB processing orders places transaction information on the audit queue. An auditing receiver reads those messages and logs the transactions. If the system becomes busy, you can run multiple instances of the auditing receiver to handle the load. Or you can decide not to run the auditing receiver until the load on the system goes down; you can then restart the auditing receiver, and it receives all messages placed on the auditing queue. The messaging server places messages in permanent storage (typically a database), holding them until the receiver is ready.

The publish-and-subscribe model comes in handy in many business-to-business cases where one business, the publisher, wants to make some information available to all its business partners, the subscribers.

8.1.3 Understanding the JMS API

The JMS API doesn't impact your choice of using a centralized or decentralized architecture for your MOM. Figure 8.4 illustrates the relationships among the various interfaces in the JMS API. All of these interfaces are in the `javax.jms` package.

You can infer the general algorithm for working with messages from the figure. For example, to receive messages, you do the following:

1. Locate a `ConnectionFactory`, typically using JNDI.
2. Use the `ConnectionFactory` to create a `Connection`.
3. Use the `Connection` to create a `Session`.
4. Locate a `Destination`, typically using JNDI.
5. Use the `Session` to create a `MessageConsumer` for that `Destination`.

Once you've done this, methods on the `MessageConsumer` enable you to either query the `Destination` for messages or to register for message notification.

Although it's not shown in the figure, each interface has both point-to-point and publish-and-subscribe interfaces that extend it. For example, the `QueueSession` interface and the `TopicSession` interface extend the `Session` interface. In addition, there are XA variations used to support messaging in a distributed transaction environment.

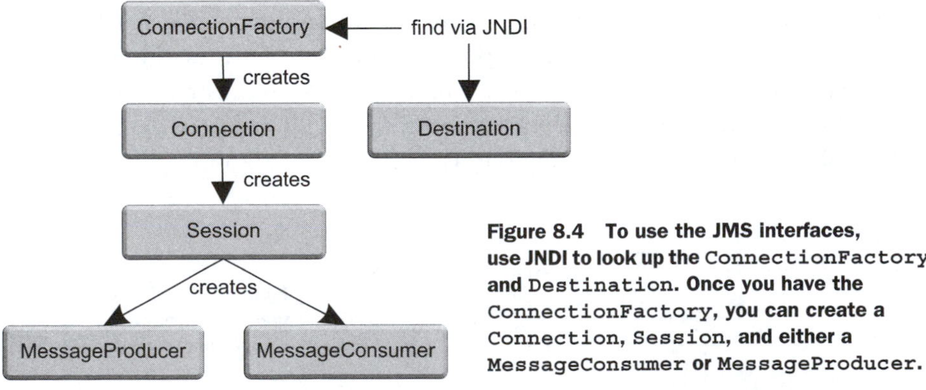

Figure 8.4 To use the JMS interfaces, use JNDI to look up the `ConnectionFactory` and `Destination`. Once you have the `ConnectionFactory`, you can create a `Connection`, `Session`, and either a `MessageConsumer` or `MessageProducer`.

These steps use the unified API introduced with the JMS 1.1 specification. This API enables the application to be agnostic in regards to working with topics or queues. If you use the various topic and queue-specific subclasses but later decide to change from using a queue to using a topic (for example), then you also have to change your code. If you use the unified API, you can easily change from using a queue to using a topic (for example) without having to change your code.

UNDERSTANDING MESSAGES

You've probably noticed that we've not yet defined what a message is—an important topic, considering that this chapter is about messaging. Although you probably already know this, a message is some data. What you want to know is: What kind of data can you send in a message? And that's the question we answer in this section.

Header	Properties	Payload

Figure 8.5 A message consists of three data areas: a header, a set of properties, and the payload.

Figure 8.5 shows the anatomy of a message, which consists of a header, properties, and a payload that contains the message data.

The header area contains a set of properties, which are required by the JMS specification and consist of values such as a unique message id, `JMSMessageId`, and the timestamp of when the message was sent, `JMSTimestamp`. Getters and setters are provided on the `javax.jms.Message` interface to access these values. We don't go into detail on the header properties and the data they provide; you can read more about them in the JMS specification.

The properties area can contain several categories of properties, as described in table 8.1. The `Message` interface provides methods to get and set the properties of a message. In addition, a message receiver or subscriber can define a message selector based on message properties so that it receives only those messages that match a certain criteria—much like using a `WHERE` clause in an SQL statement to access specific data in a database. Although you can transmit an entire message using only properties and no payload, you should place the message into the payload area and use the properties only for data that you might want to use to select messages.

Table 8.1 Message property categories

Property category	Description
JMS-defined	Optional properties described in the JMS specification. The names of these properties all begin with the string *JMSX*. Of the optional properties, JBoss Messaging provides only the `JMSXDeliveryCount` property, which identifies how many times the server attempted to deliver the message.
Vendor-specific	Properties provided by the messaging service vendor. The names of these properties all begin with the string *JMS_*, followed by the vendor name. JBoss Messaging doesn't have any vendor-specific properties.
Application	Properties provided by the client sending the message.

The payload area contains the message data. JMS defines a number of different payload types, each of which is handled by an interface. These interfaces are described in table 8.2.

Table 8.2 Message payload interfaces

Payload interface	Description
`Message`	Used for a message without any payload. This interface defines the setters and getters for the header data and properties. The other interfaces in the table extend the `Message` interface.
`BytesMessage`	Used to send an array of uninterpreted bytes. This interface is provided to support communication with external messaging systems.
`MapMessage`	Used to send a message as a set of name/value pairs. The names are strings, and the values can be any primitive type or a string.
`ObjectMessage`	Used to send a serializable Java object. The recipient must have the class for the object and all of its required supporting classes in its class path.
`StreamMessage`	Used to send a stream of Java primitives and strings.
`TextMessage`	Used to send a text string.

Now that you have an overview of JMS, let's look at how the messaging specification is implemented by JBoss Messaging.

8.1.4 Understanding the JBoss Messaging architecture

The JBoss Messaging architecture is illustrated in figure 8.6. It consists of components that reside on the server and in the client. These components work together to provide a reliable and scalable messaging system.

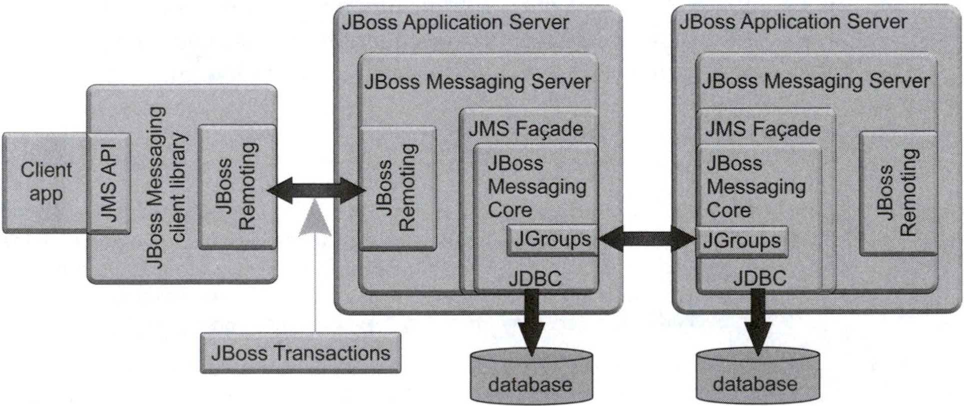

Figure 8.6 The JBoss Messaging architecture makes use of JGroups to provide a distributed, highly available messaging server. It also uses JBoss Remoting to provide an efficient transport mechanism between the client and the server.

The *JBoss Messaging Core* provides a generic messaging service that supports JMS and can be easily extended to support other types of messaging. The Core is a distributed and reliable message transport system based on JGroups. Because the Core is distributed, there's no single point of failure when multiple servers are in use. The Core uses a pluggable persistence manager to persist messages. It comes with a JDBC persistence manager, but you can provide other persistence managers to store messages in other data stores such as file-based or memory-based data stores. All messages are stored in the database as binary large objects (BLOBs); therefore, you should use a database that handles BLOBs efficiently.

In the diagram, each Core has its own database, but multiple Cores can also share a single database. *JBoss Transactions* provides two-phase commit capabilities among multiple messaging servers. The *JMS Façade* makes the Core into a JMS provider. You can provide other façades to implement other messaging systems.

The JBoss Messaging client library provides a single JAR file containing all the necessary libraries, including the JMS API used by the client application to communicate with the messaging service. *JBoss Remoting* provides the communication mechanism between the client and the server. JBoss Remoting is ideal for this task because it uses pluggable transports and data marshallers. Current transports include TCP/IP, HTTP, and a bidirectional socket transport similar to the UIL2 transport provided by JBossMQ.

8.2 Developing a JMS application

We introduce the example messaging client by describing the business problem that it solves. The Sofa Spuds video store provides a video notification service to its customers. When a new video comes in or a rental video is returned, Sofa Spuds places a message on a topic that can be subscribed to by its customers. Each customer is then notified of the new video and can react to it. The example application is a simple publish-and-subscribe client that uses the command line to govern its behavior.

8.2.1 Coding the example application

You need to write both a publisher and a subscriber, and both need to access the same topics, one to notify the customers of new videos and the other to send the customers' requests to the store. A message can identify a dynamic queue on which the receiver can reply to a message, simplifying the process; but there's a method to our madness, and you must wait until we cover message-driven beans in section 8.3 to find out why.

Figure 8.7 provides a diagram showing the interactions between the classes involved in the application. Note that the messages passed between the `Customer` and `Store` objects contain a `Video` object.

We describe the `Video` class first, then the `Store`, and finally the `Customer` class.

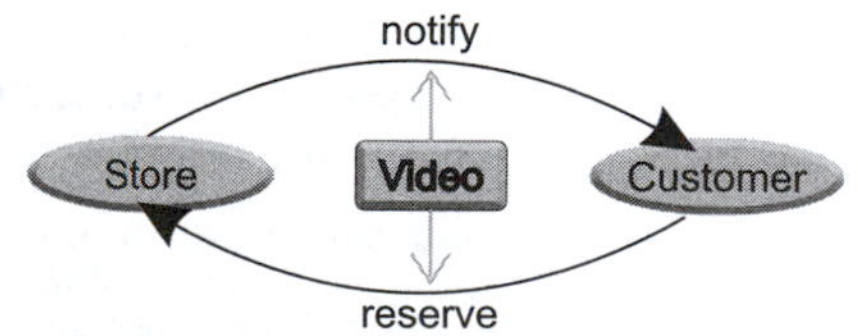

Figure 8.7 The JMS example application consists of three objects: `Store` and `Customer` objects, which pass messages containing a `Video` object between them.

CODING THE VIDEO JAVABEAN

The Video class, shown in listing 8.1, is a simple JavaBean passed in a message between the Store and Customer classes. It contains the name of the movie, its genre, and a toString method that both the Store and Customer classes will find handy.

Listing 8.1 Video.java

```
package org.jbia.jms.sofaspuds;
public class Video implements java.io.Serializable {
  private String name;
  private String genre;
  <<getters and setters>>
  @Override public String toString() {
    return name + " [" + genre + "]";
  }
}
```

Note that we omitted the code for the getters and setters; you should be able to provide those.

CODING THE STORE CLASS

The Store class goes into a loop asking for new video information and sending it to the customers via the *notification* topic. In addition, it's notified of customers' requests for videos via the *reservation request* topic. The class is long, so we present it in sections, preceding each section with a description of the purpose of the code.

The Store class implements the MessageListener interface so that it can receive asynchronous reservation requests from the customers, freeing the class from having to constantly poll the topic for such requests. The class sends messages on one thread and receives messages on a separate thread, a process which is controlled by the messaging client component. You have to do more work in the class because it uses two threads, as you'll see later in the code. In addition, you declare an input stream, which is used to get information about the video.

```
package org.jbia.jms.sofaspuds;
import java.io.*;
import javax.jms.*;
import javax.naming.*;
public class Store implements MessageListener {
 private BufferedReader rdr
  = new BufferedReader(new InputStreamReader(System.in));
```

You need only a single connection but require a session for each topic, a producer for one topic, and a consumer for the other. Use two sessions because you publish messages on one thread and receive messages on a separate thread, and each thread requires its own session; you can't access a single session from multiple threads.

```
private Connection connection;
private Session sessionProducer;
private Session sessionConsumer;
private MessageProducer producer;
private MessageConsumer consumer;
```

The run method, the main method in the class, initializes the connection to the messaging server. You have to find the connection factory and the topics; look them up using JNDI. Use a jndi.properties file so that you don't have to provide any properties to locate the initial context. There's nothing unique in the jndi.properties file, so we don't list it here; you can see one in the appendix. Once you have the initial context, you can look up the three objects by name. For now, use the topics `topic/testTopic` and `topic/testDurableTopic` that are provided by the messaging service. (You might have to get these topics from the JBoss Messaging source download; they might not be provided with JBoss AS. Look for the `destinations-service.xml` file.) Later, in section 8.5.4, we show you how to declare and use your own topics and queues.

```
private void run() throws Exception {
 try {
  Context initial = new InitialContext();
  ConnectionFactory cf =
   (ConnectionFactory)initial.lookup("ConnectionFactory");
  Destination notify =
   (Destination)initial.lookup("topic/testTopic");
  Destination request =
   (Destination)initial.lookup("topic/testDurableTopic");
```

Now that you have the connection factory, you create the connection and, from there, the producer and consumer. You're not using transactions (the `false` parameter to `createSession`), and you want the messaging client component to automatically acknowledge that it received the message (`Session.AUTO_ACKNOWLEDGE` parameter). The latter means that you don't have to acknowledge that you received the messages; accepting the message implies receipt acknowledgement. Recall that the messaging service guarantees delivery of messages; like signing for a package delivered by FedEx, the message receiver must sign that it received the message. With auto acknowledge, that signing is taken care of for you.

```
  connection = cf.createConnection();
  sessionProducer = connection.createSession(false,
   Session.AUTO_ACKNOWLEDGE);
  sessionConsumer = connection.createSession(false,
   Session.AUTO_ACKNOWLEDGE);
```

You now create the producer and consumer. Each is created from its own session to handle the issue with running multiple threads that we mentioned earlier.

```
  producer = sessionProducer.createProducer(notify);
  consumer = sessionConsumer.createConsumer(request);
```

Then establish the message listener, which receives the video reservations requests from customers, and notify the messaging service that the class is ready to work with messages. No messages are delivered until the `start` method is called.

```
  consumer.setMessageListener(this);
  connection.start();
```

The run method goes into a loop where it calls the `notifyOfVideo` method, which gets information about a video and then publishes the information. You'll see that shortly. There's a 10-second delay between loop iterations so that, when a customer responds that she wants to reserve a video, the reservation notice doesn't appear in the middle of the request for the information about the next video. Although this isn't necessary, it does make the output look cleaner when we capture the output to include in the next section.

```
while (notifyOfVideos()) {
 Thread.currentThread().sleep(10 * 1000);
}
```

Finally, any exceptions are handled by printing them out (not recommended for a production program but suitable for a simple example). And the connection is closed before the method exits. By closing the connection, the messaging client component detaches the client from both topics and removes the listener from the topic to which the code subscribed. Once the `close` method completes, the client can no longer send or receive messages.

```
} catch (Exception e) {
 e.printStackTrace();
} finally {
 if (connection != null) connection.close();
}
}
```

The first few lines of the `notifyOfVideos` method ask the user for the information about the video. If any of the information is blank, the method exits, causing the program to also exit.

```
private boolean notifyOfVideos() throws Exception {
 System.out.println("Supply info for new video:");
 System.out.print("Name: ");
 String name = rdr.readLine();
 System.out.print("Genre: ");
 String genre = rdr.readLine();
 if (name.length() == 0 || genre.length() == 0) {return false;}
```

The information gathered about the video is used to initialize the `Video` object, which is packaged into an object message and published to the notification topic. Any customers listening to the notification topic are informed of the video. The method returns `true` so that the loop in the `run` method repeats.

```
 Video video = new Video();
 video.setName(name);
 video.setGenre(genre);
 ObjectMessage om = sessionProducer.createObjectMessage(video);
 producer.send(om);
 return true;
}
```

The `onMessage` method is called when a message is placed in the topic to which the code is subscribed (in this case, the reservation request topic). The message is passed in and converted to an `ObjectMessage`, after which the `Video` object is extracted. The customer name is obtained from the message properties, and information about the reservation request is printed to the console. The `onMessage` method, because of how it's defined by the `MessageListener` interface, can't throw any exceptions, so it catches all exceptions and reports them on the command line.

```
public void onMessage(Message msg) {
 try {
  ObjectMessage om = (ObjectMessage)msg;
  Video video = (Video)om.getObject();
  String customer = om.getStringProperty("SpudsCustomer");
  System.out.println("Reservation request:");
  System.out.println("\tcustomer: " + customer);
  System.out.println("\tvideo   : " + video);
 } catch (JMSException e) {
  e.printStackTrace();
 }
}
```

The last method in the `Store` class, the `main` method, creates an instance of the class and calls the `run` method.

```
 public static void main(String[] args) throws Exception {
  new Store().run();
 }
}
```

That completes the `Store` class. Only one class is left in the example: the `Customer` class.

CODING THE CUSTOMER CLASS

The `Customer` class is also long, but it repeats much of the code already presented in the `Store` class, specifically the code that established the messaging connection. Although we could refactor the code to remove the redundancy, that would make the example more complicated. Besides, practice makes perfect, right?

The `Customer` class opens the video notification topic and waits for a message. Once a message is received, it asks the user if he would like to reserve the video; if so, it replies on the reservation request topic. The code is long, so we again present it in sections—although we don't repeat the descriptions of the message connection code because we covered that in the description of the `Store` class.

The first part of the class is the same as for the `Store` class but with two small differences. First, the class doesn't implement the `MessageListener` interface because its algorithm is simpler; it merely waits on one topic and replies on the other. Second, because the class doesn't implement the `MessageListener` interface, it doesn't need two sessions; one is sufficient.

```
package org.jbia.jms.sofaspuds;
import java.io.*;
import javax.jms.*;
import javax.naming.*;
public class Customer {
 private BufferedReader rdr =
```

```
    new BufferedReader(new InputStreamReader(System.in));
  private Connection connection;
  private Session session;
  private MessageProducer producer;
  private MessageConsumer consumer;
```

The first part of the run method is much the same as for the Store class but with three differences. First, only one session is created. Second, the producer and consumer are switched because the Customer class listens for video notifications and sends reservation requests, the opposite of the Store class. Third, the loop to listen for messages is infinite and doesn't pause between messages. The code repeatedly waits for the next message; the only way out is to Ctrl-C the program (definitely not production quality but sufficient for a simple example).

```
private void run(String customer) throws Exception {
  try {
   Context initial = new InitialContext();
   ConnectionFactory cf =
    (ConnectionFactory)initial.lookup("ConnectionFactory");
   Destination notify =
    (Destination)initial.lookup("topic/testTopic");
   Destination request =
    (Destination)initial.lookup("topic/testDurableTopic");
   connection = cf.createConnection();
   connection.setClientID(customer);
   session = connection.createSession(false,
     Session.AUTO_ACKNOWLEDGE);
   producer = session.createProducer(request);
   consumer = session.createConsumer(notify);
   connection.start();
   for (;;) {listen(customer);}
  } catch (Exception e) {
   e.printStackTrace();
  } finally {
   if (connection != null) connection.close();
  }
 }
```

The listen method waits for a video notification message to come in on the consumer destination. Once the message comes in, it extracts the Video object out of the message, prints the information about the video, and asks the user if he would like to reserve the video. If so, a response message is sent back to the store. The Video object is wrapped within an ObjectMessage wrapper and sent to the destination producer established earlier in the run method. Also, the customer name is added to the properties of the message. The name used for the property must be a valid Java name; a name such as *spuds.customer* isn't allowed. The property names can be used in message selector statements—hence, the reason that they must be valid identifiers.

```
public void listen(String customer) throws Exception {
 ObjectMessage om = (ObjectMessage)consumer.receive();
 Video video = (Video)om.getObject();
 System.out.println("New video available: " + video);
```

```
    System.out.print("Reserve a copy? ");
    String input = rdr.readLine();
    if (input.equalsIgnoreCase("y")) {
     om = session.createObjectMessage(video);
     om.setStringProperty("SpudsCustomer", customer);
     producer.send(om);
    }
   }
```

Finally, the main method verifies that the program was started with a customer name as a parameter. If not, it displays a usage message. If a customer name was given, it runs the program.

```
   public static void main(String[] args) throws Exception {
     if (args.length == 0) {
       System.out.println("usage: Customer <name>");
     } else {
       new Customer().run(args[0]);
     }
   }
 }
```

In the text, we coded the three classes that we presented in the diagram at the start of this section. Now let's look at how to package and run them.

8.2.2 Packaging and running the example application

Packaging the code is simple: compile the classes and place them into a JAR file. When compiling, make sure that the jbossall-client.jar file is in the class path. The examples of running the code assume that the resulting JAR file is named sofaspuds.jar and is in the current directory. Figure 8.8 illustrates the contents of the sofaspuds.jar file.

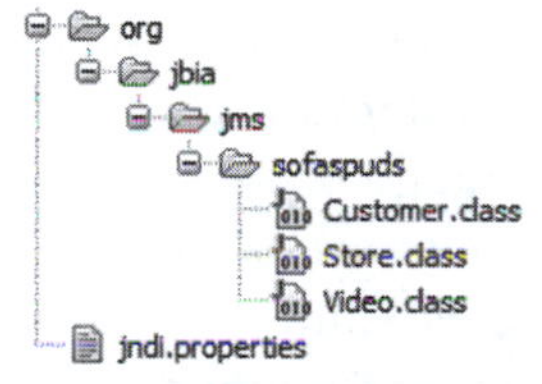

Figure 8.8 The contents of the sofaspuds.jar file consists of the three classes that make up the example application and the JNDI properties file used to access JNDI.

Before you start any of the clients, make sure that the application server is running. Because JBoss Messaging is one of the services provided automatically by the application server and because we used some predefined topics that come with JBoss Messaging, there's no need to do any other configuration or preparation.

Now that the application server is running, you start the clients. Start the customers first so that they can be notified immediately of any available videos. Open two command windows to run two customers, Natalie and Xavier, and a third command window to run the store. Once the store program starts, it asks you to enter the data for a video. Provide the requested data, and both Xavier and Natalie should be notified of the video and asked whether they want to reserve it. Respond with *n* for Xavier and *y* for Natalie. The store window should reflect the reservation request. Figure 8.9 shows screen captures that match this scenario.

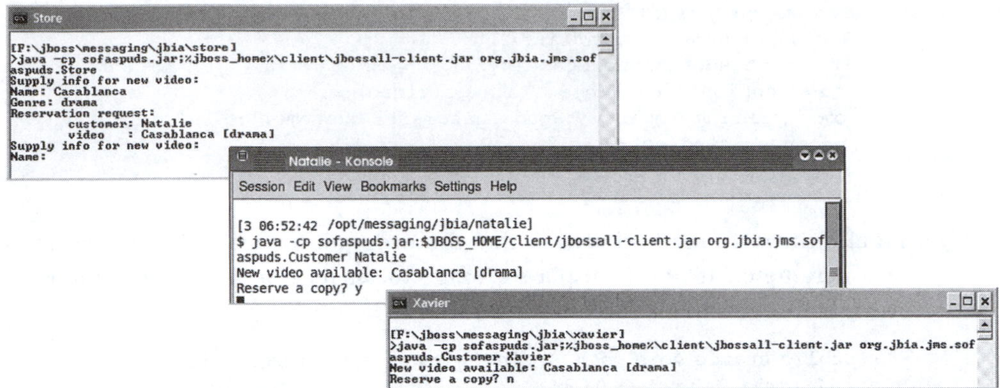

Figure 8.9 Here you see the results of running the example messaging application. The store notifies the customers that *Casablanca* is available for rental. Natalie wants to reserve a copy. Xavier doesn't. Notice that the store is notified of Natalie's request.

Now that you have the messaging clients running, let's expand the example to include a message-driven bean (MDB), and look at how to configure an MDB.

8.3 Using message-driven beans

Session EJBs can easily participate as message producers but aren't particularly suited for acting as message consumers. There are several reasons why. First, consumers typically wait for messages to arrive, and waiting on a message is something you don't want a session bean to do. You want to release a session bean as soon as possible so that it can go back into a pool. Only so many session beans are allocated in the pool; if all of them are occupied waiting for messages, then no one else can make a request that needs one of those session beans. The session bean can instead use the `receiveNoWait` method of the `MessageConsumer` interface and return immediately whether or not a message is available.

You could have the session bean register to receive notification of messages. Such notifications happen on a separate thread—another bad idea for a session bean because it could find itself processing a client request at the same time it's processing a message. In addition, because the application server creates multiple session beans, which one should register for messages? Or should they all? If only one is registered, what happens if the application server deallocates that one due to reduced request traffic?

For these reasons, the EJB 2.0 specification introduced a new type of EJB, the message-driven bean (MDB). The MDB was designed to be a message consumer. You indicate which queue or topic the MDB should subscribe to, and it processes the messages. From the messaging system point of view, the MDB is another message consumer and isn't treated any differently from other consumers.

We describe the business reason for adding an MDB to the example and show the code for it. We follow that with packaging, deploying and running the updated example, and describing configuration options.

8.3.1 Creating an MDB

Apparently, a top-secret government agency obtained a court order to monitor the videos that Natalie is watching. This agency has developed an MDB that effectively wiretaps the request topic, recording all of Natalie's video requests. We obtained the source code for this MDB, and it appears in listing 8.2.

Listing 8.2 WireTap.java

```
package org.jbia.jms.sofaspuds;
import javax.ejb.*;
import javax.jms.*;
@MessageDriven(activationConfig={                    ❶
  @ActivationConfigProperty
  (propertyName="destinationType",                   ❷
   propertyValue="javax.jms.Topic"),
  @ActivationConfigProperty
  (propertyName="destination",                       ❸
   propertyValue="topic/testDurableTopic"),
  @ActivationConfigProperty
  (propertyName="subscriptionDurability",            ❹
   propertyValue="Durable"),
  @ActivationConfigProperty
  (propertyName="messageSelector",                   ❺
   propertyValue="SpudsCustomer = 'Natalie'")
})
public class WireTap implements MessageListener {    ❻
  public void onMessage(Message msg) {               ❼
    try {
      ObjectMessage objmsg = (ObjectMessage)msg;     ❽
      Video video = (Video)objmsg.getObject();
      System.out.println("Surveillance: perp=" +
        msg.getStringProperty("SpudsCustomer") +     ❾
        ", video=" + video);
    } catch (Exception e) {                          ❿
      e.printStackTrace();
    }
  }
}
```

The @MessageDriven annotation declares this class to be a message-driven bean ❶. The bean takes a series of configuration properties to govern the handling of messages as follow:

- The destinationType property declares the destination to be a topic ❷.
- The destination property declares the JNDI name of the topic ❸.
- A durable subscription is used to access the topic ❹.
- Only reservation requests from Natalia are recorded ❺.

The WireTap class implements the MessageListener interface ❻, which requires the onMessage method ❼. Note that, without the annotation, the class looks like any other class declared as a message listener.

When the MDB receives a message, it extracts the `Video` object from the message ❽. It then prints the surveillance data ❾ to the console. And like the other message listeners we showed you before, the code is wrapped in a try-catch block because the `onMessage` method can't throw an exception ❿.

The example uses a variety of configuration properties, but many more are available to configure MDBs. The following tables describe those configuration properties. Table 8.3 lists the properties defined by the EJB3 specification and provides the default value if that option isn't specified.

Table 8.3 Standard MDB configuration properties

Property	Default	Description
`destinationType`	`javax.jms.Queue`	Identifies the destination as being `javax.jms.Queue` or `javax.jms.Topic`.
`subscriptionDurability`	`NonDurable`	Identifies the subscription to be `Durable` or `NonDurable`.
`acknowledgementMode`	`Auto-acknowledge`	Indicates if the EJB container should automatically acknowledge the message as soon as the MDB receives the message for processing (`Auto-acknowledge`) , or if the EJB container can wait until a later time to acknowledge the message, perhaps batching up acknowledgements for several messages (`Dups-ok-acknowledge`). In the latter case, the MDB must be written to handle possible duplicates, by checking the `JMSXDeliveryCount` message property, because the messaging service could redeliver the message if it doesn't receive acknowledgement from the EJB container in time.
`messageSelector`	`null`	An expression that can be used to filter the messages that are sent to the MDB.

Table 8.4 contains the extended set of properties defined by JBoss AS and provides the default value if that option isn't specified.

Table 8.4 Extended MDB configuration properties

Property	Default	Description
`destination`	`null`	JNDI name for the topic or queue.
`clientId`	`-generated-`	Used to set the `clientId` for the connection. See `javax.jms.Connection.setClientId()` for details.
`subscriptionName`	`-generated-`	The durable subscription name. See `javax.jms.Connection.createDurableConnection-Consumer()`.

Table 8.4 Extended MDB configuration properties *(continued)*

Property	Default	Description
`user`	`null`	The account name used to determine access rights to the destination. See `javax.jms.ConnectionFactory.createConnection()`.
`password`	`null`	The password used to determine access rights to the destination. See `javax.jms.ConnectionFactory.createConnection()`.
`maxMessages`	`1`	The maximum number of messages that can be assigned to a server session at one time. See `javax.jms.Connection.createDurableConnectionConsumer()`.
`minSession`	`1`	The minimum number of MDBs to keep in the pool.
`maxSession`	`15`	The maximum number of MDBs to keep in the pool.
`keepAlive`	`60000`	The amount of time to wait, in milliseconds, before removing an unused MDB from the pool.
`reconnectInterval`	`10000`	The amount of time to wait, in milliseconds, before attempting to reconnect to the messaging server if the messaging server goes away.
`providerAdaptorJNDI`	`java:/DefaultJMSProvider`	JNDI name of the JMS provider adapter that's used to create messaging resources.

Many of the extended configuration properties overwrite the values provided in the server/xxx/conf/standardjboss.xml file. Look for the commented-out <invoker-proxy-binding> tag with the name `message-driven-bean`.

8.3.2 Packaging an MDB

Include both the messaging client JAR file and the EJB3 JAR file in the class path when you compile the MDB. After compiling, place the files in a JAR file, as shown in figure 8.10. Note that we include only the required files and none of the other files, such as `Store.class`, for the example application. Drop this file into the deploy directory, and it's ready to go.

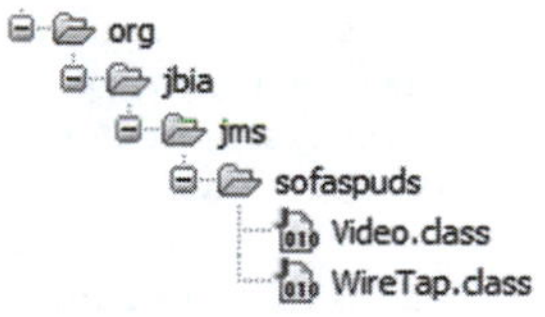

Figure 8.10 The example MDB JAR file contains two classes: the `Video` class (the object passed in the messages) and the `WireTap` class (implements the message-driven EJB).

To try it out, bring up the store and customer clients as you did before in section 8.2.2. You should see that only Natalie's video reservations are noted in the console log.

As with other EJBs, MDBs can be configured using either annotations or a deployment descriptor. The example uses annotations, so let's modify it to use a deployment descriptor instead.

8.3.3 Using a descriptor file with an MDB

Modifying the `WireTap` to use a deployment descriptor instead of annotations requires two changes. First, delete the entire `@MessageDriven` annotation along with the accompanying configuration properties. Listing 8.3 shows the updated class.

Listing 8.3 WireTap.java

```
package org.jbia.jms.sofaspuds;
import javax.ejb.*;
import javax.jms.*;
public class WireTap implements MessageListener {
  public void onMessage(Message msg) {
    <same contents as before, not shown to save space>
  }
}
```

Second, create a META-INF/ejb-jar.xml file to define the messaging properties. Listing 8.4 describes that file.

Listing 8.4 The ejb-jar.xml file

```
<?xml version="1.0"?>
<ejb-jar xmlns="http://java.sun.com/xml/ns/javaee"
  xmlns:xsi="http://www.w3.org/2001/XMLSchema-instance"
  xsi:schemaLocation="http://java.sun.com/xml/ns/javaee
   http://java.sun.com/xml/ns/javaee/ejb-jar_3_0.xsd"
  version="3.0">
<enterprise-beans>
 <message-driven>                                          ❶ Identifies MDB declaration
  <ejb-name>WireTap</ejb-name>                             ❷ Names MDB
  <ejb-class>org.jbia.jms.sofaspuds.WireTap</ejb-class>    ❸ Identifies MDB class
  <message-destination-type>
  ➥javax.jms.Topic</message-destination-type>              ❹ Indicates topic use
  <activation-config>
   <activation-config-property>
    <activation-config-property-name>
  ➥destinationType</activation-config-property-name>
    <activation-config-property-value>
  ➥javax.jms.Topic</activation-config-property-value>
   </activation-config-property>
   <activation-config-property>
    <activation-config-property-name>
  ➥destination</activation-config-property-name>           ❺ Identifies topic and properties
    <activation-config-property-value>
  ➥topic/testDurableTopic
  ➥</activation-config-property-value>
   </activation-config-property>
   <activation-config-property>
    <activation-config-property-name>
  ➥subscriptionDurability
  ➥</activation-config-property-name>
    <activation-config-property-value>
  ➥Durable</activation-config-property-value>
```

```
      </activation-config-property>
      <activation-config-property>
       <activation-config-property-name>
➥messageSelector</activation-config-property-name>
       <activation-config-property-value>
➥SpudsCustomer = 'Natalie'
➥</activation-config-property-value>
      </activation-config-property>
     </activation-config>
    </message-driven>
   </enterprise-beans>
  </ejb-jar>
```

❺ **Identifies topic and properties**

The <message-driven> node identifies this section of the file pertaining to message beans ❶. You should name the EJB in case you need to reference it elsewhere ❷. Identify the class that implements the EJB ❸, and indicate that the destination is a topic ❹. The rest of the file sets the configuration properties ❺.

The settings in the deployment descriptor override any annotations declared in the class. For example, you can keep the class as is, with the annotation, and still provide the deployment descriptor. This way you can set up the class with a default behavior and override that with the deployment descriptor. Most likely, you'd use annotations for things that usually don't change and the deployment descriptor for things that might change. For the `WireTap` MDB, you could leave the `destinationType`, `destination`, and `subscriptionDurability` settings in the class, and place the `messageSelector` in a descriptor file because that changes based on whose reservations are being monitored.

8.4 Using message-driven POJOs

Message-driven POJOs are what their name implies—POJOs that can be registered as message consumers. Message-driven POJOs are specific to JBoss AS and aren't part of either the JMS or EJB specifications; you shouldn't use them if you need your application to be application server agnostic. Also, message-driven POJOs are supported by the EJB container, meaning they can't be used on a server configuration that doesn't support EJB.

The owner of Sofa Spuds is interested in making as much money as possible (he has his eye on a solid gold Humvee). He has decided to bill customers for videos as soon as the customer requests the video. The bank provides a message-driven POJO to accept credit card charges. We show you the bank's message-driven POJO and the changes to the `Store` class to act as the message sender.

8.4.1 Implementing a message-driven POJO consumer

To define a message-driven POJO, you need both an interface and a class that implements that interface. You might wonder why an interface is required, but you have to wait until we discuss the sender. The interface for our example message-driven POJO is shown in listing 8.5.

Listing 8.5 The ICredit interface

```
package org.jbia.jms.sofaspuds;
import org.jboss.ejb3.annotation.Producer;
@Producer                                            ❶ Identifies message-driven POJO interface
public interface ICredit {
 void charge(String customer, double amount);        Defines message
}
```

The @Producer annotation identifies that this interface is used for a message-driven POJO ❶. Note that this annotation is defined in the package org.jboss; this capability is specific to JBoss AS. And now for a mystery: Why is the interface called Producer and not Consumer? We get to that in a minute.

The charge method defines the message. Not what you expected, is it? Typical message-related methods take a single message object as an argument; here, there are several arguments that are standard Java types. In fact, you can use any of the basic data types and any classes that are serializable as arguments. This makes message-driven POJOs closer in concept to asynchronous remote procedure calls (RPC), which was one of the original purposes behind messaging.

The message-drive POJO (which consumes the messages) implements the interface and contains annotations to identify the message queue. The code for that class is in listing 8.6.

Listing 8.6 The Credit class

```
package org.jbia.jms.sofaspuds;
import org.jboss.ejb3.annotation.Consumer;
import javax.ejb.*;                                  ❶ Identifies class as message consumer
@Consumer(activationConfig={
 @ActivationConfigProperty
  (propertyName="destinationType",
   propertyValue="javax.jms.Queue")                  ❷ Identifies message queue
 @ActivationConfigProperty
  (propertyName="destination",
   propertyValue="queue/testQueue")})
public class Credit implements ICredit {             ❸ Implements interface
 public void charge(String customer, double amount) {
  System.out.println("Charge to " + customer + " for " + amount);
 }
}
```

The message-driven POJO class implements the interface defined earlier ❸. The @Consumer annotation ❶, which is specific to JBoss AS, identifies this class as a consumer of messages. The @Consumer annotation uses the same @ActivationConfigProperty annotations as used by an MDB to configure the message destination ❷. All the same configuration properties supported by MDBs are supported for message-driven POJOs.

Notice the differences between this and the MDB. Although the message-driven POJO implements an interface, it's a business interface, not a framework interface, as in the case of an MDB. You can easily unit test the message-driven POJO. Second, the message consumer is coded as a typical RPC method, not as a typical message consume method. The container handles the packaging and unpacking of the messaging data, removing that chore from the business logic developer.

If you're thinking that the message sender probably also doesn't look like a typical messaging client, you're correct.

8.4.2 Implementing a message-driven POJO producer

Recall that, for the example, the customer's credit card is billed when a video request is received. The only method that has to change is the `Store.onMessage` method. Listing 8.7 shows the additional code added to that class.

Listing 8.7 The updated `Store` class

```
...
import javax.naming.*;                        ❶
import org.jboss.ejb3.mdb.*;
public class Store implements MessageListener {
  ...
public void onMessage(Message msg) {
  ProducerManager mgr = null;
  try {
   ObjectMessage om = (ObjectMessage)msg;
   Video video = (Video)om.getObject();
   String customer = om.getStringProperty("SpudsCustomer");
   System.out.println("Reservation request:");
   System.out.println("\tcustomer: " + customer);
   System.out.println("\tvideo   : " + video);
   InitialContext ctx = new InitialContext();
   ICredit card =                                          ❷
     (ICredit) ctx.lookup(ICredit.class.getName());
   ProducerObject prod = (ProducerObject) card;
   mgr = prod.getProducerManager();                   ❸
   mgr.connect();
   card.charge(customer, 4.95);         ❹
  } catch (Exception e) {e.printStackTrace();
  } finally {
   try {
     if (mgr != null) mgr.close();        ❺
   } catch (javax.jms.JMSException je) {je.printStackTrace();}
  }
 }
  ...
}
```

A few more packages are imported ❶ because you use classes from them. As with a normal message client, you have to look something up in JNDI; but instead of looking up the connection factory, you look up a proxy object that implements the business interface, `ICredit` ❷. In addition, this proxy implements the `ProducerObject` interface, which is used to establish the messaging connection ❸. It acts as both a connection factory and a connection. The call to the connect method establishes the connection. Behind the scenes, the `ProducerObject` looks up the destination defined for the message. Now you know why the `ICredit` interface used the `Producer` annotation—because it's used by the message producer to send messages. That mystery is solved.

Sending a message looks like a normal procedure call, not like a messaging call ❹. The `ProducerObject` packages the content in a form suitable for messaging and passes it off to the messaging server, which places it in the queue. Finally, the messaging connection is closed ❺.

8.4.3 Packaging a message-driven POJO

Because you've modified the `Store` class, you have to package it again; refer back to section 8.2.2 for instructions. You must include the `ICredit` class in the JAR file for the store. You can package the message-driven POJO in a JAR file, credit.jar, as shown in figure 8.11. Note that only the required files—the interface and the message-driven POJO—are listed. Drop this file into the deploy directory, and it's ready to go.

```
org
└ jbia
  └ sofaspuds
    ├ Credit.class
    └ ICredit.class
```

Figure 8.11 The message-driven POJO JAR file contains the `ICredit` interface and the `Credit` class that implements the interface.

To try it out, bring up the store and customer clients as you did in section 8.2.2. You can see each customer being charged for the video rental at the time the customer makes a reservation. The credit card charge message appears in the console log. Now that we've explored various messaging clients, let's turn our attention to various messaging configuration topics.

8.5 Configuring JBoss Messaging

We cover configuration topics such as defining new destinations, setting up a data source, securing messages, and setting up various communications mechanisms. We start with the default configuration—which is what we used for the video example—and then show how to change the configuration and update the video example to match the configuration changes.

Let's first describe the configuration changes that we intend to make. The changes are as follow:

- Replace the two built-in topics with application-specific topics.
- Add authorization and access control to the topics.
- Use the PostgreSQL database as the data store for the messages and as the location for the authentication information. You can use different databases for authentication and the messaging store; they don't have to be the same.

These changes show up in many of the same configuration files. Rather than performing the changes one at a time, we cover all three at once. Once these changes are made, we show how to secure the message text using encryption as a separate exercise later.

We cover the various descriptor file changes first, and afterwards show the changes to the example messaging application. We tackle the descriptor changes in reverse order, ending with the destination configuration because it references the security changes, which reference the data source changes.

8.5.1 Configuring a data source

The messaging service stores all messages in a database before delivering them so that it can guarantee delivery. By default, it uses the Hypersonic database that ships with the application server. Although Hypersonic is adequate for development purposes, it shouldn't be used in production. If the server crashes, all messages could be lost—undelivered—violating the guaranteed delivery contract. It also can't handle a high volume of messages.

Configuring the messaging service to use another database is easy. First, you need to select a database and configure it by defining a *-ds.xml file.

For this example, you use the PostgreSQL database, which we assume you've already installed. You need to establish a database for the messaging service and create a database user who has access to that database. If you're following along at Borders (or wherever you've lugged your laptop), run `psql` and enter the following lines (you might want to use a more secure username and password):

```
CREATE USER video WITH ENCRYPTED PASSWORD 'videopw';
CREATE DATABASE videodb WITH OWNER = video ENCODING = 'UTF8';
```

Copy the JAR file that contains the PostgreSQL JDBC driver to the server/xxx/lib directory.

Create a data source descriptor file using server/xxx/docs/examples/jca/postgres-ds.xml as an example. The descriptor should look similar to the one shown in listing 8.8. Deploy this new descriptor to JBoss AS.

Listing 8.8 video-ds.xml excerpt

```
<?xml version="1.0" encoding="UTF-8"?>
<datasources>
 <local-tx-datasource>
  <jndi-name>jdbc/VideoDS</jndi-name>        ❶
  <connection-url>
  ➥jdbc:postgresql://localhost:5432/videodb   ❷
  ➥</connection-url>
  <driver-class>org.postgresql.Driver</driver-class>
  <user-name>video</user-name>               ❸
  <password>videopw</password>
  ...
 </local-tx-datasource>
</datasources>
```

The JNDI name ❶ is important and is referenced from the postgres-persistence-service.xml file, which we cover next. As you know, the database name ❷ must match the database created earlier—ditto for the username and password ❸.

Finally, modify the persistence service descriptor, postgresql-persistence-service.xml. You can find this file in the docs/examples/jms directory. This descriptor contains the information necessary to use the database as the persistence store for the messaging service. Listing 8.9 shows only the portions of this file that you need to change and enough lines to maintain context.

Listing 8.9 postgresql-persistence-service.xml

```
<server>
 <mbean name="jboss.messaging:service=PersistenceManager" ...>
  <depends>jboss.jca:service=DataSourceBinding,name=jdbc/VideoDS
  </depends>
  <attribute name="DataSource">java:/jdbc/VideoDS</attribute>
  ...
 </mbean>
 <mbean name="jboss.messaging:service=PostOffice" ...>
  <depends>jboss.jca:service=DataSourceBinding,name=jdbc/VideoDS
  </depends>
  <attribute name="DataSource">java:/jdbc/VideoDS</attribute>
  <attribute name="Clustered">false</attribute>          Identifies data source ❶
  <!-- depends optional-attribute-name="ChannelFactoryName">
➥    jboss.jgroups:service=ChannelFactory</depends -->            ❷
  ...
 </mbean>
 </mbean>
 <mbean name="jboss.messaging:service=JMSUserManager" ...>
  <depends>jboss.jca:service=DataSourceBinding,name=jdbc/VideoDS
  </depends>
  <attribute name="DataSource">java:/jdbc/VideoDS</attribute>
  ...
 </mbean>
</server>
```

Note that the data source name appears several times, both as a JNDI name and as part of the name of the MBean that represents the data source. Also, set the `Clustered` attribute to `false` ❶ and comment out the dependency on the ChannelFactory ❷ because you're not running this example in a clustered application server. Optionally, you could remove all the attributes after the `Clustered` attribute to the end of the MBean because all those attributes are specific to clustering and you won't need them for this example. Once the file is changed, it goes into the server/xxx/deploy/messaging directory. As a final step, remove the hsqldb-peristence-service.xml file from that same directory.

8.5.2 *Configuring access control*

We cover security in detail in chapter 4, so we don't repeat that here. In the interest of completeness, we describe all the changes required, showing descriptor files and other pertinent data along the way.

CONFIGURING ACCOUNTS AND ROLES

You need two roles: one for the store and one for the customers. Each customer has his or her own account, and the store has an account. Figure 8.12 illustrates these accounts and roles.

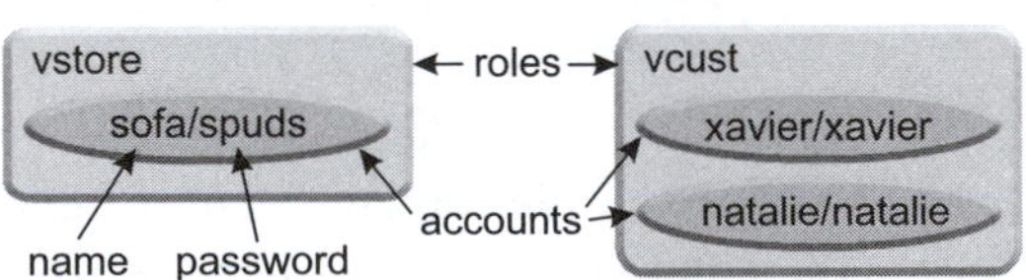

Figure 8.12 The example security configuration uses two roles: vstore and vcustomer. There's only one account for the vstore role, but each customer account is in the vcust role.

We set the passwords for the customers to the same values as their usernames, mainly to minimize the changes that are made to the example application; you should use a more secure password. Note that, when the store gets a new customer, a new account must be created and added to the vcust role.

The roles and accounts are stored in the database, in the VRole and VUser tables respectively. While logged into the videodb database—and using the video user and password set earlier—use psql to create the following SQL statements that generate the tables:

```
CREATE TABLE VUser (
  vname VARCHAR(30) NOT NULL,
  vpassword VARCHAR(250) NOT NULL,
  PRIMARY KEY(vname));
CREATE TABLE VRole (
  vname VARCHAR(30) NOT NULL,
  vrole VARCHAR(30) NOT NULL,
  PRIMARY KEY(vname));
```

And the psql statements that populate the tables:

```
INSERT INTO VUser (vname, vpassword) VALUES ('Xavier' , 'Xavier' );
INSERT INTO VUser (vname, vpassword) VALUES ('Natalie', 'Natalie');
INSERT INTO VUser (vname, vpassword) VALUES ('sofa'   , 'spuds'  );
INSERT INTO VRole (vname, vrole) VALUES ('Xavier' , 'vcust');
INSERT INTO VRole (vname, vrole) VALUES ('Natalie', 'vcust');
INSERT INTO VRole (vname, vrole) VALUES ('sofa'   , 'vstore');
```

Populating the database with the usernames and passwords is only part of the security configuration; you also need to tell the application server to look in the database for that information. For that, you need a login module, which we cover next.

CONFIGURING THE LOGIN MODULE

The messaging service uses the DatabaseServerLoginModule, which you'll also use, except you'll define another security domain and not use the domain named messaging. To do this, add a new security policy, video-realm. Make the changes in the server/xxx/conf/login-config.xml file, as shown in listing 8.10.

Listing 8.10 New security policy in login-config.xml

```
<policy>
 . . .
 <application-policy name="video-realm">      ❶
  <authentication>
   <login-module
    code="org.jboss.security.auth.spi.DatabaseServerLoginModule"
    flag="required">
    <module-option name="dsJndiName">
     java:/jdbc/VideoDS</module-option>      ❷
    <module-option name="principalsQuery">
➥SELECT vpassword FROM VUser WHERE vname=?      ❸
➥</module-option>
    <module-option name="rolesQuery">
➥SELECT vrole, 'Roles' FROM VRole WHERE vname=?      ❹
➥</module-option>
   </login-module>
```

```
   </authentication>
  </application-policy>
</policy>
```

The policy name ❶ is referenced later in the messaging-service.xml file, and the data source name ❷ comes from the *-ds.xml file defined earlier. The `principlesQuery` option ❸ and `rolesQuery` option ❹ reference the tables and columns that were created earlier.

CONFIGURING THE MESSAGING SERVICE

The final step regarding security is to configure the messaging service to use this login module. This is done in server/xxx/deploy/messaging/messaging-jboss-beans.xml, which contains two entries related to security. Listing 8.11 shows an excerpt from the updated file.

Listing 8.11 messaging-service.xml (excerpt)

```
<deployment ...>
 <bean name="SecurityStore" ...>
  <property name="defaultSecurityConfig">                 ❶ Identifies default access control
   <![CDATA[<security>
    <role name="guest" read="true"
         write="true" create="true"/>
   </security>]]>
  </property>
  <property name="securityDomain">video-realm</property>      ❷ Identifies security domain
  ...
 </bean>
 ...
</deployment>
```

We reference the new login module ❷, but we keep the `DefaultSecurityConfig` as is ❶. This entry defines the default role name and access control if no account information is provided by the client. Unlike many other services, messaging has access control turned on by default, but it also provides default access control for users that don't log on. As you can see from this example, the `default` role is `guest` and has a variety of privileges, as noted in table 8.5.

Table 8.5 Destination access modes

Access mode	Description
`read`	If `true`, then users in that role can receive messages from the destination.
`write`	If `true`, then users in that role can send messages to that destination.
`create`	If `true`, then users in that role can establish a durable topic subscription. For a durable subscription, the messaging server maintains the messages in the topic until all registered durable subscribers have received a copy of the message. A durable subscriber can exit and return later to receive any messages that have appeared since the last time it was run. This access mode is applicable only to topics and is based on the subscriber, not the publisher.

This is why the earlier example worked: All clients were given default privileges, including read and write access to all destinations. Now you also know where to go to restrict access to messaging users who don't authenticate.

8.5.3 Configuring destinations

The default destinations that come with the application server are defined in the file server/xxx/deploy/messaging/destinations-service.xml. As you can tell by the **-service.xml* suffix, this descriptor contains MBeans that define services. If you look in the file, a series of MBeans is defined; each MBean defines a destination. To create your own destinations, create a *-service.xml file and populate it with the desired MBean definitions for your destinations. Once you have the file, you can either place the file in the deploy directory or add it to your archive file, such as an EAR file, referencing it using the `<module>` and `<service>` tags in the jboss-app.xml file.

You need two topics: one for the video notification and the other for the reservation request. Give the `vstore` role the right to create a durable subscription so that customers can find out about videos that come in even when they're not online. As soon as they connect again, they're informed of said videos. The video-service.xml file containing the destinations is shown in listing 8.12.

Listing 8.12 The video-service.xml file

```
<?xml version="1.0" encoding="UTF-8"?>
<server>
 <mbean
  code="org.jboss.jms.server.destination.TopicService"          ❶
  name=" jbia.jms:service=Topic,name=Notification"          ❷
  xmbean-dd="xmdesc/Topic-xmbean.xml">
  <depends optional-attribute-name="ServerPeer">
  ➥jboss.messaging:service=ServerPeer</depends>
  <depends>jboss.messaging:service=PostOffice</depends>
  <attribute name="SecurityConfig">
   <security>
    <role name="vstore" write="true"/>                    ❸
    <role name="vcust" read="true" create="true"/>
   </security>
  </attribute>
 </mbean>
 <mbean
  code="org.jboss.jms.server.destination.TopicService"          ❹
  name="jbia.jms:service=Topic,name=Reservation"          ❺
  xmbean-dd="xmdesc/Topic-xmbean.xml">
  <depends optional-attribute-name="ServerPeer">
  ➥jboss.messaging:service=ServerPeer</depends>
  <depends>jboss.messaging:service=PostOffice</depends>
  <attribute name="SecurityConfig">
   <security>
    <role name="vstore" read="true"/>          ❻
    <role name="vcust" write="true"/>
   </security>
```

```
    </attribute>
  </mbean>
</server>
```

Declaring a destination, whether a queue or a topic, is as simple as declaring an MBean. The MBean for a topic is handled by the `org.jboss.jms.server.destination.TopicService` class (❶ and ❹). If you want to declare a queue, use the `org.jboss.jms.server.destination.QueueService` class instead.

Note that the MBean name (❷ and ❺) doesn't require any particular pattern, except for the `service=Topic` part (which would be `service=Queue` for a queue); the domain name doesn't have to be `jboss.messaging.destination`, which is used for all the example destinations. The `name=Notification` part ❷ identifies part of the JNDI name for the topic; the full name is `topic/Notification`. Similarly, if this were a queue, the full JNDI name would be `queue/Notification`.

We set up the video notification topic ❷ so that the store sends notifications and the customers obtain durable subscriptions ❸. Conversely, for the reservation topic ❺, the customers send requests, and the store reads them ❻. These are the minimum access rights required for the application. See table 8.5 for descriptions of access modes.

8.5.4 Updating the application

The `Store` class needs to reference the new destinations and use the correct account. Listing 8.13 provides excerpts from the updated `Store` class with the changes noted.

Listing 8.13 `Store.java` with authentication changes

```
...
public class Store implements MessageListener {
 ...
 private void run () throws Exception {
  ...
  Topic notify = (Topic)initial.lookup("topic/Notification");
  Topic request = (Topic)initial.lookup("topic/Reservation");
  connection = cf.createConnection("sofa", "spuds");
  ...
 }
 ...
}
```

❶ Defines new topic names

❷ Logs in using username

You change the names of the topics ❶ and log in with the appropriate username and password ❷. The changes to the customer class are similar, as shown in listing 8.14.

Listing 8.14 `Customer.java` with authentication changes

```
...
public class Customer {
 ...
 private void run (String customer) throws Exception {
  ...
  Topic notify = (Topic)initial.lookup("topic/Notification");
  Topic request = (Topic)initial.lookup("topic/Reservation");
  Connection connection =
```

Defines new topic names

```
    cf.createConnection(customer, customer);     <-- ❶ Logs in using username
    ...
  }
  ...
}
```

The customer name is used both as the login name and the password ❶. As we indicated earlier, this is done mainly to make the example simple. You should use more secure passwords.

The previous sections listed changes to a variety of configuration files. If you got lost in the shuffling of files, table 8.6 offers a recap.

Table 8.6 Files involved in configuring messaging

File usage	Location under jboss_home/server/default	Comment
Security policy definition	./conf/login-conf.xml	Add new policy or modify existing one
Messaging service configuration	./deploy/messaging/messaging-jboss-beans.xml	References new security realm and defines default access rights
Destination configuration	./deploy/video-service.xml	Defines the destinations and their access rights
PostgreSQL JDBC driver	./lib/postgresql-8.2-504.jdbc3.jar	Name varies—obtain from your JDBC driver vendor
Data source descriptor	./deploy/video-ds.xml	Create this file
Persistence service descriptor for PostgreSQL	./deploy/messaging/postgresql-persistence-service.xml	Copy from docs/examples/jms
Persistence service descriptor for Hypersonic	./deploy/messaging/hsqldb-persistence-service.xml	Delete this file

With the code changes in place, it's time to try out the example to see if the configuration changes worked.

8.5.5 Running the modified example

Start the application server and try the example program again, as shown in section 8.2.2. It should work the same way as before with the following additional features:

- *Durable subscriptions*—After running the customer the first time, bring the customer application down; then, from the store application, generate a few more video notifications. When you run the customer again, the customer is notified of all the videos.
- *Persistent storage of messages*—If the server crashes, you're notified of new videos available for rental after the server restarts.

But one thing doesn't work any more. The security changes disabled the `WireTap` MDB because we changed the topic on which the reservations are published, and added authorization to that topic. Although privacy advocates applaud this move, it could get Sofa Spuds slapped with a contempt-of-court citation. So, reluctantly, let's make the necessary changes to the `WireTap` source code.

8.5.6 Updating the MDB

To conform to these configuration changes, you need to define the new topic name, the username, and the password—all of which you can do using annotations. Listing 8.15 shows the full annotation with the updated configuration properties. The rest of the `WireTap` class is the same as from section 8.3.1.

Listing 8.15 Update annotations for the example MDB

```
@MessageDriven(activationConfig={
 @ActivationConfigProperty
 (propertyName="destinationType",propertyValue="javax.jms.Topic"),
 @ActivationConfigProperty
 (propertyName="destination",
  propertyValue="topic/Reservation"),        <-- Sets topic name
 @ActivationConfigProperty
 (propertyName="subscriptionDurability", propertyValue="Durable"),
 @ActivationConfigProperty
 (propertyName="messageSelector",
  propertyValue="SpudsCustomer = 'natalie'"),
 @ActivationConfigProperty                              | Sets user id
 (propertyName="user", propertyValue="sofa"),           |
 @ActivationConfigProperty                                  | Sets password
 (propertyName="password", propertyValue="spuds")           |
})
```

By the way, the same configuration properties apply to the message-driven POJOs; if we secured the queue used by the `Credit` POJO, we could have provided similar properties as those listed.

You can choose to modify the META-INF/ejb-jar.xml descriptor file instead of the annotations. We leave that as an exercise for you.

With this final change, all is as it was before we decided to create our own topics, secure the topics, and switch databases.

8.5.7 Configuring secure message transport

Besides access control, the other security concern is ensuring that message data isn't compromised by someone viewing the packets on the network. You can encrypt the data using SSL or a similar mechanism. In this section, we show you how.

Sofa Spuds wants to guarantee the privacy of its customers' viewing habits. After all, consider your humiliation if it became known that you rented *Gigli*. Three times. All video notifications and reservation requests need to be transported using SSL. You need to first generate a key and then configure the server and client to use the keys and pass the data using SSL.

GENERATING THE KEY

We cover public and private key pairs and certificates in chapter 4; therefore, we don't repeat that here. But to make the example complete, here are the steps to create the necessary files. First, the store needs to create a key and extract the public key. This is done in two steps.

```
keytool -genkey -alias jbiakey -keyalg RSA -validity 365
➥      -keystore server.keystore
keytool -export -alias jbiakey -keystore server.keystore
➥      -file jbiapublic.key
```

The application server uses a keystore named `server.keystore`. The customers receive a public key (or certificate) named `jbiapublic.key`. The customer takes the public key and imports it into his truststore, named `client.keystore`, using `keytool` as follows:

```
keytool -import -alias jbiakey -keystore client.keystore
➥      -file jbiapublic.key
```

Note that you need to remember the passwords you used to create the keystore and truststore for later use.

CONFIGURING THE SERVER

Now that you have a key in a keystore, you can configure the messaging server to use that keystore. The messaging service uses JBoss Remoting to pass messages between systems. A remoting service configuration file for using SSL is provided at docs/examples/jms/remoting-sslbisocket-service.xml. Copy this file to the server/xxx/default/deploy/messaging directory.

The remoting-sslbisocket-service.xml file comes with an example SSL socket builder MBean. You need to modify the MBean to use the keystore and passwords you created earlier. Listing 8.16 shows the changes required.

Listing 8.16 The SSL socket builder MBean

```
<server>
. . .
 <mbean
 name="jboss. messaging:service=SocketBuilder,type=SSL"
 ...>
  <attribute name="KeyStoreURL">                          ❶
    ${jboss.server.config.url}server.keystore</attribute>
  <attribute name="KeyStorePassword">videospuds
➥  </attribute>                                           ❷
   <attribute name="KeyPassword">videospuds</attribute>
 ...
 </mbean>
</server>
```

The `KeyStoreURL` attribute ❶ uses a system property to identify the server/xxx/conf directory so that you can place the keystore in the same directory as the rest of the general configuration files for the server. The next two entries ❷ identify the passwords used while creating the keystore and the public/private key pair.

The connector MBean in the remoting-sslbisocket-service.xml file is named `jboss.messaging:service=Connector,transport=sslbisocket`, which is different from the name used for the connector MBean in the remoting-bisocket-service.xml file. Two other configuration files reference the connector MBean; you must change both files to make use of the SSL-enabled connector. You must add a dependency to the connector MBean in the server/xxx/deploy/messaging/messaging-service.xml file, as shown in listing 8.17.

Listing 8.17 Adding a dependency on the SSL-enabled connector MBean

```
<server>
 . . .
 <mbean name="jboss.messaging:service=ServerPeer" ...>
  <depends>
➥   jboss.messaging:service=Connector,transport=bisocket</depends>
  <depends>
➥   jboss.messaging:service=Connector,transport=sslbisocket</depends>
 </mbean>
</server>
```

Notice that this file references both the SSL-enabled connector and the regular connector. You can require some clients use SSL while others don't. Whether a client must use SSL depends on the connection factory, which is configured in the server/xxx/deploy/messaging/connection-factories-service.xml file. Listing 8.18 shows the change required in that file for this example.

Listing 8.18 Setting the connection factory to use the SSL bisocket

```
<server>
 <mbean name="jboss.messaging.connectionfactory:
➥   service=ConnectionFactory" ...>
  ...
  <depends optional-attribute-name="Connector">
➥   jboss.messaging:service=Connector,transport=sslbisocket</depends>
  ...
 </mbean>
 . . .
</server>
```

Unlike the server peer, which can depend on multiple connectors, the connection factory can depend on only a single connector. Any client using this connection factory must use SSL to access the messaging service. Although it isn't shown in this listing, a connection factory has a `JNDIBindings` attribute that can be used to specify its names. You can declare multiple connection factories, using a different name for each, and each can use a different connector. The client then chooses the appropriate connection factory to use either an SSL or an unencrypted transport.

CONFIGURING THE CLIENT

Configuring the client is simple—you have to specify the following system properties when you run the client:

```
-Djavax.net.ssl.trustStore=
  ➥src/main/keystore/client.keystore
-Djavax.net.ssl.trustStorePassword=clientpwd
```

The first line identifies the location of the truststore file. The second is the password for that truststore.

RECAPPING THE CHANGES

Once again, we touched on several files. Some of them appear in the build environment and others in the application server directories. Table 8.7 lists the files that were changed in each location.

Table 8.7 Files used for configuring messaging to use an SSL transport

File usage	Location	Comment
Server keystore	server/xxx/conf/server.keystore	Keystore used by the messaging server.
Remoting configuration	docs/examples/jms/ remoting-sslbisocket-service.xml	Configures remoting to use SSL. Copied to server/xxx/ deploy/messaging.
Connection factory	server/xxx/deploy/messaging/ connection-factories-service.xml	Replaces dependency to reference SSL bisocket MBean.
Server peer	server/xxx/deploy/messaging/ messaging-service.xml	Adds dependency on SSL bisocket MBean.
Client keystore	client.keystore	Truststore used by both the store and customer clients.
Run scripts	*.bat, *.sh	If you have a script that runs the clients, add the system properties to the JVM command line.

One final note: Make sure the application server isn't running when you change the files. Once the changes are made, bring the application server up and run the clients as you did in section 8.2.2. The video notices and reservation requests should show up as they did before, but this time the messages are encrypted so that anyone monitoring the network packets doesn't know that you're once again reserving *Gigli*.

8.6 Summary

In this chapter, you learned about messaging systems in general, including a brief history of messaging and how it led to the JMS specification. Then you learned about JMS, the interfaces it defines, and how JBoss Messaging implements the JMS specification.

You then developed an example application (something a little more complex than a simple Hello World! application) that you used throughout the chapter. The application started small, consisting of two messaging clients, a producer and a consumer, and grew with the addition of another client, an MDB, and a final client implemented as a message-driven POJO. Initially, we had you rely on the default configuration as much as possible, showing you only the necessary configuration options, such as those required for the MDB.

Once the example was well established, we turned your attention toward a specific set of configuration options. We showed you how to use a database for message storage, how to define your own destinations, and how to configure authentication and authorization for those destinations. As a bonus, you used the database to store the authentication information. Finally, you changed the transport mechanism to use an SSL transport so that messages were encrypted when sent over the wire.

As with many of the other topics covered in this book, we've barely covered the surface of the capabilities of JMS. We've focused on configuring and managing JBoss Messaging. Armed with knowledge of JMS and the material covered in this chapter, you should be comfortable with developing applications that make use of messaging and with configuring JBoss Messaging to provide a robust, scalable, and high-performance messaging system.

8.7 References

The JSR-914 specification—http://jcp.org/en/jsr/detail?id=914

Monson-Haefel and Chappell's Java Messaging Service—http://www.oreilly.com/catalog/javmesser/

JBoss Messaging Documentation Library—http://www.jboss.org/jbossmessaging/docs/

Configuring Web Services

9

This chapter covers

- Understanding Web Services
- Developing a simple web service
- Developing web service clients
- Exploring JBoss Web Service-specific annotations
- Securing a web service
- Encrypting SOAP messages

It was August of 2000 in Orlando, Florida. I (Peter) recall sitting in a frigid conference room (the air conditioning was on high to combat the sweltering temperature outside) at the Professional Developer's Conference (PDC) when Microsoft rolled out their vision of the future complete with the .NET Framework and a thing called Web Services. At the time, they didn't have Visual Studio completely working with Web Services. When they did roll out the beta version of Visual Studio .NET, you could create a simple echoing web service with a few mouse clicks. The annotation capabilities in the .NET Framework made creating Web Services simple; the tools and the Framework handled the glue code that made it all possible.

The next March I attended JavaOne in San Francisco. Almost every presentation mentioned the new hot topic: Web Services. Many of the presenters pointed out that EJBs, specifically stateless session beans, were a natural fit for Web Services because they already supplied a similar capability within distributed applications.

In addition, Sun Microsystems published a document that stated how a stateless session bean could be converted into a web service endpoint. This process consisted of around a dozen steps, running a wide variety of tools and performing a wide variety of configuration steps, and only worked with Sun's application server. Needless to say, I never got my EJB-based web service working.

Development of Java-based Web Services has come a long way since then. The annotation support introduced in Java SE 5.0, and embraced by a wide variety of Java technologies, makes creating and consuming Web Services in Java as easy as in the .NET Framework.

In this chapter, we describe Web Services and present a simple web service example, showing how to develop and deploy that web service within JBoss AS. We focus on Web Services defined using the Java API for XML-based Web Services (JAX-WS) as delineated in JSR-181, implemented by JBoss Web Services 3.0, and provided in JBoss Application Server 5.0. If you're interested in the J2EE 1.4-compliant Web Services (JSR-109), see http://jbws.dyndns.org/mediawiki/index.php?title=JAX-RPC_User_Guide, where this topic is well documented. After the example, we present various configuration topics such as describing web service annotation, securing a web service, and encrypting web service messages.

If you're already familiar with Web Services or only want to learn how to configure Web Services within JBossWS, you can skip to section 9.3. If you're an administrator, you might want to skip to section 9.4 and get right into the security configuration.

9.1 Understanding Web Services

What is a web service? A cynic might say that it's nothing more than remote method invocation (RMI) performed over HTTP using a text-based (an XML document in this case) transport mechanism. And the cynic would be right. Web Services aren't necessarily a revolution but do represent an evolutionary step towards interoperability of heterogeneous systems.

There are two key concepts to Web Services. First, if two (or more) parties agree on the format for a certain type of data, then they can exchange data. For example, if hospitals and doctors agree on the layout of patient data, then a doctor could easily transfer information about a patient to the hospital where the patient is scheduled for surgery. Various industry groups have defined such data layouts for data of interest to their industries. Using XML as the basic layout for such data has increased the chances that such vertical industry data layouts will be developed and accepted.

Second, this data, which is software readable, can be transmitted over a protocol that can get through corporate firewalls. Performing standard Remote Method Invocation (RMI) between companies isn't usually possible because the firewalls block the ports used for RMI. But HTTP ports 80 and 443 are typically opened in firewalls to allow customers and other users to access a company's web site. Web servers then become responsible, not only for human-generated traffic to service web pages, but also for application-generated traffic in the form of Web Services.

9.1.1 Understanding web service terminology

As with other technologies, Web Services have their own jargon and set of mnemonics that you have to learn. Although we don't provide an exhaustive list, we do want to highlight a few of the terms that you'll encounter in this chapter. Figure 9.1 illustrates some of the relevant terminology for Web Services.

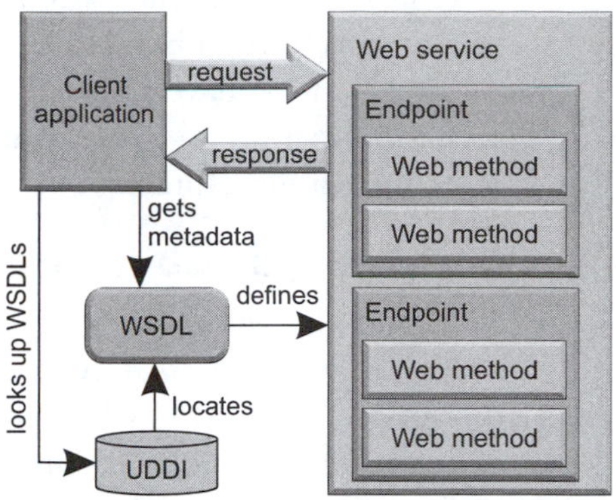

Figure 9.1 This figure illustrates Web Services terminology, showing how the client relates to the server and how Web Services are constructed within the server.

A web service is a collection of *endpoints*. Each endpoint is implemented in Java as a class. An endpoint can contain one or more *web methods*. You can also use an interface to define an endpoint and use a class to implement that endpoint. The endpoint interface is always used on the client side to construct a proxy that can marshal the arguments to the web method and unmarshal the result.

The Web Services Description Language (WSDL) file is an XML document that describes the web service. Although you can create a WSDL from scratch to define your web service and then generate the necessary stubs from it, it's usually easier to define the web service in terms of the endpoint written in Java and generate the WSDL from that. We present both mechanisms in this chapter.

The Universal Description, Discovery, and Integration (UDDI) registry is a mechanism used to publish Web Services. Think of it as a phone book with the WSDL as a phone number. If you know the phone number (WSDL), you can make the call directly. If you don't know the phone number, you can look it up in the phone book (UDDI) and then make the call.

We don't cover UDDI usage in this book because the subject of Web Services is much bigger than what can be covered easily in a single chapter. This chapter presents a simple introduction to Web Services and highlights various configuration topics when using JBossWS.

9.1.2 Understanding SOAP binding styles

SOAP is a protocol that enables the exchange of data between heterogeneous systems. It provides two different SOAP binding styles—document and Remote Procedure Call (RPC)—to pass data to a web method. In the RPC style, clients typically pass numerous parameters to a web method, and those parameters typically use simple data types such as strings and integers. Such web services tend to be chatty, or fine grained, in that the client calls on the service frequently to perform a single task.

The document style of web services tends to be coarse grained; the client packages up all the information into a single object, which is then passed to the web method. The web method has all the necessary information to perform the task. In many cases, document-style calls tend to be asynchronous; the client makes the call and then goes off to do other things. The client either checks later to see if there was a response to the call or registers to be notified when the response comes in. Asynchronous, document-style calls are preferred when using Web Services between companies.

Now that you have a basic understanding of Web Services, let's look at a simple web service, which we use as an example for the rest of the chapter when discussing various configuration topics.

9.2 Developing a web service

The example web service returns the sales tax for a purchase based on the customer's state. You input the two-character postal state code (such as CA for California), and the service returns the sales tax rate. (Don't we wish it were that easy! We don't know about other states, but in California, each county and, sometimes, even each city has its own sales tax rate. We could expand the service to also require the postal ZIP code, which would help pinpoint the exact sales tax rate. But to keep the example simple, we assume that sales tax rates are also simple, with one per state.)

Once we've shown how to code the web service, we then show how to deploy it and how to write clients to access it. Yes, we mean *clients,* as in plural. Because the biggest selling point of Web Services is interoperability among heterogeneous systems, you'll find that people who use technologies other than Java will want to access your web services. Therefore, we show you how to write clients in Java and in C# for the web service.

9.2.1 Coding the web service

There are two approaches to developing a web service, as follow:

- *The top-down approach*—You first develop the WSDL and use a utility, such as the `wsconsume` utility supplied by JBossWS, to generate the necessary glue code and stubs. You then fill in the code for the business logic in the stub classes. This approach works best when you're collaborating with various other entities to define the Web Services because the WSDL becomes the contract between those involved.
- *The bottom-up approach*—You code the web service first and then generate the WSDL from the web service. You can generate the WSDL using a utility, such as the `wsprovide` utility supplied by JBossWS, or you can package the web service and deploy it. The Web Services deployer will automatically generate the WSDL. This approach works best if you're defining a web service that you'd like others to use and there's no preexisting WSDL.

For this example, we use the bottom-up approach. Once you generate the WSDL, we briefly show how to use the WSDL for the top-down approach.

Listing 9.1 contains the code for the web service.

Listing 9.1 A simple web service

```
package org.jbia.ws;
import java.util.HashMap;
import javax.jws.*;        <-- Imports web service package
@WebService      ❶
```

```
public class SalesTax {
  private HashMap<String, Double> tax;
  public SalesTax() {init();}
  public void init() {
    tax = new HashMap<String,Double>();
    tax.put("CA", 7.75);
    tax.put("NH", 0.0);
  }
  @WebMethod
  public double getRate(String state) {
    Double rate = tax.get(state);
    if (rate == null) rate = -1.0;
    return rate;
  }
}
```

❷ (annotation on the tax initialization lines)

❸ (annotation on @WebMethod)

Returns sales tax rate

Notice the annotations, @WebService ❶ and @WebMethod ❸, which define the web service and what methods it supports. This web service is based on a POJO, and not an EJB, but you could have as easily added these annotations to a stateless session bean. We choose to use a POJO to keep the example simple.

In a real application, the code that initializes the tax rate hash table ❷ would be loaded from a database, but (again, to keep the example simple) we initialize it with a few hard-coded values. Although we could put in values for all 50 states, that would lengthen the example without adding anything to the discussion at hand.

9.2.2 *Packaging the web service*

You need to package the web service as a web application. Before you can do that, you need to create a web.xml file declaring the web service class as a servlet. The web.xml file is shown in listing 9.2.

Listing 9.2 The web.xml for the web service

```
<web-app>
  <servlet>
    <servlet-name>SalesTax</servlet-name>
    <servlet-class>org.jbia.ws.SalesTax</servlet-class>
  </servlet>
  <servlet-mapping>
    <servlet-name>SalesTax</servlet-name>
    <url-pattern>/tax</url-pattern>
  </servlet-mapping>
</web-app>
```

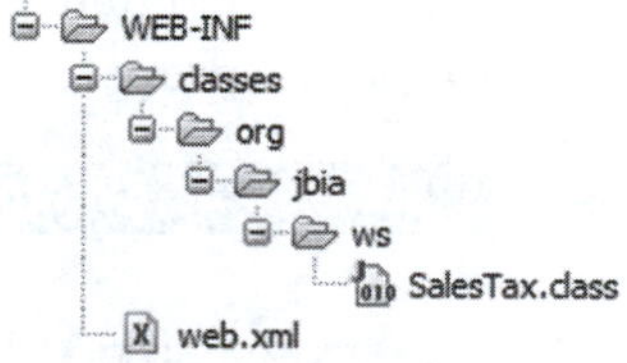

Identifies web service class

Identifies context used to access web service

You're now ready to package the web service. Create a salestax.war file as indicated in figure 9.2.

Optionally, you could package the web service in a *.wsr file. For example, instead of packaging the example in salestax.war, you could package it in salestax.wsr. What's the difference? From a content point of view, nothing. A *.wsr file has the exact same content as a *.war file. But the deployer deploys *.wsr files after *.war

Figure 9.2 The salestax.war file contains only two files: the class file that implements the web service and the standard descriptor file.

files. If it's important to have a web service deployed after the web applications, name the file *.wsr.

DEPLOYING AND ACCESSING THE WEB SERVICE

Deploying the web service is as easy as deploying any other web application; you copy the WAR file to the deploy directory. The application server creates the WSDL automatically. You can view web services deployed to the application server by going to the URL http://localhost:8080/jbossws/services. Figure 9.3 shows the resulting page with the SalesTax web service displayed.

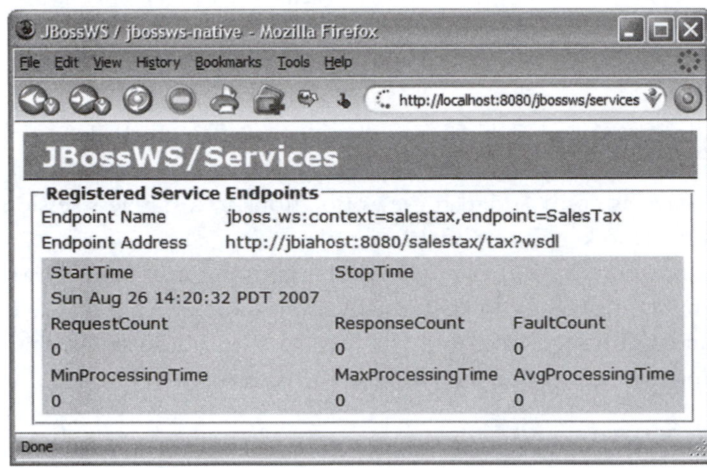

Figure 9.3 This screenshot displays information about the example web service. The Endpoint Address value is a hyperlink to the WSDL for the web service.

Click the URL identified by Endpoint Address to access the WSDL. The WSDL URL is important because you'll need it to create the client application.

9.2.3 *Manually generating the WSDL*

Instead of letting the application server generate the WSDL, you could generate it manually and include it in your WAR file. Run the `wsprovide` utility as follows:

```
wsprovide -o wsgen -c XXX -w org.jbia.ws.SalesTax
```

The `-o` option indicates that the output goes in the wsgen directory. The `-c` option provides the class path (`XXX` in the example) where you can find the endpoint class, `SalesTax` in this case. The `-w` option indicates to generate a WSDL file.

The generated WSDL contains a placeholder for the web service URL; you must supply the proper URL, as shown in listing 9.3.

Listing 9.3 Excerpt for the WSDL using an updated web service URL

```
...
<service name='SalesTaxService'>
 <port binding='tns:SalesTaxBinding' name='SalesTaxPort'>
  <soap:address location='http://localhost:8080/salestax/tax'/>
 </port>
</service>
...
```

Web service URL

The wsprovide utility is only one of many web service utilities provided by the application server. Table 9.1 lists those utilities, without the suffixes .bat and .sh, and describes their purposes. You can find the utilities in the bin directory. For usage details, run the utility passing -h as a parameter. You'll see examples of how to use each of the tools (other than wstools) in this chapter.

Table 9.1 Web service-related scripts

Script name	Purpose
wsconsume	Generates stubs or interfaces from a WSDL file. Used in top-down development.
wsprovide	Generates a WSDL file from web service classes. Used in bottom-up development.
wsrunclient	Runs a web service client and provides the necessary class path for that client.
wstools	Script used for JSR-109 Web Services development.

Now that you've generated the WSDL file, let's look at how you create a web service using the top-down approach.

9.2.4 Developing a web service using the top-down strategy

To develop a web service using a top-down approach, you need to start with the WSDL file. Then you run wsconsume to generate the class stubs from the WSDL and provide the business logic for the web methods.

To take the WSDL you generated and create the SalesTax class using the top-down approach, you generate the stubs using wsconsume as follows:

```
wsconsume -o stubs -k wsgen/SalesTaxService.wsdl
```

The -o option causes the generated files to be placed in a directory named *stubs*. The -k option indicates that the generated Java source files are to be kept; if this option isn't specified, the source files are removed and only the class files remain. Finally, the WSDL file is the one generated by wsprovide earlier.

When examining the files generated, you'll notice that one of them is called SalesTax.java. This file contains an interface that defines the web service. You need to make a few changes to the original SalesTax class to use this interface, as noted in listing 9.4.

Listing 9.4 A simple web service with top-down changes

```
package org.jbia.ws;
import java.util.HashMap;
import javax.jws.*;
@WebService(endpointInterface="org.jbia.ws.SalesTax",            ❶
        portName="SalesTaxPort",          ❷
    wsdlLocation="WEB-INF/wsdl/SalesTaxService.wsdl")            ❸
public class SalesTaxImpl implements SalesTax {          ❹
  private HashMap<String, Double> tax;
  public SalesTaxImpl() {...}
  public void init() {...}                               No WebMethod
  public double getRate(String state) {...}          <-- annotation
```

The class must be renamed to prevent the class name from clashing with the interface name, and the class must implement the interface ❹. The `@WebService` annotation must be modified to match the information in the WSDL file, so we add three elements:

- *The `endpointInterface` element* ❶—Identifies the interface that defines the web service. In the earlier bottom-up example, the class defined the web service; therefore, you didn't need this element in that example.
- *The `portName` element* ❷—Identifies the port name. You get this information from the WSDL file. If you don't provide this information, the port name is assumed to be derived from the class name (`SalesTaxImplPort` in this case).
- *The `wsdlLocation` element* ❸—Identifies the location of the WSDL file. You can specify any location within the web application, although a location within META-INF or WEB-INF is generally preferred.

Note that the `@WebMethod` annotation isn't required on the method because that annotation is already on the method in the interface. We don't show the contents of the methods because they haven't changed from the earlier example. Other than these minor changes the class remains the same.

You also have to make one change to the web.xml file, as shown in listing 9.5. Because the servlet must refer to the class and not the interface, you have to change the class name to reference `SalesTaxImpl`.

Listing 9.5 The web.xml file with top-down changes

```
<web-app...>
  <servlet>
    <servlet-name>SalesTax</servlet-name>
    <servlet-class>org.jbia.ws.SalesTaxImpl</servlet-class>    <-- The only change
  </servlet>
  ...
</web-app>
```

Now that you have all the files, compile the interface and class, and package them along with the WSDL and web.xml files in a WAR file, as illustrated in figure 9.4. You can then deploy the WAR file and access the web service.

Now that you have your web service defined using two different approaches, let's turn our attention to writing a client to access the service.

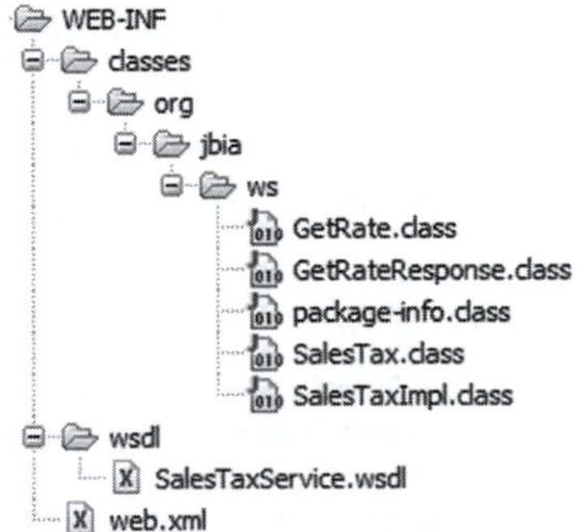

Figure 9.4 The salestax.war file contains more files when you use a top-down approach to construct web services. Compare this list of files to that shown in figure 9.2.

9.2.5 Developing the client

The example client is a simple command-line application that takes a list of state codes on the command line and prints the sales tax rate for each state. First, you generate the stubs for the client from WSDL. Note that this means that the client is coded in a top-down approach. To generate the stubs, make sure that the application server is running, the web service is deployed, and that you can access it from a browser as shown earlier in section 9.2.2. Use the wsconsume utility to generate the stub files as follows:

```
wsconsume http://localhost:8080/salestax/tax?wsdl
```

The wsconsume utility creates the stub files and compiles them. You'll need to include the generated classes in your class path when you compile the client and the classes in the final JAR file for the client. If you develop the service and the client on the same machine, make sure that the client doesn't have visibility to the files that make up the web service; otherwise, the compiler will get confused. For example, the generated files contain an interface named org.jbia.ws.SalesTax, which is the same name as the class that implements the web service if you used a bottom-up approach. If both are available to the compiler or the runtime, the wrong one might be used.

Now that you have the stubs, you can write the client. The code is shown in listing 9.6.

Listing 9.6 The web services client

```
package org.jbia.ws;
public class Client {
 public static void main(String[] args) {
  if (args.length > 0) {
   SalesTaxService svc = new SalesTaxService();      // 1 Creates service
   SalesTax tax = svc.getSalesTaxPort();             // 2 Obtains service endpoint
   for (int i = 0; i < args.length; i++) {
    double rate = tax.getRate(args[i]);              // 3 Invokes service method
    System.out.println("Sales tax for " + args[i] + " is " + rate);
}}}}
```

The first step is to declare the service ❶. Once you have it, you can obtain the service endpoint ❷ and then call the method ❸. As we mentioned earlier, the SalesTax item referenced is the interface generated by wsconsume, not the class that implements the web service.

That's all there is to it. Using a web service isn't that much different from using a local library of classes in a JAR file. The secret is that the stubs and the JAX-WS implementation within JBossWS handle all the plumbing code, enabling you to concentrate on the business logic.

PACKAGING AND RUNNING THE CLIENT

Now you're ready to compile and package the client. Remember to include the generated class files in the class path for the compiler and to add them to the JAR file, as shown in figure 9.5.

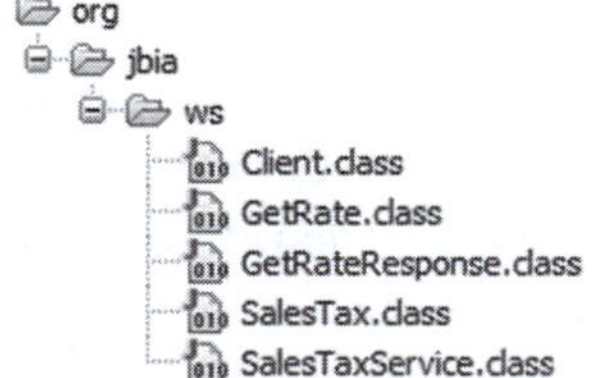

Figure 9.5 Here are the contents of the client JAR file. Only the Client.class file is hand-coded; the other files are generated by the wsconsume utility.

In the example, you coded the Client class. The wsconsume utility generated the rest of the class files.

Use the wsrunclient script to run the client. This script automatically adds to the class path the JAR files needed to run web service clients.

Here's an example of running the client:

```
>wsrunclient -classpath $JBOSS_HOME/client/jbossall-client.jar:./client.jar
➥ org.jbia.ws.Client CA NH TX
Sales tax for CA is 7.75
Sales tax for NH is 0.0
Sales tax for TX is -1.0
```

TIP Did you add logging statements to your client and provide a log4j.properties file, but the expected log file never showed up? Examine the `wsrunclient` script, and you'll see that it sets the `log4j.configuration` system property to wstools-log4j.xml, which you'll not find anywhere. It used to be in the client/jbossws-client.jar file, but now that file no longer appears. If you want to see logging output, remove that reference from the `wsrunclient` script.

Now that you have a Java client for your web service, let's look at writing a C# client.

9.2.6 Developing a C# client

The primary motivation behind Web Services is to enable organizations to exchange data among heterogeneous systems. Therefore, we now show how to consume the web service in the .NET Framework using C# and Visual Studio.

In Visual Studio, create a new C# console application project called TaxClient. Once the project is created, add a web reference to the project, as indicated in figure 9.6.

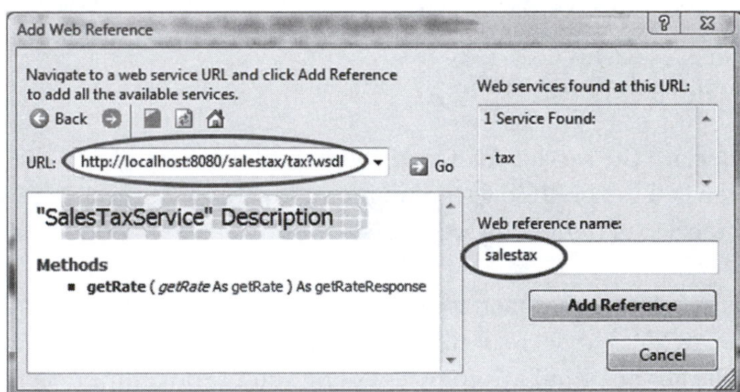

Figure 9.6 To add a web service reference to a Visual Studio project, provide the URL for the WSDL file and a name for the Web reference.

Notice that the URL used for the WSDL is that same as that used earlier for the `wsconsume` utility. By default, Visual Studio uses the hostname as the web reference name; we changed it to `salestax`.

The C# client does the same thing as the earlier Java client; it accepts state codes on the command line and prints the sales tax rate for each state. The code is given in listing 9.7.

Listing 9.7 The C# Web Services client

```
using System;
using System.Collections.Generic;
```

```
using System.Text;
using TaxClient.salestax;          ❶
namespace org.jbia.ws {
 class Client {
  static void Main(string[] args) {
   if (args.Length == 0) {
    Console.WriteLine                                    Prints usage
     ("usage: TaxClient <list-of-states>");          <-- instructions
   } else {
    SalesTaxService svc = new SalesTaxService();          ❷
    for (int i = 0; i < args.Length; i++) {
     getRate rr = new getRate();                   ❸
     rr.arg0 = args[i];
     getRateResponse resp = svc.getRate(rr);        ❹
     double rate = resp.@return;       ❺
     Console.WriteLine("Sales tax for " + args[i] + " is " + rate);
}}}}}
```

The namespace used for the web service is a combination of the name of the project and the name given to the web reference ❶. The usage instructions are slightly different because the project name is used for the program name (for readers unfamiliar with C#, the end result for a compile is an EXE file). The code then gets the web service ❷. Within the `for` loop that iterates through the command line parameters, the code builds the parameter to pass to the web method ❸, calls the web method passing the parameter ❹, and extracts the returned result ❺ before printing out the result.

9.2.7 *Revisiting the SOAP binding styles*

If you did a double take on the code because it looks a little strange, don't worry. It is strange. There are two SOAP binding styles: document and RPC. This code reflects how a C# client is coded if you're using document style. If you're wondering where the SOAP binding style was declared, recall that the web service container now provides reasonable defaults for any options you don't explicitly declare. Because you never stated which binding style to use, the web service container, when it generated the WSDL using the bottom-up approach, used the logical default—document style.

Document style makes perfect sense for the typical web services usage. For example, if the example service were for use in real-world scenarios, you'd probably code it so that it returned a collection of all sales tax rates, instead of a single rate. This way, the client could ask for the rates once when it came up and then cache the rates for repeated use. In that case, the web service would be returning a complex data type. The best way to deal with a complex data type in a heterogeneous environment is to use the document style to return a complex object and let the client extract the data from the complex type using methods or properties to get that data.

If you're dealing with simple types, such as in the example, then you could change the web service to use the RPC-style SOAP binding. Add a `@SOAPBinding` annotation to the SalesTax web service, as shown in listing 9.8.

Listing 9.8 Specifying a different SOAP binding

```
import javax.jws.soap.SOAPBinding;                    | New lines added
@SOAPBinding(style=SOAPBinding.Style.RPC)             |
@WebService()
public class SalesTax {
```

Then you rebuild and redeploy the web service. If you plan on using the Java client we showed you earlier with this web service, run the `wsconsume` utility again to generate updated stubs; fewer classes will be generated, and fewer classes will be in the client's JAR file. No change is necessary to the client source code. It still works.

For the C# client, ask Visual Studio to reload the WSDL by right-clicking the SalesTax entry under Web References within the Solution Explorer panel and selecting the Update Web Reference option. Then change the `else` clause within the client as shown in listing 9.9.

Listing 9.9 Updated C# client for RPC SOAP binding

```
} else {
 SalesTaxService svc = new SalesTaxService();
 for (int i = 0; i < args.Length; i++) {
  double rate = svc.getRate(args[i]);
  Console.WriteLine("Sales tax for " + args[i] + " is " + rate);
 }
```

Now this looks better and more closely matches the Java coding. You can run the client as follows to verify that you can access the web service properly:

```
>taxclient CA NH TX
Sales tax for CA is 7.75
Sales tax for NH is 0
Sales tax for TX is -1
```

There you have it—a Java POJO-based web service with both Java and C# clients.

9.3 Exploring JBossWS annotations

As you saw in the example, much of the configuration of Web Services can be done through annotations. Although we don't explain the annotations defined by JSR-181 (you can learn about them from the JSR-181 specification), we do want to cover the annotations provided by JBossWS itself. There are two such annotations: `@WebContext` and `@EndpointConfig`. A third annotation used with Web Services is the `@SecurityDomain` annotation, which is EJB-related.

9.3.1 Understanding the WebContext annotation

You use the `org.jboss.wsf.spi.annotation.WebContext` annotation to define items normally declared in the web.xml file. These items are identified in table 9.2.

The default column provides the value used if that element isn't specified, not the default value of the element itself; each element typically defaults to an empty string. For example, if you don't provide a `contextRoot` element, its value will be an empty string, but at the time it's used, the Web Services server will choose to use the archive name to build the context root.

Table 9.2 `WebContext` annotation elements

Element name	Default	Description
`contextRoot`	Name of JAR or EAR file	The context used in the URL to access the web service. This option is ignored if the endpoint isn't an EJB.
`virtualHosts`	-none-	Specifies the virtual hosts to which the web service is to be bound. Virtual hosts are defined in the server/ xxx/deployer/jbossweb.sar/server.xml file.
`urlPattern`	Name of the class	The name appended to the context root to form the full URL. This option is ignored if the endpoint isn't an EJB.
`authMethod`	-none-	Identifies if the client needs to be authenticated to use the web service. Valid values are `BASIC` and `CLIENT-CERT`. This option is ignored if the endpoint isn't an EJB.
`transportGuarantee`	`NONE`	Indicates the level at which the transport mechanism will guarantee that the transmitted data hasn't been tampered with. The possible values are ▪ *`NONE`*—The data is passed using plain text (not encoded). There's no guarantee that the data hasn't been tampered with. ▪ *`INTEGRAL`*—The transport mechanism guarantees that the data can't be modified while in transit. ▪ *`CONFIDENTIAL`*—The data is encrypted before being transmitted. This also guarantees that the data can't be modified. Usually, any guarantee other than `NONE` causes the data to be sent using SSL. This option is ignored if the endpoint isn't an EJB.
`secureWSDLAccess`	`True`	If the endpoint is secure (authentication is required to access the endpoint), then this indicates if authentication is also required to access the WSDL. This setting is ignored if the endpoint isn't secure.

You might have noticed that most of the annotation elements come into play only if the endpoint is also an EJB. To show how the `WebContext` annotation is used, we also must show how to convert the earlier POJO into an EJB. Let's do that next.

CONVERTING THE ENDPOINT TO AN EJB

Converting the SalesTax POJO web service into an EJB is fairly simple using annotations. Listing 9.10 highlights the changes necessary.

Listing 9.10 Implementing the endpoint as an EJB

```
import org.jboss.wsf.spi.annotation.WebContext;
import javax.ejb.Stateless;
@Stateless
@WebContext(contextRoot="/salestax", urlPattern="/tax")
@SOAPBinding(style=SOAPBinding.Style.RPC)
```

```
@WebService()
public class SalesTax {...}
```

First, the packages that contain the annotations are imported ❶, then the @Stateless annotation ❷ declares the class to be a stateless session bean, and finally the @WebContext annotation ❸ provides the context information that was supplied as part of the web application when the web service was a POJO.

Because the endpoint is now an EJB, you package it as an EJB JAR; you no longer need a web.xml file. The complete JAR file contents are given in figure 9.7. If you deploy this JAR file, remember to first undeploy the salestax.war file. Once it's deployed, the Java and C# clients should still work.

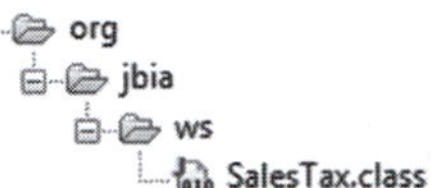

Figure 9.7 Here's the salestax.jar file containing an EJB endpoint. All you need is the class that implements the EJB.

By the way, if you didn't specify a contextRoot or urlPattern element for the WebContext annotation, the URL for the WSDL looks something like http://jbiahost: 8080/salestax/SalesTax?wsdl. The default values for contextRoot and urlPattern are salestax (the JAR filename) and SalesTax (the class name) for this example.

9.3.2 Understanding the EndpointConfig annotation

The org.jboss.ws.annotation.EndpointConfig annotation is used to identify the configuration to use with the endpoint. Table 9.3 describes the elements that can be set.

Table 9.3 EndpointConfig annotation elements

Element name	Default	Description
configName	-none-	Identifies the configuration to use.
configFile	server/xxx/deploy/jbossws.sar/META-INF/standard-jaxws-endpoint-config.xml	Identifies the file containing the endpoint configurations. This element is ignored if configName isn't supplied. If you're using the old JAX-RPC style of web services, a corresponding standard-jaxrpc-endpoint-config.xml configuration file is used instead. The location is relative to the application's location. For example, with the salestax.war file, you could place a handlers.xml file into the WEB-INF directory, in which case the value of configFile would be WEB-INF/handlers.xml.

Here's an excerpt from the default JAX-WS configuration file:

```
<jaxws-config ...>
 ...
 <endpoint-config>
  <config-name>Standard WSAddressing Endpoint</config-name>
  <pre-handler-chains>
   <javaee:handler-chain>
```

```
      <javaee:protocol-bindings>##SOAP11_HTTP
      </javaee:protocol-bindings>
      <javaee:handler>
       <javaee:handler-name>WSAddressing Handler</javaee:handler-name>
       <javaee:handler-class>
    org.jboss.ws.extensions.addressing.jaxws.WSAddressingServerHandler
       </javaee:handler-class>
      </javaee:handler>
     </javaee:handler-chain>
    </pre-handler-chains>
   </endpoint-config>
   ...
  </jaxws-config>
```

An endpoint configuration, denoted by the `<endpoint-config>` tag, has a number of attributes, as shown in table 9.4.

Table 9.4 Endpoint configuration attributes

Attribute	Description
`<config-name>`	Identifies the configuration. This name is used in the `configName` element of the `EndpointConfig` annotation.
`<pre-handler-chains>`	Identifies code that will process the message before it's passed to the endpoint. Typical handlers include the following: ▪ *Addressing service handler*—Adds the addressing information to the message context as the value for the `JAXWSAConstants.SERVER_ADDRESSING_PROPERTIES_INBOUND` property ▪ *Security handler*—Handles access control
`<post-handler-chains>`	Identifies code that processes the result after the endpoint has responded to the messages and before the response is returned to the client.
`<feature>`	Identifies particular features to use. You can use this attribute to get the Message Transmission Optimization Mechanism (MTOM) feature, which is used to more efficiently serialize messages containing the MIME types `image/jpeg`, `text/xml`, `application/xml` and `application/octet-stream`. The usage is `<feature> http://org.jboss.ws/mtom</feature>`.
`<property>`	Used to identify name/value pairs of properties.

Let's now turn our attention to securing the web service.

9.4 Securing a web service

Securing a web service includes authorization (and its companion, authentication) and encryption. We look at web service authorization and then venture into encryption.

9.4.1 Authorizing web service access

By default, anyone can call a web service. Although this might be acceptable for a web service accessed only from within a company or for a general-purpose query such as stock quotes, it's probably not the best thing for a web service that, say, obtains someone's medical records.

In this section, we show you how to secure the SalesTax web service. First, we must decide on a security realm, then define some accounts and roles in that realm, and finally use that realm to provide authentication and authorization for the web service.

9.4.2 Defining the security realm

An examination of the server/xxx/conf/login-config.xml file shows that a security realm, named `JBossWS`, is used to test security for web services. We use that realm because it's suitable for our purposes. You could easily define a security realm that uses Lightweight Directory Access Protocol (LDAP) or a database to store the authentication information.

The `JBossWS` realm uses the files server/xxx/conf/props/jbossws-users.properties and jbossws-roles.properties to define the accounts and roles. Add a role, `merchant`, and assign an account name and password to each merchant who contracts to use the SalesTax web service. Assuming two merchants have signed up, the jbossws-users.properties would contain the following (although probably with stronger passwords):

```
TJs_Pizza=password1
A1_Auto_Repair=password2
```

And the jbossws-roles.properties file would contain the following:

```
TJs_Pizza=merchant
A1_Auto_Repair=merchant
```

Now that the realm is set up, let's look into securing both the POJO and the EJB Web Services.

SECURING THE POJO WEB SERVICE

Because a POJO web service is packaged in a WAR file and uses the same descriptors. you set access control on the web service the same way as you would for a servlet or JSP. Listing 9.11 highlights the new lines you need to add to the web.xml file.

Listing 9.11 Security-related changes made to the web.xml file

```
<web-app ...>
  ...
  <security-constraint>
    <web-resource-collection>
      <web-resource-name>Secure Sales Tax</web-resource-name>
      <url-pattern>/tax</url-pattern>                          ❶ Context to secure
    <http-method>POST</http-method>                            ❷ Secures only POST requests
    </web-resource-collection>
    <auth-constraint>
      <role-name>merchant</role-name>                          ❸ Authorized role
    </auth-constraint>
  </security-constraint>
  <login-config>
    <auth-method>BASIC</auth-method>                           ❹ Uses BASIC authentication
```

```
    <realm-name>JBossWS</realm-name>
  </login-config>
  <security-role>
    <role-name>merchant</role-name>        <-- 3 Authorized role
  </security-role>
</web-app>
```

Because the web service uses the /tax context, that's the context that must be secured ❶. This is the same value that would be placed into the urlPattern element of the @WebContext annotation. The role name, merchant ❸, has to match the roles defined in the jbossws-roles.properties file. For the example, we use BASIC authentication ❹.

Only POST requests are secured ❷. The client uses POST requests to make the web service calls and a GET request to access the WSDL. The JAX-WS API doesn't provide a mechanism to specify the account name and password when the client obtains the WSDL; securing only POST requests ensures that the client still has access to the WSDL.

You need a jboss-web.xml file to identify the JNDI name for the security realm. Use the existing JBossWS realm, as follows:

```
<?xml version="1.0" encoding="UTF-8"?>
<jboss-web>
  <security-domain>java:/jaas/JBossWS</security-domain>
</jboss-web>
```

Now that you have all the files, you can package them into the WAR file and deploy it. The contents of the WAR file are illustrated in figure 9.8.

Now that you have the web service running, you need to modify the client to provide the proper credentials to access the web service. Let's do that next.

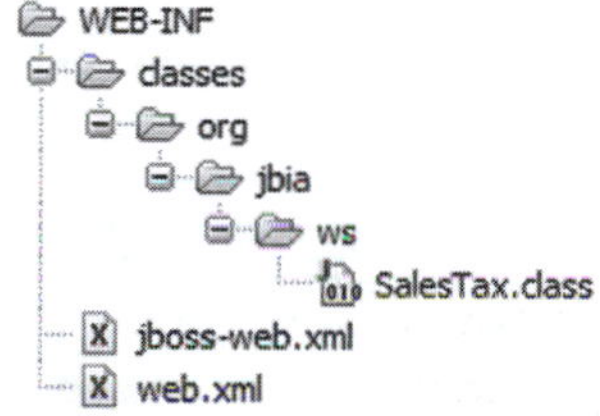

Figure 9.8 Here are the contents of the WAR file for a secured POJO web service. The only additional file, beyond what is listed in figure 9.2, is the jboss-web.xml file.

MODIFYING THE CLIENT TO ACCESS A SECURE WEB SERVICE

The client needs to supply the username and password when accessing the web service. To keep the changes to the client simple, we hard-code one of the accounts into the client. You need to add several lines right after getting the web services port. Listing 9.12 highlights the new lines in context. (The first and last lines are from the earlier example.)

Listing 9.12 Security-related changes to the client

```
...
SalesTax tax = svc.getSalesTaxPort();
BindingProvider bp = (BindingProvider)tax;                    1
Map<String, Object> rc = bp.getRequestContext();                   2
rc.put(BindingProvider.USERNAME_PROPERTY, "TJs_Pizza");          |  3
rc.put(BindingProvider.PASSWORD_PROPERTY, "password1");          |/
for (int i = 0; i < args.length; i++) {
...
```

The object returned by the getXXXPort method is versatile. Besides implementing the web service endpoint, which is SalesTax in this example, that object also implements the javax.xml.ws.BindingProvider interface ❶. This interface owns a Map containing properties used for the request ❷ where you set the username and password ❸.

Now that you have the client updated, compile it and run it as before, using the wsrunclient script. You should once again get the desired sales tax rates. To verify that the authentication is working, you can either scan the server log file looking for entries from org.jboss.security.auth.spi.UsersRolesLoginModule, or you can change the code to provide an invalid username or password—in which case, you should get an HTTP 401 error reported.

Now that the secured POJO version of the web service is running, let's turn our attention to securing the EJB version of the web service.

SECURING THE EJB WEB SERVICE

Use the WebContext annotation to define the security configuration information. Listing 9.13 shows the modified SalesTax EJB web service.

Listing 9.13 Security-related changes to the EJB web service

```
...
@WebService()
@WebContext(contextRoot = "/salestax", urlPattern = "/tax",
        authMethod = "BASIC",          ❶
        secureWSDLAccess = false)         ❷
@SecurityDomain(value = "JBossWS")        ❸
@Stateless
public class SalesTax {...}
```

You only need to change three lines to make the EJB secure. First, the authMethod element for the @WebContext annotation indicates that the BASIC authentication mechanism is used to authenticate the user ❶. This setting corresponds to the <auth-method> tag in the web.xml file for the POJO web service. The secureWSDLAccess element is set to false ❷ so that the client, and others, can access the WSDL without supplying credentials. Finally, the value element of the @SecurityDomain annotation identifies the name of the login module used ❸. This setting corresponds to the <security-domain> tag within the jboss-web.xml file used for the POJO web service, although without the java:/jaas/ prefix. You could also provide the prefix as part of the value element, such as value="java:/jaas/JBossWS", but we recommend that you don't.

Compile the source file and package the class file into salestax.jar as you did earlier. Once you deploy the JAR file (don't forget to undeploy the salestax.war file first if it's still deployed), you should be able to access the WSDL via a browser without having to log in. In addition, you should be able to run the client to access the web service.

9.5 Encrypting SOAP messages

For confidential information such as medical records, you'll want to also encrypt the message so that the contents can't be monitored during transport. In this section, we show you how to encrypt the SalesTax web service.

One of the unique aspects of encrypting a web service is that it can be done in two different ways. First, you can use SSL to transport messages using HTTPS. The mechanisms used to set this up are much the same as for using SSL with a web application. You can also use WS-Security; the contents of the message are encrypted by the JAX-WS implementation on both the client and the server. These two methods are illustrated in figure 9.9. In this chapter, we cover WS-Security only, but you can refer to chapter 6 for information on setting up SSL.

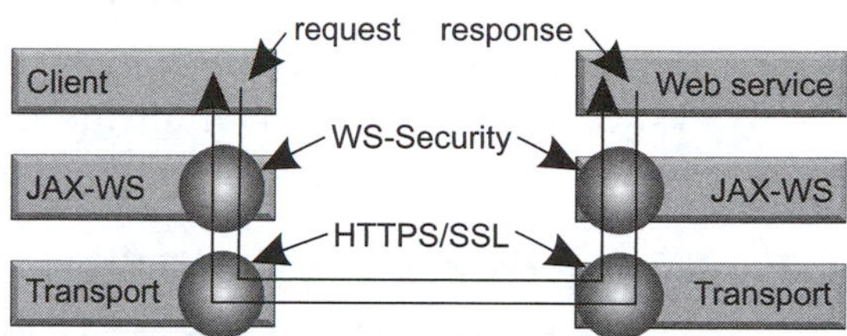

Figure 9.9 Web service requests and responses go though both the JAX-WS and transport layers, so either layer can be used to encrypt and decrypt the requests and responses.

The steps to encrypt the messages are to generate the security certificates and to configure the server and client to use those certificates. To make this example complete, we walk you through all the steps to secure the web service, even the steps to generate the certificates.

9.5.1 Generating the certificate

A web service request and response consists of two messages, each of which has to be encrypted. This is illustrated in figure 9.9. Although you could use the same certificate in both cases, you usually wouldn't want to do so in a production environment because it requires both the server and the client to have the same private key. Usually you want to keep your private key, well, *private*. Therefore, with a single client and a single server you need two certificates so that's what you generate. We discuss how you add more clients after we get the single client example working.

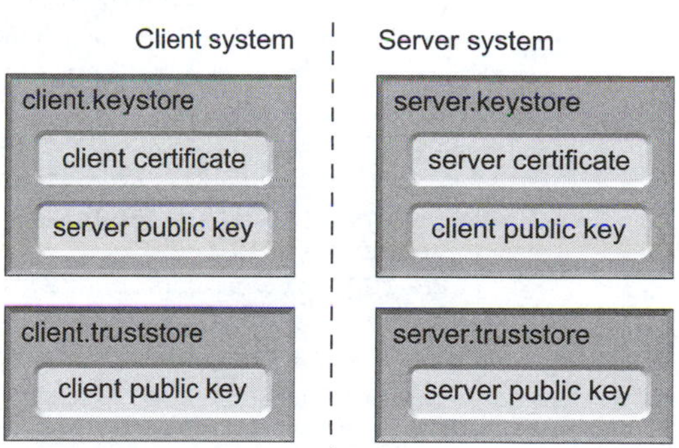

Figure 9.10 Note the relationships among the certificates stored in the keystores and truststores. The sender uses the receiver's public key, which is stored in the keystore, to encrypt the message. The receiver uses its certificate, which contains both its public and private keys, to decrypt the message.

You need two keystores and two truststores. Each keystore contains its own certificate and the public key of the certificate in the other keystore. The truststores contain the public keys of their corresponding certificates. This configuration is illustrated in figure 9.10.

Here are the commands used to set up this configuration:

```
keytool -genkey -alias server -keyalg RSA -keystore server.keystore
keytool -genkey -alias client -keyalg RSA -keystore client.keystore
keytool -export -alias server -keystore server.keystore
➥           -file server_pub.key
keytool -export -alias client -keystore client.keystore
```

```
➥           -file client_pub.key
keytool -import -alias client -keystore server.keystore
➥           -file client_pub.key
keytool -import -alias server -keystore client.keystore
➥           -file server_pub.key
keytool -import -alias client -keystore client.truststore
➥           -file client_pub.key
keytool -import -alias server -keystore server.truststore
➥           -file server_pub.key
```

When you're creating the certificates (the first two commands), the keytool command asks for a password for both for the keystore and for the certificate. Remember the passwords you used. You'll need them later.

9.5.2 Securing the server using WS-Security

For this example, we use the earlier RPC-style SalesTax POJO web service from section 9.2.7. You have to complete two steps: configure the server to use its keystore and truststore and configure the web service to use that configuration.

The jboss-wsse-server.xml file identifies the keystore and the truststore to the server. For a POJO web service, this file is placed into the WEB-INF directory; for an EJB web service, you place it into the META-INF directory. In this file, you also indicate that you want messages to be encrypted. Listing 9.14 shows the contents of the file.

Listing 9.14 Encryption-related security configuration file: jboss-wsse-server.xml

```
<jboss-ws-security
  xmlns="http://www.jboss.com/ws-security/config"
  xmlns:xsi="http://www.w3.org/2001/XMLSchema-instance"
  xsi:schemaLocation="http://www.jboss.com/ws-security/config
http://www.jboss.com/ws-security/schema/jboss-ws-security_1_0.xsd">
  <key-store-file>
  ➥WEB-INF/server.keystore</key-store-file>          ❶
  <key-store-type>jks</key-store-type>       ❷
  <key-store-password>password</key-store-password>        ❸
  <trust-store-file>
  ➥WEB-INF/server.truststore</trust-store-file>      ❹
  <trust-store-type>jks</trust-store-type>      ❺
  <trust-store-password>password</trust-store-password>        ❻
  <key-passwords>
    <key-password alias="server" password="serverpwd" />        ❼
  </key-passwords>
  <config>
    <encrypt type="x509v3" alias="client" />       ❽
    <requires>
      <encryption />       ❾
    </requires>
  </config>
</jboss-ws-security>
```

The locations of the keystore ❶ and truststore ❹ files are relative to the base directory of the WAR file. The keystore and truststore use the same password (❸ ❻); you probably want to use stronger passwords. The <key-store-type> ❷ and <trust-store-type> ❺ default to JKS, so you could leave these tags out. The server key password is provided by the `<key-passwords>` tag ❼ because that password is used to access the server certificate in the keystore. The `<encryption/>` tag ❾ requests that the message be encrypted using the alias provided by the `<encrypt>` tag ❽. The client's public key is used to encrypt the message on the server and is decrypted at the client using the client's private key from the client's keystore. You can also provide `<signature/>` and `<sign>` tags to perform authentication.

Add the `@EndpointConfig` annotation to the `SalesTax` class to indicate that you want to use WS-Security. Listing 9.15 is an excerpt from the updated `SalesTax` class, highlighting the added lines.

Listing 9.15 Encryption-related changes to the client

```
...
import org.jboss.ws.annotation.EndpointConfig;          ❶
...
@EndpointConfig(configName="Standard WSSecurity Endpoint")        ❷
public class SalesTax {...}
```

The `import` statement imports the annotation class ❶, and the `configName` element identifies the configuration you want to use ❷. The valid configurations can be found in the file server/xxx/deploy/jbossws.sar/META-INF/standard-jaxws-endpoint-config.xml. Listing 9.16 is an excerpt from that file, showing the `Standard WSSecurity Endpoint` configuration.

Listing 9.16 Endpoint-handler configuration file: standard-jaxws-endpoint-config.xml

```
<jaxws-config ...>
 ...
<endpoint-config>                                            ❶ Configuration
<config-name>Standard WSSecurity Endpoint</config-name>   <--   name
 <post-handler-chains>
  <javaee:handler-chain>
  <javaee:protocol-bindings>##SOAP11_HTTP</javaee:protocol-bindings>
   <javaee:handler>
    <javaee:handler-name>WSSecurity Handler</javaee:handler-name>
    <javaee:handler-class>
➥ org.jboss.ws.extensions.security.jaxws.
➥ WSSecurityHandlerServer         <--  WS-Security
    </javaee:handler-class>        ❷  handler class
   </javaee:handler>
  </javaee:handler-chain>
 </post-handler-chains>
</endpoint-config>
</jaxws-config>
```

The configuration name given here ❶ matches the configuration name used in the `EndpointConfig` annotation. The `WSSecurityHandlerServer` class ❷ handles the encryption and decryption of the messages.

You can add other handler chains to this configuration and even write your own handler by extending the `org.jboss.ws.core.jaxws.handler.GenericSOAPHandler` class.

Such a handler has access to and can manipulate the full SOAP message.

Now that you have all the files, you can package them into the salestax.war file, as shown in figure 9.11, and deploy the WAR file. If you have previously deployed the salestax.jar file, remember to undeploy it first.

WEB-INF
classes
org
jbia
ws
SalesTax.class
jboss-wsse-server.xml
server.keystore
server.truststore
web.xml

Figure 9.11 Here are the contents of salestax.war when using WS-Security. The additional files, beyond what you saw in figure 9.2, are the keystore, truststore, and jboss-wsse-server.xml file.

Note that the standard-jaxws-endpoint-config.xml file isn't included in the WAR file; it's picked up from its default location. If you'd like to place that file into the WAR file, you could provide the location using the `configFile` element on the `@EndpointConfig` annotation. Once the WAR file deploys, you can access the WSDL file through a browser.

ENCRYPTING AN EJB WEB SERVICE

The steps to encrypting an EJB web service are similar to that of a POJO web service, except that the configuration files and the keystore go into the META-INF directory. You'll also have to change the location of those files in the <key-store-file> and <trust-store-file> tags in the jboss-wsse-server.xml file. The packaged JAR file is shown in figure 9.12.

The configuration you have done so far means that the server won't recognize a message unless it's encrypted. You still have to make the changes to get the client to encrypt the message before sending it. Let's look at that next.

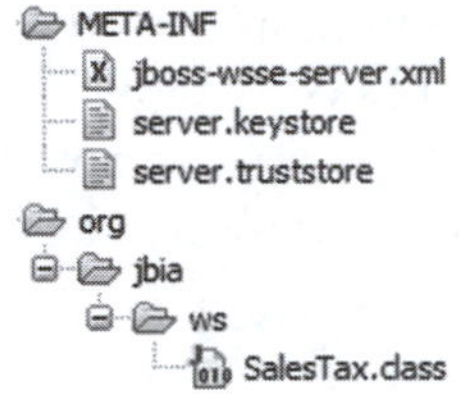

Figure 9.12 Here are the contents of salestax.jar, which contains an EJB-based endpoint, when using WS-Security. The keystore, truststore, and the jboss-wsse-server.xml file are the additional files, as in the previous figure, but the files are placed into the META-INF directory.

9.5.3 *Securing the client using WS-Security*

The client source files don't require any changes to encrypt the message, although be sure to use the earlier client from section 9.2.3 that doesn't perform any login because the server isn't expecting it. The only thing you have to do is configure WS-Security. You use two files to correspond to the two configuration files used for the server.

First, provide the information regarding the keystore and truststore. You can do this by creating a jboss-wsse-client.xml file and placing the necessary information into it, as shown in listing 9.17.

Listing 9.17 Client configuration file: jboss-wsse-client.xml

```
<?xml version="1.0" encoding="UTF-8"?>
<jboss-ws-security
 xmlns="http://www.jboss.com/ws-security/config"
```

```
xmlns:xsi="http://www.w3.org/2001/XMLSchema-instance"
xsi:schemaLocation="http://www.jboss.com/ws-security/config
http://www.jboss.com/ws-security/schema/jboss-ws-security_1_0.xsd">
 <key-store-file>
➥META-INF/client.keystore</key-store-file>
 <key-store-type>jks</key-store-type>
 <key-store-password>password</key-store-password>
 <trust-store-file>
➥META-INF/client.truststore</trust-store-file>
 <trust-store-type>jks</trust-store-type>
 <trust-store-password>password</trust-store-password>
 <key-passwords>
   <key-password alias="server"
             password="clientpwd" />        ❶ Identifies password for server key
 </key-passwords>
 <config>
   <encrypt type="x509v3" alias="server"/>   <-- Identifies certificate alias
   <requires>
     <encryption/>     <-- Requests message encryption
   </requires>
 </config>
</jboss-ws-security>
```

The contents of this file look similar to that used by the server, the only difference being that the keystore and truststore are located in the META-INF directory. The server public key ❶ is used to encrypt the message, which is decrypted at the server using the server's private key.

You can leave out the information about the keystore, truststore, their passwords, and types, and provide that information using the following system properties:

- `org.jboss.ws.wsse.keyStore`
- `org.jboss.ws.wsse.keyStorePassword`
- `org.jboss.ws.wsse.keyStoreType`
- `org.jboss.ws.wsse.trustStore`
- `org.jboss.ws.wsse.trustStorePassword`
- `org.jboss.ws.wsse.trustStoreType`

If you specify this information both in the configuration file and as system properties, the configuration file takes precedence. Additionally, because the same class handles the jboss-wsse-client.xml and jboss-wsse-server.xml files, the system properties could be used for the server also. Because the server might serve multiple Web Services, each with their own WS-Security configuration, it makes sense that the settings in the configuration file take precedence over the system properties.

You have to state that you want to use WS-Security by creating a META-INF/standard-jaxws-client-config.xml file. An example of this file can be found at server/xxx/deploy/jbossws.sar/META-INF/standard-jaxws-client-config.xml. Copy this file to your project and edit it, removing the configurations that you don't want. The only configuration you should leave is `Standard WSSecurity Client`, as shown in listing 9.18.

Listing 9.18 Client configuration file: standard-jaxws-client-config.xml

```
<?xml version="1.0" encoding="UTF-8"?>
<jaxws-config xmlns="urn:jboss:jaxws-config:2.0"
 xmlns:xsi="http://www.w3.org/2001/XMLSchema-instance"
 xmlns:javaee="http://java.sun.com/xml/ns/javaee"
xsi:schemaLocation="urn:jboss:jaxws-config:2.0 jaxws-config_2_0.xsd"
>
<client-config>
 <config-name>Standard WSSecurity Client</config-name>      <-- Configuration name
 <post-handler-chains>
  <javaee:handler-chain>
  <javaee:protocol-bindings>##SOAP11_HTTP</javaee:protocol-bindings>
   <javaee:handler>
<javaee:handler-name>WSSecurityHandlerOutbound</javaee:handler-name>
    <javaee:handler-class>
➥org.jboss.ws.extensions.security.jaxws.                       ❶ WS-Security
➥WSSecurityHandlerClient                                          handler class
    </javaee:handler-class>
   </javaee:handler>
  </javaee:handler-chain>
 </post-handler-chains>
</client-config>
</jaxws-config>
```

The `WSSecurityHandlerClient` ❶ is the client-side handler that corresponds to the `WSSecurityHandlerServer` server-side handler. Both of these classes defer to the `WSSecurityHandler` class to handle the messages.

All that's left to do is package the files into a JAR file as illustrated in figure 9.13. The classes are the same as from the earlier example; only the files in META-INF are new.

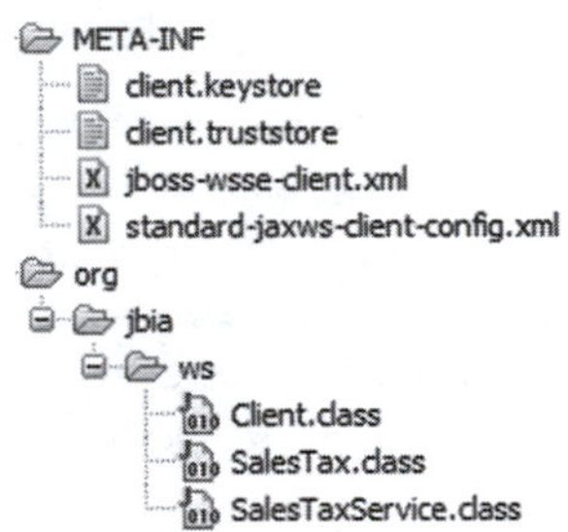

Figure 9.13 Here are the contents of the client.jar file when using WS-Security. All the classes in the META-INF directory are new.

Once you have the JAR file, you can run the client, once again using `wsrunclient`. It should work. You can verify that the messages are encrypted by turning on message tracing. Uncomment the Enable JBossWS message tracing entry in the jboss-log4j.xml file before starting the application server. Then look for the org.jboss.ws.core.MessageTrace entries in the server.log file.

9.5.4 *Signing the messages using WS-Security*

WS-Security provides a mechanism to sign a message, providing an alternate means of authenticating the user. To illustrate how this works, we modify the example that encrypts messages.

For signing a message, the sender uses his or her private key, and the receiver uses the sender's public key to verify the sender's identity. This means that both the client's public key and the server's public key must be in the server's truststore. This configuration is illustrated in figure 9.14.

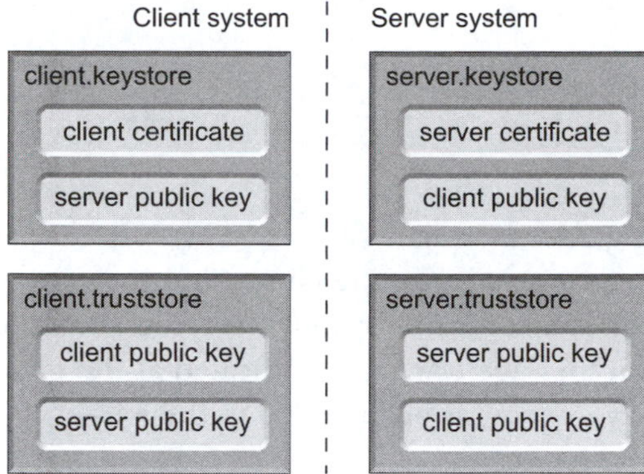

Figure 9.14 Here are the relationships among the keystores and truststores for signing messages. The only difference between this and figure 9.10 is that the other system's public key has been added to the truststore.

Assuming that the keystores and truststores are already set up for encryption, here are the additional commands used to create this configuration:

```
keytool -import -alias server -keystore client.truststore
➥           -file server_pub.key
keytool -import -alias client -keystore server.truststore
➥           -file client_pub.key
```

Once the keys are set up, you must modify the configuration files to use the keys to sign the messages. Listing 9.19 shows an excerpt from the updated jboss-wsse-server.xml file.

Listing 9.19 WS-Security configuration file, jboss-wsse-server.xml, changes

```
<jboss-ws-security ...>
  ...
  <config>
    <sign type="x509v3" alias="server" />          ❶ Identifies certificate used to sign message
    <encrypt type="x509v3" alias="client" />
    <requires>
      <signature />      Requires message to be signed
      <encryption />
    </requires>
  </config>
</jboss-ws-security>
```

The server key is used to sign messages sent by the server ❶. The keystore and truststore-related settings are the same as for the earlier encryption example; only the two lines identified were added.

The changes to the jboss-wsse-client.xml file are similar, as shown in listing 9.20.

Listing 9.20 WS-Security configuration file, jboss-wsse-client.xml, changes

```
<jboss-ws-security ...>
  ...
  <config>
    <sign type="x509v3" alias="client" />          ❶ Identifies certificate used to sign message
    <encrypt type="x509v3" alias="server" />
```

```
    <requires>
      <signature />          <-- Requires message
      <encryption />             to be signed
    </requires>
  </config>
</jboss-ws-security>
```

In this case the client key is used to sign the messages ❶.

Package up the server and deploy it, package up the client, and then run the client. The messages are now signed. You can verify this by looking at the SOAP messages in the server.log file (after turning on message tracing as indicated at the end of section 9.5.3); you'll see a <ds:Signature> entry has been added to the message.

9.6 Summary

This chapter introduced you to Web Services, including its terminology and how that terminology applied to the web service architecture. You learned terms such as endpoints, WSDL, and UDDI. You examined the different SOAP binding styles and should now know the difference between the RPC and document styles.

You built a simple web service, which you then used to examine various configuration topics. You learned how to package and deploy both POJO and EJB-style Web Services. You created Web Services using both top-down and bottom-up approaches. You learned how to use the `wsconsume`, `wsprovide`, and `wsrunclient` utilities. You explored various annotations and configuration files that you can use to configure your web service.

You created both Java and C# clients to access the web service. Working with the C# client led to a more in-depth discussion and understanding of the SOAP binding styles.

You learned how to secure your web service, using both mechanisms to secure web applications and WS-Security. You learned how to use WS-Security to encrypt a message and to sign a message, providing an alternative to standard web application authentication and authorization.

9.7 References

JSR-181, Web Services Metadata for the Java Platform, specification—http://jcp.org/en/jsr/detail?id=181

JSR-224, JAX-WS 2.0, specification—http://jcp.org/en/jsr/detail?id=224

JBossWS User Guide—http://jbws.dyndns.org/mediawiki/index.php?title=JBossWS

JAX-RPC User Guide—http://jbws.dyndns.org/mediawiki/index.php?title=JAX-RPC_User_Guide

Part 3

JBoss Portal

Let's take a break from our in-depth discussion of JBoss AS configuration and look at one of the other projects available from JBoss—the JBoss Portal. The JBoss Portal is one of the products that make up the JBoss Enterprise Middleware Suite (JEMS). The JBoss Portal is a fairly big topic, so we devote two chapters to it.

Chapter 10 describes portals in general and the JBoss Portal in particular. We explain how to install the Portal and set it up to use a database. Then, we provide an example portlet that is a little more complex than the other examples in this book because we want to highlight various portlet coding techniques. We then use the example to describe how to configure the Portal to include the portlet, using both configuration files and the Management Portlet.

In chapter 11, you'll learn how to use the Content Management System (CMS) that comes with the JBoss Portal, and how to define access control for your portal and portlets. The chapter ends with a section that puts everything you've learned together to create a custom portal.

Once you've gone through both chapters, you should feel comfortable with deploying portlets and configuring the Portal.

10 The JBoss Portal and portlets

This chapter covers

- Understanding portals
- Installing the JBoss Portal
- Developing a portlet
- Configuring a portlet
- Creating a portlet instance
- Creating a portlet window

The JBoss Portal is worthy of a book in its own right, so we can't do it complete justice in two chapters. Our aim is to introduce you to working with the Portal so that you feel familiar enough with it to tackle more in-depth portal-related topics. Portals enable you to build websites by putting together disparate pieces of code, called *portlets,* into a single page, making those separate applications appear to function as one. In addition, many portals enable users to customize the layout of their home pages to include the information they're most concerned with, making it more likely that the users will use those pages as portals into the World Wide Web.

We recommend that you read the Portal documentation, but we don't assume that you have any experience with portals. Therefore, this chapter and the next, "Configuring the JBoss Portal," can serve as an introduction into portals. But if the Portal documentation covers a particular topic—such as installation—in detail, we cover it only briefly here. In addition, the documentation that accompanies the Portal provides a good introduction to portals in general and the JBoss Portal specifically.

NOTE The code in chapters 10 and 11 has been tested with JBoss Portal 2.6.4 running in JBoss AS 4.2.2. Much of the code also works with earlier 2.6.x and 2.4.x releases but doesn't work with 2.4.0 due to various bugs, which were fixed in 2.4.1. The JBoss Portal 2.6.x doesn't run on JBoss AS 5.0.

In this chapter, we approach the Portal from the perspective of a portlet developer attempting to write, configure, and deploy a portlet to the Portal. We start with a simple, yet useful, portlet that's a step beyond the simple examples provided in the Portal documentation. We use that portlet to guide you through some aspects of portal configuration, up to the point of displaying the portlet on a portal page. Chapter 11 picks up where this chapter leaves off, introducing and expanding on the various configuration topics. But we don't ignore the portal administrator's role in managing a portal. We cover many administration topics, such as page layouts and security, in the next chapter.

10.1 Introducing the JBoss Portal

The JBoss Portal is one of many projects in JEMS. The Portal stands out because, unlike the other products that compose JEMS, the Portal is a full-blown application that can be run out of the box. It comes with an integrated RSS news reader so that you can easily set up a news feed, a Weather portlet, a basic Content Management System (CMS), and various other portlets.

Besides the included portlets, you can easily deploy many other portlets to the portal to expand its functionality—no coding necessary! The Portlet Swap website (http://labs.jboss.com/portletswap) contains various portlets—many are tutorial oriented, but some are useful out of the box, such as the IFrame portlet, which is used to easily embed other websites within the portal. The JBoss Wiki and JBoss Forums projects provide a wiki portlet and a user forums portlet, both of which can help engage users in your website. Put these portlets together and, without any programming, you can have a website ready to go in a flash.

The JBoss Portal documentation lists a large set of features provided by the Portal. We won't repeat that entire list here, but some of the features worth noting are as follow:

- Supports standards such as JSR-168, which we cover in section 10.1.1.
- Implements single sign-on using the Java Authentication and Authorization Service (JAAS). We cover this in the next chapter in section 11.4.
- Supports clustering, an advanced topic that we leave for you to explore after you've digested these two chapters.
- Works with any database because it uses Hibernate for database access. We show how to set it up for MySQL in section 10.1.3.

- Uses themes to customize or personalize the portal layout. Although we don't discuss personalization, one of the cool new features in 2.6, we do show how to customize the look of the portal in section 11.5.
- Supports hot deployment of portlets and themes. You'll make a limited use of this feature to deploy the example portlet.
- Supports internationalization of portlet content, another advanced topic we leave for you to explore.
- Supports portlets written using many industry-standard frameworks such as JSF, Struts, Spring MVC, and AJAX. The example portlet uses JSP and the JavaServer Pages Standard Tag Library (JSTL). We leave the others as advanced topics for you to explore, but be sure to check out the framework examples at the Portlet Swap website.
- Provides a basic CMS with features such as WYSIWYG editing of HTML pages, versioning of content, simple URLs to access binary content, and internationalization so that each user can see content in his language. We cover some topics related to CMS in the next chapter, section 11.3.

As you can see from the list, we cover a lot of these features in this chapter and the next. Let's get started with the first topic—JSR-168.

10.1.1 Understanding JSR-168

The Portal includes a portlet container that's an open source implementation of JSR-168, Portlet Specification. This specification provides an API that enables a portlet written to the portlet API to work with any portal that conforms to the specification.

As with all specifications, you have some leeway in implementation. For example, the specification requires certain functionality but leaves other functionality as optional, such as caching. JBoss Portal implements the full specification except the integration of custom portlet modes and custom window states. In addition, many deployment and configuration considerations are left to the portal vendor. As you read this chapter, we point out the configurations that are part of the specification and the ones that are specific to the JBoss Portal.

NOTE We recommend that you obtain the Portlet Specification document, available at http://jcp.org/en/jsr/detail?id=168. It's fairly readable and invaluable as a technical reference on a variety of topics, such as the portlet tag library and Cascading Style Sheet (CSS) style definitions.

Now that you have a basic understanding of the JSR-168 specification, let's look at some of the terminology associated with portals.

10.1.2 Understanding portal terminology

As with all technology, portal technology has its own set of terms, and any discussion of portals requires that you first understand those terms. Figure 10.1 illustrates the relationships between the various objects that make up portal technology.

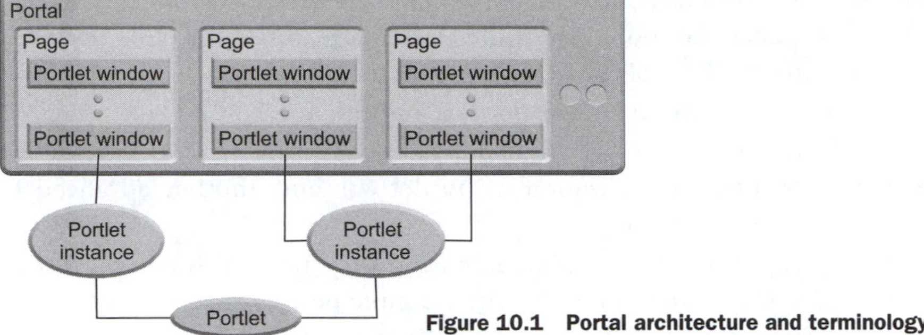

Figure 10.1 Portal architecture and terminology

And here are the definitions of the terms:

- *Portal*—A collection of pages that contain portlet windows. The JBoss Portal supports declaration of multiple portals. A portal owns pages and portlet windows but doesn't own portlet instances. A portlet instance can be viewed within multiple portal pages, possibly in multiple portals.
- *Page*—A view into the portal, containing multiple portlet windows. Corresponds to a page that a user views in a browser.
- *Portlet window*—A view into a portlet instance. You can have multiple portlet windows for a single portlet instance. The windows can be on the same or different pages or even in different portals.
- *Portlet instance*—An instantiation of a portlet. The portlet instance maintains the portlet preferences used to display data to a user. The portlet instance typically contains a global configuration, which can be further customized for a given user.
- *Portlet*—A piece of code that defines what a user can see or do. The portlet is the application code written to provide a service or capability to the user. It enables the integration of services in a portal.

We cover each of these concepts in detail in the following sections as we walk you through the example portlet. But the first thing you need to do is install the Portal.

10.1.3 Installing the JBoss Portal

You can install the Portal in the following ways:

- Via the Portal bundled with JBoss AS
- Via the binary distribution (contains the Portal only)
- Via the source distribution

Going the bundled route is the quickest way to get up and running to evaluate the Portal. You download the bundle, unzip it, and run the application server. The bundle uses a specific version of the application server and the Hypersonic database. We recommend that you switch to a different database for production use.

Going the source route is the most complicated, mainly because you must perform separate steps to build the portal and construct the database configuration. But this option is probably the most satisfying to your inner geek.

For this chapter, we go the binary route. The installation steps are as follow:

1. Download the binary distribution from http://labs.jboss.com/jbossportal/download/index.html.
2. Configure the database. See the following text for details.
3. Deploy the portal service. You copy the jboss-portal.sar directory to the server/xxx/deploy directory.

Once it's installed, run the application server and point a browser at http://localhost:8080/portal. The default portal page displays, as shown in figure 10.2.

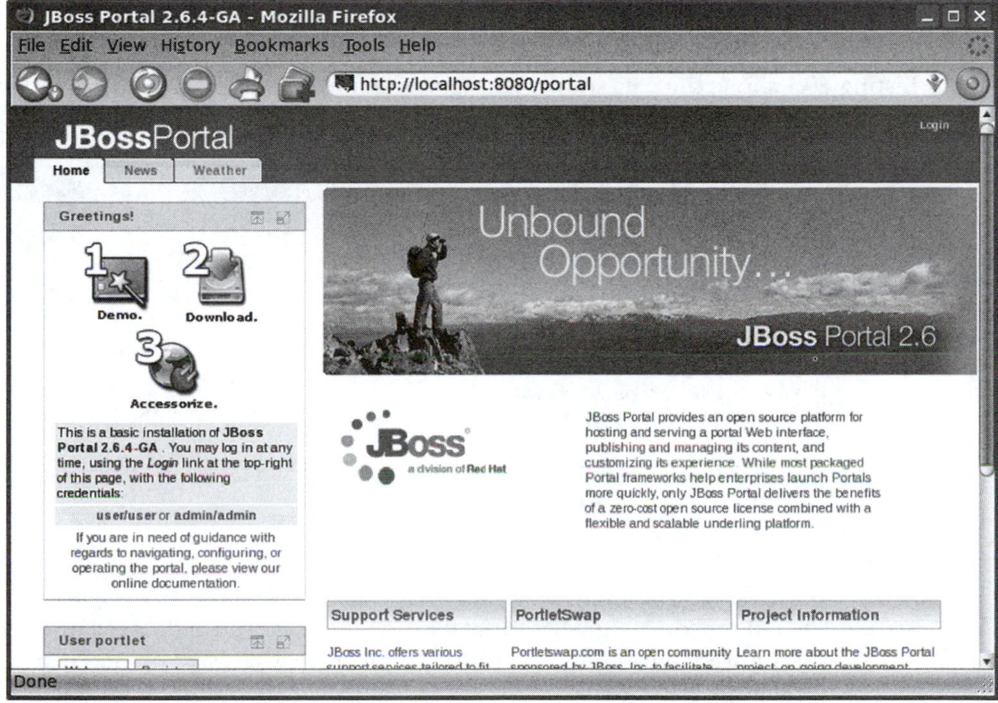

Figure 10.2 The default portal home page contains a header that shows tabs for the available pages (Home, News, and Weather). The body of the page has two columns. The left column contains a greeting and a user portlet, and the right column shows CMS content.

As stated in step 2, you need to configure a database first, so let's do that.

CONFIGURING THE DATABASE

The Portal supports any database that works with Hibernate. The setup directory in the Portal distribution contains data source configuration files for a variety of databases. Once you've selected a database, you complete the following steps:

1. Copy the JDBC driver for the database to the server/xxx/lib directory. You can obtain the JDBC driver from the database vendor.
2. Use the database's administration tools to create a database for the portal. You can name the database anything.

3 Use the database's administration tools to create a user for that database. You must give the user the ability to create tables in the database. You can use any username and password.
4 Edit the data source configuration file in the setup directory to reflect the database, username, and password you selected in the previous steps.
5 Copy the data source configuration file to the server/xxx/deploy directory.

To execute steps 2 and 3 for MySQL, run the `mysql` utility and enter the following commands:

```
CREATE DATABASE portaldb;
GRANT ALL PRIVILEGES ON portaldb.* TO 'portal'@'localhost'
➥       IDENTIFIED BY 'portalpassword' WITH GRANT OPTION;
```

Listing 10.1 shows the data source configuration file (step 4), portal-mysql-ds.xml, that matches the database and account.

Listing 10.1 Data source configuration file for MySQL

```
<?xml version="1.0" encoding="UTF-8"?>
<datasources>
 <local-tx-datasource>
  <jndi-name>PortalDS</jndi-name>
  <connection-url>
➥     jdbc:mysql://localhost:3306/portaldb
➥     ?useServerPrepStmts=false
➥     &amp;jdbcCompliantTruncation=false
➥     </connection-url>
  <driver-class>com.mysql.jdbc.Driver</driver-class>
  <user-name>portal</user-name>
  <password>portalpassword</password>
 </local-tx-datasource>
</datasources>
```

On one line, no whitespace

NOTE The 5.0 version of the MySQL database generates errors if data is truncated when stored in the database, causing a problem when storing Boolean values. The internal representation is typically all bits on, whereas the database stores only a single bit. To avoid this problem, set the `jdbcCompliantTruncation` property to `false`, as is done in the example data source configuration file, and edit the MySQL initialization file (usually named my.ini or mysql.ini) to remove the `STRICT_TRANS_TABLES` value from the `sql_mode` setting. You must restart the database to enact the latter change.

Now that you have the Portal installed and a database configured, you're almost ready to start working on the example. But before you can, you need to know how to administer the Portal because you perform several administration tasks in the next sections.

10.1.4 Administering the JBoss Portal

You must log in as an administrator to manage the portal. The default administrator username is *admin* with a password of *admin*. To log in, click the Login link located at the upper-right corner of the header (see figure 10.2). Once you're logged in, several links appear in the border on the lower-right side of the header; click the Admin link (see figure 10.3).

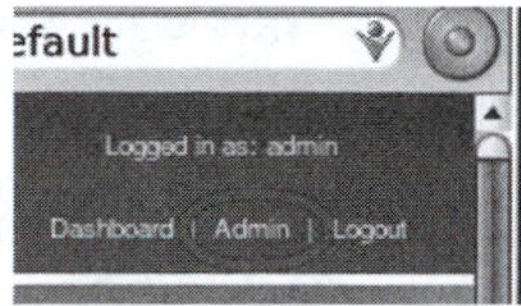

Figure 10.3 Click the Admin link in the header to get to the Admin portal.

That link takes you to the Admin portal, which contains various pages that enable you to manage the portal, as shown in figure 10.4.

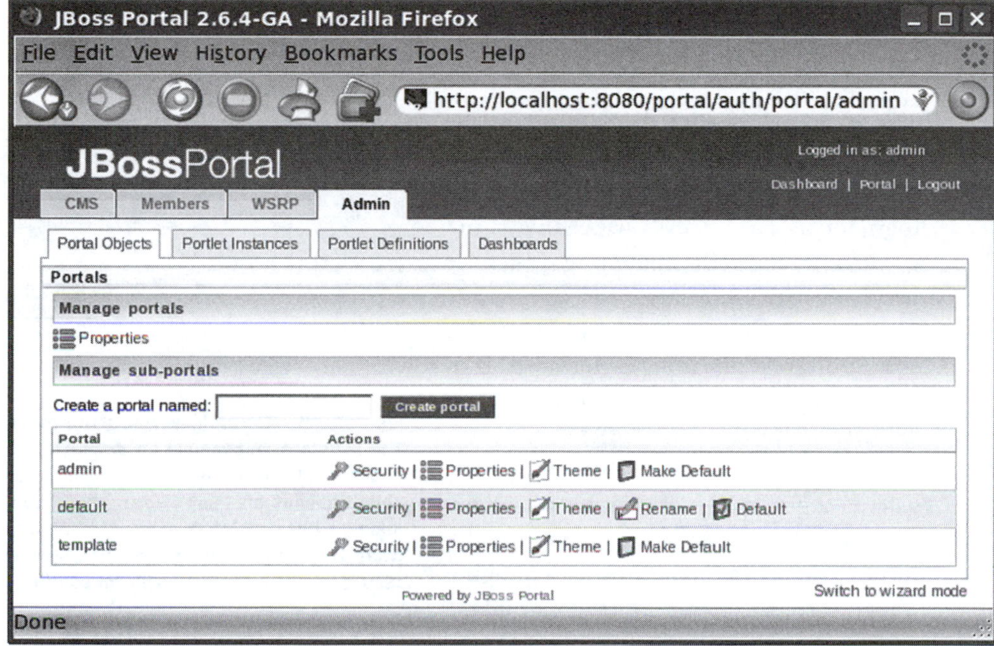

Figure 10.4 The Admin page of the Admin portal shows where you can manage portals and their pages. The other three tabs enable you to manage CMS content, users and roles (Members), and remote portlet (WSRP).

Table 10.1 describes the four tabs on the administration portal. Each page hosts one or more portlets that enable you to manage a particular resource within the portal.

Table 10.1 Understanding the pages on the administration portal

Page	Description
CMS	Contains the CMS Admin portlet, which enables you to manage the simple CMS provided with the portal.
Members	Contains the Identity Admin portlet, which enables you to manage users and roles. Users are used to define authentication. Roles are used to define access control for the pages and portlets in the portal.

Table 10.1 Understanding the pages on the administration portal *(continued)*

Page	Description
WSRP	Contains the Web Services for Remote Portlets (WSRP) Configuration portlet, which enables you to configure remote portlets.
Admin	Contains the Admin portlet, which enables you to manage portals, pages in those portals, and portlets displayed in those pages.

We return to the administration portal throughout the course of this chapter and the next as we cover various topics.

10.2 Creating a portlet

The example portlet displays an image from the web. For example, you can use the Image portlet to display the Red Hat logo, located at http://www.redhat.com/g/chrome/logo_rh_home.png, which we use as the default image.

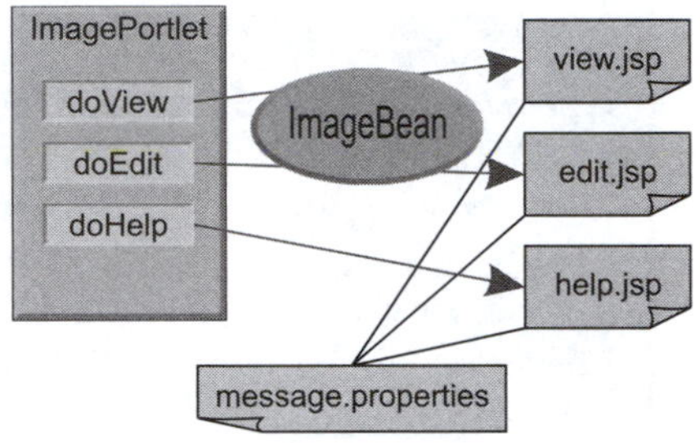

Figure 10.5 The architecture of the Image portlet. The JSPs are responsible for displaying the contents of the portlet. The `ImagePortlet` object passes an `ImageBean` object to the view and edit JSPs, which then use that data to decide what to display. All message text displayed by the JSPs is kept in a properties file for easy localization.

But you might not know the URLs for some interesting images because they change regularly. For example, one of our favorite websites is the NASA Astronomy Picture of the Day site, at http://antwrp.gsfc.nasa.gov/apod/astropix.html. Each day it displays a different picture at a different URL. To handle this changing image URL, the Image portlet can take a URL for a web page with an embedded image, and a regular expression that can extract the image URL, and then display the image using this URL. In addition, the image is presented as a hyperlink to the original web page. Using this capability, we can configure the Image portlet to display the daily astronomy picture in the portal. We don't present the code for this capability because it's outside the scope of this chapter, but the source code for the book contains many comments explaining how this works.

Figure 10.5 provides an overview of the Image portlet, showing the relationships among the various classes, JSPs, and properties files that make up the portlet.

The subsections that follow list and describe the various files that make up the portlet.

10.2.1 Coding the Image portlet

The example portlet uses JSP and JSTL, bringing up several JSP and JSTL-related topics. We don't go into detail on JSP or JSTL but focus instead on portlet-specific issues. We choose to use JSP and the JSTL, instead of a framework such as Struts or JSF, to keep the example simple and reduce the number of third-party dependencies.

The full listing for the portlet is lengthy, so we present it in sections with commentary after each section.

```
package org.jbia.portlet;
import java.io.*;
import java.net.*;
import java.net.URL;
import java.util.regex.*;
import javax.portlet.*;
public class ImagePortlet extends GenericPortlet {
```

The `ImagePortlet` class is a subclass of the `GenericPortlet` class, which provides a default implementation of the `javax.portlet.Portlet` interface. The `GenericPortlet` class determines the current display mode and calls the appropriate method. Several of the mode-related methods are implemented by the `ImagePortlet` class.

You can find the `javax.portlet` package in the jboss-portal.sar/lib/portal-portlet-jsr168api-lib.jar file. You need to include that file in the class path when you compile the portlet.

```
  private String jspView;
  private String jspHelp;
  private String jspEdit;
  @Override
  public void init(PortletConfig config) throws PortletException {
    super.init(config);
    jspView = config.getInitParameter("jsp-view");
    jspHelp = config.getInitParameter("jsp-help");
    jspEdit = config.getInitParameter("jsp-edit");
  }
```

As we mentioned, the code uses JSPs. The names of the JSPs are stored in local fields and obtained from the initialization parameters for the portlet. The `init` method, the preferred location in which to initialize local fields, is called after the portlet class is instantiated.

We could have hardcoded the JSP names in the portlet. But we didn't do so for two reasons: First, part of our objective is to teach you things about portlets, and using the `getInitParameter` method provides a convenient mechanism to introduce the concept of initialization parameters. Second, by loading the names from a configuration file you can easily move or rename the JSPs and still access them without having to modify the source code; a simple configuration change will suffice.

The portlet supports three display modes: *view*, *help*, and *edit*. Each mode has a dedicated method invoked by code in the `GenericPortlet` class. The use of each mode, as well as the code that implements each mode, is presented in the next three blocks of code.

```
  @Override
  protected void doView(RenderRequest request,
      RenderResponse response) throws PortletException, IOException{
    resolveImage(request, response, true);
    response.setContentType("text/html");
```

```
  PortletRequestDispatcher prd =
    getPortletContext().getRequestDispatcher(jspView);
  prd.include(request, response);
}
```

When a portlet is in *view* display mode, it displays its contents to the user. The `doView` method is called when the portlet is in view mode. In the example, the code calls a helper method, `resolveImage`, which we discuss later, to populate the JavaBean that it sends to the JSP. Next, the code sets the content type to indicate it will be sending an HTML document. The Portal supports only the text/HTML content type as output from portlets; you can't specify other content types, such as graphics images, like you can with servlets.

The last two statements indicate that the output generation will be performed by the JSP identified by `jspView`, which was set up as part of initialization.

```
@Override
protected void doHelp(RenderRequest request,
    RenderResponse response) throws PortletException, IOException{
  response.setContentType("text/html");
  PortletRequestDispatcher prd =
    getPortletContext().getRequestDispatcher(jspHelp);
  prd.include(request, response);
}
```

When a portlet is in *help* display mode, it displays help text to the user. The `doHelp` method is called when the portlet is in help mode. The code sets the content type to indicate it will be sending an HTML document. The last two statements indicate that the output generation will be performed by the JSP identified by `jspHelp`, which was set up as part of initialization. Except for the lack of the `resolveImage` call, the algorithm for this method is similar to that of the `doView` method that we showed earlier.

When a portlet is in *edit* display mode, it displays a form that allows users to personalize the output displayed by the portlet. The `doEdit` method, shown in listing 10.2, is called when the portlet is in edit mode.

Listing 10.2 The `doEdit` method

```
@Override
protected void doEdit(RenderRequest request,
    RenderResponse response) throws PortletException, IOException{
  ImageBean image =
   resolveImage(request, response, false);
  PortletURL action = response.createActionURL();
  action.setPortletMode(PortletMode.VIEW);               ❶
  image.setAction(action.toString());
  response.setContentType("text/html");
  PortletRequestDispatcher prd =
   getPortletContext().getRequestDispatcher(jspEdit);
  prd.include(request, response);
}
```

As with the `doView` method, the code calls the `resolveImage` helper method to populate the JavaBean that it sends to the JSP. It then calculates the URL used to send the user's changes back to the portlet and adds it to the JavaBean ❶. This URL depends on the implementation of the portal, and the `createActionURL` method enables the portlet to be portal agnostic. It sets the content type to indicate it's sending an HTML document. The last two statements indicate that the output generation will be performed by the JSP identified by `jspEdit`, which was set up as part of initialization. The algorithm for this method is similar to that of the `doView` method.

The `processAction` method, shown in listing 10.3, is called when the user submits data from the edit form.

Listing 10.3 The `processAction` method

```
@Override
public void processAction(ActionRequest request,
  ActionResponse response) throws PortletException, IOException{
 String title = request.getParameter("title");
 String url = request.getParameter("url");
 String regex = request.getParameter("regex");                ❶
 String submit = request.getParameter("submit");
 if (submit != null) {        ❷
  try {
   PortletPreferences pref = request.getPreferences();
   pref.setValue("title", title);
   pref.setValue("url", url);                                       ❸
   pref.setValue("regex", regex);
   pref.store();                                  Ignores
  } catch (ReadOnlyException e) {}          <--   exceptions
 }
 response.setPortletMode(PortletMode.VIEW);        ❹
}
```

The algorithm is simple. First, the code gets the user's input from the input parameters of the form ❶. Then it determines if the user pressed the submit button ❷ and, if so, updates the portlet preferences ❸. Note the call to the `store` method, which persists the changes. These changes are used later during view mode when resolving the image and creating the ImageBean.

You shouldn't use preferences as a database substitute. Although you, and many other hotel guests, might leave your luggage with the bell captain at the hotel for later pickup, you wouldn't consider leaving your household furnishings with the bell captain. For that you'd rent a storage space. The bell captain's storage room is similar to the space the portal provides for preferences: It's convenient, can handle small items, and is personal (each portal user can provide his own preferences). A storage area is more akin to a database and is a better solution if you need to store many things. If you decide you need a database, we recommend that you don't use the same database used by the portal; you should define your own. Defining a database for a portlet is no different than doing so for any other web application.

Preferences can be updated only when the portal calls the `processAction` method, which is called when the user enters data into a portlet in edit mode. Also, preferences can be updated only if the user is logged in. Once the preferences are saved, the code switches the portlet to view mode ❹.

We're now done with the portlet-specific methods. The rest of the methods are helper methods specific to the Image portlet, but they highlight general portlet functionality. The `resolveImage` method sets up the JavaBean passed to the JSPs. The other methods handle the disparity between providing a direct URL for the image and a URL for a web page that has an embedded image. Because the `resolveImage` method is also long, we tackle it in sections with commentary after each section.

```
private final ImageBean resolveImage(RenderRequest request,
    RenderResponse response,
    boolean isView) {
  PortletPreferences pref = request.getPreferences();
  String title = pref.getValue("title", null);
  String url = pref.getValue("url", null);
  String regex = pref.getValue("regex", null);
```

The information about what to display is stored in the preferences, so the first thing to do is to retrieve that information from the preferences.

```
  ImageBean image = new ImageBean();
```

All data displayed by the JSP is passed to the JSP in a JavaBean, so the code creates an `ImageBean` instance to hold that data. To keep this example simple, a single bean holds all possible data passed to any of the JSPs. In real life, you should have multiple beans, each with its own purpose.

```
  if (isView) {
    if (regex == null || regex.trim().length() == 0) {
      image.setUrl(url);
    } else {
      /* Refer to source for the code and description */
    }
    image.setLink(url);
```

The portlet could be in either view or edit mode. In view mode, the code determines if the URL is for the image (no `regex` given) or if it's for a web page with an embedded image (`regex` is given), and sets the bean properties accordingly. Refer to the source code for the book for the code that extracts the image URL from the web page.

```
  } else {
    image.setTitle(title);
    image.setUrl(url);
    image.setRegex(regex);
  }
```

If the portlet is in edit mode, the code sets the bean's properties.

```
  request.setAttribute("image", image);
```

The code adds the bean to the request attributes so that the JSP can access the data using the expression language.

```
  if (title != null && title.trim().length() > 0) {
    response.setTitle(title);
  }
```

If there's a title, which the code obtained from the preferences, it overrides the default title.

```
    return image;
  }
```

Finally, the code returns the bean. In edit mode, the form action URL is added to the bean, as you saw earlier in the `doEdit` method.

We're done with the source for the portlet. What do you have? You have a portlet that handles three modes: help, edit, and view. In help mode, it displays some help text. In edit mode, the portlet displays the preferences and lets you change them. In view mode, the portlet displays the image; it knows which one to display based on the preferences. In the simple case, one of the preferences is the URL of the image to show. In the more complicated case, one of the preferences is the URL of a page that contains the image, and another preference is a regular expression used to extract the URL of the image from the web page. Either way, in view mode, the image displays.

The `ImagePortlet` class isn't the only thing that you need to display the image. The code defers to JSPs for the display, and the `ImageBean` gets passed to the JSPs.

10.2.2 Coding the JSP-related source files

Before we describe the JSPs, we present the `ImageBean` containing the data the code passed to the JSPs. Once you know what that data is, we can present the JSPs.

CODING THE IMAGEBEAN

The `ImageBean` contains all the data that the portlet passes to the JSPs. We keep all the model data in a single bean to keep the example simple although, in real life, you might want to use multiple beans. The source for the bean is shown in listing 10.4.

Listing 10.4 ImageBean.java

```
package com.manning.jbia.portlet;
public class ImageBean {
 private String url;
 private String link;
 private String regex;
 private String title;
 private String action;
.<<getters and setters here>>
}
```

Table 10.2 describes how each property is used. The Mode column indicates if the property is used in the view or edit JSP.

Table 10.2 ImageBean properties

Property	Mode	Description
`url`	view, edit	In edit mode, this is the URL, either for a web page or for an image, entered by the user. In view mode, this is the URL of the image.
`link`	view	The URL used for the hyperlink to the image when displayed in view mode. Always corresponds to the URL entered by the user in edit mode.

Table 10.2 ImageBean properties *(continued)*

Property	Mode	Description
`regex`	edit	The regular expression used to extract the image from a web page.
`title`	edit	The title used when displaying the image.
`action`	edit	The value for the form action.

Now that you know what data is supplied to the JSPs, we can describe each of the JSPs.

THE VIEW MODE JSP

Figure 10.6 illustrates the view mode of the Image portlet, showing the pop-up help text that appears when you hover over the image.

The code for view.jsp is shown in listing 10.5.

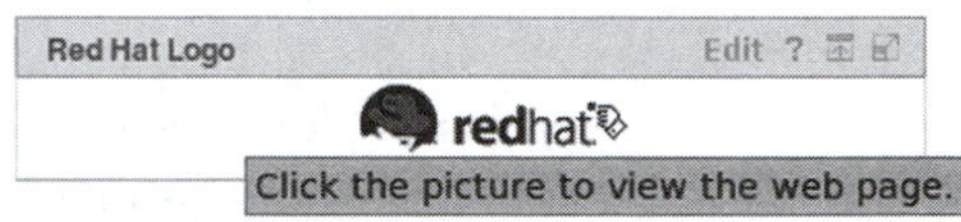

Figure 10.6 The view mode for the Image portlet, showing the tooltip for the image

Listing 10.5 view.jsp

```
<%@ page session="false"%>
<%@ taglib prefix="f" uri="http://java.sun.com/jsp/jstl/fmt"%>
<%@ taglib prefix="c" uri="http://java.sun.com/jsp/jstl/core"%>
<center>
  <a href="${image.link}" title="<f:message key='tip.link'/>"
     target="_new">
    <img src="${image.url}" style="border: 0;" />
  </a>
</center>
```

The JSP uses the JSP expression language to obtain data from the bean—for example, `${image.link}` as the `href` value for the anchor tag. The page uses the `f:message` tag to provide localized text from the message properties file defined in the web.xml file. The `style` property for the `img` tag prevents the image from being outlined because it's a hyperlink.

It's short and simple—thanks to the `ImageBean`, the expression language, and JSTL.

THE EDIT MODE JSP

Figure 10.7 illustrates the edit form displayed to the user and shows a help tip for the Regular Expression input field.

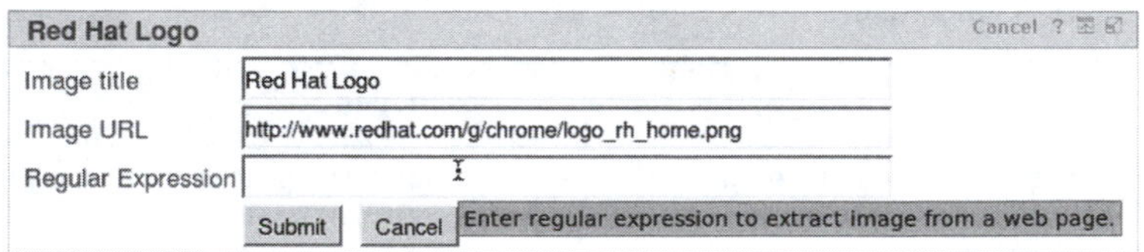

Figure 10.7 The edit mode for the Image portlet, showing the tooltip for the Regular Expression field

The JSP code, shown in listing 10.6, uses the expression language to obtain data from the bean and the `f:message` tag to provide localized text from the message properties file defined in the web.xml file. Because the portlet determines the form's action URL and supplies it as one of the bean's properties (the form's action is `${image.action}`) and because all data is provided via a bean, you don't need to declare the portlet tag library.

Listing 10.6 edit.jsp

```
<%@ taglib prefix="f" uri="http://java.sun.com/jsp/jstl/fmt"%>
<form action="${image.action}" method="post">
<table>
 <tr>
  <td><f:message key="label.title" /></td>
  <td><input type="text" size="60" name="title"
    title="<f:message key='tip.title' />" value="${image.title}"/>
  </td>
 </tr>
 <tr>
  <td><f:message key="label.url" /></td>
  <td><input type="text" size="60" name="url"
    title="<f:message key='tip.url' />" value="${image.url}" />
  </td>
 </tr>
 <tr>
  <td><f:message key="label.regex" /></td>
  <td><input type="text" size="60" name="regex"
    title="<f:message key='tip.regex' />"
    value="${image.regex}" escapeXml="false" />
  </td>
 </tr>
 <tr>
  <td> </td>
  <td><input type="submit" name="submit"
    value="<f:message key='button.submit' />" />
   <input type="submit" name="cancel"
    value="<f:message key='button.cancel' />" />
  </td>
 </tr>
</table>
</form>
```

This listing is definitely longer than the view JSP, but it's still simple. It creates a two-column table with field labels in the first column and input fields in the second column. Because there's no hardcoded text anywhere, it's easily localized.

THE HELP MODE JSP

Figure 10.8 illustrates what's displayed to the user when the Image portlet is in help mode.

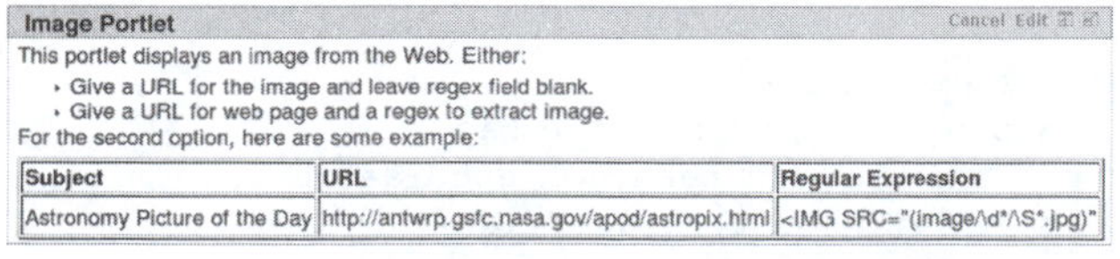

Figure 10.8 The help mode for the Image portlet, providing help text for the edit form

The JSP code shown in listing 10.7 relies on the f:message tag to show localized text.

Listing 10.7 help.jsp

```
<%@ page session="false"%>
<%@ taglib prefix="f" uri="http://java.sun.com/jsp/jstl/fmt"%>
<p><f:message key="help.intro" /></p>
<ol>
 <li><f:message key="help.option1" /></li>
 <li><f:message key="help.option2" /></li>
</ol>
<p><f:message key="help.table" /></p>
<table border="1" cellpadding="2px">
 <tr>
  <th><f:message key="help.table.subject" /></th>
  <th><f:message key="help.table.url" /></th>
  <th><f:message key="help.table.regex" /></th>
 </tr>
 <tr>
  <td><f:message key="help.table.subject.1" /></td>
  <td><f:message key="help.table.url.1" /></td>
  <td><f:message key="help.table.regex.1" /></td>
 </tr>
</table>
```

Once again, this listing creates a simple and easily localizable (thanks to the tag library) JSP.

All the JSPs use the f:message tag from the JSTL to display localized text. The message.properties file contains that text; let's look at that next.

THE MESSAGE.PROPERTIES FILE

The message.properties file, shown in listing 10.8, is referenced by both the web.xml and portlet.xml files. Only the web.xml reference is required by the JSTL; the portlet.xml file reference exists so that the portlet Java code can also access localized text.

Listing 10.8 message.properties

```
label.url=Image URL
label.regex=Regular Expression
label.title=Image title
tip.url=Enter URL for an image, or a page that contains an image.
tip.regex=Enter regular expression to extract image from a Web page.
tip.title=Enter the title for the image.
tip.link=Click the picture to view the Web page.
button.submit=Submit
button.cancel=Cancel
help.intro=This portlet displays an image from the Web. Either:
help.option1=Give a URL for the image and leave regex field blank.
help.option2=Give a URL for Web page and a regex to extract image.
help.table=For the second option, here are some example:
help.table.subject=Subject
help.table.url=URL
help.table.regex=Regular Expression
help.table.subject.1=Astronomy Picture of the Day
help.table.url.1=http://antwrp.gsfc.nasa.gov/apod/astropix.html
help.table.regex.1=&lt;IMG SRC=&quot;(image/\\d*/\\S*.jpg)&quot;
```

If you copy this file as, for example, message_de.properties and translate the text to German, anyone with a browser set to German as the preferred language will automatically see the German text.

You're familiar with the web.xml file, but what's this portlet.xml file that we mentioned? Glad you asked! Let's look at that file and the other portlet descriptors next.

10.2.3 Understanding the portlet descriptors

What do you have so far? You have the portlet, the JSPs the portlet uses to display things, the `ImageBean` used to pass data to the JSP, and a properties file for the displayed text. You have all the code you need for the portlet. Let's turn our attention toward the files needed to configure or describe the portlet. Yes, like many other Java technologies, the code to do the work isn't sufficient. You must also provide a descriptor that the portal container can use to deploy the portlet.

A variety of descriptor files are used for a portlet. One is defined by JSR-168, some are required for all web applications, and the rest are specific to the JBoss Portal. We present the contents and describe each file. In addition, all of these files are covered in detail in the documentation that comes with the JBoss Portal.

THE PORTLET.XML DESCRIPTOR FILE

The portlet.xml file is the standard portlet descriptor file defined by JSR-168. Listing 10.9 shows the entire file, but we don't go into great detail on its contents because both the JSR-168 specification and the Portal documentation cover the contents in detail. But we do highlight key nodes within the file.

Listing 10.9 The portlet.xml file for the Image portlet

```
<?xml version="1.0" encoding="UTF-8"?>
<portlet-app
 xmlns="http://java.sun.com/xml/ns/portlet/portlet-app_1_0.xsd"
 xmlns:xsi="http://www.w3.org/2001/XMLSchema-instance"
 xsi:schemaLocation=
   "http://java.sun.com/xml/ns/portlet/portlet-app_1_0.xsd"
 version="1.0">
 <portlet>
  <portlet-name>ImagePortlet</portlet-name>
  <display-name>Image Portlet</display-name>
  <description>Displays an image from the Web.</description>
    <portlet-class>
   com.manning.jbia.portlet.ImagePortlet</portlet-class>
  <init-param>
   <name>jsp-view</name>
   <value>/WEB-INF/jsp/view.jsp</value>
  </init-param>
  <init-param>
   <name>jsp-help</name>
   <value>/WEB-INF/jsp/help.jsp</value>
  </init-param>
  <init-param>
   <name>jsp-edit</name>
   <value>/WEB-INF/jsp/edit.jsp</value>
  </init-param>
```

```
      <supports>
        <mime-type>text/html</mime-type>
        <portlet-mode>VIEW</portlet-mode>
        <portlet-mode>EDIT</portlet-mode>
        <portlet-mode>HELP</portlet-mode>
      </supports>
      <resource-bundle>
        com.manning.jbia.portlet.message</resource-bundle>
      <portlet-info>
        <title>Image Portlet</title>
      </portlet-info>
      <portlet-preferences>
        <preference>
          <name>title</name>
          <value>Red Hat Logo</value>
        </preference>
        <preference>
          <name>url</name>
        <value>http://www.redhat.com/g/chrome/logo_rh_home.png</value>
        </preference>
        <preference>
          <name>regex</name>
          <value></value>
        </preference>
      </portlet-preferences>
    </portlet>
  </portlet-app>
```

Table 10.3 highlights key nodes from the portlet.xml file.

Table 10.3 Key portlet.xml file nodes

Node	Description
`<portlet-name>`	The name of the portlet. Used in various locations to reference this portlet.
`<display-name>`	The name displayed in the Admin portlet.
`<description>`	Brief text that describes the portlet. Also displayed in the Admin portlet.
`<init-param>`	Initialization parameters for the portlet. In this example, the JSP filenames for the various display modes are given.
`<supports>`	Identifies the type of output provided by the portlet (text/html, in this case) and which display modes the portlet handles.
`<resource-bundle>`	Identifies the resource bundle used for localized text.
`<portlet-info>`	The title for the portlet window. Note that the Image portlet overwrites this.
`<portlet-preferences>`	The portlet preferences. Unlike the initialization parameters, which are read-only, the preferences can be updated by the portlet, usually in response to user input in edit mode. We could omit the `regex` preference. But by providing it, it becomes available in the Admin portlet when managing portlet instances and can be overridden in the portlet-instances.xml file, which we cover later.

Now let's move on to the next descriptor file, web.xml.

THE WEB.XML DESCRIPTOR FILE

The web.xml file, shown in listing 10.10, is a standard deployment descriptor used with web applications and, for most portlets, is empty. Because the Image portlet uses JSTL, we declare the message properties file and also the 2.5 version of the servlet specification, simplifying the use of the expression language in the JSPs.

Listing 10.10 web.xml

```
<?xml version="1.0" encoding="UTF-8"?>
<web-app
  xmlns="http://java.sun.com/xml/ns/javaee"
  xmlns:xsi="http://www.w3.org/2001/XMLSchema-instance"
  xsi:schemaLocation="http://java.sun.com/xml/ns/javaee
    http://java.sun.com/xml/ns/javaee/web-app_2_5.xsd"
  version="2.5">
 <context-param>
  <param-name>
   javax.servlet.jsp.jstl.fmt.localizationContext</param-name>
  <param-value>com.manning.jbia.portlet.message</param-value>
 </context-param>
</web-app>
```

You've now seen both of the standard descriptor files. The rest of the descriptor files are specific to the JBoss Portal.

THE JBOSS-APP.XML DESCRIPTOR FILE

The jboss-app.xml file, shown in listing 10.11, defines the name of the portlet application. This name is used, along with the portlet name, as part of the identification string for the portlet.

Listing 10.11 jboss-app.xml

```
<jboss-app>
 <app-name>image</app-name>
</jboss-app>
```

If you don't provide this file with an <app-name> node, the context name is used within the portlet id. For example, if the Image portlet is packaged in a WAR file named image.war, then the text */image* is used as part of the portlet id. This point might not appear to be important now, but you'll appreciate the distinction when you use the Admin portlet to manage the portlet. Additionally, by providing an application name here, you effectively separate the portlet name from that of the WAR file.

The Document Type Definition (DTD) file that describes the layout of the jboss-app.xml file can be found at core/src/resources/dtd/jboss-app_2_0.dtd in the source download for the Portal.

THE PORTLET-INSTANCES.XML DESCRIPTOR FILE

The portlet-instances.xml file, shown in listing 10.12, describes instances of the portlet. In this case, no instances are declared. You can omit this file and the portlet still deploys.

Listing 10.12 portlet-instances.xml

```
<?xml version="1.0" encoding="UTF-8" standalone="yes"?>
<deployments>
</deployments>
```

The DTD file can be found at core/src/resources/dtd/portlet-instances_2_0.dtd in the source download for the Portal. We return to this file in section 10.3 when we declare a portlet instance.

THE *-OBJECT.XML DESCRIPTOR FILE

The *-object.xml file, shown in listing 10.13, describes portlet objects such as the windows used to display the portlet instances. The recommended convention is to use the portlet application name in this filename; therefore, the file is named image-object.xml. But the name is irrelevant; you could name the file foobar-object.xml, and it would work fine. In addition, you can have multiple *-object.xml files.

Listing 10.13 image-object.xml

```
<?xml version="1.0" encoding="UTF-8" standalone="yes"?>
<deployments>
</deployments>
```

Because no instances are declared in the portlet-instances.xml file, you don't need to declare anything in this file. If you omit this file, the portlet still deploys. Unfortunately, there's no DTD or XML Schema Definition language (XSD) file that describes the *-object.xml file. We return to this file in section 10.4 when we place the portlet on a page.

We could also provide a jboss-web.xml file, but because it doesn't play a role in the example Image portlet, we omit it.

Now what do you have? You have the portlet code, including JSPs, and you have the descriptor files. Therefore, you have the entire set of source files that you need to build the portlet.

10.2.4 Building and deploying the portlet

We need to warn you about an issue that you probably won't encounter when you deploy your own portlets, but one that occurs because we show how to configure the Image portlet in several steps, deploying it after each step. When a portlet is deployed, the Portal updates the database with the portlet deployment information. In the course of this chapter, we ask you to deploy the same Image portlet with a variety of different deployment descriptors. Each time the Image portlet is deployed, we assume that it wasn't deployed before. Therefore, you'll have to clean out the database between each Image portlet deployment. One way to do this it to stop the application server, drop the database and create it again, and then start the application server up again. The Ant script that comes with the source distribution does this for you, and contains ample documentation to explain how to use it. In a real environment, you wouldn't have to clean out the database because you'd deploy with the proper configuration to begin with. If you want to change the configuration after deploying, the Portal provides various management tools that make this easy, as you'll see in the course of this chapter and the next. With this caveat in mind, let's continue.

You package a portlet within a WAR file. Figure 10.9 illustrates the directory hierarchy for the image.war file.

Copy the WAR file to the deploy directory of the server to deploy the portlet. At this point, the portlet is ready for use in the portal.

Now that the portlet has been deployed, you might wonder where it is. It doesn't appear anywhere, even if you refresh the portal page. You can't see the portlet based on what we've told you so far because you've not yet created a portlet instance or a portlet window.

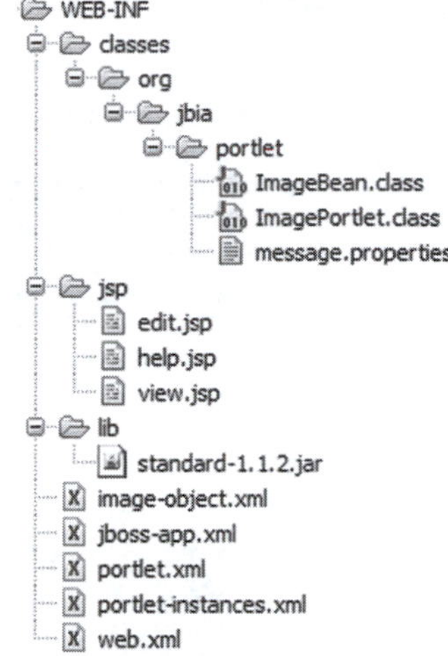

Figure 10.9 Image portlet WAR file directory hierarchy

10.3 Creating a portlet instance

You can create an instance either by providing instance information in the portlet-instances.xml file or by using the Admin portlet. We explain both. Which is the best to use? We recommend that you provide a default configuration in the portlet-instances.xml file, and then, if necessary, fine tune it in the Admin portlet. Let's look at using the portlet-instance.xml file first.

10.3.1 Creating an instance using the portlet-instance.xml file

The portlet-instances.xml file is used to identify one or more instances of a portlet. The portlet-instances.xml file shown in listing 10.14 creates a single instance of the Image portlet.

Listing 10.14 Declaring an instance in portlet-instances.xml

```
<?xml version="1.0" encoding="UTF-8" standalone="yes"?>
<deployments>
  <deployment>
    <instance>
      <instance-id>ImagePortletInstance</instance-id>
      <portlet-ref>ImagePortlet</portlet-ref>
    </instance>
  </deployment>
</deployments>
```

The name of the instance created is `ImagePortletInstance`, which is an instance of the portlet named `ImagePortlet`. The <portlet-ref> node must match the <portlet-name> node in the portlet.xml file. The instance name must be unique among all portlet instances. The name can contain any characters including special characters and spaces.

The resulting image.war file has the same set of files as mentioned earlier. When the WAR file is deployed, the instance gets created. See the warning at the start of section 10.2.4 before deploying the WAR file.

10.3.2 Creating an instance using the Admin portlet

Alternatively, you can use the Admin portlet to create an instance. Figure 10.10 illustrates this progression through the Admin portlet.

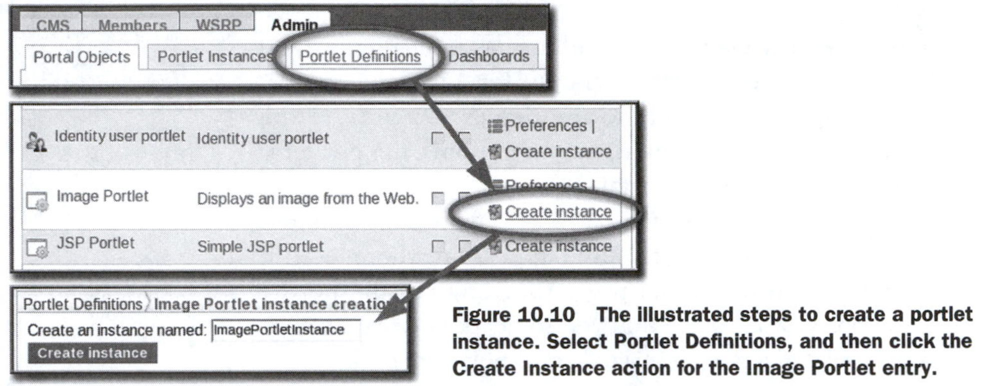

Figure 10.10 The illustrated steps to create a portlet instance. Select Portlet Definitions, and then click the Create Instance action for the Image Portlet entry.

Click the Portlet Definitions tab on the top of the Admin portlet window, and a list of deployed portlets is displayed. The portlets are displayed in alphabetical order by id, so the Image Portlet should be easy to find. In the Actions column, click the Create Instance link and fill in the instance name, such as *ImagePortletInstance*, on the resulting form. Click the Create Instance button.

You can create multiple instances of the portlet by repeating these steps, each time supplying a different name.

Even after creating a portlet instance, you'll notice that the Image portlet isn't visible. Only one more task is left—declaring the portlet window—and you'll see what you've been patiently looking for.

10.4 Declaring a portlet window

To display a portlet, you must first create an instance and then place it on a page. The previous section covered creating the instance. This section covers how to put that instance on a page—also known as *defining a portlet window*.

Once again, you can do this in two ways. If you prefer configuration files, you can describe the portlet window, or object, using the *-object.xml file. And if you prefer user interfaces, you can use the Admin portlet. We recommend providing a default configuration in the *-object.xml file, and then, if necessary, fine tuning it in the Admin portlet. We discuss the *-object.xml method first.

10.4.1 Declaring a portlet window using the *-object.xml file

The *-object.xml file defines portlet windows that display portlet instances. This file declares the portal, page, and location on the page for the portal window—also known as the *portal object*. If you change the image-object.xml file as shown in listing 10.15, then the Image portlet instance appears at the bottom of the portal home page.

Listing 10.15 Image-object.xml file with location information

```
<?xml version="1.0" encoding="UTF-8" standalone="yes"?>
<deployments>
  <deployment>
    <if-exists>keep</if-exists>
    <parent-ref>default.default</parent-ref>
    <window>
      <window-name>ImagePortletWindow</window-name>
      <instance-ref>ImagePortletInstance</instance-ref>
      <region>center</region>
      <height>1</height>
    </window>
  </deployment>
</deployments>
```

Table10.4 describes the nodes in this file.

Table 10.4 Descriptions of the nodes in the *-object.xml file

Node	Description
`<if-exists>`	Indicates what to do if the instance already exists. The value `overwrite` means to use the new data provided in the file. The value `keep` means to keep the existing instance configuration and ignore the new configuration in the file. Note that all portal information is maintained in the database, so this directive describes how the content of this file interacts with the current database contents. Experience has shown that overwriting isn't perfect, hence our warning in section 10.2.4 concerning redeploying the portlet.
`<parent-ref>`	Defines the location of the portlet instance on the page. The value is a two-part, dot-separated name. The first part identifies the portal name, and the second part identifies the page name. In our example, the instance shows up on the *default* page of the *default* portal.
`<window>`	The subnodes of this node define how the portlet window appears on the page.
`<window-name>`	Defines the name that can be used to identify the portlet window. The name must be unique among the window names on the page.
`<instance-ref>`	This matches the `<instance-id>` defined in portlet-instances.xml.
`<region>`	Identifies where on the page the portlet window appears. The values allowed depend on the layout manager for the portal. The default layout manager accepts the values `left` and `center`.
`<height>`	Identifies the relative location of this portlet window with the other portlet windows. Lower-numbered portlet windows appear above higher-numbered portlet windows.

Package this file into the image.war file, and when the WAR is deployed, the instance gets created and placed on the default page of the default portal. See the warning at the start of section 10.2.4 before deploying the WAR file. Now, when you go to the portal in your browser, you should see the Image portlet. Finally!

10.4.2 Declaring a portlet window using the Admin portlet

In section 10.3.2, you created an instance of the Image portlet using the Admin portlet. In this section, you place that instance on a page.

In the Admin portlet, click the Portal Objects tab. The Admin portlet shows a table containing the defined portals, which are Admin, Default, and Template. The names are links, so click Default, as shown in figure 10.11.

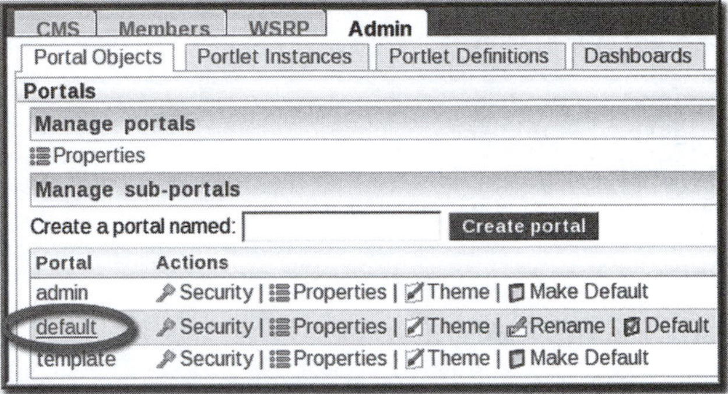

Figure 10.11 Creating a portlet window. Step 1: Choose the Default Portal.

The table now contains the names of the pages in the Default Portal; these pages are News, Weather, and Default. Notice that breadcrumbs, which identify where you are in the portal definition hierarchy, appear above the table. Once again, the page names are links, so click Default, as shown in figure 10.12.

Figure 10.12 Creating a portlet window. Step 2: Choose the Default Page.

The table now lists the portlet windows defined on that page. Click the Page Layout link that appears below the breadcrumbs, as shown in figure 10.13.

Two panels are displayed—Content Definition and Page Layout. The Page Layout panel lists the Windows in each region, Center and Left, and provides buttons to manage the region. The Content Definition panel contains a field where you can supply

Figure 10.13 Creating a portlet window. Step 3: Display the Page Layout for the Default Page.

the name for a new instance, a drop-down box for the type of content to add, and then a list of items that match the content type. If the Content Type is Portlet, then the portlet instances are shown. To create a portlet window, type in a name and click the desired portlet instance, ImagePortletInstance in this case. Note that the page refreshes when you select a portlet instance, and details about the selected instance appear above the list of instances. In addition, the selected instance is highlighted. In the Page Layout panel, click the Add button for the Center Region, as shown in figure 10.14. When the page refreshes, the new portlet window appears in the list as shown in the overlay in figure 10.14.

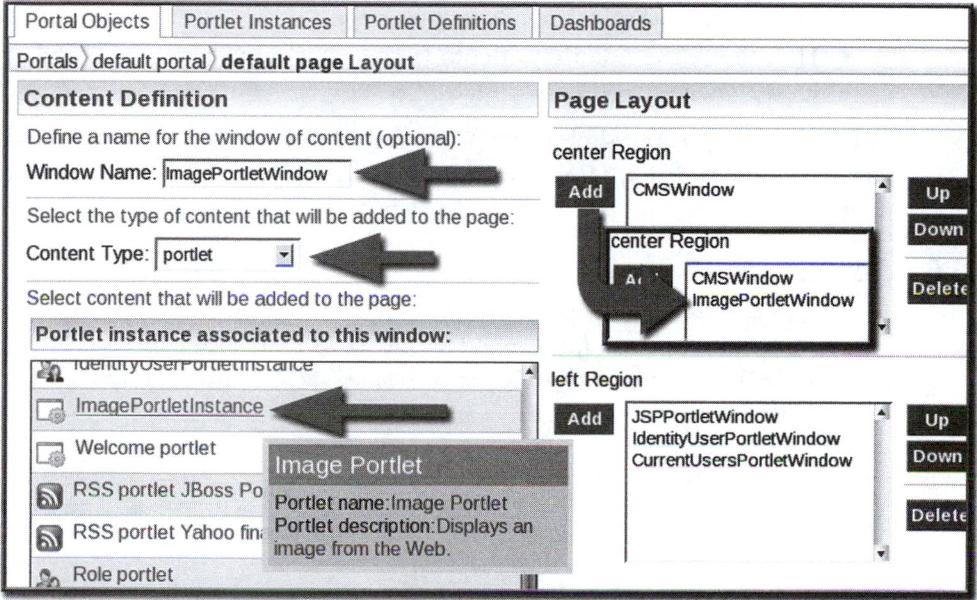

Figure 10.14 Creating a portlet window. Step 4: Create the portlet window from the portlet instance.

To view the Image portlet, click the Portal link in the right side of the header, as shown in the upper portion of figure 10.15, and the portal home page displays. The Image portlet is visible at the bottom of the page, as shown in lower portion of figure 10.15.

Our effort to create a portlet and display it in the portal is now complete.

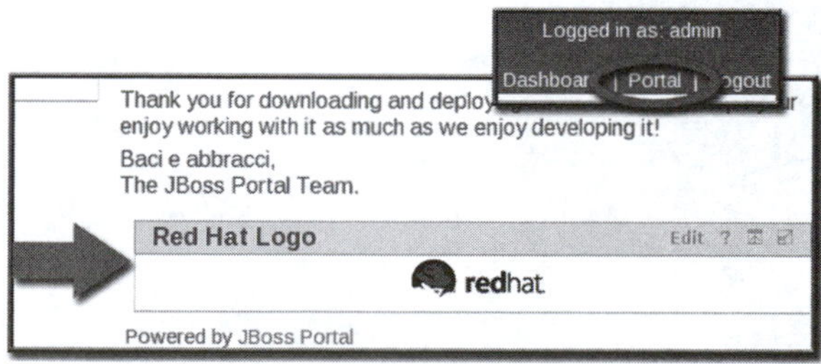

Figure 10.15 Viewing the results after creating the portlet window. The Image portlet is at the bottom of the page.

10.5 Summary

This chapter provided a brief introduction into portals and portlets. We presented the following:

- A brief description of portals and portal terminology
- A brief overview of the features provided by the JBoss Portal
- Instructions for installing the JBoss Portal, including configuring the MySQL database for use with the Portal
- An example portlet that used JSPs and JSTL to display an image to the user
- How to use the various configuration files to deploy a portlet, create a portlet instance, and display the portlet on a page
- How to use the Admin portlet to create a portlet instance and display the portlet on a page

In the next chapter, we show some of the features of the JBoss Portal, such as security and the CMS. And don't forget about the portlet you created in this chapter; you'll need it.

10.6 References

JSR-168 specification—http://jcp.org/en/jsr/detail?id=168

JBoss Portal documentation—http://labs.jboss.com/jbossportal/docs/index.html

Stefan Hepper, et al., Portlets and Apache Portals, Manning, 2005—http://www.manning.com/hepper/

11 Configuring the JBoss Portal

This chapter covers

- Configuring window appearance
- Working with multiple windows and instances
- Working with the CMS portlet
- Securing the Portal
- Developing a custom portal

In the previous chapter, you developed a simple Image portlet and deployed it to the portal. In this chapter, we describe various configuration topics including security and the CMS.

If you're new to portals and portlets and haven't read through chapter 10, "The JBoss Portal and portlets," we urge you to do so now. In that chapter, we define many terms and present many portal concepts that aren't repeated here.

We use the Image portlet from chapter 10 to illustrate several of the topics in this chapter. These topics include configuring the appearance of the portlet window, working with multiple portlet instances, and securing the portal and portlets. Along the way, we also cover the CMS that comes with the Portal. We conclude the chapter by developing and deploying a customized portal. This final topic makes use of many of the capabilities that you'll learn in this chapter, and helps you personalize the portal for your use.

11.1 Configuring window appearance

We left off in the previous chapter having finally displayed the Image portlet in a portlet window on the default page. The Image portlet window has a border and title bar. This appearance is controlled by the renderer defined for the portlet. The two basic render sets that ship with the Portal are the `div` renderer, which displays the border and title bar, and the `empty` renderer, which doesn't. In addition, there are AJAX-capable variations of each renderer, but the AJAX capabilities don't influence the window appearance. We don't cover the AJAX capabilities of the Portal in this book, but you can read about them in the Portal Reference Guide.

The renderers are defined in the file jboss-portal.sar/portal-core.war/WEB-INF/layout/portal-renderSet.xml. If you look at this file, you'll note that each renderer identifies classes that participate in the rendering of a portlet window. You could provide your own rendering classes and your own render sets. In this section, we focus our discussion on the default render sets that come with the Portal.

The Portal provides fine-grained control over the window rendering. The best way to illustrate this point is to use the Admin portlet to change the renderer used for the Image portlet window. Log in as admin, and on the Admin page with the Portal Objects tab selected, click Default portal, and then the Default page. Click the Theme link next to the ImagePortletWindow. These steps are illustrated in figure 11.1.

The three renderers can each be configured by selecting one of five rendering options. The Default option uses the renderer inherited from the parent—in this case, from the page. Although there are eight combinations (ignoring the default option because it uses the inherited renderer and ignoring the AJAX-related options because they don't affect the appearance), they result in only three usable appearances of the window, as illustrated in table 11.1.

You might wonder why anyone would want to use different renderers. If the portlet provides an edit mode and you want your users to be able to edit the preferences, then

Table 11.1 Portlet window appearances for various renderers

Window renderer	`divRenderer`	`emptyRenderer`	`divRenderer`
Decoration renderer	`divRenderer`	`emptyRenderer`	`emptyRenderer`
Portlet renderer	`divRenderer`	`emptyRenderer`	`emptyRenderer`
Description	Full window title and border	No title or border	Empty window title with border

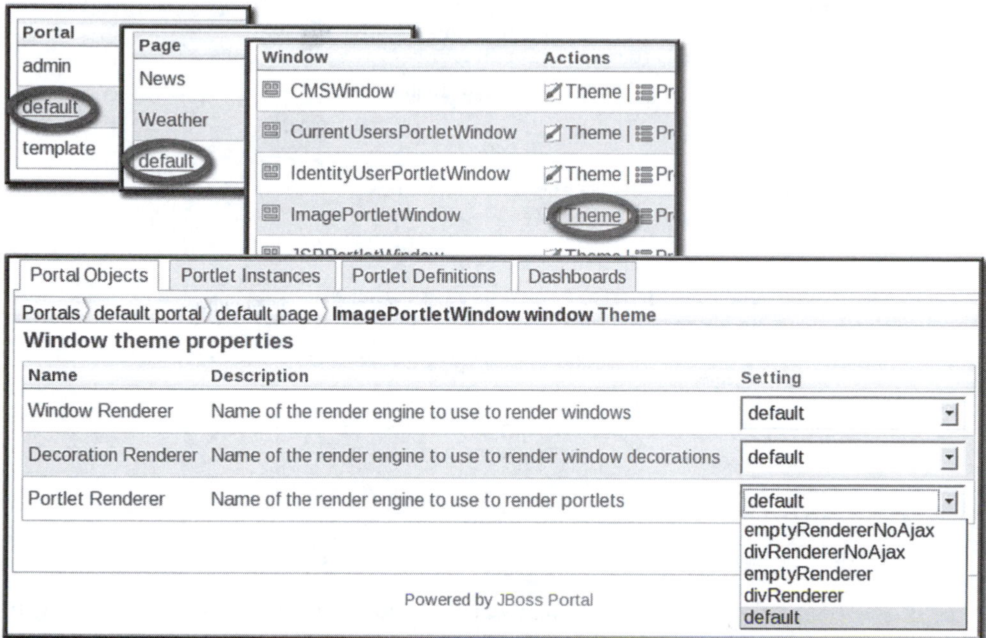

Figure 11.1 To change the portlet window renderer, click through Portal and Page to get to the list of portlet windows, and then click the Theme link next to the desired portlet window.

you should choose the option with the full window title and border. An example of this is the Weather portlet. If you want only the view mode visible, then you should choose the option with no title or border. An example of this is the CMS content that appears in the center panel of the Default portal home page. If you want to provide a frame around the portlet but prevent the user from editing, minimizing, or maximizing the portlet, then you should choose the option with the empty window title with border.

11.1.1 Configuring window appearance using *-object.xml

You can also set the renderers in the *-object.xml file—the preferred way of defining the renderers because you typically know at development time how you want the portlet window rendered.

The Image portlet displays the Red Hat logo in a window in the center panel of the portal window. But you might want to display the logo without any borders or title in the left panel. To do this, update the image-object.xml file as shown in listing 11.1.

Listing 11.1 Setting the window decorations in *-object.xml

```
<?xml version="1.0" encoding="UTF-8" standalone="yes"?>
<deployments>
 <deployment>
  <if-exists>keep</if-exists>
  <parent-ref>default.default</parent-ref>
```

```
<window>
 <window-name>ImagePortletWindow</window-name>
 <instance-ref>ImagePortletInstance</instance-ref>
 <region>left</region>
 <height>99</height>
 <properties>
  <property>
   <name>theme.windowRendererId</name>
   <value>emptyRenderer</value>
  </property>
  <property>
   <name>theme.decorationRendererId</name>
   <value>emptyRenderer</value>
  </property>
  <property>
   <name>theme.portletRendererId</name>
   <value>emptyRenderer</value>
  </property>
 </properties>
</window>
</deployment>
</deployments>
```

Changed lines (region, height)

New lines (properties)

Package this file into the image.war file, and when the WAR is deployed, the portlet window gets created and placed at the bottom of the left panel on the Default page of the Default portal. Now, when you go to the portal in your browser, you should see the logo without any title or borders at the bottom of the left panel of the window. See the warning at the start of section 10.2.4 before deploying the WAR file.

Notice that, without the title bar, the user doesn't have access to the Help or Edit button. The only way to change the image displayed is to log in as an administrator and change the preferences for the instance in the Admin portlet.

Up to this point, you've displayed the image in various locations on the page and rendered the window in a variety of ways. But you might want to show multiple images on the same page. For example, your website might use a variety of open source projects, and you'd like to acknowledge their use by displaying their "powered by" or "built by" icons. Let's look at how to display multiple windows for the same portlet next.

11.2 Working with multiple windows and instances

Try this. Using the Admin portlet, create two portlet windows for the Weather portlet on the Weather page of the Default portal. Refer back to section 10.4 if you need help doing this. Then view the Weather page. Click the Edit icon in the title bar of one of the Weather portlet windows and change the Zip Code. When you submit the changed Zip Code, the weather for that portlet changes, but the other portlet still shows the weather for Miami. So far, so good. Now, log out and log back in. Oops! Now both Weather portlet windows display the same weather for the new Zip Code! That's probably not what you wanted or expected.

The problem is that a portlet window is a window for a portlet instance; it isn't an instance itself. And the portlet instance keeps track of the preference data. When you set the preference data for the instance from one window, the preference data is picked up by the other window because that window uses the same instance. To be even more accurate, preference data is stored per user per portlet instance so that each user can personalize each portlet instance.

If you want to see the weather from two (or more) locations, you have to first create another (or several) Weather portlet instances. We'll wait while you do this. If you need a hint, go back to section 10.3. Done? Good. Now remove one of the Weather portlet windows from the Weather page. To remove a portlet window, go to the Page Layout view for the page in the Admin portlet, click the portlet window name in the list box in the Page Layout panel, and click the Delete button. Now add a window for the second Weather portlet instance and go back to the Weather page. You should be able to change the Zip Code of one of the Weather portlets without affecting the other, even if you log out and back in.

11.2.1 Configuring multiple instances and windows using the descriptor files

We want to place three images on the page. Two of the images—the Red Hat and JBoss logos—go at the bottom of the left column. Additionally, we want the astronomy picture of the day displayed on the Default page.

You should know how to place the images already. Recall that you can use the portal-instances.xml file to declare the three instances, one for each of the images. Also, you can use the *-object.xml file to position the portlet windows on the page. Although we previously showed only one instance and window, you should be able to easily figure out multiple instances and windows. But we haven't covered one area: how to change the preferences so that each window displays something different. So far, the preferences have appeared only in the portlet.xml file, which describes the portal itself, not the instances.

You can use the portlet-instance.xml file to override the default preference settings declared in portlet.xml. Note that you can't add new preferences, only override ones already declared. The full portlet-instance.xml file that contains the three desired Image portlet instances is given in listing 11.2.

Listing 11.2 Declaring multiple portlet instances

```
<?xml version="1.0" encoding="UTF-8" standalone="yes"?>
<deployments>
 <deployment>
  <instance>
   <instance-id>RedHatLogoInstance</instance-id>
   <portlet-ref>ImagePortlet</portlet-ref>
  </instance>
 </deployment>
 <deployment>
  <instance>
   <instance-id>JBossLogoInstance</instance-id>
   <portlet-ref>ImagePortlet</portlet-ref>
```

❶ First instance with RedHat logo

❷ Second instance with JBoss logo

```
    <preferences>
     <preference>
      <name>url</name>
      <value>http://www.jboss.com/themes
➥ /jbosstheme/img/logo.gif\</value>
     </preference>
    </preferences>
   </instance>
  </deployment>
  <deployment>
   <instance>
    <instance-id>AstronomyInstance</instance-id>
    <portlet-ref>ImagePortlet</portlet-ref>
    <preferences>
     <preference>
      <name>title</name>
      <value>Astronomy Picture of the Day</value>
     </preference>
     <preference>
      <name>url</name>
      <value>http://antwrp.gsfc.nasa.gov/apod
➥ /astropix.html</value>
     </preference>
     <preference>
      <name>regex</name>
      <value>IMG SRC="(image/\d*/\S*.jpg)"</value>
     </preference>
    </preferences>
   </instance>
  </deployment>
</deployments>
```

❷ Second instance with JBoss logo

❸ Third instance with astronomy picture

Notice that the first instance ❶ is declared without any preferences because it inherits the default preferences defined in the portlet.xml file. For the second instance ❷, you define a different `url` preference. You don't redefine the `title` preference because this instance is rendered without a border, hiding the title. For the third instance ❸, you set all the preferences.

That takes care of the instances; now let's look at the *-object.xml file which describes the window locations, as given in listing 11.3.

Listing 11.3 Declaring multiple portlet windows/objects

```
<?xml version="1.0" encoding="UTF-8" standalone="yes"?>
<deployments>
 <deployment>
  <if-exists>keep</if-exists>
  <parent-ref>default.default</parent-ref>
  <window>
   <window-name>RedHatLogoWindow</window-name>
   <instance-ref>RedHatLogoInstance</instance-ref>
   <region>left</region>
   <height>98</height>
   <properties>
    <property>
```

Red Hat logo on default page

```
      <name>theme.windowRendererId</name>
      <value>emptyRenderer</value>
     </property>
     <property>
      <name>theme.decorationRendererId</name>
      <value>emptyRenderer</value>
     </property>
     <property>
      <name>theme.portletRendererId</name>
      <value>emptyRenderer</value>
     </property>
    </properties>
   </window>
  </deployment>
  <deployment>
   <if-exists>keep</if-exists>
   <parent-ref>default.default</parent-ref>
   <window>
    <window-name>JBossLogoWindow</window-name>
    <instance-ref>JBossLogoInstance</instance-ref>
    <region>left</region>
    <height>99</height>
    *** same properties as above ***
   </window>
  </deployment>
  <deployment>
   <if-exists>keep</if-exists>
   <parent-ref>default.default</parent-ref>
   <window>
    <window-name>AstronomyWindow</window-name>
    <instance-ref>AstronomyInstance</instance-ref>
    <region>center</region>
    <height>99</height>
   </window>
  </deployment>
 </deployments>
```

Red Hat logo on default page

JBoss logo on default page

Astronomy picture on default page

To display the Red Hat and JBoss logos without any borders, you define the window renderer properties for them (to save space in the book, we show the rendering properties only for the first logo window). Based on the `height` setting, the Red Hat logo appears above the JBoss logo. You don't declare any rendering for the astronomy picture so that the border shows for it.

Package these files into the image.war file and when the WAR is deployed, the instances get created and placed at their respective locations. See the warning at the start of section 10.2.4 before deploying the WAR file. When you go to the portal in your browser, you should see the logos at the bottom of the left column of the window and the astronomy picture in the center column.

11.3 Working with the CMS portlet

The Portal ships with a basic Content Management System (CMS) that you can use to display static data. In addition, you can use the CMS to provide downloads of binary artifacts such as documents and images. In this section, we show you how to work with the CMS to accomplish these goals.

11.3.1 Gathering example CMS data

The first thing you need is some data to display within the CMS portlet. The software download for the book contains some simple files you can use for this purpose. Because some of the files are binary, it's difficult to provide listings for them in the book. But the content is simple, and you can make your own if you like.

The main file is a simple HTML page, as given in listing 11.4, that references two documents and a second HTML file, and contains an image.

Listing 11.4 CMS content example—index.html

```
<html>
<body>
<table border="0">
  <tr>
    <td>Some interesting documents:
    <ul>
      <li><a href="book/doc/doc_01.doc">first</a></li>
      <li><a href="book/doc/doc_02.doc">second</a></li>
    </ul>
    </td>
    <td><img src="book/image/image.gif"/></td>
  </tr>
  <tr>
    <td colspan="2"><a href="book/two.html">Next</a></td>
  </tr>
</table>
</body>
</html>
```

Each reference starts with a directory named *book*, as in book/doc/doc_01.doc, because later you'll load this content into a folder named *book* within the CMS. The second HTML file, listing 11.5, contains a link back to the first HTML page.

Listing 11.5 CMS content example—two.html

```
<html>
<body>
  <p>A lot of interesting text.</p>
  <p><a href="book/index.html">Back</a></p>
</body>
</html>
```

If you like, you can gather your own documents and your own image and use those. Either rename your files as referenced in the HTML page, or change the HTML page to reference your files. Once you have the files, package them into a zip file so that the contents are as shown in figure 11.2.

Figure 11.2 Layout of example CMS zip file

Now that you have your content, let's look at how to upload and display it in the CMS portlet.

11.3.2 Displaying the new content

Log into the portal as admin, go to the Admin portal, and go to the CMS page. The CMS page contains the CMS Administration portlet, which you can use to manage the CMS content. Initially, the content consists of a single folder named *default*. A drop-down list box presents the possible actions you can perform, including creating a new folder and uploading a file.

You need to create another folder and add the content to that folder. To do this, you complete the following steps:

1. Select the Create Folder action. The page refreshes, displaying a Confirm Directory Creation form.
2. Name the new folder *book*, and click the Create button. The page refreshes, displaying the contents of the new book folder, which is empty. Notice that breadcrumbs at the top of the portlet window indicate how deep you are in the folder structure.
3. Select the Upload Archive action. The page refreshes, displaying an Upload Archive form.

Browse for the zip file, and then click the Upload button. When the page refreshes, you'll see the two HTML files and the doc and image folders listed.

These steps and the result are illustrated in figure 11.3.

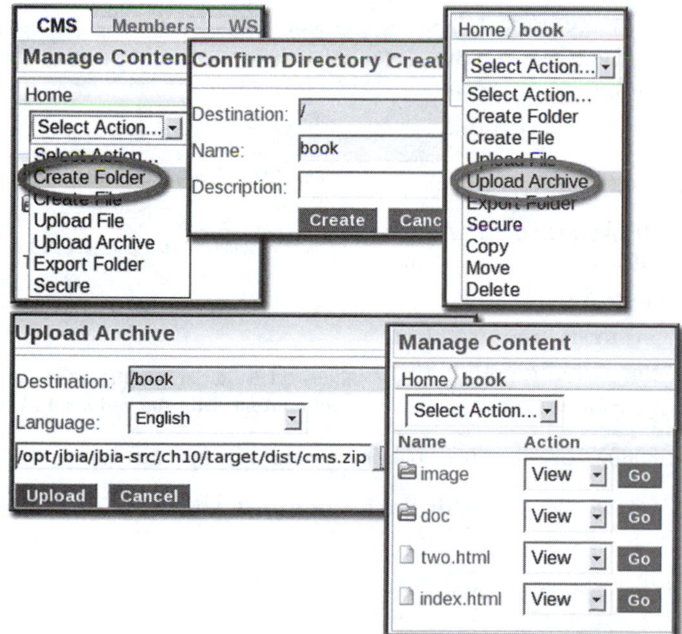

Figure 11.3 To upload content into the CMS, create a new folder for the content, and then upload a zip archive. The bottom image shows the uploaded content.

Now that you have the content loaded, let's get the CMS Window to display that content.

In the Admin portlet, drill down through the Default portal and Default page. Then click the CMSWindow link. The base CMS content, which consists of the default and book folders, appears. Notice that the Selected File attribute lists /default/index.html as the current value. Click the Book folder and then the Index.html file. When the page refreshes, the Default page contents are displayed again. Log out and log back in, and the new CMS content appears instead of the default. These steps and the final result are illustrated in figure 11.4.

When you click the two document links, you download the documents. The Next link displays the other page in the CMS portlet window.

Although this example is simple, we're sure that you can easily see the power of Portal's CMS capability. You can upload any static content and easily display it. In addition, the CMS Administration portlet provides HTML editing capabilities so that you can easily make quick modifications to the content uploaded. The HTML editor is a bit beyond what we plan to cover in this chapter, but it's fairly intuitive; you can find documentation for it in the Quick Start Guide and the User's Guide provided with the Portal.

Figure 11.4 To set the content to display in the CMS window, drill down to the CMSWindow, click it, and then drill down to the desired page to display. The bottom image shows the home page showing the new contents.

Hmm. You've uploaded an image into the CMS. The example Image portlet displays images. What would it take to get the Image portlet to display images from the CMS? Perfect segue to the next section!

11.3.3 Accessing CMS content

With the CMS portlet displaying the new content you loaded in the previous section, hover over one of the document links and note the URL, which is shown in figure 11.5.

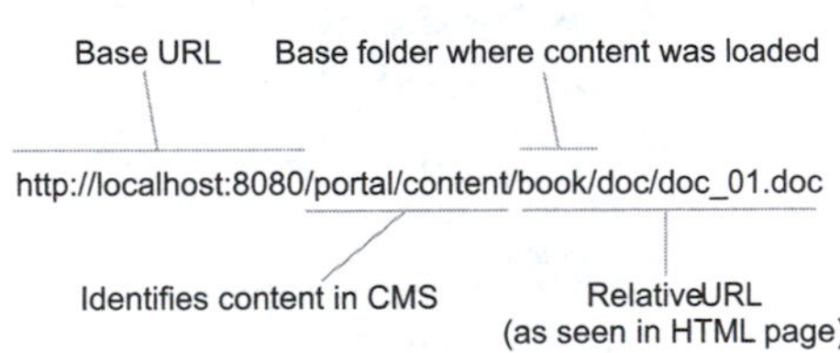

Figure 11.5 Example URL used to access CMS content, with the various parts labeled

From this, you can conclude that the URL for the image is as follows:

http://localhost:8080/portal/content/book/image/image.gif

From a portal page, you wouldn't specify the host or port; you'd use the following relative URL:

/portal/content/book/image/image.gif

Edit the URL for the astronomy Image portlet window, which you created in section 11.2. Remove the regular expression, and after you submit the changes (shown in figure 11.6), the CMS image is displayed.

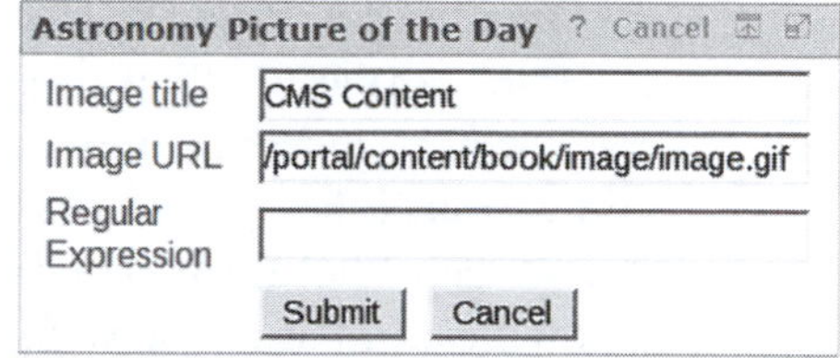

Figure 11.6 To access the CMS content from the Image portlet, change the image URL to reference the image from CMS.

This ability to access CMS content opens many possibilities. As an example, a department's website might feature a series of photographs taken at department functions. You could upload those photographs to the portal and modify the Image portlet to randomly select a photograph to display.

We've shown you how the Image portlet can access an image from the CMS. But a portlet can as easily access any content in the CMS. For example, you could modify the Image portlet to include a link to download one of the documents, opening up many possibilities for interaction between portlets and the CMS. You can directly access any non-HTML CMS content in this manner, and the content will be returned as is. If you access an HTML document in the CMS, the Portal displays the document within the CMS portlet window on the portal page that contains that window—the reason why there's only one CMS portlet instance with one window and why you can't create more instances or windows.

11.4 Securing the Portal

The Portal requires users to identify themselves, providing access to certain pages only to certain users and, at the same time, allowing access to other pages to anyone. Let's show you how to secure the information you have in the Portal and prevent unauthorized access.

As with many Java EE applications, the Portal uses role-based security. All users are assigned one or more roles, and access to content, whether portals or pages, can be granted to specific roles.

The Portal uses its database to store account information. When you install the Portal, two accounts are in this database: admin and user. The User portlet enables anyone to create a new account in the portal. In this section, we cover user management as built into the Portal. Switching to a different login module is a topic that we leave for you to explore on your own.

You can easily manage security in the Portal. We don't walk you through click-by-click steps; the Reference Guide that comes with the Portal does, and we encourage you to read the section on security. We do cover creating a new account, managing roles, and various topics related to access control.

11.4.1 Creating a new account

Any user who can access the User portlet can create an account in the portal by clicking the You Can Create An Account link in the User portlet, as shown in figure 11.7.

Once you're logged in, click the Edit Profile tab in the User portlet to edit your profile. You personalize the Portal by specifying the desired theme, language, and various other preferences. The user profile window is also where you change the password for the admin account after you've logged in as admin.

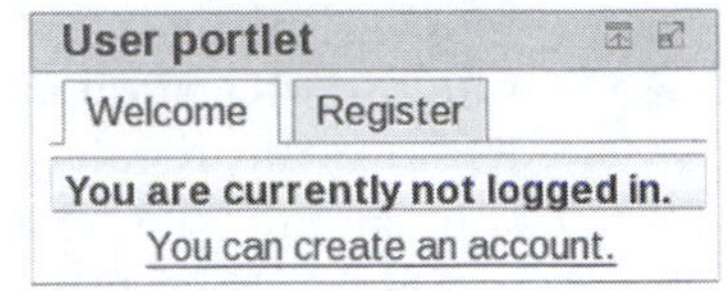

Figure 11.7 Click the You Can Create An Account link to create a new account.

If you don't want users to create accounts, you could remove the User portlet from the home page. An administrator can still create and manage accounts via the Members page on the Admin portal, but the user won't be able to edit her preferences. An alternate solution is to edit the User portlet so that it doesn't display the You Can Create An Account link. To do this, edit the jboss-portal.sar/portal-identity.sar/portal-identity.war/WEB-INF/jsf/register/overview.xhtml file; look for the identifier `IDENTITY_CREATE_ACCOUNT` and remove the `<h:commandLink>` tag containing it.

11.4.2 Managing roles

The portal comes with the three following built-in roles:

- *Admin*—Administrative role that allows users to access the Admin portal and perform functions such as defining the portal layout, assigning access control, and adding CMS content
- *User*—Standard non-administrative role for other users
- *Unchecked*—Default role that gets applied if the user doesn't fit into any other role

The Admin role contains only the admin account, and the User role contains only the user account. When an account is created, it automatically goes into the User role.

You can add new roles by using the Role Management tab on the Members page in the Admin portal. Once you create roles, you can add members, or user accounts, to the roles.

To add members to a role, you go to the Role Management tab on the Members page of the Admin portal, shown in figure 11.8. You might think that the best way to add users to a role is to click the Members tab next to the role, but if you do that, users that already have that role are displayed. For a newly created role, no users are displayed. Instead,

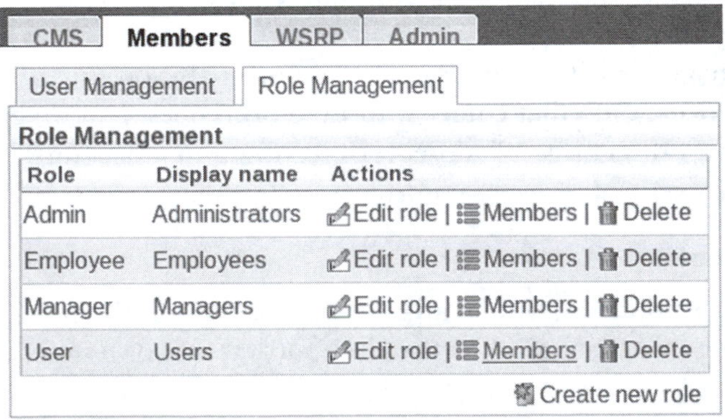

Figure 11.8 To add users to a role, click the Members link for the User role. This lists all users, which you can then assign to the desired roles.

click the Members tab next to the User role. All users are displayed. Once the users are displayed, clicking the Roles link displays a page that lets you select the roles for the user.

Now that you have a basic understanding of creating users and assigning them roles, let's look at how to define access control.

11.4.3 Understanding access control

Access control is primarily page based. A given user can interact with a particular page if the user is in a role that has the required rights to the page. The most direct way of assigning access control is via each page in the portal. The two basic access control settings are as follow:

- *View*—Allows the user to view the page
- *Personalize*—Allows the user to view and personalize the page

Let's concentrate on view access and discuss personalize access later.

In addition to the two basic access control settings, each can have a *recursive* modifier, meaning that the access control setting applies to all nested objects as well. For example, you can indirectly allow access to all the pages in a portal by specifying the view recursive access control for a given role. In this case, every user in that role has access to all pages in the portal, regardless of the access control settings on the individual pages.

We just touched on an important topic; although you can grant access, you can't withdraw access. For example, if you grant recursive view access to a portal to a specific role, you can't disallow access to any specific page in the portal to any users in that role. You should, therefore, carefully consider what access rights you want to grant and set access control accordingly. You'll find that page-level access control makes the most sense if you want to restrict any pages, whereas portal access control works well if you want to grant global access.

As an example, consider the portal named PortalA whose access control is illustrated in figure 11.9.

Portal Objects | Portlet Instances | Portlet Definitions | Dashboards

Portals > **PortalA portal Security**

Please set the portal permissions

Roles	Permissions			
Role Administrators:	☐ View	☐ View Recursive	☐ Personalize	☐ Personalize Recursive
Role Role 1:	☐ View	☑ View Recursive	☐ Personalize	☐ Personalize Recursive
Role Role 2:	☑ View	☐ View Recursive	☐ Personalize	☐ Personalize Recursive
Role Role 3:	☐ View	☐ View Recursive	☐ Personalize	☐ Personalize Recursive
Role Role 4:	☐ View	☐ View Recursive	☐ Personalize	☐ Personalize Recursive
Role Role 5:	☐ View	☐ View Recursive	☐ Personalize	☐ Personalize Recursive
Role Users:	☐ View	☐ View Recursive	☐ Personalize	☐ Personalize Recursive
Role Unchecked:	☐ View	☐ View Recursive	☐ Personalize	☐ Personalize Recursive

Update | Cancel

Figure 11.9 Portal access control example. Users in Role1 have full access to the portal, but other users not in that role might not have access.

Table 11.2 defines the full access rights for the portal (note that the first row matches the rights illustrated in figure 11.9) and its pages. An empty cell denotes that no access control is specified for that combination. For this example, we ignore the User, Admin, and Unchecked roles.

Table 11.2 Portal access control example: access control

Object	Role				
	Role1	Role2	Role3	Role4	Role5
PortalA	View Recursive	View			
Page1			View		
Page2				View Recursive	
Page3					

Table 11.3 indicates which pages in PortalA a user in a specific role can view.

Table 11.3 Portal access control example: page access

Page	Role				
	Role1	Role2	Role3	Role4	Role5
Page1	Yes	No	Yes	No	No
Page2	Yes	No	No	Yes	No
Page3	Yes	No	No	No	No

In addition, you can observe the following behaviors:

- Tabs appear in the header only for those pages to which the user has access.
- With Page1 as the default page, only users in Role1 can access the portal using the portal URL http://localhost:8080/portal/auth/portal/PortalA because only those users have access to both the portal and its default page.
- To access Page2, a user who's only in Role4 must use a URL that includes the page name http://localhost:8080/portal/auth/portal/PortalA/Page2. This user can't use the portal URL because he doesn't have access to the default page. The same is true for users in Role3 who wish to access page Page1.
- If a user is a member of multiple roles, and if any of those roles has access, the user has access.
- Users in Role2 don't have access to any pages because they're granted only view access and only at the portal level. That access isn't recursively applied to the pages in the portal.

You should now understand how to set up access rights for portal pages based on which roles you want to access which pages. So far we've talked about accessing portals and pages but what about individual portlet windows?

SETTING ACCESS CONTROL FOR PORTLET INSTANCES

Access control doesn't apply to portlet windows. If the user has view access to the page, the user can view the portlet window. To restrict access to a portlet, you must go back to the Portlet Instances list on the Admin portlet. Select one of the instances in the list, and then click the Security link next to it. You can then indicate which roles have access to the portlet instance, as is shown for the Image portlet instance in figure 11.10.

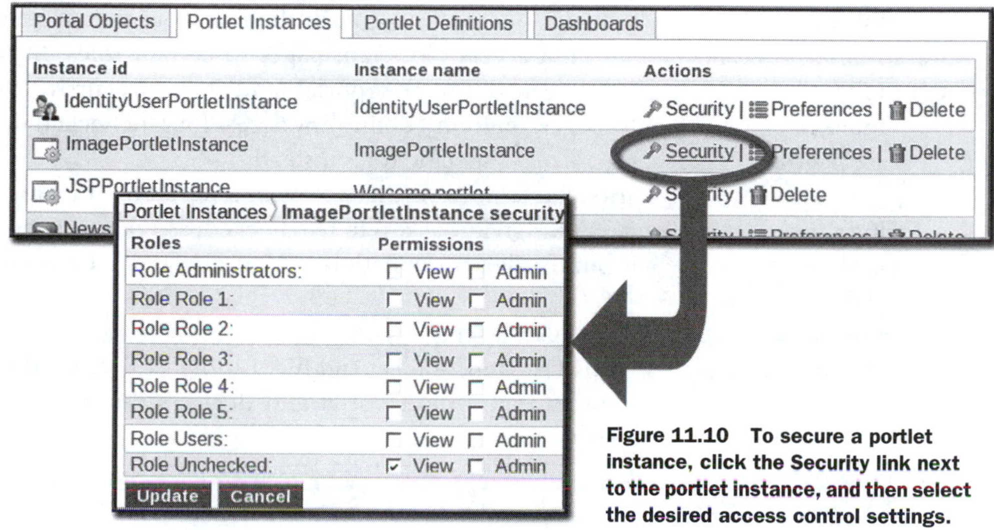

Figure 11.10 To secure a portlet instance, click the Security link next to the portlet instance, and then select the desired access control settings.

Note that this access right applies to all portlet windows defined for that instance. You usually want to restrict access to the contents displayed in a portlet, and the portlet instance decides the contents, not the portlet window, which displays those contents.

What happens if the user has access rights to a page but not to a portlet instance with a window on that page? It's simple—the portlet doesn't display.

At this time, you should be frantically waving your hand in the air because you have an important question that we've ignored. The question: What gives with the Unchecked role? It shows up in every list of roles when setting access control. Because you asked…

UNDERSTANDING THE UNCHECKED ROLE

Your initial guess might be that the Unchecked role applies to users who aren't logged in, enabling such users to view various pages. Although that guess is close, it's not quite right. The access control defined for the Unchecked role defines the default access permissions for the component in question.

Let's look at an example. In figure 11.10, Unchecked is set to View. By default, all roles have view access to the Image portlet instance. If you unselect View for

Unchecked, then no roles have access to the instance, unless such access rights are inherited from the page. Let's extend this example. If the Admin role has view access to a page containing the Image portlet, then users with that role can view the Image portlet, but other roles can't. If you also grant the Unchecked role view access to that page, all users can see that page, including users who aren't logged in.

If you don't define access control for a component, Unchecked is set to View Recursive for that component (or View for an instance). By default, all roles, including users who haven't logged into the portal, have access to the component—be it portal, page, or portlet instance.

How should you go about defining access control if you want to limit access to certain pages? There are two basic access scenarios. In the first, you want to grant access to almost everything and limit access to certain pages to certain roles. In this case, grant View access to Unchecked for the portal and View Recursive access to Unchecked for all public pages, but don't define any access for Unchecked on the private pages; assign access control to specific roles instead.

In the second scenario, you want to restrict access to a portal to only those in specific roles. In this case, don't assign any access to Unchecked; assign access only to specific roles instead. See our earlier presentation of PortalA as an example of this method.

DEFINING ACCESS CONTROL VIA DESCRIPTORS

You can define access rights using an *-object.xml file. Listing 11.6 shows the portala-object.xml file, which defines the PortalA portal and declares the roles and access rights as discussed in the previous section.

Listing 11.6 Creating a portal with access control using *-object.xml

```
<?xml version="1.0" encoding="UTF-8" standalone="yes"?>
<deployments>
 <deployment>
  <parent-ref />
  <if-exists>keep</if-exists>
  <portal>
   <portal-name>PortalA</portal-name>                    1
   <properties>
    <property>
     <name>portal.defaultObjectName</name>              2
     <value>Page1</value>
    </property>
   </properties>
   <security-constraint>
    <policy-permission>
     <role-name>Role1</role-name>
     <action-name>viewrecursive</action-name>
    </policy-permission>                                   3
    <policy-permission>
     <role-name>Role2</role-name>
     <action-name>view</action-name>
    </policy-permission>
```

```
    </security-constraint>
    <page>
     <page-name>Page1</page-name>           ❹
     <window>
      <window-name>ImageWindow</window-name>
      <instance-ref>ImagePortletInstance</instance-ref>
      <region>center</region>
      <height>0</height>
     </window>
     <security-constraint>
      <policy-permission>
       <role-name>Role3</role-name>            ❺
       <action-name>view</action-name>
      </policy-permission>
     </security-constraint>
    </page>
    <page>
     <page-name>Page2</page-name>           ❹
     <window>
      <window-name>ImageWindow</window-name>
      <instance-ref>ImagePortletInstance</instance-ref>
      <region>center</region>
      <height>0</height>
     </window>
     <security-constraint>
      <policy-permission>
       <role-name>Role4</role-name>                  ❺
       <action-name>viewrecursive</action-name>
      </policy-permission>
     </security-constraint>
    </page>
    <page>
     <page-name>Page3</page-name>           ❹
     <window>
      <window-name>ImageWindow</window-name>
      <instance-ref>ImagePortletInstance</instance-ref>
      <region>center</region>
      <height>0</height>
     </window>
     <security-constraint>
      <policy-permission />         ❻
     </security-constraint>
    </page>
   </portal>
  </deployment>
</deployments>
```

The portala-object.xml file defines a portal named PortalA ❶ whose default page is Page1 ❷ and has security settings ❸ as shown in figure 11.9. There are three pages ❹, each of which have different security constraints (❺ and ❻) as defined earlier in table 11.3.

You declare <window> entries for each page so that the portal shows something. Note that each page displays the Image portlet.

If you leave off a <security-constraint> declaration, the access control for that object defaults to `viewrecursive` for the Unchecked role. The empty <policy-permission> tag for Page3 (❻) ensures that no permissions are declared for that page.

You can't declare roles in the *-object.xml file. Even if the roles aren't defined in the portal, the access control for those roles is established so that you can define the roles later to apply the permissions. Until you define the roles, no access is possible to the objects so constrained. In this case, nobody has access to PortalA.

To deploy PortalA, add the portala-object.xml file to the WEB-INF directory of the image.war file. You can either replace the existing image-object.xml file with portala-object.xml, or you can have both files present. Nothing prevents you from having multiple *-object.xml files. Copy the WAR file to the deploy directory, once again observing the cautions noted at the start of section 10.2.4.

To access PortalA, you have to create the five roles (Role1 through Role5) and several users accounts, and add one or more accounts to each role. As an example, you could create an account named user1 and add that account to the Role1 role. When you log in as user1, you can access PortalA by entering the URL http://localhost:8080/portal/auth/portal/PortalA. A user whose only role is Role4 would have to also supply the page name http://localhost:8080/portal/auth/portal/PortalA/Page2.

Speaking of Role4, you probably notice that its access is defined as *view recursive*. You might wonder what the difference is between the *view recursive* and *view* access controls when applied to a page. Does it apply to the portlet windows on a page? No, it doesn't. You can define subpages for a page and *view recursive* propagates the access rights to those subpages. Let's take a quick look at how to define and access a subpage.

CREATING AND ACCESSING SUBPAGES

With a page selected in the Admin portlet, you can create another page which becomes a subpage of the indicated page, as seen in figure 11.11. If a role has view recursive access to a page, it has access to all subpages. For example, if page Page1 has a subpage Page1a, users in role Role3 can't view page Page1a because Role3 has only view access rights to Page1. On the other hand, if page Page2 has a subpage Page2a, users in role Role4 can view page Page2a because Role4 has view recursive access rights to Page2.

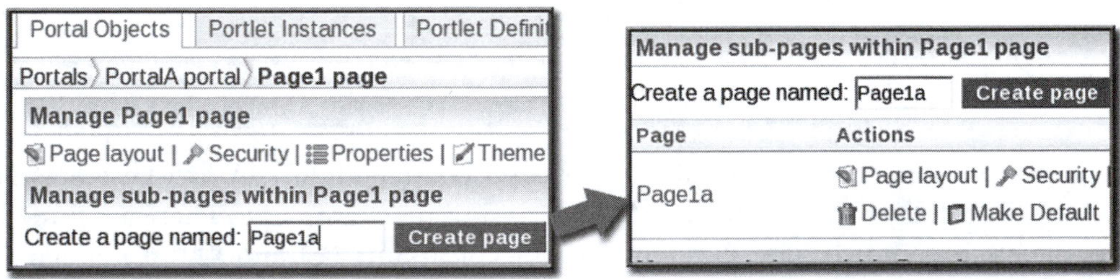

Figure 11.11 To create a subpage, drill down to the parent page, enter the subpage name, and click Add. The subpage shows up as a page on the parent page.

To access a subpage, hover over the tab that corresponds to the parent page. A drop-down menu appears that lists the subpages, as illustrated in figure 11.12. Or if you prefer to type in a URL (or need to type in a URL because you don't have access to the parent page but do have access to the subpage), you could enter a URL such as http://localhost:8080/portal/auth/portal/PortalA/Page1/Page1a.

Figure 11.12 Hover over the page tab to see a drop-down menu of subpages.

Let's look at one more thing before we leave this topic—defining a subpage with the *-object.xml file. Listing 11.7 shows an excerpt from the *-object.xml file that defines the Page1a subpage for Page1.

Listing 11.7 Creating a subpage using *-object.xml

```
<?xml version="1.0" encoding="UTF-8" standalone="yes"?>
...
 <page>
  <page-name>Page1</page-name>      <— Identifies parent page
  <page>
   <page-name>Page1a</page-name>      <— Identifies subpage
   <window>
    <window-name>ImageWindow</window-name>
    <instance-ref>JBossLogoInstance</instance-ref>
    <region>center</region>
    <height>0</height>
   </window>
    ...
  </page>
  ...
 </page>
...
```

Up to this point, we've been ignoring the personalize access right. Let's look briefly at that next.

UNDERSTANDING PERSONALIZE ACCESS

When a role is assigned *personalize* or *personalize recursive* access, that role has view and personalization ability for the portal or page. For example, you could have used personalize and personalize recursive in place of view and view recursive in the PortalA, and the access rights would be exactly the same. Therefore, personalize access provides view access, but does it grant any other access right? What does personalization mean?

At this time: nothing. Granting or refusing personalization access has no effect on what the user can do. The user can edit portlet preferences, change the theme, and manipulate the dashboard regardless of whether she has personalization access or view access.

The JBoss Portal 2.6 introduced a dashboard portal that looks like the home page. But the user can easily rearrange this portal, dragging and dropping portlets to the desired position and even adding or removing portlets. The dashboard provides personalization capabilities to all users. Note that the dashboard portal doesn't show up in the list of portals on the Admin portlet, so you can't restrict who can and who can't personalize the dashboard. We leave you to explore the dashboard on your own tour of the Portal.

11.5 Developing a custom portal

Up to this point, we've been working with the default portal that comes with JBoss Portal. Even in section 11.4, where we created a new portal to illustrate access control, the default portal was still present. Although the default portal is fine for development work, it's not what you want for production use. What you want is a customized portal that contains the pages and portlets you want to use plus a theme and color scheme that matches your identity or the identity of your company. After all, imagine deploying a portal to your customers that declares itself to be the *JBoss Portal*. Not a good thing. In this section, we show you how to create, package, and deploy a custom portal. We start with the requirements and the proposal before diving into development.

But before you get started, we should warn you that you'll modify a lot of the files that come with the Portal. You'll either want to work with a copy of the jboss-portal.sar directory or back it up first. You can also use the source code for the book and follow along with the custom portal it generates.

11.5.1 Defining the requirements

This portal must meet the following requirements:

1. It must have multiple pages.
2. It must have some, but not all, portlets that come with JBoss Portal.
3. It must have some portlets that don't come with JBoss Portal.
4. It must include only custom content in the CMS portlet.
5. The portal home page must show up as the default portal page (that is, http://hostname:8080/portal shows your portal page, not the default JBoss Portal page).
6. The portal theme must reflect your corporate or business identity.
7. The example portal must be as simple as possible—K.I.S.S.

We could add another requirement involving access control but don't do so for a few reasons. First, adding access control greatly lengthens the example, thereby violating the last requirement. Second, you should find it fairly simple to apply the recommendations in the access control section to this example. Finally, our primary intent is to show you how to package and deploy a custom portal and including access control doesn't add anything to the discussion.

11.5.2 Making the proposal

Now that we have the requirements down, we can consider how to meet them. The last requirement, simplicity, becomes the overriding factor in meeting the other requirements. Here are the proposals for meeting the requirements:

1. Create a portal with two pages. This meets both requirements 1 and 7.
2. Keep the User portlet so that users can create their own accounts and access their profiles, but put it on the second page.
3. Place the Image portlet on the second page.
4. Configure the CMS portlet to show the custom content that was presented in section 11.3. Have it be the only portlet on the first page.
5. Package the custom portal in such a way as to satisfy requirement 5. Yes, we're being vague, but we explain how to do this in detail in the following text.
6. Create a custom theme.

As you look over this list, you should have some idea on how to do some of the things. For example, you should be able to come up with the *-object.xml for the first, second, and third proposals. You might think you could do the fourth one using the CMS Administration portlet, but we'll show you a different way. And we haven't covered the fifth and sixth proposals before. Let's tackle the simplest thing first—defining the *-object.xml file.

11.5.3 *Defining the portal*

Before we get to the contents of the *-object.xml file, let's look at the portal, as shipped, to learn how the default portal is defined. If you look for *-object.xml files, you'll find them in several locations, as identified in table 11.4.

Table 11.4 Locations and usage of the *-object.xml files that ship with the portal

Location	What this file defines
jboss-portal.sar/conf/data/default-object.xml	Defines the four portals: Default, Template, Dashboard, and Admin. For Default portal, defines the default (Home) page with its three portlet windows. For Admin portal, defines the default and Members pages.
jboss-portal.sar/portal-cms.sar/portal-cms.war/ WEB-INF/default-object.xml	Adds the CMS page to the Admin portal.
jboss-portal.sar/portal-wsrp.sar/ portal-wsrp-admin.war/WEB-INF/wsrp-object.xml	Adds the WSRP page to the Admin portal.
jboss-portal.sar/samples/ portal-news-samples.war/WEB-INF/default-object.xml	Adds the News page to the Default portal.
jboss-portal.sar/samples/portal-weather-samples.war/ WEB-INF/default-object.xml	Adds the Weather page to the Default portal.

As you can see, the jboss-portal.sar/conf/data/default-object.xml file defines the basic layout for the portals, and the other *-object.xml files add to that basic definition. Knowing this, we can devise a plan to define our custom portal. We'll leave the Admin, Template, and Dashboard portals intact, modifying only the layout for the Default portal. The Default portal will declare both pages with one portlet on each page. The image-object.xml file for the Image portlet will add the Image portlet window to the second page. We also must delete the default-object.xml file for the News and Weather portlets, or those pages will show up again.

Listing 11.8 shows the full declaration of the default portal for our custom portal within the jboss-portal.sar/conf/data/default-object.xml file. The rest of the file is left untouched.

Listing 11.8 Custom portal as defined in the default-object.xml file

```
<?xml version="1.0" encoding="UTF-8" standalone="yes"?>
<deployments>
 ...
 <deployment>
  <parent-ref/>
  <if-exists>keep</if-exists>
  <portal>
   <portal-name>default</portal-name>          <-- Defines portal name
   <supported-modes>
    <mode>view</mode>
    <mode>edit</mode>
    <mode>help</mode>
   </supported-modes>
   <supported-window-states>
    <window-state>normal</window-state>
    <window-state>minimized</window-state>
    <window-state>maximized</window-state>
   </supported-window-states>
   <security-constraint>
    <policy-permission>
     <action-name>viewrecursive</action-name>
     <action-name>personalizerecursive</action-name>
     <unchecked/>
    </policy-permission>
   </security-constraint>
   <page>
    <page-name>default</page-name>          <-- Declares first page
    <properties>
     <property>
      <name>order</name>
      <value>1</value>
     </property>
    </properties>
    <window>
     <window-name>CMSWindow</window-name>          <-- Places CMS content on first page
     <content>
      <content-type>cms</content-type>
      <content-uri>/book/index.html</content-uri>          <-- Identifies custom CMS content
     </content>
     <region>center</region>
     <height>0</height>
    </window>
   </page>
   <page>
    <page-name>Astronomy</page-name>          <-- Declares second page
```

```
    <properties>
     <property>
      <name>order</name>
      <value>2</value>
     </property>
    </properties>
    <window>
     <window-name>UserPortletWindow</window-name>     ◁─ Places User portlet on second page
     <instance-ref>UserPortletInstance</instance-ref>
     <region>left</region>
     <height>1</height>
    </window>
   </page>
  </portal>
 </deployment>
 ...
</deployments>
```

Notice that this file declares the custom content for the CMS portlet window. We cover how to set up the content later. The file also defines the second page, Astronomy, but doesn't yet define the Image portlet that will reside there. Listing 11.9 shows the portlet-instances.xml file that declares the Image portlet instance. You should package this file into the image.war, as shown in section 10.2.4.

Listing 11.9 The portlet-instances.xml file for the Image portlet in the custom portal

```
<?xml version="1.0" encoding="UTF-8" standalone="yes"?>
<deployments>
 <deployment>
  <instance>
   <instance-id>AstronomyInstance</instance-id>
   <portlet-ref>ImagePortlet</portlet-ref>
   <preferences>
    <preference>
     <name>title</name>
     <value>Astronomy Picture of the Day</value>
    </preference>
    <preference>
     <name>url</name>
     <value>http://antwrp.gsfc.nasa.gov/apod/astropix.html</value>
    </preference>
    <preference>
     <name>regex</name>
     <value>IMG SRC="(image/\d*/\S*.jpg)"</value>
    </preference>
   </preferences>
  </instance>
 </deployment>
</deployments>
```

You should recognize all of this content from earlier examples, particularly from section 11.2.1. Listing 11.10 shows the image-object.xml file that places the Image portlet window on the second page of the custom portal.

Listing 11.10 The portlet-instances.xml file for the Image portlet in the custom portal

```
<?xml version="1.0" encoding="UTF-8" standalone="yes"?>
<deployments>
 <deployment>
  <if-exists>overwrite</if-exists>
  <parent-ref>default.Astronomy</parent-ref>
  <window>
   <window-name>AstronomyWindow</window-name>
   <instance-ref>AstronomyInstance</instance-ref>
   <region>center</region>
   <height>1</height>
  </window>
 </deployment>
</deployments>
```

Notice how the <parent-ref> node references the second page of the custom portal as declared in the default-object.xml file.

If this gives you the idea that you can easily and logically define separate pages for a portal in separate WAR files and then later package the desired WAR files together to build a custom portal containing only the desired pages, then go to the head of the class.

Wow, in one section with a few files, we took care of the first three requirements. Only three requirements are left.

11.5.4 Customizing the theme

We have a confession to make: we lied. For the sixth requirement regarding the portal's theme, we stated that we'd create a custom theme. Unfortunately, neither of us has a single artistic bone in our body, and we wouldn't want to foist a ghastly theme on you. Additionally, creating a theme is a major undertaking, and there's that simplicity requirement. We decided to modify an existing theme.

To do this, we made a copy of the Renaissance theme, which is the default theme for the Portal, and edited the theme using Photoshop. We used Photoshop to convert the muted blue used by Renaissance into the brownish-orange used on the cover of the book. We then got the color adjustment values from Photoshop (hue: -160, saturation: +39, lightness: +8, in case you're interested) and applied those adjustments to all the graphics files. We replaced the existing Favorites icon with one that contains part of the swordsman from the cover of the book. Finally, we also made the same color adjustments to the colors present in the stylesheet. You can observe the results of our efforts in the source code for the book.

If you decide to edit an existing theme, keep the following points in mind:

- The existing themes can be found at jboss-portal.sar/portal-core.war/themes.
- The themes have two main components: a portal_style.css stylesheet and a series of GIF files in the images directory.

You want to change the logo so that your portal doesn't advertise itself as the JBoss Portal. The logo is usually in a logo.gif file, but that's entirely up to the stylesheet, which contains a style named logoName that refers to the logo.

Many of the themes advertise their creators via a page footer using a ThemeBy style in the stylesheet. You want to change that text.

Once the modifications are complete, you need to package the theme in a WAR file. When you do so, you need to provide a WEB-INF/portal-theme.xml descriptor file for the theme. Listing 11.11 shows the contents of that file for our theme.

Listing 11.11 Contents of the portal-theme.xml file for our custom theme

```
<themes>
 <theme>
  <name>jbia</name>                              <- Defines theme name
  <link rel="stylesheet" id="main_css"
      href="/portal_style.css"                   <- ❶ Identifies stylesheet used by theme
      type="text/css"/>
  <link rel="shortcut icon"
      href="/images/favicon.ico"/>               <- Identifies icon for theme
 </theme>
</themes>
```

You might wonder why the portal-theme.xml file identifies the stylesheet ❶ but not the image directory. The stylesheet identifies the images and where they're located. Therefore, placing the stylesheet in the base directory of the WAR file and locating the images in a directory called images is merely a convention followed by the existing themes. You can place the files anywhere you like, provided the references are correct.

When you create the WAR file, it contains the files illustrated in figure 11.13. We don't list all the images, but you should get the idea. Note also that you need a web.xml file, but it can be a simple one with an empty `<web-app>` node.

Once the theme is packaged, you can test it by deploying the WAR file to the deploy directory. Then use the Admin portlet to change the theme for one of the pages and view that page to see the theme in action. We show you later how to include the theme in the customized portal distribution.

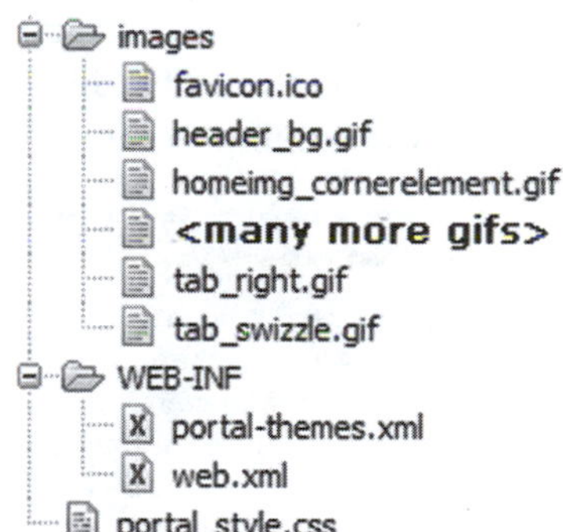

Figure 11.13 Abbreviated contents of the jbia-theme.war file. To use this theme, copy the WAR to the deploy directory.

If you do this, you'll notice something—some visual elements are still blue. Apparently, you can't change a color scheme by defining a new theme. The culprits are the CMS portlet, Admin portlet, and login dialog box. These artifacts define some of their own icons and color schemes. And the color scheme they adhere to is the one defined by Renaissance. Therefore, we changed the following files, in the same way that we changed the stylesheet and GIFs as indicated earlier:

- jboss-portal.sar/portal-admin.sar/portal-admin.war/css/style.css
- jboss-portal.sar/portal-admin.sar/portal-admin.war/img/*.gif

- jboss-portal.sar/portal-cms.sar/portal-cms.war/images/cms/admin/style.css
- jboss-portal.sar/portal-cms.sar/portal-cms.war/images/cms/*.gif
- jboss-portal.sar/portal-core.war/css/login.css
- jboss-portal.sar/portal-core.war/images/model/login-header-bg.gif
- jboss-portal.sar/portal-identity.sar/portal-identity.war/style.css
- jboss-portal.sar/portal-identity.sar/portal-identity.war/img/*.gif

With these changes, the colors are now consistent in all the pages. But there are still two slight glitches. First, although the header in the page proclaims the custom portal to be the JBIA Portal, the title bar in the browser window still references JBoss Portal. Second, the footer on each page states that the portal is *Powered by JBoss Portal*. The title and the footer are both declared in the following files:

- jboss-portal.sar/portal-core.war/layouts/generic/index.jsp
- jboss-portal.sar/portal-core.war/layouts/generic/maximized.jsp
- jboss-portal.sar/portal-core.war/layouts/3columns/index.jsp
- jboss-portal.sar/portal-core.war/layouts/1column/index.jsp

The Renaissance theme doesn't use the 3columns or 1column files, so you need to change only the generic ones. The change is the same for all three files, as follows:

```
...
  <title>JBIA Portal</title>
...
<div id="footer-container" class="portal-copyright">
Custom portal for JBoss in Action</div>
...
```

Now the customization of the theme is complete. To apply the theme to the custom portal, modify the `theme.id` property in the jboss-portal.sar/conf/data/default-object.xml, as shown in listing 11.12.

Listing 11.12 Contents of the portal-theme.xml file for our custom theme

```
<deployments>
 <deployment>
  <context>
   <context-name/>
   <properties>
    <property>
     <name>theme.id</name>
     <value>jbia</value>          <-- Identifies theme to use
    </property>
  ...
```

If you want to learn more about portal themes and how to create them, the Reference Guide contains a lengthy chapter on that topic. With the instructions that we gave you on customizing a theme, the contents of the theme chapter in the Reference Guide, and a little bit of creativity and artistic talent, you should be able to create your own themes.

We've covered requirements 1, 2, 3, and 6. Only requirement 4, replacing the default CMS content with our own content, and requirement 5, packaging, are left.

11.5.5 Customizing CMS content

Earlier we showed you how to use the CMS Admin portlet to add new content. You probably noticed that some content was already loaded. Where did that come from? To answer this, look at jboss-portal.sar/portal-cms.sar/portal/cms/conf/default-content.

There you'll see the default contents that were loaded into the portal when it first came up.

How would you supply your own default content? Simple. Copy your content to this directory and let the CMS component know about it. If you use the content from section 11.3, the default-content directory should have the files identified in figure 11.14. Note that we removed the original default content because we don't need it, but you can leave it there if you want.

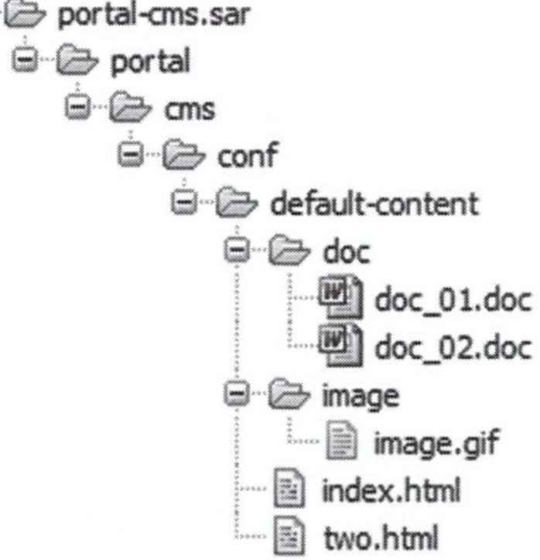

Figure 11.14 Directory and file hierarchy showing the custom default CMS content

To let the CMS component know about the new content, you need to make changes to two other files. First, there are two changes in the jboss-portal.sar/portal-cms.sar/META-INF/jboss-service.xml file. Change the `DefaultContentLocation` attribute of the `portal:service=CMS` MBean, and change the path criteria within the `DefaultPolicy` attribute of the `portal:service=Interceptor,type=Cms,name=ACL` MBean. Both changes are shown in listing 11.13.

Listing 11.13 Updated jboss-service.xml file for CMS default content

```
<server>
. . .
 <mbean name="portal:service=CMS"...>
  ...
  <attribute name="DefaultContentLocation">
[CA]portal/cms/conf/default-content/book/</attribute>
 </mbean>
 ...
 <mbean name="portal:service=Interceptor,type=Cms,name=ACL" ...>
  ...
  <attribute name="DefaultPolicy">
  <![CDATA[... <criteria name="path" value="/book"> ...]]>
  </attribute>
 </mbean>
 ...
</server>
```

For the second file, you need to modify the portlet.xml file for the CMS portlet. That file can be found at jboss-portal.sar/portal-cms.war/WEB-INF/portlet.xml, and you need to change the `indexpage` preference, as shown in listing 11.14.

Listing 11.14 Updated portlet.xml file for CMS default content

```
<portlet-app>
 . . .
 <portlet>
  <description>Content Management System Portlet</description>
  <portlet-name>CMSPortlet</portlet-name>
  . . .
  <portlet-preferences>
   <preference>
    <name>indexpage</name>
    <value>/book/index.html</value>     <-- Only change made
   </preference>
  </portlet-preferences>
 </portlet>
 . . .
</portlet-app>
```

You now have all of the files necessary for the custom portal, so let's tackle the last requirement—packaging it.

11.5.6 Packaging the portal

At this point, you have a hodgepodge of stuff all over the place. Custom CMS content here, Image portlet there, and theme elsewhere. You need to gather it into one neat little package that you can deliver to whoever will deploy the portal. And that's what we cover in this section.

You need to make a copy of the jboss-portal.sar directory because you'll be making changes to the files in that directory. For this example, copy the directory as jbia-portal.sar. All the changes you make should be done in the copy.

We start with the CMS content change because we just finished discussing that in the prior section. Change the jboss-service.xml and portlet.xml files and copy the custom content files, as we indicated in the prior section.

Next, copy the jbia-theme.war and image.war files to the jbia-portal.sar directory to make the updated theme and the Image portlet available. We recommend that you copy them as exploded WAR directories so that you can easily access the files in them, particularly the various XML descriptor files. Also, don't forget to copy the other files that contain theme-related changes. Those files were listed at the end of section 11.5.4.

If you want to, you can also include other third-party portlets. For example, the JBoss Wiki project and JBoss Forums project provide a wiki and a user forum, respectively, that you could add to the portal.

You need to replace the original jbia-portal.sar/conf/data/default-object.xml file with the default-object.xml file you created earlier in section 11.5.3.

Delete the jbia-portal.sar/samples/portal-news-samples.war/WEB-INF/default-object.xml and jbia-portal.sar/samples/portal-weather-samples.war/WEB-INF/default-object.xml files so that the News and Weather pages don't appear.

The preceding text is dense and contains many instructions. As an overview of these steps, look at figure 11.15. In the figure, we list the contents of jbia-portal.sar

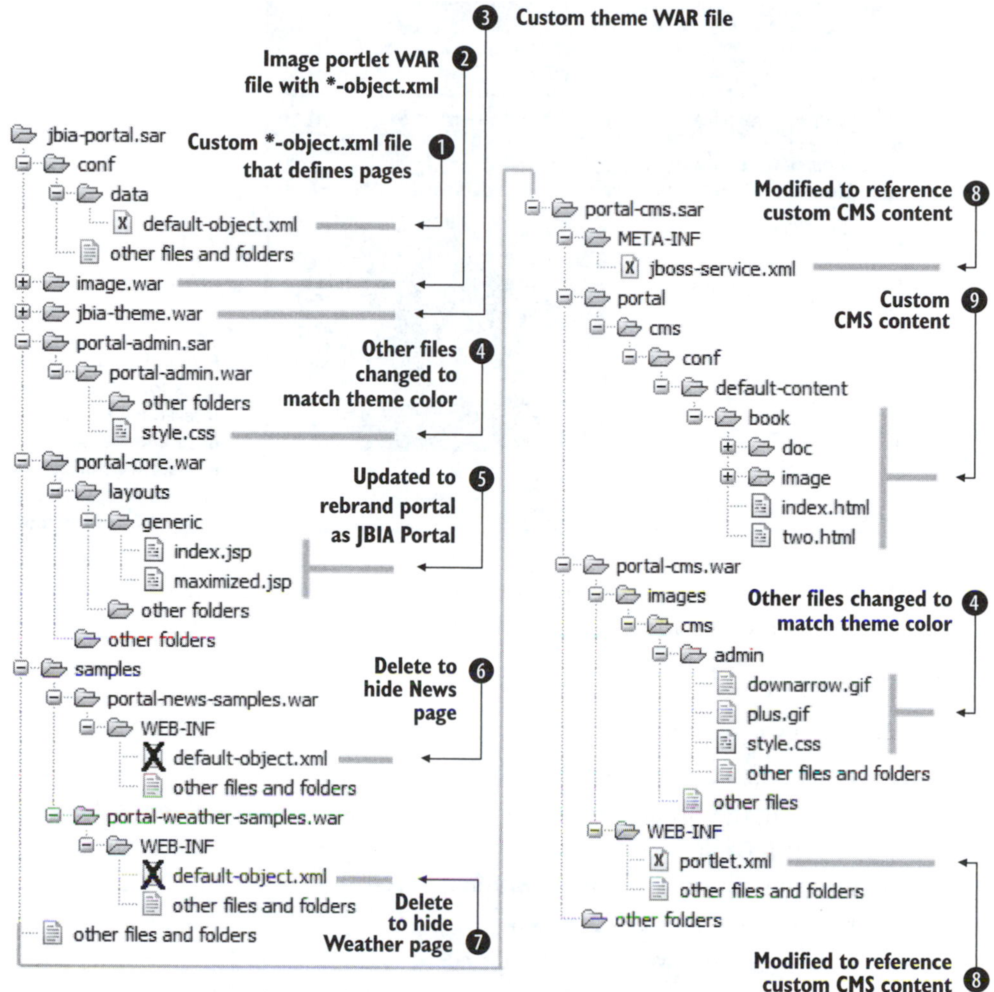

Figure 11.15 Directory and file hierarchy for the custom portal showing the files that were added, changed, and deleted

and highlight things that were changed. To keep the figure manageable, we didn't include the files and directories that didn't change; instead, we noted them with text such as *other files and folders.*

Now that you have the custom jbia-portal.sar directory, what do you do with it? Follow the JBoss Portal installation instructions, setting up JBoss AS and the database as desired. Then copy the jbia-portal.sar directory to the deploy directory. When you start the application server, the database gets initialized; when you enter the portal URL, http://localhost:8080/portal, the home page for the custom portal is displayed, as shown in figure 11.16.

Figure 11.16 The home page for the JBIA Portal. All references to JBoss Portal have been replaced. There's a custom color scheme, custom pages, and a custom favorites icon.

There you have it—a custom portal that uses many of the JBoss Portal features that you learned about in the last two chapters.

11.6 Summary

The last two chapters covered many portal topics, such as the following:

- Creating a portlet using JSPs and JSTL
- Using the Admin portlet and the descriptor files to define portlet instances and portlet windows
- Using multiple instances within a portal
- Adding content to the CMS
- Configuring window appearance
- Setting up access control for portals, pages, and windows
- Creating a custom portal

We've barely scratched the surface of the JBoss Portal, and many more features and capabilities could be explored. These chapters should give you a solid foundation so that you can venture into other topics such as using various frameworks (like Seam or JSF) to write portlets, deploying a portal in a cluster for high availability, and deploying third-party portlets to the portal. To find out more about these and other topics, refer to the Reference Guide and User's Guide that come with JBoss Portal. You can find links to them in the References section at the end of chapter 10.

Part 4

Going to production

There are many issues that you probably aren't that concerned with during development of your Java EE application; but, as you get closer to going into production, those same issues become more important. You begin to wonder: How will the application scale, can you cluster the application both to promote scaling and to provide redundancy, and what are the things you need to do before you release the application into the wild? Chapters 12 through 15 answer these questions.

We start this part of the book with two chapters on clustering. Yes, it's a big topic. Then, we turn our attention to performance, examining the different ways you can tune the application. We end with a chapter on miscellaneous things (such as replacing the Hypersonic database, changing port numbers, and running the application server as a service) that you'll want to keep in mind when putting JBoss AS into production.

12 Understanding clustering

This chapter covers

- Clustering fundamentals
- Setting up a simple cluster
- JBoss clustering
- Configuring JGroups
- Configuring JBoss Cache

A single JBoss server can handle several hundred concurrent requests; but, if your application has to scale to support multiple thousands of concurrent requests or multiple millions of requests a day, then a single application server probably won't do the trick. JBoss enables you to simultaneously run your application on multiple application servers. Requests going to your application can then be balanced across these servers, and your application can also withstand individual server failures. This deployment architecture allows you to achieve maximum scalability with minimal downtime. Clients need not know that their different requests may be handled by different servers.

Java EE doesn't specify any standards for how clustering services should work. Every application server implements clustering differently and provides a different set of clustering capabilities and services. Red Hat has set out to make cluster setup a simple task. As you'll learn in this chapter, clusters are easy to create in JBoss and require minimal configuration. Adding nodes requires no administrative management because nodes detect each other automatically over network protocols. JBoss also provides a sophisticated distributed cache that allows stateful components to replicate their states across multiple nodes in a cluster, enabling you to easily develop fault-tolerant applications, with very little code.

In this chapter, we explain the fundamentals of clustering and how to configure clustering in JBoss. We also show you how to get a simple cluster up and running to experiment with. We start with a discussion of the fundamental concepts behind clustering.

12.1 Understanding clustering

Clustering is the act of running the same application on multiple application server instances simultaneously with each application server being aware of the others in the cluster. An application server that's part of a cluster is known as a *node*. But just having nodes aware of other nodes in a cluster isn't interesting. The nodes in the cluster must be able to communicate with each other to do something useful, such as replicating state or providing failover capabilities. Before we dive into the specifics of the clustering features that JBoss offers, let's examine some of the fundamental concepts behind clustering. And, because you can't seem to talk about clustering without talking about load balancing, let's start with that.

12.1.1 Load balancing

Imagine you have a retail web application running on a single application server instance and that you average 10,000 customers a month. Your company decides to run a TV advertisement and predicts that you may start getting 100,000 customers a month. You're tasked with making sure that the application can support this number of users. In addition, your application needs to be highly available. To accomplish these goals, you have to deploy multiple application server instances and balance requests across them.

Load balancing is a way of balancing incoming load, or concurrent requests, across multiple application server instances, making your applications scalable and highly available. Scalability is a term used to describe the ability to make your application handle more user load by adding hardware and/or creating redundant instances of your application without having to change code. Load balancing can help scale your application because you can add more servers for the load balancer to balance the load across, increasing the amount of traffic your application can handle. High availability is the ability to continue processing requests in the face of server failure. We discuss high availability more in section 12.1.4.

Figure 12.1 shows you the difference between an application with and without load balancing.

The load balancer acts as a single point of entry into an application environment as well as a traffic director for requests. In the diagram found in figure 12.1, you see that the load balancer (in the middle of the figure on the right) decides which server

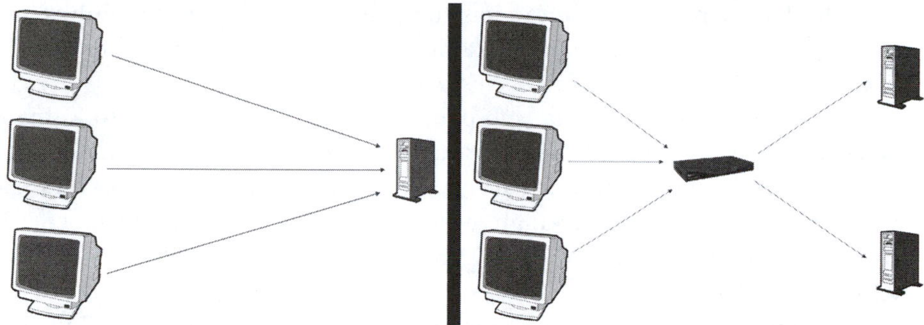

Figure 12.1 An application without load balancing (left) provides a single point of failure and a potential bottleneck, but an application with load balancing (right) can scale better and enables high availability.

to send the requests to. Because this decision happens upstream of the application server, in many cases, load balancing isn't a feature of the application or the application server and doesn't even require a cluster. Clusters are necessary when nodes need to communicate with each other, but aren't necessarily required for load balancing.

There are cases when a cluster can be used when load balancing. For example, with EJB load balancing, the client can obtain a dynamic proxy auto-populated with the names of the servers in the cluster. Although the cluster isn't used to enable the load-balancing feature, it provides information to the load balancer (the dynamic proxy) to simplify configuration.

NOTE One thing to keep in mind is that load balancing is a mechanism for scaling applications that synchronously execute code. Applications that asynchronously execute requests don't necessarily need to load balance requests. In fact, often, you want to make sure that there's only a single instance of an asynchronous application or service running to ensure that it's managing all the requests. Running a single instance allows the application or service to manage ordering and priority over all the incoming requests.

We discuss specific load-balancing features that JBoss provides in chapter 13. Now that you have a conceptual understanding of what load balancing is, let's talk about the different types of load balancers and load-balancing strategies.

TYPES OF LOAD BALANCERS

Load balancing can be done in two primary ways: with a hardware load balancer or with a software load balancer. Hardware load balancers are typically more expensive but are also more reliable.

Load balancers typically make a single IP address for a cluster visible to clients. The load balancer maintains a map of internal (or virtual) IP addresses for each machine in the cluster. When the load balancer receives a request, it rewrites the header to point to a particular machine in the cluster. If a machine in the cluster is removed or fails, the hardware load balancer has the ability to recognize the failure and avoid routing requests to it. Always having a machine available to service requests is known as *high availability*, which we discuss more in section 12.1.4.

Sometimes it's best to route subsequent requests from a client to a single server, especially if the component the user is accessing maintains state. This ability to route users back to the same server across requests is called *server affinity*. Hardware load balancers provide server affinity, high availability, and fast performance. The disadvantages are that they're very expensive and are often more difficult to set up than software load balancers.

Software load balancers come in many shapes and sizes. An OS-level load balancer, such as Microsoft's Network Load Balancing Service (NLBS), can be used to direct requests to different Windows servers. Standalone programs, such as Pure Load Balancer (PLB) for Unix, can be installed to route HTTP traffic coming into a server. But software load balancing for Java EE applications is most commonly done using a native web server such as JBoss Web Server, Apache, or IIS. Most native web servers have the capability of load balancing requests across multiple applications server instances. Most software load balancers support server affinity and high availability. Software load balancing is cheaper and easier to set up than hardware load balancing, but the load-balancing software can consume memory and CPU resources, and the performance of the software is at the mercy of other software running on the system.

Figure 12.2 shows a common topology seen in many publicly accessible applications such as public web applications. When clients access the domain name for a site, the DNS server routes the client to the load balancer. The load balancer then routes requests to the application servers running behind the firewall. The load balancer distributes the load across application servers and mitigates the security risks that exist when clients access the servers directly. In this scenario, the load balancer lives in the network's demilitarized zone (DMZ), a portion of the network that can be accessed from outside of the firewall.

Whether you use a software or hardware load balancer, there are different load-balancing strategies that you can employ. Some of the most common ones are random, round robin, and sticky session (or first available). A random load-balancing strategy sends client requests to a random server. A load balancer using a round-robin strategy sequentially sends requests to servers by going down a list of servers. With sticky-session load balancing, the load balancer sends first-time requests using a random or round-robin strategy; but, once a client has established a session with a particular server, the load balancer directs subsequent requests to the same server. There are many variations on these strategies using weight systems and other distribution policies.

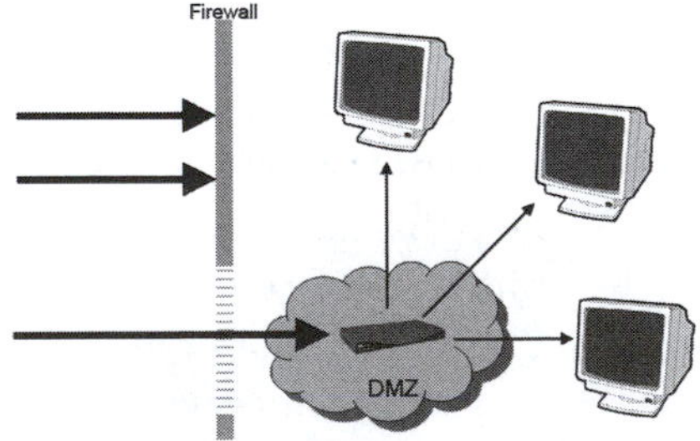

Figure 12.2 A DMZ provides a way for one or more machines or networking devices to be accessed from behind a firewall.

Round-robin DNS load balancing is another well-known software load-balancing mechanism, but we don't recommend using it. Let's discuss why.

ROUND-ROBIN DNS

Some DNS servers provide functionality for load balancing, which is often called round-robin DNS. With round-robin DNS load balancing, the DNS server is configured to maintain multiple IP addresses for a given domain name. Each time the domain name is accessed, the DNS server can return a different IP address, load balancing across the different IP addresses.

Round-robin DNS load balancing is generally simple to configure but has a few problems. First, clients (and other DNS servers) often cache IP addresses so that they can avoid doing another lookup. Caching IP addresses can lead to unbalanced load distribution where a few servers are overused and others are underused. Second, DNS servers don't have server affinity so they'll keep forwarding requests blindly, even if your server crashes. The third problem is that you don't have control over the DNS server's load-balancing policy, so you can't take advantage of things like sticky sessions and failover.

We don't recommend round-robin DNS load balancing for anything more than testing purposes. There are several different DNS servers for different server environments; if you choose to go this route, refer to your DNS server documentation for further details.

Although load balancing doesn't necessarily need a cluster, it's often discussed when talking about clustering because there are so many overlapping concepts. Let's specifically talk about clusters now and see what features they provide. We start with a discussion about cluster topology and makeup.

12.1.2 Cluster topology and makeup

Clusters can be formed with nodes running on one machine or on multiple machines. The formation of a cluster's nodes is often referred to as the cluster's *topology*. When the nodes of a cluster are on different machines, the cluster is said to be *horizontal*. When the nodes are on the same machine, the cluster is described as *vertical*. Many clusters are both horizontal and vertical, as shown in figure 12.3.

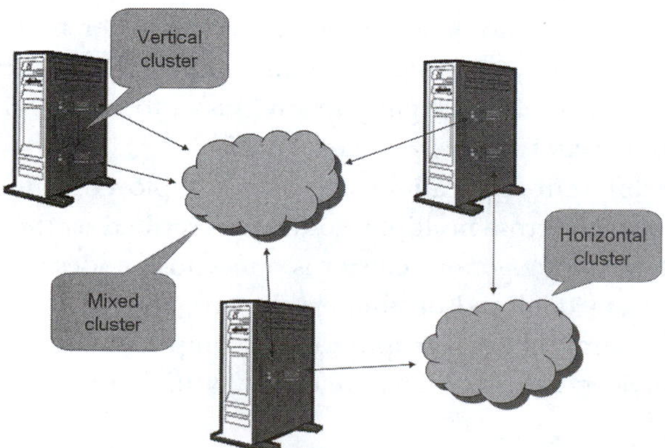

Figure 12.3 A horizontal cluster runs on multiple machines, whereas a vertical cluster runs on a single machine. Often clusters have both horizontal and vertically stacked nodes.

Two JBoss instances run on the server in the upper-left corner of this figure. These instances are configured to run in the same cluster, forming a vertical cluster. The horizontal cluster on the right is formed from one JBoss instance running on the server in the upper-left and another from the JBoss instance running on the server in the bottom of the figure. A mixed cluster can also be formed from machines on the same machine, or on different machines.

Each model has its pros and cons. It's easy to install each node of a horizontal cluster without worrying about the nodes having port conflicts or having unique directories for writing temporary files and logs. As we discuss in chapter 15, setting up multiple JBoss instances on the same machine isn't entirely trivial, but it's manageable. Vertical clusters are a little more difficult to install.

Pop quiz: Which performs better, a vertical cluster or a horizontal cluster? Sorry, this is a trick question. There's no simple answer because there are many variables. If you have a powerful server with a tremendous amount of RAM and multiple processors, a single application server instance probably won't be able to use all the hardware resources. For example, a single JVM instance can only allocate so much RAM (depending on the OS and memory addressing used). In this scenario, a vertical cluster would take better advantage of your hardware resources while avoiding network latency, allowing you to have a fast cluster.

But if you're running on a single machine whose resources are nearly consumed while running a single application server instance, running multiple application servers on that machine would surely be slow. An overused machine might drive you to buy better equipment or opt for a horizontal cluster. Horizontal clusters are also used when cluster nodes are divided across multiple geographies, but these clusters can be slow if inter-node latency is high.

The other things to consider when looking at your cluster topology are fault tolerance and scalability. In general, a horizontal cluster gives you better fault tolerance because, if a server in the cluster fails, the others can still handle requests. Scalability refers to adding hardware resources to support more request concurrency. You can only upgrade a single machine in a vertical cluster so much (scaling up). But you can always add more machines to a horizontal cluster (scaling out).

JBoss makes bringing up a vertical, horizontal, or mixed cluster fairly easy by using a feature called *automatic discovery*. Automatic discovery allows cluster nodes to discover each other without you having to configure them to know about each other. After installing all of your JBoss AS nodes, bringing up any cluster topology is relatively easy. We discuss automatic discovery further in section 12.1.3.

Cluster nodes can have different applications or services deployed to them. The likeness of applications deployed across multiple nodes is described as the makeup (or uniformity) of the cluster. A homogenous cluster is one whose nodes all have the same application or applications deployed on them. A heterogeneous cluster is one whose nodes have different applications or application components deployed on them. Certain clustering services, such as high-availability JNDI, form better when a cluster is homogenous. Heterogeneous clusters are inevitable in some production environments where hardware resources are limited and shared. As we delve into the details of each service, we discuss where the performance may become impacted by the topology of the cluster and the makeup of the cluster.

Now that you have a basic understanding of how clusters are structured, let's examine how clusters are formed and how they communicate in JBoss.

12.1.3 Automatic discovery and multicasting

As we mentioned, JBoss clustering makes it easy for nodes to self-form into clusters without the need to tell each node where the other nodes are physically located. This feature is known as automatic discovery, meaning that a node can automatically discover an existing cluster or form its own cluster and allow other nodes to its cluster. If a cluster doesn't already exist, the first node creates the cluster and become a coordinator, meaning that it manages how other nodes subscribe to the existing cluster.

The automatic-discovery features are built on top of a group-communication mechanism known as *multicast*—a method for forwarding information to a group of people where the sender is only required to send the message once and doesn't need to know the list of recipients. As long as the recipients are listening on the communication channel where the multicast was sent, then they're able to receive the communication. A real-world analogy is that of a TV or a radio—only users who are tuned in to the correct channel receive the information. Multicast is different than a multiple unicast scheme where the sender sends messages to each receiver individually.

The communication channel used for multicast communication is composed of a multicast address and a multicast port. Because multicast is used for group communication, the multicast address is also called the group address. Group members send messages to this address and subscribe to receive messages that others send. The sender's address is the address used for regular unicast communication (the regular IP address). Figure 12.4 shows three nodes that are participating in a cluster. Each node has its own IP address and is communicating with the others over a group address and port.

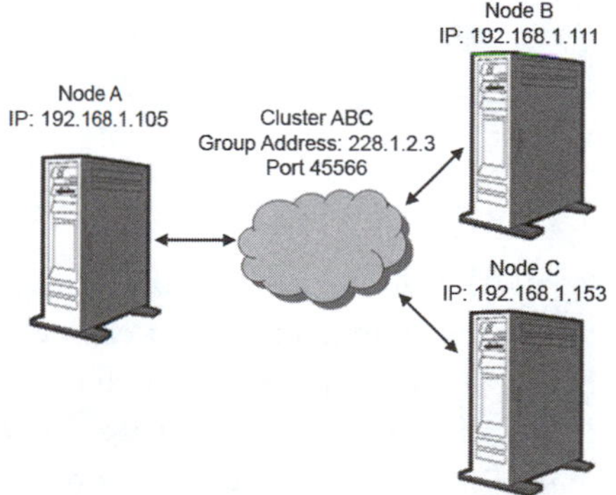

Figure 12.4 A message sent to the group address is available to any node configured to listen on that group address.

The fastest form of multicast is when the network transport protocol enables multicast, such as with UDP. If the underlying network doesn't support multicast, a multiple unicast scheme can be used in its place, but cluster performance may not be as good if there's a lot of cluster traffic.

JBoss uses a tool called JGroups to enable peer-to-peer communication between nodes. JGroups is a toolkit for reliable multicast communication. It uses existing network infrastructure and protocols to transmit multicast messages that are reliable because receivers can request retransmission of lost packets of data. JGroups enables several features used in JBoss clustering, including support for different transport protocols, automatic discovery, reliability, failure detection, and cluster membership-management services. JGroups enables you to configure multicast over UDP or a simulated multicast (using a multiple unicast) over TCP.

Understanding how automatic discovery and multicast work gives you a good sense for how clusters form and how nodes communicate. Now, let's talk about high availability.

12.1.4 High availability

Many network applications require high availability, or the ability to accept client requests with minimal downtime, while maintaining reasonable response times.

Many application vendors and service providers advertise their uptime in terms of a percentage. But achieving 100 percent availability (or uptime) is nearly impossible, so the availability is often advertised by how many nines they have. For example, 99.99 percent availability is known as four-nine availability. Table 12.1 summarizes the different uptime percentages and how they equate to actual downtime.

Table 12.1 How the various uptime percentages relate to actual time

Uptime	Availability based on number of nines	Allowed downtime per year
98%		7.3 days
99%	2-nine	87.6 hours
99.5%		43.8 hours
99.9%	3-nine	8.8 hours
99.95%		4.4 hours
99.99%	4-nine	53 minutes
99.999%	5-nine	5.3 minutes
99.9999%	6-nine	31 seconds
99.99999%	7-nine	3.1 seconds

There are two primary ways to achieve high availability. If you have a completely stateless application, you can achieve high availability through load balancing. If you are load balancing, it doesn't matter if a node goes down because clients get redirected to nodes that are still up. Load balancing provides high availability when there's no server state because it doesn't matter if requests coming from the same client go to different servers.

With stateful applications, you typically don't want clients' requests going to different servers after they've started a stateful conversation. Once a client starts talking to a server, he keeps talking to that same server. But if a server goes down you still want users to be able to continue accessing your application. Stateful architectures can achieve high availability by providing a mechanism for failover. If a client is interacting with a server for the duration of multiple requests and that server crashes, failover allows the user to work on another machine. Like load balancing, failover is the job of a hardware or software load balancer that sits upstream from your application server.

It's important to note that high availability is better achieved with horizontal clustering. Although a vertical cluster will save you if a JVM instance crashes, it won't save you if the entire server crashes due to events such as network failures, power failures, hardware crashes, or OS crashes.

You don't necessarily have to have a cluster to achieve high availability; but, if you have a stateful system, a cluster provides a great way to achieve fault tolerance.

12.1.5 Replication and fault tolerance

A fault-tolerant clustered application is one that's highly available and can continue communicating with clients without fault, even if a server crashes. The users are guaranteed correct behavior between requests, even if the server that they were communicating with has crashed. In the case of stateless architecture, fault tolerance is implied as long as the application is highly available. In the case of a stateful application, fault tolerance implies that the application fails over and that the client's state is available on the server the application failed over to.

Let's look at an example to understand fault tolerance. Imagine you're going through the checkout process on a retail website. The conversation between the browser and the server likely lasts several request/response cycles because you have to fill out multiple screens (billing information, shipment information, verifying the order, and so on), so the server has to store the state of your conversation between requests. If the server crashes in the middle of your checkout process and the cluster fails your request, but not your state, over to another node, then you wouldn't experience any downtime. But, unfortunately, you'd have to fill out your shopping cart again and redo the entire checkout procedure because your state is gone. Just because your application supports failover doesn't mean that it's fault tolerant.

Two types of data are typically associated with a user's state: session data and entity data. Session data is associated with a user and is owned by the node that the client is communicating with. Session data is maintained in memory by the application or through caching services enabled by the application server. Some examples of components that maintain session state data include HTTP sessions and SFSBs.

Entity data is owned by the database. The master copy of the data is maintained in the database although many applications keep some of the entity data in an in-memory cache for better performance. EJB3 entities are an example of components used to read and store entity data.

To be fault tolerant, state associated with an application must be redundantly available. To ensure that session data is fault tolerant, a copy of the data must be available outside of the node by which it's owned. JBoss uses a clustered cache that can replicate cached session data across nodes in a cluster. The act of replicating state data across nodes in a cluster is known as *state replication.* For session data, you can think of fault tolerance as abiding by the following equation:

fault tolerance = fail over + state replication

Figure 12.5 shows a client sending messages to a server that fails, but the server is replicating its state with another server.

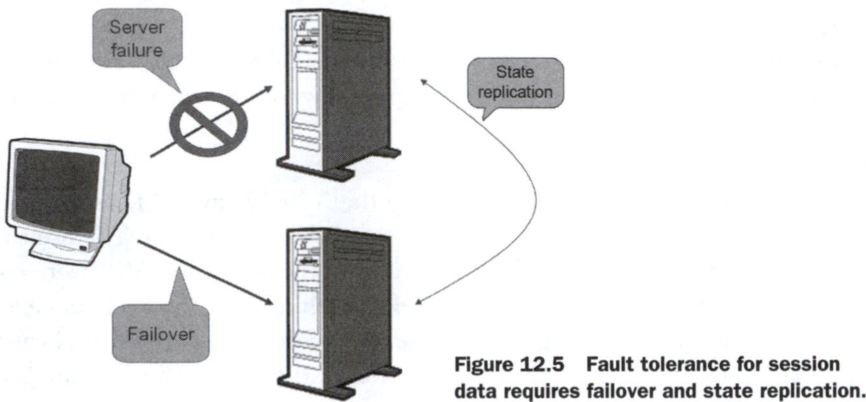

Figure 12.5 Fault tolerance for session data requires failover and state replication.

When the server fails, the client fails over to a new server instance. Because the session state was replicated to the other server before the failure, the client can continue working without losing state.

For entity data to be fault tolerant, the database must be redundantly available. Enabling database fault tolerance requires knowledge of your particular database server, and is outside the scope of this book.

State can be replicated in different ways. Let's examine these methods of state replication and talk about the differences.

TYPES OF STATE REPLICATION

There's a trade-off to having fault tolerance and, as is often the case in software development, that trade-off is performance. To guarantee fault tolerance, you must use synchronous replication—the replication has to finish before a response can be sent back to the user. If there's a lot of inter-node latency, synchronous replication can be slow, especially if the state is being replicated across all the nodes in the cluster, because your response time is always slower than the node that took the longest to replicate the state on.

Asynchronous replication is also an option—the replication is initiated when a request is received but a response is sent back to the user before replication completes. The drawback with the asynchronous-replication model is that it doesn't guarantee that the state of one request is replicated before subsequent requests are sent; there isn't a 100 percent guarantee of fault tolerance. If you're configuring state replication for a cache that holds session data, you have to decide whether you can afford this increased risk. With an entity cache, only synchronous replication ensures a consistent cache. You should only use asynchronous replication with an entity cache if you can tolerate reading stale data from your cache.

You always have the option of not replicating at all. Not replicating state in a stateful application means that your application wouldn't be fault tolerant. This sounds bad, but you have to weigh the performance gain against the potential loss of state. How often do you have a server failure? How many users would lose their sessions? What kind of state would be lost? For example, if you have a retail site with a shopping cart and, over the course of a year, only .05 percent of your users might lose their shopping cart states once, then you might be better off not replicating state and increasing your performance. If the state that you might lose relates to important financial transactions or if 10 percent of your users might be affected 2 to 3 times a month, you might want to replicate your state. Then, you have to consider whether to do synchronous or asynchronous replication.

Another scenario where you might consider skipping replication all together is if your application keeps noncritical state in memory and critical state is kept in the database. For example, if you keep your shopping cart data in the database, but the user's session information is kept in memory, the user may have to log in again if there's a server failure, but the shopping cart state would still exist.

TOTAL REPLICATION VERSUS BUDDY REPLICATION

When every node in a cluster is replicating state with every other node in the cluster, we call it *total state replication*. With total state replication, each node has to keep its own state, as well as the state that has been replicated from other nodes. In a cluster where state is replicated across all the nodes, each node has to cache the sum of the session data across all the nodes. The amount of memory needed to store all the state can add up quickly. In addition to consuming excessive memory, each node must use CPU resources in processing replication traffic from all other members in the cluster. JBoss alleviates these problems through two features: buddy replication and state passivation. We discuss state passivation in section 12.1.6.

Buddy replication is a type of replication in which state is replicated across only a subset of nodes in a cluster. Buddy replication allows you to store only the state of the subset of nodes you are buddies with, reducing the amount of memory, network traffic, and CPU usage as compared to total state replication. If a node fails, any node that a request fails over to is capable of retrieving the information from the buddy node.

In figure 12.6, you see a cluster in which each node is set to have a single buddy node. The left side of this figure shows a cluster with each node replicating to one buddy.

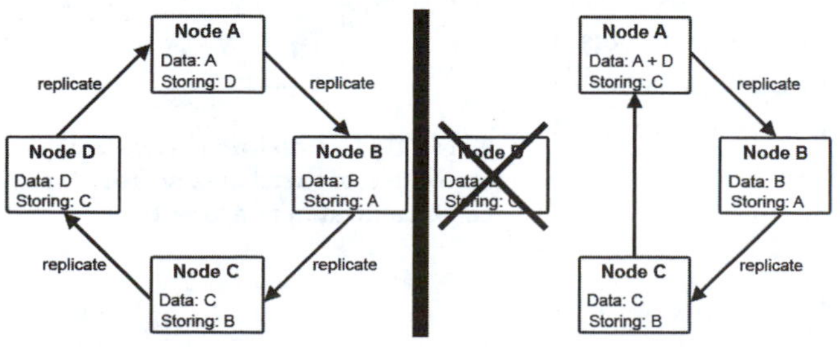

Figure 12.6 With buddy clustering, when a node fails, another node takes over as the buddy for the node that went down.

Each node maintains its own data in addition to the data for the node replicating to it. The right side of this figure shows how the cluster adapts when node D fails. Node C starts replicating data to Node A, and Node A joins its stored data with its regular data and starts storing the data that Node C starts replicating to it.

Each node maintains its own data in addition to data from another node, its buddy. For example, node A maintains its own data, replicates its data with node B, and stores data from node D. If node D goes down, node A joins its backup data from node D and its own data and starts backing up data from node C.

Buddy replication is available to anything that runs on top of JBoss Cache, so it can be used to replicate HTTP session state and SFSB state even though it's only enabled for HTTP-session replication out of the box.

INVALIDATING CACHED ENTITY DATA

As we stated earlier, entity data is owned by the database, but for performance reasons, many people make portions of the entity data available in a cache. Because all the nodes are pointing to the same database, which holds the master copy of the entity data, updates made to the entity data through one node don't necessarily have to be replicated to other nodes. An alternative is to invalidate data in the cache. Invalidation causes one node to send a message to the other nodes to let them know that they no longer have the latest copy of the entity data and should evict it from their caches. If a request is sent to another node to load that same data, it has to read it from the database.

Invalidation is faster than state replication and creates less network traffic because the messages are much smaller. Invalidation messages are smaller than replication messages, so replication traffic can be reduced greatly by using invalidation.

Earlier in this section we talked about how buddy replication can help alleviate problems associated with total state replication. Now let's discuss state passivation, the other mechanism that JBoss provides for alleviating these problems.

12.1.6 State passivation

Some applications need to keep sessions open for a long period of time. But keeping sessions open consumes memory, even when the sessions are inactive for a long time. Session passivation can be used to store inactive sessions in a secondary storage device (such as a disk, database, and so on). These sessions can then be activated if they're accessed again, or purged if they time out.

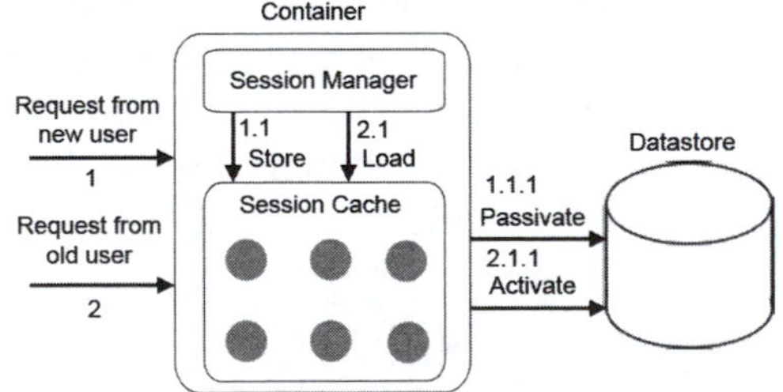

Figure 12.7 Passivation causes objects to be stored in a backend data source. These objects can be activated at a later time.

Figure 12.7 shows a cache that's already full. When a new user makes a request and the session manager tries to store it into the cache, the cache must passivate one of its older sessions into the database. When an old user whose session is passivated tries to access the session, the cache must activate the session back into the cache.

There's obviously a trade-off on the response time of a request that has to suffer the latency involved in the activation of the session. In chapter 13, we discuss SFSB passivation and HTTP session passivation.

12.1.7 Distribution versus clustering

If you're new to clustering, one important distinction to make is the difference between clustering applications and distributing application components. Distribution is the act of separating logically distinct application components onto physically separate machines—you use multiple machines to run a single application. Clustering is the act of running the same application on multiple machines simultaneously. Figure 12.8 illustrates the difference between the two.

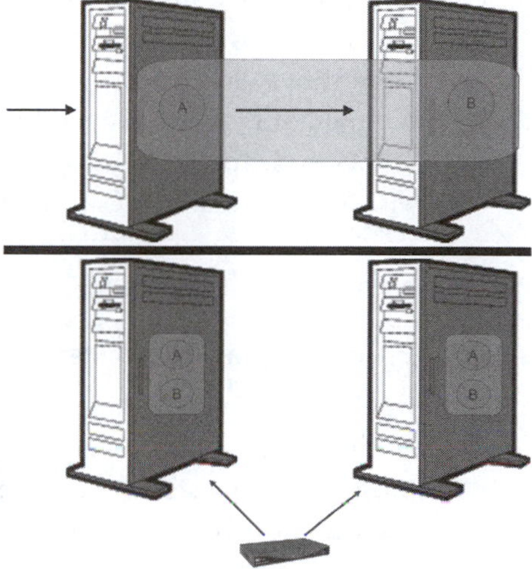

Figure 12.8 A distributed application (top) requires multiple machines, whereas a collocated application requires only a single machine (bottom) but can be clustered for scalability.

The distributed application on the top has two components, A and B. When a client accesses component A, it makes a remote call to access component B every time the component is needed. With the clustered application, the load balancer can distribute the load to one server or another in the cluster, but components A and B are collocated on each node, so no remote calls are necessary.

Many people think that distribution is a good strategy for making an application scalable. The idea is that you distribute the layers, and then you add redundant servers hosting only the layers that act as a bottleneck. For example, if your web layer acts as a bottleneck, you might add multiple servers running your web layer, load balancing across all of them, but still run a single EJB server.

The reality is that distribution is both more complicated and less performant than collocating all your application layers on one server and load balancing the entire application. Distributing different layers of your application means that every transaction has to do a remote call over a network. Even if the layers are hosted on different machines on a fast network located on the same subnet, the network latency increases your response time by orders of magnitude over an architecture where the layers are running in the same process.

A collocated architecture allows all the calls between layers to be made in the same process, making them extremely fast. Scalability can occur by load balancing across multiple nodes that run the same application, with all layers included. The moral of the story is to avoid distributed architectures and aim for a design that can be clustered easily.

At this point, you should know enough about the fundamentals of clustering to ramble on for hours. Let's put some of this knowledge to use by setting up a cluster.

12.2 Setting up a simple cluster

When I (Javid) teach JBoss courses, people seem to have the most fun during the clustering labs. My amateur psychoanalysis leads me to believe that joining into a cluster and interactively sending messages back and forth to other nodes elicits a sense of community and belonging that makes people happy. Or, it could be that they're happy that I've stopped babbling and let them do a lab.

When learning how to cluster, it's important to run a real cluster and play around with it. In this section, we walk you through setting up a simple vertical cluster on a single machine so that you can experiment with clustering on your own. Let's start by learning how to bring up a simple cluster.

12.2.1 Bringing up a JBoss cluster

In chapter 1, we explained how to start the *all* server configuration (using the `-c` all command-line switch when running the start script). The all configuration has all the JBoss clustering services enabled. Without you changing any settings, starting multiple instances of the all configuration on different machines on the same subnet should bring up a cluster.

Many JBoss users who are experimenting with clustering don't have access to multiple machines and/or a properly configured network to do so. If you only have a single machine, don't worry—you can run multiple JBoss servers on a single machine and join them into a cluster. The challenge with running multiple nodes on the same machine is that each node needs to have its own temp directories and has to bind to different ports (or the same ports on different IPs).

If you're following along with only a single machine, the simplest thing to do in Linux is to bind one cluster node to `localhost` and the other to your machine hostname. If you're using Windows, you can create a Microsoft Loopback Adapter and set it up with two IP addresses using the advanced TCP/IP settings. We have links at the end of this chapter to show you how to do these two steps in Windows, but here's a summary of the steps for Windows XP:

1. Go to Add Hardware in the Windows Control Panel.
2. Select Yes, I Have Already Connected The Hardware.
3. Scroll to the bottom of the Installed Hardware list and select Add A New Hardware Device.
4. Select the manual installation option.
5. Select Network Adapters.
6. Select Microsoft as the Manufacturer and Microsoft Loopback Adapter as the Network Adapter.

7. After it finishes adding the adapter, go to Network Connections in the Windows Control Panel and rename your newly added adapter to be something like *Loopback* for quicker identification.
8. Click the loopback adapater, go to Properties, and go to TCP/IP properties.
9. Specify a non-routable IP address (such as 192.168.1.140) with a subnet mask of 255.255.255.0.
10. Click Advanced... and add another IP address (such as 192.168.1.141) with the same subnet mask. Note that, at, this point, you may have to restart your machine.

For the remainder of this example, we use the following IP addresses: 192.168.1.140 and 192.168.1.141.

Regardless of whether you're running multiple nodes on a single machine or on separate machines, the cluster configuration should be the same. Starting with a newly unzipped copy of JBoss, navigate into the server directory and copy the all directory twice: once to a directory called node1 and once to a directory called node2. The contents of your server directory should now look like that shown in figure 12.9.

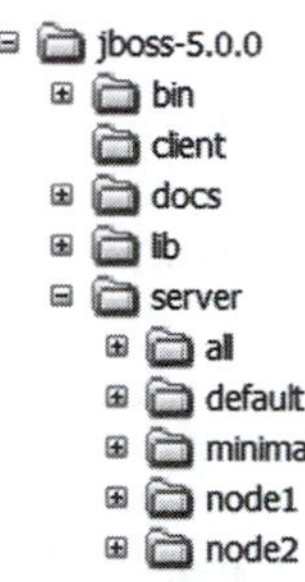

Figure 12.9 The contents of the server directory after the all configuration has been copied as node1 and node2

Now open two console windows and go to the JBoss bin directory in each. In the first window, start the JBoss instance using the following command:

```
./run.sh -c node1 -b 192.168.1.140 -Djboss.messaging.ServerPeerID=1
```

The `-c` command specifies which server configuration you're using. The `-b` command specifies the IP address to which the node will bind. We talk about binding more in chapter 15. You can change this value to match the IP address or hostname that you're using. The `-Djboss.messaging.ServerPeerID` command sets a unique ID for the node's JBoss messaging service, which is required or the clustered messaging services won't start properly.

Let that server instance start completely. Scrolling up in the console, you should see some output that looks like this:

```
[DefaultPartition] Initializing partition DefaultPartition
[DefaultPartition] Number of cluster members: 1
[DefaultPartition] Other members: 0
[DefaultPartition-HAPartitionCache] JBoss Cache version: JBossCache
   'Alegrias' 2.1.1.GA
[DefaultPartition] Fetching serviceState (will wait for 30000 milliseconds):
[DefaultPartition] State could not be retrieved (we are the first member in
   group)
```

This output tells you a few things. First, you see messages related to the `DefaultPartition`. A partition is merely another word for a cluster. Different services running in JBoss participate in different partitions. Technically, a two-node cluster may create and communicate over four or five different clusters. If you scroll back in the console, you'll see output related to other clustered services such as Messaging and HAJNDI. You also see that node1 is the first group member for this partition.

Now, in the second console, start the other server using the following:

```
./run.sh -c node2 -b 192.168.1.141 -Djboss.messaging.ServerPeerID=2
```

After the second node starts, take a look back at the first console (for node1). You should see that several additional messages have been printed. Here's part of what you should see:

```
[DefaultPartition] New cluster view for partition DefaultPartition (id: 1,
➥ delta: 1) : [192.168.1.140:1099, 192.168.1.141:1099]
```

You now have a two-node cluster. If you don't see similar output, then you may have problems with your network multicast settings. Open a web browser and visit the following URLs in different tabs or browser windows to see each node's root web application:

```
http://192.168.1.140:8080/
http://192.168.1.141:8080/
```

You may have noticed that you don't have to tell each node about the other nodes in the partition. You just started an out-of-the-box configuration of JBoss AS and the cluster formed by itself, thanks to JBoss AS's automatic-discovery feature.

OK, so you have two nodes that know about each other—so what? The fact that two nodes are communicating with each other isn't interesting unless they can do something useful, right? Well, let's make them do something. Let's create an EJB and deploy it to both servers and see how you can take advantage of the cluster.

12.2.2 Creating a clustered EJB

Let's create a simple EJB application with a client that counts from 1 to 100 and sends each number to the server to be printed on the console window. Because the server is clustered, the client's dynamic proxy calls the cluster nodes in the server using a round-robin load-balancing strategy.

Start by creating a JAR file that contains the compiled code for the interface shown in listing 12.1.

Listing 12.1 The remote interface for a clustered SLSB

```
import javax.ejb.Remote;
@Remote
public interface Counter {
  public void printCount(int messageNumber);
}
```

Then add the EJB in listing 12.2 that implements the interface.

Listing 12.2 The bean code for a clustered SLSB

```
import javax.ejb.Stateless;
import org.jboss.ejb3.annotation.Clustered;
@Stateless
```

```
@Clustered
public class CounterBean implements Counter {
  public void printCount(int countNumber) {
    System.out.println(countNumber);
  }
}
```

This code defines a SLSB that prints an integer to the standard output. Notice that the bean class has a `@org.jboss.ejb3.annotation.Clustered` annotation defined. This annotation tells the server that this bean is clustered and should be load balanced. We discuss EJB load balancing further in chapter 13.

To build this code, you need a class path that includes the client/jbossall-client.jar file. After you build the EJB, package it into an EJB-JAR file. Now you're ready to deploy it to the server. Well, actually, you're ready to deploy it to the *servers*.

12.2.3 Deploying your application

Now that you have an application archive, copy it to the server/XXX/deploy directory on both servers. If you don't want to manually copy your archive to each application server, there are several ways to do clustered deployments. JBoss provides a farming service, but it has a bad track record and most people don't rely on it in a production environment.

A popular way to handle cluster deployments is to configure the deployment scanner (described in chapter 3) so that each node points to a directory mounted on a network. On Windows, you can use Server Message Block (also known as SMB or Microsoft Windows Network) to create a mount. On Unix, you can use Network File System (NFS). Then, when an application archive is put into the network mounted directory, all the application servers will pick it up and deploy it.

Now that the server is running, let's build and execute the client code.

12.2.4 Calling the clustered EJB

Now that your application has been deployed onto both nodes of your cluster, build the client code shown in listing 12.3.

Listing 12.3 The client code that calls the clustered SFSB

```
import javax.naming.Context;
import javax.naming.InitialContext;
public class Client {
  public static void main(String[] args) throws Exception {
    InitialContext ctx = new InitialContext();
    Counter s = (Counter) ctx.lookup("CounterBean/remote");
    for (int i = 0; i < 100; i++) {
      s.printCount(i);
      Thread.sleep(1000);
    }
  }
}
```

To build this code, you need to have a class path that includes the client/jbossall-client.jar file. To run this code, you need to define the following jndi.properties file in the root of your class path:

```
java.naming.factory.initial=org.jnp.interfaces.NamingContextFactory
java.naming.factory.url.pkgs=org.jboss.naming
```

Run this code in a process running outside of your application server. When the client starts, it uses automatic discovery to find a JNDI server and then uses the JNDI server to obtain a remote interface (dynamic proxy) for a SLSB. The client simply calls the `printCount()` method on the dynamic proxy in a loop with a one-second pause between calls. Each time the `printCount()` method is executed the dynamic proxy calls the server to execute the SLSB code.

After starting the client, pull up the consoles for each node, and you should see that the messages sent from the client are being load balanced across both nodes. Table 12.2 shows you a sample of the output that you might see on the console windows.

Node 1 console output	Node 2 console output
INFO [STDOUT] 0	INFO [STDOUT] 2
INFO [STDOUT] 4	INFO [STDOUT] 7
INFO [STDOUT] 8	INFO [STDOUT] 9
INFO [STDOUT] 1	INFO [STDOUT] 3
INFO [STDOUT] 5	INFO [STDOUT] 6
INFO [STDOUT] 10	

Table 12.2 The messages that are sent from the client arrive in both nodes, showing that the clustering configuration worked.

As you can see, the dynamic proxy is directing the calls to both servers in a random fashion. Now, try bringing down one of the nodes, and you should see that load balancing allows the client requests to continue hitting the running node. The application is now fault tolerant. (Remember, stateless applications only require load balancing in order to be fault-tolerant.)

We haven't gotten into the details on how clustering is configured. Up to this point, our goal was to get something up and running so that you could get a sense of how easy it is to form JBoss AS clusters. We get into the details throughout the rest of this chapter and the next. Now that you've seen how to set up a cluster and some simple things that you can do with that cluster, let's explore how to configure and use the basic JBoss clustering services.

12.3 Understanding JBoss clustering

JBoss uses multicasting to enable automatic discovery and group communication within a cluster. All the JBoss clustering services are built on top of JGroups, as shown in figure 12.10.

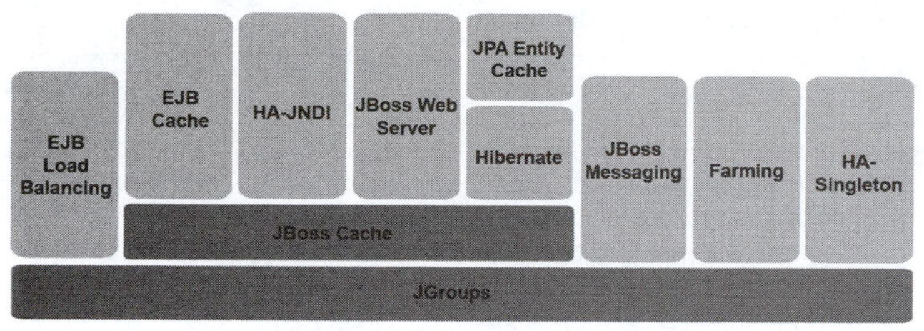

Figure 12.10 The various clustering services build on top of JGroups and JBoss Cache.

The figure shows most of the major clustering services covered in this book, as well as some services that aren't covered. As you can see, several of the services build on top of JBoss Cache, which in turn builds on top of JGroups. We talk about JBoss Cache later on in the chapter.

In the next section, we explain how JGroups works and show you how to configure it. Let's start off by building an understanding of the JGroups architecture.

12.3.1 Understanding the JGroups architecture

Two of the main architectural components in JGroups are the channel and the protocol stack. A channel provides a way for applications to connect and send messages to other members in the cluster. When a message is sent, it works its way down the protocol stack, and when it's received, it works its way up the stack. Figure 12.11 shows an application on one node of a server sending a message through JGroups to an application on another node.

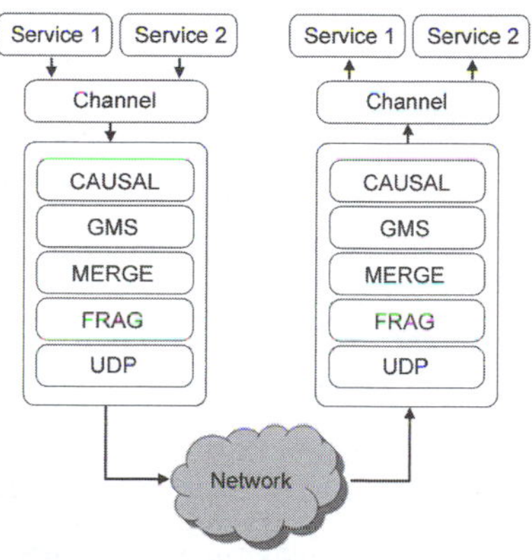

Figure 12.11 Outgoing requests go down the JGroups stack, and incoming requests go up the stack.

Each layer in the stack consists of a *protocol*. In JGroups, a protocol doesn't necessarily correspond to a transport protocol. A protocol in JGroups is a component that can send, receive, modify, reorder, pass, or drop a message. For example, the FRAG protocol can fragment outgoing messages by breaking them up into smaller parts, reassembling them into one message when they're received. Table 12.3 gives a summary of the different protocols available in JGroups.

Different services have the ability to use different channels; configuring multiple channels necessitates more threads and, in turn, more CPU context switching. It is more efficient to use a single JGroups channel that multiplexes the cluster traffic, so that's exactly what JBoss does out of the box. All the JBoss clustering services are configured to run on top of a single multiplexed JGroups channel as suggested in figure 12.11.

Let's look at the main files used to configure JBoss clustering and how to use them to define a unique cluster.

Table 12.3 The different protocols available in JGroups

Protocol category	Description	Protocols
Transport protocols	Transport protocols are found at the bottom of the stack and are responsible for sending and receiving messages to/from the network. The primary transport protocols are UDP and TCP. If firewall constraints exist, cluster traffic can be tunneled using the TUNNEL protocol.	UDP, TCP, TUNNEL, JMS, LOOPBACK
Initial membership discovery	These services are used when a node is trying to establish initial membership. A node either joins an existing cluster if one is found or decides to start its own.	PING, TCPPING, TCPGOSSIP, MPING
Fragmentation and merging	These services are used to split larger packets up into smaller ones when sending them and then reassemble them when they're received.	FRAG, FRAG2
Reliable message transmission	These services are used to ensure that packets are sent in the correct order and that all expected packets for a particular message have been received.	CAUSAL, NAKACK, pbcast.NAKACK, SMACK, UNICAST, PBCAST, pbcast.STABLE
Group membership	The group membership (GMS) protocol is used to notify the cluster when a node leaves, joins, or crashes. The MERGE protocol is used to unify groups that have been split. The VIEW_SYNC protocol causes group members to periodically synchronize their membership information.	pbcast.GMS, MERGE, MERGE2, VIEW_SYNC
Failure detection	These services are used to poll nodes in the cluster to ensure that they're still alive and active.	FD, FD_SIMPLE, FD_PING, FD_ICMP, FD_SOCK, VERIFY_SUSPECT
Security	The AUTH protocol adds a layer of security to JGroups.	AUTH
State transfer	These services are used to transfer application state to a joining member of a group.	pbcast.STATE_TRANSFER, pbcast.STREAMING_STATE_TRANSFER
Debugging	These services are used for diagnostic, performance tuning, and debugging purposes.	PERF_TP, SIZE, TRACE
Miscellaneous	The COMPRESS protocol is used to compress and decompress packets. The FLUSH protocol is used to tell a node to send all its queued messages and block it from sending more.	COMPRESS, pbcast.FLUSH

12.3.2 Configuring JBoss clustering services

Each of the clustered services in JBoss either defines its own cluster configuration or builds on top of a default cluster configuration defined in the server/all/deploy/cluster/cluster-jboss-beans.xml file. Table 12.4 summarizes the various clustering services that JBoss offers, lists the configuration files, and points you to the sections where you can find more information about the service.

Table 12.4 The various clustering service configuration files and the sections where we talk about them

Service	Configuration files[a]	Section
The JGroups protocol stack	jgroups-channelfactory.sar/META-INF/jgroups-channelfactory-stacks.xml	12.3.3
Session bean load balancing	jboss-cluster-beans.xml EJB Annotations (in your session bean)	13.3.1
SFSB replication	jboss-cache-manager.sar/META-INF/jboss-cache-configs.xml jboss-cache-manager.sar/META-INF/jboss-cache-manager-jboss-beans.xml	13.3.2
Entity cache replication	jboss-cache-manager.sar/META-INF/jboss-cache-configs.xml jboss-cache-manager.sar/META-INF/jboss-cache-manager-jboss-beans.xml	13.4
HTTP session replication & passivation	jboss-cache-manager.sar/META-INF/jboss-cache-configs.xml jboss-cache-manager.sar/META-INF/jboss-cache-manager-jboss-beans.xml war-deployers-jboss-beans.xml (under server/all/deployers/jbossweb.deployer/META-INF) WEB-INF/web.xml (in your application) WEB-INF/jboss-web.xml (in your application)	13.2
High availability naming service	cluster-jboss-beans.xml	13.5

a. All the configuration files are located under server/all/deploy/cluster unless specified otherwise.

Each clustered service must point to the channel and the protocol stack that it wants to use. The configuration is similar in each file, so let's take the cluster-jboss-beans.xml file as an example. This microcontainer configuration file defines a bean called `HAPartition`. The configuration for this bean looks something like this:

```
<bean name="HAPartition"
     class="org.jboss.ha.framework.server.ClusterPartition">
  ...
  <property name="cacheManager">
    <inject bean="CacheManager"/>        ❶
  </property>
  <property name="cacheConfigName">
    ha-partition                            ❷
  </property>
  <property name="partitionName">
    ${jboss.partition.name:DefaultPartition}     ❸
  </property>
```

The `partitionName` property ❸ defines a name for the cluster. Other configuration files might call this property `clusterName` instead of `partitionName`. We talk about the significance of this property in a bit. The `cacheManager` property ❶ points to another bean that manages JBoss Cache configurations. We talk about JBoss Cache in the next section, but we bring this up now because the cache manager has to point to the single JGroups channel that JBoss defines and each cache configuration must point to a protocol stack. The `cacheConfigName` property ❷ defines the name of the cache configuration to use. The cache manager bean is defined in server/all/deploy/cluster/jboss-cache-manager.sar/META-INF/jboss-cache-manager.beans.xml.

The cache configurations that the bean uses are defined in the jboss-cache-configs.xml file in the same directory. The cache configuration looks like this:

```
<bean name="CacheManager" >
...
 <property name="channelFactory">
  <inject bean="JChannelFactory"/>
 </property>
```

This configuration points to a bean called `JChannelFactory`, which manages the single multiplexed channel that JBoss provides and makes the protocol stacks available. The file that contains this bean is /server/all/deploy/cluster/jgroups-channelfactory.sar/META-INF/jgroups-channelfactory-jboss-beans.xml. This file has two important properties that you should know about. The first property is the `multiplexerConfig` property, which points to a file that contains all the protocol stack definitions. By default, this property points to the file jgroups-channelfactory-stacks.xml in the same directory. The second property is the `nodeAddress` property, which configures the address that the channel should bind to. By default, this is set to the `${jboss.bind.address}` variable, which can be configured at startup using the `-b` command line option. We discuss this more in chapter 15.

The cache configuration file—jboss-cache-configs.xml—points to the specific stack that the cache should use:

```
<cache-config name="ha-partition">
...
 <attribute name="MultiplexerStack">
  ${jboss.default.jgroups.stack:udp}
 </attribute>
```

The `MultiplexerStack` property references a JBoss variable called `jboss.default.jgroups.stack`, which has a default value of `udp`. All the JBoss services are configured to use the UDP protocol stack out of the box.

The following attributes must match in order for a service to form a cluster with identical services running on different nodes in a cluster:

- The multicast address
- The multicast port
- The `clusterName` or `partitionName` property

The multicast address and port are both part of the configuration for the protocol stack, which we discuss in the next section.

Changing any of these three properties is adequate for defining a new partition. To form multiple JBoss partitions within the same network, all you have to do is make sure that each partition uses a unique combination of these three values. Try it. Start the two nodes we set up in section 12.2, go into the cluster-jboss-beans.xml file for node1, and change the `partitionName` property on the `HAPartition` bean. You might

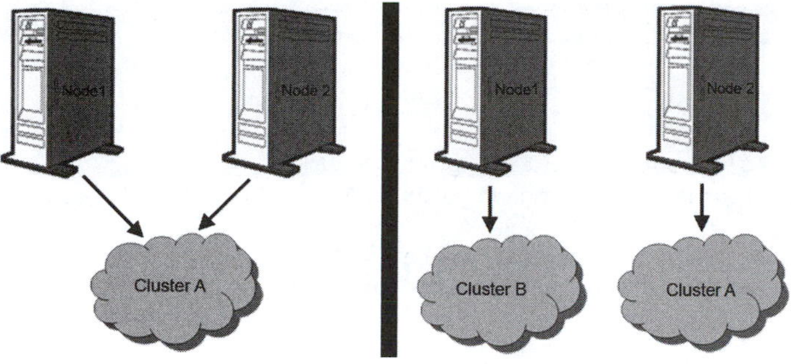

Figure 12.12 On the left, the two nodes share the same partition name, multicast port, and multicast address, so they belong to the same cluster. On the right, one or more of these three attributes differs, so the nodes aren't part of the same cluster.

have to restart the servers when you make this change. Make sure you pull up the console windows side by side and watch the output. You'll see that node1 leaves the partition it was in and starts its own partition. The output on node2 shows you that node1 has left the partition. Figure 12.12 shows you a before-and-after view of what happens when you change the partition name on one node.

WARNING Don't just change the partition name to define a new partition! Changing the multicast address and/or port in the jgroups-channelfactory-stacks.xml file is the recommended way of defining a unique partition. If you just change the partition name for one node (or service) but leave the same multicast address and port, both partitions have to filter out each other's traffic, and your clusters may be less performant.

Most of the clustering services configure the cluster names using the `jboss.partition.name` JBoss variable or name that concatenates on top of that variable. The default value for this variable is `DefaultParition`. If you want to bring up a node that uses a different partition name, you can use the `-g` command-line switch. Here's an example that would bring up the all configuration, using `MyNewPartitionName` instead of `DefaultPartition`:

```
> ./run.sh -c all -g MyNewPartitionName
```

Now that you've learned where all the configuration files for the JBoss clustering services exist and have a big picture on how to define a unique cluster, let's take a closer look at how to configure the protocol stack.

12.3.3 Configuring the protocol stack

Out of the box, several JGroups protocol stacks are available for clustering services to use. They're defined in the following file:

> server/all/deploy/cluster/jgroups-channelfactory.sar/META-INF/jgroups-channelfactory-stacks.xml

Although several stacks are available, as we mentioned earlier, all the JBoss services are preconfigured to use the UDP stack defined in this file. Listing 12.4 shows you what the UDP protocol stack looks like.

Listing 12.4 The multicast address and port of the UPD protocol stack

```
<stack name="udp">                ❶
 <config>        ❷
  <UDP
   mcast_port="${jgroups.udp.mcast_port:45688}"
   mcast_addr="${jgroups.udp.mcast_addr:228.11.11.11}"
   ... />                                                    ❸
  <PING timeout="2000" num_initial_members="3"/>
  <MERGE2 max_interval="100000" min_interval="20000"/>
  ...
 </config>
</stack>
```

Each protocol stack is defined with a `stack` element and named using the `name` attribute of the element ❶. The `config` block ❷ defines the stack. Each subelement of that block defines a new protocol ❸. These subelements are where you set the options for the protocols that JBoss supports. There are too many different protocol stacks and protocols defined in this file to discuss all of them. These protocols are well documented in the JBoss and JGroups documentation, which are referenced at the end of this chapter.

The main protocol that you configure in the stack is likely to be the transport protocol. You can only have a single transport protocol defined on the stack. The transport protocol sits at the bottom of the stack and sends and receives message from the network. You'll most likely use either the UDP or the TCP protocol, but other protocols are available as well.

When would you use TCP versus UDP? In general, the TCP protocol is more reliable than the UDP protocol and is supported by most machines connected to a WAN (for example, the internet). If you're configuring a cluster across a WAN, use the TCP protocol. Because TCP doesn't support multicasting, the TCP protocol uses multiple unicast instead of multicast. Multiple unicast is slower than multicast, so if you're running a cluster in a LAN, where UDP is supported and reliability is less of an issue, you should probably use UDP.

Let's discuss configuring the UDP protocol.

CONFIGURING THE UDP PROTOCOL

If your network supports UDP, then the default UDP stack that all the JBoss services point to should work for you. The UDP protocol configuration looks like this:

```
<UDP mcast_addr="${jgroups.udp.mcast_addr:228.11.11.11}"
   mcast_port="${jgroups.udp.mcast_port:45688}"
   ip_ttl="${jgroups.udp.ip_ttl:2}"
   loopback="true"
   .../>
```

This configuration is similar to what you see in the default JGroups configurations found in the all configuration. You can set the multicast address using the `mcast_addr` attribute and the multicast port using the `mcast_port` attribute. These attributes both have JBoss variables that you can specify at server startup time to override the default values. The `ip_ttl` value is used to set the multicast time-to-live value, which we discuss in the next subsection. If you don't wish to use multicast, you can add the `ip_mcast` attribute and set it to `false` to use multiple unicast (over UDP) instead.

Most operating systems support a loopback network interface with an address of 127.0.0.1 to facilitate IP communication without going over a real network. On most OS's, the loopback interface isn't capable of forwarding multicast packets. Real Ethernet interfaces are capable of forwarding multicast communication, but on some OS's (such as Windows), the Ethernet interfaces are disabled when you aren't connected to a real network. You can disable the Windows feature (called Media Sense) that disables the Ethernet interfaces when you aren't connected to a network. But, reportedly, many versions of Windows still won't forward multicast packets. Setting the `loopback` attribute to `true` causes a sent message to be sent back up the protocol stack to the application. Loopback is usually disabled, but on Windows machines it may be necessary to set `loopback` to `true` if you aren't connected to a network. Another way to solve this problem is to use a product called the Smartronix SuperLooper Loopback Jack & Plug by Smartronix, Inc. This is a small, inexpensive hardware loopback device that plugs into your Ethernet port. A third way is to use multiple Microsoft Loopback Adapters to run your JBoss AS cluster nodes as described earlier in the chapter.

The `ip_ttl` attribute is used to set the IP time-to-live (TTL) value. The TTL attribute is also known as a hop limit. TTL is a part of the IP protocol and is used to limit the number of network hops that a packet can make before it's discarded (with an error message sent back to the sender). Each network router that gets the message decreases the TTL value by one when it gets the message, only forwarding the message if the resulting value is greater than zero. The TTL attribute prevents packets from getting stuck in an indefinite loop inside a network.

The TTL value is equal to the number of routers that a multicast message can hop. The larger the TTL value you use, the farther the message can potentially propagate. Theoretically, if you set the TTL to a very large value, a packet could propagate across an entire network. Realistically, many routers don't forward multicast messages at all. The default TTL values are typically good enough for a LAN; but, if you have a cluster that spans multiple subnets on a WAN, you might want to increase the TTL value so that your packets don't get dropped.

The Internet Assigned Numbers Authority (IANA) controls the assignment of IP multicast addresses and has designated the range of 224.0.0.0 to 239.255.255.255 for multicast addresses. But if you're running a cluster within a LAN, you should use the range from 224.0.0.0 through 224.0.0.255. This range is reserved for local networks, so routers make sure not to forward packets sent to an address within this range outside of your network.

The default multicast addresses configured in the UDP stack is 228.11.11.11, which falls outside of the LAN range; if you're sure you're going to run in a LAN, you should change the address to fit within that range so that packets don't accidentally get routed farther than they need to. You can configure the UDP multicast address in the protocol stack or by passing in the `jgroups.udp.mcast_addr` JBoss variable at startup.

Now that you know how to configure the UDP protocol, let's see what it takes to configure the TCP protocol.

CONFIGURING THE TCP PROTOCOL

If your network doesn't support UDP or you want to create a network over a WAN, then you want to use TCP instead of UDP. You can use TCP by pointing your services to the TCP stack defined in the jgroups-channelfactory-stacks.xml file by specifying the `jboss.default.jgroups.stack` JBoss variable at startup.

You also have to make a configuration change—you have to set `initial_hosts` attribute on the TCPPING protocol. Here's an example:

```
<TCPPING timeout="3000" down_thread="false" up_thread="false"
      initial_hosts="localhost[7600],localhost[7601]"
      port_range="1"
      num_initial_members="3"/>
```

The TCP protocol doesn't support group communication like UDP does, so automatic discovery of nodes isn't possible with only TCP. If you need to use TCP and are able to use multicast as well, you can use the MPING protocol to enable multicast-based automatic discovery. If you aren't able to use multicast, you'll have to use the TCPPING protocol, which doesn't support automatic discovery.

The MPING protocol is enabled by default under the TCP stack in jgroups-channelfactory-stacks.xml file. The TCPPING protocol is available, but you must uncomment it and comment out the MPING protocol before you can use it. The TCPPING protocol has an `initial_hosts` attribute used to point to hosts that are part of the cluster. The protocol asks the hosts for information on the coordinating node for the cluster. If possible, configure this attribute to point to all the nodes in your cluster to avoid complications with orphaned coordinators. After determining who the coordinator is, the node joins the cluster by subscribing through the coordinator. If it can't determine who the coordinator is, the node itself will become the coordinator. Our example configuration merely points the initial host to two different ports on the local machine. You can also set the list of initial hosts using the `jgroups.tcpping.initial_hosts` JBoss variable.

You should now have a good idea of how to configure the UDP and TCP protocols and have a gauge of all the fundamental JBoss configuration concepts pertaining to JGroups. Now let's take a closer look at JBoss Cache to see what features it provides and how to configure it.

12.4 Configuring JBoss Cache

As we discussed earlier, stateful applications need to enable state replication in order to be fault tolerant. JBoss enables state replication using JBoss Cache, a distributed cache built on top of JGroups. JBoss Cache enables cache replication for many types of objects including SFSBs, entities, HTTP sessions, and objects placed in JNDI.

What exactly is a distributed cache? Imagine two cluster nodes where each has its own cache. When the first node writes some data to the cache, that data is replicated over the cluster to the second node. If the second node is asked for that data–say, when the first node dies and the client is failed over to the second node–then the second node already has the data available.

12.4.1 Examining the JBoss Cache configuration files

Several services in the all configuration make use of JBoss Cache. The SFSB container uses a cache to store all of its session state. The entity persistence context uses JBoss Cache as a second-level cache for entity objects. The JBoss Web Server uses a cache to store HTTP sessions. The `HAPartition` service that we talked about earlier uses a cache to enable high-availability features for clustering services such as high-availability JNDI. And the HTTP single-sign-on cache manages the distributed cache for a clustered single-sign-on service. Table 12.5 lists the files that reference configurations in the jboss-cache-configs.xml file.

Table 12.5 Where the various jboss-cache-configs.xml caches are referenced from for each service

Replicated cache	Configuration file
HA Partition Cache	deploy/cluster/cluster-jboss-beans.xml
Stateful session bean cache	Annotations on your SFSB (default annotations defined as aspects in deploy/ejb3-interceptors-aop.xml)
Entity bean cache	deployers/ejb3.deployer/META-INF/persistence.properties
HTTP session cache	deployers/jbossweb.deployer/META-INF/war-deployers-jboss-beans.xml
HTTP single-sign-on cache	Hardcoded to clustered-sso, which is aliased to ha-partition in the jboss-cache-manager-jboss-beans.xml file

These cache configurations defined in the jboss-cache-configs.xml file have various attributes that you can configure. The most common ones are shown in listing 12.5.

Listing 12.5 Common configuration elements found in JBoss Cache cache configuration

```
<cache-config name="...">
  <attribute name="MultiplexerStack">...</attribute>          ❶
  <attribute name="BuddyReplicationConfig">...</attribute>        ❷
  <attribute name="IsolationLevel">...</attribute>         ❸
  <attribute name="CacheMode">...</attribute>         ❹
  <attribute name="CacheLoaderConfig">...</attribute>        ❺
  <attribute name="EvictionPolicyConfig">...</attribute>        ❻
</bean>
```

Let's look at some of these configuration elements. We aren't going to give you an in-depth explanation of all the configuration elements for a cache configuration because the JBoss Cache documentation already does a great job of covering them. We provide you with a reference to the online JBoss Cache documentation at the end of this chapter. For many of these configuration elements, you don't even have to go that far because they are self-explanatory or documented in the configuration file itself.

CONFIGURING THE JGROUPS STACK

The `MultiplexerStack` attribute ❶ points to the JGroups protocol stack that the cache should use to communicate with other nodes when replicating. We discussed this attribute in section 12.3.

CONFIGURING BUDDY REPLICATION

By using the `BuddyReplicationConfig` property ❷, you can enable buddy replication, specify the number of buddies that a node should have, define a communication timeout, and more. The configuration details pertaining to buddy replication are covered well in the JBoss Cache documentation. To see an example of a buddy replication configuration, take a peek at the cache config with the name standard-session-cache. This configuration is used by JBoss Web Server to manage HTTP sessions replication.

The single-buddy replication configuration that we showed you in figure 12.6 can work quite well in many environments. Using this configuration with a TCP JGroups channel should give you better performance than with a UDP channel.

CONFIGURING THE ISOLATION LEVEL

The `IsolationLevel` property ❸ can be used to set the transaction isolation level for updates to the distributed cache. The isolation level's options are similar to those found in a database, as follow:

- SERIALIZABLE
- REPEATABLE_READ (the default value)
- READ_COMMITTED
- READ_UNCOMMITTED
- NONE

The trade-off between these options is also the same as that in a database. Namely, the more isolation you have (`SERIALIZABLE`), the more locking and worse performance. The less isolation you have (`NONE`), the less locking you have and more dirty data.

CONFIGURING THE CACHE MODE

The `CacheMode` property ❹ specifies the strategy that the cache uses for replicating with other nodes in the cluster. We described the various replications strategies in section 12.1.5. Table 12.6 lists the available replication modes.

Table 12.6 The different cache replication modes that can be provided to the `CacheMode` property

`cacheModeString` option	Cache mode	Summary
`REPL_SYNC`	Synchronous replication	Used for session data or cached entity data. Has the greatest fault tolerance, but is slow if the network is unreliable, if multicast can't be used, or if inter-node latency is great. High availability can be achieved by load balancing requests across all nodes in the cluster. With an entity cache, only synchronous replication ensures a consistent cache.
`REPL_ASYNC`	Asynchronous replication	Used for session data or cached entity data. Has similar performance to no replication, but doesn't guarantee fault tolerance because state replication may not have completed before failover occurs. Don't use this mode for an entity cache unless you don't care about reading stale data from your cache. Load-balancing strategies that change servers across requests, such as round-robin and random, should be avoided. Use sticky-session load balancing and failover to achieve the best possible fault tolerance.

Table 12.6 The different cache replication modes that can be provided to the `CacheMode` property *(continued)*

`cacheModeString` option	Cache mode	Summary
`INVALIDATION SYNC`	Synchronous invalidation	Used for cached entity data. Invalidation can happen much faster than replication, but at the expense of having to load data from a data source on a cache miss. With synchronous invalidation, all nodes must verify that they've been invalidated before the request can continue being processed.
`INVALIDATION ASYNC`	Asynchronous invalidation	Used for cached entity data. The invalidation happens faster when asynchronous, but cache misses still require a read from a data source.
`LOCAL`	No replication (cache is local to node)	No replication is fast, but there is no fault tolerance at all. Use sticky sessions to avoid hitting nodes that don't have the user's state. High availability can be achieved via failover.

CONFIGURING THE CACHE LOADER

The `CacheLoaderConfig` property (❺ in listing 12.5) defines a cache loader for the cache. In JBoss Cache, a cache loader is a component of the caching framework that knows how to read and write the data in a cache to and from a secondary datastore such as a database or a filesystem. In terms of clustering, cache loaders come in handy when you want to passivate session data for HTTP sessions and stateful EJBs. We talk about how to enable and configure the cache loader for HTTP sessions and stateful EJBs in chapter 13.

CONFIGURING THE EVICTION POLICY

The `EvictionPolicyConfig` property ❻ specifies the eviction policy for the cache. The policy is defined using the `policyClass` attribute under the `config` block. Here's an example that defines an LRU eviction policy:

```
<attribute name="policyClass">
   org.jboss.cache.eviction.LRUPolicy
</attribute>
```

The entity cache and SFSB cache in the all configuration both use an LRU eviction scheme by default. Table 12.7 lists the main eviction policies.

Table 12.7 The different eviction policies that can be specified in the `defaultEvictionPolicyClass` property

Eviction policy	What's evicted when thresholds are met
`org.jboss.cache.eviction.LRUPolicy`	Least recently used nodes (default)
`org.jboss.cache.eviction.LFUPolicy`	Least frequently used nodes
`org.jboss.cache.eviction.MRUPolicy`	Most recently used nodes
`org.jboss.cache.eviction.FIFOPolicy`	Creates a first-in-first-out queue and evicts the oldest nodes
`org.jboss.cache.eviction.NullEvictionPolicy`	Nothing

The cache can be broken up into regions based on cached components. Each region can specify its own configuration for the eviction policy, allowing you to evict some cached instances at a different frequency than others. Most JBoss clustering services make the regions correspond to different class or package names. By default, no regions are defined, and every cached component is bound into a region called `/_default_`.

Let's say you're configuring the entity cache and would like to make an entity called `com.manning.jbia.MyEntity` evict at a different rate than every other bean bound in the default region. You can define a region for your entity using the region element as shown in listing 12.6.

Listing 12.6 Defining different eviction policies for different regions of cache

```
<cache-config name="...">
  ...
  <attribute name="EvictionPolicyConfig">
    <config>
      <region name="/_default_"
          policyClass="org.jboss.cache.eviction.LRUPolicy">
        <attribute name="maxNodes">10000</attribute>
        <attribute name="timeToLiveSeconds">1000</attribute>      ❶
        <attribute name="minTimeToLiveSeconds">120</attribute>
      </region>
      <region name="/com/manning/jbia/MyEntity"
          policyClass="org.jboss.cache.eviction.LRUPolicy">
        <attribute name="maxNodes">100</attribute>
        <attribute name="timeToLiveSeconds">100</attribute>      ❷
        <attribute name="minTimeToLiveSeconds">50</attribute>
      </region>
    </config>
  </attribute>
</cache-config>
```

Here, two regions are defined: the default region ❶ and another for the entity ❷. The two regions define the same type of policy but have different attributes for the number of nodes and time-outs.

Knowing how to enable the cache is one thing; deciding what type of data to cache is another. Let's talk a little about that.

12.4.2 Deciding what to cache

Caches are particularly good for data that's used often by many users and seldom changes. For example, reference data, such as category lists or days of the month, would be good candidates for caching. Some bad examples would be data that changes all the time, such as financial data or data only used for an individual user.

Another particularly bad type of data to cache is anything accessed by other applications not participating in the distributed cache. Because these applications don't participate in the cache, the cache hit/miss ratio becomes much less predictable, and the cache becomes less reliable.

12.5 Summary

In this chapter, you've learned the fundamentals necessary to understand and work with clusters in JBoss. In the first section, we laid a foundation for clustering by walking you through some of the basic concepts. We started with load balancing and talked about how load balancing helps achieve high availability and fault tolerance. Next, we talked about horizontal and vertical clustering topologies and the pros and cons in terms of scalability and high availability. We also talked about the trade-offs of having a uniform cluster with all nodes having an identical set of applications deployed to them.

After that, we talked about the fundamental concepts of multicasting and automatic discovery. Then we talked about high availability and uptime, and we described how stateless applications can become highly available through load balancing, whereas stateful application can use failover to become highly available. Stateful applications may further provide fault tolerance by ensuring that the client state is available on any machine that they fail over to. We talked about the different state-replication strategies that could help enable fault tolerance. We also introduced you to the concept of buddy replication and discussed what the potential performance and high-availability trade-offs are between total and buddy replication.

We then discussed state passivation, where you learned about how to store client state for various application components in a secondary data store. Finally, we talked about application clustering versus application distribution, with a recommendation to favor clustering over distribution as a means to achieve scalability.

In the next section, we showed you how to set up a vertical cluster on a single machine. We built, deployed, and tested a clustered EJB application and showed how easy it is to take advantage of JBoss clustering.

Next, we took a closer look at how to configure a cluster. We started by looking at the JGroups architecture; then we looked at the main JBoss clustering services to see how the different components of the JGroups architecture are configured. In particular, we took a closer look at the JGroups protocol stack and how to configure it for the TCP and UDP protocols.

Many of the clustering services build on top of JBoss cache, so we devoted the last section of this chapter to JBoss Cache. We looked at the various places where JBoss cache is used and talked about how to configure buddy replication, isolation, cache loaders, and eviction policies. We then talked about how to decide what type of data is worth caching.

This chapter gave you an understanding of the basics of JBoss clusters, JBoss Cache, and JGroups, as well as the background you need to enable clustering features such as EJB load balancing and HTTP session replication. We'll dive into these topics in the next chapter, building on and referencing back to this chapter.

12.6 References

The JGroups documentation on the JGroups website—http://www.jgroups.org

A section dedicated to JGroups on the JBoss website—http://www.jboss.org/community/docs/DOC-10878

The JBoss Cache website with links to tutorials and documentation—http://labs.jboss.com/jbosscache/

How to install the Microsoft Loopback Adapter in Windows XP—http://www.windowsnetworking.com/articles_tutorials/Install-Microsoft-Loopback-adapter-Windows-XP.html

How to add Multiple IP Addresses in Windows 2000, XP, 2003—http://www.itsyourip.com/networking/how-to-add-multiple-ip-address-in-windows-2000xp2003/

Multicast Loopback—http://www.29west.com/docs/THPM/multicast-loopback.html

The Smartronix SuperLooper Loopback Jack & Plug—http://www.computercablestore.com/Smartronix_SuperLooper_Lo_PID3632.aspx

13 Clustering JBoss AS services

This chapter covers

- HTTP load balancing
- HTTP session replication
- Clustering session EJBs
- Clustering entities
- High-availability JNDI

In chapter 12, you learned about the basic concepts of clustering, experimented with a simple cluster, and learned how to configure the underlying tools that enable clustering in JBoss, such as JGroups and JBoss Cache. In this chapter, we build on top of what you learned in chapter 12 to show you how clustering applies to specific Java EE components and technologies. We explore how JBoss Cache can be used to provide state replication for web applications, SFSBs, and the Hibernate entity cache. You learn how load balancing can be enabled through an upstream hardware or software load balancer for web applications, and via dynamic proxies for EJBs. We also look at JBoss's high-availability JNDI service and see how JNDI lookups can be load balanced across a replicated JNDI cluster.

Table 13.1 The clustering requirements for various Java EE components

Object/Component	Requires load balancing?	Requires state replication?
Servlet/JSP	Yes	Yes
EJB SLSB	Yes	No
EJB SFSB	Yes[a]	Yes
EJB Entity	No[b]	Yes[c]
EJB MDB	Yes	No
JNDI object	Yes	Yes

a. You must have sticky-session load balancing.

b. EJB 2.x Entity Beans could be called remotely, but in EJB3, they can't.

c. If you're using Hibernate's 2nd level cache.

Table 13.1 lists the various Java EE application components and the clustering requirements they have.

We explore many of these clustering requirements, starting with HTTP load balancing.

13.1 HTTP load balancing

If you're hosting a web application that needs to be highly available or needs to scale to handle a large number of users, then you need to load balance requests across multiple nodes. Contrary to popular belief, load balancing a web application doesn't necessarily require a cluster. If your application is completely stateless, a cluster is unnecessary. If you have a stateful application, then you probably want to use sticky-session load balancing, but creating a JBoss cluster still isn't necessary unless you need to be fault tolerant. If your stateful application needs fault tolerance, then you need a cluster so that you can do state replication. We talk about state replication for HTTP sessions, stateful-session EJBs, and entity caches later in the chapter.

As we discussed in chapter 12, load balancing happens upstream from the systems that the load is being balanced across. To balance HTTP traffic, you must introduce a load balancer in front of your web servers. All clients direct their requests to the load balancer, which acts as a proxy to the servers running the web application.

Figure 12.2 showed you a typical network topology where a load balancer runs inside of the DMZ and forwards requests to JBoss instances that run behind the firewall. With this topology, the load balancer provides scalability while the application servers are protected by being behind the firewall. The load balancer can be a hardware load balancer or a software load balancer. Software load balancers are typically in the form of native web servers that provide a mechanism for load balancing across JBoss instances. Let's look at how to configure both hardware and software load balancers for web applications.

13.1.1 Load balancing with native web servers

As we discussed in chapter 5, Tomcat provides HTTP and AJP connectors. The AJP protocol is a TCP-based binary protocol made specifically for communicating with application servers such as JBoss Web Server. Although the AJP protocol is binary and was created to provide performance benefits over the HTTP protocol, you may not get a performance benefit in your application depending on the type of load that you have. You should test both connectors and see which one works better for you.

Most native web servers have support for the AJP protocol. Apache Web Server, IIS, and SunOne support the AJP protocol through different plug-ins or modules. A link with a list of these modules and installation instructions can be found at the end of this chapter.

Apache ships with a plug-in called mod_proxy that supports both HTTP and AJP load balancing. Many people find mod_proxy to be significantly easier to configure even though mod_jk has a longer history and is considered more stable. There are other plug-ins available as well. Each plug-in has different versions that work with different versions of the native web server that you're using. Different combinations of native web servers and plug-ins have their own unique configuration and performance pros and cons. Unfortunately, it's outside the scope of this book to explain how to install and configure the various plug-ins in the different native web servers. With a little bit of searching online, you should be able to find an article or two that cover the details of the particular web server and plug-in combination that you're trying to install. We have a few links at the end of the chapter that show you how to install some of the more popular combinations. We had good luck with Apache 2.2.9 and mod_jk 1.2.26 while testing things out for the book.

After you get the native web server installed and the appropriate plug-in configured, you're almost ready to load balance requests to JBoss. If you want your native web server to be able to use sticky-session load balancing across your JBoss instances, you must make a change in the JBoss Web Server configuration on each of the application servers you're load balancing to. In the server/xxx/deploy/jbossweb.sar/server.xml file, define a `jvmRoute` attribute on the `Engine` element, where the value of the attribute is unique among the JBoss AS server instances you're running. The `jvmRoute` setting isn't present in the server.xml file, so you'll have to add it to the `Engine` definition. After configuring the server.xml file, it should look like this:

```
<Service name="jboss.web">
   <Connector .../>
   <Connector .../>
   <Engine name="jboss.web"
         defaultHost="localhost"
         jvmRoute="node1">
```

The value of the `jvmRoute` attribute matches a logical name defined in the load-balancer configuration for the native web server plug-in. For example, if you're using mod_jk, the value of the `jvmRoute` attribute should be set to the name of the worker.

If you're trying this out with multiple JBoss instances and want to see which server is being hit on a given request, you might try uncommenting the `RequestDumperValve` in the server.xml file. Then you can watch the console output (or tail the server log) to see which JBoss AS instance is handling the request. If you don't have a `jvmRoute` specified on each JBoss AS instance, you'll see requests switch servers each time you load a page. If you define `jvmRoute` attributes and your native web server plug-in supports sticky sessions, then you should see the requests from one browser session going to the same server. But if you open a different browser or access the native web server from another machine, then you'll see the requests forward to a different JBoss AS instance.

We just showed you how to configure a native web server to perform load balancing, but you may use a hardware load balancer instead.

13.1.2 Load balancing with hardware

Load balancing can also be done with hardware. One of the more popular hardware load balancers is the F5 BIG-IP, but other brands may work just as well.

The main things to look for in a hardware load balancer are support for passive or active cookie persistence and SSL persistence. Cookie persistence is the ability for a load balancer to store a cookie on the client's web browser on the first request. The cookie helps route consecutive client calls to the same server accessed on the first request. In passive cookie persistence, the application server creates its own cookie that's passed to the client, and the load balancer uses part of the cookie to interpret the routing information. In active cookie persistence, the load balancer stores its own cookie on the client's web browser. SSL persistence is used when SSL is enabled. The load balancer handles all encryption and decryption with the client and stores a cookie on the client's browser to know which node to forward to.

Load balancing can make web applications highly available; but, if you have application state you're keeping in an HTTP session and you want to be fault tolerant, you need to enable HTTP session replication.

13.2 HTTP session replication

Web applications often keep state in HTTP session attributes. Depending on the nature of your application, you may keep all your application state here or, perhaps, only login credentials and presentation state. Nonetheless, if you want a totally fault-tolerant application, you need to make sure your web session state is replicated.

13.2.1 Configuring replication

The *all* configuration is capable of replicating HTTP session state, but you must tell your application to take advantage of this feature. To enable your web application to use session replication, you must add the `distributable` element to your application's WEB-INF/web.xml file as follows:

```
<web-app>
  <distributable/>
  ...
</web-app>
```

If you don't add this element to your application's WEB-INF/web.xml file, your application's HTTP sessions don't participate in the distributed cache, even though the distributed cache is enabled and other applications within your server may be using it.

HTTP session replication is built on top of JBoss Cache, which we discussed in chapter 12. The HTTP session cache is configured in the `standard-session-cache` cache configuration in the server/all/deploy/cluster/jboss-cache-manager.sar/META-INF/jboss-cache-configs.xml file.

This file has several configurable attributes for session replication, all of which are fairly well documented in the file comments. The preconfigured settings in the all configuration should be good enough to get you started. By default, the `CacheMode` is set to synchronize asynchronously. If you change this to be synchronous, you may want to check the `SyncReplTimeout`, which determines how long the cache will wait to timeout until other nodes confirm that they've synchronized. The default value in JBoss AS CR1 is 17500, which might be pretty high. The cache is also configured to use single-node buddy replication, which should be fine for most uses, but can be increased if necessary.

13.2.2 Understanding session usage

HTTP sessions are accessed through the Servlet API. The session provides the ability to get and set attributes (objects) stored in a map in the session with a string as the key. In the JBoss all configuration the session is backed by JBoss Cache; when one node puts an attribute into the session, it's replicated to the other nodes. Let's say you have a servlet that is reading an attribute out of the session:

```
HttpSession session = request.getSession();
Employee emp = (Employee) session.getAttribute("employee");
String firstName = emp.getFirstName();
```

Would you expect the session to replicate the attribute to other nodes in your cluster? No, because all you're doing is getting the `employee` attribute out of the session and reading values out of it. But, what if you did this:

```
HttpSession session = request.getSession();
Employee emp = (Employee) session.getAttribute("employee");
emp.setFirstName("Javid");
```

Would you expect the `employee` attribute to be replicated? Yes, you'd probably want the change to the first name replicated across the cache. In these two examples, the servlet code is interacting with the session API in the same exact way; it's just reading the attribute using the `getAttribute()` method. But the servlet code may change the object that you get out of the session, so you need a mechanism for triggering replication based on updates only.

Replication triggering can be configured in the `replication-config` element of your application's WEB-INF/jboss-web.xml file:

```
<jboss-web>
  <replication-config>
    <replication-trigger>
```

```
        SET_AND_NON_PRIMITIVE_GET
      </replication-trigger>
    </replication-config>
  </jboss-web>
```

The `replication-trigger` attribute is used to specify the type of session access that triggers a replication. The four possible values are listed in table 13.2.

Table 13.2 A summary of the various `replication-trigger` options available for HTTP session replication

Replication-trigger option	Description
`SET`	Replication occurs only if an attribute is put into the session using a set call. If you get an attribute out of the session and modify its value, the value isn't replicated.
`SET_AND_GET`	All set and get calls on any attributes trigger state replication. This option can be significantly slower than the `SET` option.
`SET_AND_NON_PRIMITIVE_GET`	Behaves the same as `SET_AND_GET` except it only replicates on a get if the attribute received isn't a wrapper for a primitive data type (for example, Integer, Long, and so on). This option is the default.
`ACCESS`	Triggers a replication on every request that accesses the session. This option is generally slow, but it ensures the session timestamp is synchronized between all nodes in a cluster, preventing the session from being evicted in one cache while remaining in others.

If you use the `SET` option, you have to make sure any objects you've retrieved from the session and updated are set back into the session.

```
HttpSession session = request.getSession();
Employee emp = (Employee) session.getAttribute("employee");
emp.setFirstName("Javid");
session.setAttribute("employee", emp);
```

The `SET_AND_NON_PRIMITIVE_GET` option is the default. There's no need to replicate when the object retrieved is a primitive wrapper type because those objects are immutable. Because they're immutable, you never run into the issue of updating a shared reference to the object. The only way to change them in the session is to do a set call:

```
HttpSession session = request.getSession();
Integer count = (Integer) session.getAttribute("count");
count = count + 1; //count is immutable; creates new object
session.setAttribute("count", count);
```

Besides determining what triggers a replication, you also have to determine what gets replicated. You could have the entire session object get replicated when the replication gets triggered, or you could replicate the modified attribute. Better yet, you could replicate a single field of the modified attribute.

The `replication-granularity` attribute in the WEB-INF/jboss-web.xml file specifies the granularity of the data that gets replicated upon a trigger:

```
<jboss-web>
  <replication-config>
    <replication-granularity>SESSION</replication-granularity>
  </replication-config>
</jboss-web>
```

The options for this attribute are shown in table 13.3.

Table 13.3 A summary of the different `replication-granularity` options available for HTTP session replication

Replication-granularity option	Description
SESSION	The entire session is replicated upon a replication trigger. This option is the default and is preferred when the sessions are generally small in size.
ATTRIBUTE	Only dirty session attributes are updated in addition to some session data (such as the `lastAccessTime`).
FIELD	Only dirty fields on an object are updated.

More information on these and other options related to replication can be found in the DTD file corresponding to the jboss-web.xml deployment descriptor. The DTD file can be found in docs/dtd/jboss-web_5_0.dtd under the top level of the JBoss installation. Field-level replication can provide significant performance advantages for many applications. Let's take a closer look.

13.2.3 Using field-level replication

Field-level replication takes advantage of JBoss Cache's fine-grained replication feature, which replicates only the changed parts of an object. If you update a field on an object, only that field is replicated. Field-level replication can tremendously cut down the amount of data replication, increasing your application's throughput. We reference an article at the end of the chapter that talks about benchmark results for different object sizes and load scenarios.

JBoss ships with a cache configuration that supports field-level replication. To enable JBoss Web Server to use this cache configuration, you have to modify the `WebAppClusteringDefaultsDeployer` bean in the server/all/deployers/jbossweb.deployer/META-INF/war-deployers-beans.xml file. In that bean, you must change the `cacheName` property from `standard-session-cache` to `field-granularity-session-cache`.

You also need to set the `replication-granularity` field in your application's WEB-INF/jboss-web.xml file as follows:

```
<jboss-web>
  <replication-config>
    <replication-granularity>FIELD</replication-granularity>
```

```
      <replication-field-batch-mode>
        true
      </replication-field-batch-mode>
    </replication-config>
  </jboss-web>
```

An additional attribute, called replication-field-batch-mode, is pertinent to field-level replication and can be set in this file (as shown in the example). This Boolean attribute specifies whether field-level replication should happen immediately or not. When set to false, replication happens immediately. When set to true—the default—the session batches all the field-level updates and replicates them all at the end of the request. We advise you to leave this attribute set to true to minimize unnecessary network traffic.

Last, you need to make sure any classes you wish to put into the session are annotated with the @org.jboss.cache.pojo.annotation.Replicable annotation, like the following:

```
@Replicable
public class Employee {
  ...
}
```

Now, let's take a look at how to enable passivation for HTTP sessions.

13.2.4 Configuring passivation

In chapter 12, we introduced you to the topic of session passivation. HTTP session passivation is enabled by default in both the standard-session-cache cache configuration and the field-granularity-session-cache cache configuration. Looking in the jboss-cache-configs.xml file, you see that both cache configurations define a CacheLoaderConfig that has passivation enabled:

```
<attribute name="CacheLoaderConfig">
  <config>
    <passivation>true</passivation>          ❶
    <shared>false</shared>       ❷
    <cacheloader>
      <class>org.jboss.cache.loader.FileCacheLoader</class>       ❸
      <properties>
        location=${jboss.server.data.dir}${/}session      ❹
      </properties>
      <async>false</async>       ❺
      ...
    </cacheloader>
  </config>
</attribute>
```

The passivation property ❶ controls how the cache interacts with the cache loader. If this property is set to true, the cache uses the cache loader to write to the secondary datastore only when a node is evicted from memory. If this property is set to false, then all changes are written as soon as they happen. Having the shared property ❷ set to false tells the cache that the cache loader isn't shared by multiple caches, but is unique to this cache. The class ❸ tells you which type of cache loader you'll use. By default the HTTP session cache loader writes to a file. The location property ❹ defines where the passivated sessions will be stored by the cache loader. By default, the cache loader is configured to read and write from a file in the configuration's data directory. The async attribute ❺ defines whether the passivation is synchronous or asynchronous.

After configuring the server to support a cache loader, you must tell your web application to enable passivation in the META-INF/jboss-web.xml file. If you don't enable passivation in a particular application, its sessions aren't passivated. To enable passivation, you must provide the following configuration:

```
<max-active-sessions>20</max-active-sessions>
<passivation-config>
  <use-session-passivation>TRUE</use-session-passivation>
  <passivation-min-idle-time>5</passivation-min-idle-time>
  <passivation-max-idle-time>10</passivation-max-idle-time>
</passivation-config>
```

The max-active-sessions property tells the web container's session manager how many sessions it should keep active in memory. The passivation-config block is necessary to enable passivation. In particular, the use-session-passivation field must be set to TRUE in order to use passivation. The min- and max-idle-time options are used to define the minimum and maximum number of seconds a session is allowed to sit idle before it's eligible for passivation.

Now that we've discussed the many aspects of HTTP session clustering, let's talk about clustering session beans.

13.3 Clustering session beans

There are two main reasons to cluster session beans. The first reason is to load balance session-bean requests across multiple EJB servers. In the discussion of HTTP, you saw that you don't need a cluster to achieve load balancing. But with session beans, the dynamic proxy acts as a load balancer, and having a cluster gives you the benefit of having the proxy automatically get updated with the list of nodes it should load balance across. Having the client receive an updated list of server nodes is useful when you're calling session beans remotely. As we talked about in chapter 12, we generally recommend not distributing the web tier and EJB tier of an application, so for many web applications, load balancing EJBs may not be necessary because load balancing occurs at the HTTP request level. But if you have a standalone client that must load-balance across EJB servers, JBoss clustering makes it easy.

Both stateful and stateless session beans make use of load balancing. SFSBs need sticky-session load balancing to achieve server affinity. SLSBs can make use of random or round-robin load balancing.

The second reason to cluster session beans is to enable state replication for SFSBs, allowing you to achieve fault tolerance for a stateful application. Let's look at how to configure both load balancing and replication for session beans, starting with load balancing.

13.3.1 Load balancing session beans

To enable a session bean to be clustered, you must run in the all configuration, and you must annotate the bean with the `@org.jboss.ejb3.annotation.Clustered` annotation. Here's an example of a clustered SLSB:

```
@Stateless
@Clustered
public class SomeBean implements SomeBusinessInterface {
  public void someWonderfulMethod() {
    // Do something cool
  }
}
```

Believe it or not, that's all you have to do so long as you want to use the default partition—specified by the `-g` command-line option as we discussed in chapter 12—and you want to use round-robin load balancing. If you want to change either of these, you can do so by passing in arguments to the annotation. Here's an example of how to use the annotation to define both the `loadBalancePolicy` and the partition:

```
@Clustered(loadBalancePolicy="RoundRobin", partition="MyPartition")
```

The `loadBalancePolicy` attribute must be a string that refers to the name of a class (without the package name) that implements the `org.jboss.ha.framework.interfaces.LoadBalancePolicy` interface. This class can be a standard JBoss load-balancing policy that exists in the `org.jboss.ha.framework.interfaces` package, or you can write your own class that implements the `LoadBalancePolicy` interface, and put the class in the same package as your bean. JBoss provides the policies in table 13.4 out of the box.

Table 13.4 The out-of-the-box load-balancing policies, which are all in the `org.jboss.ha.framework.interfaces` package

Load-balancing policy	Description
`FirstAvailable`	Each client's dynamic proxy for an EJB randomly selects a target node and sticks with that node for all calls on the proxy. If the node dies, another node is randomly selected. This load-balancing policy is also known as sticky-session load balancing.
`FirstAvailableIdenticalAllProxies`	All clients' dynamic proxies for an EJB stick with the same randomly selected node. If the node dies, another node is randomly select.
`RandomRobin`	Every request to an EJB is directed to a random node in the server.
`RoundRobin`	The dynamic proxy cycles across the list of nodes in the cluster sequentially.

When the client downloads the dynamic proxy for a clustered EJB from JNDI, the proxy already knows about all the nodes in the cluster. Every time the client makes a request to the server using the dynamic proxy, the proxy is given an updated list of nodes in the cluster. Receiving an updated list prevents the client from sending requests to nodes that are no longer available in the cluster (whether they've failed or they've purposely been removed). And because JBoss uses self-forming clusters, this happens automatically without needing to reconfigure the cluster.

13.3.2 Replicating stateful session beans

Enabling clustering on a SFSB is almost exactly the same as with a SLSB. Annotate the bean with the `@org.jboss.annotation.ejb.Clustered` annotation.

```
@Stateful
@Clustered
public class SomeBean implements SomeBusinessInterface {
  public void someMethod() {
    // Do something
  }
}
```

Just like with SLSBs, you can define the partition attribute on the `@Clustered` annotation. The only difference between specifying the `@Clustered` annotation on a stateful and a stateless session bean is that you can't use a load-balancing policy other than `FirstAvailable` with stateful beans. This value is the default, so you don't need to specify the load-balancing policy at all.

The cache used to store and replicate the state of the SFSB can be configured in the server/all/deploy/cluster/jboss-cache-manager.sar/META-INF/jboss-cache-configs.xml file, under the `sfsb-cache` cache configuration.

You can apply the `@org.jboss.ejb3.annotation.CacheConfig` annotation to your SFSB class declaration to configure entity-specific cache configuration:

```
public @interface CacheConfig
{
  String name() default "";
  int maxSize() default 10000;
  long idleTimeoutSeconds() default 300;
  boolean replicationIsPassivation() default true;
  long removalTimeoutSeconds() default 0;
}
```

The `maxSize` and `idleTimeoutSeconds` attributes control passivation. The `removalTimeoutSeconds` defines the timeout at which idle beans are removed altogether. The `replicationIsPassivation` attribute tells the container whether to invoke EJB3 `@PrePassivate` callbacks before replicating (that is, serializing) a session and `@PostActivate` after pulling it from the cache and giving it to the application. Passivation can be configured using the `cacheLoaderConfig`, which is similar to what we've already discussed for HTTP session passivation in section 13.2.4.

Now that you've learned about clustering session EJBs, let's learn about clustering entity EJBs.

13.4 Clustering entities

In previous versions of EJB, entity beans were remotely accessible (even though it wasn't generally recommended). In JPA, entities aren't accessible remotely, so you wouldn't cluster entities for the purpose of load balancing; but we do care about state replication and high availability.

The EJB3 specification says nothing about entity caching, but JBoss uses Hibernate as its JPA implementation, which has a pluggable second-level cache. By pluggable, we mean you can plug in different cache implementations that Hibernate can use. Take a wild guess which cache implementation Red Hat decided to preconfigure Hibernate/JPA with? You guessed it—JBoss Cache. Why? JBoss Cache is distributed, transactional, and is already built into JBoss.

JBoss Cache has support for caching four types of data: entities, collections, query results, and timestamps. This data is either replicated or invalidated across the cluster, dramatically reducing the number of database queries your application has to make. We have a few links at the end of the chapter that give you good background and in-depth coverage to the way Hibernate uses the second-level cache and on how to configure Hibernate with JBoss Cache.

13.4.1 Replicating the entity cache

We introduced JBoss Cache in chapter 12 and gave you an overview of how to configure it. Entities can use several cache configurations. You must configure your JPA persistence context and your beans to use the entity cache because you might not want all your entity types to participate in the cache, as we discussed in chapter 12. Queries generated by Hibernate can be cached too. Let's look at how to enable the persistence context and how to enable individual entities to use JBoss Cache.

HOOKING THE CACHE INTO JPA

Before you configure entities to use the cache, you must configure JPA to know about the cache. You can do this by specifying the following properties under the `persistence-unit` element in your application's `META-INF/persistence.xml` file:

```
<persistence-unit name="tempdb" transaction-type="JTA">
 <jta-data-source>java:/DefaultDS</jta-data-source>
 <properties>
   <property
     name="hibernate.cache.region.factory_class"
     value=
 "org.hibernate.cache.jbc2.JndiMultiplexedJBossCacheRegionFactory"/>   ❶
   <property
     name="hibernate.cache.region.jbc2.cachefactory"
     value="java:CacheManager"/>                                        ❷
   <property
     name="hibernate.cache.region.jbc2.cfg.entity"
     value="optimistic-entity"/>                                        ❸
   <property
     name="hibernate.cache.region.jbc2.cfg.collection"
     value="optimistic-entity"/>                                        ❹
```

```
    <property
      name="hibernate.cache.region.jbc2.cfg.ts"          ❺
      value="timestamps-cache"/>
    <property
      name="hibernate.cache.region.jbc2.cfg.query"       ❻
      value="local-query"/>
  </properties>
</persistence-unit>
```

The `hibernate.cache.region.factory_class` property ❶ points to the class that ties Hibernate into JBoss Cache. The `hibernate.cache.region.jbc2.cachefactory` property ❷ points to the particular JBoss Cache instance using a JNDI name. The default JNDI binding for this cache is `java:CacheManager`, as shown in the example. The JBoss Cache instance defined by ❶ has different regions for the different types of data that can be stored in the cache. Each of these data types is configured by pointing to a cache configuration. The properties for these data types are specified using ❸, ❹, ❺, and ❻.

The entity cache is used to store entity objects by id. The collection cache is used to store entity collection references. If you have an entity with a set or a list that references another entity, those references would be stored in the collection cache. The query cache is used to cache which queries and query parameters result in which entities. If the query result is available in the query cache, then it will be retrieved from the entity cache, or the database if not cached. The timestamp cache is used in conjunction with the query cache to keep track of the timestamps for the queries and the entities to make sure that query results aren't stale. Let's see what different cache configurations are available.

CHOOSING A CACHE CONFIGURATION

As with all the other cache configurations, these configurations can be found in the server/all/deploy/cluster/jboss-cache-manager.sar/META-INF/jboss-cache-configs.xml file. Table 13.5 summarizes the cache configurations that are available with JBoss AS 5 CR1.

Table 13.5 Entity cache configurations[a]

Cache configuration name	Supported data types	Best for	Cache mode	Node locking	Initial state transfer
`optimistic-entity`	Entities, collections	Entities, collections	Synchronous invalidation	Optimistic	No
`pessimistic-entity`	Entities, collections	Entities, collections	Synchronous invalidation	Pessimistic	No
`local-query`	Queries	Queries	Local	Optimistic	N/A
`replicated-query`	Queries		Asynchronous replication	Optimistic	No

a. This table is an adaptation of a table found in the Hibernate Reference found at the end of this chapter.

Table 13.5 Entity cache configurations[a] *(continued)*

`timestamps-cache`	Timestamps	Timestamps	Asynchronous replication	Pessimistic	Yes
`optimistic-shared`	Entities, collections, queries, timestamps		Synchronous replication	Optimistic	Yes
`pessimistic-shared`	Entities, collections, queries, timestamps		Synchronous replication	Pessimistic	Yes

a. This table is an adaptation of a table found in the Hibernate Reference found at the end of this chapter.

Hibernate offers a feature that enables optimistic concurrency control by adding a `version` attribute to an entity (both in the database and in the Java object). If you use this feature, the best choice for entity and collection caching is the `optimistic-entity` cache configuration. If you don't, then you should go with the `pessimistic-entity` cache configuration.

Because the database always has a valid copy of an entity, invalidation can be used with entity caches. Queries, on the other hand, have no representation in the database, so they must be replicated across a cluster to be shared—a costly endeavor. If you want to enable query caching, you'd probably get better performance using the `local-query` cache configuration over the `replicated-query` cache configuration.

The `timestamps-cache` configuration is the best choice for timestamp caching. A clustered timestamp cache is required if you want to use query caching, even if you use the nonclustered `local-query` cache configuration for query caching.

The optimistic-shared and pessimistic-shared cache configurations can be used for all the cacheable data types that Hibernate uses. The downside is that because they handle queries and timestamps, they must use replication, which will be much slower than configuring different cache configurations for the different regions.

CONFIGURING ENTITIES TO USE THE CACHE

After providing this configuration, you can tell an entity to participate in the cache by annotating the entity class. To annotate a class, you must use the `@org.hibernate.annotations.Cache` annotation. The following code shows a class called `Category` that is annotated with the `@Cache` annotation:

```
@Entity
@Table(name="CATEGORIES")
@Cache(usage=CacheConcurrencyStrategy.READ_ONLY)
public class Category implements Serializable {
  private Long jpaId;
  private String categoryName;
  // ...
}
```

Notice that the annotation takes an argument called usage of type `@org.hibernate.annotations.CacheConcurrencyStrategy`, which tells Hibernate how to treat entities of this type in the cache. The options supported by JBoss Cache are shown in table 13.6.

Table 13.6 The available `CacheConcurrencyStrategy` options you can assign to an entity

CacheConcurrencyStrategy value	Description
`READ_ONLY`	Use this option if your data never changes. Once the entity is in the cache, it isn't retrieved again unless the cache is manually evicted.
`READ_WRITE`	Use this option to cache data that's occasionally updated, but where isolation is necessary to avoid stale data. This strategy ensures read-committed isolation by maintaining a timestamp for the entity.
`NONSTRICT_READ_WRITE`	Use this option to cache data that's occasionally updated, but where some stale data can be tolerated. This mode gives no guarantee of isolation, but is faster than `READ_WRITE`.
`TRANSACTIONAL`	Guarantees full transactional isolation up to repeatable read. Use this option for data that's mostly read but where it's critical to prevent stale data if an update does occur.

Note that only the `READ_ONLY` and `TRANSACTIONAL` options are available with JBoss Cache. If you want to use `READ_WRITE` or `NONSTRICT_READ_WRITE`, you have to use a different cache implementation. The different cache implementations Hibernate supports can be found in the Hibernate documentation, which is referenced at the end of this chapter.

13.5 Clustering JNDI

In Java EE, accessing a server-side component almost always requires a JNDI lookup. JBoss provides a cluster-aware, high-availability JNDI service (called HA-JNDI) that runs on top of the existing JNDI infrastructure. In this section, we examine the architecture and see how the HA-JNDI service works and how to access it.

13.5.1 Understanding the HA-JNDI service

The HA-JNDI service is a cluster-aware naming service that runs on each node of a cluster. The service provides client applications with four main features:

- Load balancing and failover of naming requests
- The ability to search the server's local JNDI server
- Automatic discovery of naming servers
- A replicated cache

Figure 13.1 shows you a cluster running with HA-JNDI enabled.

Notice that each node has its own local JNDI service running. This local JNDI service is the standard JNDI service that runs in the default configuration. Each node also

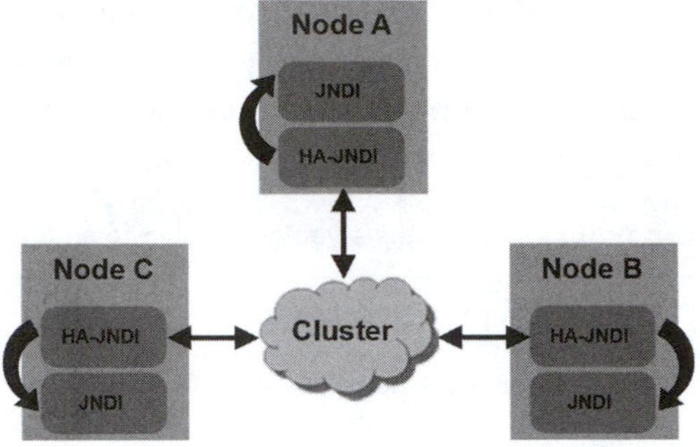

Figure 13.1 For each node in a cluster, the HA-JNDI services communicate, replicating object bindings and allowing for lookups from any node.

has a HA-JNDI service running that uses JGroups to be aware of the other HA-JNDI services running on the other nodes in the cluster.

The HA-JNDI service provides failover for client-bound objects. This feature is provided by a replicated cache implemented with JBoss Cache. This cache contains only objects bound by the client. Any objects the client binds to the HA-JNDI service are replicated across the cluster. Objects bound into a server's local JNDI service don't participate in the HA-JNDI service and don't get replicated or fail over. An EJB application deployed to a node is bound into the node's local JNDI server, excluding it from being replicated and excluding the naming lookups for the bean from failing over. But just because the JNDI binding doesn't fail over doesn't mean the EJB itself isn't able to fail over. EJB failover is a property of the dynamic proxy for the EJB and is handled by a different service.

The HA-JNDI service running on each node is aware of the node's local JNDI service, so HA-JNDI provides a way for a client to transparently look up an object from any of the local JNDI services. Figure 13.2 illustrates how this happens.

Here, node A and node B comprise a heterogeneous cluster. Node B has bound an EJB into its local JNDI server, but node A doesn't have the same EJB deployed. If a client calls node A's HA-JNDI service to do an EJB lookup, node A's HA-JNDI doesn't have the EJB and so calls node A's local JNDI service. Node A's local JNDI service doesn't have the EJB either. Subsequently, the HA-JNDI service sequentially calls each other node's HA-JNDI service, which in turn calls each node's local JNDI service until the EJB is found. The searching stops as soon as a successful lookup has occurred, so the client can call any node in the cluster to do a lookup on a locally bound object, even though the node that the call was made to may not have the object.

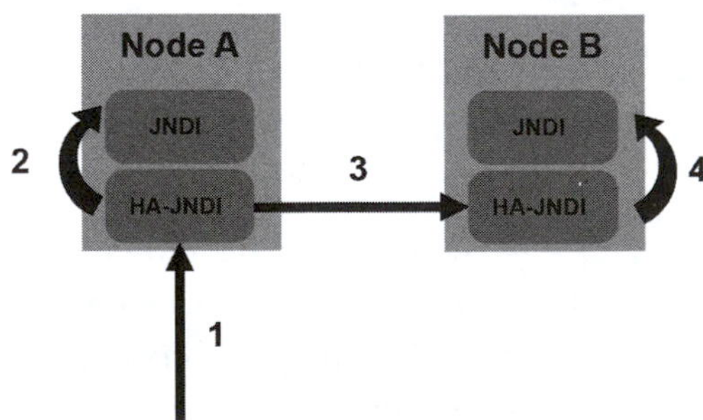

Figure 13.2 A lookup on one node's HA-JNDI and local JNDI with a lookup miss, then a call to another node's HA-JNDI, resulting in a call to the other node's local JNDI for a lookup hit

If the cluster is homogenous, then the lookup always returns from the first-called node. But if the cluster is heterogeneous, there's a performance trade-off to the transparent lookup because multiple nodes may have to be queried before the object can be found. And, in the worst case, if the object doesn't exist, all the nodes in the partition have to be called before an exception is thrown. This process can be time consuming, so you should cache the results of a JNDI query on the client side as much as possible.

Now that you have a general understanding of the HA-JNDI service architecture, let's see how you can enable the service.

13.5.2 Enabling HA-JNDI

The all server configuration comes with HA-JNDI enabled. The microcontainer bean that defines this service is the `HAJNDI` bean defined in the server/all/deploy/cluster/hajndi-jboss-beans.xml file. The `HAJNDI` bean depends on the cluster defined in the `HAPartition` bean, which is defined in the server/all/deploy/cluster/cluster-jboss-beans.xml file. We talked about the `HAPartition` bean in chapter 12.

Table 13.7 lists several properties you may want to configure on the `HAJNDI` bean in order to configure the service.

Table 13.7 A summary of the attributes that can be configured for the HA-JNDI service

Attribute	Description
`bindAddress`	The network address this service binds to in order to wait for clients to connect. The variable shown to the left populates the value of `-b` passed in on the command line. This is for a multihomed machine. Leaving it blank (the default) causes it to listen on all network interfaces. See chapter 15.
`port`	This is the port clients use to look up a naming-service dynamic proxy.
`rmiPort`	After the client looks up a dynamic proxy using the port, the dynamic proxy uses this RMI port to communicate with the JNDI server to do naming lookups.
`backlog`	Defines how many unhandled client requests are allowed to queue up on the socket before they start getting Connection Refused errors. See javadoc for java.net.ServerSocket constructor.
`discoveryDisabled`	Used to disable automatic discovery.
`autoDiscoveryBindAddress`	The network address to bind to for client auto discovery.
`autoDiscoveryAddress`	The multicast address to listen to for automatic discovery.
`autoDiscoveryGroup`	The multicast port to listen to for automatic discovery.
`autoDiscoveryTTL`	The TTL in seconds for an automatic discovery request from the client. This is similar in concept to TTL in JGroups, which we discussed in chapter 12.
`loadBalancePolicy`	The load-balancing policy to use inside the dynamic proxy downloaded by the client.

After starting the all configuration, or configuring your own configuration to start the HA-JNDI service, you need to know how to access it from a client application. Let's take a look.

13.5.3 Accessing HA-JNDI

To access the JNDI server in a single-server environment, you can provide the IP and port for the JNDI service. Here's what your jndi.properties file might look like:

```
java.naming.factory.initial=org.jnp.interfaces.NamingContextFactory
java.naming.provider.url=192.168.1.140:1099
```

And the corresponding code would simply be

```
Context ctx = new InitialContext();
```

In a clustered environment, there's no single server that you access, so you need a way for the client application to point to or discover nodes in the cluster. Both mechanisms are available in JBoss HA-JNDI.

MANUALLY SPECIFYING NODE IPS

First, you can manually specify multiple nodes within your cluster using the `java.naming.provider.url` parameter. In this case, your jndi.properties file would look like this:

```
java.naming.factory.initial=org.jnp.interfaces.NamingContextFactory
java.naming.provier.url=192.168.1.140:1100,192.168.1.141:1100,
➥   192.168.1.148:1100
```

Notice there are multiple IPs/port pairs specified, and they are comma delimited. Also notice the ports are all set to 1100, the default HA-JNDI port, rather than 1099, the default JNDI port. JBoss goes sequentially through this list to try and connect to the HA-JNDI service.

AUTO DISCOVERING NODES

The other way to connect to the cluster is to use auto discovery, a feature that utilizes JGroups' multicasting functionality to have the client automatically discover the nodes he can connect to. You enable this by specifying the initial factory property without the provider URL property:

```
java.naming.factory.initial=org.jnp.interfaces.NamingContextFactory
```

If you'd like to change the default multicast settings, you can specify a list of additional properties. The following jndi.properties file shows the properties you can set, along with their default values:

```
java.naming.factory.initial=org.jnp.interfaces.NamingContextFactory
jnp.discoveryGroup=230.0.0.4
jnp.discoveryPort=1102
jnp.disableDiscovery=false
jnp.discoveryTimeout=5000
```

Auto discovery is easier, but can perform slower.

ACCESSING HA-JNDI FROM THE SERVER

We've explored accessing HA-JNDI from a client, but what if you want to access it from the server? Creating an initial context on the server (without specifying any properties) defaults to the local JNDI server. The server doesn't have the concept of a jndi.properties file; if you want to access the HA-JNDI service from within your server code, you have to pass in the JNDI properties programmatically. Take the following code for example:

```
Hashtable<String, String> properties = new Hashtable<String, String>();
properties.put(Context.INITIAL_CONTEXT_FACTORY,
➥          "org.jnp.interfaces.NamingContextFactory");
properties.put(Context.URL_PKG_PREFIXES, "org.jboss.naming");
properties.put("jnp.partitionName", "DefaultPartition");
InitialContext ctx = new InitialContext(properties);
ctx.bind("MyJndiName","MyJndiValue");
```

Here, you populate a hash table with key-value pairs representing the properties you have to pass in to the initial context when you create it. You use static constants on the `Context` class for the keys. There's no provider URL, so automatic discovery is used. The `jnp.partitionName` property points to the partition you want to access, making sure you don't connect to the wrongly discovered cluster.

13.5.4 Deciding whether to use HA-JNDI

HA-JNDI is ideally used in a homogenous cluster where all the nodes are running within the same subnet, mainly because of performance. If the cluster is heterogeneous, then transparent lookups may have to hop between nodes. When the cluster is homogenous, transparent lookups are unnecessary because each node's local JNDI server is able to serve the objects. The only time the transparent lookups occur is when an object is nonexistent, in which case every node in the cluster is searched. This process is bad when the cluster is homogenous because you only need to search one node to see if the object exists, but the service searches every node in the cluster. Unfortunately, JBoss doesn't provide a way to disable the transparent lookups, which is what you'd want for homogenous clusters.

If the cluster nodes aren't on the same subnet then the inter-node latency is usually high. Replication occurring as a result of client-bound objects is slow, and transparent lookups are slow. The worst case is if the cluster has high inter-node latency and is heterogeneous. Table 13.8 shows you the four scenarios and describes the performance trade-offs with each.

Table 13.8 A comparison of how performance is impacted by cluster makeup and inter-node latency

	Homogenous cluster makeup	Heterogeneous cluster makeup
Low inter-node latency (same subnet)	Best case scenario! Transparent lookups are fast but unnecessary. Replication is fast.	Transparent lookups are fast and necessary. Replication is fast.

Table 13.8 A comparison of how performance is impacted by cluster makeup and inter-node latency *(continued)*

	Homogenous cluster makeup	Heterogeneous cluster makeup
High inter-node latency (nodes far apart)	Transparent lookups are slow and unnecessary (but unfortunately you can't disable them). Replication is slow.	Worst case scenario! Transparent lookups are slow and necessary. Replication is slow.

If you have a heterogeneous cluster and you have high inter-node latency, you may consider running JNDI on a single server in your cluster, but this causes you to lose out on high availability, the main benefit to running the HA-JNDI service. If you run JNDI on a single server, the only benefit you have to running HA-JNDI is the automatic discovery feature.

Another scenario where you might consider running the default JNDI service on a single node of your cluster is when you have to access an external naming or directory service. By external, we mean the naming or directory service runs outside the server's JVM process, such as an LDAP server or a DNS server. Unfortunately, one limitation of the HA-JNDI service is that you can't use an external JNDI implementation. If you have to have an external JNDI implementation such as LDAP, then you can't use HA-JNDI.

13.6 Summary

In this chapter, you learned about how to apply clustering to different application components and services including HTTP sessions, session EJBs, entity EJBs, and JNDI. We started with a discussion of HTTP load balancing and explained how you don't need a cluster to load balance HTTP requests. We talked about how to use a native web server or a hardware load balancer to load balance requests.

After that, we talked about HTTP session replication. First, you learned where to configure HTTP session replication. Then we talked about how sessions can be replicated and passivated to a secondary datastore.

Next, we covered session-bean clustering, talking about load balancing SLSBs and replicating SFSBs. After that, we covered entity clustering by discussing how to replicate the entity cache, how to hook the cache in to JPA, and how to configure entities to use the cache.

Finally, we discussed how to cluster JNDI. You learned how to enable clustered JNDI and how to access it from the client side using both manually defined IPs and auto discovery.

So far, you've learned quite a bit about how to configure JBoss to get things to work functionally. Clustering can help scale an application to help it perform better under greater loads. Often, scaling an application isn't enough to get it to perform to the extent that you want. In the next chapter, we look at ways to improve the performance of your applications and your application server.

13.7 References

Benchmark results for field-level replication—http://wiki.jboss.org/community/docs/DOC-12696

Section 19.2 (The Second Level Cache) of the Hibernate documentation—http://www.hibernate.org/hib_docs/v3/reference/en/html/

The javadocs for java.net.ServerSocket—http://java.sun.com/j2se/1.5.0/docs/api/java/net/ServerSocket.html

Apache Tomcat connectors—http://tomcat.apache.org/connectors-doc/

Using mod_jk 1.2.x with JBoss/Tomcat bundle and Apache2—http://wiki.jboss.org/communitiy/docs/DOC-12525

Using mod_proxy with JBoss/Tomcat bundle and Apache2.2.x—http://wiki.jboss.org/community/docs/DOC-12529

Using mod_jk 1.2.x with JBoss/Tomcat bundle and IIS 4.x or 5.x—http://wiki.jboss.org/community/docs/DOC-12526

Hibernate Reference: Using JBoss Cache 2 as a Hibernate Second Level Cache—http://opensource.atlassian.com/projects/hibernate/secure/attachment/13759/hibernate_reference.pdf

Hibernate: Truly Understanding the Second-Level and Query Caches—http://www.javalobby.org/java/forums/t48846.html

14 Tuning the JBoss Application Server

This chapter covers

- Defining performance
- Developing a performance tuning methodology
- Tuning the hardware and network
- Tuning the OS
- Tuning the JVM
- Tuning the application server
- Tuning your application

When I (Peter) was in high school and got my first car, it didn't have the dozens of computers that modern cars have—computers that automatically tune your engine to get the optimum performance. In those days, the engine was mostly mechanical. To keep it running at optimum performance, I used a timing strobe to make sure the spark plugs sparked at the proper instance; made sure the spark gap on the spark plug was set to the recommended distance; cleaned and adjusted the carburetor; and a whole bunch of other tasks. It wasn't enough to put gas in the car and occasionally change the oil to keep a car running efficiently.

Similarly, deploying applications to an application server and starting the server isn't sufficient to get the optimal performance from the application server. As with an older model car, you can pay someone to tune it for you, or you can learn how to tune it yourself. You're concerned that your application runs efficiently, that it doesn't consume more resources than necessary, and that the performance of the system as a whole is satisfactory to your customers. In this chapter, we tell you many of the things that you need to know to tune your applications and the application server to meet those goals.

We approach tuning from a holistic perspective, looking at all the components that make up the system and tuning those components that need it the most. For example, while much of the tuning of an older model car involves the engine and its components, anyone who knows automotive performance will tell you that the engine is only the starting point; you also need to be concerned about the transmission, rear axle, and even the tires. They all contribute to the car's overall performance.

In the course of this chapter, we examine everything from low-level details, such as the size of the CPU cache, to high-level details, such as the prepared statement cache, and a lot of details in between. In the end, you should have enough information to tackle tuning the components of your system. With each component finely tuned, you should get the best performance out of your application and customers happy with the responsiveness of the system.

We start performance tuning at the bottom of the software stack—the hardware and operating system—and work our way up through the JVM, the application server, and the application. But before we can tell you about performance tuning, we first need to define what we mean by performance.

14.1 Defining performance

There are several aspects to performance, such as *response times*, *throughput*, and the related topic of *service level agreements* (SLAs). Another aspect of performance is how well the system *scales* to meet an increased workload.

Response time relates to how quickly the system responds to a user's request. The response time can vary widely from one request to another, even if the request is the same. Therefore, it's typically better to look at the average response time for a particular request than to look at individual times. There's also the difference between the processing time and the round trip response. The *processing time* is the amount of time from when the system initially received the request until the system returns the response. The *round trip response time* includes latency, which is the time it takes to transport the user's request from the user's input device to the system and back. Therefore, the response time is always longer than the processing time and typically depends on the communications network between the user and the system.

Throughput relates to the number of requests the system can handle and is expressed as the number of requests within a given time period. For example, the throughput requirements for a system might state the system must handle 10,000 requests per hour.

An *SLA* is a contract to provide a certain level of service between a vendor, who's hosting or providing an application or system, and the customer using the system. The level of service defines a required and measurable response time, throughput, or both. The SLA guarantees that the vendor provides enough resources to process the customer's requests in a timely fashion and usually stipulates monetary compensation if the system doesn't meet the SLA goals.

Scaling relates to whether and how additional load can be added to the system. For example, a particular system might start with 100 users but later must support 1000 users. What must be done to the system to handle the extra users? There are two aspects to scaling: *scaling up* (also know as *vertical scaling*), and *scaling out* (also known as *horizontal scaling*). The term *scaling up* means adding more resources to an existing computer to handle the increased load, whereas *scaling out* means adding more computers to the system to handle the load.

Consider the aforementioned system with 100 users. Let's assume that the system consists of two computers, one for the application server and the other for the database. The computer running the application server has 512MB of RAM, a certain amount of disk space, and is dual-processor capable but contains only a single processor. If, by increasing the memory to 2GB and adding a second processor, the system can handle 1000 users, then you've successfully scaled *up* the system. If you add a second or third computer running the application server to handle the 1000 users, then you've scaled *out* the system.

Now that you understand what we mean by performance, let's describe a methodology you can use to tune your applications.

14.2 Performance tuning methodology

In this section, we define our tuning philosophy. After defining the philosophy, we show you how to set up repeatable tests you can use to measure performance and gauge the results of your tuning efforts.

14.2.1 Holistic performance tuning

Before you do any tuning, you should first have an SLA that defines throughput and/or response time requirements. Why should you have an SLA first? Because if you already meet the performance requirements that your customers demand, then you don't need to spend time and money fine-tuning your system.

NOTE The SLA is defined from the end user's point of view and encompasses the entire system: the network, the operating system, the application server, the database server, and the application.

It does no good to rewrite a sort algorithm to make it faster if that algorithm has negligible impact on the end-user experience, even if you can prove through a micro-benchmark that the new sort algorithm is 10 times more efficient. Instead, look at every part of the system and identify the main bottleneck. After identifying the bottleneck, you can either tune the component causing the bottleneck or attempt to reduce the usage of that component.

Table 14.1 Various methods that you can employ to tune an application

Tuning method	Examples
Change configuration parameter	Change an argument on the command line to the JVM. Change the size of the database connection pool in the data source configuration file.
Add or change hardware	Add a second disk controller to the database server to better parallelize access to the disk. Add more memory to the computer running the application server. Replace 100MB network cards with 1GB network cards.
Modify application or database	Change a key algorithm within the application code. Add an index to a table in the database. Deploy a cache to reduce the queries against the database.

If you want to tune the component causing the bottleneck, you typically use one or more of the methods identified in table 14.1.

When you locate bottlenecks and tune to eliminate them (or, at least, reduce them to an acceptable level), then you affect the behavior of the entire system and improve the end-user experience. Also, you don't waste your time making improvements that have little or no impact.

When we describe tuning in this chapter, we consider tuning at all levels of the software stack, as follows:

- Hardware and network
- OS
- JVM
- JBoss AS
- Your application

Even in the sections dealing with other parts of the stack, the emphasis is on the application server and the computer and JVM running it. We don't discuss tuning the database for two reasons. First, each database behaves differently and is tuned differently. Second, *books* have been written on tuning particular databases; we can't do justice to the topic in this book. We do look at some database issues as they relate to tuning the application server and your application.

Now let's look at how to set up a repeatable test to aid in performance tuning.

14.2.2 Performance analysis test cycle

The performance analysis test cycle is simple. You complete the following steps:

1. Set up the test environment.
2. Run the test.
3. Analyze the test results.
4. Tune the system.
5. Repeat from step 2.

Let's look at the details of each of these steps.

SETTING UP THE TEST ENVIRONMENT

Gather the hardware you require for the test and install the software. For example, you might have one computer for the database, another for JBoss AS, and a third to generate the simulated user traffic.

How many computers you need and the network configuration all depend on the purpose of the test. For example, if you're testing scale-out capabilities, use two or more computers running JBoss AS and, perhaps, another computer running the Apache HTTP Server to handle static content and perform load balancing between the application server computers. Also, the test system should be as close to the production system as possible because even slight differences—such as CPU speed, disk access times, or JVM version—can have significant impact on your performance results and the tuning.

> **NOTE** When testing scale-out capabilities, always take a single application server instance to its limit first, and then take two application server instances to their limits, and so on. Only then can you get a clear idea of the scale-out capabilities of your system; you'll know how much additional traffic you can support by adding another application server to the production configuration.

If your company maintains its own network, you could set up the performance test systems on that network. Doing so enables you to monitor and run the test remotely; this type of setup is handy if the test system is in a room in another part of the building. But having an isolated network where the test computers are connected via a router that's neither on the internet nor on a company-wide network is preferred. The only network traffic generated will be that of your test. Having an isolated network also prevents the embarrassment of having the network administrator appear at your door asking you why you're running a denial of service (DoS) attack against the company's computers. Ahem. Of course, we wouldn't know anything about that.

CREATING A TEST SCRIPT

You need a repeatable test script. The script must perform the exact same operations each time it's run. If you use a random number generator to vary what the script does, seed the generator with the same value each test run so that the test is repeatable. If the test isn't repeatable, you can't determine if any changes in the test results are because of the changes you made or because the script performed different operations. Ideally, if you take the resulting charts of performance data, such as CPU usage and queue depths, from several script runs and overlay corresponding charts, the charts should match exactly.

The script shouldn't be too short or too long. If the script is too short, you'll have no idea how the software behaves after it runs for a while. For example, a slow memory leak won't show up on a short run. If the script is too long, you end up waiting for test runs to complete. For example, if the test takes 8 hours to run, you can run the test only once per day. An ideal time is about 20 minutes. With a 20 minute test run, you can perform the entire performance analysis test cycle in an hour. Once you're satisfied with the performance of a 20 minute run, you can then run it for a long time, such as 24 hours, to gauge the long-term performance.

Decide what data you want to gather and set up the tools used to gather that data. You might consider using the Performance Monitor on Windows or the top utility on Linux and UNIX systems. The tools used to drive the test, such as JMeter, also provide performance data. The tools you use depend on what you have available, budget, and personal preference and familiarity. Be aware that some of these tools impact application performance. You might consider using tools that adversely impact performance only to gather data and not to measure performance against a goal.

Perform several initial runs. Use these runs to verify that the script is repeatable, that the application results are correct (for example, the database is updated as expected), and that you have all your tools in place. Don't perform any tuning between these runs. When you have three or more runs with the same results, you're ready to start the analysis cycle. Use the data from any of these runs as the baseline data.

ANALYSIS CYCLE: RUN, ANALYZE, AND TUNE

Because you've already run the test to get a baseline, examine the data gathered by that test. Based on that data, decide on what change to make to tune the system. This change can be to any part of the system. For example, you might notice that the database server was running at an average of 90 percent CPU, leading you to examine the data gathered on that server and finally causing you to conclude that a table is missing an index on one of its columns. Adding the index is the suggested tuning change.

Make only one change. This is important, so we'll repeat it: make only *one* change at a time. If you make more than one change, you'll never be able to tell which of the changes caused a change in the test results or if the changes cancelled each other out. Unless you have prior experience or knowledge to the contrary, never change more than one thing before running the test again.

Run the test again. If the performance improves, use this test run as your new baseline. If the performance worsens, keep the prior baseline.

Repeat this cycle until you run out of time (for example, the schedule allocated 2 weeks for running performance tests); you can no longer improve the performance of the system (for example, none of the recent changes have yielded any further improvements); or you're satisfied with the performance you have (for example, the goal was 10,000 requests per hour, and you achieved 3000 requests in 18 minutes).

Now that you know how to test the performance of your system, let's show you the ways that you can tune it, starting from the bottom of the stack—the hardware and network.

14.3 Tuning the hardware and network

We often see questions on the JBoss forums from people asking, "What are the hardware requirements for JBoss AS?" At one time, I was running the application server on a laptop with 512MB of RAM and a 1GHz processor. If I had more than a handful of users, the performance would've soon become unacceptable. So, what are the requirements? It depends on your needs. For example, an application server used to serve a department or company of a few dozen people could run on a computer with a 2GHz processor, 1GB RAM, and the database could run on the same computer. To service thousands of users, you might need several application server instances, a large and separate database server, and high speed connections between these components.

Let's look at some specific areas that you should consider—the network speed, the number of CPUs, and whether to use 32-bit or 64-bit CPUs.

14.3.1 Setting network card speed

Most network cards are flexible enough to run on networks of various speeds. For example, a 1 GB network card can run on a 100MB network. Unfortunately, that capability comes with a price. Most such network cards or their drivers have an auto-detect, or auto negotiation, mechanism that determines the speed of the network and adjusts the card's speed accordingly. Our tests have shown that setting the network card to run at the speed of the network, instead of using auto-detect, can boost performance by as much as 15 percent.

To set the speed of the network card on Windows, select Network Connections in the Control Panel, right-click the desired network connection, and choose Properties. In the resulting Properties dialog box, click the Configure button. The Advanced tab lists several properties (each card has its own set of properties), one of which defines the network speed. Select the speed property and choose the desired speed from the value drop-down box, as illustrated by the example in figure 14.1.

You can use the `mii-tool` or `ethtool` commands (you must be *root* to run either command) to set the speed of the network card on most Linux distributions. The discussion that follows assumes you're using the `mii-tool` command.

You can determine the current setting of your network card and the allowed network speed settings using the `-v` command line option, as shown in listing 14.1.

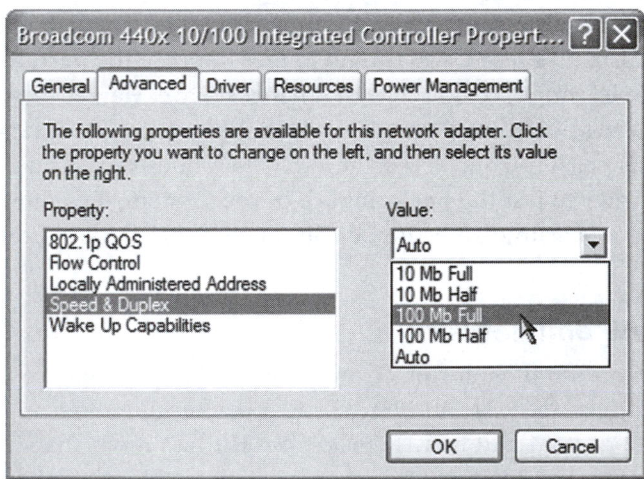

Figure 14.1 Use the Advanced tab on the NIC properties dialog box to set the speed to something other than Auto.

Listing 14.1 Running the `mii-tool` command

```
$ mii-tool -v
eth0: negotiated 100baseTx-FD, link ok
  product info: vendor 00:50:43, model 2 rev 3
  basic mode:   autonegotiation enabled              <-- Indicates card in auto-detect mode
  basic status: autonegotiation complete, link ok
  capabilities:
➥   100baseTx-FD 100baseTx-HD 10baseT-FD 10baseT-HD  <-- Lists valid speeds
  advertising:  100baseTx-FD 100baseTx-HD 10baseT-FD 10baseT-HD
                flow-control
  link partner: 100baseTx-FD 100baseTx-HD 10baseT-FD 10baseT-HD
```

Based on this output, you can set the card speed to 100 megabits per second as follows:

```
$ mii-tool -F 100baseTx-FD eth0
```

You should always set the speed to match that of the network. In this example, the network must be running at 100 megabits per second, full duplex. If the speed of the card doesn't match that of the network, you won't have network connectivity until you correct the speed.

14.3.2 Choosing the number of CPUs

Having multiple CPUs on the computer is preferred because JBoss AS uses many threads to run applications. With multiple CPUs, the threads don't have to wait as long to get time on a CPU. A two- or four-CPU computer is sufficient. You can use a computer with more CPUs such as 8 or 32, but you then must take processor affinity into account; we discuss this topic in section 14.4.1.

14.3.3 Choosing 32-bit or 64-bit

Should you use a 32-bit processor or a 64-bit processor and a corresponding JVM? From a performance viewpoint, there's little difference in the performance of an application server running on a 64-bit JVM as compared to a 32-bit JVM. Although that might sound surprising, consider that the application server, and the computer on which it runs, is only one part of a fairly large and complex system. Whereas a batch Java application that performs a lot of in-memory processing benefits significantly from 64-bit hardware, an application server spends more time waiting for other parts of the system, such as user requests or database responses, than it does processing data.

For 32-bit operating systems, if you're running only a single application server, 2 GB of RAM is usually sufficient. This enables you to assign a heap of about 1.4 GB. Even if you have more RAM, you might not be able to assign a larger heap. On a 32-bit OS, there's usually only 4 GB of address space available to each process. The OS typically reserves 2 GB of space for its own purposes such as file buffers, thread information, and all the other data necessary for it to run the process. The Java heap ends up sharing the remaining 2 GB with the JVM code and the various OS and language libraries that the JVM uses. Additionally, most JVMs require a contiguous block of memory to allocate the heap. The practical limit is usually around 1.4 GB but varies depending on the OS and its version.

For a 64-bit OS, you need more RAM because the word size is larger, so everything uses more space. As a rule of thumb, start the computer and notice the total amount of allocated memory. Add to that the heap size you want and get at least that much RAM. Usually, 4 GB is plenty. Be aware that large heaps take longer to garbage collect, possibly causing long pauses in your application.

14.4 Tuning the OS

Books have been written on tuning Windows, Linux, Solaris, and others. In general, anything that can be done to improve the performance of the OS as a whole benefits the application server. In this section, we cover a few areas that are beneficial to the application server and might not be pointed out in other books.

One obvious tuning measure is to stop all services that aren't required. All such services consume memory and processor bandwidth that can, instead, be applied to the application server. There are web sites that list the various services on Windows or daemons running on UNIX and Linux and describe the services, indicating which are necessary and which can be turned off.

While monitoring a system, ensure that the average CPU usage doesn't go over 80 percent. A range of 50 to 80 percent is usually ideal. If you push the system more than that, performance typically drops off.

If the computer running the application server contains only one or two processors, then the aforementioned advice is all that should concern you. If it has four or more processors, then you should be concerned with processor affinity.

14.4.1 Understanding processor affinity

Most OSs that support multiple processors provide a mechanism to limit the processors on which a given process runs. Such a capability is known as *processor affinity*. For example, on a multiprocessor computer running Windows, the context menu for processes in Task Manager contains a Set Affinity option, which displays a Processor Affinity dialog box, as shown in figure 14.2. Using this dialog box, you can select which processors a particular process uses.

For a multiprocessor computer running Linux, you use the `taskset` utility to set processor affinity. For example, if the application server is running as process number 9999 on an 8-CPU computer, you can declare that the application server use only four processors using the following command:

```
taskset -p 0x0f 9999
```

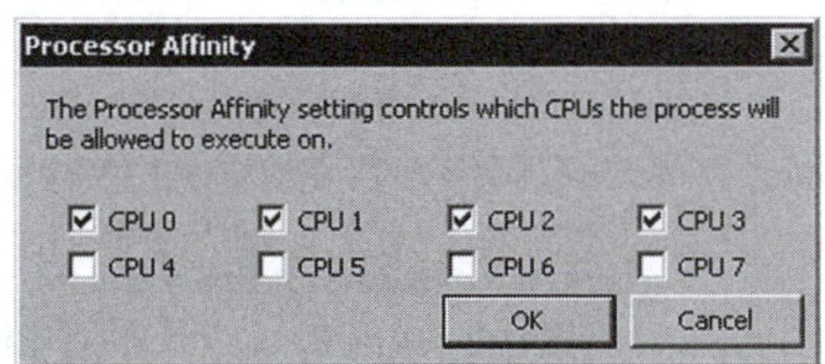

Figure 14.2 Setting processor affinity on Windows

If your computer has multiple processors, why would you want to limit the processors for a given process? To answer this question, you must first understand how a processor cache works. While the processor is executing the thread of a process, the data and code used by that thread are stored within a cache within the processor. When the thread is interrupted, because the thread either blocked while waiting on some event like I/O or used up its time allotment, another thread runs and starts to overwrite some of that cached code and data. If the cache is large enough and the thread that was running there gets back onto the same processor, then there's a good chance that some of the code or data is still cached. If the thread is assigned to a different processor, then the thread must once again try to fill the cache. And accessing cached data is many times faster than accessing data from RAM.

How does this apply to Java applications in general or application servers in particular? A Java application usually performs data access to recently created objects in the heap. Because active data is kept in the processor cache, if the thread continues to be assigned to the same processor, the cache will likely contain the data for the objects of interest. If the thread is assigned to a different processor, the thread must take the time to reload data from RAM.

SETTING PROCESSOR AFFINITY

The next question is, "What is the appropriate processor affinity for an application server?" Testing has shown that anywhere from two to four processors should be assigned to the application server for best performance. The exact number depends on the application(s) deployed to the application server. Usually, an application that has a high degree of dependency on common data performs better on two processors, whereas a more independent application performs better on four. Test your application on two, three, and four processors and select the processor affinity that works best for you.

NOTE Please don't misconstrue the advice on processor affinity as meaning that Java applications don't scale. Many Java applications do scale well up to 2, 64, or even more processors. Such applications tend to run independent threads. An application server must manage many shared objects that are accessed by all threads. It doesn't have threads dedicated to a single task (most threads handle user requests, each of which is vastly different) and has difficulty scaling higher than four processors.

You use processor affinity to run multiple application server instances on a single computer that has many processors. For example, if your application runs best using two processors and the computer has eight processors, you can run four application server instances, setting processor affinity so that each instance runs on its own pair of processors. In such a case, use a minimum of one network card for every two application server instances. Additionally, take the combined heap size into account when configuring RAM on that computer. In the example, if each application server uses a 1.4 GB heap, 8 GB of RAM is sufficient.

NOTE You might wonder how a multicore processor plays into processor affinity assignments. Our testing has shown that Java EE application servers scale well up to four physical processors, whether they're single core or dual core. If you have dual-core processors, you can scale an application server up to eight logical processors (four dual-core physical processors). When you see the term *processor* in the text, realize that we're talking about a physical processor.

You can set the processor affinity for the application server in a variety of ways, most of them difficult. The Processor Affinity dialog box on Windows enables you to set the affinity; but, as soon as you shut down the application server, you lose the setting and have to set it again. Ideally, you want a solution that automatically sets the affinity each time the application server is run.

If you have a computer with eight or more processors, the computer manufacturer or the OS vendor usually has a tool that can be used to manage processor affinity. For example, the Microsoft Windows 2000 Datacenter Server software, which runs on eight or more processors, provides the Process Manager tool, which remembers affinity settings. Unfortunately, many such tools are based on the process name, meaning that you can set only a single affinity setting for all your Java applications because they all run under the same process name. Many of the more recent tools have remedied this situation and can key off of portions of the command line. Such a capability can enable you to, for example, specify different affinity settings for multiple application server instances on the same computer. For JBoss AS, the command line key could be the name of the server configuration. Check with your OS vendor or computer manufacturer for details regarding tools that they have in this area. And keep in mind the difficulty of assigning affinity based on process name alone.

Finally, you could use a JVM that supports processor affinity, such as the Unisys JVM. With it, you can supply command line arguments to assign the desired processor affinity.

14.5 Tuning the JVM

Sun Microsystems and other JVM vendors are constantly improving the performance of their JVMs; therefore, you should prefer a later JVM over an earlier one. For example, version 6 of the Sun HotSpot JVM has significant performance improvements over the 5.0 JVM, which is significantly better than the 1.4 JVM.

There are two HotSpot JVMs, designated as the server and client virtual machines, which can be invoked using the `-client` and `-server` command line arguments. The differences between the two are mostly in how they handle compiling Java bytecode into native machine code and how they manage the heap. The client virtual machine is intended for short-running programs, and the server virtual machine is intended for longer-unning programs. For example, use the client virtual machine to run Ant, and the server virtual machine to run JBoss AS. In general, you should prefer the server virtual machine for running JBoss AS but examine the performance under both virtual machines. Be aware that a 5 or 10 minute performance test isn't adequate to judge between them. Instead, run the test for an hour or more before deciding.

TIP The Java Runtime Environment (JRE) for Windows ships with only the client virtual machine. If you want to use the server virtual machine, download and install the JDK.

Edit the `JAVA_OPTS` setting in the bin/run.bat (on Windows) or bin/run.conf (on Linux) file to set the desired virtual machine. By default, both scripts set the server virtual machine. An example setting in run.bat is as follows (note that the `-server` option must be the first option on the command line):

```
set JAVA_OPTS=-server %JAVA_OPTS% ...
```

The sections that follow concentrate on the HotSpot JVM and command line arguments used to tune that JVM. The arguments apply equally to the client and server virtual machines. Many JVM vendors (such as Apple, HP, and Unisys) license the HotSpot source code from Sun and base their JVMs on HotSpot, so the following recommendations should apply to those JVMs as well.

14.5.1 Understanding the Java heap

The JVM allocates Java objects in an area of memory known as the Java heap. You must understand how the JVM allocates objects and how it frees up heap space used by objects that are no longer in use (also known as *garbage collection*) to understand how to improve the performance of heap management. The details that follow pertain to the heap as maintained by the HotSpot Virtual Machine; other virtual machines might employ alternative heap mechanisms.

As a Java application allocates objects, the virtual machine places those objects in a heap allocated by the virtual machine. When the application no longer needs the object and removes all references to that object, that object becomes unreachable. A garbage collection typically occurs when the virtual machine runs out of room to allocate new objects.

Most objects allocated by an application have a short lifespan and are said to die young. In the HotSpot Virtual Machine, the heap is divided into the *young generation,* where new objects are placed, and a *tenured generation,* where objects that have survived several garbage collections are placed. Each generation is collected individually, and each has its own collection algorithms.

A simplified representation of the heap address space is shown in Figure 14.3. The young generation consists of the *eden space,* where all new objects are created, and two survivor spaces known as the *to space* and the *from space.* The tenured generation is also referred to as the *old generation.* The *permanent space* holds class objects, which include instances of the `java.lang.Class` class and method instances.

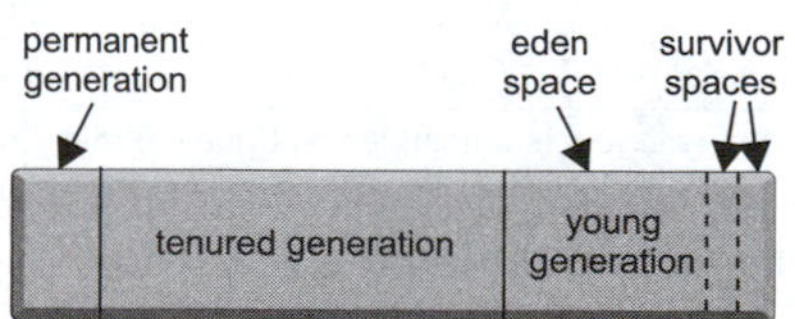

Figure 14.3 The Java heap is a generational heap with objects of different ages stored in different generations.

Table 14.2 describes the various command line arguments that can be used to set the heap sizes. The Notes column provides some

Table 14.2 JVM heap sizing arguments

Argument	Description	Notes
`-Xms<size>`[a]	Sets the minimum heap size.	In production, set the min and max heap sizes to the same value.
`-Xmx<size>`	Sets the maximum heap size.	
`-XX:NewSize=<size>`	Sets the minimum young generation size.	In production, set the min and max young generation sizes to the same value.
`-XX:MaxNewSize=<size>`	Sets the maximum young generation size.	
`-XX:NewRatio=<number>`	Sets the ratio of the size of the young generation as compared to the tenured generation. For example, a value of 2 means the tenured generation will be twice the size of the young generation.	Use either the `NewSize/MaxNewSize` arguments or the `NewRatio` argument. Don't use both.
`-XX:SurvivorRatio=<number>`[b]	Sets the ratio of the size of the eden space compared to one of the survivor spaces. For example, a survivor ratio of 8 indicates that the eden space is 8 times as large as either survivor space.	Vary the ratio based on young generation size. A ratio of 8 is good for small young generations (for example, 10MB), and 32 for larger young generations (for example, 100MB).
`-XX:+UseTLAB`	Provides each thread in the application with its own allocation area (thread-local allocation block, or TLAB) in the eden space. Note that this is a Boolean option; the plus (+) turns it on. You can use a minus (-) to turn it off: -XX:-UseTLAB.	Mainly benefits multiprocessor systems.
`-XX:TLABSize=<size>`	The size of each TLAB.	Make sure the young generation is large enough to hold all the TLABs for each thread in the application. You should try 64K, 128K, and 256K.
`-XX:MaxTenuringThreshold=<number>`	Indicates the number of minor collections that an object must survive before being automatically placed into the tenured generation.	Usually, you should use a value of 32.
`-XX:MaxPermSize=<size>`	Sets the size of the permanent generation.	Don't set this unless you run out of space (see section 14.5.4).

a. The `<size>` is a floating point number that indicates the number of bytes. It can be suffixed with the letters *K*, *M*, or *G* to represent kilobytes, megabytes, and gigabytes, respectively.

b. The `<number>` is a floating point number.

preliminary or high-level recommendations on setting some arguments. In addition, more detailed recommendations appear later in this section.

NOTE You might wonder why we didn't provide the default values for the heap sizing arguments. The defaults vary depending on the OS, the number of processors, the amount of memory, the specific version of the JVM, and even what other command line arguments you have. The defaults are sufficient to run the application server; but, if you want high performance, set these arguments to the desired values and don't let them default.

We recommend you set the minimum size and maximum size of the heap to the same value. If the values are different, the JVM takes away time from processing the application to determine if it should adjust the sizes after garbage collection. Hence the recommendation for production computers. For the same reason, we also recommend that you set the minimum and maximum young generation size to the same value. In addition, we recommend that the young generation size be one-third to one-quarter the size of the heap.

If you're running on a development machine, you may use different sizes. For example, by default, the run scripts set the application server heap to 512MB maximum and 128MB minimum. When you run the application server on your PC, you won't want it to take the entire 512MB unless it needs it because you'll probably be doing other work on the PC at the same time, such as development using an IDE.

To set these values for JBoss AS, either set the `JAVA_OPTS` environment variable or change the `JAVA_OPTS` line in the run script files. As an example, changing the `JAVA_OPTS` line in the run.bat script to the following value sets the heap to 1200MB, the young generation to 400MB, and the survivor ratio to one-thirtysecond the size of the eden space. In addition, each thread gets its own allocation block or 64K.

```
set JAVA_OPTS=%JAVA_OPTS% -Xms1200m -Xmx1200m -XX:NewSize=400M
➥     -XX:MaxNewSize=400M -XX:SurvivorRatio=32
➥     -XX:+UseTLAB -XX:TLABSize=64K
```

You might ask what the recommended values are for each of the heap settings. This example contains some initial heap settings that we've found to work well with a variety of applications deployed to an application server. Later, after we discuss garbage collection, we provide you with some tips on how to fine-tune the settings for optimum performance with your application.

14.5.2 Understanding garbage collection

There are two categories of garbage collection: minor and major. A minor collection cleans out the young generation only, whereas a major, or full, collection cleans out the tenured generation and the young generation.

When the young generation is collected, all objects still in use are moved to the survivor space designated as the *to space*. These objects are said to be alive, and objects no longer in use are dead. After the collection, the *eden space* and survivor space designated as the *from space* are empty. If the to space fills up during the collection, any excess surviving objects are placed in the tenured generation. Additionally, any objects that have survived several minor collections are also placed into the tenured generation. Once the collection is complete, the eden space and from space are empty, and within the young generation only, the to space contains in-use objects. Also, at this time, the from space and to space change designations because, after the collection, the to space is always empty.

Before the minor collection is performed, the JVM looks at the tenured generation and determines if there's ample space to hold any objects from the young generation that overflow into the tenured generation; if not, it performs a collection on the tenured generation first. This process is known as a full collection. When the tenured generation is collected, all space occupied by unreachable objects is made available again. In most cases, the tenured generation is also compacted, moving all surviving objects to one end of the tenured generation space.

UNDERSTANDING THE COLLECTOR TYPES

There are two basic types of collectors—serial and concurrent—which we compare and contrast in table 14.3. The Argument column lists the command line argument used to turn this collector on. If you want the young generation to be collected using multiple threads, also set the command line argument specified in the Parallel Collection column. Don't use a parallel collector on a system with only one processor; the garbage collection performance isn't as good as when using a single collector thread. The tenured generation is always collected with a single collector thread; there's no parallel collector for that generation.

Starting with the 5.0 release, the JVM turns on `UseParallelGC` automatically for the serial collector if the computer contains at least two processors and at least 1 GB of main memory. By default, the JVM uses one collector thread for every processor on the computer. You can adjust the number of threads using the `-XX:ParallelGCThreads=<number>` argument. Don't set this value to more than the number of processors on the computer. Also, you can turn off the parallel collector by using the argument `-XX:-UseParallelGC`, in which case only a single thread is used to collect the young generation.

Table 14.3 The basic collector types in the JVM and the arguments used to select them

Collector type	Argument	Parallel collection	Description
Serial	<none, the default>	`-XX:+UseParallelGC`	Pauses the Java application until the collection is finished. If the parallel collection argument is set, then this collector is often referred to as the *throughput collector.*
Concurrent	`-XX:+UseConcMarkSweepGC`	`-XX:+UseParNewGC`	Performs most of the collection while the Java application continues to run. The collection is performed in phases; only two short phases require the application to pause. This collector is often referred to as the *mostly concurrent collector.*

NOTE The JVM contains a variety of collectors with names such as the Concurrent Mark Sweep (CMS) collector and the Throughput Collector; each collector performs its task in a certain manner. For example, the parallel collector for CMS is different from the parallel collector used by the Throughput Collector. For our discussion, we maintain a higher-level viewpoint and consider only the basic functionality such as stop-the-world collection vs. concurrent collection and using multiple threads vs. using a single thread to do the collection.

The concurrent collector attempts to reduce the noticeable pauses in a Java application when the serial collector is used. The concurrent collector is a better choice if your application has strict SLA requirements, but the concurrent collector sacrifices throughput to perform the collection in this manner. For example, on a two processor system, one of the processors will be occupied with running the concurrent collector thread, leaving only a single processor to handle new requests; this effectively reduces throughput by 50 percent during a garbage collection. In addition, the concurrent collector takes a longer elapsed time to perform the collection than the serial collector.

Setting the concurrent collector also changes other heap settings—for example, making the survivor spaces small (64KB) and setting the tenuring threshold to 0. Any objects that survive a young generation garbage collection are promoted to the tenured generation, placing more strain on the concurrent collector because it has to collect more often. You might benefit from specifically setting the survivor ratio and the tenuring threshold to prevent this behavior. These settings must come after the `UseConcMarkSweepGC` argument.

Finally, you must be careful in setting heap sizes for the concurrent collector because, if the heap runs out of room during a concurrent collection, a costly full serial collection is performed.

Which collector should you use for your application? That depends on your application and your performance requirements. Test your application with various collection settings and use the most appropriate one. To do that, you need to know how to gather and interpret garbage collection data. Let's look at that next.

14.5.3 Gathering garbage collection data

Table 14.4 presents the various JVM arguments that can be used to gather garbage collection data.

Table 14.4 JVM arguments for gathering garbage collection data

Argument	Description	Notes
`-verbose:gc`	Generates basic garbage collection statistics: heap size before and after, and time spent in collection.	Doesn't show any statistics for the concurrent collector.
`-XX:+PrintGCDetails`	Adds data about the young generation size to that provided by `verbose:gc`.	Shows concurrent collector data.

Table 14.4 JVM arguments for gathering garbage collection data *(continued)*

Argument	Description	Notes
`-XX:+PrintHeapAtGC`	Generates detailed garbage collection statistics: sizes and percent usage of each heap space, along with heap memory addresses, before and after each collection.	Provides details on the various phases of a concurrent collection.
`-XX:+PrintGCTimestamp`	Prints the seconds that have elapsed since the start of the application.	Use in conjunction with the other print options.
`-Xloggc:<filename>`	Garbage collection statistics are placed into the file indicated by `<filename>`.	If not specified, the collection statistics are sent to standard out.

The figures 14.4 through 14.7 show example output for the various collection options. Additionally, you can supply multiple statistics arguments on the command line, in which case the various outputs are all mixed together in time order.

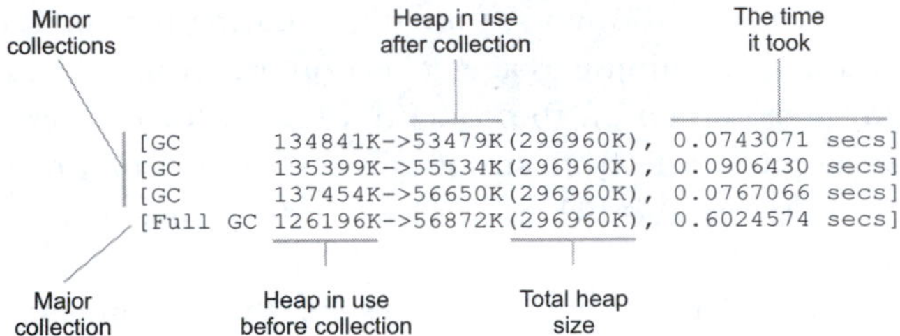

Figure 14.4 The output for `-verbose:gc` identifies if the garbage collection is a minor one or a full one. It also provides the amount of heap space in use before and after the collection, the heap size, and the time spent in collection.

The `verbose:gc` and `PrintGCDetails` outputs (figures 14.4 and 14.5) are fairly simple. The `PrintHeapAtGC` output, figure 14.6, is overwhelming at first glance, but the data is straightforward once you understand it. For each garbage collection, you see data from before the collection took place (the top half of the text in figure 14.6) and data from after the collection (the bottom half of the text in figure 14. 6).

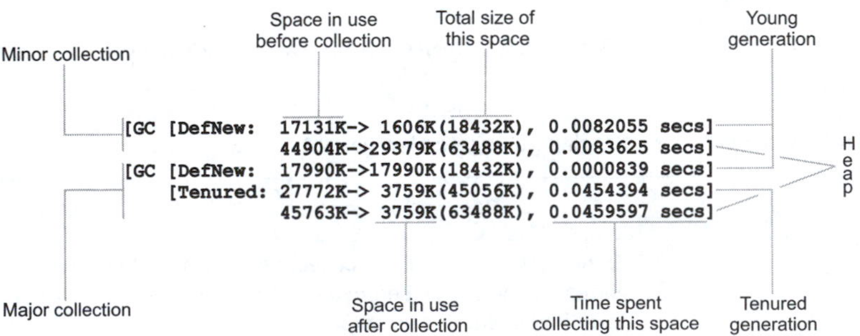

Figure 14.5 The output for `PrintGCDetails` expands on the `verbose:gc` output by providing separate data for each generation in the heap.

```
{Heap before GC invocations=422:
 Heap
 def new generation   total 18432K, used 17639K [0x6eb40000, 0x6ff40000, 0x6ff40000)
  eden space 16384K, 100% used [0x6eb40000, 0x6fb40000, 0x6fb40000)
  from space 2048K, 61% used [0x6fd40000, 0x6fe79df8, 0x6ff40000)
  to   space 2048K, 0% used [0x6fb40000, 0x6fb40000, 0x6fd40000)
 tenured generation   total 45056K, used 6403K [0x6ff40000, 0x72b40000, 0x72b40000)
  the space 45056K, 14% used [0x6ff40000, 0x70580f78, 0x70581000, 0x72b40000)
 compacting perm gen  total 8192K, used 1597K [0x72b40000, 0x73340000, 0x76b40000)
  the space 8192K, 19% used [0x72b40000, 0x72ccf598, 0x72ccf600, 0x73340000)
Heap after GC invocations=423:
 Heap
 def new generation   total 18432K, used 1197K [0x6eb40000, 0x6ff40000, 0x6ff40000)
  eden space 16384K, 0% used [0x6eb40000, 0x6eb40000, 0x6fb40000)
  from space 2048K, 58% used [0x6fb40000, 0x6fc6b4e8, 0x6fd40000)
  to   space 2048K, 0% used [0x6fd40000, 0x6fd40000, 0x6ff40000)
 tenured generation   total 45056K, used 6416K [0x6ff40000, 0x72b40000, 0x72b40000)
  the space 45056K, 14% used [0x6ff40000, 0x70584190, 0x70584200, 0x72b40000)
 compacting perm gen  total 8192K, used 1597K [0x72b40000, 0x73340000, 0x76b40000)
  the space 8192K, 19% used [0x72b40000, 0x72ccf598, 0x72ccf600, 0x73340000)
}
```

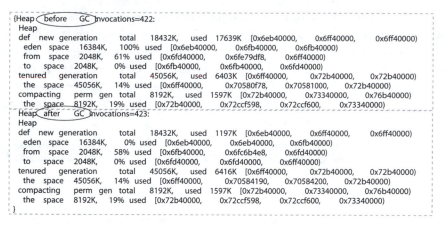

Figure 14.6 The output for `PrintHeapAtGC` provides the most data about the heap sizes both before and after a collection.

Both halves provide the same data, so figure 14.7 shows only the *before* data.

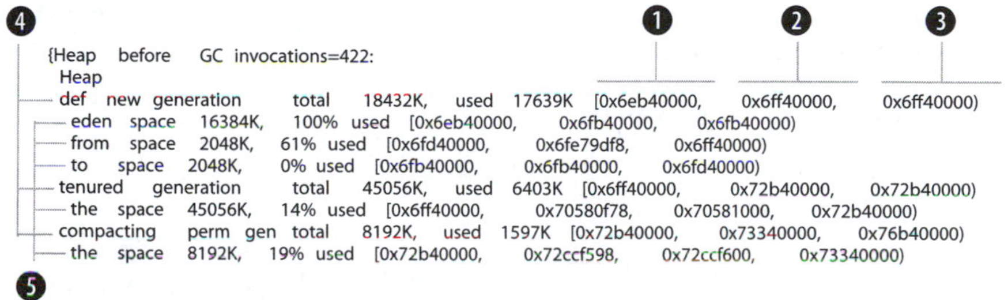

```
{Heap before GC invocations=422:
 Heap
 def new generation   total 18432K, used 17639K [0x6eb40000, 0x6ff40000, 0x6ff40000)
  eden space 16384K, 100% used [0x6eb40000, 0x6fb40000, 0x6fb40000)
  from space 2048K, 61% used [0x6fd40000, 0x6fe79df8, 0x6ff40000)
  to   space 2048K, 0% used [0x6fb40000, 0x6fb40000, 0x6fd40000)
 tenured generation   total 45056K, used 6403K [0x6ff40000, 0x72b40000, 0x72b40000)
  the space 45056K, 14% used [0x6ff40000, 0x70580f78, 0x70581000, 0x72b40000)
 compacting perm gen  total 8192K, used 1597K [0x72b40000, 0x73340000, 0x76b40000)
  the space 8192K, 19% used [0x72b40000, 0x72ccf598, 0x72ccf600, 0x73340000)
```

Figure 14.7 The output for `PrintHeapAtGC` includes the usage information for each heap generation and for each space within the generations. In addition, it provides the memory addresses of the start and end of each space and the address of the current allocation pointer.

The hex data at the end of each line provides the memory addresses for the specific generation or space: the start of memory address ❶, the end of memory address ❸, and the current allocation address ❷. For each generation ❹, you're told the total size of the generation and the amount of memory used. For each space ❺, you're told the total size of the space and the percentage of that space in use.

The various garbage collection data arguments provide a wealth of information regarding garbage collection. The main problem with the data is its volume. It's not unusual to look at thousands of lines of garbage collection data from a single application run. Additionally, it's next to impossible to see trends amid all this textual data. Let's look at how to transform this data into a format that's easier to interpret and analyze in order to tune the application.

EXTRACTING GARBAGE COLLECTION DATA

The first thing to do is extract the data of interest and convert it into a more usable form. The ideal form is one you can load into a spreadsheet or other analysis tools for further processing. Perhaps the easiest format is a comma-separated value (CSV) file. You can do this in several different ways such as using a scripting language, like Perl, that can easily parse such data. A simple Java program with a regular expression can do the same. Listing 14.2 is a Java program that converts `-verbose:gc` output into a CSV file. The nice thing about using regular expressions is that the program can generate the CSV file even if the `-verbose:gc` output is interspersed with the logging output generated by the application server.

Listing 14.2 Application to convert `verbose:gc` output to CSV

```
import java.io.*;
import java.util.regex.*;
public class Analyzer {
 public static void main(String[] args) throws Exception {
  InputStream fin = new FileInputStream(args[0]);
  int iSize = fin.available();
  byte mvIn[] = new byte[iSize];                          ❶
  fin.read(mvIn, 0, iSize);
  fin.close();
  String strText = new String(mvIn);
  PrintStream fout = new PrintStream
   (new FileOutputStream(args[0] + ".csv"));            ❷
  fout.println("Before,After,Seconds");
  Pattern p = Pattern.compile
("\\[(?:Full |)GC (\\d*)K->(\\d*)K\\(\\d*K\\), ([\\d.]*          ❸
➥   ) secs\\]");
  Matcher m = p.matcher(strText);
  while (m.find())
   fout.println(m.group(1) + "," + m.group(2) + "," + m          ❹
➥  .group(3));
  fout.close();       ❺
 }
}
```

The code reads the contents of the file containing the `-verbose:gc` output and places the contents into a string, `strText` ❶. It creates a new file to hold the comma-separated data and places titles in the headers of the three columns ❷. It declares a regular expression pattern used to match the `-verbose:gc` output and extract the data of interest ❸. Then, it iterates through the data of interest, writing the extracted data to the output file ❹. Finally, it closes the output file ❺.

For example, assume that `-verbose:gc` output is captured in a file named gcout.txt. The following command generates a CSV file named gcout.txt.csv:

```
java Analyzer gcout.txt
```

The resulting file contains data similar to the following:

```
60176,56377,0.0050069
60473,56675,0.0049446
60771,13067,0.1216777
```

The program can be easily modified to parse the output for the other garbage collection data options. Those variations are available as part of the source code for the book.

The data gathered from the `-verbose:gc` output is the heap space in use before the collection, the heap space in use after the collection, and the time it took to do the collection. If you follow the recommendation of setting the min and max heap size to the same value, the total heap size value in the `-verbose:gc` output doesn't change, and the program doesn't gather it.

PLOTTING GARBAGE COLLECTION DATA

The best way to view this data is to graph it. You can do so using your favorite spreadsheet application or a statistical analysis tool. Such applications typically accept CSV data, and once loaded, that data can be plotted in a graph. The only tricky part is that the scale of the garbage collection's elapsed time is different from the two heap-in-use values. You can compensate for this by either using a different scale for the elapsed time or first converting the elapsed time values by multiplying by a large value such as 10,000. Table 14.5 provides instructions for graphing the data in two major spreadsheet applications. Refer to the documentation for the spreadsheet for more detailed instructions on how to create charts.

Table 14.5 Graphing garbage collection data

Application	Graphing Option	Steps
Microsoft Excel	XY (Scatter)	**1** Open the CSV file. **2** Select the first column only. **3** Click Insert. On the subsequent drop-down menu, select Chart to display the Chart Wizard. **4** Choose XY (Scatter). Click Next. **5** In Step 2 of the Chart Wizard, click the Series tab. Then, click Add under the Series list box. Type the text *After* in Name field, and in the Y Values field, select the data in the second column. **6** Repeat the previous step for the third column, using *Time* as the name. Click Next. **7** On Step 3, fill out the fields as desired and click Next. **8** On Step 4, select the option to place the chart on a new sheet and click Finish. The chart is displayed on a new sheet. Note that you can edit the chart.
OpenOffice.org Calc	Chart type: lines Variant: normal	**1** Open the CSV file. **2** Select all three columns (you might want to adjust the time spent column first; see previous paragraph). **3** In the Insert menu, select Chart, and the AutoFormat Chart dialog box appears. **4** Select the option to place the chart on a new sheet and click Next. **5** Choose the Line chart with the Points Only variation. Click Next. **6** Add appropriate legends and titles and click Create. Note that you can edit the chart.

Figure 14.8 contains a typical graph created using Excel. The X-axis represents individual garbage collection instances, and the Y-axis either the heap size (in kilobytes) or the time in some factor of milliseconds. One vertical line on the graph contains the three data points for a single garbage collection. Let's look at the vertical line labeled ❶. The

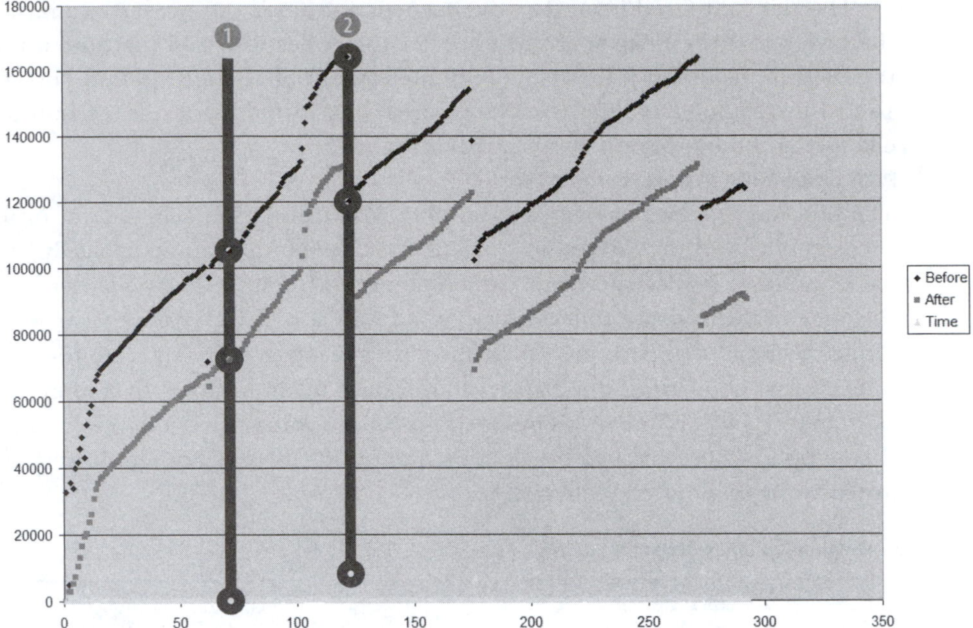

Figure 14.8 This plot of the `verbose:gc` data shows how heap usage increases as the application runs; when a major collection runs (#2), the heap usage drops. The upper lines are the heap usage before collection, the middle lines the heap usage after the collection, and the line hugging the X-axis the time spent in each collection.

topmost data point (inside the upper circle) represents the heap size before the garbage collection—approximately 115MB. The middle data point (inside the middle circle) represents the heap size after the garbage collection—approximately 81MB. The bottom data point (inside the lower circle) represents the amount of time spent in garbage collection—usually around 10 or 20 milliseconds, which is negligible.

The data points for the heap size before garbage collection, as well as the ones for after, tend to form a line with a positive slope, indicating that the tenured generation is slowly filling up with objects. The first line ❶ identifies the data points corresponding with a single garbage collection, where the heap was at around 115MB before the collection, 81MB after the collection, and the time spent was negligible.

Eventually, a full garbage collection occurs ❷. You can easily spot a full collection by noting that the data point for one collection (the middle circle) drops dramatically from the prior data point (the uppermost circle). In addition, the data point for the time spent (lower circle) is located at a higher point in the chart, in this case representing a garbage collection time of about 0.6 seconds.

Some additional data of interest are the number of garbage collections and the total amount of time spent in garbage collection. You get the latter by totaling the time spent column. If you have a repeatable performance test, you can easily determine the effect of your tuning attempts by comparing these values from one run to the next.

ANALYZING GARBAGE COLLECTION DATA

Now that the data is plotted, what should you do with it? First, you need a goal. Ideally, you want to see the following:

- *No full collections*—Full collections are expensive, as you can easily see by how much higher the dots that represent time appear during such a collection compared to the other collections.
- *As few collections as possible*—Each collection takes time. If you can cut the number of collections in half, you reduce the total amount of time running the collections by about half.

Fortunately, these goals are complementary. To reach these goals, adjust the heap sizes until you see a graph that validates that both have been achieved. A general recommendation for setting the young generation is about one-third to one-quarter the size of the heap. Figure 14.9 shows an ideal plot of garbage collection statistics.

Notice that, after 20 collections, the application reaches a steady state, as indicated by the nearly horizontal lines suggested by the *Before* and *After* data points. During steady state, 450MB of the heap is in use when a collection occurs, and about 200MB of space is used after the collection. Each collection is a minor collection. Heap usage remains fairly constant through the 70 collections charted. This graph is as ideal as you can get. You'd expect that if the application continued to run for several hours, or perhaps even days, that there wouldn't be a full collection.

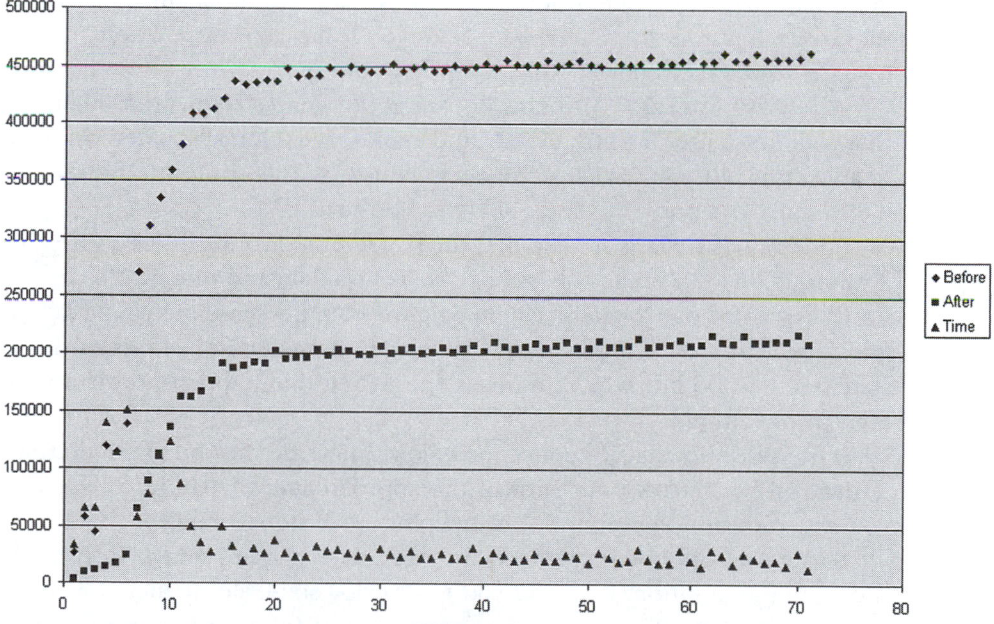

Figure 14.9 Desired garbage collection graph showing that the heap sizes before and after a collection have reached a steady state, as indicated by the nearly horizontal lines

WARNING If you see an article or paper that claims that some other technology performs better than Java EE, ask to see the Java command line used. If the young generation size hasn't been set, then the veracity of the claim is in doubt.

You might be wondering how you go about finding the ideal balance of heap size settings. Let's discuss some recommendations for setting heap sizes and look at a process for setting and adjusting the heap sizes to the ideal values for your application.

14.5.4 Choosing heap settings

Ideally, you want to allocate as much heap space to the application server as it needs but no more than that. Never set the heap to more than the available RAM on your computer—taking into account the memory used by other processes. For example, if you have 2GB of RAM and the OS and services take up 500MB, 1.5GB is the recommended maximum heap size. Additionally, 32-bit JVMs are limited on the amount of heap that can be allocated because 32-bit applications have only 2GB of data space available, some of which is occupied by system libraries. Even setting the `/3GB` boot option for Windows, or similar options for UNIX/Linux, doesn't enable you to specify a larger heap because most JVMs require contiguous memory when allocating the heap.

Although you can specify a much larger heap when using a 64-bit JVM, think twice before doing so. Allocating 20GB of heap space might seem like a good idea, but you might change your mind the first time you hit a full collection and find that the program halts for 10 or 20 minutes while the garbage collector runs. If your application requires a heap larger than 1.4GB, then you'll have to use a 64-bit JVM and set the heap to a size large enough for your application.

Where do you start? And how do you get to heap size nirvana? First, let's assume that your computer has 2GB of RAM and explore what it takes to determine the proper heap settings. If you have less memory, adjust the following numbers accordingly or install more memory (the latter being preferred).

Initially, try the largest heap that the JVM allows (around 1.4GB) with a young generation of 200MB. Gather the garbage collection data and plot it.

If the plot shows a steady state like figure 14.9, decrease the young generation size and repeat the test. Do this until you start to see major collections or that the steady state line has too much of a positive slope. When that happens, revert to the immediately prior setting.

If the plot shows major collections, slowly increase the young generation size until either you hit 500MB (one-third of the approximately 1.4GB heap, a recommended young generation-to-heap ratio) or the plot shows steady state.

Either way, once you have the young generation sized, set the heap to three times the young generation. Retest. If you lose steady state, slowly increase the heap until you have it again. The heap size is usually about three to four times the size of the young generation.

One final area to investigate is the size of the survivor spaces. The `PrintHeapAtGC` argument provides data for survivor space usage. You want to see the survivor space being anywhere from 20 to 90 percent occupied—an acceptable range. If that's what you're seeing, leave it alone. If you're seeing consistent low usage (for example, between 5 and 50 percent) or consistent high usage (for example, 90 to 99 percent), then adjust the survivor ratio until the range is acceptable. Don't forget: increasing the `SurvivorRatio` decreases the size of the survivor space and vice versa.

14.5.5 Resolving out of memory exceptions

You could get an out of memory exception for several different reasons. Your application might have a memory leak, which can occur if your application maintains references to objects that it no longer needs. As long as the application holds those references, the memory used by the objects won't be freed during a garbage collection; this applies to not only objects your application references but also any objects those objects reference. For example, assume you read-in an XML document and need to retain only one small node of data. Most likely, that node references the document root, which in turn references all the rest of the nodes in the document. Although you think you're retaining only a small portion of the XML content, you're retaining the whole document. In such a case, you should copy the required data into another object and release the whole XML document.

You can monitor the growth rate of the heap to determine if your application has a memory leak. If you see that the amount of memory in use after a full garbage collection continues to increase, then you know you have a memory leak. You can increase the heap size to forestall the problem, but the ultimate solution is to find and fix the memory leak.

If you redeploy an application to the application server often, you might eventually get an out of memory exception because the permanent generation gets filled with class objects and runs out of space. You can usually detect that the permanent generation is out of space because the heap appears to have sufficient space, and the problem usually surfaces when you redeploy an application.

You can use the `MaxPermSize` JVM argument to increase the size of the permanent generation. The default permanent generation size is usually sufficient for most needs, and the JVM will automatically adjust the permanent size if it needs more space or, even, less space. Usually, the permanent generation size remains fairly constant during the run of a Java application. If you need to set the permanent generation size, use the `PrintHeapAtGC` argument to determine the current usage of the permanent generation and then set `MaxPermSize` accordingly.

14.5.6 Exploring more tuning options

The previous sections covered the heap settings, which are the most beneficial settings when tuning a Java application. In this section, we list some other JVM command line arguments that have also proven to be beneficial.

-XX:+USESPINNING

When this option is set, if a thread finds that a resource it requires is locked, the thread goes into a busy wait (a tight loop) for a brief period to see if the resource becomes free. Although it might seem counterintuitive, on a multiprocessor machine, having the waiting thread loop for a brief time can result in better performance. Instead of having the thread give up the processor and forcing the necessary context switch to run another thread on that processor, the thread that has the resource locked might be running on another processor and soon release that resource. Don't set this option on a single-processor system.

-DSUN.RMI.DGC.CLIENT.GCINTERVAL=<INT> AND -DSUN.RMI.DGC.SERVER.GCINTERVAL=<INT>

When using RMI, which is a given when running an application server, the JVM performs a full collection every 60 seconds to free up any remote objects. Setting these system properties changes the number of milliseconds the JVM waits between performing such collections. Set these values to a large number such as 3600000 (60 minutes). You'll notice in the run scripts that these are set to 60 minutes already. Wonder how they knew to make those settings?

-XX:+DISABLEEXPLICITGC

This option forces the JVM to ignore calls to the `System.gc()` method. We discuss this further in section 14.7.1.

As you've probably noticed, you can do a lot to tune the JVM, and most of it centers around managing the heap. Now we move up to the next level in the stack—the application server.

14.6 Tuning JBoss AS

You have several opportunities for performance tuning in JBoss AS. Some of these benefit all applications, whereas others benefit only certain applications that make use of the service being tuned. Each opportunity is examined in the sections that follow.

Besides the items mentioned in this chapter, we mention several other items elsewhere in the book. One is to reduce the amount of log output; see chapter 2. Another is to remove unneeded services. Because this practice is also common in moving the server into production, we cover it in chapter 15. Yet another is to adjust the hot deployer to either turn off automatic scans or to increase the wait time between scans. See chapter 3 for details.

14.6.1 Configuring data sources

JBoss AS maintains a pool of database connections for use by applications deployed to it. In the *-ds.xml file, you can specify information about the pool size. Table 14.6 lists the pool size configuration options and how they're used.

Table 14.6 Data source pool size options

Option	Default	Description
<min-pool-size>	0	The minimum number of connections maintained to the database
<max-pool-size>	20	The maximum number of connections maintained to the database

Table 14.6 Data source pool size options *(continued)*

Option	Default	Description
`<blocking-timeout-millis>`	30 sec.	The amount of time a thread waits on a connection if all the connections are in use and the maximum connections have been allocated
`<idle-timeout-minutes>`	0	The amount of time the application server waits before deallocating a connection that's no longer needed

How big should you make the database connection pool? That depends on the application and how it's used. If each request to the application results in a database access, you need more connections than if the vast majority of requests don't access the database. Also, you don't need as many connections as users. Typically, a request holds on to a connection for a short time, so even as few as 20 connections can be sufficient to support 100 simultaneous users.

The best way to size the connection pool is to monitor the connection pool usage. When a data source is deployed, the application server creates three MBeans, one of which manages the connection pool. This MBean is named

```
Jboss.jca:name=<dsname>,service=ManagedConnectionPool
```

where `<dsname>` is the name of the data source. Monitor the key properties on this MBean, which are listed in table 14.7.

Table 14.7 Key connection pool MBean properties

Property	Description
`ConnectionCount`	The number of connections to the database
`AvailableConnectionCount`	The number of database connections not allocated to a request
`MaxConnectionsInUseCount`	The largest number of database connections ever allocated to requests
`InUseConnectionCount`	The number of database connections allocated to requests
`ConnectionCreatedCount`	The total number of connections created by the application server
`ConnectionDestroyedCount`	The total number of connections closed by the application server

If the `ConnectionCreatedCount` and `ConnectionDestroyedCount` become too high, increase the `<min-pool-size>` because the application server is spending too much time allocating, deallocating, and then reallocating connections as the number of connection requests increase and decrease. Also, increase the `<idle-timeout-minutes>` to prevent unused connections from being destroyed right before they're suddenly required again.

Don't set the pool size too high. Testing has shown that having up to 500 connections provides reasonable performance, but increasing to a higher number can adversely affect performance. Each connection in the pool uses resources in the application server and the database. Having too many connections starts to tax those resources. These recommendations are for when you have only a single data source to a single database. If you have multiple data sources or multiple databases managed by the same database server, adjust the pool sizes accordingly. For example, if the system shows performance degradation with over 500 connections and you have 2 data sources, then the maximum combined connections should be no more 500.

Finally, if your application has a consistent usage pattern, consider setting <min-pool-size> to the same value as <max-pool-size>. If not, set <min-pool-size> to handle the number of connections required when the application isn't busy.

PREPARED STATEMENT CACHE

Another configuration option in data sources is the prepared statement cache. This cache holds recently used prepared statements in case they're used again. Using a prepared statement causes the database to cache the query plan it uses to perform the query or update. Applications should always be written so that often-used SQL statements are defined using prepared statements. Table 14.8 lists the properties of the *-ds.xml configuration file that manage the prepared statement cache.

Table 14.8 Prepared statement cache properties

Option	Default	Description
<prepared-statement-cache-size>	0	The number of prepared statements to hold in the cache.
<share-prepared-statements>	False	If a request creates the same prepared statement more than once in a given request, should the same prepared statement object be used? Note that reusing the prepared statement in this case could cause the application to get unintended results if the application requested the result set from the first prepared statement after creating the second prepared statement.

Because the database also caches the SQL statements, you should coordinate the cache sizes between the database and the data source. The database typically provides statistics on the cache size and hit rates. Use that data from the database to adjust both the database and data source cache sizes.

14.6.2 Configuring the HTTP request thread pool

As with database connection pools, you can configure a pool of threads to handle HTTP requests. The HTTP request thread pool is defined in the Connector element in the server/xxx/deployer/jbossweb.sar/server.xml file. A pool exists for each connection defined. The settings of interest are listed in table 14.9.

Table 14.9 HTTP thread pool properties

Option	Default	Description
`maxThreads`	200	The maximum number of threads available to process requests. This value limits the number of requests that can be handled simultaneously.
`minSpareThreads`	4	The number of threads the web server tries to keep available above and beyond the number currently in use. The two spare threads settings are used to ensure that there are idle threads available to immediately handle future requests.
`maxSpareThreads`	50	If more threads than this are idle (not processing a request), then those threads are stopped and deallocated.
`acceptCount`	10	The maximum number of requests that can be queued, waiting for a thread to be freed. If the queue is full, the application server returns a 503 HTTP error.

Listing 14.3 shows the HTTP connector set to the default values for these properties.

Listing 14.3 Server.xml file with default thread pool property settings

```
<Server>
 . . .
 <Service name="jboss.web">
  <Connector protocol="HTTP/1.1" . . .
   maxThreads="200" minSpareThreads="4"
   maxSpareThreads="50" acceptCount="10" >
 . . .
 </Service>
</Server>
```

Although you should set `maxThreads` to a large enough number to handle your incoming requests, realize that each thread takes up system resources and each thread contends for computer resources with all the other threads. Usually, 400 threads are sufficient to handle a large number of users. If there are too many threads, performance drops. Use a combination of `maxThreads` and `acceptCount` to handle the requests.

CONFIGURING THE AJP REQUEST THREAD POOL

The AJP connector, which is defined in the server.xml file and uses port 8009 by default, also has a thread pool. Its options are the same as those for the HTTP thread pool. You should coordinate the settings for the AJP thread pool with the native web server front end such as IIS and Apache HTTP Server.

14.6.3 *Tuning the JSP servlet*

The server/xxx/deployers/jbossweb.deployer/web.xml file contains initialization parameters for the JSP servlet, `org.apache.jasper.servlet.JspServlet`. Table 14.10 lists some of the parameters that affect performance.

Table 14.10 JSP servlet properties

Parameter	Default	Description
`development`	True	If `true`, then the application server checks to see if the JSP has been updated using the modification text interval. If `false`, changed JSPs are compiled in the background using the check interval.
`checkInterval`	0	The number of seconds between checks to see if any JSPs need to be recompiled. If 0, the JSPs are never checked for changes or recompiled. Used when development is `false`.
`modificationTestInterval`	4	The number of seconds to wait before the JSP is checked for updates. If 0, the JSP is checked each time it's accessed. Used when development is `true`.
`genStrAsCharArray`	False	Generates strings as character arrays. Under some circumstances can improve performance.
`trimSpaces`	False	Removes extraneous white space from the resulting HTML text, decreasing the size of the response sent back to the client.

Listing 14.4 contains an excerpt from the web.xml file showing the declaration of the `jsp` servlet.

Listing 14.4 Web.xml file with selected tuning settings

```
<servlet>
 <servlet-name>jsp</servlet-name>
 <servlet-class>org.apache.jasper.servlet.JspServlet</servlet-class>
 . . .
 <init-param>
  <param-name>development</param-name>        ❶ Turns off
  <param-value>false</param-value>               development mode
 </init-param>
 <init-param>
  <param-name>checkInterval</param-name>        ❷ Sets modification test
  <param-value>300</param-value>                  interval to 300 seconds
 </init-param>
 . . .
</servlet>
```

Notice that development mode is turned off ❶ and a 5 minute (300 second) interval is set for rechecking the JSPs for changes ❷.

As you can see, there are a number of opportunities for tuning the application server. Now we're ready to look at the top layer of the stack—tuning the application itself.

14.7 Tuning your application

You can analyze the performance of your application use using a variety of profiling tools. These tools can identify which areas of your code could benefit from performance tuning. Both open source tools, such as the profiler that comes with IDEs (for example, NetBeans and Eclipse), and commercial tools, such as JProbe, are available. Some focus on the Java code, but others can take other parts of the system, such as the database, into account.

When using a profiler, you shouldn't run high-load tests because of the overhead of the profiler. A profiler is useful for running a handful of requests through a system and seeing the relative time those requests spend in different parts of the code. You can then pinpoint sections of your code that could benefit from improvements. When using a profiler, you might want to reduce the number of simulated users to one; otherwise, the relative times get skewed as they're divided among many threads. In general, having more than one thread also prevents you from getting useful profiling information from code that may spawn multiple execution threads.

Using a profiler and analyzing an application with it is a little beyond what we want to accomplish in this chapter. But we do want to impart some hints and tips in the sections that follow.

14.7.1 Avoiding System.gc

An application deployed to an application server should never call `System.gc()`. This method requests that the JVM perform a full garbage collection. The JVM is free to ignore this request but usually honors it. You can convince the JVM not to honor this request by using the `-XX:+DisableExplicitGC` command line argument.

There are some who recommend calling `System.gc()` at certain times during an application's execution, usually during a pause in the application or after a significant task has been finished. The theory is that if the garbage collection is performed during a quiet time that the application will be set to easily handle the next task without degrading response time. The problem with this approach in an application server is that the `System.gc()` call affects the entire application server, including all the applications deployed to it. An individual application deployed to an application server can't know when the whole application server and all its applications are in a quiescent state that warrants taking time to collect garbage.

Note that JBoss AS calls `System.gc()` at key points during initialization. It can do so because it knows the state of the applications at that time. Performing `System.gc()` during initialization makes sense because it cleans up objects necessary to start up the application server but not required to run it.

14.7.2 Taking a thread dump

Taking a thread dump helps you determine what the application server is doing at a particular moment in time. A thread dump lists all the threads in a Java application and provides a stack trace for each thread. Examining the thread dump can provide clues if the application server pauses for some reason. For example, assume that, after deploying a certain application, you find an unusual pause when the application server starts. A thread dump can help you track down the cause for the pause.

The JVM produces a thread dump when it receives a `QUIT` signal. This signal can be sent in a variety of ways but is typically sent by using a command that sends signals or by using a keystroke combination in the command window used to start the Java application. Table 14.11 lists the keystrokes and commands that are used to generate a thread dump on a variety of OSs.

Table 14.11 Taking a thread dump

OS	Keystrokes	Command
Windows	`<ctrl><break>`[a]	-none-
UNIX/Linux	`<ctrl>\`	`kill [-QUIT|-3] <process-id>`

a. In `cygwin`, this also stops the process.

You can also use another mechanism to get a thread dump: the JConsole GUI application provided with the 5.0 JDK.

USING JCONSOLE

The JConsole window contains six tabs that show various data about an application. One of those tabs, labeled Threads, provides the same information as a thread dump, as illustrated in figure 14.10.

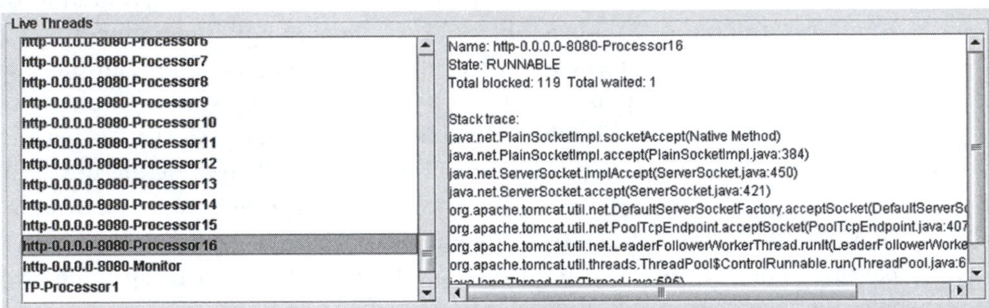

Figure 14.10 Viewing threads using JConsole

You must start the application server with the `-Dcom.sun.management.jmxremote` JVM argument to use the JConsole with the application server. You can either set the `JAVA_OPTS` environment variable or modify the run scripts. Once the application server is running, run JConsole and a dialog box appears enabling you to select the Java application to monitor. Select the application server. This technique works when JConsole and the application server run on the same computer. You can also run JConsole on a remote computer; to find out how, read the JConsole documentation.

UNDERSTANDING THREAD DUMPS

Try this. Bring up the application server but don't access it. Then take a thread dump. Notice that a lot of text is output to the command window. Either set the buffer in the command window to a large size or, when you bring up the application server, redirect the output (both standard out and standard error) to a file.

The thread dump lists every thread allocated. Each thread has a name, and most of the names provide a good hint of that thread's usage. For example, you can guess the functions of the threads named *RMI TCP Accept-4444* and *ScannerThread.* The threads at the start of the thread dump are the ones used by the application server. The threads at the end of the thread dump, from *DestroyJavaVM* on, are JVM threads. Table 14.12 lists a few threads of interest.

Table 14.12 Selected threads in a thread dump

Thread Name	Description
CompilerThread1	Used to compile Java code, usually JSPs. There could be as many of these threads as there are processors on the computer, in which case the digit at the end is different. Threads by this name aren't present when not compiling.
GC task thread#1	Used to run the garbage collection. There could be as many of these threads as there are processors on the computer, in which case the digit at the end is different. Threads by this name aren't present when not collecting garbage.
http-0.0.0.0-8080-1	Used to process requests from clients over HTTP. The IP address (0.0.0.0) changes based on the socket connection opened, and the port (8080) changes based on the HTTP port. The final digit is different for each thread handling requests.

Stack traces appear below each of the application server-related threads and a few of the JVM-related threads. Use the stack traces to determine what was going on at the time the thread dump was taken. For example, an http-0.0.0.0-8080-n thread might have a stack trace similar to the excerpt shown in listing 14.5.

Listing 14.5 Excerpt from a thread dump

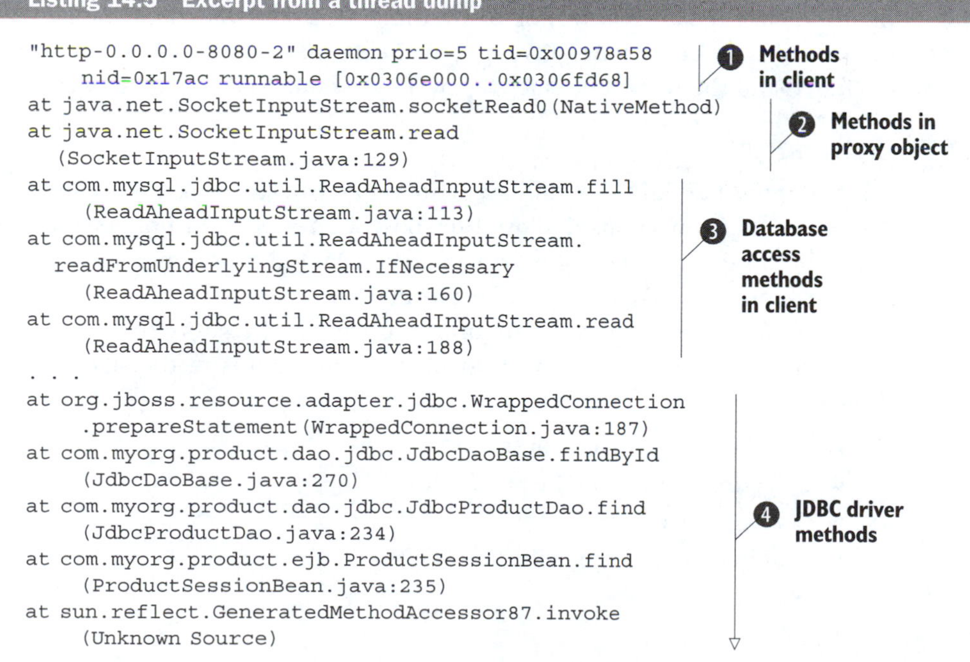

```
"http-0.0.0.0-8080-2" daemon prio=5 tid=0x00978a58
     nid=0x17ac runnable [0x0306e000..0x0306fd68]
at java.net.SocketInputStream.socketRead0(NativeMethod)
at java.net.SocketInputStream.read
   (SocketInputStream.java:129)
at com.mysql.jdbc.util.ReadAheadInputStream.fill
     (ReadAheadInputStream.java:113)
at com.mysql.jdbc.util.ReadAheadInputStream.
   readFromUnderlyingStream.IfNecessary
     (ReadAheadInputStream.java:160)
at com.mysql.jdbc.util.ReadAheadInputStream.read
     (ReadAheadInputStream.java:188)
. . .
at org.jboss.resource.adapter.jdbc.WrappedConnection
     .prepareStatement(WrappedConnection.java:187)
at com.myorg.product.dao.jdbc.JdbcDaoBase.findById
     (JdbcDaoBase.java:270)
at com.myorg.product.dao.jdbc.JdbcProductDao.find
     (JdbcProductDao.java:234)
at com.myorg.product.ejb.ProductSessionBean.find
     (ProductSessionBean.java:235)
at sun.reflect.GeneratedMethodAccessor87.invoke
     (Unknown Source)
```

```
at sun.reflect.DelegatingMethodAccessorImpl.invoke
    (DelegatingMethodAccessorImpl.java:25)
at java.lang.reflect.Method.invoke(Method.java:324)
. . .
at org.jboss.proxy.ClientContainer.invoke
    (ClientContainer.java:100)
at $Proxy64.find(Unknown Source)
at com.myorg.product.proxy.ProductProxyRemote.find
    (ProductProxyRemote.java:56)
at com.myorg.servlets.DataServletBase.doPost
    (DataServletBase.java:81)
at javax.servlet.http.HttpServlet.service
    (HttpServlet.java:717)
. . .
at org.apache.tomcat.util.net.MasterSlaveWorkerThread.run
    (MasterSlaveWorkerThread.java:112)
at java.lang.Thread.run(Thread.java:534)
```

❹ **JDBC driver methods**

❺ **Methods in socket library**

❻ **Thread identity information**

Let's examine this stack trace from the bottom to the top. The thread named http-0.0.0.0-8080-2 ❶ is processing a POST request from a client ❻. This request uses a proxy object for a remote EJB ❺ to access some data from a database using JDBC ❹. The database is MySQL ❸, and the database driver is currently waiting for the database to reply to the last request ❷.

Usually, taking one thread dump isn't sufficient. Although it provides a snapshot of what's happening at that moment, it doesn't necessarily pinpoint where a performance problem lies. Take another thread dump and, if the listed thread is still processing the request, look at what changed. If all the line numbers for each entry in the stack are the same, then the thread is still waiting for the database, in which case you should turn your attention to the database. If the line number for the `ProductSessionBean.find` method changed and everything below that line is the same, then you have a problem in the session bean code. Likewise, if the `DataServletBase.doPost` line number changed and the rest of the stack below it's the same, suspect the servlet code.

14.8 Summary

This chapter highlighted a number of areas that you can look into to improve the performance of applications deployed to JBoss AS. You should understand that performance tuning is an ongoing process, and you should have some ideas of the types of changes you can make to improve performance.

We took a holistic approach to tuning, looking at the entire software stack. We provided specific tuning areas for most of the components in the stack, including the following:

- Configuring network cards
- Selecting number and type of CPUs
- Setting processor affinity
- Monitoring garbage collection statistics
- Setting heap sizes

- Setting miscellaneous JVM options that affect performance
- Setting the various pool sizes in the application server and how to monitor the usage of the objects in the pools
- Setting miscellaneous application server options that affect performance
- Taking and interpreting a Java application stack trace

With each component finely tuned, you'll get the most performance out of the system. Also, by taking a holistic approach, you won't exert unnecessary effort in tweaking things that don't matter.

You might have noticed that we used the words *probably, usually,* and *typically* often. Because every application behaves differently, we can't tell you specifically what tuning you should do to tune your application for optimum performance. In the same way that tuning a pickup truck is different from tuning a sports car (you tune the former to improve towing power so that you can haul your boat/camper to the river/mountains/ocean, whereas you tune the latter to increase speed and acceleration), tuning one application that does one task is different from tuning another that performs some other task.

So far in this part of the book, we've covered two major topics for putting your application server into production—clustering and performance. You'll want to keep a few other things in mind when moving into production, and we cover those in the next, and final, chapter.

14.9 References

Tuning Garbage Collection with the 5.0 Java Virtual Machine—http://java.sun.com/docs/hotspot/gc5.0/gc_tuning_5.html

JConsole, Java Monitoring and Management Console—http://java.sun.com/javase/6/docs/technotes/tools/share/jconsole.html

Using JConsole to Monitor Applications—http://java.sun.com/developer/technicalArticles/J2SE/jconsole.html

15 Going to production

This chapter covers

- Selecting a platform to host JBoss AS
- Collocating multiple JBoss AS instances on the same hardware
- Removing unnecessary services
- Securing the application services
- Replacing the default Hypersonic database
- Registering the application server as a service
- Configuring JSP compilation

By this point, we hope this book has guided you through understanding the many features and idiosyncrasies of JBoss AS. We've shown you how to install JBoss AS, start it, and deploy applications into it. We've taught you how to work with the various component servers such as JBoss Web Server, the EJB server, the messaging server, and the web services container. You've also learned about the many services available to components that run in these servers, such as security, clustering, and AOP.

But if you've flipped open to this chapter, chances are that you're ready to take your application from a development environment into production. Many things in the previous chapters are useful to know when going into a production environment. For example, in the clustering chapters, we talk about deployment topologies. Picking a deployment topology and testing it for performance and scalability are important things to do before putting your application into a production environment. Enabling security and tweaking your application and server settings to enhance performance are other examples of things that must be done before going into production.

But we didn't cover everything about taking JBoss AS into a production environment in the other chapters. In this chapter, we focus on several other things important to consider for production applications, such as selecting a platform, running JBoss AS as a service, and running multiple JBoss AS instances on the same machine. We also talk about how to remove unneeded services, secure the management applications, change the default data source, and precompile JSPs.

Discussing how to select a hardware and software platform to run JBoss AS on seems like an appropriate place to start, so let's discuss that first.

15.1 Selecting a platform

Selecting a platform for development, testing, and production can be quite a daunting task. There are many decisions to make, as well as many options. Aside from selecting which version of JBoss AS you're going to use, you have to select the Java Virtual Machine (JVM), the OS, and the hardware. You also have to know how to configure each of these software and hardware components within your environment. Different components and configurations can lead to differences in performance, compatibility, reliability, and support.

15.1.1 Selecting a JVM

The JVM is a specification for an abstraction on top of a machine's hardware and OS that enables the execution of Java programs. Java programs are compiled into byte-code that can be interpreted by the virtual machine. The benefit to having a virtual machine instead of compiling code into native binaries is that the code can be more secure and portable. If you download the Java 2 Platform, Standard Edition Version 5.0 (J2SE 5.0) or the Java Standard Edition 6 (Java SE 6) from Sun, the JVM is included.

Despite having a standard specification, different vendors' JVMs can behave quite differently. The different products might have different bugs, different features, or different interpretations of ambiguities in the specification. Different vendors make JVMs, including Sun, IBM, and BEA. Sun makes the HotSpot VM which is the industry standard. You might choose the IBM VM if you're going to deploy your application on an IBM mainframe or on the AIX operating system. BEA claims that its JRockit VM has better performance and reliability on Intel platforms, and Intel seems to favor both the BEA and IBM JVMs over the Sun JVM for operation on its processors.

The Sun HotSpot JVM is installed as part of the J2SE Java Runtime Environment. You can download the installer for the either the SDK or the Java Runtime Environment (JRE). The JRE is installed as part of the SDK. JBoss AS only requires the JRE to run, but you might want to use the development tools that come with the SDK if you aren't using an IDE that has its own development tools. JBoss AS only needs JSPs to compile, but it uses the Eclipse JDT library, which is able to compile code with just a JRE.

You can evaluate these JVMs and draw your own conclusions; but, if performance isn't a concern, we recommend defaulting to the Sun HotSpot JVM because it's the most widely used, tested, and supported. The HotSpot JVM is available for Linux, Windows XP, Windows 2000, Windows NT, and Solaris. It also has support for 64-bit platforms.

JBoss AS 5 requires the Java 5 JVM at minimum. The Java 5 and Java 6 JVMs are significantly faster than previous versions and offer better support for newer libraries and APIs. We recommend going with the latest version of the Java 6 JVM; but, if you're unable to use Java 6, we strongly encourage you to select the latest version of Java 5.

JBoss AS will try to find the Java executable in the following places, in order:

- The `JAVA` environment variable
- The `JAVA_HOME` environment variable
- In a directory on your `PATH` environment variable

If the Java executable is in your path, you can check which version of Java you're running by issuing the following command at the command prompt:

```
java -version
```

If you have a `JAVA_HOME` environment variable defined, you can check the version, as follows:

```
$JAVA_HOME/bin/java -version        (on Unix)
%JAVA_HOME\bin\java -version       (on Windows)
```

The output from any of these commands is

```
java version "1.5.0_11"
Java(TM) 2 Runtime Environment, Standard Edition (build 1.5.0_11-b03)
Java HotSpot(TM) Client VM (build 1.5.0_11-b03, mixed mode, sharing)
```

This code shows you what the output might look like for the Sun's JVM, version 1.5.0. Let's talk about how to select a JBoss AS version.

15.1.2 Selecting a JBoss AS version

This book is based on JBoss AS 5, but you may not be able to use this latest version of JBoss AS in all cases. Generally, the different major versions of JBoss AS are compatible with the different J2EE (or Java EE) specifications. If you have a specific Java or J2EE version that you must remain compatible with, then you might have to choose an older version of JBoss AS. Table 15.1 shows the various JBoss AS versions and which JVMs and Java EE specifications they're associated with.

If you have no restrictions, then we recommend standardizing on JBoss AS 5, JVM 6, and Java EE 5, all of which are the latest versions of each technology available at the time this book was written. JVM 6 came out while the book was still being written; we

Table 15.1 The JVM and Java EE versions that the different JBoss AS versions support

JBoss AS version	Minimum JVM version required	J2EE/Java EE version supported
JBoss AS 3	JVM 1.3	J2EE 1.3
JBoss AS 4.0	JVM 1.4	J2EE 1.4
JBoss AS 4.2	JVM 1.5	J2EE 1.4/Java EE 5 (partial)
JBoss AS 5	JVM 1.5	Java EE 5

recommend that you use it only for JBoss AS 5 because it isn't qualified for use with earlier versions and various users have noted incompatibilities with JBoss AS 4.0.

NOTE As per the Sun web page, "The name of the Java platform for the enterprise has been simplified. Formerly, the platform was known as Java 2 Platform, Enterprise Edition (J2EE), and specific versions had 'dot numbers' such as J2EE 1.4. The '2' is dropped from the name, as well as the dot number. So the next version of the Java platform for the enterprise is Java Platform, Enterprise Edition 5 (Java EE 5)."

If you're on JBoss AS 3, we strongly encourage you to move to either JBoss AS 4 or JBoss AS 5 and switch to JVM 1.5 or JVM 1.6. If you're unable to move off of JBoss AS 4, we encourage you to try and upgrade to the latest release of JBoss AS 4.2 and switch to JVM 1.5 or JVM 1.6. If you standardize on the latest versions of both JBoss AS and the JVM, you can take advantage of the latest features and services, and you'll have an easier time migrating to future versions of each technology.

The versioning for the JBoss AS releases follows a set pattern—major branches are the first number, minor branches are the second number, and bug fix releases are the third number. For example, if you were considering using JBoss AS 5.1.2, the major branch is 5, the minor branch is 1, and the bug fix release branch is 2. Other versioning abbreviations you will run across are

- *CR*—Candidate Release (beta release)
- *DR*—Developer Release (alpha release)
- *SP*—Service Pack (patch release)
- *GA*—General Availability (final, production release)

As far as compatibility, bug-fix releases should contain only bug fixes and very minor improvements, but the JBoss AS team tends to change existing services or add new services to what could be termed bug-fix releases. For example, the plumbing to handle web services changed between 4.0.2 and 4.0.3. In many cases, you won't notice such changes; but, in the case of the web-services change, anyone using AXIS-based tools, such as AXIS-specific annotations with XDoclet, found that they could no longer compile and deploy their web services in 4.0.3. Therefore, you should thoroughly test your applications before moving up to the latest bug-fix release. We should also note that the JBoss AS team has pledged to do better in this regard, starting with the 4.2.0 release.

Minor releases are typically backward compatible, but might add new features. Backward compatibility between major versions of the JBoss AS isn't guaranteed, but migrating standard services from one version to the next is typically straightforward and mainly requires changes in configuration files. Many of the standard Java services are specified to be backward compatible, so upgrading can be quite trivial.

Upgrading JBoss AS–specific features can be more difficult than upgrading Java EE standard features, but often even these are mostly compatible. If you're using a service on one version of the JBoss ASs, that service might be replaced or updated in a future version. You might also want to update your application to take advantage of new services that a newer version of JBoss AS has to offer. In these cases, your upgrade effort might be more difficult.

UNDERSTANDING THE JBOSS ENTERPRISE APPLICATION PLATFORM (EAP)

In April of 2007, Red Hat announced a change in how the JBoss AS would be supported, using a model that Red Hat uses with its operating systems. The various JBoss projects, such as the application server, would continue to be freely available on the web and would be released as new features became available. These are the community releases, available to everyone, but provided without support. This approach is similar to the one Red Hat uses with its Fedora Core releases.

Key components are packaged together, qualified and tested, and then released under a paid support contract. These are the enterprise releases, which come with support and periodic patches to fix bugs. This approach is similar to the one Red Hat uses for its Red Hat Enterprise Linux (RHEL) releases. Table 15.2 identifies the various enterprise packages and lists the components that make up each package.

Newer platforms might contain different sets of components than what are listed in this table. Refer to the JBoss website for the exact definition of any of these platforms.

You can use the community editions for development work, and even for production, but you'll be on your own if problems come up. If you're comfortable with patching the application server or rolling your applications over to newer versions, then the community editions are for you. But, if you want more stability and prefer that someone else provide patches, then you should look into obtaining the enterprise editions.

Package name	Components
JBoss Enterprise Application Platform	JBoss AS JBoss Web Server JavaServer Faces JBoss Clustering JBoss Cache JBoss Messaging JBoss Transactions JTA Hibernate JBoss Seam
JBoss Enterprise Portal Platform	All the other components plus JBoss Portal

Table 15.2 The components that make up the Enterprise packages

15.1.3 Selecting a platform

Frequently, organizations choose a production OS and hardware for nontechnical reasons. Making these decisions for nontechnical reasons isn't unwarranted because the ability to support the environment has much to do with your current IT resources and company standards. It costs more to start supporting a technology not currently being supported within an organization.

For many applications, the technical advantages that would be evident between different hardware and OS platforms are nominal. If your application runs internal to your organization, runs behind a secure network, and doesn't necessarily need to be performant, then the OS and hardware might not matter. But, if your application runs a shopping cart that requires state management for thousands of simultaneous users, you might want a system that can support a large cache, has good memory management, can do efficient garbage collection, and has plenty of security patches in place.

WARNING Remember that End User License Agreement (EULA) that you agreed to when you first installed Windows XP or Vista (or 2000 Workstation, for that matter)? You know—the one you clicked through but didn't bother to read? Better go back and read it. It contains this little clause (actually, several of them) that effectively states that you can't host more than 10 incoming connections. If you deploy a web application, you can legally accept only 10 active users on your application. Although that number is an acceptable limit during development or for production in a small (10 people or less) office, it isn't acceptable for most enterprise software applications. To stay legal, you should deploy to Windows Server, which has no such limitation. Then again, you could always switch to Linux…

The main technical reasons for selecting one OS over another are security and performance. No matter which brand of OS you choose, the safest bet is to choose a more mature version and install all the patches and updates available from the vendor(s). Staying up to date helps minimizes security vulnerabilities. In terms of performance, you must consider how an OS manages processes/threads and memory. For many applications, you can increase your response time by caching data in memory. To handle a large in-memory cache, you need a large Java heap, which amounts to having an OS that can support large memory allocations. The largest memory allocations currently possible are available when using a 64-bit JVM, a 64-bit OS, and a 64-bit processor.

The drawback to having large memory allocations is that garbage collection becomes more costly. Multicore or dual processor CPUs can minimize the pauses that occur during garbage collection. Most JVM 5 and JVM 6 vendors have 64-bit implementations of the JVM available.

A few years ago, Intel released hyper-threading (or simultaneous multi-threading) technology into its processors. In single processor CPUs, many of the components within the processor are idle. Hyper-threading technology creates two logical processors by running multiple threads through the processor simultaneously, trying to use these idle components. Certain parts of the processor are duplicated and others are shared to facilitate multiple threads of operation. This technology is said to run faster in applications that makes use of many threads, but slower in single-threaded applications. Several hardware vendors also have multicore processors available, where there are multiple processor cores available on one processor. You must make sure that the OS that you're running supports hyper-threading and/or multiple cores if you choose to go this route.

Now that you've learned about how to select an environment, let's explore how you might run multiple JBoss AS instances on the same server.

15.2 Collocating multiple application server instances

At some point, the demands for your applications will exceed the ability of a single application server instance to handle them. For example, you might already have a large contingent of users, or the success of your business might soon cause a rapid rise in the number of visitors to your site. Either way, you should deploy a second application server. There are several ways to approach this.

First, you could purchase a new system and place another copy of the application server on that system. This is the typical usage scenario for blade systems, with a single hardware rack hosting multiple systems, each running its own application, database, or web servers.

Second, if you have a large server (say, one that has 8 CPUs), you could run virtual servers on that hardware. In this case, assuming you still have room on that server, you could easily add another virtual server on that box and deploy another instance of the application server to the new virtual server.

In either of these cases, no special configuration is required for the application server; in each case the application server runs in its own environment. We leave discussions on the pros and cons of using blades or server virtualization to the marketing departments of those companies interested in pushing one of the technologies or the other.

The third alternative, and one apropos to this chapter, is to run a second instance of the application server on the same box as an existing instance. This alternative assumes that you have a fairly decent-sized system on which you can easily run multiple application server instances. If you decide to go this route, there are a few things to keep in mind, such as the following:

- Making sure that instances do not overwrite each other's files
- Making sure that the instances don't open the same TCP ports
- Determining how to shut down each instance

These are the topics which we cover in this section.

15.2.1 Preventing file clashes

The first thing you need to realize is that you shouldn't run the same server configuration twice—that is, don't open two command prompts and enter

```
run -c myconfig
```

in both windows. The two application server instances will trip all over each other as they attempt to update the same log file, data directory, and tmp directory.

But this is a trivial problem to fix. Make a copy of your configuration directory so that you have, for example, myconfig and myconfig2. Then open two command prompts and in one enter

```
run -c myconfig
```

and in the other enter

```
run -c myconfig2
```

Now, each one uses its own configuration, which uses its own directory tree. Result: no more file clashes.

15.2.2 Preventing port clashes

If you literally followed the steps in the previous section, you'll have run into the second clash—both application server instances are attempting to use the same ports. Two mechanisms you can use to avoid a port clash are assigning different port numbers or binding to different host addresses. We cover the port binding mechanisms first and then host-address binding.

CONFIGURING PORTS

Quite a few services in the application server open ports: the HTTP port, the HTTPS port, JNDI, remoting, and so on. The ports these services use are defined in the server/xxx/conf/bindings.xml file. If you examine this file, you'll find a bean named `PortsDefaultBindings`, which has entries similar to the one shown in listing 15.1.

Listing 15.1 Port assignment example from bindings.xml

```
<bean name="PortsDefaultBindings"...>
 <constructor>
  <parameter>
   <set>
    <bean class="org.jboss.services.binding.ServiceBinding">
     <constructor>
      <parameter>jboss:service=Naming</parameter>      <-- Identifies name for port
      <parameter>Port</parameter>
      <parameter>${jboss.bind.address}</parameter>
      <parameter>1099</parameter>
     </constructor>
    </bean>
 . . .
```

This example entry defines the JNDI port used by the naming service. The naming service is defined in the server/xxx /deploy/naming-jboss-beans.xml file, which references the port defined in bindings.xml. Listing 15.2 illustrates the reference.

Listing 15.2 Reference JNDI port from naming service

```
<bean name="RemoteNamingBean" ...>
 ...
 <property name="port">
```

```
<value-factory bean="ServiceBindingManager"
           method="getIntBinding">
  <parameter>jboss:service=Naming</parameter>
  <parameter>Port</parameter>
 </value-factory>
</property>
...
```

❶ References port by name

The naming service identifies the port to use by its name in the bindings.xml file: `jboss:service=Naming` ❶. This pattern of defining the ports and their names in bindings.xml and referencing those names in the various *-service.xml configuration files for the various services is repeated for most of the ports.

One major exception is the ports defined for HTTP, HTTPS, and AJP. Those ports are handled by a transform defined by the `JBossWebConnectorXSLTConfig` bean at the end of the bindings.xml file. The transform is applied to the server/xxx/deploy/jbosssweb.sar/server.xml file. Although you could change the ports in server.xml, we recommend that you modify the ports in bindings.xml if you need to change the port assignments.

Now that you know how port assignments are made, you're probably wondering how to best assign different ports to your two application server instances. One way is to change the port numbers for each port in the `PortsDefaultBindings` bean for the second server. But there's an easier way. After the `PortsDefaultBindings` bean in the bindings.xml file, you'll find a `Ports01Bindings` bean, as shown in listing 15.3.

Listing 15.3 `Ports01Bindings` bean in bindings.xml

```
<bean name="Ports01Bindings" ...>
 <constructor>
  <parameter><inject bean="PortsDefaultBindings"/></parameter>
  <parameter>100</parameter>
  ...
 </constructor>
</bean>
```

The first parameter to the `Ports01Bindings` constructor is the `PortsDefaultBindings` bean. The second parameter, `100`, defines the increment to use when setting the port numbers. In this case, 100 is added to each port number. For example, the JNDI port becomes 1199. Another bean, named `Ports02Bindings`, adds 200 to each port number. You can declare other beans in the bindings.xml file to use other port number increments.

Earlier in the bindings.xml file, you'll find the `ServiceBindingManager` bean, which manages all the port bindings. The declaration for this bean is shown in listing 15.4.

Listing 15.4 `ServiceBindingManager` bean in bindings.xml

```
<bean name="ServiceBindingManager"...>
 <constructor>
  <parameter>${jboss.service.binding.set:ports-default}
➥ </parameter>
```

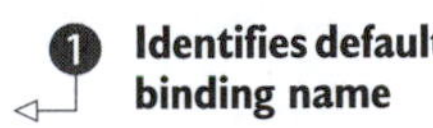

```
<parameter>
 <bean name="ServiceBindingStore"...>
  <constructor>
   <parameter>
    <map keyClass="java.lang.String"
        valueClass="java.util.Set">
     <entry>
      <key>ports-default</key>
      <value><inject bean="PortsDefaultBindings"/>
      </value>
     </entry>
     <entry>
      <key>ports-01</key>
      <value><inject bean="Ports01Bindings"/>
      </value>
     </entry>
     <entry>
      <key>ports-02</key>
      <value><inject bean="Ports02Bindings"/>
      </value>
     </entry>
    </map>
   </parameter>
  </constructor>
 </bean>
</parameter>
</constructor>
</bean>
```

❷ **Maps binding names to bindings**

The ServiceBindingManager bean contains a table that maps binding names, such as ports-01, to the binding beans we discussed earlier, such as Port01Bindings ❷. The ServiceBindingManager bean is also told which binding to use by default ❶. Notice that the default binding name is set to the value of the jboss.service.binding.set system property, with ports-default being used if that property isn't set.

To use the port assignments defined by the Ports01Bindings bean, set the jboss.service.binding.set system property to ports-01 when starting the application server. Continuing our earlier example, you'd start myconfig2 as follows:

```
run -c myconfig2 -Djboss.service.binding.set=ports-01
```

The application server uses port numbers that are 100 higher than the default port numbers to avoid conflicting port assignments when running both the myconfig and myconfig2 configurations.

BINDING TO A HOSTNAME

When you bring up the server, which IP address does it use? By default, it uses 127.0.0.1 (or ::1 if you're using IPv6), also known as localhost. But there might come a time when you want to enable access to the application server from other computers. You can accomplish this by binding the application server ports to a particular address, an approach also known as multihoming.

Down at the socket layer, binding a port requires two pieces of information: the port number and the IP address. As we said, when you start the application server, it typically binds all ports to IP address 127.0.0.1. You could, instead, bind it to the IP address 0.0.0.0 (::/128 in IPv6). This special address means "bind to all IP addresses defined to the system." If you bind to 0.0.0.0 and have a single network card and have only a single IP address on that card, all ports are bound to that one IP address. Well, not quite; you actually have two IP addresses: the one we mentioned, which is typically assigned by the Dynamic Host Configuration Protocol (DHCP) server, and 127.0.0.1, which stands for localhost and is assigned automatically.

NOTE If an award were given for the most asked question in the JBoss forums, it would go to: "Why can I access my web application using http://localhost:8080, but not when using http://myhostname:8080?" Prior to JBoss AS 4.2, the application server bound to IP address 0.0.0.0 by default; but, starting with 4.2 and continuing into 5.0, it binds to 127.0.0.1 instead, making the application server a little more secure out of the box. At one point, at least a dozen messages a week appeared with this question; and, even over a year later, there are still a few posts each week with this question—despite the fact that this configuration change, and how to deal with it, is clearly documented in the release notes that accompany the JBoss AS download, and that this issue is addressed in a FAQ on the JBoss wiki, and that there are hundreds of similar questions, all answered, on the forum.

But, if you have virtual IP addresses (multiple IP addresses for your network card) or multiple network cards, then using 0.0.0.0 as the IP address results in the ports being bound to all IP addresses. Sometimes you want this; for example, you have two network cards, and you want to access HTTP requests from both cards. Other times you don't want this; for example, you have two network cards, and you want to accept HTTP requests on only one card because the other card is connected to a database server and handles only database traffic. In this case, you don't have a reason to bind to the IP address on that second network card for HTTP requests.

To bind the application server to a particular IP address, use the `-b` option to specify the address

```
run -b <ip-address>
```

where <ip-address> is the desired IP address or hostname. For example, to bind to all IP addresses, use the following:

```
run -b 0.0.0.0
```

As another example, if the network card that accepts HTTP requests has IP address 192.168.0.100, enter

```
run -b 192.168.0.100
```

You need to be aware of one small caveat when binding to a specific IP address, such as 192.168.0.100: you can't access applications via a browser on the same system by using localhost as the hostname. For example, entering the URL

http://localhost:8080/jmx-console

doesn't bring up the JMX Console. Instead, you get an error. Why? Because localhost is IP address 127.0.0.1, and the application server doesn't bind to that IP address. Requests to that address fail. If the system is named myserver, with an IP address of 192.168.0.100, you can enter either of the following URLs to access the JMX Console:

http://myserver:8080/jmx-console
http://192.168.0.100:8080/jmx-console

As an example, let's assume you have configured two IP addresses: 192.168.0.100 and 192,168.0.101. To start both application servers, run these commands, each from its own command line:

```
run -b 192.168.0.100 -c myconfig
run -b 192.168.0.101 -c myconfig2
```

Each application server binds to its own IP address. In addition, each application server can use the same ports. For example, both can use port 8080 for HTTP requests. There's no conflict in this case because each port is bound to a different IP address.

Before we look at how to stop multiple servers, let's take a detour as we show you how to set up virtual IP addresses on your system.

DEFINING VIRTUAL IP ADDRESSES

You can define virtual IP addresses in Windows using the Advanced TPC/IP Settings dialogbox. To get to this dialog box, select Network Connections from the Control Panel, right-click the desired connection (each network card will have its own connection), select the Internet Protocol (TCP/IP) item (it might be called Internet Protocol Version 4 (TCP/IPv4) or Internet Protocol Version 6 (TCP/IPv6)) in the list of items used by that connection, and click the Properties button. On the Internet Protocol Properties dialog box, choose the Use The Following IP Address option, and then click the Advanced button. On the Advanced TCP/IP Settings dialog box, you can add additional IP addresses for the network card. We recommend that you use an IP address on the same subnet and that you first ensure that no one else on that subnet is using the same IP address. The progression through the various dialog boxes is illustrated in figure 15.1.

Note that you can't use DHCP to assign IP addresses if you want to define virtual IP addresses. Before you follow these steps, you might want to run the command `ipconfig /all` from a command prompt to get the existing IP configuration information such as your assigned IP address, the DNS IP address, the subnet mask, and so on. You'll have to enter that information into the Properties dialog box if you expect your network connection to continue working as normal.

If you'd like to use textual hostnames instead of numerical IP addresses, you can define hostnames in the c:\Windows\System32\drivers\etc\hosts file, as shown in listing 15.5.

Listing 15.5 Windows hosts file showing hostnames for virtual IP addresses

```
192.168.0.100   server1
192.168.0.101   server2
```

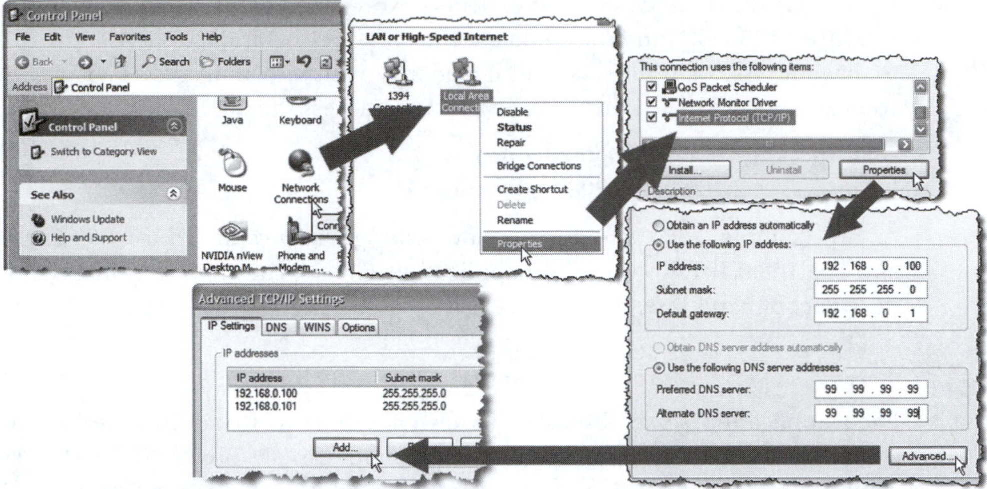

Figure 15.1 The progression of dialog boxes needed to define virtual IP addresses in Windows.

You can then use the hostname, such as `server1`, with the `-b` option to the run script in place of the IP address 192.168.0.100.

NOTE The text on configuring multiple IP address was tested on Fedora 8 and Ubuntu 8.04. Other Linux distros might provide alternate means to configure such addresses. Consult the documentation for your Linux distro for details.

You can use several mechanisms to define virtual addresses in Linux. You can use the `ifconfig` command to create a temporary virtual IP address. This address will be valid until you reboot your system or until you restart the network service. You should first run the command `ifconfig -a` to see what network interfaces are available. You'll see results that look like this:

```
>ifconfig -a
eth0     Link encap:Ethernet  HWaddr 00:12:34:56:78:9A
       inet addr:192.168.0.101  Mask:255.255.255.0 ...
. . .
```

The text `eth0` identifies an interface. You can define additional interfaces for the same network adaptor by appending a colon and a digit to the name—for example, `eth0:1` or `eth0:2`. To define an interface that uses the virtual IP address of 192.168.0.101, you could enter

```
ifconfig eth0:1 192.168.0.101 netmask 255.255.255.0 up
```

Alternately, if you're using Fedora or Red Hat Enterprise Linux you can identify permanent virtual IP addresses for your network controllers by providing network interface configuration files in the /etc/sysconfig/network-scripts directory. This directory already contains a file named ifcfg-eth0, which configures the `eth0` interface. Listing 15.6 shows an example of the contents of that file.

Listing 15.6 The ifconfig-eth0 file before editing it to support multiple IP addresses

```
# <Text that identifies the controller hardware>
DEVICE=eth0
BOOTPROTO=dhcp
ONBOOT=yes
HWADDR=00:12:34:56:78:9a
TYPE=Ethernet
```

First, you need to configure the existing interface to use a hardcoded IP address. As on Windows, using virtual IP addresses won't work with DHCP. Look back at the results from running `ifconfig -a`; the information you need for the configuration appears there. Listing 15.7 shows the updated ifcfg-eth0 file.

Listing 15.7 The ifcfg-eth0 file after editing it to support multiple IP addresses

```
# <Text that identifies the controller hardware>
DEVICE=eth0
IPADDR=192.168.0.100
NETMASK=255.255.255.0
GATEWAY=192.59.193.250
ONBOOT=yes
HWADDR=00:12:34:56:78:9a
TYPE=Ethernet
```

The ifcfg-eth0 file now has a hardcoded IP address. Now, copy this file as ifcfg-eth0:1 and change it as shown in listing 15.8.

Listing 15.8 The ifcfg-eth0:1 file that defines an additional IP address

```
# <Text that identifies the controller hardware>
DEVICE=eth0:1
IPADDR=192.168.0.101
NETMASK=255.255.255.0
GATEWAY=192.59.193.250
ONBOOT=yes
TYPE=Ethernet
```

Note that the IP address is changed and that the HWADDR entry no longer appears. If you retain the HWADDR entry, you might get only one IP address, typically the one defined in the last configuration file processed. After you create this second file, you can either reboot the system or restart the network service to register the additional network interfaces.

You can perform similar configuration magic on Ubuntu by editing the /etc/network/interfaces file, providing similar information to what we've mentioned. We refer you to the Ubuntu documentation for further details.

If you'd like to use textual hostnames instead of numerical IP addresses, you can define hostnames in the /etc/hosts file. The entries you need to make are the same as given for the Windows hosts file in listing 15.3.

Now that you know how to define multiple IP addresses and run multiple instances of the application server, each on a different IP address, you might be wondering how you shut the application servers down. We cover that next.

15.2.3 Shutting down multiple nodes

If you run each instance from a command line, type CTRL-C in each command window to bring the application server down. The application server registers a CTRL-C handler that performs an orderly shutdown, or you can use the shutdown scripts (`shutdown.bat` or `shutdown.sh`) to shut down each application server.

The shutdown scripts require that you know the hostname and the JNDI port number because they use that port number to look up the `MBeanServerConnection` object. For example, if you have two application server instances running on localhost using ports 1099 and 1199 for JNDI, you can stop both by entering

```
shutdown -s localhost:1099 -S
shutdown -s localhost:1199 -S
```

As another example, if you have two application servers bound to their own IP addresses, say 192.168.0.100 and 192.168.0.101, and both using the default JNDI port, you can stop both by entering

```
shutdown -s 192.168.0.100:1099 -S
shutdown -s 192.168.0.101:1099 -S
```

Now that you know how to work with multiple application server instances, let's turn our attention to the next topic on our going-into-production list: slimming down the application server.

15.3 Removing unwanted services

Modularity is one of the greatest features of the JBoss AS architecture. You can pick and choose which components you require, and build a configuration containing those pieces. The easiest way to do this is to use the JEMS Installer and pick only those services that you need. The installer is intelligent enough to determine any dependencies of your desired services and automatically installs those also. Alternately, if you've installed the binary distribution, you can start with a configuration that has more than what you need and remove the pieces that you don't want.

Why should you remove unneeded services? The main reason is for security. If an unneeded service opens a port, one more entry point is available to a hacker. Another reason is for performance. Services take up memory and processor time. Every service is deployed and initialized, slowing down the boot process and allocating objects, some of which aren't deallocated until the server is shut down. Additionally, some services occasionally wake up to perform periodic tasks, taking processor time away from deployed applications.

How should you go about removing unneeded services? First, choose one of the existing configurations. The primary difference between the all and default configurations is that the all configuration handles clustering and the default configuration doesn't. If you need clustering, start with the all configuration. If you don't need clustering, start with default. Once you've selected a configuration, you can remove the files used by services you don't require.

Table 15.3 lists various services that you can remove by deleting files and directories from the server/xxx/deploy and server/xxx/lib directories. There are, of course, other services that can be removed beyond those listed here.

Table 15.3 Removing unneeded services

Service	Delete these files/directories
Mail service	server/xxx/deploy/mail-service.xml server/xxx/lib/mail*.jar
Scheduler service	server/xxx/deploy/scheduler-service.xml server/xxx/deploy/schedule-manager-service.xml server/xxx/lib/scheduler-plugin*.jar
Monitoring service	server/xxx/deploy/monitoring-service.xml server/xxx/lib/Jboss-monitoring.jar
Messaging (JMS) service	server/xxx/deploy/messaging server/xxx/deploy/jms-ra.rar server/xxx/lib/jboss-messaging*.jar
Unique ID key generator	server/xxx/deploy/uuid-key-generator.sar server/xxx/lib/autonumber-plugin.jar
HTTP Invoker service	server/xxx/deploy/http-invoker.sar server/all/deploy/httpha-invoker.sar (only in the *all* configuration)
Home page	server/xxx/deploy/ROOT.war
JMX Console	server/xxx/deploy/jmx-console.war
Web Console	server/xxx/deploy/management
Quartz scheduler service	server/xxx/deploy/quartz-ra.rar

You might want use some of these services or applications, such as JMS and the JMX Console, in production. If you're going to use them, you should secure them to prevent unauthorized access.

15.4 Securing the server applications

Many people prefer not to run the prepackaged applications that ship with the application server in a production environment. Others want to be able to access the applications, but restrict that access to certain users or to users that have access to the physical server. These applications include the JMX Console, the Web Console, and the root web application. You can handle securing these applications in several ways, but here are the three most common:

- Removing the applications from the deploy directory
- Adding security to the applications
- Only allowing them to be accessed from the local machine

Let's talk about how to remove the applications from the deploy directory first.

15.4.1 Removing the server applications

If you don't need to run the server applications, you can remove them altogether. Each of the console applications is deployed as a package in the deploy directory. All you have to do is delete the correct directories and the applications are removed. Table 15.3, in the previous section, identifies which directories you should delete to remove these applications.

In chapter 5, we gave you other options for changing the root context, so if you don't want to remove the root application, you can refer there to see your other options.

If you'd rather keep the server applications available for people to access, but want to limit who can access them, you can enable security on them. Let's discuss how.

15.4.2 Adding security to the server applications

In chapter 4, we discussed how to define security domains, and in chapter 6, we discussed how to secure web applications and bind them to security domains. These chapters should give you enough background to add security to the console applications.

One thing to note is that the Web Console and the JMX Console have already done some of the legwork for you as far as enabling security. If you look in the WEB-INF directory under both of these applications, you'll see that they already have jboss-web.xml files defined with security domain references. But, because JBoss AS has security disabled by default, these security domain references are commented out. You should enable them to secure the server applications.

The security domains that these references point to (when uncommented) are already defined in the server's server/xxx/conf/login-config.xml file. In this file, you'll find both a `jmx-console` and a `web-console` security domain defined. They're both set up to use the `UsersRolesLoginModule`. The `jmx-console` security domain points to security data files in the server/xxx/conf/props directory. The `web-console` points to the security data files in the Web Console's WEB-INF/classes directory. The Web Console WAR package can be found at server/xxx/deploy/management/console-mgr.sar/web-console.war.

Aside from enabling the security domain reference in the jboss-web.xml file, you should enable the security restrictions in each application's web.xml file. The security restrictions are already available in these files also, but again, they're commented out. You can uncomment the `security-constraint` block at the bottom of each file.

15.4.3 Limiting access to the local machine

In chapter 5, we showed you how to create virtual hosts to which you could bind applications. You can create a virtual host that binds to the loopback alias available on many OS's. A loopback alias is a self-referencing name an OS defines that can be accessed only from the machine on which the OS is running.

Creating a virtual host for the loopback alias and binding an application to it allows you to limit access to the application to loopback traffic only, allowing you to access the application when you are physically accessing the machine, but not from remote machines. Restricting access in this way is useful for things such as the management console; you wouldn't want external users to be able to access this service, but you might want it running on the box so that you can monitor the system while in production.

If you want to do this, you set up a virtual host in Tomcat's server.xml file that looks something like this:

```
<Host name="loopback" autoDeploy="false"
    deployOnStartup="false" deployXML="false">
</Host>
```

You'll also have to set the `useIPVHosts` attribute to `true` on the connector that you're using (as discussed in chapter 5).Then, point your application to this virtual host by adding the following in the application's WEB-INF/jboss-web.xml file:

```
<jboss-web>
  <virtual-host>loopback</virtual-host>
</jboss-web>
```

Another common thing that you'll do when you go to production is change the default database configured for the server. Let's look at how to do this.

15.5 Changing the default database

The application server requires a database for a variety of the services that it provides. For this purpose, it comes with the Hypersonic SQL database (HSQLDB) which is an in-memory, pure Java database. Although Hypersonic is an acceptable database for development purposes, you should replace it before going into production. And, because it's so simple to replace, if you're comfortable using another database such as MySQL or PostgreSQL, or if your application will make use of features of a specific database such as Oracle, you might consider replacing Hypersonic even during development.

Switching from Hypersonic to another database requires several steps. First, you have to create a database. Because this involves database-specific steps, we refer you to the documentation for your database for performing this step. When you do this, you should record the database name, user id, and password because you'll need these in the next step.

Second, you need to create a data source descriptor file, *-ds.xml. You can have all services and applications use the same database or configure each one to use a different database. Declare the data sources you need and configure the applications and services accordingly.

Third, you need to change the configuration files for all applications that use Hypersonic to use the new database. There are two ways to accomplish this. First, when you defined the data source in the previous step, you could've named the new data source DefaultDS. If you do that, all services that used the Hypersonic database now use the new database because all application and services refer to a database via the data source JNDI name.

The second way to get the services to use the new data source is to change their configuration files to reference the new data source. Table 15.4 lists the services that use the DefaultDS data source and the configuration files that you have to change to use a different data source.

Table 15.4 Services that use the DefaultDS datasource

Service	Configuration file
Login modules	server/xxx/conf/login-config.xml
Container-Managed Persistence (EJB 2.x)	server/xxx/conf/standardjbosscmp-jdbc.xml
Timer service (EJB 2.x)	server/xxx/deploy/ejb2-timer-service.
Timer service (EJB 3)	server/xxx/deploy/ejb3-timer-service.xml
Schedule manager service	server/xxx/deploy/schedule-manager-service.xml
Messaging service	server/xxx/deploy/messaging/hsqldb-persistence-service.xml server/xxx/deploy/messaging/messaging-jboss-beans.xml
Universal Description, Discovery, and Integration (UDDI) service	server/xxx/deploy/juddi-service.sar/juddi.war/WEB-INF/jboss-web.xml server/xxx/deploy/juddi-service.sar/META-INF/jboss-service.xml
Simple Network Management Protocol (SNMP) Adaptor service	server/xxx/deploy/snmp-adaptor.sar/attributes.xml
Universally Unique ID (UUID) Key Generator service	server/xxx/deploy/uuid-key-generator.sar/META-INF/jboss-service.xml

Because the configuration files in the application server tend to change as new technologies come along and as the server is modified, you should do a text search on DefaultDS to locate all occurrences that you need to change.

Also, remove the server/xxx/deploy/hsqldb-ds.xml file. This step is crucial if, in the previous step, you named the new data source DefaultDS. But even if you went with a different name, we still recommend you remove this file so that the Hypersonic database isn't initialized. Finally, you also remove the Hypersonic JAR files, server/xxx/lib/hsqldb*.jar.

For most of the services listed in table 15.4, following these steps is sufficient. But a few services and applications require more changes. We described how to configure the messaging service to use another database in chapter 8, "JBoss Messaging" (section 8.5.1). This leaves one more service that needs special attention: the EJB3 timer service.

15.5.1 Configuring the EJB3 timer service

The EJB3 timer service uses the Quartz job scheduler from Open Symphony. The implementation of Quartz provided with JBoss AS assumes that Hypersonic will be used as the database, but the Quartz job scheduler was designed to be used with a variety of databases. So the task then becomes applying the necessary Quartz changes to the existing EJB3 timer service.

The first thing you'll need to do is download the Quartz source file that corresponds to the version provided by JBoss AS. You can determine the Quartz version by examining the META-INF/Manifest.mf file located in the server/xxx/lib/quartz.jar file.

With the Quartz source code at hand, you need to change two things in the server/xxx/deploy/ejb3-timer-server.xml file.

First, the ejb3-timer-server.xml file contains a list of Quartz properties. You're interested in this property:

```
org.quartz.jobStore.driverDelegateClass=
➥   org.quartz.impl.jdbcjobstore.HSQLDBDelegate
```

You need to change the delegate class to match the one for your database. The valid delegates can be found in the src/java/org/quartz/impl/jdbcjobstore directory of the Quartz source. For example, use the `PostgreSQLDelegate` class for a PostgreSQL database. If there's no delegate specific to your database, as is the case for MySQL, use the `StdJDBCDelegate` class. For example, for MySQL this delegate property would be

```
org.quartz.jobStore.driverDelegateClass=
➥   org.quartz.impl.jdbcjobstore.StdJDBCDelegate
```

The second change is more complicated. The `SqlProperties` attribute in the ejb3-timer-server.xml file contains a list of SQL statements used to create and initialize the tables in the database. You need to replace these SQL statements with the ones for your database. You can find the correct statements in the Quartz sources in the docs/dbTables directory. For example, use the tables_postgres.sql file for a PostgreSQL database.

When replacing the SQL statements, leave the `CREATE_*` property name on the line. For example, the property to create the job details table would look like

```
CREATE_TABLE_JOB_DETAILS = CREATE TABLE qrtz_job_details(...);
```

where the `CREATE TABLE qrtz_job_details(...);` text comes from the tables_*.sql file for your database.

For MySQL users, note that the tables_mysql.sql file uses uppercase letters for the table names. If you're running MySQL on Unix/Linux, make sure you make that change because MySQL table names are case sensitive on those platforms.

With these changes made to the EJB3 timer service, along with the other changes mentioned earlier in this section, the application server is now using a database other than Hypersonic.

15.6 Starting the application server as a service

In chapter 1, "Vote for JBoss," we showed you how to start the application server using the run scripts provided by the application server. Although this is sufficient for development work, in a production environment, you want the application server to come up at the same time the system is started. The system administrator is bound to give you a weird look if you tell her that the only way to get the application server running is to first log into the system, open a command line, and then run an application server–specific script. But never fear; with a little bit of configuration magic, the application server can be established as a system service that comes up automatically when the system is booted. Additionally, the system administrator can bring the application server up or down using the same system tools she currently uses to control other services. Let's look at how to do this for Windows and then for Linux after that. Note to our Linux readers: You'll still want to read about setting up a Windows service because we cover JBoss Native in that section.

15.6.1 Registering a service in Windows

Windows defines a specific API that must be implemented by an application that wishes to run as a service. Unfortunately, none of the Java executables implement that API. Fortunately, that fact isn't a problem because Java SE defines a standard API, the Java Native Interface (JNI), that establishes how Java code and C/C++ code interact. You're probably familiar with using JNI to access C functions from Java code, but you can also use JNI to enable C applications to host the JVM.

In fact, this is exactly how the various Java executables work. If you look in the JDK bin directory, you'll notice that all the executables are fairly small and are all almost the exact same size. These are all small C programs that take command-line parameters, load the JVM library (jvm.dll or jvm.so), and then call specific JNI functions to start the Java program. If you want to see this in action, set the `_JAVA_LOADER_DEBUG` environment variable (any value will do) and then run a Java application. You'll see output from the executable as it performs the previously mentioned steps. And another piece of trivia: All the Java executables originate from the same source code; compile-time options determine the slight variations used to create each executable.

All that's required to run a Java application as a Windows service is to provide a simple executable that follows the Windows service API specification and uses the JNI specification, or some other mechanism, to launch the JVM and the Java application. Because this is a fairly generic task, you probably expect that someone has done this already. And they have. The JBoss team provides such a tool as part of the JBoss Native package, which is part of the JBoss Web project.

USING THE JBOSS NATIVE WINDOWS SERVICE

The JBoss Native download is available at http://www.jboss.org/jbossweb/downloads/. Note that there are several variants, each for a specific OS and CPU type. Make sure you get the one that matches your platform. For example, if you're running the 64-bit version of Windows Server 2003 on an AMD or Intel EM64T CPU, download the package described as Windows 64 AMD64/EM64T Package.

Then unzip the file into your JBOSS_HOME directory. This action adds several files and a directory to the bin directory. Congratulations! You've now installed the Apache Portable Runtime files, which will improve the performance of HTTP/HTTPS requests; those requests can now be handled in native code. In addition, you'll no longer see this warning during startup:

```
INFO  [AprLifecycleListener] The Apache Tomcat Native
library which allows optimal performance in production environments
was not found on the java .library.path: .;C:\WINDOWS\system32;...
```

Note to our Linux readers: You're now excused; you may skip down to the section on setting up the Linux service.

The downloaded files in the bin directory include a readme file that describes how to install the service. It's simple—run the following command from the bin directory:

```
service install
```

This command installs a service whose short name is JBAS50SVC, and long name is JBoss Application Server 5.0. The service is set up to start automatically when the system is booted. You can use the typical Windows mechanisms, such as the Services control panel, the net command and the Get-Service cmdlet in the Windows PowerShell, to manage the service. For example, to start the service using the net command, enter the following at a command line:

```
net start jbas50svc
```

To stop the service using the Get-Service cmdlet, open a PowerShell window and enter

```
(get-service jbas50svc).stop()
```

This is all fine and good, but what if you want to run multiple application servers as services? Glad you asked.

15.6.2 Registering multiple services

To understand how to set up multiple application servers as services, you must first understand how JBoss Native handles running the application server as a service. It's very simple. An executable named jbosssvc.exe handles the requirements of the Windows service API. This executable, when asked to start the service, executes the service.bat file, which runs the run.bat file, which runs the application server. This sequence is illustrated in figure 15.2.

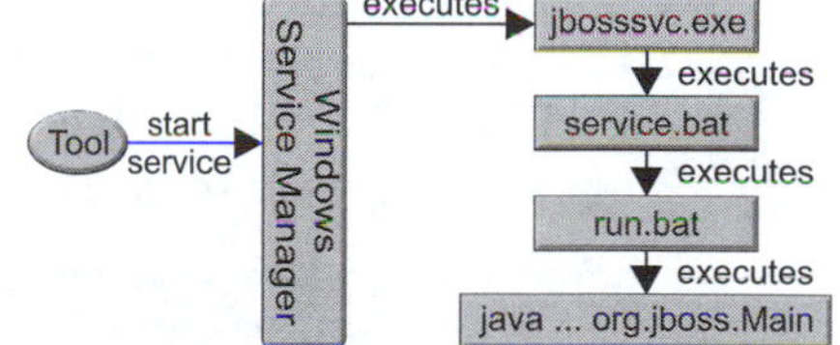

Figure 15.2 To start the application server service, the jbosssvc.exe excutable runs the service.bat script, which runs the run.bat script, which runs the application server.

This architecture gives you a lot of leeway in how to set up multiple services. We describe one such approach; you are, of course, free to try others.

We stated that the jbosssvc.exe executable runs the service.bat script. It knows to do that by the following entry in the service.bat file, which is part of the service installation process:

```
:cmdInstall
jbosssvc.exe -imwdc %SVCNAME% "%DIRNAME%" "%SVCDISP%"
➥                    "%SVCDESC%" service.bat
if not errorlevel 0 goto errExplain
echo Service %SVCDISP% installed
goto cmdEnd
```

That last parameter passed to jbosssvc.exe is the batch file to run. The service.bat script knows to start the run.bat script due to the following lines in service.bat:

```
:cmdStart
REM Executed on service start
. . .
call run.bat < .r.lock >>run.log 2>&1
. . .
goto cmdEnd
```

And service.bat script knows to use the shutdown.bat script to stop the service due to the following lines:

```
:cmdStop
REM Executed on service stop
. . .
call shutdown -S < .s.lock >>shutdown.log 2>&1
. . .
goto cmdEnd
```

There's also a restart option in service.bat, but we leave you to examine that. You now have enough information to determine how to configure multiple services. For the example, you'll define two services: Portal and Accounting.

The first step is to define to application server configurations. We covered this topic earlier in section 15.2. For our example, we assume that you've created two configurations named portal (%JBOSS_HOME%\server\portal) and accounting (%JBOSS_HOME%\server\accounting) and that you've resolved the port binding issues. Make sure that you can successfully run these configurations manually before setting them up as services.

Next, make two copies of service.bat as service_portal.bat and service_accounting.bat. Listing 15.9 shows the changes you need to make to service_accounting.bat; make similar changes to service_portal.bat.

Listing 15.9 Modifications to service_accounting.bat for the accounting service

```
...
set SVCNAME=ACCOUNTING     ❶
set SVCDISP=JBoss AS - Accounting app     ❷
set SVCDESC=Runs JBoss AS with the accounting app     ❸
set JBOSSOPT=-c accounting -b YYY     ❹
set JBOSSSTOP=-s XXX     ❺
set JAVA_HOME=C:\apps\jdk1.5.0_16     ❻
...
:cmdInstall
jbosssvc.exe -imwdc %SVCNAME% "%DIRNAME%" "%SVCDISP%"
➥              "%SVCDESC%" service_accounting.bat     ❼
...
:cmdStart
call run.bat %JBOSSOPT% >run_acct.log 2>>&1     ❽
...
:cmdStop
call shutdown %JBOSSSTOP% -S >shutdown_acct.log 2>>&1     ❾
...
```

```
:cmdRestart
call shutdown %JBOSSSTOP% -S >shutdown_acct.log 2>>&1        ❾
call run.bat %JBOSSSTOP% >>run_acct.log 2>>&1        ❽
...
```

The first three changes provide the service short name ❶, long name ❷, and description ❸. The values of the variables are arbitrary, so you can use any values you like. Be careful to use a valid name for the service and make sure that it isn't the same as an existing service. The next three lines are new. The application server is started and stopped in two locations, so it makes sense to define the start ❹ and stop ❺ options only once. In this example, the binding address (-b YYY) and the server URL (-S XXX) are undefined; you can set them based on your environment. The `JAVA_HOME` variable ❻ is declared to ensure that the application server is started with the desired JVM. Setting `JAVA_HOME` isn't necessary if it's already defined among the system environment variables.

The command that installs the service identifies the service_accounting.bat file as the script to run to manage the service ❼. The commands to start ❽ and stop ❾ the application server use the environment variables defined earlier. Note that they also redirect standard output and error to log files specific to the service.

When both of the services have been installed, you can see them in the Services control panel, as illustrated in figure 15.3.

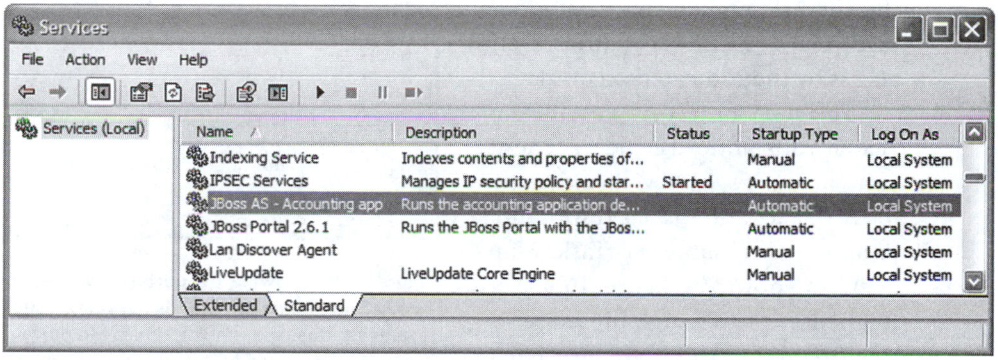

Figure 15.3 Viewing the example services in the Windows Services control panel applet

Note that the services initially aren't running, but they're configured with the automatic startup type so that they'll start when the system is booted. You can start them now if you like. You've probably noticed that the services are using the local system account, which isn't a good idea if you want to keep your system secure. Let's look at how to change that next.

USING A NON-SYSTEM ACCOUNT FOR THE SERVICE

The jbosssvc.exe executable registers the service to run with the local system account. Because that account has various special privileges, you should change the service to run with a different account. Changing the account is fairly simple to do.

First, create a new account. Don't add this account to the administrator's group. In addition, you might want to set the account so that the password never expires; otherwise, you'll notice that the service periodically stops working because it's using an expired password.

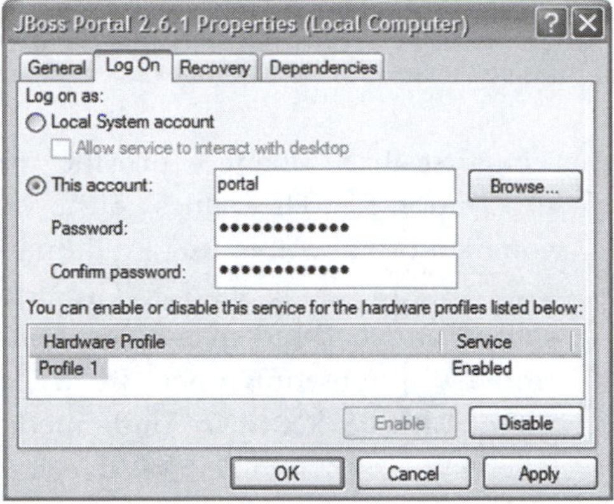

Figure 15.4 Setting the example portal service to use the restricted account named *portal*

Next, change the service to use the new account. In the Services control panel, right-click the service and select Properties. Change the account in the Log On tab of the Properties dialog box. Figure 15.4 shows using an account named *portal* to run the JBoss Portal 2.6.1 service.

Finally, ensure that the account used to run the service has access to the JBOSS_HOME directory and its subdirectories. You can also change the access control to the other directories on the system to prevent access by the indicated account.

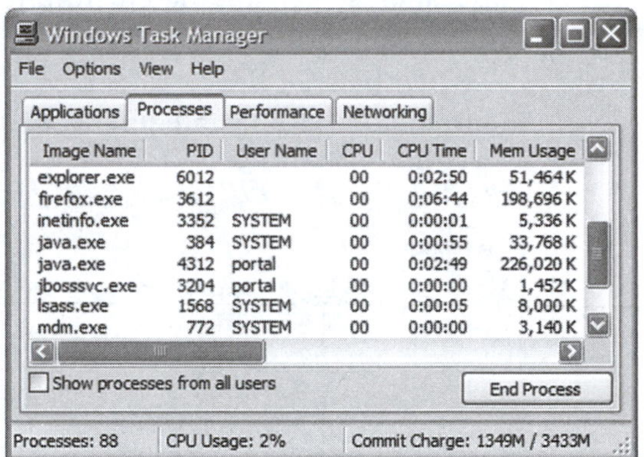

Figure 15.5 Viewing the portal service executables in Task Manager. The jbosssvc.exe and java.exe processes running under the portal account correspond to the portal service.

The next time you start the service, it runs under the new account; you can verify this by checking the jbosssvc.exe and its corresponding java.exe executable in Task Manager, as shown in figure 15.5. You might have to change the columns that are visible to see the username for each process. Note that there could be several java.exe processes running, many running under other accounts.

That covers setting up a service on Windows. Now, let's look at doing the same for Linux.

15.6.3 Registering a service in Linux

The application server comes with scripts that you can use to easily register your own service within Linux. For our example, we show you how to set up the service on Red Hat Fedora, but the same principles should apply equally to most Linux variants.

Services are defined in Linux by adding a script file to the /etc/init.d directory. These scripts must support commands to start, stop, and restart the service. The application server comes with three such scripts, named `jboss_init_*.sh`, in the bin directory. Because you're working with Fedora, use the `jboss_init_redhat.sh` script.

First, you edit the settings at the start of the script to reflect your environment. Listing 15.10 shows the changes you have to make.

Listing 15.10 Changing settings in the jboss_init_redhat.sh file

```
JBOSS_HOME=${JBOSS_HOME:-"/opt/jboss-5.0.0.GA"}        ❶
JBOSS_USER=${JBOSS_USER:-"jboss"}        ❷
JAVAPTH=${JAVAPTH:-"/usr/java/jdk1.5.0_16/bin"}        ❸
JBOSS_CONF=${JBOSS_CONF:-"default"}        ❹
JBOSS_HOST=${JBOSS_HOST:-"0.0.0.0"}        ❺
JBOSS_CONSOLE=${JBOSS_HOME:-"$JBOSS_HOME/bin/console.log"}        ❻
```

You need to change the path where JBoss AS is installed ❶, the account used to run JBoss AS ❷, and the location of the Java binary ❸. The `-c` ❹ and `-b` ❺ option values supply the server configuration name and binding address. The last line ❻ is one that you need to add to the file; it identifies the file that holds the log output that typically shows up in the command window when running the application server from a command line.

Additionally, if you later want to set this service up to start automatically when the system boots, you have to add the following comment lines to the script:

```
# chkconfig: 345 90 10
# description: Runs the JBoss Application Server
# processname: jboss
```

These lines are used by the `chkconfig` tool to identify the service and define the run level at which the script is executed. The concept of run levels is a little beyond the scope of this book, but any decent book on Linux administration can explain that topic. We discuss the `chkconfig` tool later.

Next, create a new user, named jboss to match the above settings. Don't forget to assign a password to the account. Even though the password isn't used to start the service, having a password prevents unauthorized users from gaining access to the system using that account.

Then, change the security on the files in the application server directory so that the new user has full access rights, both to run the scripts in the bin directory and to update and create files in the server directories. One way to accomplish this is to change the owner of all the files to the new user, like this (you might need to log in as root to do this if you don't own the files):

```
chown -R jboss /opt/jboss-5.0.0.GA
```

Once this is done, sign in as the new user, go to the bin directory, and run the application server. This step is more of a sanity check that this new account can be used to run the server. If it isn't successful, recheck the security permissions or fix any errors that occur. When you have the application server running, stop it; you'll restart it later as a service.

Next, copy the script to the /etc/init.d directory, renaming the script to simply jboss (or any other name you choose), mark it as executable, and register it using the chkconfig tool (you should be logged in as root). Here are the commands for these three steps:

```
cp /opt/jboss-5.0.0.GA/bin/jboss_init_redhat.sh /etc/init.d/jboss
chmod u+x /etc/init.d/jboss
chkconfig -add jboss
```

Finally, you can start the service. Enter the following (you should be logged in as root):

```
service jboss start
```

You can use the tail utility to monitor the output in the console.log file.

```
tail -f /opt/jboss-5.0.0.GA/bin/console.log
```

At this point, the service is registered to the system and starts automatically when the system restarts.

But, what if you want to run multiple instances of the application server? Easy. Make a copy of the jboss_init_*.sh file, setting the values mentioned in listing 15.8 for the second server, follow all the rest of the steps mentioned earlier, and copy the script to /etc/init.d as another name such as jboss2. You now have a second application server running as a service.

As we mentioned earlier, the example is specific to Fedora Core, but should apply equally well to other variants of Linux or Unix.

15.7 Configuring JSP compilation

By default, the JBoss Web Server doesn't compile a JSP until the first time it's accessed. After that, it checks whether the underlying JSP has changed, and recompiles it again. These are adequate settings for development purposes; but, in a production environment, these settings cause problems. First, by not compiling JSPs until the first time they're accessed in a production system, the first person who accesses the JSP has the inconvenience of waiting for it to compile. In many production environments, the best choice is to turn the lazy JSP compiling feature off all together.

The second problem with the default JSP compiler settings is that every JSP request must check whether the file has been updated in order to recompile when a JSP has been modified. Checking for file updates on each request can degrade performance in a production environment with a high load.

JSP compiling and execution is handled by a Java servlet deployed in JBoss Web Server by default when it starts up. This servlet, called the JspServlet, is configured in the global server/xxx/deployers/jbossweb.deployer/web.xml file.

The compiling configuration is done by specifying initial parameters for the servlet using <init-param> element blocks. The JspServlet is well documented in the file, so you can go in there and read about the other configuration options that you can make. As far as the compiling options go, you can configure three pertinent parameters. Table 15.5 shows you these options; the descriptions come straight from this file.

Table 15.5 The options available to configure JSP precompiling

Parameter	Description
`development`	Is Jasper used in development mode? If `true`, the frequency at which JSPs are checked for modification can be specified via the `modificationTestInterval` parameter. Default is `true`.
`checkInterval`	If `development` is `false` and `checkInterval` is greater than 0, background compilations are enabled. `checkInterval` is the time in seconds between checks to see if a JSP page needs to be recompiled. The default is 0.
`modificationTestInterval`	Causes a JSP (and its dependent files) to not be checked for modification during the specified time interval (in seconds) from the last time the JSP was checked for modification. A value of 0 causes the JSP to be checked on every access. Used in development mode only. The default value is 4.

You might have noticed that these options don't provide you with a way to precompile JSPs. You can do this in one of two ways. If you have only a few JSPs that you want to precompile, you can declare your JSP in your application's web.xml file and specify the `load-on-startup` setting.

```
<servlet>
  <servlet-name>login</servlet-name>
  <jsp-file>/login.jsp</jsp-file>
  <load-on-startup>1</load-on-startup>
</servlet>
```

If you have many JSPs in your application and you want to precompile all of them, you should use a command-line compiler. One such compiler is JSPC, which ships with JBoss Web Server. JSPC takes your JSP files and converts them into Java files. You can then use the regular Java compiler to compile the Java files. Build tools, such as Ant or Maven, simplify this process by providing build targets for you. Refer to your build tool documentation to find out more.

15.8 Summary

This chapter covered a wide range of configuration topics, but all of them were aimed at moving your application server from a development environment to a production environment. As a recap, we provide the various steps in the going-to-production checklist as, just that, a checklist:

1. Select the proper platform and JVM on which to run the application server.
2. Select a JBoss AS version, keeping in mind if you want support with that.
3. Determine if you need to run multiple instances on a single box, and if so, then creating multiple configurations and either binding the ports to unique port numbers or binding to multiple IP addresses.
4. Remove services that you don't need.

5. Secure the deployed applications and services, including the ones that come with the application server.
6. Remove the Hypersonic database, replacing it with an enterprise-class database.
7. Configure the application server to start as a service.
8. Configure the application server to precompile JSPs.

Congratulations! You now know everything necessary to roll your application server into production.

Over the course of this book, you've been introduced to a wide variety of topics concerning the JBoss AS and many of the technologies that it contains or that surround it. You should now be comfortable with performing such tasks as deploying applications, securing those applications, and various other configuration tasks. We encourage you to continue your learning by reading the documentation provided with the various JBoss technologies. With the background provided by the book, you should now find that documentation easier to comprehend. And finally, we hope that now you too will vote for JBoss!

15.9 Resources

Precompiling JSPs using ANT—http://scriptlandia.blogspot.com/2006/04/how-to-pre-compile-jsp-pages-for.html

JBoss Native website—http://www.jboss.org/jbossweb/downloads/jboss-native/

Quartz job scheduler—http://www.opensymphony.com/quartz/

appendix A: JNDI namespaces

This appendix covers

- Understanding the Enterprise Naming Context
- Examining common JNDI namespaces

As we discussed in chapter 7, EJBs are automatically bound into a JNDI server when they're deployed to the application server. The JBoss JNDI naming server is called JBossNS. Every application server binds beans into naming contexts of the application server's own choice. For example, as you saw in chapter 7, if you deploy an EAR file, JBoss will bind the beans into a context relative to the EAR file name. JBoss uses this convention, but other application servers may or may not use different strategies. In this appendix, we'll explore how JBoss does JNDI binding and how to generically bind your applications in JNDI, making them more portable across application servers.

A.1 Understanding the enterprise naming context

Some problems arise when you write code that references EJBs bound to the JNDI context that a particular vendor chooses. First, if you decide to migrate an application from one application server to another, your code has to be modified. For example, if you're running on WebLogic and decide to migrate to JBoss, you have to update all your JNDI references in your code to use the JBoss convention rather than the WebLogic convention. This task might not be bad, but some people have JNDI references hardcoded throughout their code, making it a little more difficult.

Another problem comes up when your application must be supported on multiple application servers. Many vendor product developers have this requirement. It doesn't make sense to keep separate versions of your code base for each application server when the only difference is the JNDI naming convention.

A third problem arises when you change the name of a bean and are then forced to change the reference to that bean in your code. For example, imagine that you have a session bean that reads data from a database, and you want to swap it out for a bean that reads the same data from a different database or, perhaps, a web service. It would be nice if your code could use a logical name to reference the bean rather than referencing it by its actual name.

The Java EE specification provides a mechanism for logically referencing beans, EJBs, and resources using the *Environment Naming Context (ENC)*. You'll also hear the ENC referred to as the component local namespace. The ENC is a private JNDI namespace available to EJBs. This private (or local) namespace is standard across all Java EE application servers and is mapped to the application server's proprietary (or global) namespace using the application server's proprietary deployment descriptor file, which is META-INF/jboss.xml in the case of JBoss.

Figure A.1 shows you how the ENC maps a local component name to the global component name.

In this figure a servlet is trying to access an EJB proxy through the ENC. The servlet looks up the EJB's proxy object using a local name defined in the web application's WEB-INF/web.xml file. We know the name is local because it starts with `java:/comp/env`, which is the standard prefix defined in the Java EE specification. This lookup

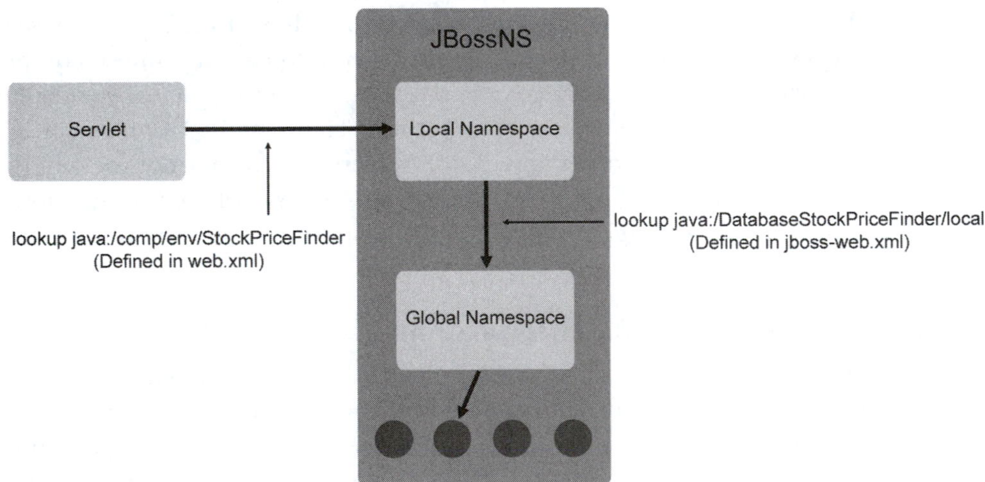

Figure A.1 Web applications can access resources by their local JNDI names, which are mapped to their global JNDI names.

causes a JNDI lookup to occur in JBossNS's global namespace. The global JNDI name for the EJB is defined in the WEB-INF/jboss-web.xml file. When the EJB is deployed, JBossNS creates a mapping between the local and the global name. JBossNS uses that mapping to locate the global name and then the proxy so that it can send it back to the servlet.

You can also do the same thing for a data source. For example, each application server vendor may bind its default data source to a different part of its global namespace. But, you can have your code and your standard deployment descriptors refer to the component local name. In a web application, you might configure your web.xml file to point to the local name java:comp/env/jdbc/DataSourceName using the following configuration:

```
<web-app>
  ...
  <resource-ref>
    <res-ref-name>jdbc/DataSourceName</res-ref-name>
    <res-type>javax.sql.DataSource</res-type>
    <res-auth>Container</res-auth>
    <res-sharing-scope>Shareable</res-sharing-scope>
  </resource-ref>
  ...
</web-app>
```

The local name is referenced using the `res-ref-name` element. The `java:comp/env` portion of the name is implied and doesn't need to be included. Then, you might map this local name to JBoss AS's default data source, using the default data source's global name, `java:DefaultDS`. This configuration would go in your WEB-INF/jboss-web.xml file.

```
<jboss-web>
  ...
  <resource-ref>
    <res-ref-name>jdbc/DataSourceName</res-ref-name>
    <jndi-name>java:DefaultDS</jndi-name>
  </resource-ref>
  ...
<jboss-web>
```

The `res-ref-name` element points to the local name, and the `jndi-name` element defines the mapping to the global name for the data source.

A.2 Examining the JNDI namespaces

The namespaces in JNDI fall into two main categories: global or local. Access to the local namespace (also called the `java:` namespace) is limited to the local JBoss instance. Access to the global namespace is open to remote clients as well. Table A.1 shows you some examples of what can be found in these namespaces.

Notice that the `java:/comp/env` namespace—the ENC—is under the local namespace (`java:`). Access to the ENC is not only restricted to local access within the JBoss instance, but is also limited to the EJB for which it's defined.

Table A.1 Examples of contexts and resources that are bound in the global and local namespaces in JBossNS

Global namespace	Description
`ConnectionFactory`	The context in which the JMS client connection manager gets bound
`Queue`	The context in which JMS queues get bound
`Topic`	The context in which JMS topics get bound
`Jmx`	The context in which JMX protocol adapters get bound
java:/comp/env	The context in which components (for example, session EJBs) will bind their proxies
java:/jaas	The context in which security domains get bound
java:DefaultDS	A reference to the default data source

You can see what's bound in JNDI by going to the JMX Console (http://localhost:8080/jmx-console/) and clicking the `service=JNDIView` link under the `jboss` domain. Then click the `invoke` button for the `list` operation; this will forward you to a screen that looks like figure A.2.

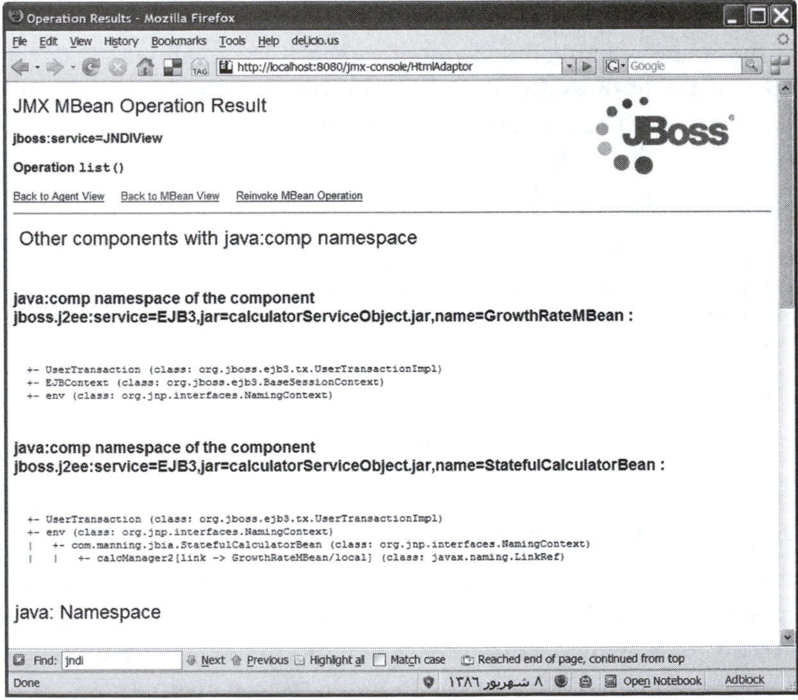

Figure A.2 The JNDI view in the JMX console shows you the various components bound in the local and global namespaces.

This view will show you everything in the local namespace and the global namespace (not seen in the screenshot). It will also break down the contents of each component bound into the ENC. Figure A.2 shows two beans bound into the ENC.

Understanding what gets bound into JNDI and how to look up objects in JNDI is helpful when configuring applications. Many questions on the JBoss forums are about or related to JNDI, so it would be well worth your time to dig through the JNDI view and learn what's there.

appendix B: Change is inevitable

This appendix covers

- Jopr and the new administration console
- JBoss Portal 2.7.0
- The default/lib directory
- The *web* configuration
- The profile service repository
- The `jboss.server.log.threshold` system property

Things do not change; we change.

—Henry David Thoreau

Thoreau was wrong, mainly because he never knew of any open source Java projects! To give you a little history, we finished writing the book in August of 2007. At that time, JBossAS 5.0.0 was at Beta 2 and GA was scheduled for that December. So we put the book on the shelf and awaited CR1. It was a long wait. As Beta 3, Beta 4, and then CR1 came out, we scrambled to update the book and source code to reflect the changes in each release. Then CR2 came out near the end of making text changes based on CR1, so we revalidated on CR2 and started sending chapters to the typesetter confident that the content would match GA very well. Considering the changes we saw in CR2, and with assurances from key members of the JBossAS development team that there would be no more changes, this seemed a reasonable assumption. There were few configuration changes in CR2; instead, it mostly fixed things that were broken in earlier versions, such as the port binding service that had been broken since Beta 1.

But soon we heard about other changes such as the release of the long-awaited Administration Console and the creation of the common/lib directory. Unfortunately, the chapters had already been typeset—hence, this appendix was born.

This appendix contains changes that came after CR2 and before the book went to the printer. Any changes after that will appear on the book's website. So without further ado, let's look at what's changed.

B.1 Jopr and Embedded Jopr

One of the important announcements during the JBoss World conference in Orlando in February 2008 was that an open source version of JBoss ON would be released, and that a subset of the functionality of that product would be used to create an Administration Console for JBoss AS. In October of 2008, the JBoss team made available Jopr—which is the open source version of JBoss ON—and Embedded Jopr—which is the Administration Console.

Jopr enables management of an entire datacenter, and can be used to manage and monitor a number of services running on each host, services such as databases, JBoss AS, Tomcat, operating systems, and so on. In addition, you can use Jopr to administer any instance of JBoss AS running in your data center, doing such things as deploying applications and defining data sources. Jopr is typically installed on a separate box, comes with its own application server, and connects to a database to store its data. You can use the JBoss ON documentation for Jopr; that documentation describes installation, configuration and usage, so we won't delve into Jopr in this book.

Embedded Jopr, on the other hand, is a web application that runs with a copy of JBoss AS, and can administer only that application server. You can use it to monitor the application server; but, unlike Jopr which provides graphs for performance data, Embedded Jopr provides only text. You can also use it to manage applications, data sources, message destinations, and other things.

In this appendix, we focus on Embedded Jopr, giving you a quick tour through its capabilities.

B.1.1 Installing and configuring Embedded Jopr

Installing Embedded Jopr is simple. First, download and unzip the zip file—it contains the admin-console.war file. You can copy the WAR file to the server/xxx/deploy directory, but we recommend unpacking the WAR file and deploying it as an exploded directory.

NOTE We aren't sure of the name for this WAR file. As of this writing, the WAR file in the downloaded zip file is named embedded-jopr.war. But this WAR file works only with JBoss AS 4.2.x. On the other hand, the source obtained from the Subversion repository builds both 4.2.x and 5.0 variations of Embedded Jopr and names both WAR files admin-console.war, which seems like a more reasonable name; that's the name we use in this appendix.

Embedded Jopr uses the jmx-console security domain for access control. This security domain uses the server/xxx/conf/props/jmx-console-roles.xml and jmx-console-users.xml files to manage the users and the roles. In JBoss AS, these files are set up to accept a username and password of admin/admin. In JBoss EAP, these files by default don't contain any valid roles—the admin user is commented out. If you're using JBoss EAP, make sure to set up valid usernames. For example, you could uncomment the admin user.

That's all that there is to installation. Start the app server, enter the URL http://localhost:8080/admin-console into your browser, provide the username and password to log in, and you'll see the page shown in figure B.1.

The top of the page is a header that identifies the Admin Console and contains a logout link. The left side of the page contains a tree view showing the components

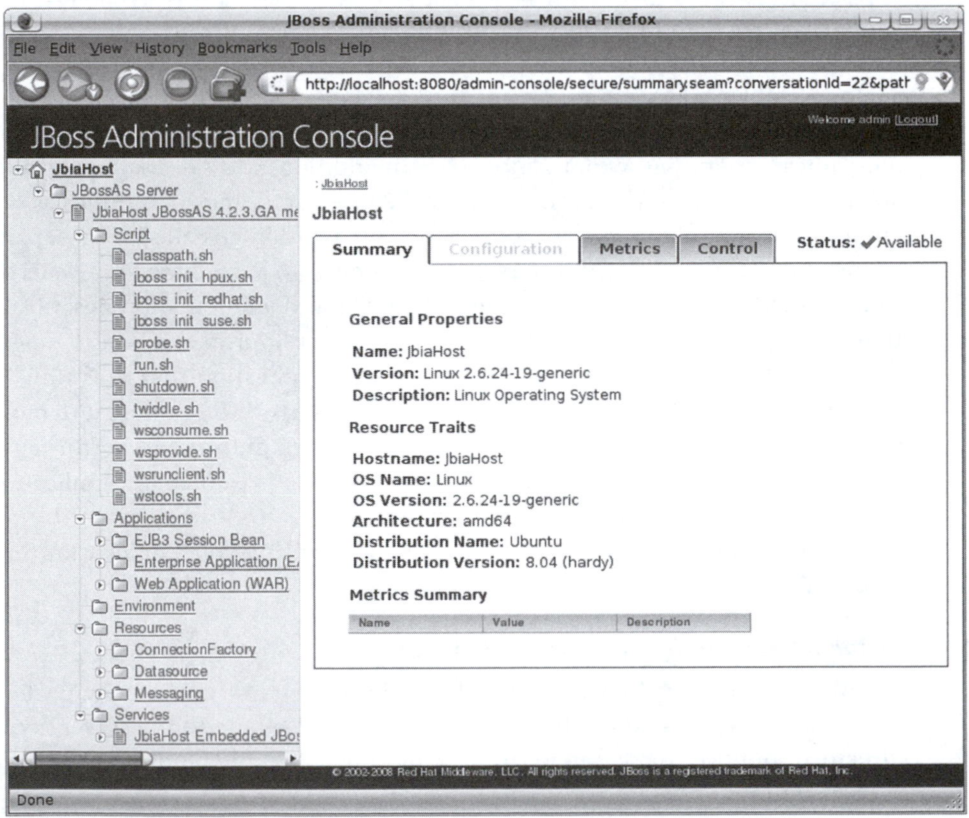

Figure B.1 The home page of the Amin Console

that can be managed. The right side of the page contains details about the component selected in the tree view.

The top of the detail panel contains breadcrumbs that identify your location within the component hierarchy. It also has four tabs used to group information about, or capabilities of, the component. Let's explore a few of the components, examining the tabs as we do so.

UNDERSTANDING THE SUMMARY TAB

The Summary tab provides information about the component. The Summary tab is always available, unlike the other tabs that, although they're always displayed, aren't always available. In figure B.1, the Summary tab is currently selected, the Configuration tab is unavailable, and the Metrics and Control tabs are available.

For a component that has no subcomponents, the Summary tab displays general information about the component, as you can see in the home page shown in figure B.1, which shows information about the host running the application server.

For a component that has subcomponents, the Summary tab displays a table of the subcomponents, as you can see in figure B.2, where the Datasource component is selected.

You can use the Delete button to remove the subcomponent. For a data source, if you click that button, the *-ds.xml file is removed from the deploy directory. You can use the Add A New Resource button to create a new subcomponent. For a data source, you're presented with a form into which you can enter the data source configuration information. This information is stored into a *-ds.xml file that's placed into the deploy directory. Similarly, if you create a new message destination, a *-destination-service.xml file for the

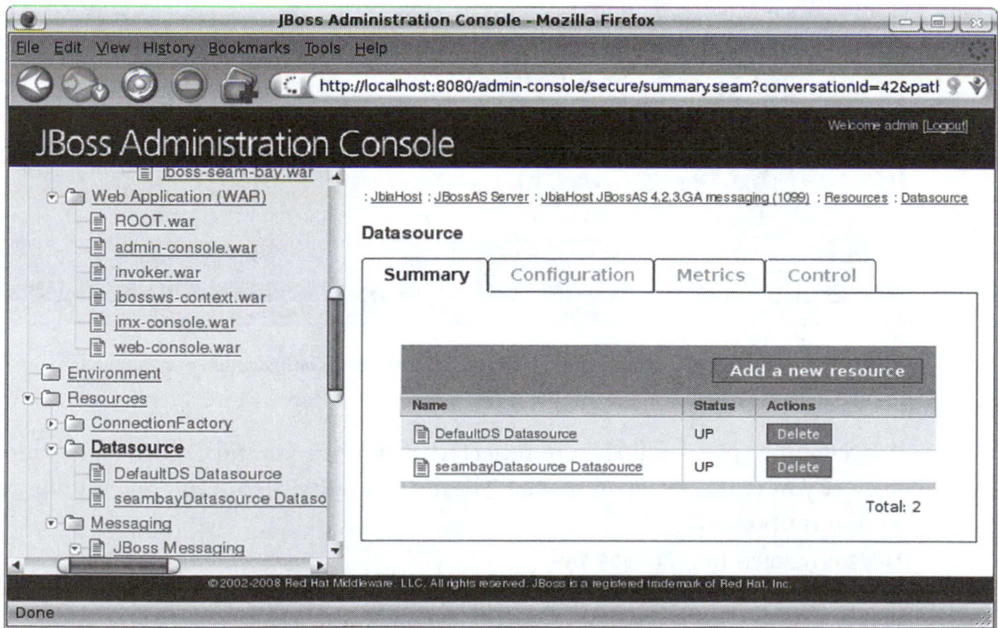

Figure B.2 The Summary tab for the data source component shows a table of data sources.

destination appears in the deploy directory. For a web application or enterprise application, the Add A New Resource button takes you to a form where you can specify the application's archive filename and indicate if the application should be deployed as an exploded directory. The application archive file is uploaded to the application server and deployed in the deploy directory. You always use the buttons on the Summary tab to create or delete a component.

UNDERSTANDING THE CONFIGURATION TAB

The Configuration tab displays a form you can use to modify the properties of the component. This tab is active when you select a data source or destination, for example. Figure B.3 shows the Configuration tab contents for a data source.

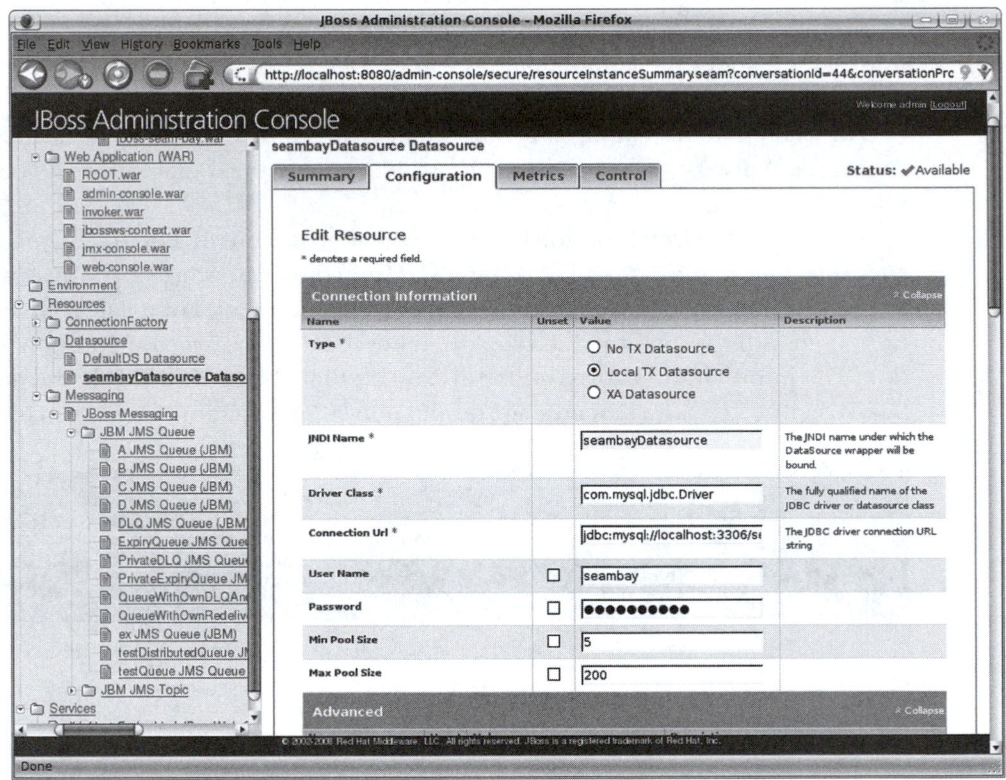

Figure B.3 The Configuration tab enables you to modify the configuration of a component.

Any changes that you make are reflected in the *-ds.xml file for the data source. Similarly, if you edit a destination, the *-destination-service.xml file containing that destination is updated.

UNDERSTANDING THE METRICS TAB

The Metrics tab displays a table showing the metrics captured for the component. Figure B.4 shows the metrics gathered for a web application.

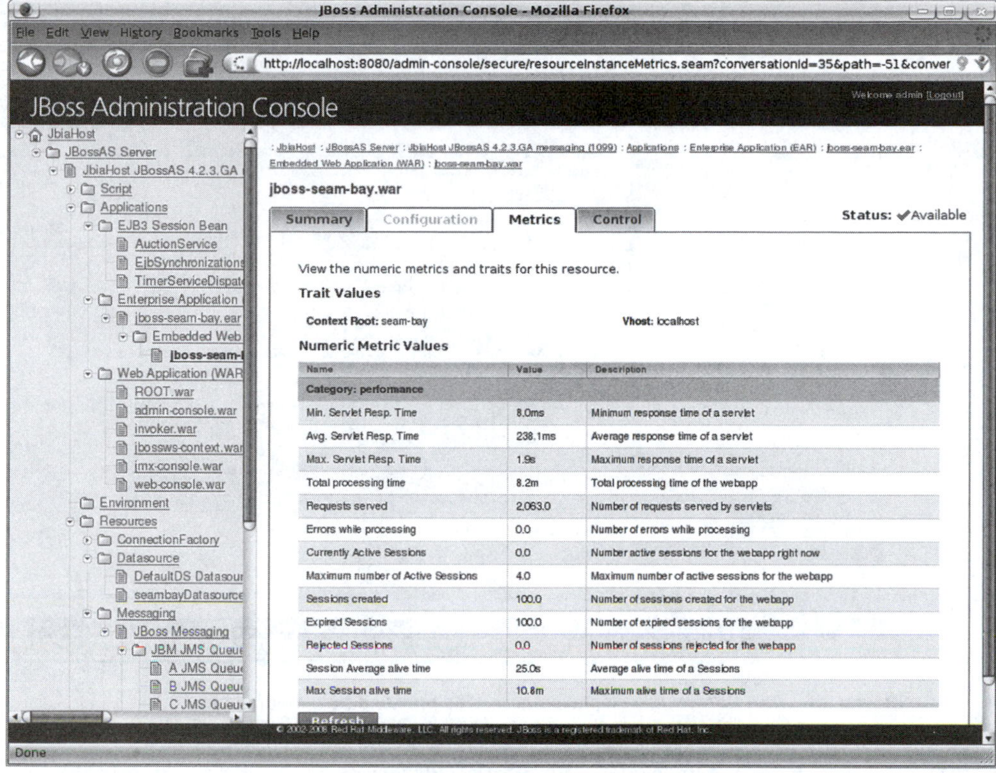

Figure B.4 The Metrics tab displays metrics gathered for a component.

You can use the refresh button, which is barely visible at the bottom of the figure, to gather the metrics again—the Admin Console doesn't automatically update the metrics.

UNDERSTANDING THE CONTROL TAB

The Control tab displays a button for each operation provided by the component, along with a description of what the operation does. Figure B.5 shows the Control tab for a web application.

And so ends our quick tour through the Admin Console. You've learned most of its capabilities and explored details regarding some of the components. We now leave you to explore the rest of the functionality and capabilities offered to you by the Admin Console.

B.1.2 JBoss Portal 2.7.0

The JBoss Portal 2.7.0.GA release adds Portlet 2.0 support, as defined by JSR-286, to JBoss Portal. The Portlet 2.0 specification addresses many issues that came up as people attempted to build and deploy portlet applications, such as inter-portlet communication, sharing global parameters, serving content other than HTML text, and input and output filtering. Please read the Portlet 2.0 specification to learn more about

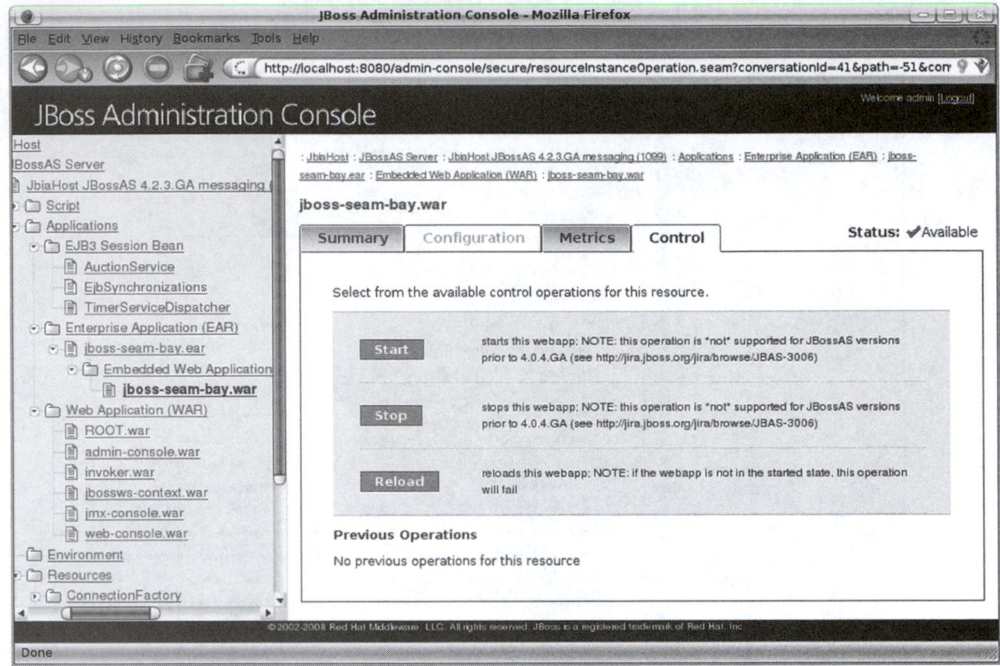

Figure B.5 The Control tab displays operations provided by a component.

these features. The rest of this section describes issues that you might encounter as you work your way through chapters 10 and 11.

Portal 2.7.0 requires a larger permanent generation space than prior versions of the Portal. You need to edit the run scripts (run.bat on Windows, run.conf on Unix/Linux/Mac) to set a maximum permanent generation size. For example, on Windows, change the line that sets the heap sizes as follows:

```
set JAVA_OPTS=%JAVA_OPTS% -Xms128m -Xmx512m -XX:MaxPermSize=128m
```

The rest of the issues relate to creating a custom portal (section 11.5).

Table 11.1 lists the *-object.xml files that ship with the portal. In 2.7.0, yet another one is located at jboss-portal.sar/samples/portal-portlet-samples.war/WEB-INF/default-object.xml. This *-object.xml file creates the Samples tab on the default page. You should remove this file if you don't want the tab to show up in the custom portal.

Portal 2.7.0 uses the new renew theme as the default theme. This shouldn't cause any problems when creating the theme for the custom portal because we create a new theme named jbia from the renaissance theme, so our existing instructions still work.

B.1.3 *The common/lib directory*

If you've used prior versions of JBoss AS, you'll have noticed that the lib directories under server/xxx contain almost the same JAR files. With only three configurations, this wasn't that much of a problem; but, when JBoss EAP came out, it included a fourth configuration named production. Now the binary download zip file was bloating due to duplicate JAR files. Additionally, the JBoss AS team wanted to add a few more configurations—which would lead to even more bloat.

To solve this problem, the JBoss AS team decided to move the common JAR files found in the configurations to a common location called common/lib. If you look at server/default/lib, you'll see that the directory is empty; server/all/lib contains the extra JAR file required for clustering.

The following system properties were introduced to identify this directory:

- *jboss.common.base.url*—Identifies the location of the common directory
- *jboss.common.lib.url*—Identifies the location of the common/lib directory

As with the other system properties, you can set these on the command line to change the location of the directories.

B.1.4 The web configuration

As you read the prior section, one question probably popped to mind: what new configurations? One of the common requests on the JBoss user's forums is to slim down the default configuration to remove things such as web services and messaging support, leaving only the servlet container. The web configuration provides such a slimmed-down servlet container configuration. Now you no longer have to slim down the default configuration by hand—a ready-made servlet container configuration is there waiting to be used.

Looking at the web configuration, you might think that it supports EJBs because it contains the directory server/web/deployers/ejb3.deployer. But, that deployer only supports annotations for EJB client, such as the @EJB annotation. The web configuration does support JCA, so you can deploy *-ds.xml files for your data sources.

B.1.5 The profile service repository

The new profile service manages application lifecycles and performs such tasks as deploying and undeploying applications. As of this writing, there's scant documentation on this service. (JIRA issue JBAS-6070, which addresses this, is unresolved.)

Two configuration files govern how the profile service works: one for the repository-based profile service and the other for the non-repository-based profile service. There's even less information on what distinguishes these. The repository-based profile service enables you to hook different repositories into JBoss AS, where a repository is a mechanism to locate the various applications and configurations used to run the application server. The 5.0 release ships with a file-based repository that uses the typical set of directories found within a configuration—such as the conf, lib, and deploy directories—to locate resources.

After the CR2 release, the repository-based profile service became the default, and configuration files in the server/xxx/conf directory were renamed. The file that used to be called bootstrap.xml is now called bootstrap-norepo.xml, and the file that used to be called bootstrap-repo.xml is now called boostrap.xml. In addition, there's a bootstrap-minimal.xml file, which doesn't work at this time because it's missing the include statements for the virtual filesystem and the port bindings. The file named bootstrap.xml is the default configuration file used to define the POJOs managed by the microcontainer. The new boostrap.xml file includes the profile-repository.xml file. In addition, all the bean configuration files, such as profile-repository.xml, were moved to the server/xxx/conf/bootstrap directory.

So what does all this have to do with you? It means that table 3.3 is now incorrect. Well, not entirely incorrect—table 3.3 still describes the beans declared in profile.xml, although some of those have moved to other files. By default, these beans are no longer used. Instead, the beans declared in profile-repository.xml are used.

Perhaps the best way to highlight the changes is to identify either where the beans went or what beans in profile-repository.xml provide the same or similar functionality to the beans in profile.xml (table B.1).

Table B.1 Mapping beans that were in profile.xml to their new location or replacement in profile-repository.xml

Old profile.xml bean	Old bean's property	Comment on new location
`MainDeployer`	-all-	Moved to deployers.xml.
`DeploymentFilter`	-all-	Also appears in profile-repository.xml.
`VFSDeploymentScanner`	`URIList`	`SerializableDeploymentRepositoryFactory` bean, `applicationURIs` property.
	`URIs`	You can provide each directory location as its own `<value>` entry. See listing B.1 and the following text.
	`recursiveSearch`	Not supported.
`VFSBootstrapScanner`	-	Replaced by `ProfileServiceBootstrap` bean but without any of the properties, such as URIs, supported by `VFSBoostrapScanner`. `SerializableDeploymentRepository` bean provides the location of the bootstrap directory; it's hardcoded and can't be changed.
`VFSDeployerScanner`	-	The `SerializableDeploymentRepository` bean provides the location of the deployers directory; it's hardcoded and can't be changed.
`HDScanner`	-all-	Moved to server/xxx/deploy/profileservice-hdscanner-jboss-beans.xml.

If you need to deploy applications from a location other than server/xxx/deploy, you can add more `<value>` entries to the `applicationURIs` property, as shown in the example in listing B.1.

Listing B.1 Adding more deployment directories in profile-repository.xml

```
<deployment ...>
  ...
  <bean name=" SerializableDeploymentRepositoryFactory " ...>
    ...
    <property name="applicationURIs">
      <array elementClass="java.net.URI">
        <value>${jboss.server.home.url}deploy</value>
        <value>file:///c:/temp/deploy</value>
        <value>file:///c:/temp/alternate/</value>
      </array>
    </property>
  </bean>
</deployment>
```

Unlike the `URIList` property for the `VFSDeploymentScanner` bean, the `applicationURIs` property accepts only directory names—you can't specify a package name such as a specific WAR file or exploded WAR directory. In addition, as shown in the example, it doesn't matter if you end the directory name with a slash, or if you leave it off.

B.1.6 The jboss.system.log.threshold system property

In prior releases of JBoss AS, the server.log file logged all messages with a threshold of TRACE or higher. The 5.0 release uses the `jboss.system.log.threshold` system property to define the level. This system property is set to DEBUG by default. You can easily override the setting by passing a value for the property on the command line, such as the followng:

```
run -Djboss.system.log.threshold=WARN
```

You can also change the default by editing the server/xxx/conf/jboss-service.xml file. Look for the attribute named `DefaultJBossServerLogThreshold` on the logging service MBean.

B.1.7 References

Jopr home page—http://www.jboss.org/jopr/

JBoss ON Documentation—https://docs.jbosson.redhat.com/confluence/display/JON2/Home

JSR-286 specification—http://jcp.org/en/jsr/detail?id=286

index

Symbols

A

K

L

Q

R

S

T

U

V

W

X

Y

Z